Phil Edmonston
LEMON-AID

1990-2015

NEW AND USED
CARS AND TRUCKS

DUNDURN
TORONTO

Editor: Catherine Leek of Green Onion Publishing
Design: Kim Monteforte of WeMakeBooks.com
Printer: Webcom

ISBN: 978-1-45971-940-8 (pb)
ISBN: 978-1-45971-942-2 (pdf)
ISBN: 978-1-45971-943-9 (epub)

1   2   3   4   5   17   16   15   14   13

Conseil des Arts du Canada — Canada Council for the Arts — Canadä — ONTARIO ARTS COUNCIL CONSEIL DES ARTS DE L'ONTARIO

We acknowledge the support of the **Canada Council for the Arts** and the **Ontario Arts Council** for our publishing program. We also acknowledge the financial support of the **Government of Canada** through the **Canada Book Fund** and **Livres Canada Books**, and the **Government of Ontario** through the **Ontario Book Publishing Tax Credit** and the **Ontario Media Development Corporation**.

Visit us at
Dundurn.com | @dundurnpress | Facebook.com/dundurnpress
Pinterest.com/dundurnpress

Dundurn	Gazelle Book Services Limited	Dundurn
3 Church Street, Suite 500	White Cross Mills	2250 Military Road
Toronto, Ontario, Canada	High Town, Lancaster, England	Tonawanda, NY
M5E 1M2	LA1 4XS	U.S.A. 14150

CONTENTS

CONTENTS

CONTENTS

KEY DOCUMENTS

European Vehicles

KEY DOCUMENTS

BUY A MILLIONAIRE'S CAR

Easy Money

Luxury models led the list of the 10 most popular cars for people earning over $250,000: The Mercedes E-class, Lexus RX 350, BMW 5 Series and 3 Series had the top four spots. But most surprising is the cars that rounded out the top 10: Three Hondas, a Toyota, an Acura and a Volkswagen. Not a single domestic vehicle in the bunch, though Cadillac has at least grown in popularity among the rich for the past two years.

www.forbes.com/sites/joannmuller/2011/12/30/what-the-rich-people-really-drive/

Women ask the important questions and listen. Men get "gadget-giddy." Take your mother, wife, or sister along.

QUALITY IS PRICELESS

Forget that old adage that "you get what you pay for." Whether buying new or used, the quality of a vehicle has nothing to do with how much it costs. Take a look at J. D Power, *Consumer Reports*, and *Lemon-Aid* new car ratings over the past four decades and you will see some of the cheapest cars remain the most reliable. Millionaires know this, too. That's why 38 percent polled in *The Millionaire Next Door* said they buy only used cars.

This year's *Lemon-Aid* breaks with tradition and rates, for the first time, both new and used cars built over the past 25 years. Why go so far back? Simple.

- There are more cheap, reliable. and safe vehicles on the market.
- Hard times give "beaters" a nouveau-frugal cachet.
- Seniors want collector cars they couldn't afford when they were younger.

2014 new car buyers will see fewer bargains due to the pent up demand for new cars following the recent economic recession. American and Japanese automakers are leading the charge with predicted increased prices in the 4 to 7 percent range, while ailing European manufacturers will likely stand pat on prices and "goose" sales through regional incentives, low interest rates, leasing discounts, and free maintenance. The South Koreans, just coming off a record-breaking sales year, are expected to increase prices modestly and offer more sales incentives early in 2014.

WHAT'S NEW IN THIS YEAR'S GUIDE?

This year's guide rates more cars, trucks, SUVs, and vans than ever before. We give you each car's residual value, crashworthiness ratings, real interior space, and fuel economy figures you can count on. We also revisit hybrid and electric cars to see if the fuel savings claims are legitimate or just hot air. And speaking of hot air, *Lemon-Aid* looks into whether tire fill-ups with nitrogen gas are a fuel-saver or a scam.

We show what to look for in a new or used vehicle that most buyers miss, like "chin-to-chest" head restraints, blinding dash reflections, dash gauges that can't be seen in sunlight, and the painful wind-tunnel roar if the rear windows are opened while underway.

DON'T BE SILLY. THAT'S CAUSED BY BIRD DROPPINGS!

INADEQUATE PRIMER CAUSED MY PAINT TO PEEL!

"Secret" Warranties

Of course what would *Lemon-Aid* be without its annual roundup of secret warranties that provide for free repairs to those customers who scream the loudest (or who read *Lemon-Aid*). These arbitrary and little-known warranty extensions are often called "goodwill" policies by automakers and are used to placate some customers when poor-quality components fail after the warranty expires. Dealership mechanics often blame the problem on road salt, bird droppings, or poor maintenance – never on a factory screw-up.

This practice has nothing to do with goodwill. It's simply a cynical way to transform the factory's mistake into a selling tool for the dealer. The reasoning is simple – customers will stay loyal to a dealer who pretends to bend the rules by offering a free repair. Four recent examples: Audi and VW biodegradable DSG powertrains; Chrysler defective wheel bearings; GM failure-prone catalytic converters; and Nissan faulty transmissions. In Part Three of this guide we have an extensive, revised list of secret warranties that are still in effect for thousands of 1995-2012 cars, trucks, SUVs, and vans.

WARRANTY EXTENSION FOR CERTAIN 2007-2010 MODEL YEAR VOLKSWAGEN VEHICLES EQUIPPED WITH A DSG TRANSMISSION

DATE: DECEMBER 2009

Dear Volkswagen Owner:

As part of our ongoing commitment to customer satisfaction, we are pleased to inform you of our decision to extend the warranty that covers the DSG gearbox transmission in your vehicle to 10 years or 100,000 miles, whichever occurs first, from the vehicle's original in-service date.

The vehicle's original in-service date is defined as the date the vehicle was delivered to either the original purchaser or the original lessee; or if the vehicle was first placed in service as a "demonstrator" or "company" car, on the date such vehicle was first placed in service.

Should you ever have an issue with the DSG transmission in your vehicle, your authorized Volkswagen dealer will diagnose and repair it at no cost to you, as long as your vehicle is within the time and mileage limit of this warranty extension. Please keep this letter with your Warranty booklet and deliver it to any new owner, along with the owner's manual.

Audi was later included in the above announcement. Benefits are not as extensive as Nissan's (below) but once negligence is admitted, second owners and all expenses flowing from the failure are covered. Plus a small claims court judge can expand the models covered, years, and mileage parameters.

CHRYSLER MINIVAN 5-YEAR EXTENDED WARRANTY

NUMBER: 02-004-12

DATE: DECEMBER 2009

CHRYSLER

GROUP: Front Suspension
SUBJECT: Growling and/or humming sound at the front wheel bearings (5yr./ 90,000 Mile/145,000 Km) Warranty Extension); **OVERVIEW:** This bulletin involves road testing and if necessary removing and replacing both front wheel bearings; **MODELS:** 2008-2010 Caravan /Town & Country.

SPECIAL COVERAGE ADJUSTMENT – CATALYTIC CONVERTER WARRANTY EXTENSION

BULLETIN NO.: 10134

DATE: NOVEMBER 17, 2010

2006–07 Chevrolet Malibu equipped with 2.2L Engine (L61)
2006–07 Pontiac G6 equipped with 2.4L Engine (LE5)

CONDITION: Some customers of 2006–07 model year Chevrolet Malibu vehicles with a 2.2L engine (L61) and Pontiac G6 vehicles equipped with a 2.4L engine (LE5) may comment about the illumination of the indicator lamp. This may be due to erosion of the mat within the catalytic converter.

SPECIAL COVERAGE ADJUSTMENT: This special coverage covers the condition described for a period of 10 years or 120,000 miles (193,000 km), whichever occurs first, from the date the vehicle was originally placed in service, regardless of ownership. The repairs will be made at no charge to the customer.

GM Catalytic Converter ten-year Extended Warranty. Shhh ... GM will replace your $600 catalytic converter for free, for up to ten years, whether you bought the car new or used.

NISSAN CVT – CUSTOMER SATISFACTION PROGRAM

The following is a list of vehicles included in the Nissan CVT Warranty Extension program:

2007	2008	2009	2010
Murano	–	Murano	Murano
–	Rogue	Rogue cube®	Rogue cube®
Sentra	Sentra	Sentra	Sentra
Versa 1.8SL	Versa 1.8SL	Versa 1.8SL	Versa 1.8SL
Maxima	Maxima	Maxima	Maxima
Altima	Altima	Altima	Altima
Altima Coupe	Altima Coupe	Altima Coupe	Altima Coupe
Altima Hybrid	Altima Hybrid	Altima Hybrid	Altima Hybrid

Nissan's generous offer covers almost any eventuality and is a benchmark for claims relative to similar failures by vehicles from any carmaker. Both letters nail down what the industry accepts as "reasonable durability" (ten years).

OTHER *LEMON-AID* HIGHLIGHTS

1. Fire-prone Jeeps: Would Fiat or Chrysler lie to 2.7 million owners?
2. New and used vehicle prices, including the dealer's markup.
3. Vehicles with the best and worst residual value and return on investment.
4. National Highway Traffic Safety Administration and Insurance Institute for Highway Safety latest crashworthiness ratings (front, front-quarter, side, rear, and roof).
5. "Infotainment" features: Not entertaining, nor informing; glitch-prone and distracting.

6. *Lemon-Aid's* Endangered Species List: Jaguar, Land Rover, and the Smart Car.
7. Why Audis are beautiful to behold, but hell to own (biodegradable transmissions, rodent-snack wiring, and mind-boggling depreciation).
8. New jurisprudence that holds automakers liable for occupant injuries caused by faulty airbags and imposes tougher misleading advertising penalties for false gas-mileage claims.
9. Luxury "dream cars" that can turn into nightmares (like "deadly" DSG trannies on Audis and VWs).
10. Ford's poor EcoBoost engine/transmission performance and infotainment glitches.
11. Electric cars and hybrids: A mixture of hype and hope. Why electric, ethanol, and hybrid fuel-saving claims have more in common with Harry Potter than the Society of Automotive Engineers.
12. How to get a refund if your vehicle burns more fuel than promised.
13. Best cars for seniors, families, and young drivers, along with lists of the optional features that are worth the extra cash – and the ones that aren't recommended.
14. Hundreds of new confidential service bulletins and safety complaints.
15. Easy-to-write complaint letters covering misrepresentation, poor service, and factory-related defects.

Make *Lemon-Aid 2014* part of your car's tool kit. No experience needed.

Phil Edmonston
October 2013

Part One
NEW WHEELS AND OLD DEALS

"YESSIR, THE CAR IS HOT AND IT GLOWS IN THE DARK."

A GOOD TIME TO BUY

There are lots of reasons why 2014 is a good year to buy a new car or truck – as long as you stay away from some of the rotten products and knock down the boosted prices by about 10 percent. Although there's not a lot of new product coming out this year, Detroit carmakers are doing what they have always done – "selling the sizzle." They're tweaking rebates, adding standard equipment and two-years of free maintenance, plus $500 pre-paid gas cards, 3,000 Air Miles points, zero percent financing, *and* car loans for up to 96 months. Of course the longer the loan the more the vehicle costs, but this isn't of much consequence if you beat the depreciation demons by keeping the vehicle at least eight years.

Prices are higher this year due to the pent up demand for cars following the 2009 recession when payrolls shrank, deficits grew, and credit was scarce.

Fortunately, the bad economic times have moderated and North American sales have returned to within 15 percent of their pre-recession level, while auto sales in Europe and Asia continue to slide.

10 Buying Tips

Now's a good time to be a contrarian.

For example, higher oil prices are driving down large, fully-loaded truck and SUV prices. Savings of 20 percent or more are commonplace and will probably be more as we go into the winter and summer months. With the money saved, the fuel penalty is softened and depreciation isn't as steep because of the discounted purchase price.

1. Buy a vehicle that is relatively uncomplicated, is easy to service, and has been sold in large numbers. This will ensure that cheaper, independent garages can provide service and parts.
2. Look for a vehicle that's finishing its model run, but steer clear of models that were axed because of poor reliability or mediocre performance, like GM's front-drive minivans or the Nissan Quest.
3. Don't buy European offerings, unless you *know* local servicing is competent and reasonably priced. Dealership networks are notoriously weak for these cars, parts are inordinately expensive and hard to find, and few independent garages will invest in the expensive equipment needed to service complicated emissions and fuel-delivery systems. The old axiom that there is a right way, a wrong way, and a European way to troubleshoot a car still holds true.
4. Don't buy a hybrid or electric model. They give a poor return on investment, are complicated to service, dealer-dependent, and they don't always provide the fuel economy or savings they hype. A VW diesel is far more reliable and gives you a greater return on investment (see chart below). However, other diesel models are arriving this year and should be treated with caution during their first year in Canada.

VW's Jetta Diesel TDI: A gas-sipper with a biodegradable transmission.

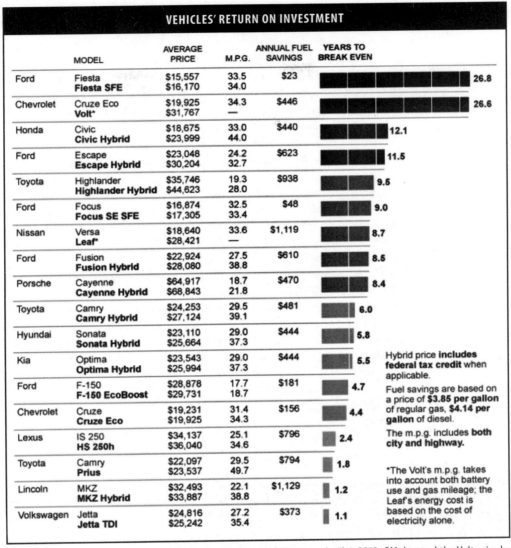

VEHICLES' RETURN ON INVESTMENT

	MODEL	AVERAGE PRICE	M.P.G.	ANNUAL FUEL SAVINGS	YEARS TO BREAK EVEN
Ford	Fiesta **Fiesta SFE**	$15,557 $16,170	33.5 34.0	$23	26.8
Chevrolet	Cruze Eco **Volt***	$19,925 $31,767	34.3 —	$446	26.6
Honda	Civic **Civic Hybrid**	$18,675 $23,999	33.0 44.0	$440	12.1
Ford	Escape **Escape Hybrid**	$23,048 $30,204	24.2 32.7	$623	11.5
Toyota	Highlander **Highlander Hybrid**	$35,746 $44,623	19.3 28.0	$938	9.5
Ford	Focus **Focus SE SFE**	$16,874 $17,305	32.5 33.4	$48	9.0
Nissan	Versa **Leaf***	$18,640 $28,421	33.6 —	$1,119	8.7
Ford	Fusion **Fusion Hybrid**	$22,924 $28,080	27.5 38.8	$610	8.5
Porsche	Cayenne **Cayenne Hybrid**	$64,917 $68,843	18.7 21.8	$470	8.4
Toyota	Camry **Camry Hybrid**	$24,253 $27,124	29.5 39.1	$481	6.0
Hyundai	Sonata **Sonata Hybrid**	$23,110 $25,664	29.0 37.3	$444	5.8
Kia	Optima **Optima Hybrid**	$23,543 $25,994	29.0 37.3	$444	5.5
Ford	F-150 **F-150 EcoBoost**	$28,878 $29,731	17.7 18.7	$181	4.7
Chevrolet	Cruze **Cruze Eco**	$19,231 $19,925	31.4 34.3	$156	4.4
Lexus	IS 250 **HS 250h**	$34,137 $36,040	25.1 34.6	$796	2.4
Toyota	Camry **Prius**	$22,097 $23,537	29.5 49.7	$794	1.8
Lincoln	MKZ **MKZ Hybrid**	$32,493 $33,887	22.1 38.8	$1,129	1.2
Volkswagen	Jetta **Jetta TDI**	$24,816 $25,242	27.2 35.4	$373	1.1

Hybrid price **includes federal tax credit** when applicable.

Fuel savings are based on a price of **$3.85 per gallon** of regular gas, **$4.14 per gallon** of diesel.

The m.p.g. includes **both city and highway.**

*The Volt's m.p.g. takes into account both battery use and gas mileage; the Leaf's energy cost is based on the cost of electricity alone.

Note: After these figures were published in the New York Times on April 4, 2012, GM dropped the Volt price by $10,000(U.S.) and Nissan cut the Leaf's MSRP by $15,000.

Source: *www.truecar.com*

5. Be wary of Chrysler, Dodge, or Jeep models. Chrysler is the weakest of the Detroit Three and its lineup has a sad history of serious safety- and performance-related defects, and its automatic transmissions, brakes, and air conditioners are particularly troublesome. The diesel-powered Ram truck is the best of a bad lot.

6. Don't buy General Motors (2014 Impala excepted) or Chrysler front-drive models or vehicles made in China. Crash test ratings for many China-made

vehicles are listed as "Poor," and their assembly quality is neanderthal, at best. Jacob George, vice-president of China operations for J. D. Power Asia Pacific, says China-built vehicles won't match American average initial quality before 2016. As a rule, GM front-drives are less reliable than the rear-drives and have poorly performing powertrains and brakes. Start shopping for a GM car or truck in the first quarter of 2014, when the auto show hoopla has died down and General Motors' sweetened rebates drive prices downward.

7. Consider Ford, except for its small cars and new EcoBoost turbocharged engines which are plagued with chronic loss of power, stalling on-road bucking, and surging.

8. Don't buy from dual dealerships. Parts inventories at many dealerships may have been depleted due to slow sales, and qualified mechanic may be in short supply. The represented auto companies see the dealerships as less than loyal and will cut them little slack in vehicle deliveries and warranty assistance.

9. Don't buy any vehicle that requires an extended warranty due to a reputation for past failures. Instead, choose a better car.

10. Use your credit card for the down payment, and put down as little money as possible. Use credit instead of cash to pay for repairs and maintenance charges. If you want to cancel a sales contract or work order, it's easier to do with a credit card than with cash.

Buying a New Car, Truck, SUV, or Van

I remember in the '70s, American Motors gave away free TVs with each new car purchase, just before shutting its doors. In the past decade, General Motors gave away free Dell computers and VW hawked free guitars with its cars. The Detroit Three automakers continue to build poor-quality cars and trucks, although there appears to be some improvement over the past three years. The gap between Asian and American automobile quality has narrowed; however, this may reflect only a lowered benchmark following recent Honda, Nissan, and Toyota powertrain, electrical system, and body fit glitches and a substantial increase in recalls. Nevertheless, Asian makes continue to dominate J.D. Power and Associates' dependability surveys, while other American and European models are mostly ranked below the industry average, but are trending upward.

Incidentally, Ford, long the darling for improved quality scores during the past five years, has crashed in the latest ratings charts due to chronic infotainment electronic failures, faulty EcoBoost (turbocharged) powertrains, and false fuel-economy ratings with its C-Max hybrid and Fusion compact. Ford is being sued by owners of the 2013 Fusion Hybrid and C-Max Hybrid, who say the company's official fuel economy claims are exaggerated.

Ford Fusion Hybrid

Ford C-Max Hybrid

In a class-action petition filed in Philadelphia last April 2013, the owners claim:

Plaintiffs are some of the tens of thousands of consumers who purchased a Fusion Hybrid or C-Max Hybrid, only to be stuck with under-performing, less-valuable vehicles that inflict higher fuel costs on their owners. Both cars are rated at 47 mpg in all three EPA categories (city, highway, combined), but in *Consumer Reports'* full test, the Fusion Hybrid returned 39 mpg, while the C-Max Hybrid returned 37 mpg.

Ford denied all allegations, but six months later settled the suits out of court and announced a $500 compensation refund for all affected North American owners.

Step 1: Keep it Simple

First, keep in mind that you are going to spend much more money than you may have anticipated – almost $31,000 for the average vehicle transaction, according to Dennis DesRosiers, a Toronto-based auto consultant. The many hidden fees, like freight charges and so-called administrative costs, are added to the bottom line. But, with cut-throat discounts and armed with tips from this guide, you can bring that amount down considerably.

According to the Canadian Automobile Association (CAA), the average household owns two vehicles, which are each driven about 20,000 km annually and cost an average of $800 a year for maintenance; DesRosiers estimates $1,100.

Do Toyota hybrids really save you money over a similar gasoline-engine-equipped small car? Not according to the CAA. The auto association says in its *2010 Driving Costs* brochure that Toyota's Prius hybrid costs more to drive than an equivalent Chevrolet Cobalt. Total cost of driving a 2010 Toyota Prius 32,000 km is $10,783, while the 2010 Chevrolet Cobalt LT would cost slightly less at $10,694. The cost rises to $14,363 for a 2010 Dodge Grand Caravan.

Keep in mind that it's practically impossible to buy a bare-bones car or truck because automakers know this is a seller's market until early 2014, so they tend to cram new cars with costly, non-essential performance and convenience features in order to maximize their profits. Nevertheless, money-wasting features like electronic navigation, self-parking, camera vision, digital screens, and voice-command capability can easily be passed up with little impact on safety or convenience. In fact, voice command and in-dash computer screens can be very distracting while driving – producing a negative safety effect. Full-torso side curtain airbags and electronic stability control (ESC), however, are important safety options that are well worth the extra expense.

Our driving needs are influenced by where we live, our lifestyles, and our ages (see pages 33-38 for a discussion of vehicles best suited to mature drivers). The ideal car should be crashworthy and easy to drive, have minimal high-tech features to distract and annoy, and not cost much to maintain.

In the city, a small wagon or hatchback is more practical and less expensive than a mid-sized car like the Honda Accord or Toyota Camry. Furthermore, have you seen the newer Civic and Elantra? What once were small cars are now quite large, relatively fuel-efficient, and equipped with more horsepower than you'll ever likely need. Nevertheless, if you're going to be doing a lot of highway driving, transporting small groups of people, or loading up on accessories, a medium-sized sedan, wagon, or small sport-utility could be the best choice for price, comfort, and reliability.

Don't let spikes in fuel prices stampede you into buying a vehicle unsuitable to your driving needs. If you travel less than 20,000 km per year, mostly in the city, choose a small car or SUV equipped with a 4-cylinder engine that produces about 140 hp to get the best fuel economy without sacrificing performance. Anything more powerful is just a waste. Extensive highway driving, however, demands the cruising performance, extra power for additional accessories, and durability of a larger, 6-cylinder engine. Believe me, fuel savings will be the last thing on your mind if you buy an underpowered vehicle.

Be especially wary of the towing capabilities bandied about by automakers. They routinely exaggerate towing capability and seldom mention the need for expensive optional equipment, or that the top safe towing speed may be only 72 km/h (45 mph). Generally, 3-3.8L V6 engines will safely accommodate most towing needs. The 4-cylinder engines may handle light loads, but will likely offer a white-knuckle experience when merging with highway traffic or travelling over hilly terrain.

Remember, you may have to change your driving habits to accommodate the type of vehicle you purchase. Front-drive braking is quite different from braking with a rear-drive, and braking efficiency on ABS-equipped vehicles is compromised if you pump the brakes. Also, rear-drive vans handle like trucks, and you may scrub the right-rear tire during sharp right-hand turns until you get the hang of making wider turns. Limited rear visibility is another problem with larger vans, forcing drivers to carefully survey side and rear traffic before changing lanes or merging.

Step 2: Be Realistic

Don't confuse styling with needs (do you have a bucket bottom to conform to those bucket seats?) or trendy with essential (will a cheaper down-sized SUV like a Hyundai Tucson or Subaru Forester suit you as well as, or better than, a mid-sized car?). Visiting the showroom with your spouse, a level-headed relative, or a sensible friend will help you steer a truer course through all the non-essential options you'll be offered.

Getting a female perspective can be really helpful. Women don't generally receive the same welcome at auto showrooms as men do, but that's because they make the salesmen (yes, usually less than 10 percent of the sales staff are women) work too hard to make a sale. Most sales agents admit that female shoppers are far more knowledgeable about what they want and more patient in negotiating contract details than men, who tend to be mesmerized by many of the techno-toys available.

In increasing numbers, women have discovered that minivans, SUVs, and small pickups are more versatile than passenger cars and station wagons. And, having spotted a profitable trend, automakers are offering increased versatility combined with unconventional styling in so-called "crossover" vehicles. These blended cars are part sedan and part station wagon, with a touch of sport-utility added for function and fun. For example, the 2014 Ford Flex is a smaller, sporty crossover vehicle that looks like a miniature SUV. First launched as a 2009 model, the Flex comes in an entry-level SE trim line that brings down the starting price a bit.

Small South Korean SUVs like this Hyundai Tucson ($20,000) are ideal for small families and light commuting. Remember, Hyundai owns Kia and their vehicles are quite similar. So, if a Hyuundai dealer doesn't have the model or offer the price you want, go to a Kia outlet.

TSB Number	TSB Date	TSB Title
13-4-16	04/25/2013	A/T Controls – Intermittent, No Upshift, No DTCs Stored
13-4-19	04/25/2013	Body/Exhaust – Exhaust Sulfur Odour After Hard Acceleration
13-3-11	03/21/2013	Navigation/GPS – Unale to Locate Vehicle or GPS Concerns
13-3-9	03/15/2013	Body – Water Leak from Roof Opening Panel
13-2-6	02/14/2013	Interior – Rattle or Scratching Noise from the Headliner Area
12A04S2	01/14/2013	Campaign – SYNC(R) MyFord/My Lincoln Touch(R) Upgrades
13-1-1	01/10/2013	Memory Sys – Incorrect Easy Entry/Exit Steering Column Position
12-12-11	12/31/2012	Interior – Front Seat Heaters Don't Get Warm Enough
12-11-8	11/15/2012	Audio System – Display Stays On 20-30 seconds After Key Off
12-11-1	11/05/2012	My Ford/Lincoln Touch(R) – Various Issues
12-7-3	07/19/2012	Engine Controls – Missing PIDS

For the past three years, My Ford/Lincoln Touch infotainment systems have morphed into Hal, the evil computer in *2001, A Space Odyssey*. And, like Dave, the endangered astronaut in the film, Ford has found the perfect solution – disconnect some of the system, and bring back knobs. What will they think of next, eh?

Step 3: What Can I Afford?

Determine how much money you can spend, and then decide which vehicles in that price range interest you. Have several models in mind so that the overpriced one won't tempt you too much. As your benchmarks, use the ratings, alternative models, estimated purchase costs, and residual value figures shown in Part Four of this guide. Remember, logic and prudence are the first casualties of showroom hype, so carefully consider what you actually need and how these things will fit into your budget before comparing models and prices at a dealership.

Write down your first, second, and third choices relative to each model and the equipment offered. Browse the automaker websites both in Canada and in the States, and consult *www.unhaggle.com* for the Canadian manufacturer's suggested retail price (MSRP), promotions, and package discounts. Look for special low prices that may apply only to Internet-generated referrals. Once you get a good idea of the price variations, get out the fax machine or PC at home or work (a company letterhead is always impressive) and then make the dealers bid against each other (see page 73). Call the lowest-bidding dealership, ask for an appointment to be assured of getting a sales agent's complete attention, and take along the down-loaded price info from the Canadian and American automaker websites to avoid arguments.

Sometimes a cheaper "twin" will fit the bill. Twins are nameplates made by different auto manufacturers, or by different divisions of the same company, that are virtually identical in body design and mechanical components, like the Chevrolet Silverado and GMC Sierra pickups.

Let's look at the savings possible with "twinned" Chrysler minivans. A 2009 Grand Caravan SXT that was originally listed for $31,395 is now worth about $7,000. An upscale 2009 Town & Country Limited that performs similarly to the Grand Caravan, with just a few additional gizmos, first sold for $42,995 and is now worth about $11,500. Where once almost $11,500 separated the two minivans, the price difference is now only $4,500 – and you can expect the gap to close to almost nil over the next few years. Did the little extras really justify the Town & Country's higher price, or make it a better buy than the Grand Caravan? Obviously, the marketplace thinks not.

And don't get taken in by the "Buy Canadian!" chanting from Chrysler, Ford, General Motors, and the Canadian Auto Workers. It's pure hokum. While Detroit-based automakers are beating their chests over the need to buy American, they buy Asian automakers and suppliers and then market the foreign imports as their own. This practice has resulted in bastardized nameplates whose parentage isn't always easy to nail down. For example, is the Aveo a Chevy or a Daewoo? (For the record, it's a Daewoo, and not that reliable, to boot.) Beyond car makes, imported Chinese auto parts have had a poor reliability record over the past decade running the gamut of leaking tire valve stems to grenading transmissions.

Vehicles that are produced through co-ventures between Detroit automakers and Asian manufacturers have better quality control than vehicles manufactured by companies that were bought outright, and this looks like one of the factors that may save the American auto industry. For example, Toyota and Pontiac churned out identical Matrix and Vibe compacts in Ontario and the U.S.; however, the cheaper, Ontario-built Matrix has the better reputation for quality. On the other hand, Jaguar and Volvo quality declined when Ford bought the companies and Volvo is still struggling under new Chinese ownership. GM-owned Saab has gone bankrupt, although General Motors still pledges to honour all warranties on Saabs it sold. As for Daimler's shotgun wedding with Chrysler, apart from dissension, what did they really build together – certainly no innovative, high-quality products.

Sometimes choosing a higher trim line that packages many options as standard features will cost you less when you take all the features into account separately. It's hard to compare these bundled prices with the manufacturer's base price and added options in Canada, though, U.S. automaker websites often provide more details. All of the separate prices are inflated and must be negotiated downward individually, while fully equipped vehicles don't allow for options to be deleted or priced separately. Furthermore, many of the bundled options are superfluous, and you probably wouldn't have chosen them to begin with.

Minivans, SUVs and pickups, for example, often come in two versions: A base commercial (or cargo) version and a more luxurious model for private use. The commercial version doesn't have as many bells and whistles, but it's more likely to be in stock and will probably cost much less. And if you're planning to convert it, there's a wide choice of independent customizers that will likely do a better – and less expensive – job than the dealer. Of course, you will want a written guarantee from the dealer or customizer, or sometimes both, that no changes will invalidate the manufacturer's warranty. Also, look on the lot for a low-mileage (less than 10,000 km) 2013 demonstrator that is carried over unchanged as a 2014 version. You will get an end-of-model-year rebate, a lower price for the extra mileage, and sundry other sales incentives that apply. Remember, if the vehicle has been registered to another company or individual, it is no longer a demo and should be considered used and be discounted accordingly (by at least 25 percent). You will also want to carry out a CarProof (*www.carproof.com*) VIN search and get a complete printout of the vehicle's service history.

WHEN AND WHERE TO BUY

When to Buy

Start doing your research now, but wait until the first quarter of 2014 to get a more reasonable price. And shoppers who wait until next summer or early fall can double-dip from additional automakers' dealer incentive and buyer rebate programs. Honda, Nissan, and Toyota will likely pour the most money into sales incentives in an effort to recapture market share lost through reduced production during the natural disasters of 2011 and 2012. Remember, too, that vehicles made between March and August offer the most factory upgrades and fewer factory-related glitches.

Visit the showroom at the end of the month, just before closing, when the salesperson will want to make that one last sale to meet the month's quota. If sales have been terrible, the sales manager may be willing to do some extra negotiating in order to boost sales staff's morale.

Where to Buy

Large cities have more selection, and dealers offer a variety of payment plans that will likely suit your budget. Prices are also very competitive as dealers use sales volume to make most of their profit.

But, price isn't everything and good dealers aren't always the ones with the lowest prices. Buying from someone you know gives honest and reliable service is just as important as getting a low price. Check a dealer's honesty and reliability by talking with motorists in your community who drive vehicles purchased from the local dealer (identified by the nameplate on the vehicle's trunk). If these customers have been treated fairly, they'll be glad to recommend their dealer. You can also check the dealer's thoroughness in new-vehicle preparation and servicing by renting a vehicle for a weekend, or by getting your trade-in serviced.

How can you tell which dealers are the most honest and competent? Well, judging from the thousands of reports I receive each year, dealerships in small suburban and rural communities are often fairer than big-city dealers because they're more vulnerable to negative word-of-mouth testimonials and to poor sales – when their vehicles aren't selling, good service picks up the slack. Their prices may also be more competitive, but don't count on it. Unfortunately, as part of their bankruptcy restructuring, Chrysler and General Motors closed down many dealerships in suburban and rural areas because the dealers couldn't generate sufficient sales volume to meet the automakers' profit targets.

Dealers that sell more than one manufacturer's product line present special problems. Their overhead can be quite high, and the cancellation of a dual dealership by an automaker in favour of setting up an exclusive franchise elsewhere is an ever-present threat. Parts availability may also be a problem because dealers with two separate vehicle lines must split their inventory and may, therefore, have an inadequate supply on hand (read: Smart/Mercedes and former Mitsubishi/Chrysler partnerships).

The quality of new-vehicle service is directly linked to the number and competence of dealerships within the network. If the network is weak, parts are likely to be unavailable, repair costs can go through the roof, and the skill level of the mechanics may be subpar, since better mechanics command higher salaries. Among foreign manufacturers, Asian automakers have the best overall dealer representation across Canada, except for Mitsubishi and Kia.

Kia's dealer network is adequate and growing through strong sales after having been left by its owner, Hyundai, to fend on its own. Mitsubishi, on the other hand, was floundering several years ago, despite having a good array of quality products. Its major problem has always been insufficient product and a weak dealer network paired with outlets, like Chrysler, that sold other makes. As many dealers closed their doors when Chrysler and General Motors went bankrupt, Mitsubishi thought seriously of leaving the North American market. Instead, the company scurried around picking up abandoned dealers who hadn't been gobbled up by Hyundai, Kia, and Mazda. Fortunately, a surge during 2011-13 in small car sales has helped Mitsu's bottom line tremendously, forcing the automaker to rethink its North American strategy and stay put.

Except for the VW Group and BMW, European automaker profits aren't expected to grow much throughout 2013 as Europe's economic troubles cut auto sales by about 15 percent. Still, higher fuel prices, and the quest for better highway performers in North America are driving shoppers to small European imports like the BMW 1 Series and the European-based Ford Fiesta. Servicing, however, will continue to be problematic, inasmuch as many good mechanics left the business during the 2008-09 economic downturn.

Although it sells well in Canada, the $43,200 BMW 135i Coupe has had some serious reliability problems relative to the fuel and electrical systems, engine, and body fit and finish. Fuel and electrical deficiencies seem to be a common complaint among owners of other BMWs, as well.

Despite these drawbacks, you can always get better treatment by going to dealerships that are accredited by auto clubs such as the CAA or consumer groups like the Automobile Protection Association (APA) or Car Help Canada. Auto club accreditation is no ironclad guarantee that a dealership will be honest or competent; however, if you're insulted, cheated, or given bad service by one of their recommended garages (look for the accreditation symbol in a dealer's phone book ads, on the Internet, or on their shop windows), the accrediting agency is one more place to take your complaint to apply additional mediation pressure. And, as you'll see in Part Three, plaintiffs have won substantial refunds by pleading that an auto club is legally responsible for the actions of a garage it recommends.

Automobile Brokers and Vehicle-Buying Services

Brokers are independent agents who act as intermediaries to find the new or used vehicle you want at a price below what you'd normally pay. They have their smartphone contact lists, speak the sales lingo, know all of the angles and scams, and can generally cut through the bull to find a fair price – usually within days. Their services may cost a few hundred dollars, but you may save a few thousand. Additionally, you save the stress and hassle associated with the dealership experience, which for many people is like a trip to the dentist.

Brokers get new vehicles through dealers, while used vehicles may come from dealers, auctions, private sellers, and leasing companies. The broker's job is to find a vehicle that meets a client's expressed needs and then to negotiate its purchase (or lease) on behalf of that client. The majority of brokers tend to deal exclusively in new vehicles, with a small percentage dealing in both new and used vehicles. Ancillary services vary among brokers and may include such things as comparative vehicle analysis and price research.

The cost of hiring a broker can be charged either as a flat fee of a few hundred dollars or as a percentage of the value of the vehicle (usually 1-2 percent). The flat fee is usually best because it encourages the broker to keep the selling price low. Reputable brokers are not beholden to any particular dealership or make, and they'll disclose their flat fee up front or tell you the percentage amount they'll charge on a specific vehicle. Brokers employed to purchase cars in the States may charge a few thousand dollars, seriously cutting into the savings you may get from a lower purchase price. Seriously consider doing the transaction without a broker. It's that easy.

Finding the right broker

Good brokers are hard to find, particularly in western Canada. Buyers who are looking for a broker should first ask friends and acquaintances if they can recommend one. Word-of-mouth referrals are often the best because people won't refer others to a service with which they were dissatisfied. Your local credit union or the regional CAA office is also a good place to get a broker referral. For instance, Alterna Savings recommends a car-buying service called Dealfinder.

Dealfinder

For most buyers, going into a dealer showroom to negotiate a fair price is intimidating and confusing. Numbers are thrown at you, promises are made and broken, and after getting the "lowest price possible," you realize your neighbour paid a couple thousand dollars less for the same vehicle.

No wonder smart consumers are turning away from the "showroom shakedown" and letting professional buyers, like Ottawa-based Dealfinder Inc. (*www. dealfinder.ca*), separate the steak from the sizzle and real prices from "come-ons." In fact, simply by dealing with the dealership directly, Dealfinder can automatically save you the $200+ sales agent's commission before negotiations even begin.

For a $159 (plus tax) flat fee, Dealfinder acts as a price consultant after you have chosen the vehicle you want. The agency then shops dealers for the new car or truck of your choice in any geographic area you indicate. It gets no kickbacks from retailers or manufacturers, and if you can negotiate and document a lower price than Dealfinder gets, the fee will be refunded. What's more, you're under no obligation to buy the vehicle they recommend, since there is absolutely no collusion between Dealfinder and any manufacturer or dealership.

Dealfinder is a small operation that has been run by Bob Prest for over 19 years. He knows the ins and outs of automobile price negotiation and has an impressive list of clients, including some of Canada's better-known credit unions. His reputation is spread by word-of-mouth recommendations and the occasional media report. He can be reached by phone at 1-800-331-2044, or by e-mail at dealfinder@ magma.ca.

Hidden Costs: Freight Fees

Lemon-Aid has always cautioned new-car buyers against paying transportation and PDI (pre-delivery inspection) fees or suggested they be whittled down by about half. This advice worked well until a couple of years ago when charges ballooned to $1,400–$2,000 and automakers made them part of the MSRP instead of listing the item separately. When rolled into the MSRP, the freight charge/PDI often goes undetected, making it difficult to oppose or rollback the extra fee.

Interestingly, provincial and federal government agencies are pressuring car dealers and travel agencies to adopt a "truth in pricing" code, where all the "extra" fees and taxes are clearly indicated.

"FLEECING" BY LEASING

Why Leasing Costs More

In 2005 leasing represented 45 percent of all vehicle sales; now that figure has declined to less than 20 percent. Nevertheless, even though Detroit automakers have backed away from leases, leaving the market to the Asians and Europeans, it's still a fairly popular option, leading to 60-month leases and a proliferation of leasing deals on high-end sports and luxury cars and fully-loaded trucks and SUVs. Insiders say that almost all vehicles costing $60,000 or more are leased vehicles.

Yet, there are many reasons why leasing is a bad idea. It's often touted as an alternative used to make high-cost vehicles more affordable, but for most people, it's really more expensive than buying outright. Lessees usually pay the full MSRP on a vehicle loaded with costly options, plus hidden fees and interest charges that wouldn't be included if the vehicle was purchased instead of leased. Researchers have found that some fully loaded entry-level cars leased with high interest rates and deceptive "special fees" could cost more than what some luxury models would cost to buy. A useful website that takes the mystery out of leasing is *www.federal-reserve.gov/pubs/leasing* (see Leasing under the Consumer Information tab), run by the U.S. Federal Reserve Board. It goes into incredible detail comparing leasing versus buying, and has a handy dictionary of the terms you're most likely to encounter.

Decoding "Lease-Talk"

Take a close look at the small print found in most leasing ads. Pay particular attention to words relating to the model year, condition of the vehicle ("demonstration" or "used"), equipment, warranty, interest rate, buy-back amount, down payment, security payment, monthly payment, transportation and preparation charges, administration fees ("acquisition" and "disposal" fees), insurance premiums, number of free kilometres, and excess-kilometre charges.

Leasing Advantages

Experts agree: If you must lease, keep your costs to a minimum by leasing for the shortest time possible, by assuming the unexpired portion of an existing lease, and by making sure that the lease is close-ended (meaning that you walk away from the vehicle when the lease period ends) – an option used by 75 percent of lessees, according to the CAA.

Leasing does have a few advantages, though. First, it saves some of your capital, which you can invest to get a return greater than the leasing interest charges. Second, if you are taking a chance on a new model that hasn't been proven, you know that yours can be dumped at the dealer when the lease expires.

But taking a chance on an unproven model raises several questions. What are you doing choosing such a risky venture in the first place? And will you have the patience to wait in the service bay while your luxury lemon waits for parts or a mechanic who's ahead of the learning curve? Plus, suppose you want to keep the car after the lease expires. Your guaranteed buy-out price will likely cost 10-15 percent more than what the vehicle is worth on the open market.

Some Precautions and an Alternative

On both new and used purchases and leases, be wary of unjustified hidden costs, like a $495 "administrative" or "disposal" fee, an "acquisition" charge, or boosted transport and freight costs that can collectively add several thousand dollars to a vehicle's retail price. Also, look at the lease transfer fee charged by the leasing company, the dealer, or both. This fee can vary considerably.

Instead of leasing, consider purchasing used. Look for a three- to five-year-old off-lease vehicle with 60,000-100,000 km on the clock and some of the original warranty left. Such a vehicle will be just as reliable for less than half the cost of one bought new or leased. Parts will be easier to find, independent servicing should be a breeze, insurance premiums will come down from the stratosphere, and your financial risk will be lessened considerably if you end up with a lemon.

Breaking a Lease

Not an easy thing to do, and you may wind up paying $3,000-$8,000 in cancellation fees.

The last thing you want to do is stop your payments, especially if you've leased a lemon. The dealer can easily sue you for the remaining money owed, and you will have to pay the legal fees for both sides. You won't be able to prove the vehicle was defective or unreliable, because it will have been seized after the lease payments stopped. So there you are, without the vehicle to make your proof and on the receiving end of a costly lawsuit.

There are several ways a lease can be broken. First, you can ask for free Canadian Motor Vehicle Arbitration Plan (CAMVAP) arbitration (see page 134) if you believe you have leased a lemon. A second recourse, if there's a huge debt remaining, is to send a lawyer's letter cancelling the contract by putting the leasing agency and automaker on notice that the vehicle is unacceptable. This should lead to some negotiation. If this fails, inspect the vehicle, take pictures of any defects, have it legally tendered back to the dealer, and then sue for what you owe plus your inconvenience and assorted sundry expenses. You can use the small claims court on your own if the amount in litigation is less than the court's claim limit ($7,000 in Quebec; $25,000–$30,000 elsewhere).

The leasing agency or dealer may claim extra money when the lease expires, because the vehicle may miss some original equipment or show "unreasonable" wear and tear (dings, paint problems, and excessive tire wear are the most common reasons for extra charges). Prevent this from happening by having the vehicle inspected by an independent retailer and taking pictures of the vehicle prior to returning it.

BUYING THE RIGHT CAR OR TRUCK

Front-Drives

Front-drives direct engine power to the front wheels, which pull the vehicle forward while the rear wheels simply support the rear. The biggest benefit of front-drives is foul-weather traction. With the engine and transmission up front, there's lots of extra weight pressing down on the front-drive wheels, increasing tire grip in snow and on wet pavement. But when you drive up a steep hill, or tow a boat or trailer, the weight shifts and you lose the traction advantage.

Although I recommend a number of front-drive vehicles in this guide, I don't like them as much as rear-drives. Granted, front-drives provide a bit more interior room (no transmission hump), more car-like handling, and better fuel economy than do rear-drives, but damage from potholes and fender-benders is usually more extensive, and maintenance costs (especially premature suspension, tire, and brake wear) may be a bit higher than with rear-drives.

Rear-Drives

Rear-drives direct engine power to the rear wheels, which push the vehicle forward. The front wheels steer and also support the front of the vehicle. With the engine up front, the transmission in the middle, and the drive axle in the rear, there's plenty of room for larger and more durable drivetrain components. This makes for less crash damage, lower maintenance costs, and higher towing capacities than with front-drives.

On the downside, rear-drives don't have as much weight over the front wheels as do the front-drives and, therefore, they can't provide as much traction on wet or icy roads and tend to fishtail unless they're equipped with an expensive traction-control system.

Ford's rear-drive 2013 Mustang ($24,000) comes with a V6 that's almost as powerful as its earlier V8. Used, you can get it for $4,000 less with lots of warranty coverage remaining.

Four-Wheel Drive (4×4)

Four-wheel drive (4×4) directs engine power through a transfer case to all four wheels, which pull and push the vehicle forward, giving you twice as much traction. On most models, the vehicle reverts to rear-drive when four-wheel drive isn't engaged. The large transfer-case housing makes the vehicle sit higher, giving you additional ground clearance.

Keep in mind that extended driving over dry pavement with 4×4 engaged will cause the driveline to bind and result in serious damage. Some buyers are turning instead to rear-drive pickups equipped with winches and large, deep-lugged rear tires.

Many 4×4 customers driving SUVs set on truck platforms have been turned off by the typically rough and noisy driveline, a tendency for the vehicle to tip over when cornering at moderate speeds, vague or truck-like handling, high repair costs, and poor fuel economy.

All-Wheel Drive (AWD)

Subaru has used AWD since 1972, but it became a standard feature on all Subarus beginning with the 1996 lineup. AWD is four-wheel drive that's on all the time. The lone exception is the rear-drive BRZ introduced in 2012. Used mostly in sedans and minivans, AWD never needs to be deactivated when running over dry pavement and doesn't require the heavy transfer case that raises ground clearance and cuts fuel economy. AWD-equipped vehicles aren't recommended for off-roading because of their lower ground clearance and fragile driveline parts, which aren't as rugged as 4×4 components. But, you shouldn't be off-roading in a car or minivan in the first place.

SAFETY

Which Safety Features Are Best?

Automakers have loaded 2013-14 models with features that wouldn't have been imagined several decades ago, because safety devices appeal to families and some, like airbags, can be marked up by 500 percent. Yet some safety innovations, such as anti-lock brake systems (ABS) and adaptive cruise control (ACC), don't deliver the safety payoffs promised by automakers and may create additional dangers. For example, ABS often fail and are expensive to maintain, while ACC may slow the vehicle down when passing another car on the highway. Some of the more-effective safety features are head-protecting side airbags, ESC, adjustable brake and accelerator pedals, standard integrated child safety seats, seat belt pretensioners, adjustable head restraints, and sophisticated navigation and communication systems.

Seat belts provide the best means of reducing the severity of injury arising from both low- and high-speed frontal collisions. In order to be effective, though, seat belts must be adjusted properly and feel comfortably tight without undue slack. Owners often complain that seat belts don't retract enough for a snug fit, are too tight, chafe the neck, or don't fit children properly. Some automakers have corrected these problems with adjustable shoulder-belt anchors that allow both tall and short drivers to raise or lower the belt for a snug, more comfortable fit. Another important seat belt innovation is the pretensioner (not found on all seat belts), a device that automatically tightens the safety belt in the event of a crash.

Crashworthiness

A vehicle with a high crash protection rating is a lifesaver. In fact, crashworthiness is the one safety improvement over the past 40 years that everyone agrees has paid off handsomely without presenting any additional risks to drivers or passengers. By surrounding occupants with a protective cocoon and deflecting crash forces away from the interior, auto engineers have successfully created safer vehicles without increasing vehicle size or cost. And purchasing a vehicle with the idea that you'll be involved in an accident someday is not unreasonable. According to IIHS (see below), the average car will likely have two accidents before ending up as scrap, and it's twice as likely to be in a severe front-impact crash as a side-impact crash.

Since some vehicles are more crashworthy than others, and since size doesn't always guarantee crash safety, it's important to buy a vehicle that gives you the best protection from frontal, frontal offset, side, and rear collisions while keeping its rollover and roof-collapse potential to a minimum.

Two Washington-based agencies monitor how vehicle design affects crash safety: The National Highway Traffic Safety Administration (NHTSA) and the Insurance Institute for Highway Safety (IIHS). Crash information from these two groups doesn't always correspond because tests and testing methods vary.

NHTSA crash-test results for vehicles and tires are available at *www.safercar.gov/Safety+Ratings*. Information relating to safety complaints, recalls, defect investigations, and service bulletins can be found at *www.safercar.gov /Vehicle+Owners*. IIHS results may be found at *www.iihs.org/ratings*.

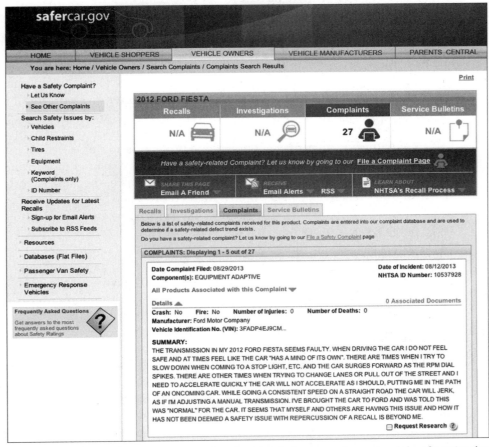

NHTSA's (*safercar.gov*) 2012 Ford Fiesta complaint log (above) gives you early warning and confirmation that a failure is the manufacturer's fault, widespread, and which fixes did or did not work. In this case, we see the same tranny glitch that also affects VW/Audi DSG dual-clutch units. This site is a great tool for negotiating settlements, or prompting recalls.

Don't get taken in by the five-star crash rating hoopla touted by automakers. Except for the Tesla electric car, few vehicles can claim a prize for being the safest. Vehicles that do well in NHTSA side and front crash tests may not do very well in IIHS offset crash tests, or may have poorly designed head restraints that can increase the severity of neck injuries. Or a vehicle may have a high number of airbag failures, such as the bags deploying when they shouldn't or not deploying when they should.

Before making a final decision on the vehicle you want, look up its crashworthiness and overall safety profile in Part Four.

Cars versus trucks

Occupants of large vehicles have fewer severe injury claims than do occupants of small vehicles. This was proven conclusively in a 1996 NHTSA study showing that collisions between light trucks or vans and small cars resulted in the car occupants having an 81 percent higher fatality rate than the occupants of the light trucks or vans.

Vehicle weight offers the most protection in two-vehicle crashes. In a head-on crash, for example, the heavier vehicle drives the lighter one backward, which decreases forces inside the heavy vehicle and increases forces in the lighter one. All heavy vehicles, even poorly designed ones, offer this advantage in two-vehicle collisions. However, they may not offer good protection in single-vehicle crashes.

Crash test figures show that SUVs, vans, and trucks also offer more protection to adult occupants than do passenger cars in most crashes because their higher set-up allows them to ride over other vehicles (Ford's 2002 4×4 Explorer lowered its bumper height to prevent this hazard). Conversely, because of their high centre of gravity, easily overloaded tires, and unforgiving suspensions, these vehicles have a disproportionate number of single-vehicle rollovers, which are far deadlier than frontal or side collisions. In the case of the early Ford Explorer, Bridgestone/Firestone CEO John Lampe testified in August 2001 that 42 of the 43 rollovers involving Ford Explorers in Venezuela were on competitors' tires – shifting the rollover blame to the Explorer's design and crashworthiness.

Interestingly, a vehicle's past crashworthiness rating doesn't always guarantee that subsequent model years will be just as safe or safer. Take Ford's Escort as an example. It earned five stars for front-passenger collision protection in 1991 and then earned fewer stars every year thereafter, until the model was discontinued in 2002. The Dodge Caravan is another example. It was given five stars for driver-side protection in 2000, but earned only four stars ever since, until taken off the market in 2007. The Grand Caravan, though, has consistently earned five stars in the same category.

Rollovers

Although rollovers represent only 3 percent of crashes (out of 10,000 annual U.S. road accidents), they cause one-third of all traffic deaths from what are usually single-vehicle accidents.

Rollovers occur less frequently with passenger cars and minivans than with SUVs, trucks, and full-sized vans (especially the 15-passenger variety). That's why electronic vehicle stability systems aren't as important a safety feature on passenger cars as on minivans, vans, pickups, and SUVs.

More Safety Considerations

Unfortunately, there will never be enough simple safety solutions to protect us from ourselves. According to NHTSA's figures, seat belts prevented 75,000 deaths between 2004 and 2008, while over 40 percent of passengers killed in accidents in 2007 were not wearing seat belts. NHTSA has also discovered that kids wear their seat belt 87 percent of the time if their parents do, and that 60 percent of children killed on the roads in 2005 were not wearing a seat belt.

Although there has been a dramatic reduction in automobile accident fatalities and injuries over the past three decades, safety experts feel that additional safety features will henceforth pay small dividends, and they expect the highway death and injury rate to start trending upward. They say it's time to target the driver. NHTSA believes that we could cut automobile accident fatalities by half through 100 percent seat belt use and the elimination of drunk driving. The entirely preventable epidemic of drunk driving is responsible for 33.8 percent of motor vehicle fatalities in Canada, according to a 2002 Transport Canada study (*www.tc.gc.ca/media/documents/roadsafety/tp11759e_2000.pdf*).

This means that safety programs that concentrate primarily on motor vehicle standards won't be as effective as measures that target both the driver and the vehicle – such as more sophisticated "black box" data recorders, more-stringent licensing requirements, including graduated licensing and de-licensing programs directed at teens and seniors, and stricter law enforcement.

Incidentally, police studies have shown that there's an important side benefit to arresting traffic-safety scofflaws. They often net dangerous career criminals or seriously impaired drivers before they have the chance to harm others. Apparently, sociopaths and substance abusers don't care which laws they break.

Beware of unsafe designs

Although it sounds hard to believe, automakers will deliberately manufacture a vehicle that will kill or maim simply because, in the long run, it costs less to stonewall complaints and pay off victims than to make a safer vehicle. I learned this lesson after listening to the court testimony of GM engineers, who deliberately placed fire-prone "sidesaddle" gas tanks in millions of pickups to save $3 per vehicle, and after reading the court transcripts of *Grimshaw v. Ford* (fire-prone Pintos) from 1981. Reporter Anthony Prince wrote the following assessment of Ford's indifference in an article titled "Lessons of the Ford/Firestone scandal: Profit motive turns consumers into road kill," *People's Tribune* (Online Edition), Vol. 26, No. 11, November 2000:

> Rejecting safety designs costing between only $1.80 and $15.30 per Pinto, Ford had calculated the damages it would likely pay in wrongful death and injury cases and pocketed the difference. In a cold and calculating "costs/benefits" analysis, Ford projected that the Pinto would probably cause 180 burn deaths, 180 serious burn injuries, [and] 2,100 burned vehicles each year. Also, Ford estimated civil suits of $200,000 per death, $67,000 per injury, [and]

$700 per vehicle for a grand total of $49.5 million. The costs for installing safety features would cost approximately $137 million per year. As a result, the Pinto became a moving target, its unguarded fuel tank subject to rupture by exposed differential bolts shoved into it by rear-end collisions at speeds of as little as 21 miles per hour [34 km/h]. Spewing gasoline into the passenger compartment, the car and its passengers became engulfed in a raging inferno.

And here are more recent examples of corporate greed triumphing over public safety: "Exploding" pre-1997 airbag designs that maim or kill women, children, and seniors; ABS that don't brake; flimsy front seats and seatbacks; the absence of rear head restraints; and fire-prone GM pickup fuel tanks and Ford cruise-control deactivation switches. Two other examples of hazardous engineering designs that put profit ahead of safety are failure-prone Chrysler, Ford, and GM minivan sliding doors and automatic transmissions that suddenly shift into Neutral, allowing the vehicle to roll away when parked on an incline or lose power on the highway.

Active safety

Advocates of active safety stress that accidents are caused by the proverbial "nut behind the wheel" and believe that safe driving can be best taught through schools or private driving courses. Active safety components are generally those mechanical systems, such as ABS, high-performance tires, and traction control, that may help a driver to avoid accidents if they're skillful and mature.

I am not a fan of ABS. The systems are often ineffective, failure-prone, and expensive to service. Yet they are an essential part of most systems' ESC, which is a proven lifesaver. Essentially, ABS prevents a vehicle's wheels from locking when the brakes are applied in an emergency situation, thus reducing skidding and the loss of directional control. When braking on wet or dry roads, your stopping distance will be about the same as with conventional braking systems. But in gravel, slush, or snow, your stopping distance will be greater.

The theory of active safety has several drawbacks. A recent study of seriously injured drivers at the Shock Trauma Center in Maryland showed that 51 percent of the sample tested positive for illegal drugs while 34 percent tested positive for alcohol (*www.druggeddriving.org/ddp.html*). Drivers who are under the influence of alcohol or drugs cause about 40 percent of all fatal accidents. All the high-performance options and specialized driving courses in the world will not provide much protection from impaired drivers who draw a bead on your vehicle. And, because active safety components get a lot of use – you're likely to need ABS 99 times more often than you'll need an airbag – they have to be well designed and well maintained to remain effective. Finally, consider that independent studies show that safe driving taught to young drivers doesn't necessarily reduce the number of driving-related deaths and injuries (*Lancet*, July 2001; 1978 DeKalb County, Georgia, Study):

The DeKalb Study compared the accident records of 9,000 teens that had taken driver education in the county's high schools with 9,000 teens that had no formal driver training. The final results showed no significant difference between the two groups. In other words, DeKalb County, Georgia, paid a large amount of money for absolutely no value.

Passive safety

Passive safety assumes that you will be involved in life-threatening situations and should be either warned in time to avoid a collision or automatically protected from rolling over, losing traction, or bearing the brunt of collision forces. Head-protecting side airbags, ESC, brake override systems, daytime running lights, and a centre-mounted third brake light are five passive safety features that have paid off handsomely in reduced injuries and lives saved.

Passive safety features also assume that some accidents aren't avoidable and that, when those accidents occur, vehicles should provide as much protection as possible to drivers, passengers, and other vehicles that may be struck – without depending on the driver's reactions. Passive safety components that have consistently been proven to reduce vehicular deaths and injuries are seat belts, laminated windshields, and vehicle structures that enhance crashworthiness by absorbing or deflecting crash forces away from the vehicle's occupants.

Driving while distracted is a major cause of automobile accidents that can be prevented by driver's using common sense (active safety) – which isn't very likely. Yet, the danger is real. For example, a driver talking with other passengers in the car is said to be the cause of 81% of auto crashes. Auto accident statistics show that other significant causes of car accidents are listening to or changing the radio stations (involved in 66% of all accidents) and talking on cell phones (25%).

Interestingly, a 2006 University of Utah study compared cell phone use to drunk driving (*www.distraction.gov/research/PDF-Files/Comparison-of-CellPhone-Driver-Drunk-Driver.pdf*). Researchers found impairments associated with using a cell phone while driving can be as profound as those associated with driving with a blood alcohol level at 0.08%.

What about stricter law enforcement? Don't get your hopes up. A 2010 study carried out by the Highway Loss Data Institute reviewed insurance claims in New York, Connecticut, and California and compared the data to other areas without cell phone bans. The conclusion? Laws banning the use of hand-held devices while driving did not reduce the rate of accidents in the three states and the District of Columbia (*www.cnn.com/2010/US/01/29/cellphone.study/index.html*).

SAFETY FEATURES THAT KILL

In the late '60s, Washington forced automakers to include essential safety features like collapsing steering columns and safety windshields in their cars. As the years have passed, the number of mandatory safety features increased to include seat belts, airbags, and crashworthy construction. These improvements met with public approval until quite recently, when reports of deaths and injuries caused by ABS and airbag failures showed that defective components and poor engineering negated the potential life-saving benefits associated with having these devices.

For example, one out of every five ongoing NHTSA defect investigations concerns inadvertent airbag deployment, deactivation of the front passenger airbag, failure of the airbag to deploy, or injuries suffered when the bag did go off. In fact, airbags are the agency's single largest cause of current investigations, exceeding even the full range of brake problems, which runs second.

Side Airbags – Good and Bad

Side and side curtain airbags are designed to protect drivers and passengers in rollovers and side-impact crashes, which are estimated to account for almost one-third of vehicular deaths. They have also been shown to help keep unbelted occupants from being ejected in rollovers. Head-protecting side airbags can reduce serious crash injuries by 45 percent. Side airbags without head protection reduce injuries by only 10 percent. Ideally, you want a side airbag system that protects both the torso and head.

Percent driver side airbag availability by protection area

		2012	2011	2010	2009	2008	2007	2006	2005	2004	2003	2002	2001	2000	1999	1998	1997	1996	1995
Head/torso	Standard	83.9	83.2	77.0	64.5	58.9	47.6	38.3	31.9	27.0	22.1	20.3	18.6	10.1	5.4	1.3			
	Optional	4.5	2.4	0.8	5.3	6.8	11.5	15.3	15.6	12.3	10.3	8.8	9.4	6.9	2.2				
Head only	Standard	7.6	7.4	10.4	11.9	9.8	3.7	1.9	1.8	1.7	1.5	0.4							
	Optional	1.7	2.8	2.2	6.9	9.7	15.1	14.8	13.6	8.4	6.2	3.7	1.4						
Torso only	Standard	.08	1.0	1.1	1.0	2.0	2.3	5.6	5.6	5.4	8.0	13.4	9.6	12.8	12.5	13.7	3.6		0.4
	Optional					0.1	0.1	3.3	5.7	10.8	10.9	4.6	4.3	2.4	2.6	1.9	0.4	1.3	
Not available		1.5	3.2	8.4	10.3	12.6	19.7	20.8	25.8	34.4	41.0	48.9	56.8	67.7	77.3	83.1	96.0	98.7	99.6

Source: IIHS at *www.iihs.org/ratings/side_airbags/side_airbags.aspx*

There's a downside to increased side airbag protection. Sit properly in your seat, or face serious injury from the deploying side airbag. Preliminary safety studies show that side airbags may be deadly to children or to any occupant sitting too close to the airbag, resting his or her head on the side pillar, or holding onto the roof-mounted assist handle. Research carried out in 1998 by safety researchers (Anil Khadikar of Biodynamics Engineering Inc. and Lonney Pauls of Springwater Micro Data Systems, *Assessment of Injury Protection Performance of Side Impact Airbags*) shows there are four hazards that pertain to most airbag systems:

1. Inadvertent airbag firing (short circuits, faulty hardware or software);
2. Unnecessary airbag firing (sometimes the opposite-side airbag will fire; the airbag may deploy when a low-speed side-swipe wouldn't have endangered occupant safety);
3. A small child, say, a three-year-old, restrained in a booster seat could be seriously injured; and
4. Out-of-position restrained occupants could be seriously injured.

The researchers conclude with the following observation, "Even properly restrained vehicle occupants can have their upper or lower extremities in harm's way in the path of an exploding [side] airbag."

The 1998 study and dozens of other scientific papers confirm that small or tall restrained drivers face death or severe injury from frontal and side airbag deployments for the simple reason that they are outside of the norm of the 5'8", 180-pound, male test dummy.

And don't forget NHTSA's side airbag warning issued on October 14, 1999:

> Side impact airbags can provide significant supplemental safety benefits to adults in side impact crashes. However, children who are seated in close proximity to a side airbag may be at risk of serious or fatal injury, especially if the child's head, neck, or chest is in close proximity to the airbag at the time of deployment.

Protecting yourself

Because not all airbags function, or malfunction, the same way, *Lemon-Aid* has done an exhaustive analysis of American and Canadian recalls, crash data, and owner complaints to determine which vehicles and which model years use airbags that may seriously injure occupants or deploy inadvertently. That data can be found in Part Four's model ratings.

Additionally, you should take the steps below to reduce the danger from airbag deployment.

- Buy a vehicle with head-protecting side curtain airbags for front and rear passengers.
- Make sure that seat belts are buckled and all head restraints are properly adjusted (to about ear level).
- Choose vehicles with head restraints that are rated "Good" by IIHS (see Part Four).
- Insist that passengers who are frail or short or who have recently had surgery sit in the back and properly position themselves away from side airbags.
- Ensure that the driver's seat can be adjusted for height and has tracks with sufficient rearward travel to allow short drivers to remain at a safe distance (over 25 cm (10 in.)) away from the bag's deployment and still be able to reach the accelerator and brake.

- Consider buying pedal extensions to keep you at a safe distance away from a deploying airbag if you are short-statured.

Top 20 Safety Defects

The U.S. government's online safety complaints database contains well over 100,000 entries, going back to vehicles made in the late '70s. Although the database was originally intended to record only incidents of component failures that relate to safety, you will find every problem imaginable dutifully recorded by clerks working for NHTSA.

A perusal of the listed complaints shows that some safety-related failures occur more frequently than others and often affect one manufacturer more than another. Here is a summary of the most commonly reported failures.

1. Sudden unintended acceleration
2. Total brake failure; wheel lock-up
3. Airbag malfunctions
4. Tire-tread separation
5. Electrical/fuel-system fires
6. Sudden stalling
7. Sudden electrical failures
8. Erratic transmission engagements
9. Unintended transmission shifts
10. Steering and suspension failures
11. Seat belt malfunctions
12. Collapsing seatbacks
13. Defective sliding doors and locks
14. Poor headlight illumination; glare
15. Dash reflecting onto windshield
16. Hood flying up
17. Wheel falling away
18. Steering wheel lifting off
19. Transmission lever pulling out
20. Exploding windshields

COMFORT

Do You Feel Comfortable in the Vehicle?

The advantages of many sports cars and minivans quickly pale in direct proportion to your tolerance for a harsh ride, noise, a claustrophobic interior, and limited visibility. Large minivans, SUVs and trucks often have awkwardly high step-ups, auto-regulated interior temperatures that range from Siberian to Death Valley, lots of buffeting from wind and passing trucks, and poor rear visibility. With these drawbacks, many buyers find that after falling in love with the showroom image, they end up hating their purchase – all the more reason to test drive your choice over a period of several days to get a real feel for its positive and negative characteristics.

Check to see if the vehicle's interior is user-friendly. For example, can you reach the sound system and AC controls without straining or taking your eyes off the road? Are the controls just as easy to operate by feel as by sight? What about dash glare onto the front windshield, and headlight aim and brightness? Can you drive with the window or sunroof open and not be subjected to an ear-splitting roar? Do rear-seat passengers have to be contortionists to enter or exit, as is the case with many two-door vehicles?

To answer these questions, you need to drive the vehicle over a period of time to test how well it responds to the diversity of your driving needs, without having some impatient sales agent yapping in your ear. If this isn't possible, you may find out too late that the handling is less responsive than you'd wanted and that the infotainment electronics create an Orwellian environment.

You can conduct a few showroom tests. Adjust the seat to a comfortable setting, buckle up, and settle in. Can you sit 25 cm (10 in.) away from the steering wheel and still reach the accelerator and brake pedals? Do the head restraints force your chin into your chest? When you look out the windshield and use the rear- and side-view mirrors, do you detect any serious blind spots? Will optional mirrors give you an unobstructed view? Does the seat feel comfortable enough for long trips? Can you reach important controls without moving your back from the seatback, or taking your eyes off the road? If not, shop for something that better suits your needs.

VEHICLES FOR OLDER DRIVERS

Drivers over 80 are the fastest-growing segment of the driving population. According to Candrive, the Canadian Driving Research Initiative for Vehicular Safety in the Elderly, there are currently about 3 million senior drivers in Canada, and their numbers are expected to double by 2040. A quarter of Canadians 85 and older now have a driver's licence, and 105 licences have been issued to centenarians in Ontario and Manitoba alone. By 2030, it's estimated that there will be roughly 15,000 centenarians driving in Canada – approximately three times as many as there are today. Husbands do the bulk of family driving, which usually involves short trips (11-17 km (6-10 mi) per day, on average) for medical appointments and visits to family, friends, and shopping malls. This puts older women, who tend to outlive their husbands, in a serious bind because of their lack of driving experience – particularly in rural areas, where driving is a necessity rather than a choice.

I'm 69, so I know that older drivers, like most other drivers, want cars that are reliable, relatively inexpensive, and fuel efficient. Additionally, we require vehicles that compensate for some of the physical challenges associated with aging (I'm getting fatter, slower, and much more taciturn, I'm told) and provide protection for accidents more common with mature drivers (side impacts, for example). Furthermore, as drivers get older, they find that the very act of getting into a car (sitting down while moving sideways, without bumping their heads or twisting their necks) demands considerable acrobatic skill. And don't even ask about shoulder pain when reaching up and over for the shoulder belt!

It seems each decade brings me new infirmities that I have to compensate for in my daily life. But, I'm *alive* – not a bad trade-off – when you consider the alternative.

Driving Through the Ages

Accident death rates are much higher for older occupants than for younger age groups. This is because our fragility increases as we age, and our ability to withstand the forces involved in crashes become much lower. Of course, our driving skills also deteriorate as we age, although most of us are reluctant to admit it.

- **At age 40:** Thought processing starts slowing down, multi-tasking becomes more difficult, night and peripheral vision worsens, and glare blinds you for a longer period of time.
- **At age 50:** Nine in 10 people use bifocals, reaction time slows, and distractions increase.
- **At age 60:** Muscle strength and range of motion decrease by as much as 25 percent. Hearing acuity is reduced.
- **At age 70:** Arthritic joints may make movement painful and restrict mobility, and conditions such as stroke, Parkinson's disease, hypertension, and diabetes may impair cognitive ability or affect behaviour.

Safety Features

So, how do we protect ourselves – from ourselves?

First off, older drivers need a better view of what's ahead, beside, and behind them. The driver's seat should be mounted high enough to give a commanding view of the road (with slower reaction times, seniors need earlier warnings), an expansive view of both sides, and a rear view unhampered by rear seat head restraints or a high deck lid. A camera-assisted rear-view is helpful when parking due to the limited range of neck rotation experienced by many older drivers.

Driver's seats must offer enough rearward travel to attenuate the force of an exploding airbag, which can be particularly hazardous to older or small-statured occupants, children, or anyone recovering from surgery. Adjustable gas and brake pedals are a must for short-legged drivers.

And while we're discussing airbags, remember that they are calibrated to explode during low-speed collisions (at less than 10 km/h (6 mph)) and that reports of injuries caused by their deployment are commonplace. Therefore, always put at least 25 cm (10 in.) between your upper torso and the steering wheel.

Look for handles near the door frame that can be gripped for support when entering or leaving the vehicle, bright dashboard gauges that can be seen in sunlight, and instruments with large-sized controls.

Remote-controlled mirrors are a must, along with adjustable, unobtrusive head restraints, and a non-reflective front windshield (many drivers put a cloth on the dash-top to cut the distraction).

As far as safety features are concerned, a superior crashworthiness rating is essential, as well as torso- and head-protecting side airbags, since most intersection collisions involving mature drivers occur when drivers are making a turn into oncoming traffic. The extra head protection can make a critical difference in side impacts. For example, Toyota's RAV4 with head-protecting side airbags earned a "Best Pick" designation from the IIHS. When tested without the head protection, it received a "Poor" rating in the side test.

Don't be overly impressed by ABS, since their proper operation (no tapping on the brakes) runs counter to everything you have been taught, plus they aren't that reliable. And make sure that the brake and accelerator pedals aren't mounted too close together.

Look for headlights that give you a comfortable view at night, as well as easily seen and heard dash-mounted turn signal indicators.

Ensure that the vehicle's knobs and switches are large and easy to identify and that the gauges are sufficiently backlit that they don't wash out in daylight. Also, be sure to check that the dash doesn't cause windshield glare (a common problem with light-coloured dash panels).

Having an easily accessed, full-sized spare tire and a user-friendly lug wrench and jack stand is also important.

Access and Comfort

I've been told that some drivers with arthritic hands have to insert a pencil into their key ring to twist the key in the ignition. Make sure your ignition lock doesn't require that much effort. Power locks and windows are a must, especially if the vehicle will be operated with hand controls. A remote keyless entry will allow entry without having to twist a key in the door lock.

A vehicle equipped with a buttonless shifter will be less difficult to activate for arthritis sufferers and drivers with limited upper-body mobility. Cruise control can be helpful for those with lower-body mobility challenges.

 Get a vehicle that's easy to enter and exit. Check for door openings that are wide enough to get into and out of easily, both for you and for any wheelchairs or scooters that may need to be loaded. Make sure the door catches when opened on a slight incline so that it doesn't close as you are exiting. If necessary, your trunk or rear cargo area should have a low liftover and room to stow your wheelchair or scooter. Bench seats are preferable because they're roomier and easier to access; getting a power-adjustable driver's seat with memory is also a good idea. Make sure the seat is comfortable and has plenty of side bolstering.

Forget minivans, unless you invest in a step-up, choose one with an easily reached inside-grip handle, and don't mind bumping the left-side steering-column stalk with your knee each time you slide into the driver's seat. Incidentally, GM's 2009 minivans offered a Sit-N-Lift option: A motorized, rotating lift-and-lower passenger seat that's accessed through the middle door and can be taken out when not needed.

Drivers with limited mobility, or those who are recovering from hip surgery, give kudos to the Cadillac Escalade SUV and GM Venture/Montana minivans; Toyota's Echo, Yaris, Matrix, and Avalon; and small SUVs such as the Honda CR-V, Hyundai Tucson, and Toyota RAV4. Of this group, only the discontinued GM minivans give me cause for concern, because of their poor reliability.

To help cover the costs of installing adaptive driving aids or mobility assistance equipment, the Toyota Mobility Program offers a $1,000 allowance to physically-challenged customers who purchase or lease a new Toyota vehicle. This allowance is in addition to any customer incentives that may be available from Toyota at the time of delivery.

Most people prefer the versatility of a van like the Toyota Sienna or the full-sized GM Express/Savana, but well-equipped smaller versions can accommodate the physically-challenged, just as well.

Qualified customers will receive a Toyota Mobility Program Allowance Application from the salesperson at the time of vehicle delivery. The applicant must present a record of their physically challenged condition, in the form of a doctor's note or government certificate. Customers then have up to four months to complete the application and return it to Toyota Canada, along with proof of vehicle modification in the form of a payment receipt or work order from the installer. Adaptive driving or passenger equipment includes, but is not limited to, wheelchair or other lift equipment, hand or other driving controls, and lifts or cart storage. Upon verification of the claim, a cheque will be mailed directly to the customer.

Adaptive Aids

For most people, driving a motor vehicle has become essential to the tasks of everyday living – commuting to work, running errands, or taking children to school for example – and synonymous with freedom, independence, and self-sufficiency. Driving in vehicle-congested areas is challenging enough for drivers without disabilities; for a person with a physical disability, driving to the local grocery store can be downright daunting. But it can be done. After rehabilitative assessment and evaluation, the driving needs of people with temporary or permanent disabilities can be accommodated through the use of adaptive vehicle equipment, safe driver training, or both.

Many persons with physical disabilities can safely drive using some of the considerable variety of adaptive devices available today. Some of these devices are found in almost all vehicles and are used by people with and without physical disabilities.

For example, some of the commonly found adaptive aids are:

- Left foot accelerator – eliminates left leg cross-over;
- Right hand turn signals – eliminate right hand cross-over;
- Foot pedal extensions – raise height of brake and accelerator pedals;
- Hand controls – operate horn, wipers, turn signals, dimmer switch; can also operate brake and accelerator;
- Steering devices – allow steering by spinner knobs, amputee ring, quad fork, or tri-pin;
- Custom seating – creates balance, positioning, and stability; and
- Lifts and ramps – permit access into and out of the vehicle.

Adaptive aids compensate for the disability or inability to perform the needed function. For example, if a driver is missing a right leg, a left foot gas pedal allows him to drive with his left foot.

Simple assistive devices are available to make driving safer and easier. Items such as seat belt adjusters, handibars, or expanded mirrors are available either in home catalogues or at medical supply or auto parts stores. Other items that do not require a specialist to install are easy-locking seat belts, visor extenders, steering wheel covers to improve grip, seat and back support cushions to relieve back pain or improve the ability to see over the steering wheel, keyless ignitions, and doors that automatically lock and open (see *www.colonial medical.com*).

To begin adaptive-on-the-road driving, a person should first become familiar with the current state-of-the-art adaptive vehicle equipment and rehabilitative driver training available in their province. A good place to start is by calling your local automobile dealer or e-mailing automobile manufacturers (with Google, put in the name of the car company followed by @ca or simply type GM Mobility, for example) or non-profit organization representing the physically handicapped. One Ottawa-based national group that works with many regional associations is: Independent Living Canada, 214 Montreal Road, Suite 402, Ottawa ON Canada K1L 8L8; Phone: 613/563.2581; TTY/TDD: 613/563.4215; E-mail: info@ilc-vac.

Where to Go for More Information

Another good source of information is the National Highway Traffic Safety Administration's brochure entitled "Adapting Motor Vehicles for People with Disabilities" found at *www.nhtsa.dot.gov:* select "Disability Information"). Here are some other websites that may be helpful.

- The National Mobility Equipment Dealers Association (NMEDA) supports the use of safe, reliable vehicles and modifications to enhance accessibility for people with special needs (see: *www.nmeda.org.*).

- The National Highway Traffic Safety Administration (NHTSA) addresses automotive safety issues for persons with disabilities (see: *www.nhtsa.dot.gov/ cars/rules/adaptive*).

- AAA "Safe Features for Mature Drivers" (see: *www.aaaexchange.com/Main/ Default.asp?CategoryID=18&SubCategoryID=86&ContentID=388*).

- AAA list of vehicles and their options suitable for seniors can be accessed at: *www.aaapublicaffairs.com/Assets/Files/20083211031180.SFMD-VehicleListv6.2.pdf*.

OTHER BUYING CONSIDERATIONS

When "New" Isn't New

Nothing will cause you to lose money more quickly than buying a new car that's older than advertised, has previously been sold and then taken back, has accident damage, or has had the odometer disconnected or turned back.

Even if the vehicle hasn't been used, it may have been left outdoors for a considerable length of time, causing the deterioration of rubber components, premature body and chassis rusting, or severe rusting of internal mechanical parts, which leads to brake malfunction, fuel line contamination, hard starting, and stalling.

You can check a vehicle's age by looking at the date-of-manufacture plate usually found on the driver-side door pillar. If the date of manufacture is 7/13 or earlier, your vehicle was probably one of the last 2013 models made before the September changeover to the 2014s. Redesigned vehicles or those new to the market are exceptions to this rule. They may arrive at dealerships in early spring or mid-summer and are considered to be next year's models. They also depreciate more quickly owing to their earlier launching, but this difference narrows over time.

Sometimes a vehicle can be too new and cost you more in maintenance because its redesign glitches haven't yet been worked out. As Honda's North American manufacturing chief, Koki Hirashima, so ably put it, carryover models generally have fewer problems than vehicles that have been significantly reworked or just introduced to the market. Newly redesigned vehicles get quality scores that are, on average, 2 percent worse than vehicles that have been around for a while, says J.D. Power. Some surprising poor performers have been the Honda Civic, Jaguar X-Type, Nissan Altima and Quest, and Toyota Corolla and Tundra.

Because they were the first off the assembly line for that model year, most vehicles assembled between September and February are called "first-series" cars. "Second-series" vehicles, made between March and August, incorporate more assembly-line fixes and are better built than the earlier models, which may depend on ineffective "field fixes" to mask problems until the warranty expires. Second-series vehicles will sell for the same price or less, but they will be a far better buy because of their assembly-line upgrades and more generous rebates. Service bulletins for Chrysler's new Caliber and Charger; GM's Solstice, Torrent, and Sky roadsters; and the Ford Fusion, Zephyr, and Milan show these vehicles all had serious quality shortcomings during their first year on the market. It usually takes a couple of years for the factory to get most of the quality glitches corrected.

There's also the very real possibility that the new vehicle you've just purchased was damaged while being shipped to the dealer and was later fixed in the service bay during the PDI. It's estimated that this happens to about 10 percent of all new vehicles. Although there's no specific Canadian legislation allowing buyers of vehicles damaged in transit to cancel their contracts, B.C. legislation says that dealers must disclose damages of $2,000 or more. In a more general sense, Canadian common-law jurisprudence does allow for cancellation or compensation whenever the delivered product differs markedly from what the buyer expected to receive. Ontario's revised *Consumer Protection Act* is particularly hard-nosed in prohibiting this kind of misrepresentation.

Fuel Economy Follies

Poor gas mileage is one of the top complaints among owners of new cars and minivans. Drivers say gas mileage is seldom as high as it's hyped to be; in fact, it's likely to be 10-20 percent less than advertised with most vehicles. (Gas mileage, measured in mpg, is the opposite of metric fuel consumption, measured in L/100 km. In other words, you want gas mileage to be high and consumption to be low.) *Consumer Reports* magazine once estimated that 90 percent of vehicles sold don't get the gas mileage advertised.

Why such a contradiction between promise and performance?

It's simple; automakers cheat on their tests. They submit their own test results to the government after testing under optimum conditions. Transport Canada then publishes these self-serving "cooked" figures as its own research. One Ford service bulletin is remarkably frank in discounting the validity of these tests:

> Very few people will drive in a way that is identical to the EPA [sanctioned] tests. These [fuel economy] numbers are the result of test procedures that were originally developed to test emissions, not fuel economy.

Stephen Akehurst, a senior manager at Natural Resources Canada, which tests vehicles and publishes the annual *Fuel Consumption Guide*, admits that his lab tests vehicles under ideal conditions. He says that actual driving may burn about 25 percent more fuel than what the government tests show. Too bad we never see this fact hyped in the automakers' fuel economy ads.

Keep in mind that although good fuel economy is important, it's hardly worth a harsh ride, excessive highway noise, side-wind buffeting, anemic acceleration, and a cramped interior. You may end up with much worse gas mileage than advertised and a vehicle that's underpowered for your needs.

If you never quite got the hang of metric fuel economy measurements using the Canadian Imperial gallon, click on the fuel conversion tool found at *www.euronet. nl/users/grantm/frans/fuel.html* to see how many miles to a U.S. gallon of gas your vehicle provides. A listing of the fuel consumption of all vehicles sold in Canada since 1995 is provided in miles per gallon and the metric Imperial gallon equivalent can be found at *oee.nrcan.gc.ca/transportation/tools/fuelratings/ratings-search.cfm*. A listing by city and province of gas prices can be found at *gasbuddy.com*. It lists the best and worst corner gas stations to buy fuel and is updated daily.

"Miracle" Fuels

The lure of cheap, "clean" fuel has never been stronger, and the misrepresentations as to the advantages of different fuels have never been greater. Take a look at the following list of flavour-of-the-month alternate fuels that have been proposed by politicians and businesses, and consider that, except for diesel, not a single other alternate fuel is economically viable.

Ethanol and flex-fuel vehicles (FFVs)

Ethanol is the trendy "fuel of the year" for automakers, oil companies, and politicians who have their heads stuck up their tailpipes. All three groups recite the mantra that increased ethanol use will cut fuel costs, make us less dependent on foreign oil sources (goodbye, Big Oil; hello, Big Corn), and create a cleaner environment. Unfortunately, this is simply not true. It's reminiscent of the misguided embrace of the 1997 Kyoto Accord by governments who promised they would be effective in cutting emissions that lead to global warming. Ironically, research now shows signatories to the Accord produce more emissions than non-signatories.

FFVs are all the rage with the Detroit Three, and they're being promoted over hybrids and diesel engines because the switchover is less costly for automakers. They only have to modify the fuel-delivery system on their vehicles and then lobby the federal government to pay billions of dollars for new pipelines, tankers, and gas stations. Millions of their vehicles are already on the market and can run on a mixture of 85 percent ethanol and 15 percent gasoline (called E85), but oil companies limit the supply of ethanol available because charging high gasoline prices is more profitable. Furthermore, governments won't pony up the billions of dollars needed to construct new ethanol pipelines (at an estimated cost of $1.6 million per km for 322,000 km) and to convert filling stations (at an estimated cost of $240,000 per new tank and pump) just to provide real competition for traditional gas-selling stations. At the moment, many E85 FFVs are gasoline-powered because few E85 commercial retailers can be found in Canada (only four stations existed in 2009), though there are over 1100 stations selling E10 (only 2,414 out of 168,987 filling stations sell E85 ethanol in the States). Yet the auto-makers get important tax credits because they have converted much of their production to run on ethanol fuel (in theory), though most of the vehicles stay on a pure gasoline diet or drink E10.

Indeed, ethanol is smokeless, burns cleaner, and (theoretically) leads to less engine maintenance. Plus, you can drink it (diluted, or with a chaser). But will the increased use of ethanol make North America much less dependent on gasoline? No way – not if you do the math. About 4 billion gallons of ethanol are produced annually in the U.S., but they burn an average of 140 billion gallons of gasoline each year.

Accepting that E85 filling stations are practically nonexistent and are expected to stay that way, here are some other jaw-dropping facts that ensure ethanol won't be the fuel of the future: The fuel costs almost as much as gasoline in some places (unless you distill it yourself); gas mileage *drops* by up to 30 percent when ethanol is used; cold-weather performance is mediocre; and the product is highly corrosive, with a particular fondness for snacking on plastic and rubber components.

Hybrids

After reading the CAA's findings that a 2010 Toyota Prius hybrid will cost slightly more to run than a $15,496 2010 Chevrolet Cobalt (see page 11), it's hard to comprehend how the $26,100 hybrid can be called a money-saver.

As practical as the promise of ethanol fuel for everybody seemed to be at first, hybrids use a pie-in-the-sky alternative fuel system that requires expensive and complex electronic and mechanical components to achieve the same fuel economy that a bare-bones Honda Civic can achieve for about two-thirds the cost of the Prius – and without polluting the environment with exotic toxic metals leached from battery packs and powertrain components.

Four years before the CAA findings, Consumer Reports tested six pairs of vehicles, with each pair including a conventional vehicle and the equivalent hybrid model, and published the astounding results in its April 2006 edition. *CR* found that in each category of car, truck, and SUV, the extra cost for the hybrid version was unacceptably *higher* than the cost of the same vehicle equipped with a conventional propulsion system.

Other disadvantages of hybrids are their mechanical and electronic com-plexities, dependence on specialized dealers for basic servicing, high depreciation rates and insurance costs, overblown fuel-efficiency numbers (owners report getting 40 percent less mileage than promised), and the $3,000 cost to replace their battery packs.

Finally, consider that Hybrid vehicles like the Toyota Prius use rare-earth minerals such as lanthanum, scandium, and yttrium mixed oxides and aluminas (which are used in almost all automotive emissions control systems). Neodymium is another rare element needed for the lightweight permanent magnets that power hybrid motors. It's a radioactive substance mined almost exclusively in China, which has threatened to restrict its sale for domestic use and slapped on heavy export duties. And there's a good reason why mining has been mostly restricted to China – the government there doesn't care if the mining and refining of these toxic minerals poisons the environment and sickens villagers – something North American "green" advocates overlook.

Western nations simply cannot afford to mine and refine neodymium within their borders due to the enormous environmental toxicity that mining it produces. In a sense, China is not cornering the neodymium market using their mineral reserves, but rather their willingness to sacrifice their environment and expose their populace to a higher cancer rate. In the end, North American motorists may trade a dependence on Middle Eastern oil for a troubling dependence on Chinese-sourced neodymium that's poisoning the Chinese people in the process.

Diesels

Diesel fuel is cleaner these days and far more fuel-efficient than ever before. Among the alternative fuels tested by independent researchers, diesel comes closest to the estimated fuel economy figures. It's also widely available and requires neither a steep learning curve in the service bay nor exotic replacement parts. Additionally, unlike hybrids, diesel-equipped vehicles are reasonably priced and hold their value quite well.

Except for Chrysler's Cummins diesel, most Detroit-made vehicles equipped with diesel engines are a big letdown. Owners report horrendously expensive maintenance costs, considerable repair downtime, and the worsening of the diesel's poor reliability trend, which was seen over the past decade with Ford's Powerstroke and GM's Duramax. Additionally, many of the diesel engines now require that owners regularly fill up with urea – an unexpected extra expense and annoyance.

To pee or not to pee? Recent model diesels, like the Mercedes' Bluetec, inject a urea solution – known as AdBlue – into the exhaust to reduces nitrous oxide (NOx) emissions. Audi, BMW, VW, and the Detroit Three also use urea injection under different names.

A yearly urea refill can be expected since the urea tank contains roughly 8 gallons (U.S.), which is good for about 19,300 km (12,000 miles) of standard operation. Generally, automakers will add the urea solution at every scheduled maintenance visit.

Mercedes-Benz Blutec diesels will not run if the urea tank doesn't contain a certain amount. If the tank reaches one gallon, the car notifies the driver. It does so again with only 20 starts remaining. To reset the system, at least two gallons of AdBlue – or four half-gallon bottles at $7.75 each – must be added. Not a lot to clean the environment, you say? Read on.

Consumer Reports was charged an outrageous $317 to put 7.5 gallons of AdBlue in its Mercedes GL320 test car at $32/gallon for the fluid, even though 7.5 gallons would only cost $116.25 in half-gallon bottles elsewhere. So, what can you do if your car or truck is urea-immobilized, there is no dealership around, or you refuse to pay through the nose for a simple fill-up?

That brings us back to our original question: "To pee or not to pee?"

Don't pee, at least not into the urea tank. Yes, human urine contains 2-4 percent urea, but modern diesels won't use your pee because it's too diluted and full of other substances like salts, toxins, bile pigments, hormones, and up to 95 percent water. AdBlue, TDI, and other urea products have a concentration of 32.5 percent urea mixed with deionized water. If you put anything else in the urea tank, your car or truck won't start.

Fuel economy misrepresentation

So if you can't make a gas-saving product that pours into your fuel tank or attaches to the fuel or air lines, you have to use that old standby and, well, lie. Hell, if automakers and government fuel-efficiency advocates can do it, why not dealers?

Fuel economy misrepresentation is actionable, and there is Canadian jurisprudence that allows for a contract's cancellation if the gas-mileage figures are false (see Part Three). Most people, however, simply keep the car they bought and live with the fact that they were fooled.

There are a few choices you can make that will lower fuel consumption. First off, choose a smaller version of the vehicle style you are interested in buying. Second, choose a manual transmission or an automatic with a fuel-saving fifth or sixth gear. Third, an engine with a cylinder-deactivation feature or variable valve timing will increase fuel economy by 8 and 3 percent, respectively.

Excessive Maintenance Fees

Maintenance inspections and replacement parts represent hidden costs that are usually exaggerated by dealers and automakers to increase their profits on vehicles that either rarely require fixing or are sold in insufficient numbers to support a service bay.

Alan Gelman, a well-known Toronto garage owner and co-host of Toronto AM740's "Dave's Corner Garage," warns drivers:

> There are actually two maintenance schedules handed out by car companies and dealers. The dealer inspection sheets often call for far more extensive and expensive routine maintenance checks than what's listed in the owner's manual. Most of those checks are padding;

smart owners will stick with the essential checks listed in the manual and have them done by cheaper, independent garages.

Getting routine work done at independent facilities will cost about one-third to one-half the price usually charged by dealers. Just be sure to follow the automaker's suggested schedule so no warranty claim can be tied to botched servicing. Additionally, an inexpensive ALLDATA service bulletin subscription (see Appendix IV) will keep you current as to your vehicle's factory defects, required check-ups, and recalls; tell you what's covered by little-known "goodwill" warranties; and save you valuable time and money when troubleshooting common problems.

Choosing a Reliable, Cheap Vehicle

Overall vehicle safety and body fit and finish on both domestic and imported vehicles are better today than they were three decades ago. Premature rusting is less of a problem, and reliability is improving. Repairs to electronic systems and powertrains, however, are outrageously expensive and complicated. Owners of cars and trucks made by General Motors, Ford, and Chrysler still report serious engine and automatic transmission deficiencies, often during the vehicle's first year in service. Other common defects include electrical system failures caused by faulty computer modules; malfunctioning ABS systems; brake rotor warpage; early pad wearout; failure-prone air conditioning and automatic transmissions; and faulty engine head gaskets, intake manifolds, fuel systems, suspensions, and steering assemblies.

Nothing shows the poor quality control of the Detroit Three automakers as much as the poor fit and finish of body panels. Next time you're stuck in traffic, look at the trunk lid or rear hatch alignment of the vehicle in front of you. Chances are, if it's a Detroit-bred model, the trunk or hatch will be so misaligned that there will be a large gap on one side. Then look at most Asian products. Usually, you will see perfectly aligned trunks and hatches without any large gaps on either side.

That, in a nutshell, is Detroit's problem, although, Ford has come a long way over the past few years improving fit and finish.

Detroit's "Good" Products

Don't get the impression that Detroit automakers can't make reasonably good vehicles, though. Ford's Mustang still gives you a big bang for your buck (some owners say that bang could be the Chinese-built manual transmission); GM's full-sized rear-drive vans are good buys; and its Acadia, Enclave, Equinox, Terrain, and Traverse SUVs also perform well,

General Motors' products are quite a mixed bag. Its full-sized vans, SUVs, small cars, and joint ventures with Toyota and Suzuki have all done well, but its recent mid-sized family cars (think Malibu and Impala) are mediocre, at best.

Most studies done by consumer groups and private firms show that, in spite of improvements attempted over the past two decades, vehicles made by Chrysler, General Motors, and (to a lesser extent) Ford still don't measure up to Japanese and some South Korean products, such as Hyundai, in terms of drivetrain quality and technology. This is particularly evident in SUVs and minivans, where Honda and Toyota have long retained the highest reliability and dependability ratings, despite some powertrain and brake deficiencies.

Chrysler

Chrysler doesn't have much product that's popular. It will be relying mostly on its new Fiat, the Chrysler 200, and its reworked Jeep Grand Cherokee. Nevertheless, like General Motors, it does have pockets full of cash thanks to the Japanese post-earthquake sales losses and many months of outstanding sales.

The Chrysler/Fiat merger has been a lifesaver for – Fiat.

This will be the crunch time to see if Detroit's weakest automaker can turn itself around and make these new models a success, without any more help from Mother Nature.

Don't buy a Chrysler unless it's a well-inspected Ram pickup with a manual transmission and a diesel engine. Rams so equipped can be excellent buys from a reliability and durability standpoint. As far as Jeeps are concerned, they are excellent off-roaders – when they aren't off-road at the repair bay.

Ford

Ford sold off most of its assets and borrowed billions of dollars just before the recession hit. The fact that it didn't go bankrupt means that Ford not only kept its own loyal customers and critical rural dealers but is also well poised to poach Chrysler, General Motors, Honda, Nissan, and Toyota sales.

Ford's management is only marginally less dysfunctional and more focused than Chrysler, while General Motors has improved dramatically. Moreover, the company has improved its quality control during the past several years and brought out popular new products like the Edge and Fusion. Lincoln's reliable and profitable Town Car will likely remain for a few more years as Ford's only rear-drive Lincoln, due to its popularity with seniors and fleet managers.

What models not to buy from Ford this year? The redesigned Explorer, for one. It was glitch-prone when first launched in 1990 and will likely be troublesome during the first year as a revamped model. Early tests by *Consumer Reports* point out that its powertrain runs roughly, the transmission is slow to downshift, and engine braking on hills is too abrupt. Overall handling isn't very agile, marked by slow steering response and limited road feedback, plus there's some body lean when cornering. Inside the cabin, the driver will find narrow seats with an under-sized bottom cushion, limited footroom and the gas and brake pedals positioned too close together. Finally, Ford's much-touted Sync-voice-command feature isn't user-friendly for giving simple commands.

General Motors

GM is back to making bundles of money, thanks to what's become a seller's market with the Japanese rebuilding their factories and re-jigging their supply lines and General Motors' outstanding sales in China (second only to VW). It intends to pay off most of its bailout debt this year and invest money in new products, as well as in better quality control of existing vehicles, which trail Ford for overall reliability and durability. The company's eight divisions have been whittled down to a more manageable four (it sold Saab, Hummer, and Saturn; and Pontiac has been successfully shut down).

Major quality deficiencies still affect most of General Motors' lineup, notably American-built front-drives and imported pickups. Owners cite unreliable powertrains, poor braking performance, electrical problems, and subpar fit and finish as the main offenders. The revamped 2014 Malibu looks bland and hasn't impressed most car critics, however this year's Impala has impressed most independent consumer groups.

The company's increased reliance on factories in China to build economy cars for North America is pretty scary. Imagine, not only are North Americans' bailout funds being used to create jobs in China, but we also will have the dubious pleasure of driving some of the worst-made automobiles in the world, imported from the country that sold us lead-laced-paint-coated kids' toys and poisoned pet food ingredients. Move over, Fiat! Here come the China-sourced Chery econobox and Brilliance luxury sedan – two cars that are cheap and not so crashworthy. (Don't just take my word that these are bad cars – watch the crash videos.)

An interesting conclusion relative to Chinese manufacturing, according to several independent studies – like those done by Christensen Associates, Inc. (*www.camcinc.com/library/SoYou'reBuyingFromChina.pdf*) and by Paul Midler in *Poorly Made in China: An Insider's Account of the Tactics Behind China's Production Game* (John Wiley & Sons, 2009) – is that safety and quality are trumped by price. Your car has no brakes? No problem. We'll give you a 10 percent discount and shoot the factory foreman.

Asian Automakers

Almost all of the Asian automakers make exceptionally good cars and weathered the poor 2008-2011 sales period better than most. The only exceptions are Mitsubishi,

Suzuki, and Kia; the first two automakers were crippled by an almost nonexistent dealer network and Suzuki had little product and an equally weak dealer body. Early this year Suzuki pulled out of Canada to concentrate upon other world markets.

Kia has done extremely well during the last two years selling its full lineup amid accolades for improved quality coming from independent auto reviewers. As for Hyundai, its parent company, sales are just as good and quality is a notch better. The Accent and Elantra are a big hit and good stand-ins for Honda, Mazda, Nissan, and Toyota small and family-sized cars.

Don't buy into the myth that parts for imports are overpriced or hard to find. It's actually easier to find parts for Japanese and South Korean vehicles than for domestic ones because of the large number of units produced, the ease with which relatively simple parts can be interchanged among different models, and the large reservoir of used parts available.

Sadly, customer relations have been the Japanese automakers' Achilles' heel. Dealers are spoiled rotten by decades of easy sales and have developed a "take it or leave it" showroom attitude, which is often accompanied by a woeful ignorance of their own model lineups. This was once a frequent complaint of Honda and Toyota shoppers, though recent APA undercover surveys show a big improvement among Toyota dealers.

There's no problem with discourteous or ill-informed South Korean automakers. Instead, poor quality has been their bugaboo. Yet, like Honda's and Toyota's recoveries following start-up quality glitches, Hyundai (South Korea's biggest automaker) has made considerable progress in bringing quality up almost to Toyota's and Honda's level.

Up to the mid-'90s, South Korean vehicles were merely cheap, poor-quality knock-offs of their Japanese counterparts. They would start to fall apart after their third year because of subpar body construction, unreliable automatic transmission and electrical components, and parts suppliers who put low prices ahead of reliability and durability.

Hyundai Accent: Cheap, reliable, and easily serviced.

Hyundai Elantra: All of the Accent's attributes, plus more power and interior room.

This was particularly evident with Hyundai's Pony, Stellar, Excel, and early Sonata models. During the past decade, though, Hyundai's product lineup has been extended and refined, and quality is no longer a worry. In fact, Hyundai's 2014 upscale Genesis is a top-performing $39,999 (watch out for the $1,800 freight fee) luxury sedan that's recommended by *Consumer Reports* and *Lemon-Aid*. Also, Hyundai's comprehensive base warranty protects owners from most of the more expensive breakdowns that may occur.

Hyundais are easily repaired by independent garages, and their rapid depreciation doesn't mean much; they cost so little initially, and entry-level buyers are known to keep their cars longer than most, thereby easily amortizing the higher depreciation rate.

Kia, a struggling, low-quality, small South Korean compact automaker bought by Hyundai in October 1998, has come a long way. At first, it languished under Hyundai's "benign neglect," as Hyundai spent most of its resources on its own cars and SUVs. But, during the past few years, Hyundai has worked hard to improve Kia reliability and fit and finish by using more Hyundai parts in each Kia redesign and by improving quality control on the assembly line.

A good rule of thumb at this stage is to stick with Kia small cars and the Sportage SUV. Give the other models time to incorporate better quality control. Kia's Forte, Optima, Rondo, Soul, and Sportage are the models with the fewest quality problems, while the Sorento and Sedona are riddled with drivetrain, electrical, brake, and fuel system defects, in addition to poor fit and finish.

European Models

Lemon-Aid doesn't recommend many European cars; there are way too many with serious and expensive quality and servicing problems. Heck, even the Germans have abandoned their own products. For example, a 2002 J.D. Power survey of 15,000 German car owners found that German drivers are happiest at the wheel of a Japanese Lexus. This survey included compact and luxury cars as well as off-roaders. Toyota won first place on quality, reliability, and owner satisfaction, while Nissan's Maxima headed the luxury class standings. BMW was the first choice among European offerings.

For those who feel the German survey was a fluke, there's also a 2003 study of

In Europe and North America, the BMW is the German sales leader ($42,450 BMW X3 shown above).

34,000 car owners with vehicles up to eight years old, published by Britain's Consumers' Association. It found that less than half of British owners would recommend a British-made Rover or Vauxhall to a friend. The most highly rated cars in the study were the Japanese Subaru, Isuzu, and Lexus; over 85 percent of drivers would recommend them.

And there's more. In 2005, Britain's Warranty Direct, a third-party warranty provider, checked the cost of repairs and reliability of 250 of the most popular models sold in the British Isles. It found the Honda Accord to be the most reliable and the Fiat Punto to be the least reliable in its survey. (Are you listening, Chrysler?) Overall, Asian cars fared best in reliability and cost of repair ratings.

Honda was the brand least likely to require repairs, with Mazda, Toyota, Subaru, Nissan, Mitsubishi, and Lexus all top-ranking. Smart, Mini, and Porsche were the only European nameplates in the top ten.

Another poor performer was Land Rover. It recorded a horrendous warranty claim rate of 47 percent in an average year. This was followed up by Renault and Saab, both with a 38 percent chance of requiring a repair in an average year, while Jeep scored similarly low on the reliability index. Other reliability "bottom feeders" were Audi, Volvo, Chrysler, and Mercedes-Benz.

Mercedes not "world-class"

Here's another surprise. Although it builds some of the most expensive cars and SUVs in the world, Mercedes' quality isn't always first class. After stumbling badly when it first launched its rushed-to-production American-made SUV for the 1998 model year, the automaker sent out many urgent service bulletins that sought to correct a surprisingly large number of production deficiencies affecting its entire lineup, including C-Class and, to a lesser extent, E-Class models.

Mercedes' executives admit that the company's cars and SUVs have serious quality shortcomings, and have vowed to correct them. But such a turnaround is complicated by M-B's huge financial losses from Chrysler and Smart. The "oh, so cute" Smart division has lost billions and doesn't compare with the more-refined and safer Asian competition.

While Mercedes sorts through its woes, shoppers who can't resist having a European nameplate should buy a VW Jetta (but not the cheapened base version).

Ready for another shocker? Volkswagen's quality is much better than Mercedes', and its sales have been on the upswing for a long time. Granted, VW has always been early on the scene with great concepts that have often been accompanied by poor execution and a weak servicing network – think hippy-era minivans and the Thing, a Jurassic-era compact SUV built on a Beetle platform and sold with a folding cloth top, removable doors and a bare-metal interior. (The Thing was discontinued in the U.S. after the 1974 model year, falling victim to federal vehicle safety standards and good taste.)

With its failure-prone and under-serviced Eurovan and Camper, the company hasn't been a serious minivan player since the late '60s, and VW's Rabbit and Golf small cars were resounding duds. Even the company's forays into luxury cruisers have been met with underwhelming enthusiasm and general derision.

But, Wolfsburg has bounced back during the past decade from both a quality and performance perspective. For 2014, VW's small cars and diesel-equipped models will continue to be strong sellers. Resale values are strong, and prices will be even more competitive via $1,000 cash rebates in North America to compensate for VW's mediocre sales in Europe.

Nevertheless, with European models, your service options are limited and customer-relations staffers can be particularly insensitive and arrogant. You can count on lots of aggravation and expense because of the unacceptably slow distribution of parts and their high markups. Because these companies have a quasi-monopoly on replacement parts, there are few independent suppliers you can turn to for help. And auto wreckers, the last-chance repository for inexpensive car parts, are unlikely to carry European parts for vehicles that are either more than three years old or manufactured in small numbers.

These vehicles also age badly after the five-year mark. The weakest areas remain the drivetrains, electronic control modules, electrical and fuel systems, brakes, accessories (including the sound system and AC), and body components.

Cutting Costs

Watch the Warranty

There's a big difference between warranty promise and warranty performance. Most automakers offer bumper-to-bumper warranties that are good for at least the first 3 years/60,000 km, and most models get powertrain coverage up to 5 years/100,000 km, although Mitsubishi offers a 5-year/100,000 km base warranty and a 10-year/160,000 km powertrain warranty. It's also becoming an industry standard for car companies to pay for roadside assistance, a loaner car, or hotel accommodations if your vehicle breaks down while you're away from home and it's still under warranty. This assistance may be for as long as five years, without any kilometre restriction. *Lemon-Aid* readers report few problems with these ancillary warranty benefits.

Don't buy a car that's warranty-dependent

If you pick a vehicle rated Recommended by *Lemon-Aid*, the manufacturer's warranty won't be that important and you won't need to spend money on additional warranty protection. On those vehicles that have a history of engine and transmission breakdowns, but the selling price is too good to turn down, budget about $1,500 for an extended powertrain warranty backed by an insurance policy. If the vehicle has a sorry overall repair history, you will likely need a $2,000 comprehensive warranty. But first ask yourself this question, "Why am I buying a vehicle that's so poorly made that I need to spend several thousand dollars to protect myself until the warranty company grows tired of seeing my face?"

Just like the weight-loss product ads you see on TV, what you see isn't always what you get. For example, bumper-to-bumper coverage usually excludes stereo components, brake pads, clutch plates, and many other expensive parts. And automakers will pull every trick in the book to make you pay for their factory screw-ups. These tricks include blaming your driving or your vehicle's poor maintenance, penalizing you for using an independent garage or the wrong fuel, or simply stating that the problem is "normal" and it's really you who is out of whack.

Part Three has all the answers to the above lame excuses. There, you will find plenty of court decisions and sample claim letters that will make automakers and their dealers think twice about rejecting your claim.

Don't pay for repairs covered by "secret" warranties

Automobile manufacturers are reluctant to publicize their secret warranty programs because they feel that such publicity would weaken consumer confidence in their products and increase their legal liability. The closest they come to an admission is to send out a "goodwill policy," "special policy," or "product update" service bulletin intended for dealers' eyes only. These bulletins admit liability and propose free repairs for defects that include faulty paint, air conditioning malfunctions, and engine and transmission failures.

If you're refused compensation, keep in mind that secret warranty extensions are, first and foremost, an admission of manufacturing negligence. You can usually find them in technical service bulletins (TSBs) that are sent daily to dealers by automakers. Your bottom-line position should be to accept a pro-rata adjustment from the manufacturer, whereby you, the dealer, and the automaker each accept a third of the repair costs. If polite negotiations fail, challenge the refusal in court on the grounds that you should not be penalized for failing to make a reimbursement claim under a secret warranty that you never knew existed!

Service bulletins are written by automakers in "mechanic speak" because service managers relate better to them that way. They're great guides for warranty inspections (especially the final one), and they're useful in helping you decide when it's best to trade in your car. Manufacturers can't weasel out of their obligations by claiming that they never wrote such a bulletin.

If your vehicle is passed warranty, show these bulletins to less-expensive, independent garage mechanics so they can quickly find the trouble and order the most recent upgraded part, ensuring that you don't replace one defective component with another.

Canadian service managers and automakers may deny at first that the bulletins even exist, or they may shrug their shoulders and say that they apply only in the States. However, when they're shown a copy, they usually find the appropriate Canadian part number or bulletin in their files. The problems and solutions don't change from one side of the border to another. Imagine American and Canadian tourists' cars being towed across the border because each country's technical service bulletins were different? Mechanical fixes do differ in cases where, for example, a bulletin is for California only, or it relates to a safety or emissions component used only in the U.S. But these instances are rare, indeed. What is quite gratifying is to see some automakers, like Honda, candidly admit in their bulletins that "goodwill" repair refunds are available. What a shame other automakers aren't as forthcoming!

The best way to get bulletin-related repairs carried out is to visit the dealer's service bay and to attach the specific ALLDATA-supplied service bulletin covering your vehicle's problems to a work order.

Getting your vehicle's service bulletins

Free summaries of automotive recalls and technical service bulletins listed by year, make, model, and engine can be found at the ALLDATA (*www.alldata.com/TSB*) and NHTSA (*www.safercar.gov*) websites. But, like the NHTSA summaries, ALLDATA's summaries are so short and cryptic that they're of limited use. You can download the complete contents of all the bulletins applicable to your vehicle from ALLDATA at *www.alldatadiy.com* if you pay the $26.95(U.S.) annual subscription fee. Many bulletins offering "secret warranty" coverage are reproduced in Part Four. (See below for sample bulletin summaries for the 2013 Dodge Grand Caravan minivan and the Chevrolet Silverado 1500.)

2013 Dodge Grand Caravan V6-3.6L

TSB Number	TSB Date ▼	TSB Title
23-014-13A	04/19/2013	Body – Sunroof Opens but Won't Close, Cycle Back to Open
08-016-13	03/19/2013	Collision Avoidance – Blind Spot Monitor ON or Flashing
18-007-13A	03/06/2013	Fuel System – MIL ON, DTC P0300, Engine Runs Rough
17-003-13	02/08/2013	Suspension – Rear End Noise at Low Speeds on Uneven Surfaces
09-001-13	02/06/2013	Engine – Gasoline Engine Diagnostic Inspection Procedure
CAN-M38	02/04/2013	Canada – Campaign – ECM Update for Improved A/T Shift Quality
M38	02/04/2013	Campaign – ECM Update for Improved A/T Shift Quality
23-003-13A	01/29/2013	Interior – Rear Speaker Bolster Raised at Quarter Panel Trim
31-001-13	01/11/2013	Body – Paint Overspray Removal Procedures
21-012-12B	11/29/2012	A/T, Engine Controls – A/T Shift Improvements
08-053-12	11/15/2012	Audio, Cell Phone – Various Issues, Complaints
08-059-12	10/23/2012	Body – Power Sliding Door Won't Close/Clicking Noises

TSB Number	TSB Date ▼	TSB Title
31-007-12	08/14/2012	Body/Frame – Welded Sheet Metal Repairs and Replacements
31-005-12	08/03/2012	Body – Don't Apply Corrosion Protection on Plastic Panels
31-004-12	07/27/2012	Body – Front Bumper Fascia Repair for License Bracket Holes
09-001-12	06/27/2012	Engine – Oil Consumption Guideline

For over two decades, Chrysler minivan sliding doors open when they should close, and close when they should open, injuring adults and children. The tragedy is that this danger is industry-wide and affects particularly Ford, GM, Honda, Nissan, and Toyota minivans. Look at the *Sharman* court decision against the Ford Windstar sliding door in Part Three. There, a former customer relations agent for Ford in Oakville, won punitive damages for the "mental distress" caused by driving his children in a minivan with doors that could open at anytime. He no longer works at Ford.

2013 Chevy Truck Silverado 1500 2WD V6-4.3L

TSB Number	TSB Date ▼	TSB Title
06-03-09-004E	05/03/2013	Suspension – Squeaking Noise from Rear of Vehicle
99-04-20-002H	04/11/2013	Drivetrain – Information on Driveline Clunk Noise
12-08-132-001A	03/26/2013	Electrical – Power Outlet and Trailer Lighting Fuse Replacement
10-08-61-001C	03/22/2013	Body – Body Mounts Stripped, Will Not Loosen
13-08-116-001A	03/22/2013	Electrical – Aftermarket Interface Devices Causing Issues
06-00-89-029I	03/22/2013	Interior – Cleaning Instrument Panel, Interior Trim
00-03-10-002G	03/04/2013	Wheels – Chromed Aluminum Wheel Staining/Pitting/Corrosion
06-08-44-012F	02/28/2013	Navigation System – DVD Navigation Update Program
99-08-51-001C	02/25/2013	Body – Paint-less Dent Repair Process
12-02-32-001A	02/21/2013	Steering – Fluid Leak at Hose Connection to Rack
10-08-45-001D	02/14/2013	Electrical – Ground Repair Information
06-08-43-003D	02/12/2013	Wipers/Washers – Windshield Wiper Performance Information
09-08-57-002D	02/04/2013	Body/Frame – General Water Leak Diagnostic Guide
00-03-10-006I	01/28/2013	Tires/Wheels – Information on Tire Radial Force Variation (RFV)
08-08-48-00G	01/28/2013	Body – Tapping/Clicking/Ticking Noise at Windshield Area
08-08-51-002A	01/16/2013	Body – Pre-Painting/Cleaning Process for TPO Plastic Fascias
09-08-66-011B	01/16/2013	Body – Pickup Box Accessory Mounting Points

TSB Number	TSB Date ▼	TSB Title
12331A	01/04/2013	Recall – Steering Column Replacement
NHTSA13V001000	01/02/2013	Recall 13V001000 – Steering Column Replacement
11-00-90-001A	12/21/2012	Engine – GM Dexos 1(R) and Dexos 2(R) Oil Specifications/Info
11-00-90-001A	12/20/2012	Engine – GM Dexos 1(R) and 2(R) Oil Specifications
12-03-10-003	12/07/2012	Wheels/Tires – Vibration Issue Diagnostic Tips
08-08-46-004A	11/30/2012	Electrical – Aftermarket Devices May Interfere with OnStar(R)
00-00-89-027G	11/28/2012	Interior – Eliminating Unwanted Odours in Vehicles
12-03-10-002	11/26/2012	Wheels/Tires – Proper Wheel Installation/Wheel Torque Technique
10-00-89-010B	11/13/2012	Locks – Key Code Security Rules, Key Code Look Up
10-05-23-001C	10/29/2012	Brakes – Vibration/Rumble on Downhill Braking
07-08-42-006G	10/16/2012	Body Controls – BCM Update for Bulb Outage Detection
12-06-01-008A	09/27/2012	Vehicle – Engine and Sub Systems Flushing Info (CANADA)
04-06-01-029G	09/27/2012	Vehicle – Engine and Sub-Systems Flushing Recommendations
05-03-10-020D	09/18/2012	Wheels/Tires – Use of Nitrogen Gas in Tires
07-08-49-020G	09/17/2012	Instruments – IPC Odometer Programming Method
00-00-90-002K	09/14/2012	Tires – Information on Proper Tire Pressure
03-06-04-030H	08/28/2012	Fuel System – Driveability Concerns/MIL ON/Multiple DTCs
12-02-32-003	08/09/2012	Suspension/Steering – Pop, Click, or Clunk Noise at Low Speeds
06-08-64-027K	08/07/2012	Body – LH/RH Outside Rearview Mirror Glass Shake/Flutter
03-03-10-007G	07/13/2012	Tires/Wheels – OE Tire Shake/Vibration Information
10-08-44-004B	06/26/2012	Audio – Information on USB/Multimedia Player
09-08-44-013D	06/26/2012	Audio System – USB/Multimedia Interface Information
00-06-01-012D	10/25/2011	Engine – Use of 'Surface Conditioning Disks'

For over three decades, GM is unique in telling owners a tranny shift clunk noise is "normal."
Also, its steering fluid leak bulletin covers most 2007-13 trucks and SUVs. Seven model years.
How's that for a confidence-builder?

Trim Insurance Costs

Insurance premiums can average between $900 and $2,000 per year, depending on the type of vehicle you own, your personal statistics and driving habits, and whether you can obtain coverage under your family policy.

There are some general rules to follow when looking for insurance savings. For example, vehicles older than five years do not necessarily need collision coverage, and you may not need loss-of-use coverage or a rental car. Other factors that should be considered are noted below.

- When you phone for quotes, make sure you have your serial number in hand. Many factors, such as the make of the car, the number of doors, if there's a sports package, and the insurer's experience with the car, can affect the quote. And be honest, or you'll find your claim denied, the policy cancelled, or your premium cost boosted.

- Where you live and work also determine how much you pay. In the past, auto insurance rates have been 25-40 percent lower in London, Ontario, than in downtown Toronto because there are fewer cars in London and fewer kilometres to drive to work. Similar disparities are found in B.C. and Alberta.

- Taking a driver-training course can save you thousands of premium dollars.

- You may be able to include your home or apartment insurance as part of a premium package that's eligible for additional discounts.

InsuranceHotline.com, based in Ontario but with quotes for other provinces, says that it pays to shop around for cheap auto insurance rates. The group has found that the same insurance policy could vary in cost by a whopping 400 percent.

In Part Two, we take a closer look at reducing your insurance premium through avoiding "captive" insurance brokers, buying the right kind of vehicle, and getting your insurance coverage from online underwriters. Plus, tips for staying off the list of cars that thieves adore. (See page 94.)

"Hidden" Costs

Depreciation

Depreciation is the biggest – and most often ignored – expense that you encounter when you trade in your vehicle or when an accident forces you to buy another vehicle before the depreciated loss can be amortized. Most new cars depreciate a whopping 30-45 percent during the first two years of ownership.

The best way to use depreciation rates to your advantage is to choose a vehicle listed as being both reliable and economical to own and then keep it for ten years or more. Generally, by choosing a lower-depreciating vehicle – such as one that keeps at least half its value over four years – you are storing up equity that will give you a bigger down payment and fewer loan costs with your next purchase.

Gas Pains

With gas prices once again headed toward the $1.30 a litre mark, motorists are scratching their heads trying to find easy ways to cut gas consumption. Here are three simple suggestions (and 20 more tips are found in Appendix II).

1. Buy a used compact car for half its original price. Savings on taxes, freight fees, and depreciation is about $15,000.
2. Find low-cost fuel referrals on the Internet (*www.gasbuddy.com*). You can save about 15 cents a litre.
3. Keep your vehicle properly tuned for a 10 percent savings from improved fuel economy.

More dirt on diesels

The only reasons to buy a diesel-equipped vehicle are for their potential to deliver outstanding fuel economy and for their much lower maintenance and repair costs when compared with similar-sized vehicles powered by gasoline engines. Unfortunately, independent data suggests that both claims by automakers may be false.

Let's examine the fuel-savings issue first. In theory, when compared with gasoline powerplants, diesel engines are up to 30 percent more efficient in a light vehicle and up to 70 percent cheaper to run in a heavy-duty towing and hauling truck or SUV. They become more efficient as the engine load increases, whereas gasoline engines become less so. This is the main reason diesels are best used where the driving cycle includes a lot of city driving – slow speeds, heavy loads, frequent stops, and long idling times. At full throttle, both engines are essentially equal from a fuel-efficiency standpoint. The gasoline engine, however, leaves the diesel in the dust when it comes to high-speed performance.

On the downside, fleet administrators and owners report that diesel fuel economy in real driving situations is much less than what's advertised – a complaint also voiced by owners of hybrids. Many owners say that their diesel-run rigs get about 30 percent less mileage than what the manufacturer promised.

Also undercutting fuel-savings claims is the fact that, in some regions, the increased cost of diesel fuel – because of high taxes and oil company greed, some say – makes it more expensive than regular fuel.

The diesel engine's reputation for superior reliability may have been true in the past, but no longer. This fact is easily confirmed if you cross-reference owner complaints with confidential automaker service bulletins and independent industry polling results put out by J.D. Power and others, a task done for you in Part Four's ratings section.

Many owners of diesel-equipped vehicles are frustrated by chronic breakdowns, excessive repair costs, and poor road performance. It's practically axiomatic that bad injectors have plagued Ford Power Stroke, GM Duramax engines, and (to a lesser extent) Dodge Cummins diesels.

In the past, defective injectors were often replaced at the owner's expense and at a cost of thousands of dollars. Now, General Motors and Ford are using "secret warranty" programs to cover replacement costs long after the base warranty has expired (11-13 years). Chrysler has been more recalcitrant in making payouts, apparently because fewer vehicles may be involved and costs can be quite high (expensive lift pumps and injectors may be faulty).

Hybrid cars

Automakers are offering hybrid vehicles, like the Toyota Prius and Honda Civic and Accord, that use an engine/electric motor for maximum fuel economy and low emissions while providing the driving range of a comparable small car. Yet this latest iteration of the electric car still has serious drawbacks, which may drive away even the most green-minded buyers.

- Real-world fuel consumption may be 20 percent higher than advertised.
- Cold weather and hilly terrain can cut fuel economy by almost 10-30 percent.
- AC and other options can increase fuel consumption even more.
- Interior cabin heat may be insufficient.
- Electrical systems can deliver a life-threatening 275-500 volts if tampered with through incompetent servicing or during an emergency rescue.
- Battery packs can cost up to $3,000(U.S.), and fuel savings almost equal the hybrid's extra costs only after about 32,000 km of use.
- Hybrids cost more to insure, and they depreciate just as quickly as non-hybrid vehicles that don't have expensive battery packs to replace.
- Hybrids make you a captive customer where travel is dependent on available service facilities.

If you find the limitations of an electric hybrid too daunting, why not simply buy a more fuel-efficient small car? Or, get a comfortable higher line of used car? Here are some environmentally friendly cars recommended by Toronto-based Environmental Defence Canada (*www.environmentaldefence.ca)* and by *Lemon-Aid*:

- Honda Civic and Fit
- Hyundai Accent and Tucson
- Mazda3 and Mazda5
- Nissan Sentra and Versa (although the Versa received a two-star crash rating)
- Toyota Corolla and Yaris
- VW Golf/Jetta TDI

Test for "Real" Performance

Take the phrase "car-like handling" with a large grain of salt. A van isn't supposed to handle like a car. Since many rear-drive models are built on a modified truck chassis and use steering and suspension components from their truck divisions, they tend to handle more like trucks than cars, in spite of automakers' claims to the contrary. Also, what you see isn't necessarily what you get when you buy or lease a new sport-utility, van, or pickup, because these vehicles seldom come with enough standard features to fully exploit their versatility. Additional expensive options are usually a prerequisite to make them safe and comfortable to drive or capable of towing heavy loads. Consequently, the term "multipurpose" is a misnomer unless you are prepared to spend extra dollars to outfit your car or minivan. Even fully equipped, these vehicles don't always provide the performance touted by automakers.

Rust Protection

Most vehicles built today are much less rust-prone than they were several decades ago, thanks to more-durable body panels and better designs. When rusting occurs now, it's usually caused by excessive environmental stress (road salt, etc.), a poor paint job, or the use of new metal panels that create galvanic corrosion or promote early paint peeling – the latter two causes being ones that are excluded from most rustproofing warranties.

Invest in undercoating, and remember that the best rustproofing protection is to park the vehicle in a dry, unheated garage or under an outside carport and then wash it every few weeks. Never bring it in and out of a heated garage during the winter months, since it is most prone to rust when temperatures are just a bit above freezing; keep it especially clean and dry during that time. If you live in an area where roads are heavily salted in winter, or in a coastal region, have your vehicle's undercoating sprayed annually.

Annual undercoating, which costs around $150, will usually do as good a job as rustproofing. It will protect vital suspension and chassis components, make the vehicle ride more quietly, and allow you to ask a higher price at trade-in time. The only downside, which can be checked by asking for references, is that the undercoating may give off an unpleasant odour for months, and it may drip, soiling your driveway.

Whether you are rustproofing the entire vehicle or just undercoating key areas, make sure to include the rocker panels (make a small mark inside the door panels on the plastic hole plugs to make sure that they were removed and that the inside was actually sprayed), the rear hatch's bottom edge, the tailgate, and the wheelwells. It's also a smart idea to stay at the garage while some of the work is being done to see that the overspray is cleaned up and all areas have been covered.

SURVIVING THE OPTIONS JUNGLE

The best options for your buck are a 5- or 6-speed automatic transmission, an anti-theft immobilizer, air conditioning, a premium sound system, and higher-quality tires – features that may bring back one-third to half their value come trade-in time. Rustproofing can also make cars easier to sell in some provinces where there's lots of salt on the roads in the winter, but paint protection and seat sealants are a waste of money. Most option packages can be cut by 20 percent, while extended warranties are overpriced by about 75 percent.

Dealers make more than three times as much profit selling options as they do selling most cars (50 percent profit versus 15 percent profit). No wonder their eyes light up when you start perusing their options list. If you must have some options, compare prices with independent retailers and buy where the price is lowest and the warranty is the most comprehensive. Buy as few options as possible from the dealer, since you'll get faster service, more comprehensive guarantees, and lower prices from independent suppliers. Remember, extravagantly equipped vehicles hurt your pocketbook in three ways: They cost more to begin with but return only a fraction of what they cost when the car is resold; they drive up maintenance costs; and they often consume extra fuel.

A heavy-duty battery and suspension, and perhaps an upgraded sound system, will generally suffice for American-made vehicles; most imports already come well equipped. An engine block heater with a timer isn't a bad idea, either. It's an inexpensive investment that ensures winter starting and reduces fuel consumption by allowing you to start out with a semi-warm engine.

When ordering parts, remember that purchases from American outlets can be slapped with a small customs duty if the part isn't made in the U.S. And then you'll pay the inevitable GST or HST levied on the part's cost and customs duty. Finally, your freight carrier may charge a $15-$20 brokerage fee for representing you at the border.

Smart Options

The problem with options is that you often can't refuse them. Dealers sell very few bare-bones cars and minivans, and they option-pack each vehicle with features that can't be removed. You'll be forced to dicker over the total cost of what you are offered, whether you need the extras or not. So it isn't a case of "yes" or "no," but more a decision of "at what cost?"

Adjustable Pedals and Extensions

This device moves the brake and accelerator pedals forward or backward about 10 cm (4 in.) to accommodate short-statured drivers and protect them from airbag-induced injuries.

If the manufacturer of your vehicle doesn't offer optional power-adjustable pedals, there are several companies selling inexpensive pedal extensions through the Internet; for example, go to HDS Specialty Vehicles' website at *hdsmn.stores.yahoo.net*. If you live in Toronto or London, Ontario, check out Kino Mobility (*www.kinomobility.com*).

Adjustable Steering Wheel

This option allows easier access to the driver's seat and permits a more-comfortable driving position. It's particularly useful if more than one person will drive the vehicle.

Air Conditioning

AC systems are far more reliable than they were a decade ago, and they have a lifespan of five to seven years. Sure, replacement and repair costs can hit $1,000, but that's very little when amortized over an eight- to ten-year period. AC also makes your car easier to resell.

Does AC waste or conserve fuel when a vehicle is driven at highway speeds? Edmunds, a popular automotive information website, conducted fuel-efficiency tests and concluded that there wasn't that much difference between open or closed windows, a finding confirmed by *Consumer Reports*. See *www.edmunds.com/advice/ fueleconomy/articles/106842/article.html*:

> While the A/C compressor does pull power from the engine wasting some gas, the effect appears to be fairly minimal in modern cars. And putting the windows down tends to increase drag on most cars, canceling out any measurable gain from turning the A/C off. But this depends on the model you're driving. When we opened the sunroof in our SUV, the mileage did decrease even with the A/C off. Still, in our experience, it's not worth the argument because you won't save a lot of gas either way. So just do what's comfortable.

AC provides extra comfort, reduces wind noise (from not having to roll down the windows), and improves window defogging. Factory-installed units are best, however, because you'll get a longer warranty and improve your chances that everything was installed properly.

Anti-Theft Systems

You'd be a fool not to buy an anti-theft system, including a lockable fuel cap, for your much-coveted-by-thieves Japanese compact or sports car. Auto break-ins and thefts cost Canadians more than $400 million annually, meaning that there's a one in 130 chance that your vehicle will be stolen but only a 60 percent chance that you'll ever get it back.

Since amateurs are responsible for stealing most vehicles, the best theft deterrent is a visible device that complicates the job while immobilizing the vehicle and sounding an alarm. For less than $150, you can install both a steering wheel lock and a hidden remote-controlled ignition disabler. Satellite tracking systems like GM's OnStar feature are also very effective.

Battery (Heavy-Duty)

The best battery for northern climates is the optional heavy-duty type offered by many manufacturers for about $100. It's a worthwhile purchase, especially for vehicles equipped with lots of electric options. Most standard batteries last only two winters; heavy-duty batteries give you an extra year or two for about 20 percent more than the price of a standard battery.

Make sure your new vehicle comes with a fresh battery – one manufactured less than six months earlier. Batteries are stamped with a date code, either on the battery's case or on an attached label. The vital information is usually in the first two characters – a letter and a numeral. Most codes start with a letter indicating the month: A for January, B for February, and so forth. The numeral denotes the year, say, 0 for 2000. For example, "B3" stands for February 2003.

Don't order an optional battery with cold cranking amps (CCA) below the one specified for your vehicle, or one rated 200 amps or more above the specified rating. It's a waste of money to go too high. Also, buy a battery with the longest reserve capacity you can find; a longer capacity can make the difference between driving to safety and paying for an expensive tow.

Replacement batteries are very competitively priced and easy to find. Sears' DieHard batteries usually get *Consumer Reports*' top ratings. A useful link for finding the right battery with the most CCA for your car and year is *www.autobatteries. com/basics/selecting.asp*.

Central Locking Control

Costing around $200, this option is most useful for families with small children, car-poolers, or drivers of minivans who can't easily slide across the seat to lock the other doors.

Child Safety Seat (Integrated)

Integrated safety seats are designed to accommodate any child more than one year old or weighing over 9 kg (20 lb.). Since the safety seat is permanently integrated into the seatback, the fuss of installing and removing the safety seat and finding someplace to store it vanishes. When not in use, it quickly folds out of sight, becoming part of the seatback. Two other safety benefits: You know that the seat has been properly installed, and your child gets used to having his or her "special" seat in back, where it's usually safest to sit.

Electronic Stability Control (ESC)

The latest IIHS studies conclude that as many as 10,000 fatal crashes could be prevented if all vehicles were equipped with ESC. Its June 2006 report concluded that stability control is second only to seat belts in saving lives because it reduces the risk of fatal single-vehicle rollovers by 80 percent and the chance of having other kinds of fatal collisions by 43 percent.

ESC was first used by Mercedes-Benz and BMW on the S-Class and 7 Series models in 1995 and then was featured on GM's 1997 Cadillacs and Corvettes. It helps prevent the loss of control in turns, on slippery roads, or when you must make a sudden steering correction. The system applies the brakes to individual wheels or cuts back the engine power when sensors find the vehicle is beginning to spin or skid. It's particularly useful in maintaining stability with SUVs, but it's less useful with passenger coupes and sedans.

The steady increase in ESC-equipped vehicles has been ushered along by a 2007 U.S. federal mandate requiring automakers to install electronic stability systems on all passenger cars, SUVs, vans, and pickup trucks manufactured on or after September 1, 2011. The mandate included a phase-in schedule culminating in 100% compliance for all model-year 2012 vehicles.

Not all ESC systems have worked as they should in the past and the federal standard has gone far in improving their overall performance from 2012 on. In tests carried out by *Consumer Reports* on 2003 models, the stability control system used in the Mitsubishi Montero was rated "unacceptable," BMW's X5 3.0i system provided poor emergency handling, and Acura's MDX and Subaru's Outback VDC stability systems left much to be desired. Smart shoppers counting on an effective ESC system would be wise to stick with 2012-14 models.

Engines (Cylinder Deactivation)

Choose the most powerful 6- or 8-cylinder engine available if you're going to be doing a lot of highway driving, if you plan to carry a full passenger load and luggage on a regular basis, or if you intend to load up the vehicle with convenience features like air conditioning. Keep in mind that minivans, SUVs, and trucks with 6-cylinder or larger engines are easier to resell and retain their value the longest. For example, Honda's '96 Odyssey minivan was a sales dud in spite of its bulletproof reliability, mainly because buyers didn't want a minivan with an underpowered 4-cylinder powerplant. Some people buy underpowered vehicles in the mistaken belief that increased fuel economy is a good trade-off for decreased engine performance. It isn't. That's why there's so much interest in peppy 4-cylinders hooked to 5- or 6-speed transmissions and in larger engines with a "cylinder deactivation" feature.

In fact, cylinder deactivation is one feature that appears more promising than most other fuel-saving add-ons. For example, *AutoWeek* magazine found the overweight Jeep Commander equipped with a "Multiple Displacement System" still managed a respectable 13.8 L/100 km (17 mpg) on the highway in tests published in its March 2006 edition.

Honda employs a similar method, which cuts fuel consumption by 20 percent on the Odyssey. It runs on all six cylinders when accelerating, and on three cylinders when cruising. So far, there have been neither reliability nor performance complaints.

Engine and Transmission Cooling System (Heavy-Duty)

This relatively inexpensive option provides extra cooling for the transmission and engine. It can extend the life of these components by preventing overheating when heavy towing is required. It's a must-have feature for large cars made by Chrysler, Ford, or General Motors.

Extended Warranties

A smart buy if the dealer will discount the price by 50 percent and you're able to purchase the extra powertrain coverage only. However, you are throwing away $1,500-$2,000 if you buy an extended warranty for cars, vans, or trucks rated Recommended in *Lemon-Aid* or for vehicles sold by automakers that have written "goodwill" warranties covering engine and transmission failures. If you can get a great price for a vehicle rated just Average or Above Average but want protection from costly repair bills, patronize garages that offer lifetime warranties on parts listed in this guide as being failure-prone, such as powertrains, exhaust systems, and brakes.

Buy an extended warranty only as a last resort, and make sure you know what it covers and for how long. Budget $1,000 after dealer discounting for the powertrain warranty. Incidentally, auto industry insiders say the average markup on these warranties varies from 50-65 percent, which seems almost reasonable when you consider that appliance warranties are marked up from 40-80 percent.

Keyless Entry (Remote)

This safety and convenience option saves you from fiddling with your key in a dark parking lot, or taking off a glove in cold weather to unlock or lock the vehicle. Try to get a keyless entry system combined with anti-theft measures, such as an ignition kill switch or some other disabler. Incidentally, some automakers no longer make vehicles with an outside key lock on the passenger's side.

Paint Colour

Choosing a popular colour can make your vehicle easier to sell at a good price. DesRosiers Automotive Consultants say that blue is the preferred colour overall, but green and silver are also popular with Canadians. Manheim auctioneers say that green-coloured vehicles brought in 97.9 of the average auction price, while silver ones sold at a premium 105.5 percent. Remember that certain colours require particular care.

- **Black (and other dark colours):** These paints are most susceptible to sun damage because of their heavy absorption of ultraviolet rays.

- **Pearl-toned colours:** These paints are the most difficult to work with. If the paint needs to be retouched, it must be matched to look right from both the front- and side-angle views.
- **Red:** This colour also shows sun damage, so keep your car in a garage or shady spot whenever possible.
- **White:** Although grime looks terrible on a white car, white is the easiest colour to care for. But the colour is also very popular with car thieves, because white vehicles can be easily repainted another colour.

Power-Assisted Sliding Doors, Mirrors, Windows, and Seats

Merely a convenience feature with cars, power-assisted windows and doors are a necessity with minivans – crawling across the front seat a few times to roll up the passenger-side window or to lock the doors will quickly convince you of their value. Power mirrors are convenient on vehicles that have a number of drivers, or on minivans. Power seats with memory are particularly useful, too, if more than one person drives a vehicle. Automatic window and seat controls currently have few reliability problems, and they're fairly inexpensive to install, trouble-shoot, and repair. As a safety precaution, make sure the window control has to be lifted. This will ensure no child is strangled from pressing against the switch. Power-sliding doors on minivans are even more of a danger. They are failure-prone on all makes and shouldn't be purchased by families with children.

Side Airbags

A worthwhile feature if you are the right size and properly seated, side airbags are presently overpriced and aren't very effective unless both the head and upper torso are protected. Side airbags are often featured as a $700 add-on to the sticker price, but you would be wise to bargain aggressively.

Suspension (Heavy-Duty)

Always a good idea, this inexpensive option pays for itself by providing better handling, allowing additional ride comfort (though a bit on the firm side), and extending shock life by an extra year or two.

Tires

There are three rules to remember when purchasing tires. First, neither brand nor price is a reliable gauge of performance, quality, or durability. Second, the cheapest prices are offered by tire discounters like Tire Rack (*www.tirerack.com*), and Discount Tire Direct (*www.discounttiredirect.com*), and their Canadian equivalents like Canadian Tire and TireTrends (*www.tiretrends.com/index.php3*). Third, choosing a tire recommended by the automaker may not be in your best interest, since traction and long tread life are often sacrificed for a softer ride and maximum EPA (Environmental Protection Agency) mileage ratings.

Two types of tires are generally available: All-season and performance. "Touring" is just a fancier name for all-season tires. All-season radial tires cost from $90-$150 per tire. They're a compromise since, according to Transport Canada, they won't get you through winter with the same margin of safety as snow tires will and they don't provide the same durability on dry surfaces as do regular summer tires. In areas with low to moderate snowfall, however, these tires are adequate as long as they're not pushed beyond their limits.

Mud or snow tires provide the best traction on snowy surfaces, but traction on wet roads is actually decreased. Treadwear is also accelerated by the use of softer rubber compounds. Beware of using wide tires for winter driving; 70-series or wider give poor traction and tend to float over snow.

Remember, too, that buying slightly larger wheels and tires may improve handling – but there's a limit. For example, many cars come with 16-in. (40.64-cm) original equipment (OE) tires supplied by the carmaker. Moving up to a slightly larger size, say a 17-in. (43.18-cm) wheel, could improve your dry and wet grip handling. Getting any larger wheels can have serious downsides, though, like making the vehicle harder to control, providing less steering feedback, making the car more subject to hydroplaning ("floating" over wet surfaces), and causing SUVs and pickups to roll over more easily.

Don't over-inflate tires to lower their rolling resistance for better fuel economy. The trade-off is a harsher ride and increased risk of a blowout when passing over uneven terrain. Excessive tire pressure may also distort the tread, reducing contact with the road and increasing wear in the centre of the tread. Under-inflation is a far more common occurrence. Experts agree that tire life decreases by ten percent for every ten percent the tire is under-inflated, sometimes through lack of maintenance or due to the perception that an under-inflated tire improves traction. Actually, an under-inflated tire makes for worse traction. It breaks traction more easily than a tire that is properly inflated, causing skidding, pulling to the side when braking, excessive wheelspin when accelerating, and tire failure due to overheating.

Spare tires

Be wary of space-saver spare tires. They often can't match the promised mileage, and they seriously degrade steering control. Furthermore, they are usually stored in spaces inside the trunk that won't hold a normal-sized tire. The location of the stored spare can also have safety implications. Watch out for spares stowed under the chassis or mounted on the rear hatch. Frequently, the attaching cables and bolts rust out or freeze, so the spare falls off or becomes next to impossible to use when you need it.

Self-sealing and run-flat tires

Today, there are two technologies available to help maintain vehicle mobility when a tire is punctured: Self-sealing and self-supporting/run-flat tires.

SELF-SEALING: Ideal if you drive long distances. Punctures from nails, bolts, or screws up to 3/16 of an inch (0.48 cm) in diameter are fixed instantly and permanently with a sealant. A low air-pressure warning system isn't required. Expert testers say a punctured self-sealing tire can maintain air pressure for up to 200 km (124.5 mi) – even in freezing conditions. The Uniroyal Tiger Paw NailGard ($85-$140, depending on the size) is the overall winner in a side-by-side test conducted by Tire Rack (*www.tirerack.com*).

SELF-SUPPORTING/RUN-FLAT: Priced from $175-$350 per tire, 25-50 percent more than the price of comparable premium tires, Goodyear's Extended Mobility Tire (EMT) run-flat tires were first offered as an option on the 1994 Chevrolet Corvette and then became standard on the 1997 model. These tires reinforce the side wall so it can carry the weight of the car for 90 km (55 mi), or about an hour's driving time, even after all air pressure has been lost. You won't feel the tire go flat; you must depend on a $250-$300 optional tire-pressure monitor to warn you before the side wall collapses and you begin riding on your rim. Also, not all vehicles can adapt to run-flat tires; you may need to upgrade your rims. Experts say run-flats will give your car a harder ride, and you'll likely notice more interior tire and road noise. The car might also track differently. The Sienna's standard Dunlop run-flat tires have a terrible reputation for premature wear. At 25,000 km (15,534 mi), one owner complained that her Sienna needed a new set at $200 each. You can expect a backlog of over a month to get a replacement. Goodyear and Pirelli run-flat tires have been on the market for some time now, and they seem to perform adequately.

"Green" tires

No, these tires aren't coloured differently; they're simply tires with a lower rolling resistance that have been proven (through independent tests) to save fuel, which saves you money, and contributes to lower greenhouse gas emissions. One recently-found fuel-efficient tire make that provides good traction, reasonable tread life, and low rolling resistance is the Continental Pro-Contact EcoPlus.

In the discussion above, the Michelin's Energy Saver A/S ranked highest for fuel savings; the Cooper GFE also gave good fuel economy, but its overall performance was only average. The Department of Transportation says fuel savings can be substantial, depending on the tire, knocking down fuel consumption by 4 percent in city driving and 7 percent on the highway. *Consumer Reports* magazine pegs the annual savings at $100 per set. Lower rolling resistance tires may also produce less road noise and have a longer tread life.

Nitrogen air refills

The NHTSA has seen reduced aging of tires filled with nitrogen. Claims have also been made that nitrogen maintains inflation pressure better than air. Though the data technically does support that passenger car tires could benefit from being filled with nitrogen, tire manufacturers say that they already design tires to perform well with air inflation. And while nitrogen will do no harm, manufacturers say that they don't see the need to use nitrogen, which generally adds $5 or more per tire charge.

Consumer Reports says consumers can use nitrogen and might enjoy the slight improvement in air retention provided, but you can do just as well without paying an extra penny by performing regular inflation checks.

Which tires are best?

There is no independent Canadian agency that evaluates tire performance and durability. However, the U.S.-based NHTSA rates tread wear, traction, and resistance to sustained high temperatures; etches the ratings onto the side walls of all tires sold in the States and Canada; and regularly posts its findings on the Internet (*www.safercar.gov*). NHTSA also logs owner complaints relative to different brands. *Lemon-Aid* summarizes these complaints in the ratings of specific models in Part Four.

You can get more-recent complaint postings, service bulletins, and tire recall notices at the same government website, and check out independent owner performance ratings as compiled by Tire Rack, a large tire retailer, at *www.tirerack. com/tires/surveyresults/index.jsp.*

Traction Control

This option limits wheelspin when accelerating. It is most useful with rear-drive vehicles and provides surer traction in wet or icy conditions.

Trailer-Towing Equipment

Just because you need a vehicle with towing capability doesn't mean that you have to spend big bucks. But you should first determine what kind of vehicle you want to do the job and whether your tires will handle the extra burden. For most towing needs (up to 900 kg/2,000 lb.), a passenger car, small pickup, or minivan equipped with a 6-cylinder engine will work just as well as a full-sized pickup or van (and will cost much less). If you're pulling a trailer that weighs more than 900 kg, most passenger cars won't handle the load unless they've been specially outfitted according to the automaker's specifications. Pulling a heavier trailer (up to 1,800 kg/4,000 lb.) will likely require a large vehicle equipped with a V8 powerplant.

Automakers reserve the right to change limits whenever they feel like it, so make any sales promise about towing an integral part of your contract. A good rule of thumb is to reduce the promised tow rating by 20 percent. In assessing towing weight, factor in the cargo, passengers, and equipment of both the trailer and the towing vehicle. Keep in mind that five people and luggage add 450 kg (almost 1,000 lb.) to the load, and that a full 227L (60 gal.) water tank adds another 225 kg (almost 500 lb.). The manufacturer's gross vehicle weight rating (GVWR) takes into account the anticipated average cargo and supplies that your vehicle is likely to carry.

Automatic transmissions are fine for trailering, although there's a slight fuel penalty. Manual transmissions tend to have greater clutch wear caused by towing than do automatic transmissions. Both transmission choices are equally acceptable. Remember, the best compromise is to shift the automatic manually for maximum performance going uphill and to maintain control, while not overheating the brakes, when descending mountains.

Unibody vehicles (those without a separate frame) can handle most towing chores as long as their limits aren't exceeded. Front-drives aren't the best choice for pulling heavy loads in excess of 900 kg (2,000 lb.), since they lose some steering control and traction with all the weight concentrated in the rear.

Whatever vehicle you choose, keep in mind that the trailer hitch is crucial. It must have a tongue capacity of at least 10 percent of the trailer's weight; otherwise, it may be unsafe to use. Hitches are chosen according to the type of tow vehicle and, to a lesser extent, the weight of the load. Most hitches are factory-installed, even though independents can install them more cheaply. Expect to pay about $200 for a simple boat hitch and a minimum of $600 for a fifth-wheel version.

Equalizer bars and extra cooling systems for the radiator, transmission, engine oil, and steering are prerequisites for towing anything heavier than 900 kg (2,000 lb.). Heavy-duty springs and brakes are a big help, too. Separate brakes for the trailer may be necessary to increase your vehicle's maximum towing capacity.

Transmissions

Despite its many advantages, the manual transmission is an endangered species in North America, where manuals equip only 8-10 percent of all new vehicles (mostly econocars, sports cars, and budget trucks), and that figure is slated to fall as more vehicles adopt fuel-saving CVT transmissions, among other powertrain innovations. One theory on why the manual numbers keep falling: North American drivers are too busy with cell phones, text messaging, and cappuccinos to shift gears. Interestingly, European buyers opt for a manual transmission almost 90 percent of the time. (And they also drink cappuccinos, but usually not in 20 oz. paper takeout cups.)

Automakers are currently offering hybrid manumatic transmissions that provide the benefits of an automatic transmission while also giving the driver the

NASCAR-styled fun of clutchless manual shifting. Or, if all you want is fuel savings, there are now 5- and 6-speed automatic models – and even 7- and 8-, and 9-speed versions – all reputedly fuel-sippers – with long-term reliability still unproven.

Some considerations: The brake pads on stick-shift vehicles tend to wear out less rapidly than those on automatics; a transmission with five or more forward speeds is usually more fuel-efficient than one with three forward speeds (hardly seen anymore); and manual transmissions usually add a mile or two per gallon over automatics, although this isn't always the case, as *Consumer Reports* recently discovered. Their road tests found that the 2008 Toyota Yaris equipped with an automatic transmission got slightly better gas mileage than a Yaris powered by a manual tranny.

UNNECESSARY OPTIONS

All-Wheel Drive (AWD)

Mark Bilek, editorial director of *Consumer Guide*'s automotive website (*consumer-guideauto.howstuffworks.com*), is a critic of AWD. He says AWD systems generally encourage drivers to go faster than they should in adverse conditions, which creates trouble stopping in emergencies. Automakers like AWD as "a marketing ploy to make more money," Bilek contends. My personal mechanic adds, "Four-wheel drive will only get you stuck deeper, farther from home."

Anti-Lock Brakes (ABS)

Like ACC and backup warning devices, ABS is another safety feature that's fine in theory but often impractical under actual driving conditions. The system maintains directional stability by preventing the wheels from locking up. This will not reduce the stopping distance, however. In practice, ABS is said to make drivers overconfident. Many still pump the brakes and render them ineffective; total brake failure is common; and repairs are frequent, complicated, and expensive to perform.

Cruise Control

Automakers provide this $250-$300 option, which is mainly a convenience feature, to motorists who use their vehicles for long periods of high-speed driving. The constant rate of speed saves some fuel and lessens driver fatigue during long trips. Still, the system is particularly failure-prone and expensive to repair, can lead to driver inattention, and can make the vehicle hard to control on icy roadways. Malfunctioning cruise-control units are also one of the major causes of sudden acceleration incidents. At other times, cruise control can be very distracting, especially to inexperienced drivers who are unaccustomed to sudden speed fluctuations.

ACC is the latest evolution of this feature. It senses a vehicle ahead of you and then automatically downshifts, brakes, or cuts your vehicle's speed. This commonly occurs when passing another car or when a car passes you, and it can make for a harrowing experience, especially when you are in the passing lane.

Electronic Instrument Readout

If you've ever had trouble reading a digital watch face or resetting your VCR, you'll feel right at home with this electronic gizmo. Gauges are presented in a series of moving digital patterns that are confusing, distracting, and unreadable in direct sunlight. This system is often accompanied by a trip computer and vehicle monitor that indicate average speed, signal component failures, and determine fuel use and how many kilometres you can drive until the tank is empty. Figures are frequently in error or slow to catch up.

Fog Lights

A pain in the eyes for some, a pain in the wallet for others who have to pay the high bulb replacement costs. Fog lights aren't necessary for most drivers who have well-aimed original-equipment headlights on their vehicles.

Gas-Saving Gadgets and Fuel Additives

Ah, the search for the Holy Grail. Magic software and miracle hardware that will turn your gas-hungry Hummer into a fuel-frugal Prius when the right additive is poured into your fuel tank.

The accessory market has been flooded with hundreds of atomizers, magnets, and additives that purport to make vehicles less fuel-thirsty. However, tests on over 100 gadgets and fuel or crankcase additives carried out by the EPA have found that only a handful produce an increase in fuel economy, and the increase is tiny. These gadgets include warning devices that tell the driver to ease up on the throttle or shift to a more fuel-frugal gear, hardware that reduces the engine power needed for belt-driven accessories, cylinder deactivation systems, and spoilers that channel airflow under the car. The use of any of these products is a quick way to lose warranty coverage and fail provincial emissions tests.

GPS Navigation Systems

This navigation aid links a Global Positioning System (GPS) satellite unit to the vehicle's cellular phone and electronics. Good GPS devices cost $125-$1,500(U.S.) when bought from an independent retailer. As a dealer option, you will pay $1,000-$2,000(U.S.). For a monthly fee, the unit connects drivers to live operators who will help them with driving directions, give repair or emergency assistance, or relay messages. If the airbag deploys or the car is stolen, satellite-transmitted signals are automatically sent from the vehicle to operators who will notify the proper authorities of the vehicle's location.

Many of the systems' functions can be performed by a cellular telephone, and the navigation screens may be obtrusive, distracting, washed out in sunlight, and hard to calibrate. A portable Garmin GPS unit is more user-friendly and much cheaper.

High-Intensity Headlights

These headlights are much brighter than standard headlights, and they cast a blue hue. Granted, they provide additional illumination of the roadway, but they are also annoying to other drivers, who will flash their lights – or give you the middle finger – thinking that your high beams are on. These lights are easily stolen and expensive to replace. Interestingly, European versions have a device to maintain the light's spread closer to the road so that other drivers aren't blinded.

ID Etching

This $150-$200 option is a scam. The government doesn't require it, and thieves and joyriders aren't deterred by the etchings. If you want to etch your windows for your own peace of mind, several private companies will sell you a $15-$30 kit that does an excellent job (try *www.autoetch.net*), or you can wait for your municipality or local police agency to conduct one of their periodic free VIN ID etching sessions in your area.

Paint and Fabric Protectors

Selling for $200-$300, these "sealants" add nothing to a vehicle's resale value. Although paint lustre may be temporarily heightened, this treatment is less effective and more costly than regular waxing, and it may also invalidate the manufacturer's guarantee at a time when the automaker will look for any pretext to deny your paint claim.

Auto fabric protection products are nothing more than variations of Scotchgard, which can be bought in aerosol cans for a few dollars – a much better deal than the $50-$75 charged by dealers.

Power-Assisted Minivan Sliding Doors

Not a good idea if you have children. These doors have a high failure rate, opening or closing for no apparent reason and injuring children caught between the door and post.

Reverse-Warning System

Selling for about $500 as part of an option package, this safety feature warns the driver of any objects in the rear when backing up. Although a sound idea in theory, in practice the device often fails to go off or sounds an alarm for no reason. Drivers eventually either disconnect or ignore it.

Rollover-Detection System

This feature makes use of sensors to determine if the vehicle has leaned beyond a safe angle. If so, the side airbags are automatically deployed and remain inflated to make sure occupants aren't injured or ejected in a rollover accident. This is a totally new system that has not yet been proven. It could have disastrous consequences if the sensor malfunctions, as has been the case with front and side airbag sensors over the past decade.

Rooftop Carrier

Although this inexpensive option provides additional baggage space and may allow you to meet all your driving needs with a smaller vehicle, a loaded roof rack can increase fuel consumption by as much as 18 percent. An empty rack can increase your gas bill by about 10 percent.

Rustproofing

Rustproofing is no longer necessary, since automakers have extended their own rust warranties. In fact, you have a greater chance of seeing your rustproofer go belly up than having your untreated vehicle ravaged by premature rusting. Even if the rustproofer stays in business, you're likely to get a song and dance about why the warranty won't cover so-called internal rusting, or why repairs will be delayed until the sheet metal is actually rusted through.

Be wary of electronic rustproofing. Selling for $425-$700, these electrical devices claim to inhibit vehicle corrosion by sending out a pulse current to the grounded body panels, protecting areas that conventional rust-inhibiting products can't reach. There is much debate as to whether these devices are worth the cost, or if they work at all.

Seat Warmers

Over the last 20 years, the NHTSA has logged over 1,260 complaints on seat heaters, the complaint charging overheating in almost every case, resulting in 287 injuries and over 500 fires.

Sunroof

Unless you live in a temperate region, the advantages of having a sunroof are far outweighed by the disadvantages. You aren't going to get better ventilation than a good AC system would provide, and a sunroof may grace your environment with painful booming wind noises, rattles, water leaks, and road dust accumulation.

A sunroof increases gas consumption, reduces night vision because overhead highway lights shine through the roof opening, and can cost you several centimetres of headroom. Worst of all, sunroofs have a nasty habit of suddenly shattering for no apparent reason. Automakers have dropped their "road debris" mantra and now simply shrug their shoulders as they send you off to make an insurance claim. (Don't do it!)

Tinted Glass

On the one hand, tinting jeopardizes safety by reducing your night vision. On the other hand, it does keep the interior cool in hot weather, reduces glare, and hides the car's contents from prying eyes. Factory applications are worth the extra cost, since cheaper aftermarket products (costing about $150) distort visibility and peel away after a few years. Some tinting done in the States can run afoul of provincial highway codes that require more transparency.

CUTTING THE PRICE

Bidding by Fax or E-mail

The process is quite easy: Simply fax or e-mail an invitation for bids to area dealerships, asking them to give their bottom-line price for a specific make and model. Be clear that all final bids must be sent within a week. When all the bids are received, the lowest bid is sent to the other dealers to give them a chance to beat that price. After a week of bidding, the lowest price gets your business. Incidentally, with the Canadian loonie headed to parity with the American dollar, try doing an Internet search for American prices and then using that lower figure to haggle with Canadian dealers.

Dozens of *Lemon-Aid* readers have told me how this bidding approach has cut thousands of dollars from the advertised price and saved them from the degrading song-and-dance routine between the buyer, sales agent, and sales manager ("he said, she said, the sales manager said").

A *Lemon-Aid* reader sent in the following suggestions for buying by fax or e-mail.

First, I'd like to thank you for writing the *Lemon-Aid* series of books, which I have used extensively in the fax-tendering purchase of my '99 Accord and '02 Elantra. I have written evidence from dealers that I saved a bare minimum of $700 on the Accord (but probably more) and a whopping $900 on the Elantra through the use of fax-tendering, over and above any deals possible through Internet-tendering and/or showroom bargaining.

Based on my experience, I would suggest that in reference to the fax-tendering [or e-mail-tendering] process, future *Lemon-Aid* editions emphasize the issues below.

Casting a wide geographical net, as long as you're willing to pick the car up there. I faxed up to 50 dealerships, which helped tremendously in increasing the number of serious bidders. One car was bought locally in Ottawa, the other in Mississauga.

Unless you don't care much about what car you end up with, be very specific about what you want. If you are looking at just one or two cars, which I recommend, specify trim level and all extended warranties and dealer-installed options in the fax letter. Otherwise, you'll end up with quotes comparing apples and oranges, and you won't get the best deal on options negotiated later. Also, specify that quotes should be signed. This helps out with errors in quoting.

Dealerships are sloppy. There is a 25-30 percent error rate in quotes. Search for errors and get corrections, and confirm any of the quotes in serious contention over the phone.

Phone to personally thank anyone who submits a quote for their time. Salespeople can't help themselves, they'll ask how they ranked, and often want to then beat the best quote you've got. This is much more productive than faxing back the most competitive quote (I know, I've tried that too).

Another reader, in B.C., was successful with this approach.

I purchased your 2005 edition *SUVs, Vans, and Trucks* earlier this year from Chapters. Thanks for all the information that helped me decide to purchase a new Honda Odyssey EX-L for a super price from a good dealer.

After completing my research (and vacillating for a few weeks) I ended up issuing a faxed "request for quotation" (RFQ) from several dealerships. I can tell you that some of them were not happy and tried to tell me that Honda Canada was clamping down on this activity. In the end, one dealership did not respond and one "closer" salesperson called to attempt to get me in their dealership so he could "assess my needs." I told him that my needs were spelled out very specifically in my request but he refused to give me a price.

In the end, I received five quotations by phone, fax, and e-mail. I purchased my van in Chilliwack for about $2,200 off list. It turned out that the salesperson just started selling cars two months ago and was very appreciative of my business. The whole deal was completed in half an hour. I was in full control but treated every respondent fairly. I did not play dealers off one another and went with the lowest first offer.

GETTING A FAIR PRICE

"We Sell Below Cost"

This is no longer a bait-and-switch scam. Many dealers who are going out of business are desperate to sell their inventory, sometimes for 40 percent below the MSRP. Assuming the vehicle's cost price was 20 percent under the MSRP, astute buyers are getting up to a 20 percent discount. The chart lists the profit margins for various vehicle categories, excluding freight, PDI, and administrative fees, which you should bargain down or not pay at all. In addition to the dealer's markup, some vehicles may also have a 3 percent carryover allowance paid out in a dealer incentive program. Finance contracts may also tack on a 2 percent dealer commission.

Holdback

Ever wonder how dealers who advertise vehicles for "a hundred dollars over invoice" can make a profit? They are counting mostly on the manufacturer's holdback.

In addition to the MSRP, the invoice price, dealer incentives, and customer rebates (available to Canadians at *www.apa.ca*), another key element in every dealer's profit margin is the manufacturer's holdback – the quarterly payouts dealers depend on when calculating gross profit.

The holdback was set up over 45 years ago by General Motors as a guaranteed profit for dealers tempted to bargain away their entire profit to make a sale. It usually represents 1-3 percent of the sticker price (MSRP) and is seldom given out by Asian or European automakers, which use dealer incentive programs instead. There are several free Internet sources for holdback information. The most recent and comprehensive are *www.edmunds.com* and *www.kbb.com*, two websites geared toward American buyers. Although there may be a difference in the holdback percentage between American automakers and their Canadian subsidiaries, it's usually not significant.

Some GM dealers maintain that they no longer get a holdback allowance. They are being disingenuous – the holdback may have been added to special sales "incentive" programs, which won't show up on the dealer's invoice. Options are the icing on the cake, with their average 35-65 percent markup.

Can You Get a Fair Price?

Yes, but you'll have to keep your wits about you and time your purchase well into the model year – usually in late winter or spring.

New-car negotiations aren't wrestling matches where you have to pin the sales agent's shoulders to the mat to win. If you feel that the overall price is fair, don't jeopardize the deal by refusing to budge. For example, if you've brought the contract price 10 percent or more below the MSRP and the dealer sticks you with a $200 "administrative fee" at the last moment, let it pass. You've saved money and the sales agent has saved face.

Of course, someone will always be around to tell you how he or she could have bought the vehicle for much less. Let that pass, too.

To calculate a fair price, subtract two-thirds of the dealer's markup from the MSRP and then trade the carryover and holdback allowance for a reduced delivery and transportation fee. Compute the options separately, and sell your trade-in privately. Buyers can more easily knock $4,000 off a $20,000 base price if they wait until Chrysler and General Motors hold their new year "fire" sales in early 2014 and ratchet up the competition. Remember, choose a vehicle that's in stock, and resist getting unnecessary options.

Beware of Financing and Insurance Traps

Once you and the dealer have settled on the vehicle's price, you aren't out of the woods yet. You'll be handed over to an F&I (financing and insurance) specialist, whose main goal is to convince you to buy additional financing, loan insurance, paint and seat cover protection, rustproofing, and extended warranties. These items will be presented on a computer screen as costing only "a little bit more each month."

Compare the dealer's insurance and financing charges with those from an independent agency that may offer better rates and better service. Often, the dealer gets a kickback for selling insurance and financing. And guess who pays for it? Additionally, remember that if the financing rate looks too good to be true, you're probably paying too much for the vehicle. The F&I closer's hard-sell approach will take all your willpower and patience to resist, but when he or she gives up, your trials are over.

Add-on charges are the dealer's last chance to stick it to you before the contract is signed. Dealer PDI and transportation charges, "documentation" fees, and extra handling costs are ways that the dealer gets extra profits for nothing. Dealer preparation is often a once-over-lightly affair, with a car seldom getting more than a wash job and a couple of dollars' worth of gas in the tank. It's paid for by the factory in most cases, but when it's not, it should cost no more than 2 percent of the car's selling price. Reasonable transportation charges are acceptable, although dealers who claim that the manufacturer requires the payment often inflate them.

"No Haggle" Pricing Is "Price Fixing"

All dealers bargain. They hang out the "No dickering; one price only" sign simply as a means to discourage customers from asking for a better deal. Like parking lots and restaurants that claim they won't be responsible for lost or stolen property, they're bluffing. Still, you'd be surprised by how many people believe that if it's posted, it's non-negotiable.

Price Guidelines

When negotiating the price of a new vehicle, remember that there are several price guidelines and dealers use the one that will make them the most profit on each transaction. Two of the more common prices quoted are the MSRP (what the automaker advertises as a fair price) and the dealer's invoice cost (which is supposed to indicate how much the dealer paid for the vehicle). Both price indicators leave considerable room for the dealer's profit margin, along with some extra padding in the form of inflated transportation and preparation charges. If you are presented with both figures, go with the MSRP, since it can be verified by calling the manufacturer. Any dealer can print up an invoice and swear to its veracity. If you want an invoice price from an independent source, contact *www. apa.ca* or *www.carhelpcanada.com*.

Buyers who live in rural areas or in western Canada are often faced with grossly inflated auto prices compared to those charged in major metropolitan areas. A good way to get a more competitive price without buying out of province is to check online to see what prices are being charged in different urban areas. Show the dealer printouts that list selling prices, preparation charges, and transportation fees, and then ask for his or her price to come closer to the advertised prices.

Another tactic is to take a copy of a local competitor's car ad to a competing dealer selling the same brand and ask for a better price. Chances are they've already lost a few sales due to the ad and will work a little harder to match the deal; if not, they're almost certain to reveal the tricks in the competitor's promotion to make the sale.

Dealer Incentives and Customer Rebates

Sales incentives haven't changed much in the past 30 years. When vehicles are first introduced in the fall, they're generally overpriced; early in the new year, they'll sell for about 20-30 percent less. After a year, they may sell for less through a combination of dealer sales incentives (manufacturer-to-dealer), cash rebates (manufacturer-to-customer), zero percent interest financing (manufacturer's-finance-company-to-customer), and discounted prices (dealer-to-customer).

In most cases, the manufacturer's rebate is straightforward and mailed directly to the buyer from the automaker. There are other rebate programs that require a financial investment on the dealer's part, however, and these shared programs tempt dealers to offset losses by inflating the selling price or pocketing the manufacturer's rebate. Therefore, when the dealer participates in the rebate program, demand that the rebate be deducted from the MSRP, not from some inflated invoice price concocted by the dealer.

Some rebate ads will include the phrase "from dealer inventory only." So if your dealer doesn't have the vehicle in stock, you won't get the rebate.

Sometimes automakers will suddenly decide that a rebate no longer applies to a specific model, even though their ads continue to include it. When this happens, take all brochures and advertisements showing your eligibility for the rebate plan to provincial consumer protection officials. They can use false advertising statutes to force automakers to give rebates to every purchaser who was unjustly denied one.

If you are buying a heavily discounted vehicle, be wary of "option packaging" by dealers who push unwanted protection packages (rustproofing, paint sealants, and upholstery finishes) or who levy excessive charges for preparation, filing fees, loan guarantee insurance, and credit life insurance.

Price Swings

This year, the best prices will come early in the first quarter of 2014 and will continue through the summer. This includes Ford's 2013 and 2014 Mustang. On the other hand, if your choice has an unusually low sticker price, find out why it's so unpopular and then decide if the savings are worth it. Vehicles that don't sell because of their weird styling are no problem, but poor quality control (think Chrysler's cars and some compact Fords) can cost you big bucks.

Leftovers

The 2013 leftovers are being picked clean as the 2014s arrive this fall. They are good buys, if you can amortize the first year's depreciation by keeping the vehicle for eight years or more. But if you're the kind of driver who trades every two or three years, you're likely to come out a loser by buying an end-of-the-season vehicle. The simple reason is that, as far as trade-ins are concerned, a leftover is a "used" vehicle that has depreciated at least 20 percent in its first year. The savings the dealer gives you may not equal that first year's depreciation (a cost you'll incur without getting any of the first year's driving benefits). If the dealer's discounted price matches or exceeds the 30 percent depreciation, you're getting a pretty good deal.

Ask the dealer for all work orders relating to the vehicle, including the PDI checklist, and make sure that the odometer readings follow in sequential order. Remember as well that most demonstrators should have less than 5,000 km (3,100 mi) on the ticker and that the original warranty has been reduced from the day the vehicle was first put on the road. Also, make sure the vehicle is relatively "fresh" (about three months old) and check for warranty damage. With demos, have the dealer extend the warranty or lower the price about $100 for each month of warranty that has expired. If the vehicle's file shows that it was registered to a leasing agency or any other third party, you're definitely buying a used vehicle disguised as a demo. You should walk away from the sale – you're dealing with a crook.

CASH VERSUS FINANCING

Up until this year, car dealers preferred financing car sales instead of getting cash, because of the 1-2 percent kickbacks lenders gave them. This is less the case now, because fewer companies are lending money, and those that do are giving back very little to dealers and don't want to give loans for more than two-thirds of the purchase price. Dealers are scrambling for equity and will sell their vehicles for less than what they cost if the buyer pays cash. Cash is, once again, king.

If you aren't offered much of a discount for cash, financial planners say it can be smarter to finance the purchase of a new vehicle if a portion of the interest is tax deductible. The cash that you free up can then be used to repay debts that aren't tax deductible (mortgages or credit card debts, for example).

Rebates Versus Low or Zero Percent Financing

Low-financing programs have a number of disadvantages.

- Buyers must have exceptionally good credit.
- Shorter financing periods mean higher payments.
- Cash rebates are excluded.
- Only fully equipped or slow-selling models are eligible.
- Buyers pay full retail price.

The above stipulations can add thousands of dollars to your costs. Remember, to get the best price, first negotiate the price of the vehicle without disclosing whether you are paying cash or financing the purchase (say you haven't yet decided). Once you have a fair price, you can then take advantage of the financing.

Getting a Loan

Borrowers must be at least 18 years old (the age of majority), have a steady income, prove that they have discretionary income sufficient to make the loan payments, and be willing to guarantee the loan with additional collateral or with a parent or spouse as a co-signer.

Before applying for a loan, you should have established a good credit rating via a paid-off credit card and have a small savings account with your local bank, credit union, or trust company. Prepare a budget listing your assets and obligations. This will quickly show whether or not you can afford a car. Next, prearrange your loan with a phone call. This will protect you from much of the smoke-and-mirrors showroom shenanigans.

Incidentally, if you do get in over your head and require credit counselling, contact Credit Counselling Service (CCS), a not-for-profit organization located in many of Canada's major cities (*www.creditcanada.com*).

Hidden Loan Costs

The APA's undercover shoppers have found that most deceptive deals involve major banking institutions rather than automaker-owned companies.

In your quest for an auto loan, remember that the Internet offers help for people who need an auto loan and want quick approval, but don't want to face a banker. The BMO (Bank of Montreal: *www.bmo.com*), RBC (Royal Bank of Canada: *www.rbc.com*), and other banks allow vehicle buyers to post loan applications on their websites. Loans are available to any web surfer, including those who aren't current BMO or RBC customers.

Be sure to call various financial institutions to find out the following:

- The annual percentage rate on the amount you want to borrow, and the duration of your repayment period;

- The minimum down payment that the institution requires;
- Whether taxes and licence fees are considered part of the overall cost and, thus, are covered by part of the loan;
- Whether lower rates are available for different loan periods, or for a larger down payment; and
- Whether discounts are available to depositors, and, if so, how long you must be a depositor before qualifying.

When comparing loans, consider the annual rate and then calculate the total cost of the loan offer – that is, how much you'll pay above and beyond the total price of the vehicle.

Dealers may be able to finance your purchase at interest rates that are competitive with the banks' because of the rebates they get from the manufacturers and some lending institutions. Don't believe dealers who say they can borrow money at as much as 5 percentage points below the prime rate. Actually, they're jacking up the retail price to more than make up for the lower interest charges. Sometimes, instead of boosting the price, dealers reduce the amount they pay for the trade-in. In either case, the savings are illusory.

When dealing with banks, keep in mind that the traditional 36-month loan has now been stretched from 60-96 months. Longer payment terms make each month's payment more affordable, but over the long run, they increase the cost of the loan considerably. Therefore, take as short a term as possible or make sure you keep the car far longer than the term of the loan.

Be wary of lending institutions that charge a "processing" or "document" fee ranging from $25-$100. Sometimes consumers will be charged an extra 1-2 percent of the loan up front in order to cover servicing. This is similar to lending institutions adding "points" to mortgages, except that with auto loans, it's totally unjustified. In fact, dealers in the States are the object of several state lawsuits and class actions for inflating loan charges.

Some banks will cut the interest rate if you're a member of an automobile owners' association or if loan payments are automatically deducted from your chequing account. This latter proposal may be costly, however, if the chequing account charges exceed the interest-rate savings.

Loan Protection

Credit insurance guarantees that the vehicle loan will be paid if the borrower becomes disabled or dies. There are three basic types of insurance that can be written into an installment contract: Credit life, accident and health, and comprehensive. Some car companies, like Hyundai, will make some of your loan payments if you become unemployed. Most bank and credit union loans are already covered by some kind of loan insurance, but dealers sell the protection separately at an extra cost to the borrower. For this service, the dealer gets a hefty 20 percent commission. The additional cost to the purchaser can be significant.

Collecting on these types of policies isn't easy. There's no payment if your unemployment was due to your own conduct or if an illness is caused by some condition that existed prior to your taking out the insurance. Generally, credit insurance is unnecessary if you're in good health, you have no dependants, and your job is secure. Nevertheless, if you need to cancel your financial obligations, the same company that started LeaseBusters now offers FinanceBusters (*www.financebusters.com*). They provide a similar service to a lease takeover, but for customers who have vehicle loans.

Personal loans from financial institutions (particularly credit unions) now offer lots of flexibility, like fixed or variable interest rates, a choice of loan terms, and no penalties for prepayment. Precise conditions depend on your personal credit rating.

Leasing contracts are less flexible. There's a penalty for any prepayment, and rates aren't necessarily competitive.

Financing Scam: "Your Financing Was Turned Down"

This may be true, now that credit has become more difficult to get. But watch out for the scam that begins after you have purchased a vehicle and left your trade-in with the dealer. A few days later, you are told that your loan was rejected and that you now must put down a larger down payment and accept a higher monthly payment. Of course, your trade-in has already been sold.

Protect yourself from this rip-off by getting a signed agreement that stipulates that financing has been approved and that monthly payments can't be readjusted. Tell the dealer that your trade-in cannot be sold until the deal has closed.

The Contract

How likely are you to be cheated when buying a new car or truck? APA staffers posing as buyers visited 42 dealerships in four Canadian cities in early 2002. Almost half the dealers they visited (45 percent) flunked their test, and (hold onto your cowboy hats) auto buyers in western Canada were especially vulnerable to dishonest dealers. Either dealer ads left out important information or vehicles in the ads weren't available or were selling at higher prices. Fees for paperwork and vehicle preparation were frequently excessive.

Now, 11 years later, we know dealers are much more honest. Ahem ... maybe.

The Devil's in the Details

Watch what you sign, since any document that requires your signature is a contract. Don't sign anything unless all the details are clear to you and all the blanks have been filled in. Don't accept any verbal promises that you're merely putting the vehicle on hold. And when you are presented with a contract, remember it doesn't have to include all the clauses found in the dealer's pre-printed form. You and the sales representative can agree to strike some clauses and add others.

When the sales agent asks for a deposit, make sure that it's listed on the contract as a deposit, try to keep it as small as possible (a couple hundred dollars at most), and pay for it by credit card – in case the dealer goes belly up. If you decide to back out of the deal on a vehicle taken from stock, let the seller have the deposit as an incentive to cancel the contract (believe me, it's cheaper than hiring a lawyer and probably equal to the dealer's commission).

Scrutinize all references to the exact model (there's a heck of an upgrade from base to LX or Limited), prices, and delivery dates. Make sure you specify a delivery date in the contract that protects the price.

Contract Clauses You Need

You can put things on a more equal footing by negotiating the inclusion of as many clauses as possible from the sample of additional contract clauses found on page 83. To do this, write in a "Remarks" section on your contract and then add, "See attached clauses, which form part of this agreement." Then attach a photocopy of the "Additional Contract Clauses" and persuade the sales agent to initial as many of the clauses as possible. Although some clauses may be rejected, the inclusion of just a couple of them can have important legal ramifications later if you want a full or partial refund.

"We Can't Do That"

Dealers and automakers facing bankruptcy can do almost anything to get your business. Don't take the dealer's word that "We're not allowed to do that" – heard most often in reference to reducing the PDI or transportation fee. Some dealers have been telling *Lemon-Aid* readers that they are "obligated" by the automaker to charge a set fee and could lose their franchise if they charge less. This is pure hogwash. No dealer has ever had their franchise licence revoked for cutting prices. Furthermore, the automakers clearly state that they don't set a bottom price, since doing so would violate Canada's *Competition Act* – that's why you always see them putting disclaimers in their ads saying the dealer can charge less.

The Pre-delivery Inspection

The best way to ensure that the PDI (written as "PDE" in some regions) will be completed is to write in the sales contract that you'll be given a copy of the completed PDI sheet when the vehicle is delivered to you. Then, with the PDI sheet in hand, verify some of the items that were to be checked. If any items appear to have been missed, refuse delivery of the vehicle. Once you get home, check the vehicle more thoroughly, and send a registered letter to the dealer if you discover any incomplete items from the PDI.

1. **Original contract:** This is the ONLY contract; i.e., it cannot be changed, retyped, or rewritten, without the specific agreement of both parties.
2. **Financing:** This agreement is subject to the purchaser obtaining financing at _____% or less within _____ days of the date below.
3. **"In-service" date and mileage:** To be based on the closing day, not the day the contract was executed, and will be submitted to the automaker for warranty and all other purposes. The dealership will have this date corrected by the automaker if it should become necessary.
4. **Delivery:** The vehicle is to be delivered by _____, failing which the contract is cancelled and the deposit will be refunded.
5. **Cancellation:**
   (a) The purchaser retains the right to cancel this agreement without penalty at any time before delivery of the vehicle by sending a notice in writing to the vendor.
   (b) Following delivery of the vehicle, the purchaser shall have two days to return the vehicle and cancel the agreement in writing, without penalty. After two days and before thirty-one days, the purchaser shall pay the dealer $25 a day as compensation for depreciation on the returned vehicle.
   (c) Cancellation of contract can be refused where the vehicle has been subjected to abuse, negligence or unauthorized modifications after delivery.
   (d) The purchaser is responsible for accident damage and traffic violations while in possession of the said vehicle.
6. **Protected price:** The vendor agrees not to alter the price of the new vehicle, the cost of preparation, or the cost of shipping.
7. **Trade-in:** The vendor agrees that the value attributed to the vehicle offered in trade shall not be reduced, unless it has been significantly modified or has suffered from unreasonable and accelerated deterioration since the signing of the agreement.
8. **Courtesy car:**
   (a) In the event the new vehicle is not delivered on the agreed-upon date, the vendor agrees to supply the purchaser with a courtesy car at no cost. If no courtesy vehicle is available, the vendor agrees to reimburse the purchaser the cost of renting a vehicle.
   (b) If the vehicle is off the road for more than two days for warranty repairs, the purchaser is entitled to a free courtesy vehicle for the duration of the repair period. If no courtesy vehicle is available, the vendor agrees to reimburse the purchaser the cost of renting a vehicle of equivalent or lesser value.
9. **Work orders:** The purchaser will receive duly completed copies of all work orders pertaining to the vehicle, including warranty repairs and the pre-delivery inspection (PDI).
10. **Dealer stickers:** The vendor will not affix any dealer advertising, in any form, on the vehicle.
11. **Fuel:** Vehicle will be delivered with a free full tank of gas.
12. **Excess mileage:** New vehicle will not be acceptable and the contract will be void if the odometer has more than 200 km at delivery/closing.
13. **Tires:** Original equipment Firestone or Bridgestone tires are not acceptable.

_____   _____   _____
　　　　　Date　　　　　　　　　　　Vendor's Signature　　　　　　　Buyer's Signature

Selling Your Trade-In

When to Sell

Used cars are worth more than ever because new cars are suspect (in terms of price and insecurities about warranties being honoured and dealer/automaker backup). New prices are lower than ever before, and used prices are rising. This makes it hard for most owners to figure out the best time to buy another vehicle. It doesn't take a genius to figure out that the longer one keeps a vehicle, the less it costs to own.

If you're happy with your vehicle's styling and convenience features and it's safe and dependable, there's no reason to get rid of it. But when the cost of repairs becomes equal to or greater than the cost of payment for a new car, you need to consider trading it in. Shortly after your vehicle's fifth birthday (or whenever you start to think about trading it in), ask a mechanic to look at it to give you some idea of what repairs, replacement parts, or maintenance work it will need in the coming year. Find out if dealer service bulletins show that it will need extensive repairs in the near future (see Appendix IV for how to order bulletins from ALLDATA). If it's going to require expensive repairs, you should trade the vehicle right away; if expensive work isn't predicted, you may want to keep it. Auto owners' associations provide a good yardstick. They figure that the annual cost of repairs and preventive maintenance for the average vehicle is about $800. If your vehicle is five years old and you haven't spent anywhere near $4,000 in maintenance, it would pay to invest in your old vehicle and continue using it for another few years.

Consider whether your vehicle can still be serviced easily. If it's no longer on the market, the parts supply is likely to dry up and independent mechanics will be reluctant to repair it.

Don't trade for fuel economy alone. Most fuel-efficient vehicles, such as front-drives, offset the savings through higher repair costs. Also, the more fuel-efficient vehicles may not be as comfortable to drive because of their excessive engine noise, lightweight construction, stiff suspension, and torque steer.

Reassess your needs. Has your family grown to the point that you need a new vehicle? Are you driving less? Are you taking fewer long trips? Let your car or minivan show its age, and pocket the savings if its deteriorating condition doesn't pose a safety hazard and isn't too embarrassing. If you're in sales and are constantly on the road, it makes sense to trade every few years – in that case, the vehicle's appearance and reliability become a prime consideration, particularly since the increased depreciation costs are mostly tax deductible.

Getting the Most for Your Trade-In

Customers who are on guard against paying too much for a new vehicle often sell their trade-ins for too little. Before agreeing to any trade-in amount, read Part Four of this guide to compare the dealer price and what the vehicle is worth in a private sale.

Now that you've nailed down your trade-in's approximate value, here are some tips on selling it with a minimum of stress.

- Never sign a new vehicle sales contract unless your trade-in has been sold – you could end up with two vehicles.

- Negotiate the price from retail (dealer price) down to wholesale (private sales).

If you haven't sold your trade-in after two weekends, you might be trying to sell it at the wrong time of year or have it priced too high.

Make Money – Sell Privately

If you must sell your vehicle and want to make the most out of the deal, consider selling it yourself and putting the profits toward your next purchase. You'll likely come out hundreds of dollars ahead – buyers will pay more for your vehicle because they know cars sold by owners cost less. The most important thing to remember is that there's a large market for used vehicles in good condition in the $5,000-$7,000 range. Although most people prefer buying from individuals rather than from used-car lots, they may still be afraid that the vehicle is a lemon. By using the suggestions below, you should be able to sell your vehicle quite easily.

1. Know its value. Study dealers' newspaper ads and compare them with the prices listed in *Lemon-Aid*. Undercut the dealer's price by $300-$800, and be ready to bargain down another 10 percent for a serious buyer. Remember, prices can fluctuate wildly depending on which models are trendy, so watch the want ads carefully.

2. Enlist the aid of the salesperson who's selling you your new car. Offer him or her a few hundred dollars to find you a buyer. The fact that one sale hinges on the other, along with the prospect of making two commissions, may work wonders.

3. Post notices on bulletin boards at your office or local supermarkets, and place a "For Sale" sign in the window of the vehicle itself. Place a newspaper ad only as a last resort.

4. Don't give your address right away to a potential buyer responding to your ad. Instead, ask for the telephone number where you may call that person back.

5. Be wary of selling to friends or family members. Anything short of perfection, and you'll be eating Christmas dinner alone.

6. Don't touch the odometer. If you do, you may get a few hundred dollars more – and a criminal record.

7. Paint the vehicle. Some specialty shops charge only $300 and give a guarantee that's transferable to subsequent owners.

8. Make minor repairs. This includes a minor tune-up and patching up the exhaust. Again, if any repair warranty is transferable, use it as a selling point.

9. Clean the vehicle. Go to a reconditioning firm, or spend the weekend scrubbing the interior and exterior. First impressions are important. Clean the chrome, polish the body, and peel off old bumper stickers. Remove butts from the ashtrays and clean out the glove compartment. Make sure all tools and spare parts have been taken out of the trunk. Don't remove

the radio or speakers – the gaping holes will lower the vehicle's worth much more than the cost of the sound equipment. Replace missing or broken dash knobs and window cranks.

10. Change the tires. Recaps are good buys.
11. Let the buyer examine the vehicle. Insist that it be inspected at an independent garage, and then accompany the prospective buyer to the garage. This gives you protection if the buyer claims you misrepresented the vehicle.
12. Don't mislead the buyer. If the vehicle was in an accident or some financing is still to be paid, admit it. Any misleading statements may be used later against you in court. It's also advisable to have someone witness the actual transaction in case of a future dispute.
13. Keep important documents handy. Show prospective buyers the sales contract, repair orders, owner's manual, and all other documents that show how the vehicle has been maintained. Authenticate your claims about fuel consumption.
14. Write an effective ad, if you need to use one.

Selling to Dealers

Selling to a dealer means that you're likely to get 20 percent less than if you sold your vehicle privately, unless the dealer agrees to participate in an accommodation sale based on your buying a new vehicle from them. Most owners will gladly pay some penalty to the dealer, however, for the peace of mind that comes with knowing that their eventual buyer won't lay a claim against them. This assumes that the dealer hasn't been cheated by the owner. If the vehicle is stolen, isn't paid for, has had its odometer spun back (or forward to a lower setting), or is seriously defective, the buyer or dealer can sue the original owner for fraud. Sell to a dealer who sells the same make. He or she will give you more because it's easier to sell your trade-in to customers who are interested in only that make of vehicle.

Drawing Up the Contract

The province of Alberta has prepared a useful bill of sale applicable throughout Canada that can be accessed at *www.servicealberta.gov.ab.ca/pdf/mv/BillOfSaleReg3126.pdf.* Your bill of sale should identify the vehicle (including the serial number) and include its price, whether a warranty applies, and the nature of the examination made by the buyer.

The buyer may ask you to put in a lower price than what was actually paid in order to reduce the sales tax. If you agree to this, don't be surprised when a Revenue Canada agent comes to your door. Although the purchaser is ultimately the responsible party, you're an accomplice in defrauding the government. Furthermore, if you turn to the courts for redress, your own conduct may be put on trial.

SUMMARY

Purchasing a used vehicle and keeping it at least five years saves you the most money. It takes about eight years to realize similar depreciation savings when buying new. Giving the biggest down payment you can afford, using zero percent financing programs, and piling up as many kilometres and years as possible on your trade-in are the best ways to save money with new vehicles. Remember that safety is another consideration that depends largely on the type of vehicle you choose.

Buy Safe

Here are some safety features to look for.

1. High NHTSA and IIHS crashworthiness ratings for front, offset, and side collisions (pay particular attention to the side rating if you are a senior driver) and roof strength, plus a low rollover potential due to ESC
2. Good-quality tires; be wary of "all-season" tires and Bridgestone/Firestone makes and follow *www.tirerack.com* consumer recommendations
3. Three-point seat belts with belt pretensioners and adjustable shoulder belt anchorages
4. Integrated child safety seats and seat anchors, safety door locks, and over-ride window controls
5. Depowered dual airbags with a cut-off switch; side airbags with head protection; unobtrusive, effective head restraints that don't push your chin into your chest; and pedal extenders
6. Front driver's seat with plenty of rearward travel and a height adjuster
7. Good all-around visibility; a dash that doesn't reflect onto the windshield
8. An ergonomic interior with an efficient heating and ventilation system
9. Headlights that are adequate for night driving and don't blind oncoming traffic
10. Dash gauges that don't wash out in sunlight or produce windshield glare
11. Adjustable head restraints for all seating positions
12. Delaminated side-window glass
13. Easily accessed sound system and climate controls
14. Navigation systems that don't require a degree from MIT to calibrate
15. Manual sliding doors in vans (if children are being transported)

Buy Smart

1. Buy the vehicle you need and can afford, not the one someone else wants you to buy, or one loaded with options that you'll probably never use. Take your time. Price comparisons and test drives may take a month, but you'll get a better vehicle and price in the long run.

2. Buy in winter or later in the new year to double-dip from dealer incentives and customer rebate or low-cost financing programs.
3. Sell your trade-in privately.
4. Arrange financing before buying your vehicle.
5. Test drive your choice by renting it overnight or for several days.
6. Buy through the Internet or by fax, or use an auto broker if you're not confident in your own bargaining skills, you lack the time to haggle, or you want to avoid the "showroom shakedown."
7. Ask for at least a 25 percent discount off the MSRP, and cut PDI and freight charges by at least 50 percent. Insist on a specific delivery date written in the contract, as well as a protected price in case there's a price increase between the time the contract is signed and when the vehicle is delivered. Also ask for a free tank of gas.
8. Order a minimum of options, and seek a 30-40 percent discount on the entire option list.
9. Put the vehicle's down payment on your credit card.
10. Avoid leasing. If you must lease, choose the shortest time possible, drive down the MSRP, and refuse to pay an "acquisition" or "disposal" fee.
11. Look at Asian vehicles made in North America, co-ventures with American automakers, and rebadged imports. They often cost less than imports and are just as reliable. However, some European imports may not be as reliable as you might imagine – Mercedes' M-Class sport-utilities, for example. Get extra warranty protection from the automaker if you're buying a model that has a poorer-than-average repair history. Use auto club references to get honest, competent repairs at a reasonable price.

Now you know how to get a reliable new car for much less than its advertised selling price. Part Two will show you how to cut that price in half and save up to $10,000 by buying a three-year-old used car.

Part Two

USED WHEELS AND BETTER DEALS

Common Sense

When buying a used car, punch the buttons on the radio. If all the stations are rock and roll, there's a good chance the transmission is shot.

Larry Lujack

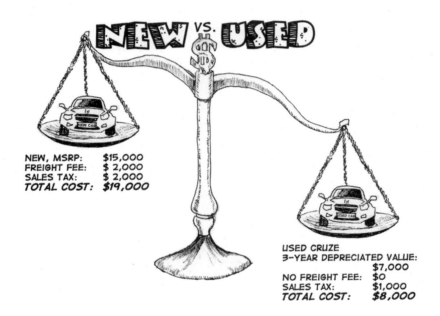

NEW VS. USED

NEW, MSRP: $15,000
FREIGHT FEE: $ 2,000
SALES TAX: $ 2,000
TOTAL COST: *$19,000*

USED CRUZE
3-YEAR DEPRECIATED VALUE:
                   $7,000
NO FREIGHT FEE: $0
SALES TAX: $1,000
TOTAL COST: *$8,000*

"Half-Price" — With Free Delivery

Most cars sold in Canada are used. While new-car sales surged to 1.67 million units in 2012, that's still a bit short of 2003's peak of 1.70 million (U.S. sales reached 15.3 million vehicles). Used-car sales, though, are going through the roof. In fact, the 2.89 million previously owned "bargains" and "beaters" sold in 2010 was an all-time high. Indeed, almost two-thirds of the cars sold in Canada were used, up from about 56 percent just a decade ago.

Blame it on increased longevity – of the driver – and of the car (or more so, the truck). We discussed the phenomenon of senior drivers populating our highways in the previous chapter, but we also should mention that many older drivers own "senior" cars. More than 6 million of the 21.4 million cars on the road are ten years old or older and R.L Polk Data says that 54.2 percent of all the cars manufactured in the last 25 years are still on the road today.

Trucks last almost three times longer than cars, with 17.9 percent of the light trucks manufactured in the last two-and-a-half decades still on the road. By brand segment, 21.7 percent of all the Chevrolet pickups sold 25 years ago are still chugging along our highways and Chrysler and Ford pickups aren't far behind.

Buying a used vehicle is easier than buying new and with a little bit of homework and patience you can find reliable wheels for less than half what the car originally cost. Plus, there is less of a showroom shakedown – confusing figures, payment plans, and costly "extras" – awaiting you. You get a car that has already been scratched, dented, and corroded, but this saves you from that sickening feeling when new-car imperfections first appear. The transformation from new to used occurs as soon as the sales title passes from dealer to a second owner, thus throretically making every car sold a used vehicle. The beauty of this instant morphing from new to used is that it creates a huge pool of inexpensive used vehicles and competing sellers who expect you to haggle.

And price haggling is encouraged because depreciation gives buyers a large margin to bring prices down. In fact, most private owners discover they can get about 20 percent more by selling their trade-in privately than what most dealers would offer. Dealers also make more money selling used vehicles than they make selling new cars and trucks, and they aren't burdened by such things as the manufacturer's suggested retail price, freight charges, options loading, high floor plan interest rates, reduced commissions, and warranty charge-backs. The savings generated by these simpler transactions often go straight into the dealer's and buyer's pockets.

Why Smart Canadians Buy Used

It simply costs too much to own a new car or SUV. In fact, many of my readers tell me that the cost of their new car exceeded the downpayment on their first mortgage. No wonder that of the 4.4 million automobiles that were sold in Canada in 2010, most were second-hand (2.9 million).

Read on for more reasons why Canadians increasingly prefer to buy used vehicles rather than new ones.

Less Initial Cash Outlay, Slower Vehicle Depreciation, "Secret" Warranty Repair Refunds, and Better and Cheaper Parts Availability

New-vehicle prices average around $31,000 and insurance can cost almost $2,000 a year for young drivers. Canadian Automobile Association (CAA) calculates that once you add financing costs, maintenance, taxes, and a host of other expenses, the yearly outlay in 2012 for a small-sized car, like a Honda Civic LX driven 18,000 km a year, is $8,761, or 49 cents per km; a Camry LE driven the same distance may cost about $10,452.40 a year, or 58 cents per km; and, not surprisingly, a Chevrolet Equinox SUV will cost $11,751.52, a year, or 65 cents per km.

For a comprehensive comparative analysis of all the costs involved in owning a vehicle over one- to 10-year periods, access Alberta's consumer information website at *www.agric.gov.ab.ca/app24/costcalculators/vehicle/getvechimpls.jsp*.

Don't forget the savings. Used vehicles aren't sold with $1,600-$2,000 transport fees or $495 "administration" charges, and you can legally avoid paying some sales tax when you buy privately. That's right! You'll pay at least 10 percent less than the dealer's price, and you may avoid the federal Goods and Services Tax that in some provinces applies to dealer sales only.

Depreciation works for you

If someone were to ask you to invest in stocks or bonds guaranteed to be worth less than half their initial purchase value after three to four years, you'd probably head for the door. But this is exactly the trap you're falling into when you buy a new vehicle that will likely lose up to 60 percent of its value after three years of use.

When you buy used, the situation is altogether different. That same vehicle can be purchased three years later, in good condition, and with much of the manufacturer's warranty remaining for less than half its original cost.

Secret warranty refunds

Almost all automakers use secret "goodwill" warranties to cover factory-related defects long after a vehicle's original warranty has expired. This creates a huge fleet of used vehicles that are eligible for free repairs (see pages 157-162).

We're not talking about merely a few months' extension on small items. In fact, some free repairs – like those related to Audi, Nissan, and VW transmissions – are authorized up to ten years under a variety of "goodwill" programs (see Introduction). Still, most secret warranty extensions hover around the five- to seven-year mark and seldom cover vehicles exceeding 160,000 km (almost 100,000 mi). Yet there are exceptions, like the secret catalytic converter warranty that will pay for the converter's replacement up to ten years, or 193,000 km (120,000 mi), on many Chevrolet models.

Incidentally, automakers and dealers claim that there are no "secret" warranties, since they are all published in service bulletins. Although this is technically correct, have you ever tried to get a copy of a service bulletin? Or, if you did manage to get a copy, did the dealer or automaker say the benefits are applicable only in the States? Pure weasel speak!

Parts

Used parts can have a surprisingly long lifespan. Generally, a new gasoline-powered car or minivan can be expected to run with few problems for at least 200,000-300,000 km (125,000-200,000 mi) in its lifetime and a diesel-powered vehicle can easily double those figures. Some repairs will crop up at regular intervals along with preventive maintenance, and your yearly running costs should average about $1,000. Buttressing the argument that vehicles get cheaper to operate the longer you keep them, the U.S. Department of Transportation points out that the average vehicle requires one or more major repairs after every five years of use. Once these repairs are done, however, the vehicle can then be run relatively trouble-free for another five years or more, as long as the environment isn't too hostile. In fact, the farther west you go in Canada, the longer owners keep their vehicles – an average of ten years or more in some provinces, like British Columbia, Manitoba, and Saskatchewan.

Time is on your side in other ways, too. Three years after a model's launch, the replacement parts market usually catches up to consumer demand. Dealers stock larger inventories, and parts wholesalers and independent parts manufacturers expand their output.

Used replacement parts are unquestionably easier to come by after this three-year point through bargaining with local garages, carefully searching of auto wreckers' yards, or looking on the Internet. And a reconditioned or used part usually costs one-third to half the price of a new part. There's generally no difference in the quality of reconditioned mechanical components, and they're often guaranteed for as long as, or longer than, new ones. In fact, some savvy shoppers use the ratings in Part Four of this guide to see which parts have a short life and then buy those parts from retailers who give lifetime warranties on their brakes, exhaust systems, tires, batteries, and so on.

Buying from discount outlets or independent garages, or ordering through mail-order houses, can save you big bucks (30-35 percent) on the cost of new parts and another 15 percent on labour when compared with dealer charges. Mass merchandisers like Costco are another good source of savings; they cut prices and add free services and lifetime warranties (on brakes, mufflers, and transmissions).

Body parts are a different story. Although car company repair parts cost 60 percent more than certified generic aftermarket parts, buyers would be wise to buy only original equipment manufacturer (OEM) parts supplied by automakers in order to get body panels that fit well, protect better in collisions, and have maximum rust resistance, says *Consumer Reports* magazine. Insurance appraisers often substitute cheaper, lower-quality aftermarket body parts in collision repairs, but *Consumer Reports* found that 71 percent of those policyholders who requested OEM parts got them with little or no hassle. The magazine suggests that Canadian consumers complain to their provincial Superintendent of Insurance if OEM parts aren't provided.

With some European models, you can count on a lot of aggravation and expense caused by the unacceptably slow distribution of parts and by the high markup. Because these companies have a quasi-monopoly on replacement parts, there are few independent suppliers you can turn to for help. And junkyards, the last-chance repository for inexpensive car parts, are unlikely to carry foreign parts for vehicles that are more than three years old or are manufactured in small numbers.

Finding parts for Asian and domestic cars and trucks is no problem because of the large number of vehicles produced, the presence of hundreds of independent suppliers, the ease with which relatively simple parts can be interchanged from one model to another, and the large reservoir of used parts stocked by junkyards.

Insurance Costs Less

The price you pay for insurance can vary significantly, not only between insurance companies but also within the same company over time. But one thing does remain constant – the insurance for used vehicles is a lot cheaper than new-car coverage, and through careful comparison shopping, insurance premium payouts can be substantially reduced.

Beware of "captive" brokers

Although the cost of insurance premiums for used cars is often one-third to half the cost of the premiums you would pay for a new vehicle, using the Internet to find the lowest auto insurance quote and accepting a large deductible are critical to keeping premiums low.

Use InsuranceHotline.com

InsuranceHotline.com is the largest online quoting service for car insurance in Canada. *InsuranceHotline.com* represents 80 percent of the Canadian auto insurance, home insurance, and life insurance market for consumers searching for the lowest rate. At no charge, the agency will run applicants' profiles through its database of 30 insurance companies to find the insurer with the lowest rate.

Surprisingly, some of the vehicles with the poorest reliability, durability, and fuel economy ratings, such as GM's Hummer, have good insurance rates and don't see the same multiplication of premiums in the case of a ticket or accident (in which case, your premiums can almost quadruple). When rates for a Hummer and a Honda Civic were calculated, the Civic driver saved only $49 compared to the Hummer premium. But add a police ticket and accident to the equation, and the Civic owner could pay over $2,500 more.

Here are some other *InsuranceHotline.com* findings.

- A family car under $35,000 can cost more to insure than one over $35,000.
- SUVs under $35,000 don't always cost more to insure than a family car or a small luxury model.
- Luxury cars mean luxury premiums, costing on average about $500 more annually to insure than family cars, SUVs, muscle cars, or hybrids.
- Hybrids' fuel savings can be wiped out by higher-cost insurance premiums that rival what you would pay to insure a muscle car.

Auto theft in Canada: The list you don't want to be on

According to the Insurance Bureau of Canada, automobile theft costs Canadians close to $1 billion every year, including $542 million for insurers to fix or replace stolen cars, $250 million in police, health care, and court system costs, and millions more for correctional services.

Thieves generally steal cars for one of four reasons.

1. **For sale abroad:** Stolen cars are often immediately packed – with their vehicle identification numbers (VINs) still intact – and shipped abroad, where they are sold for many times their original market value.
2. **For sale to unsuspecting consumers:** Stolen cars may be given a new identity with false vehicle identification plates, and then sold to unsuspecting consumers. They can also be dismantled and sold for parts.
3. **To get somewhere:** This is commonly, but inappropriately, referred to as "joyriding." Auto theft of any kind is still a crime, and innocent people do get hurt or killed as a result.
4. **To commit another crime:** Stolen cars used to commit other crimes are often recovered – abandoned and badly damaged – within 48 hours of their theft.

"Although many high-end, four-wheel-drive vehicles like the BMW X6, Toyota RAV4, and Lexus RX350 don't appear in the top ten," says Rick Dubin, Vice-President, Investigations at the Insurance Bureau of Canada, "thieves are stealing them in greater numbers than ever before. There is a demand for vehicles like these in Ghana, Nigeria, Dubai, Lebanon, the Middle East, and Eastern Europe. Organized criminals are shipping the vehicles overseas, and as a result, the recovery rate for stolen vehicles in Canada continues to decline, even though there are fewer thefts in total."

The Insurance Bureau of Canada claims that individuals steal less expensive cars because they are easier to steal and tend not to have alarm systems. More data on which vehicles are stolen the most and the least and accident claims stats on a model and year basis are just a click away at *www.ibc.ca*.

Insured collision repairs

The Automobile Repair Regulatory Council says the owner of a motor vehicle damaged in an accident has the right to choose the shop that will do the repairs. Do not waste your time or that of several shops getting several estimates. Select a repair facility you feel comfortable with, then notify your agent or insurance company, or ask the shop to call on your behalf. Your insurance adjuster may require that the damage to the vehicle be inspected. This can be done at an insurance drive-in claim centre or at the shop you have chosen.

Here are some things to inspect yourself, before driving away with your repaired car.

- Check the appearance of the repaired area close up and at a distance.
- Examine the paint for colour match, texture, and overspray.
- Take a test drive to check mechanical repairs.
- Check that the vehicle is clean.

If you are not satisfied, mention your concerns immediately and follow up with a written claim (copy your insurer) and a time period for the work to be completed.

Notify your insurance company

Before you sign any work orders, notify your insurance company or agent, and tell them where the damaged vehicle can be inspected. Most collision and repair centres guarantee their work to some degree, which may not include the paint job. Ask to see a copy of the shop's guarantee and have any information you do not understand clarified. As for the paint warranty, try to get at least a one-year guarantee.

Choosing a qualified repair shop

Look for signs that indicate repair technician certification and training. Membership in professional trade associations indicates that the shop is keeping up with the latest repair procedures. Also, affiliation with automobile associations like the CAA, Alberta Motor Association (AMA), or British Columbia Automobile Association (BCAA) is a plus, because you can use the association to exert pressure when the repair takes too long, or the work isn't done properly. In Part Three you will find jurisprudence where one auto club was found liable for the negligence of one of its member garages (see page 172-173).

Defects Can't Hide

You can easily avoid any nasty surprises by having your chosen used vehicle checked out by an independent mechanic (for $85-$100) before you purchase. This examination protects you against any of the vehicle's potential hidden defects. It's also a tremendous negotiating tool, since you can use the cost of any needed repairs to bargain down the purchase price.

It's easier to get permission to have the vehicle inspected if you promise to give the seller a copy of the inspection report should you decide not to buy it. If you still can't get permission to have the vehicle inspected elsewhere, walk away from the deal, no matter how tempting the selling price. The seller is obviously trying to put one over on you. Ignore the standard excuses that the vehicle isn't insured, that the registration plates have expired, or that the vehicle has a dead battery.

You Know the Past, Present, and Future

Smart customers can easily run an Internet history check on a vehicle and its previous owners through CarProof ($49.95, or $69.95 if you want Insurance Corporation of British Columbia (ICBC) vehicle claims history info, as well) and then read through *Lemon-Aid* to get answers to the following questions before signing a contract: What did the vehicle first sell for, and what is its present insured value? Who serviced it? Has it had accident repairs? Are parts easily available? How much of the original warranty or repair warranties are left? Does the vehicle have a history of costly performance-related defects? What free repairs are available through "goodwill" warranty extensions? (See "Secret Warranties/Internal Bulletins" in Part Four.)

Quick and Cheap Justice

Lawyers win, regardless of whether you win or lose. And you're likely to lose more than you'll ever get back using the traditional court system in a used-car dispute.

But if you're just a bit creative, you'll discover there are many federal and provincial consumer-protection laws that go far beyond whatever protection may be offered by the standard new-vehicle warranty. While Nova Scotia has introduced a "lemon law," Manitoba is the only province with regulations in effect. Furthermore, buyers of used vehicles don't usually have to conform to any arbitrary rules or service guidelines to get this protection.

Let's say you do get stuck with a vehicle that's unreliable, has undisclosed accident damage, or doesn't perform as promised. Fortunately, small claims courts have a jurisdiction limit of $10,000-$30,000 – more than enough to cover the cost of repairs, or compensate you if the vehicle is taken back. That way, any dispute between buyer and seller can be settled within a few months, and without lawyers or excessive court costs. Furthermore, you're not likely to face a battery of lawyers standing in for the automaker and dealer in front of a stern-faced judge. You may not even have to face a judge at all, since many cases are settled through court-imposed mediators at a pretrial meeting that's usually scheduled a month or two after filing.

Car dealers get their vehicles from fleets, lessees, wholesalers, trade-ins, and private sales. Some of the less reputable dealers will buy at auction vehicles that other dealers unloaded because they weren't good enough to sell to their own customers. Other dealers will set up "curb-sider" scams where they sell used vehicles from private homes, using their employees as shills.

Going into 2014, Chrysler, Ford, and General Motors dealers have an abundance of "young" three-year-old off-lease vehicles at unusually low prices because the buy-back prices at lease end were set low as the recession loomed. On the other hand, dealers now selling import brands are chronically short of product because owners keep these vehicles three to four years longer and use the buy-back option for themselves. The majority of private sales are comprised of vehicles six years or older, while independent used-car dealers get most of their profit from selling anything that can be driven away.

Asian Prices

Although used models may cost more this year, they won't cost that much more. We are heading into a seller's new car market which will free up more used cars as buyers return to new cars. Asian new-car prices will only be about 5 percent higher this year due to increased Detroit competition. Only the South Koreans are holding the line on price increases on all but their most popular models. Detroit auto manufacturers, awash in profits from record sales, will stoke the incentive fires with rebate and other sales incentives that will include free two-year maintenance programs and 96-month financing.

Buying strategies

As new cars remain affordable, used cars become even more attractive. Used Honda Civics are more in demand than ever before now that the redesigned 2012 has been trashed by both independent consumer rating groups and a coterie of car columnists. Toyota has regained its sales footing after being mauled by incessant safety recalls, but its halo has been tarnished, resulting in more reasonable new and used prices. Meanwhile, South Korean automakers like Hyundai and Kia have been riding a surge of record sales over the past few years thanks to *Consumer Reports* recommending most of Hyundai's cars and SUVs and a few (OMG!) Kias.

Used Hondas are least likely to have servicing problems since 92 percent of Honda's Canadian sales came from domestically manufactured cars like the Civic, Acura, and Ridgeline pickup. Mazda Canada is also well situated to service its products. Its two best-selling models in Canada, the Mazda3 and Mazda5, have been on the market long enough to build up a large supply of replacement parts and used models aren't hard to find at reasonable prices. Subarus (especially, the Forester), on the other hand, are over-priced due to a combination of their standard AWD, strong reliability ratings, and exceptional road performance. With the revamped 2014 Forester's arrival, used models will cost a bit less, but not by much. Suzuki has left the North American market, and used prices have tumbled. Inasmuch as Suzukis have always been reliable buys, smart consumers may wish to take advantage of the cars' depressed prices and uncomplicated servicing by independent garages.

LUXURY LEMONS

But let's not pick on just Ford, General Motors, and Chrysler. European automakers make their share of lemons as well. If you have been a steady reader of *Lemon-Aid* since 1991, you've been made wary of Mercedes' poor quality for over two decades and probably saved money buying a Lincoln Town Car or Toyota Avalon instead. Furthermore, BMW owners have proven to be some of the most satisfied with their cars' overall dependability when compared with most other European makes, including Audi, Jaguar, Porsche, Saab, Volkswagen, and Volvo.

Lincoln's front-drive Continental (a failure-prone Taurus in disguise) and Mercedes' unreliable luxury cars and SUVs are proof positive that there's absolutely no correlation between safe, dependable transportation and the amount of money a vehicle costs, especially with most front-drive Lincoln and Cadillac luxury cars. Rear-drive Lincolns and Cadillacs, however, have always performed well after many years of use.

Chrysler "luxury" means beautiful styling and lousy quality control. Its luxury rear-drives, like the 300 and Magnum that once sold at a 10 percent premium, are now piling up on dealers' lots due to their reputation as gas-guzzlers with serious automatic transmission, fuel, and suspension system problems, as well as body deficiencies. It's hard to believe, but a 2009 Chrysler 300 Touring that originally sold for $32,095 is now worth barely $8,500. Depreciation also takes a pretty big bite out of Asian luxury car values, with a 2008 Lexus IS 250 that once cost $31,900 now selling for $15,000.

FOUR DECADES OF HITS AND MISSES

Hits

Acura – CL Series, Integra, and Legend; **Audi** – A3, A4, A6, R8, S4, S6, TT, TTs, TTRS; **BMW** – 135i, 3 Series, and 5 Series; **Chrysler** – Colt, 2000 and later Neons, Stealth, 2014 Ram, and Tradesman vans (invest in an extended warranty for the automatic transmission); **Ford** – Crown Victoria, Econoline vans, Escape, 1991 and later Escorts, Freestyle/Taurus X, Grand Marquis, Mustang V6, and Ranger; **GM** – Cruze, 2014 Impala, Enclave, Equinox, Express, Firebird, Rainier, Savana, Terrain, Traverse, and Vandura; **Honda** – Accord, Civic, CR-V, Element, Fit, Odyssey, Pilot, and Ridgeline; **Hyundai** – Accent, Elantra, Genesis, Santa Fe, Tiburon, Tucson, Velostar, and Veracruz; **Kia** – Forte, Rondo, and Soul; **Lexus** – All models; **Lincoln** – Mark series and Town Car; **Mazda** – 323, 626, Mazda3, Mazda5, Mazda6, Miata, Protegé, and Tribute; **Mitsubishi** – Outlander and Spyder; **Nissan** – Frontier, GT-R, Leaf, Rogue, Sentra, Versa, Xterra, and X-Trail; **Subaru** – Impreza, Legacy, Outback, and Forester; **Suzuki** – Aerio, Esteem, Kizashi, Swift, and SX4; **Toyota** – Avalon, Camry, Corolla, Cressida, Echo, Highlander, Matrix, Sienna, Sequoia, Tercel, and Venza; **VW** – Jetta TDI (without DSG trannies).

Misses

Audi – A8, and Q7; **BMW** – 7 Series, Mini Cooper, and X5; **Chrysler** – 200, 300, Avenger, Caravan, Charger, Dakota, Durango, Grand Caravan, Intrepid, LHS, Magnum, Neon, New Yorker, Pacifica, PT Cruiser, Sebring, Sprinter, and Town & Country; **Daewoo** – All models; **Fiat** – 500; **Ford** – Aerostar, Contour, Explorer, F-150, 2003 and later Focus, Mystique, Sable,

Owning a GM front-drive minivan is akin to owning beachfront property in Louisiana.

Taurus, Tempo, Topaz, and Windstar/Freestar; **GM** – Avalanche, Aveo, Canyon, Catera, Cimarron, Cobalt, Colorado, CTS, Envoy, Fiero, G6, Grand Prix, HHR, Impala (through 2013), the Lumina/Montana/Relay/Silhouette/Terraza/Trans Sport/Venture/Uplander group of minivans, Malibu, SRX, STS, TrailBlazer, and Volt; **Hyundai** – Excel, Pony, pre-2006 4-cylinder Sonatas, and Stellar; **Infiniti** – G20; **Jaguar** – All models; **Jeep** – Cherokee, Commander, Compass, Grand Cherokee, Journey, and Patriot; **Kia** –Sedona, Sephia, Sorento, Spectra, and 2006 and earlier Sportages; **Lada** – All models; **Land Rover** – All models; **Lincoln** – Continental front-drive; **Mercedes-Benz** – 190, B-Class, C-Class, CLK, GL-Class (V8), M series, R-Class, S-Class, and SLK; **Merkur** – All models; **Nissan** – 240Z, 250Z, 260Z, pre-2005 Altimas, Armada, Cube, Juke, Quest, Titan; **Porsche** – All models; **Saab** – All models; **Saturn** – L-Series, ION, Relay, S-Series, and VUE; **Suzuki** – Forenza, Samurai, Verona, and X-90; **Toyota** – Previa; **VW** – EuroVan, Passat, Golf, Rabbit, and Touareg (with DSG transmissions).

Note in the list above how many so-called premium luxury brands have fallen out of favour and have been orphaned by shoppers and then abandoned by the automakers themselves. Their hapless owners are left with practically worthless, unreliable cars that can't be serviced properly.

Also, keep in mind that some Japanese makes from Honda, Lexus, Mazda, Nissan, and Toyota have had a resurgence of engine and transmission problems, in addition to an apparent overall decline in reliability and safety.

For example, Nissan engineers have worked overtime during the past seven years to correct Quest glitches, and Toyota's Tacoma and Tundra pickups have such serious corrosion problems (covered by a 15-year secret warranty that includes buying back the pickups at 150 percent of their resale value), and sudden acceleration, drivetrain, and suspension defects that the automaker has continually recalled the vehicles or extended their warranties to compensate owners.

Chrysler Automatic Transmissions

Since the early '90s, practically all models in Chrysler's front-drive lineup have had disposable automatic transmissions. What adds insult to injury, though, is that Chrysler regularly stiffs its customers with transmission repair bills that average about $3,000 – about half the average vehicle's worth after five years – when the warranty expires. Since this is far less than what a new car or minivan would cost, most owners pay the bill and then hop onto the transmission merry-go-round, replacing the same transmission at regular intervals. Go ahead, ask any transmission shop.

Keep in mind that during the past few years Chrysler has changed over to a new powertrain hookup with a re-engineered transmission that includes 8-speed gearing and a new Pentastar V6 engine.

The 2014 Jeep Cherokee is on track to be the first light vehicle in the world with a 9-speed transmission – beating Land Rover, which promised to have a 9-speed on the market earlier. Chrysler says increasing the number of gears from six to nine helps to reduce emissions, improve fuel efficiency by 45 percent, and adds to the vehicle's off-road capability, all claims that are yet to be proven.

Has the 6-speed automatic coupled to a Pentastar 3.6L V6 engine introduced on most 2011 models cured the company's age-old powertrain deficiencies? Preliminary data says it hasn't, as the following owner review in *www.Edmunds.com clearly shows:*

We bought our 2011 Grand Cherokee Laredo 4X4 in December 2010 and it has been in the shop on and off for weeks since we bought it, with major engine-related problems. It only has 13000 km on it, but it blows black smoke out of the exhaust when it is started and sounds like an old diesel engine when it runs. The front crankshaft pulley came apart grinding the remaining pulley against the engine block (Chrysler called it "engine crankshaft damper problems" and "harmonizer balancer issues") and most recently the engine was "pulling in too much fuel" and Chrysler informed us the oil separator and PVC valve would need to be replaced. The gear shifter has broken, and was further damaged by the dealer 4 months ago and still has not been repaired due to "a lack of replacement parts." The engine has had declining performance since about 5000 km.

We didn't just get a lemon because we found out that in fact other 3.6-liter Pentastar V6 engines have come in with the same problems and there have been technical service bulletins released by Chrysler on these issues and on other Grand Cherokees.

This engine is scheduled to go into many more models in 2012 and I would strongly recommend avoiding this engine at all costs. Chrysler supposedly spent years developing this new engine and have high hopes it will pull this automaker out of financial ruin but they should have spent a little more time because it is full of problems and will no doubt cost anyone unfortunate enough to buy one a fortune. Chrysler hasn't been willing to do anything to help and we continue to have out of pocket costs add up.

FAVORITE FEATURES: Looks good but runs terrible. If you just want to park it in your yard and look at it, it is great but if you plan on driving it, forget it, as this is beyond what it can handle. Oh yeah, the stereo sounds good, since there is no road noise in my driveway.

And from *www.dodgeforum.com:*

According to *Consumers Reports*, the transmission is "clunky" in their tests. Well, it is, especially when cold. It wants to get into 2nd and 3rd so quickly, that the shift is a bit jerky . . .
I bought my 2011 Dodge Grand Caravan in May and as soon as it hit 5000 miles, I noticed a bang between 1st and 2nd gear. It took 4 days to get an appointment at the local dealer. I told them I shouldn't be driving the car with this shifting problem, they didn't seem to be worried. I brought the van in and they had to wait 5 days for a part to come in for it. I got the van back to find out I had no reverse and the check engine light came on. Brought the van back the next morning and they told me they had done a complete rebuild on the transmission and that a pump had gone. Got the van back a week later and noticed the same banging from 1st to 2nd gear and a shudder when in reverse. Brought it back again, and just picked the van up today to find out it was low on transmission fluid. There is no dipstick, and the service manager said the only way to know the fluid is low is by going on the computer. The van still has the hesitation from 1st to 2nd but I have only driven it about 10 miles today.

Well, after driving the van for a week, out of the economy mode, it happened again. I was backing down a steep driveway and when I put it into drive it hopped and had about a 3-second delay, while on-coming traffic was approaching me at 50mph! Pretty scary. So I put it back into economy mode to have the same jerky shifting. Later that afternoon, I pulled out of my parking lot and it banged in between 1st and 2nd gear again. This is unacceptable. Calling the dealer today for the 4th fix on this tranny.

Diesel Defects

All three Detroit manufacturers have had serious injector problems with their newest diesel engines. Ford is covering repair costs through a variety of "goodwill" programs, while General Motors and Chrysler argue that their recent bankruptcy absolves them from any liability.

Nevertheless, J.D. Power's 2004 Vehicle Dependability Study found that Ford and Chevrolet diesel pickups were worse performers than similar gas models, while Dodge and GMC trucks were better overall. Owners of Volkswagen diesels reported up to twice as many engine problems as did owners of VWs that burn gas.

Chrysler

Although Chrysler's Cummins engine has been the most reliable diesel sold by American automakers, it also has had some serious manufacturing flaws, involving lift-pump failures that compromise injector-pump performance. Here's how independent mechanic Chuck Arnold (*chuck@thepowershop.com*) describes the problem.

Low fuel pressure is very dangerous because it is possible for the engine to run very well right up to the moment of failure. There may be no symptom of a problem at all before you are walking. If you notice extended cranking before startup of your Cummins 24-Valve engine you should get your lift pump checked out fast. Addition of fuel lubricant enhancing additives to every tank of fuel may minimize pump damage and extend pump life. Finally, Cummins and Bosch should re-engineer their injector pump to make it less sensitive to low-fuel-pressure-induced failure. Existing safety systems designed to limit performance or signal engine trouble need to be redesigned to work when fuel pressure is inadequate so that very expensive injector pumps are not destroyed without warning.

Ford

F-Series equipped with the 6.0L Power Stroke diesel engine were so badly flawed that they couldn't be fixed, forcing Ford to buy back over 500 units. Wary customers are snapping up Ford's earlier 7.3L diesels, which are apparently more reliable, though less powerful (275 hp versus 325 hp). Power Strokes have a history of fuel injectors that leak into the crankcase, and, on the 7.3L diesel, water can leak into the fuel tank, causing the engine to seize. Other glitches affect the turbocharger, the fuel injection control pressure sensor, and the engine control software.

> The 6-liter Power Stroke diesel V8, built by a unit of Navistar for Ford, commands nearly half the U.S. market for diesel pickups. But a raft of problems and repeat trips to dealerships for repairs has left some owners upset, threatening Ford's efforts to rebuild a reputation for quality vehicles.
>
> Soon after the new engines went on sale in November in heavy-duty Ford pickups and the Ford Excursion sport-utility vehicle, owners started reporting problems. Among the costliest is fuel seeping into the engine's oil supply in amounts large enough to ruin the engine. Other complaints included engines that ran roughly or stalled, lack of power at low speeds and harsh shifts.
>
> JUSTIN HYDE
> *REUTERS*, AUGUST 20, 2003

> We're pulling heads off of a 6.0 now with 4,000 miles [6,400 km] on it. All these problems I've mentioned are on trucks with less than 20,000 miles [32,000 km]. My diesel tech constantly wishes that since they had worked all the kinks out of the 7.3, Ford would have kept it. So far, we've had six buybacks. The one we're pulling the heads off of now will be the next. Before this, I only had one buyback, in four years.

After years of stonewalling and rejecting *Lemon-Aid*'s criticism and owners' refund claims for faulty 6.0L diesel truck engines, Ford now agrees that its engines were crap and has demanded that the supplier of these engines, International Engine Group, pay the automaker compensation for the defective diesels. Ironic, isn't it? Ford has done to International what many angry owners of Power Stroke 6.0L-diesel-equipped trucks threatened to do to Ford. And, as in the Ford Explorer/Firestone tire debacle, neither company will admit guilt, or even apologize to owners for their shoddy product.

Ford's 6.4L diesels are continuing to use faulty fuel injectors that may leak fuel into the engine crankcase, causing the oil level to rise and possibly damage the engine. Ford set up a "goodwill" warranty extension (Campaign 09B08) to replace these leaking injectors for free, but that program expired in September 2010.

Nevertheless, Ford is now paying for replacements under a "goodwill" warranty on a case-by-case basis. What does all this mean? Don't take no for an answer.

Also, both Ford and General Motors have had problems with snow accumulation in the air filter element, restricting air passage to the engine and possibly causing severe engine damage. Both companies are liable for the free repair of any damage caused by this poor design. Or did they imagine Canada was a snow-free zone?

General Motors

GM's diesel engine failures primarily affect the 6.5L and 6.6L Duramax engine. The 6.5L powerplants are noted for cracked blocks, broken cranks, cracks in the main webbing, cracked cylinder heads, coolant in the oil, loss of power, hard starting, low oil pressure, and oil contamination. Duramax 6.6L engines have been plagued by persistent oil leaks and excessive oil burning, and by defective turbo-chargers, fuel-injection pumps, and injectors, causing seized engines, chronic stalling, loss of power, hard starts, and excessive gas consumption. Finally, anecdotal reports from diesel owners tell *Lemon-Aid* that engine head gasket repairs or replacements are covered by a "goodwill" policy for up to 7 years/160,000 km.

SAFETY FIRST

Looking through Part Four can help you make a list of safe and reliable used car buys to consider before you even leave the house.

The best indicator of a car's overall safety is National Highway Traffic Safety Administration (NHTSA) and Insurance Institute for Highway Safey (IIHS) crashworthiness ratings, applicable to most vehicles made and

Volkswagen 2012 CC: A four-door becomes a three-door.

sold over the past several decades in North America. IIHS uses more severe standards and rates head restraint effectiveness, roof crush resistance, and front-quarter protection as well. Results from these two agencies are posted for each model rated in Part Four. For readers who wish to go directly to the respective website of either safety group, see *safercar.gov* or *www.iihs.org/ratings*.

However, there are many other national and international testing agencies that you may consult, and they can be found at *www.crashtest.com/netindex.htm*. This site shows the results of early crash tests of cars that were sold in Australia, Europe, and Japan and that are just now coming to the North American market. Take the

Mercedes Smart Car as an example. Nowhere in Mercedes' or Chrysler's sales brochures did I see a reference to the Smart's unimpressive "Acceptable" frontal crash test rating for early models, or any mention that during the 2008 Smart Fortwo's side-impact test, the driver-side door unlatched and opened. A door opening during a side-impact crash increases the likelihood of occupant ejection and massive injuries or death.

Of course, no one expects to be in a collision, but NHTSA estimates that every vehicle will be in two accidents of varying severity during its lifetime. So why not put the averages on your side?

WHEN AND WHERE TO BUY

When to Buy

In the fall, dealer stocks of quality trade-ins and off-lease returns are at their highest level, and private sellers are moderately active. Prices are higher, but you'll have a greater choice of vehicles. In winter, prices decline substantially, and dealers and private sellers are generally easier to bargain with because buyers are scarce and weather conditions don't allow sellers to present their wares in the best light. In spring and summer, prices go up a bit as private sellers become more active and increased new-car rebates bring more trade-ins.

Private Sellers

Private sellers are your best source for a cheap and reliable used vehicle because you're on an equal bargaining level with a vendor who isn't trying to profit from your inexperience. A good private sale price would be about 5 percent *more* than the rock-bottom wholesale price, or approximately 20 percent *less* than the retail price advertised by local dealers. You can find estimated wholesale and retail prices in Part Four.

Remember, no seller, be it a dealer or a private party, expects to get his or her asking price. As with price reductions on home listings, a 10-20 percent reduction on the advertised price is common with private sellers. Dealers usually won't cut more than 10 percent off their advertised price.

It is also a good idea to draw up a bill of sale that gives all the pertinent details of your used-car transaction. (See the following page for one that you may use as your guide *www.registryedmonton.com/uploads/BillOfSaleReg3126.pdf.*)

BUYING WITH CONFIDENCE

No matter whom you're buying a used vehicle from, there are a few rules you should follow to get the best deal.

PLEASE PRINT CLEARLY

Bill of Sale

- **Sections 1 and 2 must be completed** in order to make this Bill of Sale acceptable for vehicle registration. Completion of section 3, on the back of this form, is optional.
- Two copies of this Bill of Sale should be completed. The buyer keeps the original and the seller keeps the copy.
- Alterations or corrections made while completing the vehicle information section should be initialled by the buyer and seller.

SECTION 1

SELLER(S) INFORMATION		
Name(s) *(Last, First, Second)*		Telephone Number
Address Street	City / Town Province / State	Postal Code / Zip Code
Personal Identification:		

VEHICLE INFORMATION			
Year	Make	Model or Series	Style
Vehicle Identification Number (VIN) / Serial Number	Body Color	Roof Color	Odometer Reading

BUYER(S) INFORMATION		
Name(s) *(Last, First, Second)*		Telephone Number
Address Street	City / Town Province / State	Postal Code / Zip Code
Personal Identification:		

This vehicle was sold for the sum of:

_____ Dollars $ _____
(Sum written in full)

(Subject to the terms and special conditions which appear in Section 3 on the back of this form)

SECTION 2

GENERAL INFORMATION

Dated at: _____
               City / Town   Province / State   Country

on _____ .

I certify that all information shown above is true to the best of my knowledge.

_____   _____
Signature of Buyer   Signature of Seller

_____   _____
Signature of Buyer   Signature of Seller

_____   _____
Signature of Witness   Signature of Witness

REG3126 (2011/01)

SECTION 3 (OPTIONAL)

SPECIAL CONDITIONS OF SALE

1. The vehicle described on the front of this form is:
   Check the appropriate box(es)

   a) Free of all liens and encumbrances: ☐ Yes ☐ No   If No, please give names of lien holders:

   _____

   b) Being paid for in full: ☐ Yes ☐ No

   Being paid by: ☐ Cash ☐ Cheque ☐ Money Order ☐ Other *(please specify):* _____

2. Payment Terms: _____

3. Vehicle was last registered in: _____

                                       Province / State   Country

4. Special conditions of sale *(if any)*: _____

   _____

   _____

   _____

General Information:

- The law in the Province of Alberta requires a vehicle to be insured prior to registration. Documentary proof of vehicle insurance is required. Legislation allows a person to whom a valid licence plate is issued to transfer the licence plate to a newly purchased vehicle to be registered within 14 days of the date on their Bill of Sale.

  The above does not apply to commercial vehicles used for the transportation of goods or passengers for compensation.

- A vehicle entering Alberta from another jurisdiction requires a safety inspection. Information can be obtained from a Registry Agent. A listing of local Registry Agents can be found in the telephone directory under Licence and Registry Services; or visit Service Alberta's website at www.servicealberta.gov.ab.ca for comprehensive registries and consumer information and services.

- In addition to the Bill of Sale, other identification is required to obtain Alberta registration. Where possible, obtain Section 2 of the previous Alberta vehicle registration certificate.

- The prospective purchaser can determine whether a vehicle is free of liens and encumbrances in Alberta by contacting a Registry Agent.

  In order to perform a search, a Registry Agent will require the vehicle identification number (VIN) / serial number of the vehicle. A request for a search can be made in person or in writing. There is a fee for this service.

- Vehicle Information Reports are available from a Registry Agent. There is a fee for each service.

- The buyer must produce a copy of a properly completed Bill of Sale, that includes the same information as shown on this standardized form, in order to register and licence a vehicle in Alberta.

This form is provided as a courtesy by Service Alberta to ensure that sufficient information is contained within the Bill of Sale to permit licensing and registration of the described vehicle by the new owner.

No liability attaches to the Crown through the use of this document in respect of the sale of this vehicle. Any dispute arising from the sale becomes a civil matter among the parties named in this document.

REG3126 (2011/01)

Source: Alberta government site: www.registryedmonton.com/uploads/BillOfSaleReg3126.pdf.

First, have a good idea of what you want and the price you're willing to pay. If you have a preapproved line of credit, that will keep the number crunching and extra fees to a minimum. Finally, be resolute and polite, but make it clear that you are a serious buyer and won't participate in any "showroom shakedowns."

Here's a successful real-world technique used by Kurt Binnie, a frequent *Lemon-Aid* tipster.

> Imagine the surprise of the used-car salesman when I pulled out my BlackBerry and did a VIN search right in front of him using Carfax [*Lemon-Aid* recommends the Canadian firm CarProof]. Threw him right off balance. Carfax results for Ontario vehicles give a good indication, but not the complete MTO [Ministry of Transportation, Ontario] history. I bought the UVIP [Used Vehicle Information Package] ... before closing the deal. For the car I ended up buying, I didn't even tell the sales staff that I was running the VIN while I was there. I was able to see it wasn't an auction vehicle or a write-off. This technique should work with pretty much any WAP [Wireless Application Protocol] enabled phone.

Kurt's letter goes on to describe how he avoids negotiations with sales staff and managers. He figures out the price he's willing to pay beforehand, using a combination of book values and the prices listed at *www.autotrader.ca*. He then test drives the vehicle, runs the VIN through his BlackBerry, and then makes a point-blank, one-time offer to the dealer. He has also found that used-car staff often have no knowledge about the vehicles on their lots beyond their asking price, and they make no distinction between cars manufactured early or late in the model year. An alert buyer could get a car built in August 2002 for the same price as one from September 2001, since they are both used 2002 cars.

Primary Precautions

Get a printed sales agreement, even if it's just handwritten, that includes a clause stating that there are no outstanding traffic violations or liens against the vehicle. It doesn't make a great deal of difference whether the car will be purchased "as is" or certified under provincial regulation. A vehicle sold as safety certified can still turn into a lemon or be dangerous to drive. The certification process can be sabotaged if a minimal number of components are checked, the mechanic is incompetent, or the instruments are poorly calibrated. "Certified" is not the same as having a warranty to protect you from engine seizure or transmission failure. It means only that the vehicle met the minimum safety standards on the day it was tested.

Make sure the vehicle is lien-free and has not been damaged in a flood or written off after an accident. Flood damage can be hard to see, but it impairs ABS, power steering, and airbag functioning (making deployment ten times slower).

Canada has become a haven for rebuilt American wrecks. Write-offs are also shipped from provinces where there are stringent disclosure regulations to provinces where there are lax rules or no rules at all.

If you suspect your vehicle is flood-damaged, is a rebuilt wreck from the States, or was once a taxi, there's a useful Canadian search agency called CarProof that can give you a complete history of any vehicle within a day.

CarProof (www.carproof.com)

Operating out of London, Ontario, CarProof's services cost between $34.95 and $69.95, plus taxes, per report. Information requests can be completed overnight – or sometimes within minutes – online. Contact the company through its website, or if you prefer to talk, call 519-675-1415.

In most provinces, you can do a lien and registration search yourself, but it's hardly worth the effort considering the low cost and comprehensive nature of CarProof's services.

If a lien does exist, you should contact the creditor(s) listed to find out whether any debts have been paid. If a debt is outstanding, you should arrange with the vendor to pay the creditor the outstanding balance, or agree that you can put the purchase price in a trust account to pay the lender. If the debt is larger than the purchase price of the car, it's up to you to decide whether you wish to complete the deal. If the seller agrees to clear the title personally, make sure that you receive a written relinquishment of title from the creditor before transferring any money to the seller. Make sure the title doesn't show an "R" for "restored," since this indicates that the vehicle was written off as a total loss and may not have been properly repaired.

Even if all documents are in order, ask the seller to show you the vehicle's original sales contract and a few repair bills in order to ascertain how well it was maintained. The bills will show you if the odometer was turned back and will also indicate which repairs are still guaranteed. If none of these can be produced, leave. If the contract shows that the car was financed, verify that the loan was paid. If you're still not sure that the vehicle is free of liens, ask your bank or credit union manager to check for you. If no clear answer is forthcoming, look for something else.

DON'T PAY TOO MUCH

Prices for used large- and mid-sized cars, trucks, and SUVs are falling as gas prices go higher. But this price drop hasn't been as severe with small cars and trucks, mini-minivans, downsized SUVs, or wagon crossovers. Their prices on the used-car market are relatively stable and are expected to stay that way through the summer.

If you'd like to save even more when buying used, consider the tips below.

- Choose a vehicle that's five years old or more and has a good reliability and durability record. Don't buy an extended warranty that may become worthless. The money you save from the extra years' depreciation and lower insurance premiums will make up for some additional maintenance costs.

- Look for discounted off-lease vehicles with low mileage and a good reputation.
- Buy a vehicle that's depreciated more than average simply because of its bland styling, unpopular colour (dark blue, white, and champagne are out; silver is in), lack of high-performance features, or discontinuation.
- Buy a cheaper twin or rebadged model like a fully loaded Camry instead of a Lexus ES, a Toyota Matrix in lieu of a Pontiac Vibe, or a Chevrolet Silverado instead of a GMC Sierra.
- Buy a fully equipped gas hog. Your $30,000 savings on a large SUV or pickup will pay the gas bill many times over, and the vehicle can be easily resold a few years down the road, with only moderate depreciation.

Price Guides

The best way to determine the price range for a particular model is to read the *Lemon-Aid* values found in Part Four. From there, you may wish to get a free second opinion by accessing Vehicle Market Research International's Canadian used-car prices at *www.vmrcanada.com*. It is one of the few free sources that list wholesale and retail values for used cars in Canada. The site even includes a handy calculator that adjusts a vehicle's value according to model, mileage, and a variety of options.

Black Book and *Red Book* price guides, found in most libraries, banks, and credit unions, are essential to anyone buying or selling a used vehicle. Both guides are easily accessible on the Internet. To read the *Canadian Black Book* values, simply copy the following URL into your web browser: *www.canadianblackbook.com/used-cars.html*. This site lists the vehicle's trade-in and future value, as well as the asking price based upon your Canadian postal code. No other identification is required.

Now, if you want to use the *Canadian Red Book Vehicle Valuation Guide*, which seems more attuned to Quebec and Ontario sales, you can order single copies of their used car and light truck wholesale and retail price guide for $19.95 at *www.canadianredbook.com* (an annual subscription costs $105). There are no restrictions as to who may subscribe.

You may also go to *Auto Trader* magazine's website at *www.autotrader.ca* to see at what prices other Canadians are trying to sell your chosen vehicle.

Don't be surprised to find that many national price guides have an Eastern Ontario and Quebec price bias, especially the *Red Book*. They often list unrealistically low prices compared with what you'll see in the eastern and western provinces and in rural areas, where good used cars are often sold for outrageously high prices or are simply passed down through the family for an average of eight to ten years. Other price guides may list prices that are much higher than those found in your region. Consequently, use whichever price guide lists the highest value when selling your trade-in or negotiating a write-off value with an insurer. When buying, use the guide with the lowest values as your bargaining tool.

Cross-Border Sales

Shopping in the States for a used car or truck won't save you much money with cheaper, entry-level small cars. However, sports cars, luxury vehicles, SUVs, large trucks, and vans bought in the U.S. can save you tens of thousands of dollars, now that the Canadian dollar is flirting with parity to the American greenback.

Here's what to do.

1. Check with Ottawa to see if the used vehicle you covet can be imported into Canada (call the Registrar of Imported Vehicles at 1-888-848-8240, or visit their website at *www.riv.ca*).
2. Take a trip across the border to scout out what is available from all dealers. Compare your findings with what's offered by Canadian cross-border brokers.
3. Verify if the price is fair once taxes and transport charges are considered.

Hire a broker or deal directly with the dealer. Be wary of private sellers, because your legal rights may be more limited in cross-border transactions.

Rental and Leased Vehicles

Next to buying privately, the second-best choice for getting a good used vehicle is a rental company or leasing agency. Due to our slumping economy, Budget, Hertz, Avis, and National are selling, at cut-rate prices, vehicles that have one to two years of service and approximately 80,000-100,000 km (approximately 50,000-60,000 mi) on the odometer. These rental companies will gladly provide a vehicle's complete history and allow an independent inspection by a qualified mechanic of the buyer's choice, as well as arrange for competitive financing.

Rental vehicles are generally well maintained, sell for a few thousand dollars more than privately sold vehicles, and come with strong guarantees, like Budget's 30-day money-back guarantee at some of its retail outlets (including three in B.C.). Rental-car companies also usually settle customer complaints without much hassle so as to not tarnish their images with rental customers.

Rental agencies tend to keep their stock of cars on the outskirts of town near the airport (particularly in Alberta and B.C.) and advertise in the local papers. Sales are held year-round as inventory is replenished. Late summer and early fall are usually the best times to see a wide selection because the new rentals arrive during this time period.

Vehicles that have just come off a three- or five-year lease are much more competitively priced than rentals, generally have less mileage, and are usually as well maintained. You're also likely to get a better price if you buy directly from the lessee, rather than going through the dealership or an independent agency. But remember that you won't have the dealer's leverage to extract post-warranty "goodwill" repairs from the automaker.

Repossessed Vehicles

Repossessed vehicles frequently come from bankrupt small businesses or subprime borrowers who failed to make their finance payments. They are usually found at auctions, but finance companies and banks sometimes sell them as well. Canadian courts have held that financial institutions are legally responsible for defects found in what they sell, so don't be at all surprised by the disclosure paperwork that will be shoved under your nose. Also, as with rental car company transactions, the combination of these companies' deep pockets and their abhorrence of bad publicity means you'll likely get your money back if you make a bad buy. The biggest problem with repossessed sport-utilities and pickups is that they may have been damaged by off-roading or neglected by their financially troubled owners. Although you rarely get to test drive or closely examine these vehicles, a local dealer may be able to produce a vehicle maintenance history by running the VIN through their manufacturer's database.

New-Car Dealers

New-car dealerships aren't bad places to pick up good used cars or trucks. Sure, prices are about 20 percent higher than those for vehicles sold privately, but rebates and zero percent financing plans can trim used-car prices dramatically. Plus, dealers are insured against selling stolen vehicles or vehicles with finance or other liens owing. They also usually allow prospective buyers to have the vehicle inspected by an independent garage, offer a much wider choice of models, and have their own repair facilities to do warranty work. In addition, if there's a possibility of getting post-warranty "goodwill" compensation from the manufacturer, your dealer can provide additional leverage, particularly if the dealership is a franchisee for the model you have purchased. Finally, if things do go terribly wrong, dealers have deeper pockets than private sellers, so there's a better chance of winning a court judgment.

Provinces are also cracking down on dealers who sell defective used cars. In addition to Manitoba's recently enacted "lemon law," Alberta now requires a thorough mechanical inspection of every used car sold by dealers. Under the revised regulations, a mechanical assessment will be completed by a licensed journeyman technician with a trade certificate as an Automotive Service Technician or Heavy Equipment Technician under the *Apprenticeship and Industry Training Act.*

A mechanical fitness assessment will be valid for 120 days from the time of completion. This is a change from 14 days for the previous certificate. The extended time period recognizes the broader nature of the assessment. More information about the amendments to the vehicle inspection regulation is available on the Alberta Transportation website at *www.transportation.alberta.ca* (under the "Drivers and Vehicles" tab).

"Certified" vehicles

The word "certified" doesn't mean much. Ideally, it tells us the vehicle has undergone some reconditioning that was monitored by the manufacturer. Of course, some dealers don't do anything but slap a "certified" sticker on the car and then inflate the selling price. Sometimes, an auto association will certify a vehicle that has been inspected and has had the designated defects corrected.

Used-car leasing

It isn't a good idea to lease either new or used vehicles. Leasing has been touted as a method of making the high cost of vehicle ownership more affordable, but don't you believe it. Leasing is generally costlier than an outright purchase, and, for most people, the pitfalls far outweigh any advantages. If you must lease, do so for the shortest time possible and make sure the lease is close-ended (meaning that you walk away from the vehicle when the lease period ends). Also, make sure there's a maximum mileage allowance of at least 25,000 km (about 15,500 mi) per year and that the charge per excess kilometre is no higher than 8-10 cents. (For information on leasing see "Fleecing" by Leasing in Part One.)

Used-Car Dealers

Used-car dealers usually sell their vehicles for a bit less than what new-car dealers charge. However, their vehicles may be worth a lot less because they don't get the first pick of top-quality trade-ins. Many independent urban dealerships are marginal operations that can't invest much money in reconditioning their vehicles, which are often collected from auctions and new-car dealers reluctant to sell the vehicles to their own customers. And used-car dealers don't always have repair facilities to honour the warranties they do provide. Often, their credit terms are easier (but more expensive) than those offered by franchised new-car dealers.

That said, used-car dealers operating in small towns are an entirely different breed. These small, often family-run businesses recondition and resell cars and trucks that usually come from within their communities. Routine servicing is usually done in-house, and more complicated repairs are subcontracted out to specialized garages nearby. On one hand, these small outlets survive by word-of-mouth advertising and wouldn't last long if they didn't deal fairly with local townsfolk. On the other hand, their prices will likely be higher than elsewhere due to the better quality of their used vehicles and the cost of reconditioning and repairing what they sell under warranty.

Auctions

First of all, make sure it's a legitimate auction. Many are fronts for used-car lots where sleazy dealers put fake ads in complicit newspapers, pretending to hold auctions that are no more than weekend selling sprees.

Furthermore, you'll need lots of patience, smarts, and luck to pick up anything worthwhile. Government auctions – places where the mythical $50 Jeeps are sold – are fun to attend but highly overrated as places to find bargains. The odds against you: It's impossible to determine the condition of the vehicles put up for bid, prices can go way out of control, and auction employees, professional sellers, their relatives, and their friends usually pick over the good stuff long before you ever see it.

To attend commercial auctions is to swim with the piranhas. They are frequented by "ringers" who bid up the prices, and by professional dealers who pick up cheap, worn-out vehicles unloaded by new-car dealers and independents. There are no guarantees, cash is required, and quality is likely to be as low as the price. Remember, too, that auction purchases are subject to provincial and federal sales taxes, the auction's sales commission (3-5 percent), and, in some cases, an administrative fee of $75-$100.

If you are interested in shopping at an auto auction, remember that certain days are reserved for dealers only, so call ahead. You'll find the vehicles locked in a compound, but you should have ample opportunity to inspect them and, in some cases, take a short drive around the property before the auction begins.

The Internet

The Internet is a risky place to buy a used car. You don't know the seller, and you know even less about the car. It's easy for an individual to sell a car they don't own, and it's even easier to create a

Used car predators are ready to pounce on the unwary.

virtual dealership, with photos of a huge inventory and a modern showroom, when the operation is likely made up of one guy working out of his basement.

Rating systems are unreliable too. Ratings from "happy customers" may be nothing but ploys – fictitious postings created by the seller to give out five-star ratings and the appearance that the company is honest and reliable.

If you must use the Internet, get the seller's full name and a copy of their driver's licence, plus lots of references. Then go see the vehicle, take a road test, and have a mechanic verify if the car is roadworthy and able to pass a safety inspection.

Although you take an even bigger risk buying out-of-province or in the States, there are a few precautions you can take to protect yourself. First off, compare shipping fees with a Canadian automobile transporter like Hansen's (*www.lhf.com*), and put your money into an escrow account until the vehicle is delivered in satisfactory condition.

If the car is located in the States, print out the tips found on eBay's website at *pages.ebay.ca/ebaymotors/explained/checklist/howtobuyUS.html*. The website takes you through each step in detail and will tell you if the vehicle is permitted in Canada and the likely modification requirements. If the vehicle needs alteration, you should check with a mechanic for an estimate. You will also need to get a recall clearance letter from the dealer or automaker in order to pass federal inspection. Additional information can be obtained from the Registrar of Imported Vehicles (1-888-848-8240 or *www.riv.ca*).

Beware of phony eBay solicitations that are sent via doctored e-mails selling out-of-province vehicles. In the e-mail the "owner" will even promise to deliver the car to you at no extra cost. Rather than paying through the relatively secure PayPal used in most legitimate transactions, you will be instructed to send payment through a Western Union or MoneyGram money transfer.

How prevalent is this scam? About a third of the ads in *Canadian Auto Trader* checked out several years ago by the non-profit Automobile Protection Association turned out to be phony. The most obvious indications these ads were placed by scam artists is that the same e-mail address kept reappearing, or the listed phone number was a dummy.

Most of the fraudulent advertisements were placed outside Canada, apparently without the knowledge of the online sites that published them. Nevertheless, it's hard not to suspect some complicity because the ads are quite easy to verify by the hosting site. For example, *Wheels.ca* staffers refuse advertisers with an IP address outside of Canada and ad claims and contact information are constantly checked.

Another fraud is committed by phony overseas used-car buyers when they take delivery of the car and pay for it with a worthless cashier's cheque. Again, using PayPal will protect you from this scam.

There is some government help available to catch Internet used-car swindlers. PhoneBusters, the federal-provincial agency set up to deal with telephone and Internet scams (1-888-495-8501) has ties to the RCMP and OPP, and will investigate and arrest these high-tech crooks.

Here are some more tips for selling or purchasing vehicles online.

- Check out the listed phone number and ask for an address and independent reference.
- Insist that the car be inspected by a third party before closing the deal.
- Search the VIN or ad description using Google or *www.carproof.com*. Often the same wording or VIN will appear on different sites.
- Never use a money transfer service.
- Call the online escrow agency and speak with a representative before divulging any personal financial information.
- Be skeptical of eBay "second chance" offers.

- Always use the eBay "contact seller" process.
- Report all shady deals to the local RCMP detachment. Then, file a complaint with your local police service and at the same time voice your concerns with the Internet service provider (ISP) hosting the offensive material. The Canadian Association of Internet Providers (*www.caip.ca*) would also welcome your comments or concerns in regards to Canadian ISPs.

Canadian car sales websites

- *AMVOQ.ca* – Quebec used-car classifieds (in French)
- *AutoHunter.ca* – Alberta used-car classifieds
- *Autonet.ca* – New and used cars and trucks, new-car dealers, new-car prices, and reviews
- *AutoTrader.ca* – Used-car classifieds from all across Canada
- *BuySell.com* – Classifieds from all across Canada
- eBay Motors Canada (*cars.eBay.ca*) – The premiere site for used cars located in Canada or anywhere in the world
- North American Automobile Trade Association (*www.naata.org*) – This trade association lists dealers and brokers who will help you find a new or used cross-border bargain
- *RedFlagDeals.com* – A compendium of shopping tips, as well as advice on dealing with the federal and provincial governments
- Used Cars Ontario (*www.usedcarsontario.com*) – Used-car classifieds for major cities in Ontario, with links and articles

U.S. car sales websites

- *AutoTrader.com* – New- and used-car classifieds
- *Cars.com* – Ditto, except there's an "Advanced Search" option
- *CarsDirect.com* – One of the largest car-buying sites
- eBay Motors U.S. (*www.motors.ebay.com*) – Similar to the Canadian site
- *Edmunds.com* – Lots of price quotes and articles
- The Big Lot! (*www.thebiglot.com*) – Another large car-buying site

FINANCING CHOICES

You shouldn't spend more than 30 percent of your annual gross income on the purchase of a new or used vehicle. By keeping the initial cost low, there is less risk to you, and you may be able to pay mostly in cash. This can be an effective bargaining tool to use with private sellers, but dealers are less impressed by cash sales because they lose their kickbacks from the finance companies.

Credit Unions

A credit union is the best place to borrow money for a used car at competitive interest rates and with easy repayment terms. In fact, credit unions are jumping into car financing as the major automakers pull back. You'll have to join the credit union or have an account with it before the loan is approved. You'll also probably have to come up with a larger down payment.

Banks

Financing a car through a bank can mean either applying for a car loan or a line of credit. A loan will require a lien on your car and fixed monthly payments until the end of the term. Interest rates on car loans often vary considerably. According to *www.bankrate.com/,* the cost of a used-car loan taken out for four years in the States on June 2013 is 2.7 percent. The average new-car loan interest rate offered by Bank of America in Fort Lauderdale is 2.14 percent.

In Canada, as of June 2013, the cheapest used car loans vary between 4.99 and 7.89 percent (*money.canoe.ca/rates/en/carloans.html*).

You can get a good idea of the different car-loan interest rates through an online comparison of bank rates. For purchases in the States, go to *www.bankrate.com*; Canadian loan interest rates are updated by the individual banks and credit unions who mostly ask you to call toll-free to get a quote.

The National Bank of Canada is more upfront with their interest rates, even to the point of hustling their profitable eight-year car loan for its "reasonable" monthly payment (see next page).

Since you are already online, e-mail the lowest-interest lenders and get a loan commitment first, before you start shopping and the dealer's sales agent starts throwing different figures at you. Simply Google the bank's name and add "car loan interest rates."

Lines of credit, on the other hand, require no lien and offer the ability to pay a minimum each month, or as much as you can afford. The rates are often lower than traditional bank loans and there are no penalties for paying it off early, making it the preferred route for many car buyers.

Banks are always leery of financing used cars, but they generally charge rates that are competitive with what dealers offer.

In your quest for a bank loan, keep in mind that the loan officer will be impressed by a prepared budget and sound references, particularly if you seek out a loan before choosing a vehicle. If you don't have a preapproved loan, it wouldn't hurt to buy from a local dealer, since banks like to encourage businesses in their area.

The Internet offers help for people who need an auto loan and want quick approval but don't want to face a banker. For example, the Royal Bank website has a selected list of dealers who are empowered to process Royal Bank loans at their dealerships (see *www.rbcroyalbank.com/products/personalloans/installment_loan.html*).

Let's assume that your monthly budget is $400. The following table shows you the cost of the vehicle you can afford based on different repayment periods.

Monthly Payment	Loan Term	Interest Rate and APR[3]	Loan Amount
$400	4 years	7.59%[4]	$16,514.65
	5 years	7.49%[5]	$19,966.86
	6 years	7.49%[6]	$23,141.09
	7 years	7.49%[7]	$26,086.94
	8 years[2]	7.49%[8]	$28,820.85

As you can see, with an eight-year car loan[2], you can buy a more expensive vehicle while sticking to your monthly budget.

[2]Subject to credit approval by National Bank. Certain conditions apply.

[3]APR means "Annual Percentage Rate" and represents the total interest and fees charged by the Bank, expressed as an annual percentage. It corresponds to the annual interest rate if the cost of borrowing is comprised exclusively of interest.

[4]Example based on financing of $16,514.65, with a four-year term and a hypothetical rate of 7.59%.

[5]Example based on financing of $19,966.86, with a five-year term and a hypothetical rate of 7.49%.

[6]Example based on financing of $23,141.09, with a six-year term and a hypothetical rate of 7.49%.

[7]Example based on financing of $26,086.94, with a seven-year term and a hypothetical rate of 7.49%.

[8]Example based on financing of $28,820.85, with an eight-year term and a hypothetical rate of 7.49%.

Source: National Bank of Canada: www.nbc.ca.

Dealers

Cash may be king with some Canadian retailers, but not at your local car dealership. It's a myth that dealers will treat you better if you pay cash. Dealers want you to buy a fully loaded vehicle and finance the whole deal. And, now that auto loans are easier to get than they were in 2008 and 2009, dealers are financing everything in sight – especially used cars.

Still, not that many buyers have that kind of extra green lying around. Fewer than 8 percent of all car sales are cash deals, so that leaves financing through the dealer or a bank as the only option for most of us.

Dealer financing isn't the rip-off it once was, but still be watchful for all the expensive little extras the dealer may try to pencil into the contract, because, believe it or not, dealers make far more profit on used-car sales than on new-car deals. Don't write them off for financing, though – if they want to, dealers can finance your purchase at rates that compete with those of banks and finance companies, because they agree to take back the vehicle if the creditor defaults on the loan. Some dealers mislead their customers into thinking they can get financing at rates far below the prime rate. Actually, the dealer jacks up the base price of the vehicle to compensate for the lower interest charges. As bank and other financing choices dry up in some areas, a credit union or cash may be your only alternatives.

DEALER SCAMS

Most dealer sales scams are so obvious, they're laughable. But like the "Nigerian lost fortune" e-mail rip-off, enough imprudent people get sucked in to make these flim-flam practices profitable.

One of the more common tricks is to not identify the previous owner because the vehicle was used commercially, was problem-prone, or had been written off as a total loss after an accident. It's also not uncommon to discover that the mileage has been turned back, particularly if the vehicle was part of a company's fleet. Your best defence? Demand the name of the vehicle's previous owner and then run a VIN check through CarProof as a prerequisite for purchasing.

It would be impossible to list all the dishonest tricks employed in used-vehicle sales. As soon as the public is alerted to one scheme, crooked sellers use other, more elaborate frauds. Nevertheless, under industry-financed provincial compensation funds, buyers can get substantial refunds if defrauded by a dealer.

Here are some of the more common fraudulent practices you're likely to encounter.

Evading Sales Tax by Trimming the Price

Here's where your own greed will do you in. In a tactic used almost exclusively by small, independent dealers and some private sellers, the buyer is told that he or she can pay less sales tax by listing a lower selling price on the contract. But what if the vehicle turns out to be a lemon, or the sales agent has falsified the model year or mileage? The hapless buyer is offered a refund on the fictitious purchase price indicated on the contract. If the buyer wanted to take the dealer to court, it's quite unlikely that he or she would get any more than the contract price. Moreover, both the buyer and dealer could be prosecuted for making a false declaration to avoid paying sales tax.

Phony Private Sales ("Curbsiders")

Individual transactions account for about three times as many used-vehicle sales as dealer sales, and crooked dealers get in on the action by posing as private sellers.

Called "curbsiders," these scammers lure unsuspecting buyers through lower prices, cheat the federal government out of tax money, and routinely violate provincial registration and consumer protection regulations. Bob Beattie, executive director of the Used Car Dealers Association of Ontario (*www.ucda.org*), once estimated that about 20 percent of so-called private sellers in Ontario are actually curbsiders. Dealers in large cities like Toronto, Calgary, and Vancouver believe curbsiders sell half of the cars advertised in the local papers. This scam is easy to detect if the seller can't produce the original sales contract or show repair bills made out over a long period of time in his or her own name. You can usually identify a car dealer in the want ads section of the newspaper – just check to see if the same telephone number is repeated in many different ads. Sometimes you can trip up a curbsider by requesting information on the phone, without identifying the specific vehicle. If the seller asks you which car you are considering, you know you're dealing with a curbsider.

Legitimate car dealers claim to deplore the dishonesty of curbsider crooks, yet they are their chief suppliers. Dealership sales managers, auto auction employees, and newspaper classified ad sellers all know the names, addresses, and phone numbers of these thieves but don't act on the information. Newspapers want the ad dollars, auctions want the action, and dealers want someplace they can unload their wrecked, rust-cankered, and odometer-tricked junkers with impunity. Talk about hypocrisy, eh?

Curbsiders are particularly active in Western Canada, importing vehicles from other provinces where they were sold by dealers, wreckers, insurance companies, and junkyards (after having been written off as total losses). They then place private classified ads in B.C. and Alberta papers, sell their stock, and then import more.

Buyers taken in by these scam artists should sue in small claims court both the seller and the newspaper that carried the original classified ad. When just a few cases are won in court and the paper's competitors play up the story, the practice will cease.

"Free-Exchange" Privilege

Dealers get a lot of sales mileage out of this deceptive offer. The dealer offers to exchange any defective vehicle for any other vehicle in stock. What really happens, though, is that the dealer won't have anything else selling for the same price and so will demand a cash bonus for the exchange – or you may get the dubious privilege of exchanging one lemon for another.

"Money-Back" Guarantee

Once again, the purchaser feels safe in buying a used car with this kind of guarantee. After all, what could be more honest than a money-back guarantee? Dealers using this technique often charge exorbitant handling charges, rental fees, or mechanical repair costs to the customer who bought one of these vehicles and then returned it.

"50/50" Guarantee

This can be a trap. Essentially, the dealer will pay half of the repair costs over a limited period of time. It's a fair offer if an independent garage does the repairs. If not, the dealer can always inflate the repair costs to double their actual worth and then write up a bill for that amount (a scam sometimes used in "goodwill" settlements). The buyer winds up paying the full price of repairs that would probably have been much cheaper at an independent garage. The best kind of used-vehicle warranty is 100 percent with full coverage for a fixed term, even if that term is relatively short.

"As Is" and "No Warranty"

You will see from the jurisprudence in Part Three that these phrases are pure bluff, whether used in a dealer or private sale. Sellers insert these clauses much like parking lot owners or coat checkers at restaurants when they post warnings that they have no responsibility to indemnify your losses. In fact, when you pay for a custodial service or a used vehicle, the commission the seller of that service or product receives requires that you be protected.

Remember, every vehicle carries a provincial legal warranty protecting you from misrepresentation and the premature failure of key mechanical or body components. Nevertheless, sellers often write "as is" or "no warranty" in the contract in the hope of dissuading buyers from pressing legitimate claims.

Generally, when "as is" has been written into the contract or bill of sale, it usually means that you're aware of mechanical defects, you're prepared to accept the responsibility for any damage or injuries caused by the vehicle, and you're agreeing to pay all repair costs. However, the courts have held that the "as is" clause is not a blank cheque to cheat buyers, and must be interpreted in light of the seller's true intent. Was there an attempt to deceive the buyer by including this clause? Did the buyer really know what the "as is" clause could do to his or her future legal rights? It's also been held that the courts may consider oral representations ("parole evidence") as an expressed warranty, even though they were never written into the formal contract. So, if a seller makes claims as to the fine quality of the used vehicle, these claims can be used as evidence. Courts generally ignore "as is" clauses when the vehicle has been intentionally misrepresented, when the dealer is the seller, or when the defects are so serious that the seller is presumed to have known of their existence. Private sellers are usually given more latitude than dealers or their agents.

Odometer Fraud

Who says crime doesn't pay? It most certainly does if you turn back odometers for a living in Canada.

Estimates are that each year close to 90,000 vehicles with tampered odometers reach the Canadian marketplace – at a cost to Canadians of more than $3.56

million. This is about double the incidents one would expect based on a 2002 U.S. NHTSA study that pegs odometer fraud at 450,000 vehicles annually. NHTSA estimates that half of the cars with reset odometers are relatively new, high-mileage rental cars or fleet vehicles.

Odometer fraud is a pernicious crime that robs thousands of dollars from each victim it touches. See, for example, *United States v. Whitlow*, 979 F.2d 1008 (5th Cir. 1992), at 1012 (under sentencing guidelines, the court affirmed the estimate that consumers lost $4,000 per vehicle). The television news magazine *60 Minutes* once characterized odometer scams as the largest consumer fraud in America. Victims of this fraud are commonly the least able to afford it, since buyers of used cars include large numbers of low-income people. In addition, consumers generally are unaware of being victimized.

Odometer tampering involves several interrelated activities. Late-model, high-mileage vehicles are purchased at a low price. The vehicles are "reconditioned" or "detailed" to remove many outward appearances of long use. Finally, odometers are reset, typically removing more than 64,000 km (40,000 mi).

In addition to the cosmetic "reconditioning" of the car, the odometer tamperer "reconditions" the car's paperwork. Automobile titles include a declaration of mileage statement to be completed when ownership is transferred. To hide the actual mileage that is declared on the title when the car is sold to an odometer tamperer, the tamperer must take steps to conceal this information. These steps vary from simple alteration of mileage figures to creating transfers to fictitious "straw" dealerships to make it unclear who was responsible for the odometer roll-back and title alteration. Alternatively, the odometer tamperers frequently destroy original title documents indicating high mileage and obtain duplicate certificates of title from state motor vehicle departments, upon which the false, lower mileage figures are entered.

Odometer fraud is practiced by a variety of people, including:

- Organizations that roll back (or "clock") the odometers on thousands of cars, wholesaling them to dealers who resell them to the public;
- Groups of individuals (commonly called "curbstoners") who buy cars, clock them, and sell them through the classifieds, passing them off as cars of a friend or relative ("I'm selling Aunt Sally's Buick for her"); and
- Individuals who only clock their own car to defeat a lease provision or cheat on a warranty.

Gangs of odometer scammers ply their trade in Canada because it seems as if no one cares what they do, and they stand to gain thousands of dollars, or 10 cents profit for each mile erased from the odometer on the resale value of a doctored car. Moreover, electronic digital odometers make tampering child's play for anyone with a laptop computer, or anyone who has sufficient skill to simply replace the dashboard's instrument panel.

Think: When was the last time you heard of a Canadian dealership being charged with odometer fraud? Probably a long time ago, if at all. And what is the punishment for those dealers convicted of defrauding buyers? Not jail time or loss of their franchise. More than likely, it'll be just a small fine.

Not so in the States. Many victims can get compensation from dealers who sold cars with altered odometers, regardless of who was responsible for the alteration. For business and legal reasons, dealers frequently compensate consumers who purchased vehicles with altered odometers. U.S. federal law permits consumers to obtain treble damages or $1,500, whichever is greater, when they are victims of odometer fraud (49 U.S.C. section 32710). The courts have been liberal in protecting consumers in these kinds of lawsuits against dealers.

How to spot a car that's been to a "spin doctor?"

- When calling a supposedly private seller, ask to see the car in the ad, without specifying which one.

- Ask the seller for a copy of the contract showing the name of the selling dealer and previous owner.

- Check the history of the car through CarProof.

- Look for uneven paint or body panels that don't line up. Do the doors, hood, and trunk open and close easily? Do the bumpers and fenders sit squarely?

- Examine brake and gas pedal wear as well as the driver's door sill. Does their wear match the kilometres? An average tire lasts 80,000 kilometres; any premature wear signals an odometer turnback or chassis misalignment.

- On older vehicles that don't use a digital odometer, check to see if the numbers on the odometer are lined up and snug. If they jiggle when you bang your hand on the dash, have an expert check for fraud.

- Have the car inspected by a franchised dealer for that make of vehicle, and ask for a copy of the service records, noting the mileage each time the vehicle was serviced.

Misrepresentation

Used vehicles can be misrepresented in a variety of ways. A used airport commuter minivan may be represented as having been used by a Sunday school class. A mechanically defective sports car that's been rebuilt after several major accidents may have plastic filler in the body panels to muffle the rattles or hide the rust damage, heavy oil in the motor to stifle the clanks, and cheap retread tires to eliminate the thumps. Your best protection against these dirty tricks is to have the vehicle's quality completely verified by an independent mechanic before completing the sale. Of course, you can still cancel the sale if you learn of the misrepresentation only after taking the vehicle home, but your chances of successfully doing so dwindle as time passes.

Both the federal and provincial governments have scored impressive victories resulting in fines of up to $10 million and personal damage awards of $15,000 against General Motors, *Time Magazine,* and Bell Telephone for misrepresenting their products. I'm not sure that these court decisions will create a cottage industry of misleading advertising plaintiffs, but Canadian businesses are terrified that it will (see pages 128-130).

Private Scams

A lot of space in this guide is dedicated to describing how used-car dealers and scam artists cheat uninformed buyers. Of course, private individuals can be dishonest, too. In either case, protect yourself at the outset by keeping your deposit small and by getting as much information as possible about the vehicle you're considering. Then, after a test drive, you may sign a written agreement to purchase the vehicle and give a deposit of sufficient value to cover the seller's advertising costs, subject to cancellation if the automobile fails its inspection. After you've taken these precautions, watch out for the following private sellers' tricks.

Vehicles that Are Stolen or Have Finance Owing

Many used vehicles are sold privately without free title because the original auto loan was never repaid. You can avoid being cheated by asking for proof of purchase and payment from a private seller. Be especially wary of any individual who offers to sell a used vehicle for an incredibly low price. Check the sales contract to determine who granted the original loan, and call the lender to see if it's been repaid. Place a call to the provincial Ministry of Transportation to ascertain whether the car is registered in the seller's name. Find out if a finance company is named as beneficiary on the auto insurance policy. Finally, contact the original dealer to determine whether there are any outstanding claims.

In Ontario, all private sellers must purchase a Used Vehicle Information Package at one of 300 provincial Driver and Vehicle Licence Issuing Offices, or online at *www.mto.gov.on.ca/english/dandv/vehicle/used.htm*. This package, which costs $20, contains the vehicle's registration history in Ontario; the vehicle's lien information (i.e., if there are any liens registered on the vehicle); the fair market value on which the minimum tax payable will apply; and other information such as consumer tips, vehicle safety standards inspection guidelines, retail sales tax information, and forms for bills of sale.

In other provinces, buyers don't have easy access to this information. Generally, you have to contact the provincial office that registers property and then pay a small fee for a computer printout that may or may not be accurate. You'll be asked for the current owner's name and the car's VIN, which is usually found on the driver's side of the dashboard.

There are two high-tech ways to get the goods on a dishonest seller. First, have a dealer of that particular model run a vehicle history check through the automaker's online network. This will tell you who the previous owners and dealers were, what warranty and recall repairs were carried out, and what other free repair programs may still apply. Second, you can use CarProof (*www.carproof.com*) to carry out a background check.

Wrong Registration

Make sure the seller's vehicle has been properly registered with provincial transport authorities; if it isn't, it may be stolen, or you could be dealing with a curbsider.

SUMMARY: BE TOUGH AND FAIR

Don't treat your used-car negotiation like a World Wrestling Federation title bout. You are no Vince McMahon and most private sellers are simple, honest folk. Dealers, on the other hand, will use every trick in the book to maximize their profit, but you will likely still get a good deal if the price and inspection results are acceptable. You will end up with a reliable used car, truck, or minivan at a reasonable price – through patience and homework.

Nevertheless, prevent potential headaches and hassles by becoming thoroughly familiar with your legal rights, as outlined in Part Three, and by buying a vehicle recommended in Part Four.

Here are the steps to take to keep your level of risk to a minimum.

1. Keep your present vehicle for at least 10 years. Don't get panicked over high fuel costs – depreciation is a greater threat to your pocketbook.
2. Sell to a dealer if the reduction in applicable taxes on your next purchase is greater than the potential profit of selling privately.
3. Sell privately if you can get at least 15 percent more than what the dealer offered.
4. Buy from a private party, rental car outlet, or dealer – in that order.
5. Use an auto broker to save time and money, but pay a set fee, not a commission.
6. Buy only a *Lemon-Aid*-recommended three- to five-year-old vehicle with some original warranty left that can be transferred.
7. Carefully inspect front-drive vehicles that have reached their fifth year. Pay particular attention to the engine intake manifold and head gasket, CV joints, steering box, and brakes. Make sure the spare tire and tire jack haven't been removed.
8. Buy a full-sized, rear-drive delivery van and then add the convenience features that you would like (seats, sound system, etc.) instead of opting for a more-expensive, smaller, less-powerful minivan.
9. Buy a vehicle recommended by *Lemon-Aid*, thereby foregoing the need to purchase a $1,500–$2,000 extended warranty; many of these warranty providers may be headed for bankruptcy.
10. Have maintenance repairs done by independent garages that offer lifetime warranties on brakes, exhaust systems, and automatic transmissions.

11. Install used or reconditioned mechanical parts, demand that original parts be used for body repairs, and insist upon choosing your own repairer.

12. Keep all the previous owner's repair bills to facilitate warranty claims and to let mechanics know what's already been replaced or repaired.

13. Upon delivery, adjust mirrors to reduce blind spots and adjust head restraints to prevent your head from snapping back in the event of a collision. On airbag-equipped vehicles, move the seat backward more than half its travel distance and sit at least 30 cm away from the airbag housing.

14. Ensure that the side airbags include head protection.

15. Make sure that both the dealer and automaker have your name in their computers as the new owner of record. Ask for a copy of your vehicle's history, which is stored in the same computer.

16. Go to *www.safercar.gov* and look up all the free confidential service bulletins applicable to your vehicle and compare that to the free ALLDATA index of bulletins at *www.alldatadiy.com/recalls/index.html*. Get true copies of all the recalls and service bulletins that are particularly significant to your needs from ALLDATA's site (*www.alldatadiy.com/buy*). The cost is $26.95(U.S.) for a one-year subscription, or $44.95 for five years. A one-year subscription for additional vehicles costs $16.95 per vehicle. Overnight, you will be sent an Internet download or data disc of all your vehicle's service bulletins going back to 1982. This will keep you current as to the latest secret warranties, recalls, and troubleshooting tips for correcting factory screw-ups.

3

Part Three

DENY, LIE, AND CRY

Crime in the Suites

First they ignore. Next they deny and bury. Then they minimize. Finally, they shout about freedom — and how politicians are taking it away. These are, to the best of our reckoning, the four stages of corporate response when the public and political leaders start demanding restrictions on products that make us sick or do us harm.

William L. Haar
May 22, 2013
www.forbes.com/.../ignore-evidence-deny-science-minimize-problems

NHTSA said at least 32 fatal rear-impact fire crashes involving Grand Cherokees have resulted in 44 deaths, and at least five fatal rear-impact crashes involving the Liberty have resulted in seven fatalities. (*www.detroitnews.com/article/20130605/*)

LIAR, LIAR, JEEP'S ON FIRE

Chrysler Group CEO Sergio Marchionne's embarrassment was palpable. Two weeks after taking a tough public stand against recalling 2.7 million fire-prone Jeeps, he caved in to U.S. government and media pressure and reversed his decision. On June 18 he announced Chrysler would, indeed, recall 1.56 million 1992-1998 Jeep Grand Cherokees and 2002-07 Libertys. Chrysler also promised to set up a free "customer service program" to install gas-tank protective hitches where needed on 1.2 million 1999-2004 Grand Cherokees.

As part of his deal with Washington, Marchionne, ever-mindful of the eight lawsuits over Jeep fires filed against his company, had just one request, "Don't call the gas-tank safety issue a 'defect.'"

However, Washington isn't through with the Jeep fire-tank investigation. It is still testing those models that are part of the "service program" and may still hold public hearings and file lawsuits to extend its partial recall.

The Department of Transportation's smackdown of Chrysler would never have occurred a decade ago, when auto safety was put on the back burner (no pun intended) and many "sweetheart" deals were done by top-drawer, K-street auto lobbyists. Toyota literally got away with murder with massive brake failures and cars that would suddenly accelerate out of control.

Fortunately, times have changed as our governments and courts become more responsive to consumer issues and less tolerant of corporate crime. Small-claims "people's courts" allow claims for as much as $30,000. We have multi-million dollar class actions, government-run auto insurance, and more aggressive government regulators that ensure our rights are respected. Yes, there's a new sheriff in town.

FALSE ADVERTISING, NEXT

Following the American government's lead on better auto safety enforcement, Canada's courts have made a full-court press against misleading advertising in our country. The Supreme Court has ruled that the omnipresent misleading advertising that has bombarded us in print, over the airwaves, and on the Internet for what seems forever must stop. In two powerful decisions, originating from Ontario and Quebec, Bell Canada and *Time* magazine were exposed as flim-flam hypocrites and hit with a record-breaking fine and precedent-setting damages.

On June 28, 2011, Bell Canada consented to pay a $10-million settlement (the first time that the maximum penalty for misleading advertising has ever been imposed) and change its advertising after the Canadian Competition Bureau said its ads were contrary to the *Competition Act's* civil prohibition against making representations that are false or misleading.

Bell lied continuously in its ads for over five years about the prices at which certain of its services were available (including home phones, Internet, satellite television, and wireless services). Bell's representations gave the "general impression" that the advertised monthly price for the services was sufficient, when in fact Bell used a variety of "fine-print disclaimers" to "hide" additional mandatory fees that made the actual price paid by consumers higher than the advertised price (in one instance 15% higher than advertised). According to the *Competition Act's* misleading advertising provisions, the "general impression" conveyed by the advertisement to the average consumer, as well as its literal meaning, were considered in determining that the representations made were false or misleading. (The settlement between Bell and the Bureau is set out in a "consent agreement" found at *www.ct-tc.gc.ca*.)

As with most businesses caught scamming the public, Bell maintained it did no wrong. Nevertheless, the company paid the $10-million fine and agreed to drop all non-compliant advertising within 60 days. In particular, Bell agreed not to use small print or other ancillary disclosures that contradict the general impression of its price representations. Bell also agreed to pay the Competition Bureau $100,000 to cover the costs of the Bureau's investigation.

Automobile Advertising Deception

Ottawa's position is similar to Quebec's – if qualifying information is necessary to prevent a representation from being false or misleading when read on its own, then that information should be presented clearly and conspicuously. "Fine print," which is the bread and butter of auto advertising, won't do.

Car newspaper ads and television commercials say one thing, but mean another, especially when the details are scrutinized. Read the car ads in any Canadian newspaper. Can you see, let alone understand, the cryptic abbreviations at the bottom of each dealer/automaker ad? Or, what about the blue lettering on a darker blue or other colour background? What brave journalist would submit his or her own newspaper ads to the provincial order of opthamologists and lawyers to confirm readability and clarity?

VEHICLE PRICING IS NOW EASIER TO UNDERSTAND BECAUSE ALL OUR PRICES INCLUDE FREIGHT, PDI AND MANDATORY GOVERNMENT LEVIES. Consumers may be required to pay up to $599 for Dealer fees.***
Prices do not include applicable taxes and PPSA.

Wise customers read the fine print: ❖, *, ˘, ✦, †, ±, § Save the Freight Event offers apply to retail deliveries of sele... applies on up to 1,000 2010 Grand Caravan SE Plus and SXT models offered through Ontario Dealers. Chrysler Canad... retailer for complete details. Price includes freight; air tax, tire levy and OMVIC fee. Price excludes licence, insurance, CVP and Caliber SE PLUS and Sprinter models. Bonus Cash is a manufacturer-to-retailer incentive which will be dedu... by vehicle. See your retailer for complete details. †0% purchase financing for 36 months available to qualified custome... Sprinter and Ram Chassis Cab. Example: 2010 Dodge Caravan SE Plus with purchase price of $22,799, including $6,0... and registration, any retailer administration fees, other retailer charges and other applicable fees and taxes. Retailer ... Variable rate is TD Prime Rate and fluctuates accordingly. Payments and financing term may increase or decrease with ... including applicable Consumer Cash Discount/Bonus Cash Offer: $26,355. Price includes freight ($1,400), air tax, tir... ratings published by Natural Resources Canada. Transport Canada test methods used. Your actual fuel consumption ma...

Hmmm…GM Canada also includes the freight charge in the manufacturer's suggested retail price (MSRP) and only mentions $599 in extra dealer fees.

YOU HAVE JUST WON $1 MILLION DOLLARS,
IF YOU SUBSCRIBE TO TIME...HOLD YOUR BREATH FOR FIVE
MINUTES, SING ALL STANZAS OF "O'CANADA" IN BOTH
LANGUAGES, AND TELL US WHERE SENATOR MIKE DUFFY LIVES.

Angry consumer reading *Time* letter. "GRRRRRR!"

Not the *Globe and Mail*. Not *La Presse*, and, most certainly, not the *Toronto Star*.

Television commercials are more deceptive. You get twenty seconds of praise for the vehicle and then ten seconds of small type scrolled down the screen at breakneck speed telling you all of the exceptions to the foregoing. In effect, fine-print "truth" flashes.

What brave Canadian journalist would care to take this mission into the realm of media misrepresentation?

On February 12, 2012, Canada's Supreme Court judges took up this challenge and stomped where investigative media fear to tiptoe. The judges threw the book at *Time* magazine for lying to readers in order to sell subscriptions. Yes, the same *Time* that pillories politicians for being untruthful has used its subscription sales department for years to give consumers false expectations that they have won a sweepstakes prize.

The ruling endorses Quebec's "seller beware" mindset in its precedent-setting judgment relating to false and misleading representations under the province's *Consumer Protection Act*. In *Richard v. Time Inc.* (*scc.lexum.org/decisia-scc-csc/scc-csc/ scc-csc/en/7994/1/document.do*), the Court held that a representation should be judged simply by what a credulous and inexperienced consumer would believe to be true – a position long held by the courts in matters relating to misleading advertising charges filed under the federal *Competition Act*.

The Court also stated that if a prohibited business practice exists, there is no need to prove actual damages; an irrefutable presumption of prejudice exists. This opens the door to punitive damages, even where the circumstances do not justify a compensatory award.

Although punitive, or exemplary damages, can go as high as $1 million (Cdn.) (see pages 151 and 546: *Whiten v. Pilot*), *Time* magazine was ordered to pay (to the plaintiff, yippee!) only $15,000. Yet, the impact of this award has been far greater than the amount, as it serves as a reminder to business and government that lies won't be tolerated in Ottawa – except in Parliament.

THE ART OF COMPLAINING

Most Canadian consumers don't like to complain or get involved with the legal system. And, they have reason to be wary. Blood pressure rises, heated words are exchanged, and you always think of a better argument after the discussion is over.

Yet there are some complaint strategies that aren't hard to employ and that are often successful.

Cold-calling

Phone the seller or automaker, but don't expect to get much out of the call. Private sellers won't want to talk with you, and service managers will simply apply the dealership's policy, knowing that 90 percent of complainers will drop their claims after venting their anger.

Still, try to work things out by contacting someone higher up who can change the policy to satisfy your request. In your attempt to reach a settlement, ask only for what is fair and don't try to make anyone look bad.

Speak in a calm, polite manner, and try to avoid polarizing the issue. Talk about cooperating to solve the problem. Let a compromise emerge – don't come in with a rigid set of demands. Don't insist on getting the settlement offer in writing, but make sure that you're accompanied by a friend or relative who can confirm the offer in court if it isn't honoured. Be prepared to act upon the offer without delay so that your hesitancy won't be blamed if the seller or automaker withdraws it.

Service manager help

Service managers have more power than you may realize. They make the first determination of what work is covered under warranty or through post-warranty "goodwill" programs, and they are directly responsible to the dealer and manufacturer for that decision (dealers hate manufacturer audits that force them to pay back questionable warranty decisions). Service managers are paid both to save the dealer and automaker money and to mollify irate clients – almost an impossible balancing act.

Nevertheless, when a service manager agrees to extend warranty coverage, it's because you've raised solid issues that neither the dealer nor the automaker can ignore. All the more reason to present your argument in a confident, forthright manner with your vehicle's service history and *Lemon-Aid*'s "Reasonable Part Durability" table on hand (refer to page 137). Also, bring as many technical service bulletins (TSBs) and owner complaint printouts as you can find from National Highway Traffic Safety Administration's (NHTSA) website and similar sources. It's not important that they apply directly to your problem; they establish parameters for giving out after-warranty assistance, or "goodwill."

Don't use your salesperson as a runner, since the sales staff are generally quite distant from the service staff and usually have less pull than you do. If the service manager can't or won't set things right, your next step is to convene a mini-summit with the service manager, the dealership principal, and the automaker's service rep, if he or she represents that make. Regional service representatives are technicians who are regularly sent out by the manufacturer to help dealers with technical problems. By getting the automaker involved, you can often get an agreement where the seller and the automaker pay two-thirds of the repair cost, even when the vehicle was bought used.

Get an independent estimate

Dealers who sell a brand of vehicle used that they don't sell new will give you less latitude. You have to make the case that the vehicle's defects were present at the time of purchase or should have been apparent to the seller, or that the vehicle doesn't conform to the representations made when it was purchased. Emphasize that you intend to use the courts if necessary to obtain a refund – most sellers would rather settle than risk a lawsuit with all the attendant publicity. An independent estimate of the vehicle's defects and repair costs is essential if you want to convince the seller that you're serious in your claim and that you stand a good chance of winning your case in court. Come prepared with an estimated cost of repairs to challenge the dealer who agrees to pay half the repair costs and then jacks up the price 100 percent so that you wind up paying the whole shot.

Create a paper trail

If you haven't sent a written claim letter, fax, or e-mail, you really haven't complained – or at least, that's the auto industry's mindset. If your vehicle was misrepresented, has major defects, or wasn't properly repaired under warranty, the first thing you should do is give the seller a written summary of the outstanding problems and stipulate a time period within which the seller can fix the vehicle or refund your money. Follow the format of the sample complaint letter on page 151.

Remember, you can ask for compensation for repairs that have been done or need to be done, insurance costs while the vehicle is being repaired, towing charges, supplementary transportation costs such as taxis and rented cars, and damages for inconvenience. If no satisfactory offer is made, ask for mediation, arbitration, or a formal hearing in your provincial small claims court. Make the manufacturer a party to the lawsuit, especially if the emissions warranty, a secret warranty extension, a safety recall campaign, or extensive chassis rusting is involved.

Mediation and Arbitration

If the formality of a courtroom puts you off, or you're not sure that your claim is all that solid and you don't want to pay legal costs to find out, consider using mediation or arbitration. These services are sponsored by the Better Business Bureau, the Automobile Protection Association, the Canadian Automobile Association, the Canadian Automobile Manufacturers Arbitration Plan, and by many small claims courts where compulsory mediation is a prerequisite to going to trial.

Mandatory arbitration clauses

The Supreme Court of Canada in *Seidel v. Telus Communications Inc.* (2011 SCC 15), recently struck down mandatory arbitration clauses in "contracts of adhesion" in a narrow 5-4 split decision. Seidel signed a cell phone contract with TELUS and she was being charged for connection time and ring time instead of just the actual talking time. Seidel claimed that TELUS engaged in deceptive and unconscionable practices contrary to the British Columbia *Business Practices and Consumer Protection Act*. She also sought certification to act as a representative of a class of allegedly overcharged customers under the *Class Proceedings Act*.

Contracts of adhesion are standard form contracts drafted by sellers and signed by customers without negotiation and usually without even being read. The arbitration clauses say that in the event of a dispute, the parties agree to submit their dispute to arbitration rather than to the courts. Some provincial legislatures, however, have enacted laws to invalidate these arbitration clauses thereby allowing consumers to pursue class actions. Also, lower courts in several provinces have made rulings that invalidate arbitration clauses where they would prevent consumers from pursuing class proceedings.

Dealers and automakers favour arbitration because it's relatively inexpensive, decisions are rendered more quickly than through regular litigation, there is a less formalistic approach to the rules of evidence, jurisprudence isn't created, and they can dodge bad publicity.

The disadvantages to binding arbitration are many and include the following: Loss of recourse to the courts, no appeals, no jurisprudence to guide plaintiffs as to the rules of law used in prior decisions (which often leads to quicker settlements or encourages litigants to stand by their principles), and the chumminess that often develops between arbiters and dealer/automaker defendants who may meet often over similar issues throughout the year – a familiarity that breeds contempt.

Automakers want binding arbitration clauses in sales contracts because they can use them to oppose class actions related to their products and can more easily cover up design or production defects that are carried over year

Automakers know judges can't be hood-winked.

after year, since plaintiff's must file their cases individually and cannot pool their resources, or drum up media support.

Another drawback is that the defendant can refuse to take back the car or pay the cost of repairs simply by arguing that the arbitration process was flawed because the arbitrator exceeded his or her mandate. This objection puts the arbitration in the regular court system where each side has lawyers' fees and a final decision may take two years. This is what Ford of Canada did in refusing to take back a 2010 Focus that had abraded paint. Ford's appeal against the Canadian Motor Vehicle Arbitration Plan (CAMVAP) was tossed out of court.

Don't get the impression that binding arbitration is a useless tool to get redress. CAMVAP has worked fairly well with some new car disputes. On the other hand it proved woefully ineffective in resolving the "death wobble" on Dennis Warren's 2007 Dodge Ram 2500 (see *www.cbc.ca/m/touch/news/story/2011/05/16/bc-dodgeproblem.html*).

Two Warranties

Defects are covered by two warranties. The *expressed* or *written* warranty, which has a fixed time limit, and the *implied* or *legal* warranty, the application of which is entirely up to a judge's discretion based upon the vehicle's cost, how it was maintained, manufacturer and dealer assertions, the severity of the failure, and the extent of that failure's consequences.

Expressed

The expressed warranty given by the seller is often full of empty promises, and it allows the dealer and manufacturer to act as judge and jury when deciding whether a vehicle was misrepresented or is afflicted by defects they'll pay to correct. Rarely does it provide a money-back guarantee.

Some of the more familiar lame excuses used in denying expressed warranty claims are "You abused the car," "It was poorly maintained," "It's normal wear and tear," "It's rusting from the outside, not the inside," and "It passed the safety inspection." Ironically, the expressed warranty sometimes says there is no warranty at all, or that the vehicle is sold "as is." Fortunately, courts usually throw out these exclusions by upholding two legal concepts.

1. The vehicle must be fit for the purpose for which it was purchased.
2. The vehicle must be of merchantable quality when sold.

Not surprisingly, sellers use the expressed warranty to reject claims, while smart plaintiffs ignore the expressed warranty and argue for a refund under the implied warranty instead.

Implied

The implied warranty ("of fitness") is your ace in the hole. As clearly stated in the under-reported Saskatchewan decision *Maureen Frank v. General Motors of Canada*

Limited, in which the judge declared that paint discoloration and peeling shouldn't occur within 11 years of the purchase of the vehicle, the implied warranty is an important legal principle. It is solidly supported by a large body of federal and provincial laws, regulations, and jurisprudence, and it protects you primarily from hidden defects that may be either dealer- or factory-related. But the concept also includes misrepresentation and a host of other scams.

This warranty also holds dealers to a higher standard of conduct than private sellers because, unlike private sellers, dealers and auto manufacturers are presumed to be aware of the defects present in the vehicles they sell. That way, they can't just pass the ball to the previous owner and then walk away from the dispute.

Dealers are also expected to disclose defects that have been repaired. For instance, in British Columbia, provincial law (the *Motor Dealer Act*) says that a dealer must disclose damages that cost more than $2,000 to fix. This is a good law to cite in other jurisdictions.

In spite of all your precautions, there's still a 10 percent chance you'll buy a lemon, says mobility services company Runzheimer International (a figure also cited by former GM VP Bob Lutz, who confirms that one out of every 10 vehicles produced by the Detroit automakers is likely to be a lemon).

Why the implied warranty is so effective

1. It establishes the concept of reasonable durability (see "How Long Should a Part or Repair Last?" below), meaning that parts are expected to last for a reasonable period of time, as stated in jurisprudence, judged by independent mechanics, or expressed in extended "goodwill" warranties given by automakers in the past (examples: 10 years/193,000 km for catalytic converters; 7 years/200,000 miles for diesel injectors as expressed in one U.S. service bulletin; and 7 years/160,000 km for engines and transmissions).
2. It covers the entire vehicle and can be applied for whatever period of time the judge decides.
3. It can order that the vehicle be taken back, or a major repair cost be refunded. One *Lemon-Aid* reader writes:

   I wanted to let you and your readers know that the information you publish about Ford's paint failure problem is invaluable. Having read through your "how-to guide" on addressing this issue, I filed suit against Ford for the "latent" paint defect. The day prior to our court date, I received a settlement offer by phone for 75 percent of what I was initially asking for.

4. It can order that plaintiffs be given compensation for supplementary transportation, inconvenience, mental distress, missed work, screwed-up vacations, insurance paid while the vehicle was in the repair shop, repairs done by other repairers, and exemplary, or punitive, damages in cases where the seller was a real weasel.
5. It is often used by small claims court judges to give refunds to plaintiffs "in equity" (out of fairness), rather than through a strict interpretation of contract law.

How Long Should a Part or Repair Last?

If you wish to use the legal, *implied* warranty to get a refund for a faulty part or unsatisfactory repair, there has to be some independent benchmark as to what is normally expected of that part or repair. You'll have to show what the auto industry considers to be "reasonable durability," however. This isn't all that difficult if you use the guide that automakers, mechanics, and the courts have recognized over the years (see page 137).

Much of the chart's guidelines are extrapolated from the terms of automaker payouts to dissatisfied customers and from Chrysler's original seven-year powertrain warranty. Other sources:

- Ford and GM transmission warranties, which are outlined in their secret warranties,
- Ford, GM, and Toyota engine "goodwill" programs, which are laid out in their internal service bulletins, and
- Court judgments where judges have given their own guidelines as to what constitutes reasonable durability.

Unsafe Vehicles

As mentioned earlier, incidents of airbags that deploy for no reason, or don't deploy when they should, sudden unintended acceleration, and brake failure are among the top most frequent complaints logged by Transport Canada and NHTSA. However, the cause of these failures can be very difficult to diagnose, and individual cases are treated very differently by federal safety agencies. Sudden acceleration is considered to be a safety-related problem – stalling isn't always given the same priority. Never mind that a vehicle's sudden loss of power on a busy highway (as happens with 2001-05 Toyota and Lexus models) puts everyone's lives at risk. The same problem exists with engine and transmission powertrain failures, which are only occasionally considered to be safety-related. Anti-lock Braking Systems (ABS) and airbag failures are universally considered to be life-threatening defects and jury awards can be quite substantial as the *Duncan v. Hyundai* decision shows (No. CL-10-0503 (Va. Cir. 2013)).

In this recent judgment, Hyundai was ordered to pay $14 million to a Virginia man who suffered traumatic brain damage in a car accident after the side airbags in his 2008 Hyundai Tiburon failed to deploy. The plaintiffs said the airbags did not deploy because Hyundai had put its side airbag sensors in the wrong location, under the driver's seat, instead of further out on the car. Hyundai had conducted studies and knew about the potentials risks with the sensor location, the lawsuit alleged. Apparently, 2003-08 Tiburons used the same airbag sensor before Hyundai dumped the Tiburon after 2008.

REASONABLE PART DURABILITY

Accessories

Air conditioner	7 years
Cruise control	7 years/140,000 km
GPS	7 years
Headlights (HID)	5 years/100,000 km
Hybrid battery	11 years
Power doors, windows	5 years
Power seats, locks	5 years
Radiator	5 years/100,000 km
Radio	7 years
Tire pressure sensor	5 years

Body

Door handles	10 years/160,000 km
Liftgate struts	7 years
Paint (peeling)	7-11 years
Rust (perforations)	7-11 years
Rust (surface)	5 years
Water/wind/air leaks	5 years

Brake System

ABS	100,000 km
ABS computer	10 years/200,000 km
Brake drum	120,000 km
Brake drum linings	35,000 km
Brake rotor	60,000 km
Brake calipers/pads	30,000 km
Master cylinder	100,000 km
Wheel cylinder	80,000 km

Engine and Drivetrain

CV joint	6 years/120,000 km
Differential	7 years/140,000 km
Engine (diesel)	15 years/300,000 km
Engine (gas)	7 years/140,000 km
Engine block	7 years/no mileage
Engine control module	15 years/300,000 km

Engine and Drivetrain (cont.)

Engine turbocharger	7 years/140,000 km
Fuel pump module	10 years/200,000 km
Oxygen sensor	10 years/200,000 miles
Transfer case	10 years/200,000 km
Transmission (auto.)	10 years/200,000 km
Transmission (man.)	12 years/240,000 km
Transmission oil cooler	10 years/200,000 km

Exhaust System

Catalytic converter	10 years/200,000 km
Exhaust manifold	10 years/200,000 km
Muffler	3 years/60,000 km
Tailpipe	5 years/100,000 km

Ignition System

Cable set	60,000 km
Electronic module	5 years/100,000 km
Retiming	20,000 km
Spark plugs	20,000 km
Tune-up	20,000 km

Safety Components

Airbags	life of vehicle
Seat belts	life of vehicle
Stability control	5 years/100,000 km

Steering and Suspension

Alignment	1 year/20,000 km
Ball joints	10 years/200,000 km
Coil springs	10 years/200,000 km
Power steering	5 years/100,000 km
Shock absorber	3 years/60,000 km
Struts	5 years/100,000 km
Tires (radial)	5 years/100,000 km
Truck tie-rod ends	5 years/100,000 km
Wheel bearings	3 years/60,000 km

If your vehicle has a safety-related failure of any kind, here's what you need to do.

1. Get independent witnesses to confirm the problem exists. Confirmation includes verification by an independent mechanic, passenger testimony, downloaded data from your vehicle's data recorder, and lots of Internet browsing using *www.lemonaidcars.com* and a search engine like Google. Notify the dealer or manufacturer by fax, e-mail, or registered letter that you consider the problem to be a factory-induced, safety-related defect. Make sure you address your correspondence to the manufacturer's product liability or legal affairs department. At the dealership's service bay, make sure that every work order clearly states the problem as well as the number of previous attempts to fix it. (You should end up with a few complaint letters and a handful of work orders confirming that this is an ongoing deficiency.) If the dealer won't give you a copy of the work order because the work is a warranty claim, ask for a copy of the order number "in case your estate wishes to file a claim, pursuant to an accident." (This will get the service manager's attention.) Leaving a paper trail is crucial for any later claim, because it shows your concern and persistence and clearly indicates that the dealer and manufacturer had ample time to correct the defect.

2. Note on the work order that you expect the problem to be diagnosed and corrected under the emissions warranty or a "goodwill" program. It also wouldn't hurt to add the phrase on the work order or in your claim letters that "any deaths, injuries, or damage caused by the defect will be the dealer's and manufacturer's responsibility" since this work order (or letter, fax, or e-mail) constitutes you putting them on formal notice.

3. If the dealer does the necessary repairs at little or no cost to you, send a follow-up confirmation saying that you appreciate the assistance. Also, emphasize that you'll be back if the problem reappears, even if the warranty has expired, because the repair renews your warranty rights applicable to that defect. In other words, the warranty clock is set back to its original position. You won't likely get a copy of the repair bill, because dealers don't like to admit that there was a serious defect present. Keep in mind, however, that you can get your complete vehicle file from the dealer and manufacturer by issuing a subpoena, which costs about $75 (refundable), if the case goes to small claims or a higher court. This request has produced many out-of-court settlements when the internal documents show extensive work was carried out to correct the problem.

4. If the problem persists, send a letter, fax, or e-mail to the dealer and manufacturer saying so, look for ALLDATA service bulletins to confirm that your vehicle's defects are factory-related, and call Transport Canada or NHTSA, or log onto NHTSA's website, to report the failure. Also, contact the Center for Auto Safety in Washington, D.C. at 202-328-7700 or visit

www.autosafety.org for a lawyer referral and an information sheet covering the problem. To find an expert Canadian lawyer familiar with auto defects and sales scams, contact the non-profit Automobile Protection Association (contact info available at *www.APA.ca*).

5. Now come two crucial questions: Should you repair the defect now or later, and should you use the dealer or an independent? Generally, it's smart to use an independent garage if you know the dealer isn't pushing for free corrective repairs from the manufacturer, if weeks or months have passed without any resolution of your claim, if the dealer keeps claiming that it's a maintenance item, or if you know an independent mechanic who will give you a detailed work order showing the defect is factory-related and not a result of poor maintenance. Don't mention that a court case may ensue, since this will scare the dickens out of your only independent witness. The bonus of using an independent garage is that the repair charges will be about half what a dealer would demand. Incidentally, if the automaker later denies warranty "goodwill" because you used an independent repairer, use the argument that the defect's safety implications required emergency repairs to be carried out by whoever could see you first.

6. Take note of the manufacturer's own safety warnings. Dashboard-mounted warning lights usually come on prior to airbags suddenly deploying, ABS brakes failing, or engine glitches causing the vehicle to stall out. (Sudden acceleration, however, usually occurs without warning.) Automakers consider these lights to be critical safety warnings and generally advise drivers to immediately have the vehicle serviced to correct the problem (advice that can be found in the owner's manual) when any of the above lights come on. This bolsters the argument that your life was threatened, emergency repairs were required, and your request for another vehicle or a complete refund isn't out of line.

7. Use the balance of probabilities. Sudden acceleration can have multiple causes, is difficult to prove because it isn't easy to duplicate, and is often blamed on the driver mistaking the accelerator for the brakes or failing to perform proper maintenance. Yet NHTSA data shows that factory-related defects are often the culprit. For example, 1997-2004 Lexus ES 300/330s and Toyota Camrys may have a faulty transmission that may cause engine surging. So how do you satisfy the burden of proof showing that the problem exists and is the automaker's responsibility? Use the legal doctrine called "the balance of probabilities" by eliminating all of the possible dodges the dealer or manufacturer may employ. Show that proper maintenance has been carried out, that you're a safe driver, and that the incident occurs frequently and without warning.

8. If any of the above defects causes an accident, the airbag fails to deploy, or you're injured by its deployment, ask your insurance company to have

the vehicle towed to a neutral location and clearly state that neither the dealer nor the automaker should touch the vehicle until your insurance company and Transport Canada have completed their investigation. Also, get as many witnesses as possible and immediately go to the hospital for a check-up, even if you're feeling okay. You may be injured and not know it because the adrenalin coursing through your veins is masking your injuries. A hospital exam will easily confirm that your injuries are related to the accident, which is essential in court or for future settlement negotiations.

9. Peruse NHTSA's online accident database to find reports of other accidents caused by the same failure.

10. Don't let your insurance company settle the case if you're sure the accident was caused by a mechanical failure. Even if an engineering analysis fails to directly implicate the manufacturer or dealer, you can always plead the aforementioned balance of probabilities. If the insurance company settles, your insurance premiums will probably increase.

Airbags

Airbags usually carry a five-year/100,000 km (about 62,000 mi) warranty in Canada; however, automakers routinely offer "goodwill" warranty extensions for up to 10 years/191,000 km (almost 119,000 mi). Mercedes-Benz Canada, for example, sent off a dealer notification on December 2010 advising dealers that it would cover airbag replacement or correct a faulty wiring harness connection for free on 2005 through 2008 models up to 10 years or 160,000 km (100,000 mi). The affected vehicles are model years 2005-06 ML (164), SLK (171), C (203), CLK (209), E (211), CLS (219), R (251), and 2005-08 G (463).

Owners who paid for the repair will be refunded their money upon presentation of an acceptable receipt from a Mercedes-Benz dealer. Independent garage receipts will likely be accepted if you push hard enough.

Here is part of a letter that was sent out to U.S. owners.

Dear Mercedes-Benz Owner,

In our continuing efforts to assure the proper performance of Mercedes-Benz products and to ensure the satisfaction of our customers, Mercedes-Benz USA, LLC (MBUSA) has decided to extend the warranty for the driver's air bag wiring ... from the original 4 years/50,000 miles (whichever occurs first) to 10 years/100,000 miles (whichever occurs first). This warranty extension applies to these vehicles regardless of ownership. If, during this period, your vehicle should experience an illumination of the "Air Bag" light as described above, this warranty extension would cover the necessary repairs to correct those conditions.

RALPH S. FISHER
MERCEDES-BENZ USA, LLC
GENERAL MANAGER, CUSTOMER ASSISTANCE CENTER
DECEMBER 2010

Mercedes-Benz's admission that airbag systems should be trouble-free for 10 years/160,000 km (100,000 mi) serves as an important benchmark for owners experiencing airbag-related failures. Owners of any make or model of vehicle can use this durability standard (what the automaker considers "reasonable durability") to haggle for a "goodwill" settlement or to win a small claims court petition.

Airbags cost thousands of dollars to fix or replace. Their complexity makes them one of of the most failure-prone components reported to government and consumer protection agencies. Insurance companies won't cover their replacement or repair cost unless a collision is involved. But even if they did refund the repair cost, why should you pay a higher insurance fee for a failure caused by the automaker's poor design or use of inferior quality electronics?

Inadvertent deployment may occur after passing over a bump in the road or slamming the car door. At other times the airbag doesn't deploy when it should. Both failures are common, judging by the hundreds of recalls and thousands of complaints recorded on the NHTSA website.

Forget the assurances of auto manufacturers and the safety establishment. Airbag deployment can cause massive face and chest trauma, ruin your hearing and eyesight, and break bones. Granted, any personal injuries or cabin-area damages caused by airbag deployment are covered by your accident insurance policy. However, if the airbag fails to deploy, or there is a sudden deployment for no apparent reason, the automaker and the dealer should be held jointly responsible for all injuries and damages caused by the failure.

How do you prove that the airbag deployed improperly? Download the data from your "black box" Electronic Data Recorder (EDR) *immediately* after the incident. Further driving of the vehicle may cause the EDR crash data record to be overwritten by the addition of new data.

You can use the car's data recorder (see pages 156–157) to prove that the airbag, brakes, and/or throttle control failed prior to an accident. Simply hook a computer up and then download the data from your vehicle's EDR. This will likely lead to a more generous settlement from the two parties and will prevent your insurance premiums from being jacked up. (Appendix IV lists two apps to download data via cell phone.)

Once you get all of your proof assembled, including photos of interior damage or injuries caused by the airbag's inadvertent deployment or non-deployment, file suit in provincial court if it's obvious no settlement is in the offing. If your insurance company decides to pay all of your damages and doesn't want to subrogate your case before the courts, make sure you state that they cannot raise your rates following their decision not to sue.

If you do decide to sue, copy the following template Edmonton lawyers have used in their Statement of Claim against Toyota for inadvertent airbag deployment and read the recent Calgary court judgment in *Hutton v. General Motors*. (This lengthy judgment cites much case law favourable to plaintiffs. It can be accessed for free online at *www.canlii.org*.)

Emissions Components

Car companies have repeatedly gotten themselves into hot water for refusing to replace emissions parts free of charge. These parts are covered by the emissions warranty, a relatively generous warranty set up several decades ago by automakers with the approval of the U.S. Environmental Protection Agency (EPA), which also monitors how fairly the warranty is applied. Canada has approved the same warranty, but leaves enforcement to the States and the courts. The EPA has fined both Ford and Chrysler for rejecting legitimate claims for failed emissions parts covered by the EPA and thereby violating the warranty's provisions. The EPA has aggressively gone after other automakers and entered into consent agreements with them to respect owner warranty rights.

Use the manufacturer's emissions warranty as your primary guideline for the expected durability of high-tech electronic and mechanical pollution-control components, such as powertrain control modules and catalytic converters. These guidelines are usually found in bulletins dealing with sudden acceleration, stalling, hard starts, foul exhaust odours, and excessive tailpipe emissions. First look at your owner's manual for an indication of which parts on your vehicle are covered. Buttress that information with what the U.S. government's online copy of the service bulletin says is covered (the service bulletins are available under the "Vehicle Owners" tab at *www.safercar.gov*). If you don't come up with much detailed parts information, ask the dealer's service manager or automaker for a list of specific components covered by the emissions warranty. If you're stonewalled, invest $26.95 (U.S.) in an ALLDATA service bulletin subscription (available for 1982-2011 models).

Many of the confidential TSBs listed in Part Four show parts failures that are covered under an eight-year emissions warranty, even though motorists are routinely charged for their replacement. This excerpt from the Mazda Owners Manual is a typical example.

> The basic warranty for Mazda vehicles covers all parts found to be factory defective for 36 Months or 80,000 km (60,000 km for the B-Series), whichever comes first. Additional warranties cover powertrain components for a period of 5 years or 100,000 km whichever comes first. The 2004-2011 RX-8 rotary short engine (engine core only) is covered for an additional period ending at 96 months or 160,000 km. Body sheet metal perforation for 8 years and unlimited mileage (on 2013 model year and newer) and specific emission control components for up to 8 years or 128,000 km.

Make sure to get your emissions system checked out thoroughly by a dealer or an independent garage before the emissions warranty expires and before having the vehicle inspected by provincial emissions inspectors. In addition to ensuring you pass provincial tests, this precaution could save you up to $1,000 if both your catalytic converter and other emissions components are faulty.

Paint and Body Defects

The following tips on making a successful claim apply mainly to paint defects, water and air leaks, and subpar fit and finish, but you can use the same strategy for any other vehicle defect that you believe is the automaker's or dealer's responsibility. If you're not sure whether the problem is a factory-related deficiency or a maintenance item, have it checked out by an independent garage or get a TSB summary for your vehicle. The summary may include specific bulletins relating to the diagnosis, correction, and ordering of upgraded parts needed to fix your problem.

1. If you know that your vehicle's paint problem is factory-related, take your vehicle to the dealer and ask for a written, signed estimate. When you're handed the estimate, ask if the paint job can be covered by some "goodwill" assistance. (Ford's euphemism for this secret warranty is "Owner Notification Program" or "Owner Dialogue Program;" GM's term is "Special Policy;" and Chrysler simply calls it an "Owner Satisfaction Notice." Don't use the term "secret warranty" yet. You'll just make everyone angry and evasive.)

2. Your request will probably be met with a refusal, an offer to repaint the vehicle for half the cost, or (if you're lucky) an agreement to repaint the vehicle free of charge. If you accept the half-the-cost offer, make sure that it's based on the original estimate you have in hand, since some dealers jack up their estimates so that your 50 percent is really 100 percent of the true cost.

3. If the dealer or automaker has already refused your claim and the repair hasn't been done yet, get an additional estimate from an independent garage that shows the problem is factory-related.

4. If the repair has yet to be done, mail or fax a registered claim to the automaker (and send a copy to the dealer) claiming the average of both estimates. If the repair has been done at your expense, mail or fax a registered claim with a copy of your bill.

5. If you don't receive a satisfactory response within a week, deposit a copy of the estimate or paid bill and claim letter/fax before the small claims court and await a trial date. This means that the automaker/dealer will have to appear, no lawyer is required, and costs should be minimal (under $100). Usually, an informal pretrial mediation hearing with the two parties and a court clerk will be scheduled within a few months, followed by a trial a few weeks later (the time varies depending on region). Most cases are settled at the mediation stage. You can help your case by collecting photographs, maintenance work orders, previous work orders dealing with your problem, TSBs, and by speaking to an independent expert (the garage or body shop that did the estimate or repair is best, but you can also

use a local teacher who instructs automotive repair). Remember, service bulletins can be helpful, but they aren't critical to a successful claim.

Other situations

- If the vehicle has just been repainted or repaired but the dealer says that "goodwill" coverage was denied by the automaker, pay for the repair with a certified cheque and write "under protest" on the cheque. Remember, though, if the dealer does the repair, you won't have an independent expert who can affirm that the problem was factory-related or that it was a result of premature wear. Plus, the dealer can say that you or the environment caused the paint problem. In these cases, TSBs can make or break your case.
- If the dealer or automaker offers a partial repair or refund, take it. Then sue for the rest. Remember, if a partial repair has been done under warranty, it counts as an admission of responsibility, no matter what "goodwill" euphemism is used. Also, the repaired component or body panel should be just as durable as if it were new. Hence the clock starts ticking from the time of the repair until you reach the original warranty parameter – no matter what the dealer's repair warranty limit says.

Very seldom do automakers contest these paint claims before small claims court, instead opting to settle once the court claim is bounced from their customer relations people to their legal affairs department. At that time, you'll probably be offered an out-of-court settlement for 50-75 percent of your claim.

Stand fast, and make reference to the service bulletins you intend to subpoena in order to publicly contest in court the unfair nature of this "secret warranty" program (automakers' lawyers cringe at the idea of trying to explain why consumers aren't made aware of these bulletins) – 100 percent restitution will probably follow.

Four favourable paint judgments

In *Dunlop v. Ford of Canada* (No. 58475/04; Ontario Superior Court of Justice, Richmond Hill Small Claims Court; January 5, 2005; Deputy Judge M.J. Winer), the owner of a 1996 Lincoln Town Car, purchased used in 1999 for $27,000, was awarded $4,091.64. Judge Winer cited the *Shields* decision (following) and gave these reasons for finding Ford of Canada liable:

Evidence was given by the Plaintiff's witness, Terry Bonar, an experienced paint auto technician. He gave evidence that the [paint] delamination may be both a manufacturing defect and can be caused or speeded up by atmospheric conditions. He also says that [the paint on] a car like this should last ten to 15 years, [or even for] the life of the vehicle....

It is my view that the presence of ultraviolet light is an environmental condition to which the vehicle is subject. If it cannot withstand this environmental condition, it is defective in my view.

In *Shields v. General Motors of Canada* (No. 1398/96; Ontario Court, General Division; Oshawa Small Claims Court; July 24, 1997; Deputy Judge Robert Zochodne), the owner of a 1991 Pontiac Grand Prix purchased the vehicle used with over 100,000 km on its odometer. Beginning in 1995, the paint began to bubble and flake and eventually peeled off. Deputy Judge Robert Zochodne awarded the plaintiff $1,205.72 and struck down every one of GM's environmental/acid rain/UV rays arguments. Here are the other important aspects of this 12-page judgment that General Motors did not appeal.

1. The judge admitted many of the TSBs referred to in *Lemon-Aid* as proof of GM's negligence.
2. Although the vehicle already had 156,000 km on it when the case went to court, GM still offered to pay for 50 percent of the paint repairs if the plaintiff dropped his suit.
3. The judge ruled that the failure to protect the paint from the damaging effects of UV rays is akin to engineering a car that won't start in cold weather. In essence, vehicles must be built to withstand the rigours of the environment.
4. Here's an interesting twist: The original warranty covered defects that were present at the time it was in effect. The judge, taking statements found in the GM technical service bulletins, ruled that the UV problem was factory-related, existed during the warranty period, and represented a latent defect that appeared once the warranty expired.
5. The subsequent purchaser was not prevented from making the warranty claim, even though the warranty had long since expired from a time and mileage standpoint and he was the second owner.

The small claims judgment in *Bentley v. Dave Wheaton Pontiac Buick GMC Ltd. and General Motors of Canada* (Victoria Registry No. 24779; British Columbia Small Claims Court; December 1, 1998; Judge Higinbotham) builds on the Ontario *Shields v. General Motors of Canada* decision and cites other jurisprudence as to how long paint should last on a car. If you're wondering why Ford and Chrysler haven't been hit by similar judgments, remember that they usually settle out of court. (See also *Maureen Frank v. General Motors of Canada Limited* (No. SC#12 (2001); Saskatchewan Provincial Court; October 17, 2001; Provincial Court Judge H.G. Dirauf), discussed on page 134.)

Other paint and rust cases

In *Whittaker v. Ford Motor Company* ((1979), 24 O.R. (2d) 344), a new Ford developed serious corrosion problems in spite of having been rustproofed by the dealer. The court ruled that the dealer, not Ford, was liable for the damage for having sold the rustproofing product at the time of purchase. This is an important judgment to use when a rustproofer or paint protector goes out of business or refuses to pay a claim, since the decision holds the dealer jointly responsible.

The original owner of a 1981 Honda Civic sought compensation for the premature "bubbling, pitting, [and] cracking of the paint and rusting of the Civic after five years of ownership." Judge Sigurdson agreed with the owner and ordered Honda to pay $1,163.95 in Martin v. Honda Canada Inc. (Ontario Small Claims Court, Scarborough; March 17, 1986; Judge Sigurdson).

This Mazda owner (in *Thauberger v. Simon Fraser Sales and Mazda Motors* (3 B.C.L.R. 193)) sued for damages caused by the premature rusting of his 1977 Mazda GLC. The court awarded him $1,000. Thauberger had previously sued General Motors for a prematurely rusted Blazer truck and was also awarded $1,000 in the same court. Both judges ruled that the defects could not be excluded from the automaker's expressed warranty or from the implied warranty granted by British Columbia's *Sale of Goods Act*.

See also:

- *Danson v. Chateau Ford (1976) C.P.* (No. 32-00001898-757; Quebec Small Claims Court; 1976; Judge Lande)
- *Doyle v. Vital Automotive Systems* (Ontario Small Claims Court, Toronto; May 16, 1977; Judge Turner)
- *Lacroix v. Ford* (Ontario Small Claims Court, Toronto; April 1980; Judge Tierney)
- *Marinovich v. Riverside Chrysler* (No. 1030/85; District Court of Ontario; April 1, 1987; Judge Stortini)

Broken Promises

New or used vehicles can turn out to be bad buys for various reasons. They were misrepresented by the seller, who sold for the wrong model year ("redated"), covered up damage, turned back the odometer, inflated their fuel economy, lied about its previous use (not really driven only on Sundays by a little old lady, etc.), or they are afflicted with factory-induced defects like sudden acceleration or brake failures. In some cases, abusive driving or poor maintenance by the previous owner can make a vehicle unreliable or dangerous to drive. Misrepresentation is relatively easy to prove. You simply have to show the vehicle doesn't conform to the oral or written sales representations made before or during the time of purchase. These representations include sales brochures and newspaper, radio, television, and Internet ads. Omission of key information can also fall under misrepresentation.

Private sales can easily be cancelled if the vehicle's mileage has been turned back, if accident damage hasn't been disclosed, or if the seller is really a dealer pretending to be a private seller ("curbsiding" (see Part Two)). Even descriptive phrases like "well-maintained," "driven by a woman" (whatever *that*'s supposed to imply), or "excellent condition" can get the seller into trouble if misrepresentation was intended.

To get compensation or to have the car taken back, defects need to be confirmed by an independent garage examination that shows either that the deficiencies are premature, factory-related, or not maintenance-related or that they were hidden at the time of purchase. You can also make your proof by showing repetitive repairs for the same problem over a short period of time. It doesn't matter if the vehicle was sold new or used. In fact, many of the small claims court victories against automakers relating to defective paint, engines, and transmissions were won by owners who bought their vehicles used and then sued both the seller and the automaker.

Sure, automakers will sometimes plead they are not part of the chain of responsibility because they didn't sell the product to the plaintiff. Fortunately, as you will learn reading this section, Canadian judges do not buy that argument. Particularly if the defect was obviously factory-related and caused an injury or death.

Cases involving these kinds of failures are not that difficult to win in Canada under the doctrine of *res ipsa loquitur*, meaning "the thing speaks for itself," or in negligence cases, the liability is shown by the failure itself. Planes shouldn't fall and cars shouldn't suddenly accelerate or fail to stop. Under *res ipsa loquitur*, you don't have to pinpoint the exact cause of the failure, and judges are free to award damages by weighing the "balance of probabilities" as to fault.

This advantage found in Canadian law was laid out succinctly in the July 1, 1998, issue of the *Journal of Small Business Management* in its comparison of product liability laws on both sides of the border (see "Effects of Product Liability Laws on Small Business" at *www.allbusiness.com*).

> Although in theory the Canadian consumer must prove all of the elements of negligence (*Farro v. Nutone Electrical Ltd. 1990*; Ontario Law Reform Commission 1979; Thomas 1989), most Canadian courts allow injured consumers to use a procedural aid known as *res ipsa loquitur* to prove their cases (*Nicholson v. John Deere Ltd. 1986; McMorran v. Dom. Stores Ltd. 1977*). Under *res ipsa loquitur*, plaintiffs must only prove that they were injured in a way that would not ordinarily occur without the defendant's negligence. It is then the responsibility of the defendant to prove that he was not negligent. As proving the negative is extremely difficult, this Canadian reversal of the burden of proof usually results in an outcome functionally equivalent to strict product liability (*Phillips v. Ford Motor Co. of Canada Ltd. 1971; Murray 1988*). This concept is reinforced by the principal that a Canadian manufacturer does not have the right to manufacture an inherently dangerous product when a method exists to manufacture that product without risk of harm. To do so subjects the manufacturer to liability even if the safer method is more expensive (*Nicholson v. John Deere Ltd. 1986*).

In *Jarvis v. Ford* (United States Second Circuit Court of Appeal, February 7, 2002), a judgment was rendered in favour of a driver who was injured when her six-day-old Ford Aerostar minivan suddenly accelerated as it was started and put into gear. What makes this decision unique is that the jury had no specific proof of a defect. The Court of Appeal agreed with the jury award, and Justice Sotomayor (now a Supreme Court Justice) gave these reasons for the court's verdict:

> A product may be found to be defective without proof of the specific malfunction:
>
> It may be inferred that the harm sustained by the plaintiff was caused by a product defect existing at the time of sale or distribution, without proof of a specific defect, when the incident that harmed the plaintiff:

(a) was of a kind that ordinarily occurs as a result of product defect; and

(b) was not, in the particular case, solely the result of causes other than product defect existing at the time of sale or distribution.

Restatement (Third) of Torts: Product Liability §3 (1998). In comment c to this section, the Restatement notes:

[There is] *no requirement that plaintiff prove what aspect of the product was defective.* The inference of defect may be drawn under this Section without proof of the specific defect. Furthermore, quite apart from the question of what type of defect was involved, the plaintiff need not explain specifically what constituent part of the product failed. For example, if an inference of defect can be appropriately drawn in connection with the catastrophic failure of an airplane, the plaintiff need not establish whether the failure is attributable to fuel-tank explosion or engine malfunction.

The jury awarded Ms. Jarvis $24,568 in past medical insurance premiums, $340,338 in lost earnings, and $200,000 in pain and suffering. For future damages, the jury awarded $22,955 in medical insurance premiums, $648,944 in lost earnings, and $300,000 for pain and suffering.

GETTING OUTSIDE HELP

Don't lose your case because of poor preparation. Ask government or independent consumer protection agencies to evaluate how well you've prepared before going to your first hearing. Also, use the Internet to ferret out additional facts and gather support (*www.lemonaidcars.com* and its links are good places to start).

Pressure Tactics

You can put additional pressure on a seller or garage, and have fun at the same time, by putting a lemon sign on your car and parking it in front of the dealer or garage, by creating a "lemon" website, or by forming a self-help group. Angry Chrysler and Ford owners, for example, have received sizeable settlements in Canada by forming the Chrysler Lemon Owners Group and Ford Lemon Owners Group.

Often, simply calling a press conference will short-circuit the no-sayers and quickly bring out competent company agents who will correct the problem. It worked beautifully for Apple Inc. co-founder Steve Wozniak. He repeatedly called Toyota over the course of several months to report brake failures with his Prius. Toyota officials ignored him. However, when he mentioned the problem in an aside during an Apple press conference, all hell broke loose. Toyota officials returned his call, apologized, fixed the brakes, and promptly recalled thousands of cars.

Use your website and social media (Twitter, Facebook, Yelp, etc.) to gather data from others who may have experienced a problem similar to your own. This can help you organize other auto owners for class action and small claims court lawsuits and it pressures the dealer or manufacturer to settle. Public demonstrations (picketing, decorating your car with lemons, etc.), websites and Twitter "buzz" often generate news stories that will take on a life of their own as others join the movement or add depth and breadth to the campaign.

Here's some more advice from this consumer advocate with hundreds of pickets and mass demonstrations under his belt. Keep a sense of humour, and never break off the negotiations.

Finally, don't be scared off by threats that it's illegal to criticize a product or company. Unions, environmentalists, and consumer groups do it regularly (it's called informational picketing), and the Supreme Court of Canada in *R. v. Guinard* reaffirmed this right in February 2002 (see [2002] 1 S.C.R. 472). In that judgment, an insured posted a sign on his barn claiming the Commerce Insurance Company was unfairly refusing his claim. The municipality of Saint-Hyacinthe, Quebec, told him to take the sign down. He refused, maintaining that he had the right to state his opinion. The Supreme Court agreed.

This judgment means that consumer protests, signs, and websites that criticize the actions of corporations or government cannot be shut up or taken down simply because they say unpleasant things. However, what you say must be true, and your intent must be to inform, without malice.

Even if you do respectfully protest your treatment following a used car purchase from a dealer, on rare occasions that dealer may file suit against you for defamation or libel. Generally, Canadian courts take a dim view of consumers and non-government organizations, like unions and environmental groups, being sued for protesting, or even picketing. Nevertheless, some dealers will sue.

Fortunately, two other Supreme Court decisions buttress a citizen's right to engage in information protests or picketing. This assumes the protest is done without infringing upon the rights of others through actions such as assault, restricting access, defacing property, or harassing others.

The first decision overturned a lower court award of $1.5 million to a forestry executive who sued *The Toronto Star*. The *Star* alleged he had used political connections to get approval for a golf course expansion (*Grant v. Torstar Corp.*, [2009] 3 S.C.R. 640).

The Supreme Court struck down the judgment against the newspaper because that judgment had failed to give adequate weight to the value of freedom of expression. The court announced a new defense of "responsible communication on matters of public interest." In the court's opinion, anyone (journalists, bloggers, unions, picketers, etc.) can avoid liability if they can show that the information they communicated – whether true or false – was of public interest and they tried their best to verify it.

In another case, again involving a major Canadian newspaper, a former Ontario police officer sued *The Ottawa Citizen* after it reported he had misrepresented his search-and-rescue work at Ground Zero in New York City after the attacks of September 11, 2001. The Supreme Court reversed the $100,000 jury award because the judges felt the article was in the public interest (*Quan v. Cusson*, [2009] 3 S.C.R. 712).

CONTACT THE RIGHT PEOPLE

Before we go any further, let's get one thing straight – a telephone call to a service manager or automaker may only be marginally effective. Auto manufacturers and their dealers want to make money, not give it back. Customer service advisors are paid to *apply* the warranty policy; don't expect them to *make* policy due to your claim's extenuating circumstances.

To get action, if you suspect a secret warranty applies or that your vehicle has an independently-confirmed factory-related defect, you have to kick your claim upstairs, where the company representatives have more power. This can usually be accomplished by sending your claim to the legal affairs department (typically found in Ontario). It should be a registered letter, fax, or e-mail – something that creates a paper trail and gets attention. What's more, that letter must contain the threat that you will use the implied warranty against the dealer and manufacturer and cite convincing jurisprudence to win your small claims court action in the same region where that business operates.

On the opposite page is a sample complaint letter that shows the type of ammunition you'll need in order to invoke the implied warranty and get a refund for a bad car or ineffective repairs.

MORE WARRANTY RIGHTS

The manufacturer's or dealer's warranty is a written legal promise that a vehicle will be reasonably reliable, subject to certain conditions. Regardless of the number of subsequent owners, this promise remains in force as long as the warranty's original time/kilometre limits haven't expired. Tires aren't usually covered by car manufacturers' warranties; they're warranted instead by the tiremaker on a prorated basis. This isn't such a good deal, because the manufacturer is making a profit by charging you the full list price. If you were to buy the same replacement tire from a discount store, you'd likely pay less, without the prorated rebate.

But consumers have gained additional rights following Bridgestone/Firestone's massive recall in 2001 of its defective ATX II and Wilderness tires. Because of the confusion and chaos surrounding Firestone's handling of the recall, Ford's 575 Canadian dealers stepped into the breach and replaced the tires with any equivalent tires they had in stock, no questions asked. This is an important precedent that tears down the traditional wall separating tire manufacturers from automakers in product liability claims. In essence, whoever sells the product can now be held liable for damages. In the future, Canadian consumers will have an easier time holding the dealer, the automaker, and the tire manufacturer liable, not just

New or Used Vehicle Complaint Letter/E-mail/Fax

Without Prejudice

[Date]

[Dealer and Automaker]

[Your Address and Phone #]

Gentlemen,

Please be advised that I am dissatisfied with my vehicle, a [model and VIN], for the following reasons:

1. _____.

2. _____.

3 _____.

In compliance with consumer protection laws and the "implied warranty" set down by the Supreme Court of Canada in Donoghue v. Stevenson and Kravitz v. GM, I hereby request that these defects be repaired in the near future without charge or the vehicle be taken back and my money refunded.

This vehicle has not been reasonably durable and is, therefore, not as represented to me.

Should you fail to repair these defects in a satisfactory manner and within a reasonable period of time, I reserve the right to have the repairs done elsewhere by an independent garage and claim reimbursement in court without further delay. I also reserve my rights to punitive damages up to $1 million, pursuant to the Canadian Supreme Court's ruling in Whiten v. Pilot (February 22, 2002).

I believe your company wants to deal with its clients in an honest, competent manner and trust that my claim is the exception and not the rule.

A positive response within the next five (5) days would be appreciated.

Sincerely,

[signed with telephone, e-mail address, or fax #])

for recalled products but also for any defect that affects the safety or reasonable durability of that product.

This is particularly true now that the Supreme Court of Canada (*Winnipeg Condominium v. Bird Construction*, [1995] 1 S.C.R. 85) has ruled that defendants are liable in negligence for any designs that result in a risk to the public's safety or health. Sometimes automakers plead that their compliance with federal automobile safety laws immunizes them from product liability claims, but this argument has been shot down countless times by the courts. (Type "auto safety standards liability" into an Internet search engine to find such cases.)

Other Warranties

In the United States, safety restraints such as airbags and safety belts have warranty coverage extended for the lifetime of the vehicle, following an informal agreement made between automakers and NHTSA. In Canada, however, some automakers have tried to dodge this responsibility, alleging that they are separate entities, their vehicles are different, and no U.S. agreement or service bulletin can bind them. That distinction is both disingenuous and dishonest and wouldn't likely hold up in small claims court – probably the reason why most automakers relent when threatened with legal action.

Aftermarket products and services – such as gas-saving gadgets, rustproofing, and paint protectors – can render the manufacturer's warranty invalid, so make sure you're in the clear before purchasing any optional equipment or services from an independent supplier.

How fairly a warranty is applied is more important than how long it remains in effect. Once you know the normal wear rate for a mechanical component or body part, you can demand proportional compensation when you get less than normal durability – no matter what the original warranty says. Some dealers tell customers that they need to have original equipment parts installed in order to maintain their warranty. A variation on this theme requires that the selling dealer does routine servicing, including tune-ups and oil changes (with a certain brand of oil), or the warranty is invalidated. Nothing could be further from the truth. Canadian law stipulates that whoever issues a warranty cannot make that warranty conditional on the use of any specific brand of motor oil, oil filter, or any other component, unless it's provided to the customer free of charge.

Sometimes dealers will do all sorts of minor repairs that don't correct the problem, and then after the warranty runs out, they'll tell you that major repairs are needed. You can avoid this nasty surprise by repeatedly bringing your vehicle to the dealership before the warranty ends. During each visit, insist that a written work order include the specific nature of the problem, as you see it, and a statement that this is the second, third, or fourth time the same problem has been brought to the dealer's attention. Write this down yourself, if need be. This allows you to show a pattern of non-performance by the dealer during the warranty period and establishes that the problem is both serious and chronic. When the warranty expires, you have the legal right to demand that it be extended on those items consistently reappearing on your handful of work orders. *Lowe v. Fairview Chrysler* (see page 173) is an excellent judgment that reinforces this important principle. In another lawsuit, *François Chong v. Marine Drive Imported Cars Ltd. and Honda*

Canada Inc. (see page 173), a Honda owner forced the company to fix his engine six times – until they got it right.

A retired GM service manager suggests another effective tactic when you're not sure that a dealer's warranty "repairs" will actually correct the problem for a reasonable period of time after the warranty expires. Here's what he says you should do.

> When you pick up the vehicle after the warranty repair has been done, hand the service manager a note to be put in your file that says you appreciate the warranty repair, however, you intend to return and ask for further warranty coverage if the problem reappears before a reasonable amount of time has elapsed – even if the original warranty has expired. A copy of the same note should be sent to the automaker.... Keep your copy of the note in the glove compartment as cheap insurance against paying for a repair that wasn't fixed correctly the first time.

Extra-Cost Warranties

When a company goes bankrupt, its extended warranties become worthless unless successfully litigated. At best, payouts will be parsimonious. Supplementary warranties providing extended coverage may be sold by the manufacturer, the dealer, or an independent third party and are automatically transferred when the vehicle is sold. They cost between $1,500 and $2,000 and are usually a waste of money. You can protect yourself better by steering clear of vehicles that have a reputation for being unreliable or expensive to service (see Part Four ratings), and using the threat of small claims courts when factory-related trouble arises. Don't let the dealer pressure you into deciding right away.

Generally, you can purchase an extended warranty any time during the period in which the manufacturer's warranty is in effect or, in some cases, shortly after buying the vehicle from a used-car dealer. An automaker's supplementary warranty will likely cost about a third more than warranties sold by independents. And in some parts of the country, notably B.C., dealers have a quasi-monopoly on selling warranties, with little competition from the independents.

Dealers love to sell extended warranties, whether you need them or not, because dealer markup represents up to 60 percent of the warranty's cost. Out of the remaining 40 percent comes the sponsor's administration costs and profit margin, calculated at another 15 percent. What's left to pay for repairs is a paltry 25 percent of the original amount. The only reason that automakers and independent warranty companies haven't been busted for this "Ponzi scheme" is that only half of the car buyers who purchase extended service contracts actually use them.

It's often difficult to collect on supplementary warranties because independent companies frequently go out of business or limit the warranty's coverage through subsequent mailings. Provincial laws cover both situations. If the bankrupt warranty company's insurance policy won't cover your claim, take the dealer to small claims court and ask for repair costs and the refund of the original warranty payment. Your argument for holding the dealer responsible is a simple one. By accepting a commission to act as an agent of the defunct company, the dealer took on the obligations of the company as well. As for limiting the coverage after you have bought the warranty policy, this is illegal, and it allows you to sue both the dealer and the warranty company for a refund of both the warranty and the repair costs.

FREE RECALL REPAIRS

Vehicles are recalled for one of two reasons – either they are potentially unsafe or they don't conform to federal pollution control regulations. Whatever the reason, recalls are a great way to get free repairs – if you know which ones apply to you and you have the patience of Job.

In North America, NHTSA has been involved in 17,000 separate recalls involving about 500 million vehicles, since American recall legislation was passed in 1966 (a weaker Canadian law was enacted in 1971). During that time, about one-third of the recalled vehicles never made it back to the dealership for repairs, because owners were never informed, didn't consider the defect to be that hazardous, or gave up waiting for corrective parts.

Subsequent American legislation targets automakers who drag their feet in making recall repairs. Owners on both sides of the border may wish to cite the NHTSA guidelines for support.

If you've moved or bought a used vehicle, it's smart to pay a visit to your local dealership, give them your address, and get a report card on which recalls, warranties, and free service campaigns apply to your vehicle. Simply give the service advisor the vehicle identification number – found on your insurance card, or on your dash just below the windshield on the driver's side – and have the number run through the automaker's computer system. Ask for a computer printout of the vehicle's history (have it e-mailed to you or a friend), and make sure you're listed in the automaker's computer as the new owner. This ensures that you'll receive notices of warranty extensions and emissions and safety recalls.

Regional Recalls

In order to cut recall costs, many automakers try to limit a recall to vehicles in a certain designated region. This practice doesn't make sense, since cars are mobile and an unsafe, rust-cankered steering unit can be found anywhere – not just in certain rust-belt provinces or American states. For instance, in 2001, Ford attempted to limit to five American states its recall of faulty Firestone tires. Public ridicule of the company's proposal led to an extension of the recall throughout North America.

Common safety defects

Wherever you live or drive, don't expect to be welcomed with open arms when your vehicle develops a safety- or emissions-related problem that's not yet part of a recall campaign. Even if it is covered by a recall, carmakers have a lot of wiggle room to delay the repairs.

Under U.S. safety regulations and Canadian law, carmakers can't be forced to recall unsafe vehicles until NHTSA calls public hearings into the issue and orders a recall, backed up by a court order to enforce it. However, manufacturers can be shamed into bringing their cars in for a free fix through bad publicity and class action lawsuits predicated upon NHTSA's statistical and engineering findings that the Jeep SUVs are unsafe.

Automobile manufacturers and dealers take a restrictive view of what constitutes a safety or emissions defect and frequently charge for repairs that should be free under federal safety or emissions legislation. To counter this tendency, look at the following list of typical defects that are clearly safety-related. If you experience similar problems to these, insist that the automaker fix the problem at no expense to yourself, including paying for a car rental while corrective repairs are done:

A fatal fire involving a 1999 Jeep Grand Cherokee that was rear-ended by a pickup.

- Airbag malfunctions;
- Corrosion affecting the safe operation of the vehicle;
- Disconnected or stuck accelerators;
- Electrical shorts;
- Faulty windshield wipers;
- Fuel leaks;
- Problems with orginal axles, driveshafts, seats, seat recliners, or defrosters;
- Seat belt problems;
- Stalling, or sudden acceleration;
- Sudden steering or brake loss;
- Suspension failures;
- Tire pressure monitor systems (TPMS);
- Tire valve airleaks; or
- Trailer coupling failures.

Voluntary service campaigns, called by some "phantom recalls," are a real problem. The government doesn't monitor the notification of owners; dealers and automakers routinely deny there's a recall, thereby dissuading most claimants; and the company's so-called fix, not authorized by any governing body, may not correct the hazard at all. Also, the service program may leave out many of the affected models, or unreasonably exclude certain owners.

Safety Defect Information

If you wish to report a safety defect or want recall info, you may access Transport Canada's website at *www.tc.gc.ca/roadsafety/recalls/search_e.asp*. Recall information is available in French and English, as is general information relating to road safety and importing a vehicle into Canada. Web surfers can now access the recall database for 1970-2013 model year vehicles, but, unlike NHTSA's website, the Transport Canada website doesn't list owner complaints, doesn't disclose defect investigations, doesn't show "voluntary warranty extensions" (read "secret warranties"), and doesn't provide service bulletin summaries. You can also call Transport Canada at 1-800-333-0510 (toll-free within Canada) or 613-993-9851 (within the Ottawa region or outside Canada) to get additional information.

If you aren't happy with Ottawa's treatment of your recall inquiry, try NHTSA's website. It's more complete than Transport Canada's (NHTSA's database is updated daily and covers vehicles built since 1952). You can search the database for your vehicle or tires at *safercar.gov*. You'll get immediate access to four essential database categories applicable to your vehicle and model year – the latest recalls, current and past defect investigations, complaints reported by other owners, and a brief summary of TSBs.

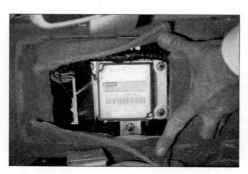

"Black box" data can prove that the brakes, airbag, or another component failed.

"BLACK BOX" DATA RECORDERS

If your car has an airbag, it's probably spying on you. And if you get into an accident caused by a mechanical malfunction, you will be glad that it is.

Event data recorders (EDRs) the size of a VCR tape have been hidden near the engine, under the seat, or in the centre consoles of about 30 million airbag-equipped Ford and GM vehicles since the early '90s. Almost all domestic and imported cars now carry them. To find out if your car or truck carries an EDR, read your owner's manual, contact the regional office of your car's manufacturer, or go to *www.harristechnical.com/down loads/cdrlist.pdf*.

EDRs operate in a similar fashion to flight data recorders used in airplanes. They record data from the last five seconds before impact, including the force of the collision, the airbag's performance, when the brakes were applied, engine and vehicle speed, gas pedal position, and whether the driver was wearing a seat belt.

Getting EDR Data

In the past, automakers have systematically hidden their collected data from government and insurance researchers, citing concerns for drivers' privacy. This argument, however, has been roundly rejected by law enforcement agencies, the courts, and car owners who need the independent information to prove negligence or simply to keep track of how and where their vehicles are driven. Car owners, rental agencies, and fleet administrators are also using EDR data to pin legal liability on automakers for accidents caused by the failure of safety components, such as airbags that don't deploy when they should (or do deploy when they shouldn't) and anti-lock brakes that don't brake. Car owners who wish to dispute criminal charges, oppose their insurer's decision as to fault, or hold an automaker responsible for a safety device's failure (airbags, seat belts, or brakes) will find this data invaluable (see "GoPointe" app at page 550) – if the data hasn't been wiped clean by the dealer!

Psst ... "Secret" Warranties Are Everywhere

Toyotas needing new pistons and rings, Ford Focuses with steering issues, and VWs that leak when it rains are among the vehicles covered in the latest TSBs unearthed by *Lemon-Aid*.

Automakers are reluctant to make free repair programs public because they feel that doing so would weaken confidence in their product and increase their legal liability. The closest they come to an admission is sending a "goodwill policy," "product improvement program," or "special policy" TSB to dealers or first owners of record. Consequently, the only motorists who find out about these policies are the original owners who haven't changed their addresses or leased their vehicles. The other motorists who get compensated for repairs are the ones who read *Lemon-Aid* each year, staple TSBs to their work orders, and yell the loudest.

Remember, vehicles on their second owners and repairs done by independent garages are included in these secret warranty programs. Large, costly repairs, such as blown engines, burned transmissions, and peeling paint, are often covered. Even mundane little repairs, which can still cost you $100 or more, are frequently included in these programs. If you have a TSB but you're still refused compensation, keep in mind that secret warranties are an admission of manufacturing negligence. Owners who have been refused compensation should send an e-mail claim to the automaker and selling dealer and then file a small claims court claim if no settlement is reached within a week.

Here are a few examples of secret warranties that may save you thousands of dollars. More extensive listings are found in Part Four's model ratings.

ALL YEARS, ALL MODELS

Problem: Faulty automatic transmissions that self-destruct, shift erratically, gear down to "limp mode," are slow to shift in or out of Reverse, or are noisy. **Warranty coverage:** If you have the assistance of your dealer's service manager, or some internal service bulletin that confirms the automatic transmission may be defective, expect an offer of 50-75 percent (about $2,500) if you threaten to sue in small claims court. Acura, Honda, Hyundai, Lexus, and Toyota coverage varies between seven and eight years.

Problem: Premature wearout of brake pads, calipers, and rotors. Produces excessive vibration, noise, and pulling to one side when braking. **Warranty coverage:** *Calipers and pads:* "Goodwill" settlements confirm that brake calipers and pads that fail to last 2 years/40,000 km will be replaced for half the repair cost; components not lasting 1 year/20,000 km will be replaced for free. *Rotors:* If they last less than 3 years/60,000 km, they will be replaced at half price; replacement is free up to 2 years/40,000 km.

ACURA

2007-09 MDX; 2009-10 RL; and 2009-11 TL

Problem: Fix for a transmission judder. **Warranty coverage:** 8 years/169,000 km (105,000 mi) radiator assembly and automatic transmission warranty extension, which covers "damage, repairs, replacement, and related towing resulting from this issue." Original and subsequent owner coverage and retroactive reimbursement.

BMW

2004-06 models

Problem: Premature failure of the seat airbag occupant detection mat. **Warranty coverage:** BMW has extended the warranty to 10 years/unlimited mileage.

FORD

2009-2011 Escape, Mariner; 2010-2011 Fusion and Milan vehicles equipped with a 2.5L or 3.0L engine built on or before 03/04/2011

Problem: A leaking/stuck canister purge valve. This condition may cause various intermittent driveability symptoms. **Warranty coverage:** 8 years under the Emissions Warranty.

2009-11 Edge, Flex; 2011 Explorer; 2010–11 MXS; 2009-2011 MKX; 2010-11 MKT

Problem: Sluggish transmission. **Warranty coverage:** Change the valve body calibration under the 8-year Emissions Warranty.

2011-14 models equipped with the MyFord Touch touch screen entertainment and navigation system

Problem: Poor cell phone and Bluetooth compatibility; doesn't recognize voice commands; slow to respond; and not user-friendly. **Warranty coverage:** Ford Motor Co. will upgrade and extend the warranty. Ford is also extending the warranty on the system in its Ford brand vehicles to five years with unlimited miles, up from three years and 58,000 km (36,000 mi). The software on Lincoln vehicles will now be covered for six years with unlimited miles, up from four years and 80,000 km (50,000 mi).

GENERAL MOTORS

2000–03 GM S10 and Sonoma models

Problem: Corroded, fractured tailgate cables. **Warranty coverage:** GM warranty extension to 12 years/no mileage limitation.

2005-06 G6, Malibu, and Malibu Maxx; 2008 G6, Malibu, Malibu Maxx, and Aura

Problem: Loss of power-steering assist. **Warranty coverage:** Under Special Coverage Adjustment #10183, dated July 20, 2010, GM will replace the failed components free of charge up to 10 years/160,000 km (100,000 mi.).

2006-07 Cobalt, G4/G5, and Ion

Problem: A faulty fuel pump module may produce a fuel odour or spotting on the ground. **Warranty coverage:** GM has extended the fuel pump warranty to 10 years/ 193,000 km (120,000 mi.), says TSB #09275A, issued March 3, 2010.

2006-07 Malibu and G6

Problem: Catalytic Converter failure. **Warranty coverage:** Under Special Coverage Adjustment #10134, dated November 17, 2010, GM will replace the converter free of charge up to 10 years/193,000 km (120,000 mi.).

2006-07 Buick Terraza; 2010 Buick Lucerne; 2006-07 Chevrolet Monte Carlo; 2006-08 Chevrolet Uplander; 2006-10 Chevrolet Impala; 2008-09 Chevrolet Malibu; 2006-08 Pontiac Montana SV6; 2006-09 Pontiac G6; 2006-08 Saturn Relay; 2007-09 Saturn AURA; all equipped with a 3.5L or 3.9L Engine

Problem: Some customers may comment on a coolant leak. The comments may range from spots on the driveway to having to add more coolant. If the coolant leak is coming from the front (accessory drive end) of the engine, the coolant crossover gaskets should be replaced. If the leak is found to be coming from a cylinder head gasket, the gasket must be replaced. **Warranty coverage:** GM's 8-year Emissions Warranty.

2006-09 Cadillac STS-V, XLR, XLR-V; 2007-08 Cadillac Escalade, Escalade ESV, Escalade EXT, XLR; 2006-09 Chevrolet Corvette; 2007-08 Chevrolet Silverado; 2008 Chevrolet Suburban; 2007-08 GMC Sierra, Sierra Denali, Yukon Denali, Yukon XL Denali; 2008 GMC Yukon XL; 2008-09 HUMMER H2; and 2008-09 Pontiac G8

Problem: Slips in Reverse or Third, Delayed Reverse or Drive Engagement, DTC P0776, P2715, P2723, Harsh 2-3 Shifts (Inspect 1-2-3-4/3-5-R housing and pump seal rings). **Warranty coverage:** GM's base warranty. Eligible for "goodwill" consideration since the housing and pump seal rings weren't reasonably durable.

2006-11 models

Problem: Engine Oil Consumption on Aluminum Block/Iron Block Engines with Active Fuel Management. Install AFM Oil Deflector and Clean Carbon from Cylinder and/or Install Updated Valve Cover. **Warranty coverage:** The 8-year Emissions Warranty.

2007-12 Chevrolet Silverado and GMC Sierra

Problem: Excessive rear interior wind noise, which GM attributes to "a void in the body filler within the C-pillar" or "a result of the design of the body rear panel acoustic insulator that is mounted behind the rear seat. The insulator could be one of several early designs which demonstrated a lesser success of minimizing wind noise (Bulletin No.: 10-08-58-001F). **Warranty coverage:** GM will add padding in the cab area on a case-by-case basis at no charge under a "goodwill" policy. *GM P/N 12378195 is not available in Canada. However several equivalents such as Evercoat (Q-Pads) P/N 100116 and Dominion Sure Seal (Sound Deadener Pads) BSDE Part 110900 are available through NAPA Auto Parts retailers. Information for finding your local retail location can be obtained online at *www.napacanada.com*. Dominion Sure Seal (sound deadener pads) BSDE Part 110900 can be obtained by contacting Dominion Sure Seal at 1-800-265-0790.

HONDA

2000-02 Accords; 2001-04 Civics; 2002-04 CR-Vs; 2003 Elements; 2002 Odysseys; and 2003-04 Pilots

Problem: Failure of the airbag occupant position detection system. **Warranty coverage:** Honda has extended the emissions warranty to 10 years/241,000 km (150,000 mi).

2006-08 Civics, except GX, Hybrid, and Si

Problem: Engine overheats or leaks coolant due to the engine block cracking at the coolant passages. Install a new engine block assembly. **Warranty coverage:** Repair may be eligible for goodwill consideration by the District Parts and Service Manager or the Zone Office.

2006-09 Civic

Problem: The sun visor may come apart or split with use. **Warranty coverage:** Honda has extended the warranty to 10 years/161,000 km (100,000 mi).

2006-09 Civic

Problem: Engine overheats or leaks coolant because the engine block is cracking at the coolant passages. **Warranty coverage:** Honda will install a new engine block assembly free of charge under a "goodwill policy," as stated in its TSB #10-048, issued August 17, 2010.

2007-09 Civics

Problem: An engine oil leak from the front of the timing chain case cover on the oil pump assembly. **Warranty coverage:** Post-warranty free repairs may be eligible for goodwill consideration by the District Parts and Service Manager or your Zone Office.

2008-09 Accord

Problem: The leather seat covers may crack or paint rub off, delaminate, or peel. Honda attributes the problem to "an insufficient buffing process and material problem." **Warranty coverage:** Honda will replace the seat-back or seat cushion cover.

LEXUS

2007-13 Lexus ES; 2006-12 Lexus IS; and 2013 Lexus GS models

Problem: Emergency trunk release can break, trapping an occupant inside. **Warranty coverage:** Trunk release will be replaced; no time or ownership limitation.

MAZDA

2007-11 CX7 and CX-9

Problem: These Mazdas may leak oil from the rear differential seal. In TSB 0300411, Mazda says the differential breather was placed too low and could easily become clogged by snow or water. **Warranty coverage:** A new differential with a raised breather covered by the breather boot will be installed for free on a case-by-case basis.

MERCEDES

Model Year 2005-06 ML (164), SLK (171), C (203), CLK (209), E (211), CLS (219), R (251), and Model Year 2005-08 G (463)

Problem: Faulty airbag wiring may cause the airbag warning light to remain lit. **Warranty coverage:** Mercedes has extended the warranty to 10 years/161,000 km (100,000 mi).

2005-08 models

Problem: Inaccurate fuel sending unit. **Warranty coverage:** Nissan extended the warranty to 7 years/116,000 km (72,000 mi).

2005-10 Frontier, Pathfinder, and Xterra models

Problem: Coolant may leak into the five-speed transmission. **Warranty coverage:** 8 years/129,000 km (80,000 mi) torque converter coverage for the original owner and any subsequent owners. Owners who already had the radiator or transmission repaired would be eligible for reimbursement.

2007-12 Altimas and Sentras and 2008-12 Rogues with 4-cylinder engines

Problem: A leak from the oil cooler may be a problem on some Nissans. In TSB NTB11015A, Nissan says the leak is from the upper end of the oil cooler. **Warranty coverage:** Removing the cooler and replacing the gaskets are covered under an undefined extended warranty.

USING THE COURTS

Nova Scotia's Used-Car "Lemon Law"

In 2010, Nova Scotia became the first Canadian province to pass legislation requiring that used-car dealers identify rebuilt or previously damaged vehicles by placing labels on their windshields.[1] Acting on consumer complaints, the provincial government introduced changes to the *Motor Vehicle Act* to ensure consumers know a used vehicle's history before they buy it.

Under the new law, dealers must clearly label vehicles that have been deemed unrepairable, are manufacturers' buybacks, or have been involved in a serious collision in Canada or the U.S. Sellers who do not comply with the new legislation will be fined up to $1,000 per vehicle.

Unfortunately, the fines are ridiculously low and the new rules will not apply to private auto sales or trade-ins.

Sue as a Last Resort

If the seller you've been negotiating with agrees to make things right, give him or her a deadline and then have an independent garage check the repairs. If no offer is made within ten working days, file suit in court. Make the manufacturer a party to the lawsuit only if the original, unexpired warranty was transferred to you; if your claim falls under the emissions warranty, a TSB, a secret warranty extension,

---

[1] S.N.S. 2010, c. 60. The statute received Royal Assent on December 10, 2010, but at the time of writing has not yet been proclaimed in force. There is some limited legislation in Manitoba (S.M. 2008, c. 30).

or a safety recall campaign; or if there is extensive chassis rusting due to poor engineering.

Choosing the Right Court

You must decide what remedy to pursue – a partial refund or a cancellation of the sale. To determine the refund amount, add the estimated cost of repairing existing mechanical defects to the cost of prior repairs. Don't exaggerate your losses or claim for repairs that are considered routine maintenance. A suit for cancellation of sale involves practical problems. The court requires that the vehicle be "tendered," or taken back to the seller, at the time the lawsuit is filed. This means that you are without transportation for as long as the case continues, unless you purchase another vehicle in the interim. If you lose the case, you must then take back the old vehicle and pay storage fees. You could go from having no vehicle to having two, one of which is a clunker.

Generally, if the cost of repairs or the sales contract amount falls within the small claims court limit, file the case there to keep costs to a minimum and to get a speedy hearing. Small claims court judgments aren't easily appealed, lawyers aren't necessary, filing fees are minimal (about $125), and cases are usually heard within a few months.

Watch what you ask for. If you claim more than the small claims court limit, you'll have to go to a higher court – where costs quickly add up and delays of a few years or more are commonplace.

Small Claims Courts

Crooked automakers scurry away from small claims courts like cockroaches from bug spray, not because the courts can issue million-dollar judgments or force litigants to spend millions in legal fees (they can't), but because they can award sizeable sums to plaintiffs ($25,000-$30,000) and make jurisprudence that other judges on the same bench are likely to follow.

For example, in *Dawe v. Courtesy Chrysler* (SCCH #206825; Dartmouth Nova Scotia Small Claims Court; July 30, 2004), Judge Patrick L. Casey, Q.C., rendered an impressive 21-page decision citing key automobile product liability cases over the past 80 years. He awarded $5,037 to the owner of a new 2001 Cummins-equipped Ram pickup that suffered from myriad ailments. The truck shifted erratically, lost braking ability, wandered all over the road, lost power or jerked and bucked, bottomed out when passing over bumps, allowed water to leak into the cab, produced a burnt-wire and oil smell as the lights would dim, and produced a rear-end whine and wind noise around the doors and under the dash. Dawe had sold the vehicle and reduced his claim to meet the small claims threshold.

There are small claims courts in most counties of every province, and you can make a claim either in the county where the problem happened or in the county where the defendant lives and conducts business. Simply go to the small claims court office and ask for a claim form. Instructions on how to fill it out accompany the form. Remember, you must identify the defendant correctly, and this may require some help from the court clerk or a law student because some automakers name local attorneys to handle suits (look for other recent lawsuits naming the same party). Crooks often change their company's name to escape liability; for example, it would be impossible to sue Joe's Garage (2008) if your contract is with Joe's Garage Inc. (2004).

At this point, it wouldn't hurt to hire a lawyer or a paralegal for a brief walk-through of small claims procedures to ensure that you've prepared your case properly and that you know what objections the other side will likely raise. If you'd like a lawyer to do all the work for you, there are a number of law firms around the country that specialize in small claims litigation. "Small claims" doesn't mean small legal fees, however. In Toronto, some law offices charge a flat fee of $1,000 for a basic small claims lawsuit and trial.

Remember that you're entitled to bring to court any evidence relevant to your case, including written documents such as a bill of sale, receipt, contract, or letter. If your car has developed severe rust problems, bring a photograph (signed and dated by the photographer) to court. You may also have witnesses testify, but it's important to discuss witness testimony prior to the court date. If a witness can't attend the court date, he or she can write a report and sign it for representation in court. This situation usually applies to an expert witness, such as an independent mechanic who has evaluated your car's problems.

If you lose a case in spite of all your preparation and research, some small claims court statutes allow cases to be retried, at a nominal cost, in exceptional circumstances. If a new witness has come forward, additional evidence has been discovered, or key documents that were previously not available have become accessible, apply for a retrial. In Ontario, this little-known provision is Rule 18.4(1)B.

Alan MacDonald, a *Lemon-Aid* reader who won his case in small claims court, gives the following tips on beating Ford (*MacDonald v. Highbury Ford Sales Limited* (Court File #0001/00; Ontario Superior Court of Justice in the Small Claims Court London; June 6, 2000; Judge J. D. Searle):

In 1999 after only 105,000 km the automatic transmission went. I took [my 1994 Ford Taurus wagon] to Highbury Ford to have it repaired. We paid $2,070 to have the transmission fixed, but protested and felt the transmission failed prematurely. We contacted Ford, but to no avail: their reply was we were out of warranty period. The transmission was so poorly repaired (and we went back to Highbury Ford several times) that we had to go to Mr. Transmission to have the transmission fixed again nine months later at a further $1,906.02. . . .

My observations with going through small claims court involved the following: I filed in January of 2000, the trial took place on June 1 and the judgment was issued June 6.

At pretrial, a representative of Ford (Ann Sroda) and a representative from Highbury Ford were present. I came with one binder for each of the defendants, the court, and one for myself (each binder was about 3 inches thick — containing your reports on Ford Taurus automatic transmissions, ALLDATA Service Bulletins, [and extracts from the following websites:]

Taurus Transmissions Victims (Bradley website), Center for Auto Safety ... Read This Before Buying a Taurus ... and the Ford Vent Page....

The representative from Ford asked a lot of questions (I think she was trying to find out if I had read the contents of the information I was relying on). The Ford representative then offered a 50 percent settlement based on the initial transmission work done at Highbury Ford. The release allowed me to still sue Highbury Ford with regards to the necessity of going to Mr. Transmission because of the faulty repair done by the dealer. Highbury Ford displayed no interest in settling the case, and so I had to go to court.

For court, I prepared by issuing a summons to the manager at Mr. Transmission, who did the second transmission repair, as an expert witness. ... Next, I went to the law school library in London and received a great deal of assistance in researching cases pertinent to car repairs. I was told that judgments in your home province (in my case, Ontario) were binding on the court; that cases outside of the home province could be considered, but not binding, on the judge.

The cases I used for trial involved *Pelleray v. Heritage Ford Sales Ltd.*, Ontario Small Claims Court (Scarborough) SC7688/91 March 22, 1993; *Phillips et al. v. Ford Motor Co. of Canada Ltd. et al*, Ontario Reports 1970, 15th January 1970; *Gregorio v. Intrans-Corp.*, Ontario Court of Appeal, May 19, 1994; *Collier v. MacMaster's Auto Sales*, New Brunswick Court of Queen's Bench, April 26, 1991; *Sigurdson v. Hillcrest Service & Acklands (1977)*, Saskatchewan Queen's Bench; *White v. Sweetland*, Newfoundland District Court, Judicial Centre of Gander, November 8, 1978; *Raiches Steel Works v. J. Clark & Son*, New Brunswick Supreme Court, March 7, 1977; *Mudge v. Corner Brook Garage Ltd.*, Newfoundland Supreme Court, July 17, 1975; *Sylvain v. Carroseries d'Automobiles Guy Inc. (1981)*, C.P. 333, Judge Page; and *Gagnon v. Ford Motor Company of Canada, Limited et Marineau Automobile Co. Ltée. (1974)*, C.S. 422–423.

In court, I had prepared the case, as indicated above, and had my expert witness and two other witnesses who had driven the vehicle (my wife and my 18-year-old son). As you can see by the judgment, we won our case and I was awarded $1,756.52, including prejudgment interest and costs.

Legal "Secrets" Only Lawyers Know

Send a claim letter to both the seller (if it's a dealer) and the automaker to let them work out together how much they will refund to you. Make sure you keep plenty of copies of the complaint and indicate how you can most easily be reached.

Unfair Contract Clauses

Don't let anyone tell you that contracts and warranties are iron-clad and cannot be broken. In fact, a judge can cancel an unfair sales contract or extend your warranty at any time, even though corporate lawyers spend countless hours protecting their clients with one-sided, standard-form contracts. Judges look upon these agreements, called "contracts of adhesion," with a great deal of skepticism. They know these loan documents, insurance contracts, automobile leases, and guarantees grant consumers little or no bargaining power. So when a dispute arises over terms or language, provincial consumer protection statutes require that judges interpret these contracts in the way most favourable to the consumer. Simply put, ignorance can sometimes be a good defence.

Hearsay and Courtroom Tactics

Judges have considerable latitude in allowing hearsay evidence if it's introduced properly. But it is essential that printed evidence and/or witnesses (relatives are not excluded) be available to confirm that a false representation actually occurred, that a part is failure-prone, or that its replacement is covered by a secret warranty or internal service bulletin alert. If you can't find an independent expert, introduce this evidence through the automaker reps and dealership service personnel who have to be at the trial anyhow. They know all about the service bulletins and extended warranty programs cited in *Lemon-Aid* and will probably contradict each other, particularly if they are excluded from the courtroom prior to testifying. Incidentally, you may wish to have the court clerk send a subpoena requiring the deposition of the documents you intend to cite, all warranty extensions relevant to your problem, and other lawsuits filed against the company for similar failures. This will make the fur fly in Oshawa, Oakville, and Windsor, and will likely lead to an out-of-court settlement. Sometimes, the service manager or company representative will make key admissions if questioned closely by you, a court mediator, or the trial judge. Here are three important questions to ask: Is this a common problem? Do you recognize this service bulletin? Is there a case-by-case "goodwill" plan covering this repair?

Automakers often blame owners for having pushed their vehicle beyond its limits. Therefore, when you seek to cancel the contract or get repair work reimbursed, it's essential that you get an independent mechanic or your co-workers to prove the vehicle was well maintained and driven prudently.

Reasonable Diligence

When asking for a refund, keep in mind the "reasonable diligence" rule that requires that a suit be filed within a reasonable amount of time after the purchase, which usually means less than a year. Because many factory-related deficiencies take years to appear, the courts have ruled that the reasonable diligence clock starts clicking only after the defect is confirmed to be manufacturer- or dealer-related (powertrain, paint, etc.). For powertrain components like engines and transmissions, this allows you to make a claim seven to ten years after the vehicle was originally put into service, regardless of whether it was bought new or used. Body failures like paint delamination (see *Frank v. GM* at page 134) are reimbursable for up to 11 years. If there have been negotiations with the dealer or the automaker, or if either the dealer or the automaker has been promising to correct the defects for some time or has carried out repeated unsuccessful repairs, the deadline for filing the lawsuit can be extended.

KEY COURT DECISIONS

The following Canadian and U.S. lawsuits and judgments cover typical problems that are likely to arise. Use them as leverage when negotiating a settlement or as a reference should your claim go to trial. Legal principles applying to Canadian and American law are similar; Quebec court decisions, however, may be based on legal principles that don't apply outside of that province. Nevertheless, you can find a comprehensive listing of Canadian decisions from small claims courts all the way to the Supreme Court of Canada at *www.legalresearch.org* or *www.canlii.org*.

You can find additional court judgments in the legal reference section of your city's main public library or at a nearby university law library. Ask the librarian for help in choosing the legal phrases that best describe your claim. LexisNexis (*www.lexisnexis.com*) and FindLaw (*www.findlaw.com*) are two useful Internet sites for legal research. Their main drawback, though, is that you may need to subscribe or use a lawyer's subscription to access jurisprudence and other areas of the sites.

Some of the small claims court cases cited in *Lemon-Aid* may not be reported. If that happens, contact the office of the presiding judge named in the decision and ask his or her assistant to send you a copy of the judgment. If the judge or assistant isn't available, ask for the court clerk of that jurisdiction to search for the case file and date referenced in *Lemon-Aid*.

An excellent reference book that will give you plenty of tips on filing, pleading, and collecting your judgment is Judge Marvin Zuker's *Ontario Small Claims Court Practice 2013* (Carswell, 2013). Judge Zuker's 1,360-page book is easily understood by non-lawyers and uses court decisions from across Canada to help you plead your case successfully in almost any Canadian court. It costs $97 (Cdn.) and can be ordered from *www.carswell.com* (1-800-387-5164).

Product Liability

Almost three decades ago, in *Kravitz v. GM* (the first case where I was called as a *pro bono* expert witness), the Supreme Court of Canada clearly affirmed that automakers and their dealers are jointly liable for the replacement or repair of a vehicle if independent testimony shows that it is afflicted with factory-related defects that compromise its safety or performance. The existence of a secret warranty extension or TSB also helps prove that the vehicle's problems are the automaker's responsibility. For example, in *Lowe v. Fairview Chrysler* (see page 173), TSBs were instrumental in showing an Ontario small claims court judge that Chrysler's history of automatic transmission failures went back to 1989.

In addition to replacing or repairing the vehicle, an automaker can also be held responsible for any damages arising from the defect. This means that loss of wages, supplementary transportation costs, and damages for personal inconvenience can be awarded. In the States, product liability damage awards often exceed millions of dollars. Canadian courts, however, are far less generous.

Implied Warranty Rulings

Reasonable durability

As outlined near the beginning of this Part, this is that powerful "other" warranty that they never tell you about. It applies during and after the expiration of the manufacturer's or dealer's expressed or written warranty and requires that a part or repair will last a reasonable period of time. What is reasonable depends in a large part on benchmarks used in the industry, the price of the vehicle, and how it was driven and maintained. Look at the "Reasonable Part Durability" table on page 137 for some guidelines as to what you should expect. Judges usually apply the implied or legal warranty when the manufacturer's expressed warranty has expired and the vehicle's manufacturing defects remain uncorrected.

Chevrier v. General Motors du Canada (No. 730-32-004876-046; Quebec Small Claims Court, Joliette District (Repentigny); October 18, 2006; Justice Georges Massol) (you can find the full judgment (French) at *www.canlii.org.*): The plaintiff leased and then bought a 2000 Montana minivan. At 71,000 km the automatic transmission failed and two GM dealers estimated the repairs to be between $2,200 and $2,500. They refused warranty coverage because the warranty had expired after the third year of ownership or 60,000 km of use. The owner repaired the transmission at an independent garage for $1,869 and kept the old parts, which GM refused to examine.

A small claims court lawsuit was filed, and Judge Massol gave the following reasons for ruling against GM's two arguments that (1) there was no warning that a claim would be filed, and (2) all warranties had expired:

1. GM filed a voluminous record of jurisprudence in its favour, relative to other lawsuits that were rejected because they were filed without prior notice. The judge reasoned that GM could not plead a "failure to notify," because the owner went to several dealers who were essentially agents of the manufacturer.

2. The judge also reasoned that the expiration of GM's written warranty does not nullify the legal warranty set out in articles 38 and 39 of the *Consumer Protection Act*. The legal warranty requires that all products be "reasonably durable," which did not appear to be the case with the plaintiff's vehicle, given its low mileage and number of years of use.

GM was ordered to pay the entire repair costs, plus interest, and the $90 filing fee.

Dufour v. Ford Canada Ltd. (No. 550-32-008335-009; Quebec Small Claims Court, Hull; April 10, 2001; Justice P. Chevalier): Ford was forced to reimburse the cost of engine head gasket repairs carried out on a 1996 Windstar 3.8L engine – a vehicle not covered by the automaker's Owner Notification Program, which cut off assistance after the '95 model year.

Schaffler v. Ford Motor Company Limited and Embrun Ford Sales Ltd. (Court File No. 59-2003; Ontario Superior Court of Justice; L'Orignal Small Claims Court; July 22, 2003; Justice Gerald Langlois): The plaintiff bought a used 1995 Windstar in 1998. Its engine head gasket was repaired for free three years later, under Ford's seven-year extended warranty. In 2002, at 109,600 km, the head gasket failed again, seriously damaging the engine. Ford refused a second repair. Justice Langlois ruled that Ford's warranty extension bulletin listed signs and symptoms of the covered defect that were identical to the problems written on the second work order ("persistent and/or chronic engine overheating; heavy white smoke evident from the exhaust tailpipe; flashing 'low coolant' instrument panel light even after coolant refill; and constant loss of engine coolant"). Judge Langlois concluded that "the problem was brought to the attention of the dealer well within the warranty period; the dealer was negligent." The plaintiff was awarded $4,941 plus 5 percent interest. This judgment included $1,070 for two months' car rental.

John R. Reid and Laurie M. McCall v. Ford Motor Company of Canada (Claim No: #02-SC-077344; Superior Court of Justice; Ottawa Small Claims Court; July 11, 2003; Justice Tiernay): A 1996 Windstar, bought used in 1997, experienced engine head gasket failure in October 2001 at 159,000 km. Judge Tiernay awarded the plaintiffs $4,145 for the following reason:

> A Technical Service Bulletin dated June 28, 1999, was circulated to Ford dealers. It dealt specifically with "undetermined loss of coolant" and "engine oil contaminated with coolant" in the 1996-98 Windstar and five other models of Ford vehicles. I conclude that Ford owed a duty of care to the Plaintiff to equip this vehicle with a cylinder head gasket of sufficient sturdiness and durability that would function trouble-free for at least seven years, given normal driving and proper maintenance conditions. I find that Ford is answerable in damages for the consequences of its negligence.

Dawe v. Courtesy Chrysler (SCCH #206825; Dartmouth Nova Scotia Small Claims Court; July 30, 2004; Judge Patrick L Casey, Q.C.): "Small claims" doesn't necessarily mean small judgments. This 21-page, unreported Nova Scotia small claims court decision is impressive in its clarity and thoroughness. It applies *Donoghue*, *Kravitz*, and *Davis, et al.*, in awarding a 2001 Dodge Ram owner over $5,000 in damages. Anyone with engine, transmission, and suspension problems or water leaking into the interior will find this judgment particularly useful.

Fissel v. Ideal Auto Sales Ltd. ((1991), 91 Sask. R. 266): Shortly after the vehicle was purchased, its motor seized and the dealer refused to replace it, even though the car was returned on several occasions. The court ruled that the dealer had breached the statutory warranties in sections 11(4) and (7) of the *Consumer Products Warranties Act*. The purchasers were entitled to cancel the sale and recover the full purchase price.

Friskin v. Chevrolet Oldsmobile (72 D.L.R. (3d) 289): A Manitoba used-car buyer asked that his contract be cancelled because of his car's chronic stalling problem.

The garage owner did his best to correct it. Despite the seller's good intentions, the *Manitoba Consumer Protection Act* allowed for cancellation.

Graves v. C&R Motors Ltd. (British Columbia County Court; April 8, 1980; Judge Skipp): The plaintiff bought a used car on the condition that certain deficiencies be remedied. They never were, and he was promised a refund, but it never arrived. The plaintiff brought suit, claiming that the dealer's deceptive activities violated the provincial *Trade Practices Act*. The court agreed, concluding that a deceptive act that occurs before, during, or after the transaction can lead to the cancellation of the contract.

Hachey v. Galbraith Equipment Company ((1991), 33 M.V.R. (2d) 242): The plaintiff bought a used truck from the dealer to haul gravel. Shortly thereafter, the steering failed. The plaintiff's suit was successful because expert testimony showed that the truck wasn't roadworthy. The dealer was found liable for damages for being in breach of the implied condition of fitness for the purpose for which the truck was purchased, as set out in section 15(a) of the New Brunswick *Sale of Goods Act*.

Henzel v. Brussels Motors ((1973), 1 O.R. 339 (County Court)): The dealer sold a used car, brandishing a copy of the mechanical fitness certificate as proof that the car was in good shape. The plaintiff was awarded his money returned because the court held the certificate to be a warranty that was breached by the car's subsequent defects.

Johnston v. Bodasing Corporation Limited (No. 15/11/83; Ontario County Court, Bruce; February 23, 1983; Judge McKay): The plaintiff bought a used 1979 Buick Riviera that was represented as being "reliable" for $8,500. Two weeks after purchase, the motor self-destructed. Judge McKay awarded the plaintiff $2,318 as compensation to fix the Riviera's defects. One feature of this particular decision is that the trial judge found that the *Sale of Goods Act* applied, notwithstanding the fact that the vendor used a standard contract that said there were no warranties or representations. The judge also accepted the decision in *Kendall v. Lillico* (1969) (2 Appeal Cases 31), which indicates that the *Sale of Goods Act* covers not only defects that the seller ought to have detected but also latent defects that even his or her utmost skill and judgment could not have detected. This places a very heavy onus on the vendor, and it should prove useful in actions of this type in other common-law provinces with laws similar to Ontario's *Sale of Goods Act*.

General Motors Products of Canada Ltd. v. Kravitz ((1979), 1 S.C.R. 790): The court said the seller's warranty of quality was an accessory to the property and was transferred with it on successive sales. Accordingly, subsequent buyers could invoke the contractual warranty of quality against the manufacturer, even though they did not contract directly with it. This precedent was then codified in articles 1434, 1442, and 1730 of Quebec's *Civil Code*.

Morrison v. Hillside Motors (1973) *Ltd.* ((1981), 35 Nfld. & P.E.I.R. 361): A used car advertised to be in "A1" condition and carrying a 50/50 warranty developed a number of problems. The court decided that the purchaser should be partially compensated because of the ad's claim. In deciding how much compensation to award, the presiding judge considered the warranty's wording, the amount paid for the vehicle, the model year of the vehicle, the vehicle's average life, the type of defect that occurred, and the length of time the purchaser had use of the vehicle before its defects became evident. Although this judgment was rendered in Newfoundland, judges throughout Canada have used a similar approach for more than a decade.

Neilson v. Maclin Motors (71 D.L.R. (3d) 744): The plaintiff bought a used truck on the strength of the seller's allegations that the motor had been rebuilt and that it had 210 hp. The engine failed. The judge awarded damages and cancelled the contract because the transmission was defective and the motor had not been rebuilt and did not have 210 hp.

Parent v. Le Grand Trianon and Ford Credit (C.P., 194; Quebec Provincial Court; February 1982; Judge Bertrand Gagnon): Nineteen months after paying $3,300 for a used 1974 LTD, the plaintiff sued the Ford dealer for his money back because the car prematurely rusted out. The dealer replied that rust was normal, there was no warranty, and the claim was too late. The court held that the garage was still responsible. The plaintiff was awarded $1,500 for the cost of rust repairs.

Narbonne v. Glendale Recreational Véhicules (Reference: 2008 QCCQ 5325; Quebec Small Claims Court; June 2, 2008; Judge Richard Landry): Three years after the plaintiff purchased a travel trailer, the manufacturer sent a recall notice to the wrong address. Seven years after that, the vehicle broke down when the recalled part failed. The manufacturer said it had done its part in sending out the recall notice. The judge disagreed, and found the company responsible for the full cost of the repairs, lodging, and $500 for general inconvenience, for a total of $5,792.

"As is" clauses

Since 1907, Canadian courts have ruled that a seller can't exclude the implied warranty as to fitness by including such phrases as "there are no other warranties or guarantees, promises, or agreements than those contained herein." See *Sawyer-Massey Co. v. Thibault* ((1907), 5 W.L.R. 241).

Adams v. J&D's Used Cars Ltd. ((1983), 26 Sask. R. 40 (Q.B.)): Shortly after the plaintiff purchased a car, its engine and transmission failed. The court ruled that the inclusion of "as is" in the sales contract had no legal effect. The dealer breached the implied warranty set out in Saskatchewan's *Consumer Products Warranties Act*. The sale was cancelled, and all monies were refunded.

Leasing

Ford Motor Credit v. Bothwell (No. 9226-T; Ontario County Court, Middlesex; December 3, 1979; Judge Macnab): The defendant leased a 1977 Ford truck that had frequent engine problems, characterized by stalling and hard starting. After complaining for one year and driving 35,000 km, the defendant cancelled the lease. Ford Credit sued for the money owing on the lease. Judge Macnab cancelled the lease and ordered Ford Credit to repay 70 percent of the amount paid during the leasing period. Ford Credit was also ordered to refund repair costs, even though the corporation claimed that it should not be held responsible for Ford's failure to honour its warranty.

Salvador v. Setay Motors/Queenstown Chev-Olds (Case No.1621/95; Hamilton Small Claims Court): The plaintiff was awarded $2,000, plus costs, from Queenstown Leasing. The court found that the company should have tried harder to sell the leased vehicle, and at a higher price, when the "open lease" expired.

Schryvers v. Richport Ford Sales (No. C917060; B.C.S.C.; May 18, 1993; Justice Tysoe): The court awarded $17,578.47, plus costs, to a couple who paid thousands of dollars more in unfair and hidden leasing charges than if they had simply purchased their Ford Explorer and Escort. The court found that this price difference constituted a deceptive, unconscionable act or practice, in contravention of the *Trade Practices Act* (R.S.B.C. 1979, c. 406).

Judge Tysoe concluded that the total general damages awarded to the Schryvers for both vehicles would be $11,578.47. He then proceeded to give the following reasons for awarding an additional $6,000 in punitive damages:

> Little wonder Richport Ford had a contest for the salesperson who could persuade the most customers to acquire their vehicles by way of a lease transaction. I consider the actions of Richport Ford to be sufficiently flagrant and high handed to warrant an award of punitive damages.
>
> There must be a disincentive to suppliers in respect of intentionally deceptive trade practices. If no punitive damages are awarded for intentional violations of the legislation, suppliers will continue to conduct their businesses in a manner that involves deceptive trade practices because they will have nothing to lose. In this case I believe that the appropriate amount of punitive damages is the extra profit Richport Ford endeavoured to make as a result of its deceptive acts. I therefore award punitive damages against Richport Ford in the amount of $6,000.

See also:

- *Barber v. Inland Truck Sales* (11 D.L.R. (3d) 469)
- *Canadian-Dominion Leasing v. Suburban Super Drug Ltd.* ((1966), 56 D.L.R. (2d) 43)
- *Neilson v. Atlantic Rentals Ltd.* ((1974), 8 N.B.R. (2d) 594)
- *Volvo Canada v. Fox* (No. 1698/77/C; New Brunswick Court of Queen's Bench; December 13, 1979; Judge Stevenson)
- *Western Tractor v. Dyck* (7 D.L.R. (3d) 535)

Repairs: Faulty Diagnosis

Davies v. Alberta Motor Association (No. P9090106097; Alberta Provincial Court; Civil Division; August 13, 1991; Judge Moore): The plaintiff had the AMA's Vehicle Inspection Service check out a used 1985 Nissan Pulsar NX prior to buying it. The car passed with flying colours. A month later, the clutch was replaced and numerous electrical problems ensued. At that time, another garage discovered that the car had been involved in a major accident, had a bent frame, a leaking radiator, and was unsafe to drive. The court awarded the plaintiff $1,578.40 plus three years' interest. The judge held that the AMA set itself out as an expert and should have spotted the car's defects. The AMA's defence – that it was not responsible for errors – was thrown out. The court held that a disclaimer clause could not protect the association from a fundamental breach of contract.

Secret Warranty Rulings

It's common practice for manufacturers to secretly extend their warranties to cover components with a high failure rate. Customers who complain vigorously get extended warranty compensation in the form of "goodwill" adjustments.

François Chong v. Marine Drive Imported Cars Ltd. and Honda Canada Inc. (No. 92-06760; British Columbia Provincial Small Claims Court; May 17, 1994; Judge C.L. Bagnall): The plaintiff was the first owner of a 1983 Honda Accord with 134,000 km on the odometer. He had six engine camshafts replaced – four under Honda "goodwill" programs, one where he paid part of the repairs, and one via this small claims court judgment.

In his ruling, Judge Bagnall agreed with Chong and ordered Honda and the dealer to each pay half of the $835.81 repair bill for the following reasons:

> The defendants assert that the warranty, which was part of the contract for purchase of the car, encompassed the entirety of their obligation to the claimant, and that it expired in February 1985. The replacements of the camshaft after that date were paid for wholly or in part by Honda as a "goodwill gesture." The time has come for these gestures to cease, according to the witness for Honda. As well, he pointed out to me that the most recent replacement of the camshaft was paid for by Honda and that, therefore, the work would not be covered by Honda's usual warranty of 12 months from date of repair. Mr. Wall, who testified for Honda, told me there was no question that this situation with Mr. Chong's engine was an unusual state of affairs. He said that a camshaft properly maintained can last anywhere from 24,000 to 500,000 km. He could not offer any suggestion as to why the car keeps having this problem.
>
> The claimant has convinced me that the problems he is having with rapid breakdown of camshafts in his car is due to a defect, which was present in the engine at the time that he purchased the car. The problem first arose during the warranty period and in my view has never been properly identified nor repaired.

Automatic Transmission Failures (Chrysler)

Lowe v. Fairview Chrysler-Dodge Limited and Chrysler Canada Limited (No. 1224/95; Ontario Court, General Division; Burlington Small Claims Court; May 14, 1996;): This judgment, in the plaintiff's favour, raises important legal principles relative to Chrysler.

- TSBs are admissible in court to prove that a problem exists and that certain parts should be checked out.
- If a problem is reported prior to a warranty's expiration, warranty coverage for the problematic component(s) is automatically carried over after the warranty ends.
- It's not up to the car owner to tell the dealer/automaker what the specific problem is.
- Repairs carried out by an independent garage can be refunded if the dealer/automaker unfairly refuses to apply the warranty.
- The dealer/automaker cannot dispute the cost of the independent repair if they fail to cross-examine the independent repairer.
- Auto owners can ask for and win compensation for their inconvenience, which in this judgment amounted to $150.

Court awards quickly add up. The plaintiff was given $1,985.94, with the addition of court costs and prejudgment interest, plus costs of inconvenience fixed at $150. The final award amounted to $2,266.04.

Tire Failures: Premature Wear

Blackwood v. Ford Motor Company of Canada Ltd., 2006 (Docket: PO690101722; Provincial Court of Alberta, Civil Division; Registry: Canmore; December 8, 2006; Honourable J. Shriar): This four-page judgment gives important guidelines as to how a plaintiff can successfully claim a refund for a defective tire.

The plaintiff bought a new 2005 Ford Focus. After ten months and 22,000 km, his dealer said all four tires needed replacing at a cost of $560.68. Both the dealer and Ford refused to cover the expense under the 3-year/60,000 km manufacturer's tire warranty, alleging that the wear was "normal wear and tear." Judge Shriar disagreed and awarded the plaintiff the full cost of the replacement tires, plus the filing fee and costs related to the registered mail and corporate records address check. An additional $100 was awarded for court costs, plus interest on the total amount from the date of the filing.

False Advertising

Misrepresentation

Goldie v. Golden Ears Motors (1980) Ltd (Case No. CO8287; Port Coquitlam, British Columbia Small Claims Court; June 27, 2000; Justice Warren): In a well-written, eight-page judgment, the court awarded plaintiff, Goldie, $5,000 for engine repairs on a 1990 Ford F-150 pickup in addition to $236 court costs. The dealer was found to have misrepresented the mileage and sold a used vehicle that didn't meet Section 8.01 of the provincial *Motor Vehicle Act Regulations* due to its unsafe tires and defective exhaust and headlights.

In rejecting the seller's defence that he disclosed all information "to the best of his knowledge and belief" as stipulated in the sales contract, Justice Warren stated:

> The words "to the best of your knowledge and belief" do not allow someone to be willfully blind to defects or to provide incorrect information. I find as a fact that the business made no effort to fulfill its duty to comply with the requirements of this form.... The defendant has been reckless in its actions. More likely, it has actively deceived the claimant into entering into this contract. I find the conduct of the defendant has been reprehensible throughout the dealings with the claimant.

This judgment closes a loophole that sellers have used to justify their misrepresentation, and it allows for cancellation of the sale and damages if the vehicle doesn't meet highway safety regulations.

MacDonald v. Equilease Co. Ltd. (Ontario Supreme Court; January 18, 1979; Judge O'Driscoll): The plaintiff leased a truck that was misrepresented as having an axle stronger than it really was. The court awarded the plaintiff damages for repairs and set aside the lease.

Seich v. Festival Ford Sales Ltd.((1978), 6 Alta. L.R. (2d) 262): The plaintiff bought a used truck from the defendant after being assured that it had a new motor and transmission. It didn't, and the court awarded the plaintiff $6,400.

Used car sold as new (demonstrator)

Bilodeau v. Sud Auto (No. 09-000751-73; Quebec Court of Appeal; 1973; Judge Tremblay): This appeals court cancelled the contract and held that a car can't be sold as new or as a demonstrator if it has ever been rented, leased, sold, or titled to anyone other than the dealer.

Rourke v. Gilmore (January 16, 1928; as found in *Ontario Weekly Notes*, vol. XXXIII, at p. 292): Before discovering that his new car was really used, the plaintiff drove it for over a year. For this reason, the contract couldn't be cancelled. However, the appeals court instead awarded damages for $500, which was quite a sum in 1928!

Vehicle not as ordered

Whether you're buying new or used, the seller can't misrepresent the vehicle. Anything that varies from what one would commonly expect, or from the seller's representation, must be disclosed prior to signing the contract. Typical misrepresentation scenarios include odometer turnbacks, undisclosed accident damage, used or leased cars being sold as new, new vehicles that are the wrong colour or the wrong model year, and vehicles that lack promised options or standard features.

Chenel v. Bel Automobile (1981) Inc. (Quebec Superior Court, Quebec City; August 27, 1976; Judge Desmeules): The plaintiff didn't receive his new Ford truck with the Jacob brakes essential for transporting sand in hilly regions. The court awarded the plaintiff $27,000, representing the purchase price of the vehicle less the money he earned while using the truck.

Lasky v. Royal City Chrysler Plymouth ((1987), 59 O.R. (2d) 323 (H.C.)): The plaintiff bought a 4-cylinder 1983 Dodge 600 that was represented by the salesman as being a 6-cylinder model. After putting 40,000 km on the vehicle over a 22-month period, the buyer was given her money back, without interest, under the provincial *Business Practices Act.*

Used car fuel-economy misrepresentation

Sidney v. 1011067 Ontario Inc. (c.o.b. Southside Motors) (Ontario Provincial Court): The court ruled that fuel economy misrepresentation can lead to a contract's cancellation if the dealer gives a higher-than-actual figure, even if it's claimed it was an innocent misrepresentation. In this case, the buyer was awarded $11,424.51 plus prejudgment interest because of a false representation made by the dealer regarding fuel efficiency. The plaintiff claimed that the defendant advised him that the vehicle could run 800-900 km per tank of fuel, when in fact the maximum distance was only 500 km per tank.

Car owners, panicked over soaring fuel prices, have been scammed by carmakers and dealers alike with bogus fuel economy claims.

Fortunately, the courts are cracking down on sellers who use false gas consumption figures to sell both new and used cars. For example, Ontario's revised *Consumer Protection Act*, 2002 (available through the province's searchable law database, *www.e-laws.gov.on.ca*), lets consumers cancel a contract within one year of entering into the agreement if a dealer makes a false, misleading, deceptive, or unconscionable representation. This includes false fuel economy claims.

Dealers cannot make the excuse that they were fooled or that they were simply providing data supplied by the manufacturer. The law clearly states that both parties are jointly liable, and therefore the dealer is presumed to know the history, quality, and true performance of what is sold.

Extra, Punitive Damages

Yes, you can claim some personal expenses, like hotel and travel costs, research reports, witness travel, compensation for general inconvenience, and even missed work days. Fortunately, when legal action is threatened – usually through small claims court – automakers quickly up their out-of-court offer to include most of the owner's expenses because they know the courts will be far more generous. For example, a British Columbia court's decision gave $2,257 for hotel and travel costs, and then capped it off with a $5,000 award for "inconvenience and loss of enjoyment of their luxury vehicle" to a motorist who was fed up with his lemon Cadillac (see *Wharton v. Tom Harris Chevrolet Oldsmobile Cadillac Ltd. and General Motors of Canada Limited* ([2002] B.C.J. No. 233, 2002 BCCA 78 (S.C.)).

On March 19, 2005, the Supreme Court of Canada confirmed that car owners can ask for punitive, or exemplary, damages when they feel the seller's or the automaker's conduct has been so outrageously bad that the court should protect

In *Prebushewski v. Dodge City Auto (1985) Ltd. and Chrysler Canada Ltd.*, the Supreme Court ordered Chrysler to pay $25,000 in punitive damages for denying a Saskatoon Dodge Ram owner's refund request.

society by awarding a sum of money large enough to dissuade others from engaging in similar immoral, unethical conduct. In *Prebushewski v. Dodge City Auto (1984) Ltd. and Chrysler Canada Ltd.* (2001 SKQB 537 (S.C.)), the plaintiff got $25,000 in a judgment handed down December 6, 2001, in Saskatoon. The award followed testimony from Chrysler's expert witness that the company was aware of many cases where daytime running lights shorted and caused 1996 Ram pickups to catch fire. The plaintiff's truck had burned to the ground, and Chrysler refused the owner's claim, saying it had fulfilled its expressed warranty obligations, in spite of its knowledge that fires were commonplace. The plaintiff sued on the grounds that there was an implied warranty that the vehicle would be safe. Justice Rothery gave this stinging rebuke in his judgment against Chrysler and its dealer:

> Not only did Chrysler know about the problems of the defective daytime running light modules, it did not advise the plaintiff of this. It simply chose to ignore the plaintiff's requests for compensation and told her to seek recovery from her insurance company. Chrysler had replaced thousands of these modules since 1988. But it had also made a business decision to neither advise its customers of the problem nor to recall the vehicles to replace the modules. While the cost would have been about $250 to replace each module, there were at least one million customers. Chrysler was not prepared to spend $250 million, even though it knew what the defective module might do.
>
> Counsel for the defendants argues that this matter had to be resolved by litigation because the plaintiff and the defendants simply had a difference of opinion on whether the plaintiff should be compensated by the defendants. Had the defendants some dispute as to

the cause of the fire, that may have been sufficient to prove that they had not willfully violated this part of the *Act*. They did not. They knew about the defective daytime running light module. They did nothing to replace the burned truck for the plaintiff. They offered the plaintiff no compensation for her loss. Counsel's position that the definition of the return of the purchase price is an arguable point is not sufficient to negate the defendants' violation of this part of the *Act*. I find the violation of the defendants to be willful. Thus, I find that exemplary damages are appropriate on the facts of this case.

In this case, the quantum ought to be sufficiently high as to correct the defendants' behaviour. In particular, Chrysler's corporate policy to place profits ahead of the potential danger to its customers' safety and personal property must be punished. And when such corporate policy includes a refusal to comply with the provisions of the *Act* and a refusal to provide any relief to the plaintiff, I find an award of $25,000 for exemplary damages to be appropriate. I therefore order Chrysler and Dodge City to pay: Damages in the sum of $41,969.83; Exemplary damages in the sum of $25,000; Party and party costs.

Canadian courts have become more generous in awarding plaintiffs money for mental distress experienced when defects aren't repaired properly under warranty. In *Sharman v. Formula Ford Sales Limited, Ford Credit Limited, and Ford Motor Company of Canada Limited* (No.: 17419/02SR; Ontario Superior Court of Justice; October 7, 2003), Justice Shepard of the Ontario Superior Court in Oakville awarded Mr. Sharman (a Ford of Canada customer relations staffer in Oakville) $7,500 because Ford had breached the implied warranty of fitness and made him fearful his children would fall out of his 2000 Windstar due to a faulty sliding door. Another $7,207 was given for breach of contract and breach of warranty because the minivan's sliding door wasn't secure and still leaked air and water after many attempts to repair it.

The plaintiff and his family have had three years of aggravation, inconvenience, worry, and concern about their safety and that of their children. Generally speaking, our contract law did not allow for compensation for what may be mental distress, but that may be changing. I am indebted to counsel for providing me with the decision of the British Columbia Court of Appeal in *Wharton v. Tom Harris Chevrolet Oldsmobile Cadillac Ltd.*, [2002] B.C.J. No. 233, 2002 BCCA 78. This decision was recently followed in *T'avra v. Victoria Ford Alliance Ltd.*, [2003] BCJ No. 1957.

In *Wharton,* the purchaser of a Cadillac Eldorado claimed damages against the dealer because the car's sound system emitted an annoying buzzing noise and the purchaser had to return the car to the dealer for repair numerous times over two and a half years. The trial court awarded damages of $2,257.17 for breach of warranty with respect to the sound system, and $5,000 in non-pecuniary damages for loss of enjoyment of their luxury vehicle and for inconvenience, for a total award of $7,257.17. The Court of Appeal upheld the decision of the trial judge and Levine J.A. spent considerable time reviewing the law, but in particular the law relating to damages for breach of implied warranty of fitness: "The principles applicable to an award of damages for mental distress resulting from a breach of contract were thoroughly and helpfully analyzed in the recent judgment of the House of Lords in *Farley v.*

Skinner, [2001] 3 W.L.R. 899, [2001] H.L.J. No. 49, affirming and clarifying the decision of the English Court of Appeal in *Watts v. Morrow,* [1991] I W.L.R. 142 1. Both of those cases concerned a claim by a buyer of a house against a surveyor who failed to report matters concerning the house as required by the contract. In *Watts,* the surveyor was negligent in failing to report defects in the house, and non-pecuniary damages of $6,750 were awarded to each of the owners for the inconvenience and discomfort experienced by them during repairs. In *Farley,* the surveyor was negligent in failing to discover, as he specifically undertook to do, that the property was adversely affected by aircraft noise. The House of Lords upheld the trial judge's award of non-pecuniary damages of $610,000, reversing the Court of Appeal, principally on the grounds that the object of the contract was to provide 'pleasure, relaxation, peace of mind, or freedom from molestation' and also because the plaintiff had suffered physical discomfort and inconvenience from the aircraft noise."

. . .

The reasons for judgment in *Farley* provide a summary and survey of the law as it has developed, in England, to date. They are helpful in analyzing and summarizing the principles derived from *Watts,* which are, in my view, applicable to the case at bar. In summary they are (borrowing the language from both *Watts* and *Farley*):

(a) A contract-breaker is not in general liable for any distress, frustration, anxiety, displeasure, vexation, tension, or aggravation which the breach of contract may cause to the innocent party.

(b) The rule is not absolute. Where a major or important part of the contract is to give pleasure, relaxation or peace of mind, damages will be awarded if the fruit of the contract is not provided or if the contrary result is instead procured.

(c) In cases not falling within the "peace of mind" category, damages are recoverable for inconvenience and discomfort caused by the breach and the mental suffering directly related to the inconvenience and discomfort. However, the cause of the inconvenience or discomfort must be a sensory experience as opposed to mere disappointment that the contract has been broken. If those effects are foreseeably suffered during a period when defects are repaired, they create damages even though the cost of repairs are not recoverable as such.

Application of Law to the Facts of this Case

In the *Wharton* case (see page 176), the respondent contracted for a "luxury" vehicle for pleasure use. It included a sound system that the appellant's service manager described as "high end." The respondent's husband described the purchase of the car in this way:

[W]e bought a luxury car that was supposed to give us a luxury ride and be a quiet vehicle, and we had nothing but difficulty with it from the very day it was delivered with this problem that nobody seemed to be able to fix. . . . So basically we had a luxury product that gave us no luxury for the whole time that we had it.

It is clear that an important object of the contract was to obtain a vehicle that was luxurious and a pleasure to operate. Furthermore, the buzzing noise was the cause of physical, in the sense of sensory, discomfort to the respondent and her husband. The trial judge found it inhibited listening to the sound system and was irritating in normal conversation. The respondent and her husband also bore the physical inconvenience of taking the vehicle to the appellant on numerous occasions for repairs. The inconvenience and discomfort was, in my view, reasonably foreseeable, if the defect in the sound system had been known at the date of the contract. The fact that it was not then known is, of course, irrelevant.

The award of damages for breach of the implied warranty of fitness satisfies both exceptions from the general rule that damages are not awarded for mental distress for breach of contract, set out in *Watts* as amplified in *Farley* (both cases discussed in the excerpt to this case, above).

The justice continued and said (at para. 63), "...awards for mental distress arising from a breach of contract should be restrained and modest."

The court upheld the trial judge's award of $5,000 in *Wharton* where the issue was a buzzing in the sound system.

In my view, a defect in manufacture which goes to the safety of the vehicle deserves a modest increase. I would assess the plaintiff's damage for mental distress resulting from the breach of the implied warranty of fitness at $7,500. Judgment to issue in favour of the plaintiff against the defendants, except Ford Credit, on a joint and several basis for $14,707, plus interest and costs.

Provincial business practices acts and consumer protection statutes prohibit false, misleading, or deceptive representations and allow for punitive damages should the unfair practice toward the consumer amount to an unconscionable representation (see *Canadian Encyclopedic Digest* (3d) s. 76, pp. 140-45). "Unconscionable" is defined as "where the consumer is not reasonably able to protect his or her interest because of physical infirmity, ignorance, illiteracy, or inability to understand the language of an agreement or similar factors." This concept has been successfully used in consumer, environmental, and labour law.

- Exemplary damages are justified where compensatory damages are insufficient to deter and punish. See *Walker v. CFTO Ltd.* ((1978), 59 O.R. (2d) 104 (C.A.)).

- Exemplary damages can be awarded in cases where the defendant's conduct was "cavalier." See *Ronald Elwyn Lister Ltd. v. Dayton Tire Canada Ltd.* ((1985), 52 O.R. (2d) 89 (C.A.)).

- The primary purpose of exemplary damages is to prevent the defendant and all others from doing similar wrongs. See *Fleming v. Spracklin* (1921).

- Disregard of the public's interest, lack of preventive measures, and a callous attitude all merit exemplary damages. See *Coughlin v. Kuntz* ((1989), *2 C.C.L.T. (2d) (B.C.C.A.)*).

- Punitive damages can be awarded for mental distress. See *Ribeiro v. Canadian Imperial Bank of Commerce* ((1992), 13 O.R. (3d) 278 (C.A.), leave to appeal to

Supreme Court of Canada refused [1993] 2 S.C.R. x)) and *Brown v. Waterloo Regional Board of Commissioners of Police* ((1983), 43 O.R. (2d) 113, affirming in part (1982), 37 O.R. (2d) 277).

In the States, punitive damage awards have been particularly generous. Whenever big business complains of an "unrestrained judiciary," it trots out a 20-year-old case where an Alabama BMW 500 series owner was awarded $4 million because his new car had been repainted before he bought it and the seller didn't tell him. Under appeal, the owner was offered $50,000.

The case was *BMW of North America, Inc. v. Gore* (517 U.S. 559, 116 S. Ct. 1589 (S.C. (1996))). In this case, the Supreme Court cut the damages award and established standards for jury awards of punitive damages. Nevertheless, million-dollar awards continue to be quite common. In the following example, an Oregon dealer learned that a $1-million punitive damages award was not excessive under *Gore* and under Oregon law.

The Oregon Supreme Court determined that the standard it set in *Oberg v. Honda Motor Company* (888 P.2d 8 (Or. Sup. Ct. (1996))), on remand from the Supreme Court, survived the Supreme Court's subsequent ruling in *Gore.* The court held that the jury's $1-million punitive damages award, 87 times larger than the plaintiff's compensatory damages in *Parrott v. Carr Chevrolet, Inc.* (2001 Ore. LEXIS), wasn't excessive. In that case, Mark Parrott sued Carr Chevrolet, Inc., over a used 1983 Chevrolet Suburban under Oregon's *Unlawful Trade Practices Act.* The jury awarded Parrott $11,496 in compensatory damages and $1 million in punitive damages because the dealer failed to disclose collision damage to a new-car buyer.

See also:

- *Vlchek v. Koshel* ((1988), 44 C.C.L.T. 314 (B.C.S.C.))
- *Granek v. Reiter* (No. 35/741; Ontario Court, General Division)
- *Morrison v. Sharp* (No. 43/548; Ontario Court, General Division)
- *Schryvers v. Richport Ford Sales* (B.C.S.C., No. C917060; May 18, 1993; Judge Tysoe)
- *Varleg v. Angeloni* (No. 41/301; B.C.S.C.)
- *Grabinski v. Blue Springs Ford Sales, Inc.* (U.S. App. LEXIS 2073 (8th Cir. W.D. MO (2000))

Some Canadian law firms who have been successful in automobile class actions:

Stevensons LLP
144 Front Street, Suite 400
Toronto, ON M5J 2L7
Phone: 416-599-7900
E-mail: *cstevenson@stevensonlaw.net*
bkirkland@stevensonlaw.net (647-847-3811)

Koskie Minsky LLP
20 Queen Street West, Suite 900, Box 52
Toronto, Ontario, M5H 3R3
Phone: (416) 977-8353
Class Actions Department
Kirk Baert: kbaert@km*law.ca*

Class Action Abuses – by Lawyers

For several decades class-action legislation in Canada has helped motorists recover milions of dollars in refunds from deep-pocket car makers. Costs are cheap and lawyer contingency fees take the sting out of court costs. All well and good.

Unfortunately, a new ambulance-chasing, quick-settlement-hunting lawyer rank has emerged from the sewers to skim fees off of Canadian actions that are no more than copies of American lawsuits that are at the point of settlement.

For example, Toyota USA announced last December a $1.2-billion sudden acceleration settlement that resulted in American lawyers getting over $200 million in fees for research and other original work. On the other hand, Toyota Canada offered Canadians a measly $600,000 separate settlement shortly thereafter. The settlement offers Canadian lawyers a quick $11.9-million fee for their work that consisted of copying and filing much that was in the American lawsuit.

Apparently, the class-action tool set up in Canada to provide quick and fair compensation to consumers has become a giant teat which some lawyers rush to suckle by piggy-backing separate Canadian class actions on American litigation and billing huge fees in return. Sad.

Part Four

1990-2015 RATINGS ("BRINGING IN THE CHEAP")

Used Car Prices Falling

This year's spike in new car sales is good news for used car buyers. As more people opt for new cars, more vehicles will become available on the used car market, lowering their prices. According to Kelley Blue Book, wholesale auction prices for used cars were at a three-year low as of April, and the average price for a one-year-old used car is 18.5 percent lower than it is for the same model new.

Bill Vlasic
New York Times, June 5, 2013

Going "Car-less"

Before we go into what makes a good car buy and lead you through the jungle of new and used choices, I'll take one last stab at explaining why a car isn't a smart buy, at all.

Let's do the math: Figure $8,000 a year as your average new car expense, including a $200 monthly finance payment. Consider that just the extra cost for the freight/administrative fee of $2,000 is almost as much as one year's financing, plus the fee has to be paid up front.

Now, as mentioned in Part Two, you can buy a used car and cut the $8,000 to $4,000 annual costs and ditch the freight charge. So, that's by far a better buy.

But, here's the kicker. Don't buy a car.

Instead, budget $10 each weekday for public transportation to work or school, or for downtown entertainment or strolling. That's $50 weekly or $200 a month – equal to the cost of financing a new car, or paying just its freight cost. For special occasions, splurge with a $100 rental.

There are also lots of advantages to being "car-less."

- The savings can pay down college costs or a home mortgage – both good investments.
- Car pooling builds social skills and makes for lasting friendships.
- You're in tune with the environment; you see more, hear more, and know more.
- Forget Al Gore. *You* have the secret to achieving zero emissions. Even if you relent and buy used, you're not adding another vehicle to the mix. How's that for going "green?"
- Less worry in bad weather over starting, driving, parking, and windshield ice.
- More relaxed commuting; no anger in traffic jams; free to read, write, or nap.

What's a "Good" Car?

Interestingly, buyers looking for the best new or use car choice don't put safety or crashworthiness at the top of their list. Price is the primary motivator, especially with used vehicles, probably because the used-car buyer has less spendable income to start with. Also, advanced technology wasn't a consideration a decade ago. Now, car buyers want connectivity with smartphones, the Internet, and any devices that can transform their vehicles into mobile offices.

1. **A good investment:** It should have a reasonable purchase price, low down payment, reasonable monthly payments, low-cost financing, a high resale value, and provide good gas mileage (in the 6-7L/100km (30-40 mpg) range). Gas mileage now ties with reliability and durability in terms of importance in what buyers want.

2. **Above average reliability and durability:** This includes few factory-related defects, comprehensive warranty coverage, no-hassle servicing, and a 15-year lifespan.

3. **Performance, comfort, and cachet:** Buyers want no-surprise acceleration, stopping, steering, shifting, or jostling. Exterior styling should focus on functionality and interior amenities must be practical, comfortable, and convenient to access.

4. **Advanced technology:** Drivers want the latest electronic safety gear and the most advanced and reliable infotainment features available. Unfortunately, the desire for optimum "connectivity" has resulted in dangerously distracted drivers and failure-prone electronic features like Ford's "MyFordTouch" on its 2011-13 models. The Ford brand fell to 27th last year in J.D. Power & Associates' new-car quality survey, from fifth several years ago, largely because of complaints with MyFord Touch and the Sync software which underpins it.

5. **Safety:** Once one of the top three considerations, car buyers now take safety features for granted. They presume their car will have a high crash-test score and be equipped with fail-safe accelerators, electronic steering control, and safe fuel tanks.

No matter if you buy American, Asian, or European, new or used, you are taking on someone else's problems – the dealer's and automaker's, or the previous owner's. Fortunately, you likely already saved $10,000 (on the average three-year-old American family sedan) if you bought used, so you'll have plenty of cash reserve to repair run-of-the-mill glitches at cheaper, independent shops.

Plus, there's not much that can surprise you on a well-inspected vehicle that has been widely sold and can be easily serviced. There's a safety advantage as well, since the vehicle's crashworthiness has likely been tested and retested by a handful of different agencies and about 75 percent of the recalls have been carried out. Best of all, there's the peace of mind knowing you won't get left in the lurch if the dealer or automaker goes bust – again.

Let's take a look at this year's bestselling vehicles in Canada through April-May 2013 (Sources: Manufacturers, *goodcarbadcar.com*, *Consumer Reports*, *Lemon-Aid Used Car and Truck Guide 2013*, and *Automotive News* Data Center). Those models marked with an * are considered "good" buys. The ideal vehicle will have low sales and a Good rating, like the Honda Civic, Hyundai Accent, Kia Forte, and VW Jetta. Low sales will attract rebates and other sales incentives.

2013 Bestselling Cars in Canada

Sales	Model	Sales	Model	Sales	Model
#1	Hyundai Elantra*	#8	Toyota Camry*	#15	Nissan Sentra*
#2	Honda Civic*	#9	Ford Fusion	#16	Chrysler 200
#3	Toyota Corolla*	#10	Hyundai Accent*	#17	Toyota Matrix*
#4	Mazda3*	#11	Honda Accord*	#18	Chrysler 300
#5	Chevrolet Cruze*	#12	Kia Forte*	#19	Ford Mustang*
#6	Ford Focus	#13	Hyundai Sonata	#20	Dodge Avenger
#7	VW Jetta*	#14	Kia Rio*		

2013 Bestselling Minivans

Sales	Model	Sales	Model	Sales	Model
#1	Chevy Orlando	#5	Kia Rondo*	#9	Toyota Sienna*
#2	Chrysler T & C	#6	Kia Sedona*	#10	VW Routan
#3	Grand Caravan	#7	Mazda5*		
#4	Honda Odyssey*	#8	Nissan Quest		

2013 Bestselling Pickups

Sales	Model	Sales	Model	Sales	Model
#1	Ford F-Series*	#6	Toyota Tundra	#11	Cadillac Escalade EXT*
#2	Dodge Ram*	#7	Nissan Titan*	#12	Chevrolet Colorado
#3	GMC Sierra	#8	Chevrolet Avalanche*	#13	GMC Canyon
#4	Chevrolet Silverado	#9	Nissan Frontier*		
#5	Toyota Tacoma	#10	Honda Ridgeline*		

2013 Bestselling SUVs

Sales	Model	Sales	Model	Sales	Model
#1	Ford Escape*	#4	Dodge Journey	#7	Chevrolet Equinox*
#2	Toyota RAV48*	#5	Hyundai Santa Fe*	#8	Mazda CX-5*
#3	Honda CR-V*	#6	Jeep Wrangler	#9	Ford Edge

Sales	Model	Sales	Model	Sales	Model
#10	Nissan Rogue*	#14	Jeep Grand Cherokee	#18	Jeep Compass
#11	Kia Sorento*	#15	Ford Explorer	#19	Lexus RX*
#12	Hyundai Tucson*	#16	Subaru Forester*	#20.1	Lexus RX350*
#13	GMC Terrain*	#17	Mitsubishi RVR	#20.2	Lexus RX450h*

*Indicates a good buy, new or used

Buy one of the above designated vehicles new, if you must, but be mindful that it should be kept ten years or longer to compensate for the upfront depreciation and freight fee. A new, well-equipped compact car or small SUV will run between $18,000 and $25,000. The same three- to five-year-old used car or SUV will cost about one-third to one-half of its original selling price ($7,000-$15,000).

New or used, the vehicle must meet your everyday driving needs and have high crashworthiness and reliability scores. Annual maintenance should cost no more than the Canadian Automotive Association (CAA) and DesRosiers' estimated average of $800-$1,100, and parts and servicing costs shouldn't be excessive either, which means checking out maintenance costs from Internet owner forums before you buy. Finally, the depreciation rate should have levelled off, so that subsequent years won't cut the car's price by more than a couple thousand dollars over the next few years, leaving you with some resale equity.

The best values come from South Korea, followed by Japan. European vehicles (mostly BMW and Volkswagen) and American models bring up the rear, led by General Motors, followed closely by Ford. Chrysler/Fiat comes a distant third, a ranking it has won for several decades.

Small cars and family sedans give the most performance and reliability for the price. Some of the better choices are Honda's Fit, Civic (except for the 2012) and Accord; the Chevrolet Cruze and Impala; Hyundai's Accent and Elantra; the Subaru Legacy; and Volkswagen's diesel-equipped TDI (without the DSG transmission).

Luxury models, large cars and minivans, and mid-sized and large SUVs represent the worst values among used vehicles. If interior room is your paramount concern, consider a Mazda5 microvan, a Subaru Outback or Forester, or a down-sized Hyundai Tucson or Toyota RAV4.

The best values for your purchasing dollar among luxury cars are the BMW 3 Series, including the X3, Acura RDX and MDX, Infiniti EX, and all of the Lexus lineup. Luxury vehicles that don't provide much value are models built by Cadillac, Jaguar, Land Rover, and Lincoln.

Fuel economy isn't all that important when you are buying used, since all of your other savings should easily compensate for the extra fuel costs.

We don't recommend most gas-electric engine hybrids. Their retail prices are mostly high-end and long-term reliability can be problematic. *Consumer Reports'* April 2013 issue targets the 2009 Honda Civic Hybrid as the worst of a bad lot:

[It] has a big problem with the drive battery. The 2009 model was the worst: almost one in five owners needed a replacement hybrid battery in our 12-month survey period ... more than ten percent of owners of the 2003, 2004, and 2010 models also needed one.

Honda provided a software update to owners of 2006-08 Civic Hybrids to help extend the life of the IMA battery and issued a technical service bulletin (TSB) for the States in late 2012 which extends the IMA battery warranty. Batteries that were once covered for 10 years/100,000 miles (almost 161,000 km) are now warranteed for 11 years/137,000 miles (more than 220,000 km); vehicles covered for 8 years/80,000 miles (almost 130,000 km) are now covered for 9 years/96,000 miles (more than 154,000 km); and replacement batteries that were bought are covered for 36,000 miles (58,000 km), or 3 years. Furthermore, imagine looking for a replacement battery while in another town or on vacation. As for guaranteeing the $3,000 replacement up to the equivalent of three years driving? Thanks, but no thanks.

Honda Civic Hybrid (above). Sure, check the tires – oh! – and replace the battery ($2,000-$4,000 U. S.).

Hybrid fuel sipping can be as advertised – 4.5L/100km (about 52 mpg) (2013 Toyota Prius), or much less – with some owners claiming a 40 percent reduction in the fuel economy hyped by automakers. There have also been reports that hybrid motors have a high failure rate due to corrosion; battery replacement costs are estimated to run as high as $3,000(U.S.) for the Toyota Prius and up to $10,000 for other makes. Furthermore, hybrid resale values are no better than similar vehicles equipped with conventional engines. Look again at a 2007 Toyota Prius that originally sold for $31,280. It is now valued at a disappointing $9,000, less than a third of its original price (and less than two years before the expiration of the battery-pack warranty).

Incidentally, Honda switched to a new lithium-ion battery pack for the 2012-2013 Civic Hybrid (as well as Acura ILX Hybrid). Already, two incidents have been reported in Japan where lithium-ion batteries in Japanese cars caught fire or melted. A similar failure was experienced with Boeing's 787 Dreamliner when the overheating of lithium-ion batteries on two planes in January led regulators to ground all 787s worldwide for about three months.

Don't Believe in the "Fuel Fairy"

Take our Part Four fuel economy estimates with a large grain of salt and blame it on the feds, since Ottawa is in cahoots with automakers through bailouts, tax exemptions, "green car" rebates, and fanciful fuel economy ratings. It's not a criminal conspiracy; it's just lazy complacency that they are just now correcting. Nevertheless, until last year, the Canadian mileage figures were "cooked" by as much as 22 percent.

In November of 2011, CBC News and the Automobile Protection Association (APA) compared the Canadian and American fuel consumption ratings of various 2012 models. The survey showed that Canadian fuel-economy estimates were inflated by 16-22 percent compared to the U.S. estimates, for the same vehicles. Since this is L/100km, a lower number is better.

More accurate U.S. fuel economy figures for 2012 and earlier models can be found at: *www.fueleconomy.gov*, while the puffed-up Canadian figures reside at *oee. nrcan.gc.ca/transportation/tools/fuelratings/ratings-search.cfm*.

APA President, George Iny, says Canadian numbers are generated by the industry from standardized lab tests, not real-life road conditions. Back in 2008 the American government got rid of the test Canada's carmakers were still using to generate their estimates.

Since then, American cars have been more rigorously tested for real life conditions and the Environmental Protection Agency (EPA) said some cars use 30 percent more gas than the previous tests showed.

Depreciation Is Your Friend

Not all cars and trucks are born with equal attributes, and they age (depreciate) at different rates. When buying new, you want a reliable model that depreciates slowly; when buying used, consider a vehicle that has prematurely lost much of its value but is still dependable and inexpensive to maintain. Fortunately, there are plenty of the latter on the market due to poor vehicle sales during the 2008 and 2009 model years, which have put lots of good four- and five-year-old vehicles on used car lots.

During the past year, rebates, cut-rate financing, subsidized leasing, and fluctuating fuel costs, along with poor reputations for quality, have depressed the residual values of most American cars and trucks. According to the *Automotive Lease Guide* (*www.alg.com*), Detroit-made vechicles, like the 2012 Ford Fusion SE, come off their leases barely keeping 33 percent of their sticker value after four years, while the average 2012 Subaru is predicted to keep 46 percent of its value after four years. Residual values can be accessed free of charge at *www.cars.com/go/alg/index.jsp*.

HOW *LEMON-AID* PICKS THE "BEST" AND "WORST"

Lemon-Aid doesn't give a rating for every vehicle make sold in Canada. We focus primarily on new and used vehicles, sold in relatively large numbers, considered to be the best and worst buys. Additionally, we may suggest buying a high-ranking, used car that hasn't been redesigned to take advantage of a much lower price (the Audi TT Coupe is a good example).

If you have a question about a vehicle not found in *Lemon-Aid,* send us an e-mail at *lemonaid@earthlink.net.* We will be glad to send you a free update with the information we have available.

Lemon-Aid has been giving honest, independent, and dependable auto ratings for over four decades by following these simple rules.

- Ratings should be used primarily as a comparative database when the low-ranked or recommended models reappear in different driving tests and owner surveys. The best rating approach is to combine a driving test with an owners' survey of past models (only *Consumer Reports* does this).

- We use the database of owner complaints collected by the National Highway Traffic Safety Administration (NHTSA) at *safercar.gov* site. It's a treasure trove of auto-failure anecdotes that show which cars have repeated failures or outstanding recalls, or are part of an ongoing safety probe, and which particular component is faulty. It even suggests ways to get a free warranty extension to cover the repair, or to get a free replacement part.

- The responses must come from a large owner pool (over 1.2 million responses from *Consumer Reports* subscribers, for example). Anecdotal responses should then be cross-referenced, updated, and given depth and specificity through NHTSA's safety complaint prism. Responses must be cross-referenced again through automaker internal service bulletins to determine the extent of the defect over a specific model and model-year range and to alert owners to problems likely to occur.

- Rankings should be predicated on important characteristics measured over a significant period of time, unlike Car of the Year contests, owner-perceived values, or J.D. Power-surveyed problems assessed after only three months of ownership.

- Ratings must come from unimpeachable sources. There should be no conflicts of interest due to ties with advertisers or consultants, and no results gathered from self-serving tests done under ideal conditions, like previous years' Transport Canada fuel economy tests.

- Tested cars must be bought, not borrowed, and serviced, not pampered as part of a journalists' fleet lent out for ranking purposes. Also, all automakers need to be judged equally. (Toyota at one time boycotted weekend car journalist "roundup" tests as invalid tests and refused to lend its vehicles to the events; thus, they were penalized.) Automakers must not be members of the ranking body.

- Again, we are wary of self-administered fuel economy ratings used by automakers in complicity with the federal government and some car enthusiast magazines. *Automotive News* added its name to the list of skeptics when it found that Honda and Toyota hybrids get 20-40 percent less real-world gas mileage than advertised. The car industry publication discovered that hybrids need to be driven in a particular way in order to be fuel efficient, use more fuel than ordinary cars on short trips or when using air conditioning, and are affected by colder climates, resulting in increased fuel consumption way beyond what the ratings figures indicate. The EPA has admitted its fuel economy calculations were overestimated and has set up a website at *www.fueleconomy.gov* that contains recalculated figures for 1985-2007 model year vehicles that will leave you scratching your head.

DEFINITION OF TERMS

We rate vehicles on a scale of one to five stars, with five stars being our top ranking. Models are designated as "Recommended," "Above Average," "Average," "Below Average," or "Not Recommended," with the most recent year's rating indicated by the number of stars beside the vehicle's name.

Recommended

We don't give this rating out very often, and we are quick to drop it if safety, servicing, or overall quality control decline. We don't believe for one moment that the more you spend, the better performing, more reliable, or safer the vehicle. For example, most Hondas are as good as Acuras, which cost thousands of dollars more for their luxury cachet. The same is true when you compare Toyota and Lexus. Even more surprising, some luxury makes, such as Jaguar, are "pseudo-luxe," because the older models may be merely dressed-up Fords sold at a luxury-car price. The extra money only buys you more features of dubious value and newer, failure-prone electronic gadgetry.

In fact, the simplest choice is often the best buy. Ford's Mustang, Chevrolet's Cruze, Hyundai's Elantra and Tucson and the Mazda3 get positive ratings because they are easy to find, fairly reliable, and reasonably priced – not the case with many overpriced Hondas and Toyotas. The above vehicles are good buys new and used, however, some model years are more troublesome than others, like the recently redesigned Mustangs with made-in-China "grenading" manual transmissions.

Above Average/Average

Vehicles that are given an Above Average or Average rating are good second choices if a Recommended vehicle isn't your first choice, isn't available, or isn't within budget.

Below Average/Not Recommended

Many vehicles are given a Below Average rating by *Lemon-Aid* because we know they will likely be troublesome; however, we also believe their low price and reasonably priced servicing may make them acceptable buys to some do-it-yourselfers who have put aside sufficient money saved from the transaction to cover expected failures.

Vehicles with a history of unforeseeable, recurring, and expensive defects are most likely to be given a Not Recommended rating. They are best avoided altogether, no matter how low the price, because they're so likely to suffer from many durability and performance problems that you may never stop paying for repairs. Sometimes, however, a Not Recommended model will improve over several model years and garner a better rating (as the Ford Focus and Hyundai's Sonata – 2012 excepted – and SUVs have done).

Incidentally, for those owners who wonder how I can stop recommending model years I once recommended, let me clarify. As vehicles age, their ratings change to reflect new information from owners, service bulletins relating to durability, and the automaker's warranty performance. For example, Nissan's Quest, Toyota's Sienna, and BMW's Mini have been downgraded for some years because new service bulletins and additional owner complaints show some disturbing trends in dependability and servicing performance. Unlike car columnists who can't change their ratings due to automaker pressure, I quickly warn shoppers of rating downgrades as soon as they're made through subsequent editions of *Lemon-Aid* and updates to my website, *www.lemonaidcars.com*, and alerts on Twitter (*@lemonaidcars*).

For 43 years, I have been an active consumer advocate, not a *passive* auto journalist. When I uncover fraud, unsafe designs, or failure-prone components, I first denounce the problem. Then I take a second step, one rarely taken by journalists: I become part of the story by mobilizing owners, lawyers, and independent mechanics to force automaker recalls or set up reimbursement programs.

My proudest achievement? Getting GM Canada, five years ago, to pay back millions of dollars to Canadian car owners stuck with "cooked" V6 engines afflicted by warped intake manifold gaskets in GM's 1995-2005 models. GM paid Canadians an estimated $40 million in repairs because the automaker used faulty engine gaskets made out of plastic to save a few pennies per car.

Throughout the year, I get refunds for buyers cheated by dealers and automakers. I lobby automakers to compensate owners of out-of-warranty vehicles either through formal warranty extension programs or on a case-by-case basis. I also publish little-known lawsuits, judgments, and settlements in *Lemon-Aid* to help car owners win their cases or get a fair settlement without my personal assistance.

Reliability data is compiled from a number of sources, including confidential technical service bulletins, owner complaints sent to me each year by *Lemon-Aid* readers, owners' comments posted on the Internet, and survey reports and tests done by auto associations, consumer groups, and government organizations. Some auto columnists feel this isn't a scientific sampling, and they're quite right. Nevertheless, the results have been mostly on the mark over the past four decades. Like the weather forecast, it may or may not rain, but carry an umbrella (*Lemon-Aid*), just in case.

Not all cars and trucks are profiled; those that are new to the market or relatively rare may receive only an abbreviated mention until sufficient owner or service bulletin information becomes available. Best and worst buys from each automaker are listed in a summary at the beginning of each rating section. Some cars aren't profiled at all due to page limitations.

Strengths and Weaknesses

ALERT! We have added an **ALERT!** section to clearly point out those vehicles that may be exceptional buys, or are seriously flawed, or require special maintenance.

With the Detroit automakers, engine head gasket, automatic transmission, brake, steering, and electrical failures are omnipresent. Ford infotainment systems are chaotic and annoying. South Korean vehicles have weak transmissions, electrical systems, and electronic control modules. Japanese makes are noted mostly for their brake, door, AC, window, sound system, electrical, and fuel delivery glitches, though engine and transmission failures have been appearing more frequently, especially with Toyota and Lexus models built during the past decade. Finally, the European automakers are in a high-tech bind. Like Ford, electronic demons constantly bedevil Audi, BMW, Jaguar, Land Rover, Mercedes, and VW high-end products, making them unreliable and costly to service after only a few years of ownership; plus, these vehicles are so complicated to diagnose and service that many mechanics simply throw up their hands in dismay.

Unlike other auto guides, *Lemon-Aid* knows where automotive skeletons are buried and pinpoints potential parts failures, explains why those parts fail, and advises you as to your chances of getting a repair refunded under a "goodwill warranty" program. We also give parts numbers for upgraded parts (why replace poor-quality brake pads with the same failure-prone part?) and offer troubleshooting tips direct from the automakers' bulletins so that your mechanic won't replace parts unrelated to your troubles before coming upon the defective component that is actually responsible.

Parts supply can be a real problem. It's a myth that automakers have to keep a supply of parts sufficient to service what they sell, as any buyer of a Chevrolet/Daewoo Aveo, a front-drive Lincoln Continental, or a Ford Windstar/Freestar will quickly tell you. Additionally, apart from *Lemon-Aid*, there's no consumer database that warns prospective purchasers as to which models are "parts-challenged."

The "Secret Warranties/Internal Bulletins" sections and vehicle profile tables show a vehicle's overall reliability and safety, providing details as to which specific model years pose the most risk and why. This helps you direct an independent mechanic to check out the likely trouble spots before you make your purchase.

Major Redesigns

This section outlines a vehicle's differences between model years, including major redesigns and other modifications. If a model is unchanged from one model year to the next, why pay a premium for it simply because it is one year newer? Or, if a vehicle was redesigned a few years ago, don't you want that vehicle a year after the redesign, when most of the factory kinks have been ironed out?

Safety

Here we list safety failures reported by owners and ongoing safety investigations. NHTSA complaints are summarized by model year, even though they aren't all safety-related. This summary can help you prove that a part failure is widespread and factory-related and then use that information for free "goodwill" repairs or in litigation involving accident damage, injuries, or death.

NHTSA records indicate other common safety-related failures that include vehicles with collapsing axles (Ford Windstar/Freestar, *et al.*), vehicles rolling away with the transmission in Park, sliding minivan doors that don't open when they should or open when they shouldn't, or electronic computer modules that cause a vehicle to "lag and lurch" (the vehicle won't accelerate from a stop for a few seconds, and then it will lurch out into traffic after the accelerator has been floored to get the vehicle out of harm's way).

Be wary. You are dealing with an industry that ignores cars suddenly accelerating out of control with no brakes, pickups that corrode so badly their suspension is unsafe, steering wheels that fly off, and, with GM Corvettes, steering assemblies that suddenly lock up and roofs that take flight once the car is underway.

In a nutshell, the auto industry continues to put profits before safety, unions value jobs over integrity, and all that governments care about is getting back their auto bailout investment.

If *Lemon-Aid* doesn't list a problem you have experienced, go to the NHTSA website's database at *www.safercar.gov/Vehicle+Owners* or *www.safercar.gov/Vehicle+Shoppers* for an update. Your vehicle may be currently under investigation, or may have been recalled since this year's guide was published.

Automotive News says an estimated 72 percent of the 25 million vehicles recalled in 2005 were fixed. *Lemon-Aid* doesn't list most recalls because there are so many, and the information can be easily obtained either from NHTSA at the above-listed sites or from Transport Canada (*www.tc.gc.ca/roadsafety/recalls/search_e.asp*). Dealers willingly give out recall info when they run a vehicle history search through their computers, since they hope to snag the extra repair dollars. Just make sure you ask the dealer to also check for a "customer satisfaction program," a "service policy," a "goodwill" warranty extension, or a free emissions warranty service.

Secret Warranties/Internal Bulletins

It's not enough to know which parts on your vehicle are likely to fail. You should also know which repairs will be done for free by the dealer and automaker, even though you aren't the original owner and the manufacturer's warranty has long since expired.

Welcome to the hidden world of secret warranties, found in confidential technical service bulletins (TSBs) published in *Lemon-Aid* or gleaned from owners' feedback from Internet auto forums.

Almost all automakers have "secret warranty" or "warranty adjustment" programs. Under these programs, the manufacturer will do free repairs on vehicles with persistent problems, even after the warranty expires, in order to avoid a recall, bad press, or a small claims court lawsuit. According to the Center for Auto Safety (*www.autosafety.org/secret-warranties*), at any given time there are approximately 500 secret warranty programs available through automobile manufacturers.

For years, NHTSA has declined to post on its website complete service buletins from automakers about problems with their cars and about specialized warranty extensions that could save car owners thousands of dollars on repairs. Usually, what you will find on NHTSA's website (*www.safercar.gov*) is a cryptic reference to some service campaign or the bulletin itself. As for Transport Canada's help, don't hold your breath.

NHTSA says automakers have warned it that service bulletins are copyrighted and cannot be reproduced. Yet, *Alldata.com* has sold bulletins online to car owners for over two decades, without a peep from any car manufacturer. Even more damning, several leading automakers interviewed by the *New York Times* said that either they did not copyright their bulletins or that they would not object to publication by NHTSA. Those automakers are BMW, Chrysler, General Motors, Honda, Hyundai, Nissan, Subaru, and Volvo.

In five states, California, Connecticut, Maryland, Virginia, and Wisconsin, manufacturers are required to tell eligible consumers about secret warranty programs – usually within 90 days of adopting the program.

Wisconsin has the most comprehensive "secret" warranty law in the States. It allows the consumer to collect double the cost of repairs when the law is violated:

WISCONSIN SECRET WARRANTY LAW
218.0172 Motor vehicle adjustment programs.

(1) Definitions. In this section:

    (a) "Adjustment program" means an extended policy program under which a manufacturer undertakes to pay for all or any part of the cost of repairing, or to reimburse purchasers for all or any part of the cost of repairing, any condition that may substantially affect motor vehicle durability, reliability or performance. "Adjustment program" does not include service provided under a written warranty provided to a consumer, service provided under a safety or emission-related recall program or individual adjustments made by a manufacturer on a case-by-case basis.

    (b) "Consumer" has the meaning given in s. 218.0171(1)(b).

    (c) "Manufacturer" has the meaning given in s. 218.0171(1)(c).

    (d) "Motor vehicle" has the meaning given in s. 218.0171(1)(d).

    (e) "Motor vehicle dealer" means a motor vehicle dealer, as defined in s. 218.0101(23)(a), that sells new motor vehicles.

(2) Disclosure requirements.

    (a) A manufacturer shall do all of the following:

        1. Establish a procedure to inform a consumer of any adjustment program applicable to the consumer's motor vehicle and, upon request, furnish the consumer with any document issued by the manufacturer relating to any adjustment program.

        2. Notify, by 1st class mail, a consumer who is eligible under an adjustment program of the condition in the motor vehicle that is covered by the adjustment program and the principal terms and conditions of the adjustment program within 90 days after the date on which the adjustment program is adopted.

        3. Notify its motor vehicle dealers, in writing, of all the terms and conditions of an adjustment program within 30 days after the date on which the program is adopted.

        4. If a consumer is a purchaser or lessor of a new motor vehicle, notify the consumer, in writing, of the consumer's rights and remedies under this section. The notice shall include a statement in substantially the following language: "Sometimes.... (manufacturer's name) offers a special adjustment program to pay all or part of the cost of certain repairs beyond the terms of the warranty. Check with your motor vehicle dealer to determine whether any adjustment program is applicable to your motor vehicle."

    (b) If a motor vehicle dealer has been informed of an adjustment program under par. (a) 3., the motor vehicle dealer shall disclose to a consumer seeking repairs for a condition covered by the adjustment program the terms and conditions of the adjustment program.

(3) Adjustment program reimbursement.

    (a) A manufacturer who establishes an adjustment program shall implement procedures to assure reimbursement of each consumer eligible under an adjustment program who incurs expenses for repair of a condition subject to the program before acquiring knowledge of the program. Reimbursement shall be consistent with the terms and conditions of the particular adjustment program.

(b) A consumer shall make a claim for reimbursement under par. (a) in writing to the manufacturer within 2 years after the date of the consumer's payment for repair of the condition. The manufacturer shall notify the consumer within 21 business days, as defined in s. 421.301 (6), after receiving a claim for reimbursement if the claim will be allowed or denied. If the claim is denied, the specific reasons for the denial shall be stated in writing.

(4) Remedies. In addition to pursuing any other remedy, a consumer may bring an action to recover damages caused by a violation of this section. A court shall award a consumer who prevails in such an action twice the amount of any pecuniary loss, together with costs, disbursements and reasonable attorney fees, notwithstanding s. 814.04 (1), and any equitable relief the court determines appropriate.

HISTORY: 1999 A. 31 S. 288; STATS. 1999 S. 218.0172.

Canada has nothing like Wisconsin's law.

That's why I pore over thousands of bulletins each year and summarize or reproduce the important ones in *Lemon-Aid* for each model year, along with improved parts numbers. These bulletins target defects related to safety, emissions, and performance that service managers would have you believe either don't exist or are your responsibility to fix. If you photocopy the applicable service bulletin included in *Lemon-Aid*, you'll have a better chance of getting the dealer or automaker to cover all or part of the repair costs. Bulletins taken from *Lemon-Aid* have also been instrumental in helping claimants win in small claims court mediation and trials. (Remember, judges like to have the bulletins validated by an independent mechanic or by the dealer or automaker you are suing.)

Service bulletins listed in *Lemon-Aid* cover repairs that may be eligible for express or implied warranty coverage in one or more of the following five categories (although the description of the repairs is not always specific):

1. Emissions *expressed warranty (5-8 years/80,000-130,000 km (50,000-80,000 mi))*;
2. Safety component expressed warranty (this covers seat belts, ABS, and airbags, and usually lasts from eight years to the lifetime of the vehicle);
3. Body expressed warranty (paint: six years; rust perforations: seven years);
4. An implied warranty used as a secret benchmark among automakers (coverage varies from five to ten years); or
5. An *implied* legal warranty used as a benchmark by judges, mostly in small claims court trials or during mediation (depends on mileage, use, and repair cost; may be as high as 11 years, according to GM paint delamination jurisprudence).

Use these bulletins to get free repairs – even if the vehicle has changed hands several times – and to alert an independent mechanic about defects to look for. They're also great tools for getting compensation from automakers and dealer service managers after the warranty has expired, since they prove that a failure is factory-related and, therefore, not part of routine maintenance or caused by a caustic environmental substance such as bird droppings or acid rain. In small claims court, the argument that bird droppings caused a paint problem usually loses credibility when only certain models or certain years are shown to be affected, pointing the finger at the paint process and quality.

Automakers' "bird poop" defence doesn't explain why birds apparently defecate only on certain model vehicles (Chrysler Caravans and GM minivans, etc.). Nevertheless, the implied warranty requires that all automakers use the same durability standard or disclose at the time of sale that their vehicles aren't "bird-proofed."

In *Maureen Frank v. General Motors of Canada Limited,* the Saskatchewan small claims court judge ruled that paint finishes should last for 11 years. Three other Canadian small claims judgments have likewise extended the benchmark for second owners and to pickups. In those cases, the courts judged that seven years was an appropriate extension. Automakers will offer a free paint job or partial compensation for up to six years (no mileage limitation). Thereafter, most manufacturers will offer 50-75 percent refunds on the small claims courthouse's front steps.

The diagnostic shortcuts and lists of upgraded parts found in many service bulletins make them invaluable in helping mechanics and do-it-yourselfers to troubleshoot problems inexpensively and to replace the correct part the first time. Auto owners can also use the TSBs listed here to verify that a repair was diagnosed correctly, that the correct upgraded replacement part was used, and that the labour costs were fair.

Summaries of service bulletins relating to 1982-2013 vehicles can be obtained for free from the ALLDATA or NHTSA websites, but they are worded so cryptically that you really need the bulletins themselves. If you have a vehicle that's off warranty, you should get copies of the hundreds of pages of bulletins applicable to your model year, listing factory-related defects and diagnostic shortcuts. These bulletins can be ordered and downloaded from the Internet for $26.95 (U.S.) through

ALLDATA at *www.alldatadiy.com/buy/index.html*. Or you can get the bulletin title for free from ALLDATA and then search for it on the Internet.

Vehicle Profile Tables

These tables cover the various aspects of vehicle ownership at a glance. Included are reliability and crashworthiness scores, the manufacturer's suggested retail price, and used values for 2004-12 cars, trucks, SUVs, and vans. Models that were axed, low-volume sellers, or sold several decades ago are rated in the Reviews section of Appendix 1.

Prices

Dealer profit margins on new and used cars vary considerably, giving lots of room to negotiate a fair price if you take the time to find out what the vehicle is really worth. A new vehicle's selling price as suggested by the manufacturer (MSRP) is just that – a suggestion. Most savvy buyers beat the MSRP by at least 10 percent by shopping when inventories pile up and automakers/dealers double-down on sales incentives (usually during the first quarter of the year).

Used prices are based on sales recorded as of August 2013. Prices are for the lowest-priced standard model that is in good condition with a maximum of 20,000 km (almost 12,500 mi) for each calendar year. Watch for price differences reflecting each model's equipment upgrades, designated by a numerical or alphabetical abbreviation. For example, L, LX, and LXT usually mean more standard features are included, progressively, in each model. Numerical progression usually relates to engine size.

Prices reflect the auto markets in Quebec and Ontario, where the majority of used-vehicle transactions take place. Residents of Eastern Canada should add 10 percent, and Western Canadians should add at least 15-20 percent to the listed price. Why the higher costs? Less competition, combined with inflated new-vehicle prices in these regions. Don't be too disheartened, though; you'll recoup some of what you overpaid down the road when you sell the vehicle.

Why are *Lemon-Aid*'s prices sometimes lower than the prices found in dealer guides such as *Red Book*? The answer is simple: Much like a homeowner selling a house, dealers inflate their prices so that you can bargain the price down and wind up convinced that you made a great deal.

I use newspaper classified ads from Quebec, Ontario, and B.C., as well as auction reports, to calculate my used-vehicle values. I then check these figures against *Red Book* and *Black Book* estimates. I don't start with *Red Book*'s retail or wholesale figures because their prices are inflated about 10-20 percent. I then project what the value will be by mid-model year, and that lowers my prices further. I'll almost always fall way under *Red Book*'s appraisals, but not far under *Black Book*'s prices.

Since no evaluation method is foolproof, check dealer prices against newspaper- and Internet-sourced private classified ads and then add the option values listed in the table below to come up with a fairly representative offer. Don't forget to bargain the price down further if the odometer shows a cumulative reading of more than 20,000 km per calendar year.

It will be easier to match the indicated used prices if you buy privately. Dealers rarely sell much below the maximum prices; they claim that they need the full price to cover the costs of reconditioning and paying future warranty claims. If you can come within 5-10 percent of this guide's price, you'll have done well.

In the table below, take note that some options – such as paint protector, rust-proofing, and tinted windows – have little worth on the resale market, though they may make your vehicle easier to sell.

Value of Options by Model Year

OPTION	2004	2005	2006	2007	2008	2009	2010	2011	2012
Air conditioning	$200	$200	$250	$300	$350	$400	$500	$600	$750
Radio & CD player	100	100	100	150	175	200	300	500	600
Anti-lock brakes	50	50	100	125	150	175	300	300	400
Automatic transmission	250	250	300	325	375	400	500	600	750
Cruise control	75	50	50	75	100	125	225	300	350
Electric six-way seat	50	50	100	125	150	175	200	400	450
GPS	50	50	100	100	100	150	150	200	300
Leather upholstery	50	100	200	225	325	400	500	800	900
Paint protector	50	50	50	50	50	50	50	50	50
Power antenna	0	0	0	0	0	75	75	75	75
Power door locks	50	50	100	125	150	175	200	250	250
Power windows	50	50	100	125	150	175	225	250	250
Rustproofing	50	0	0	0	25	25	50	50	50
Stability control	100	125	150	150	150	175	225	275	300
Sunroof	50	50	50	75	125	150	300	500	500
T-top roof	150	200	300	400	500	700	800	1,000	1,000
Tilt steering	0	50	50	75	75	100	175	250	200
Tinted windows	0	0	0	0	25	50	50	50	50
Tires (Firestone)	−100	−100	−100	−100	−100	−150	−150	−150	−150
Traction control	50	100	125	150	175	275	400	500	500
Wire wheels/locks	50	75	100	125	150	175	275	300	350

NOTE: Dealer-installed GPS/Navigation systems may cost $2,000 to $6,000 and not work as well as smartphones, which provide continuous traffic and road construction updates. Hence, the rapid depreciation of this optional feature.

Reliability

The older a vehicle gets (at five to seven years old), the greater the chance that major components, such as the engine and transmission, will fail as the result of high mileage and environmental wear and tear. Surprisingly, a host of other expensive-to-repair failures are just as likely to occur in new vehicles as in older ones. The air conditioning, electronic computer modules, electrical systems, and brakes are the most troublesome components, manifesting problems early in a vehicle's life. Other deficiencies that will appear early, due to sloppy manufacturing and harsh environments, include failure-prone body hardware (trim, finish, locks, doors, and windows), susceptibility to water leakage or wind noise, and peeling and/or discoloured paint. A "star score" in the Profile shows a model year's degree of overall reliability and recommendation.

| NOT RECOMMENDED | BELOW AVERAGE | AVERAGE | ABOVE AVERAGE | RECOMMENDED |

Crashworthiness

Some of the main factors weighed in the safety ratings are a model's crashworthiness, its front and rear visibility, and the availability of safety features such as seat belt pretensioners, depowered airbags, airbag disablers, adjustable brake and accelerator pedals, integrated child safety seats, effective head restraints, and assisted stability and traction control.

- **NHTSA CRASH TESTS:** Front, side, and roof crash protection figures are taken from NHTSA's New Car Assessment Program. For the front crash test, vehicles are crashed head-on at 57 km/h (35 mph) into a fixed barrier. NHTSA uses star rankings to show the likelihood, expressed as a percentage, of belted occupants surviving a crash without serious injury – the higher the number, the greater the protection.

- **SIDE CRASHWORTHINESS:** NHTSA's side crash test represents an intersection-type collision with a 1,368 kg (3,015 lb.) barrier moving at 62 km/h (38.5 mph) into a standing vehicle. The moving barrier is covered with material that has give in order to replicate the front of a car. This test result is especially important to senior drivers who often misjudge the speed of oncoming cars when turn into an intersection.

- **ROOF STRENGTH:** Roofs of light passenger vehicles weighing up to 2,722 kg (6,000 lb.) are required to withstand up to three times the weight of the vehicle. Heavier light-duty vehicles weighing 2,722-4,536 kg (6,000-10,000 lb.) need only withstand 1.5 times their own weight on the roof.

- **IIHS CRASH TESTS:** The Insurance Institute for Highway Safety (IIHS) rates vehicles' frontal offset, front overlap, side, head-restraint/rear crash, and roof protection as "Good," "Acceptable," "Marginal," or "Poor."

In the Institute's 64 km/h (40 mph) frontal offset test, 40 percent of the total width of each vehicle strikes a barrier on the driver's side. The barrier's deformable face makes the forces in the test similar to those involved in a frontal offset crash between two vehicles of the same weight, each going just less than 64 km/h.

IIHS's 50 km/h (31 mph) side-impact test is carried out at a slower speed than NHTSA's test; however, the barrier uses a front end that is shaped to simulate the typical front end of a pickup or SUV, which is deemed to give truer results.

- **SMALL OVERLAP FRONT CRASH TEST:** This is IIHS's newest test – and the crash that's the hardest to survive. Two-thirds of the vehicles had poor ratings for structure, and about half of them were poor or marginal for restraints and kinematics, meaning the dummy's movements weren't well-controlled to prevent contact with hard surfaces.

IIHS added the small overlap test to its lineup of vehicle safety evaluations last year. It replicates what happens when the front corner of a vehicle strikes another vehicle or an object like a tree or a utility pole.

In one example of poor structure, the front pillar of the Nissan Rogue's door frame was pushed far inside the occupant compartment and after the crash was almost touching the driver seat. The 2013 Jeep Patriot was among the worst for restraints and kinematics. The dummy's head slid off the frontal airbag as the steering wheel moved 8 inches up and nearly 6 inches to the right. The side curtain airbag didn't deploy, and the safety belt allowed the dummy's head and torso to move too far forward.

The Forester and the Outlander Sport crash scores were outstanding. Of the 2013 small SUV test group, nine earned *TOP SAFETY PICK*, including the BMW X1 and the Buick Encore, Ford's Escape, the Honda CR-V, the Hyundai Tucson and its twin, the Kia Sportage, the Mazda CX-5, the Toyota RAV4, and Volkswagen Tiguan and the redesigned 2014 Patriot.

- **ROLLOVERS:** A vehicle's rollover resistance rating is an estimate of its risk of rolling over in a single-vehicle crash, not a prediction of the likelihood of a crash. The lowest-rated vehicles (one star) are at least four times more likely to roll over than the highest-rated vehicles (five stars) when involved in a single-vehicle crash.

AMERICAN MODELS

Carlos Gomes, Scotiabank senior economist, said the strong performance this spring has led him to increase his forecast for Canadian auto sales for 2013 as a whole to 1.72 million units from 1.69 million units previously. "After a sluggish start to the first quarter, the industry really did come out and enhanced incentives beginning in April," he said. "The market has obviously responded." Most automakers have really started to push aggressive incentives again to purchase new vehicles, including 0% financing and increasing the cashback they were offering for trade-ins, he said.

Scott Deveau
Financial Post, June 27, 2013

Despite "happy-face" press conferences, the Chrysler/Fiat
marriage is rocky at best. Or, should I say "lacks "AMORE" Or,
"We ain't got a barrel of money … We may be ragged and funny…"

CHRYSLER/FIAT/JEEP

Chrysler is out of crisis mode for the time being, thanks to its bankruptcy filing, bailouts by Ottawa and Washington, and the purchase of the company by Fiat.

The Fiat "rescue" is all the more ironic now that the Italian automaker needs cash from Chrysler to support its lagging European sales.

The Chrysler/Fiat plan is to give Chrysler responsibility for large cars, trucks, SUVs, and vans and leave the smaller vehicles to Fiat. Chrysler will handle engines larger than 2.0L, hybrids, and electrics, while Fiat will handle smaller engines and small- to mid-sized diesels. For 2014, Chrysler is focused on tweaking its powertrains, slightly restyling some models like the Dodge Durango, offering a wider range of standard equipment, and dropping the Avenger. The 200 model will be reworked in 2015.

Jeep

Jeep's Compass and Patriot both get a Hyundai-sourced, 6-speed automatic and a high-performance Magna all-wheel drive system, shown to respond more quickly than the CVT-based one used in earlier model Jeeps. A new 2014 Jeep Cherokee debuts with a 2.4L 4-cylinder and a 3.2L V6, in addition to FWD, AWD, and 4x4 powertrains, that will include a 9-speed ZF automatic transmission. The 2014 Grand Cherokee gets an 8-speed automatic; has a restyled front end, interior and exterior; and a 3.0L diesel powerplant. Wagoneer fans will see a new model in 2015, while the Wrangler continues mostly unchanged until 2016.

Culture clash? No doubt this is a European van with its close pedals, faraway steering wheel, and minuscule Uconnect centre console display.

Nudging $29,000 (U.S.) and equipped with a standard 280 hp, 3.6L V6 (or a 3.0L diesel turbo) hooked to a 6-speed automatic transmission, Ram's new ProMaster cargo van is for businesses that were poorly served by the big, expensive, inefficient, and unreliable Sprinter. Essentially an Americanized modified version of the Fiat Ducato (think of an old Dodge Tradesman with Italian components and styling), the ProMaster slots between the old Sprinter and Ford's new Transit – with plenty of cargo space for businesses.

Ram pickups "Recommended"

Another shocker? The Ram 1500 was named number-one in *Consumer Reports* magazine's July 2013 pickup comparison test, and given a coveted "Recommended" rating. The award was a stunner to the assembled car critics and Chrysler, as well, who had grown accustomed to seeing the "Not Recommended" Ram anchor CR's annual performance and quality ratings.

"The Ram 1500 is surprisingly luxurious and refined – but still fully capable of doing hard work when needed," said Jake Fisher, director of *Consumer Reports'* Auto Test Center. "Continued interior and powertrain improvements make the Ram a particularly well-rounded choice," he said.

Although, J. D. Power still ranks Ram at the bottom of its ratings this year, *CR* says that the Ram delivers one of the best rides of any pickup, thanks to its unique coil spring rear suspension. It also has an exceptionally quiet, spacious crew cab, and the Uconnect infotainment feature (a Ford failing) can't be beat.

The Ram pickup lineup adopted many fuel-saving features (stop/start, 8-speed automatic transaxles, and lighter components) that are seen on the 2014s. Heavy-duty models get an optional 6.4L engine coupled to a new Aisin transmission which, hopefully, will end Chrysler's premature automatic transmission failures. Handling should be considerably improved with the optional air suspension setup and the advent of Long Hauler improvements. This should mean less white-knuckle driving when going over uneven pavement and potholes, resulting in the infamous "Death Wobble" (Google "Chrysler death wobble").

Fiat

The 2014 Fiat 500L ("large"), a four-door crossover, arrives in North America this fall. It comes with two more doors than the base 500 hardtop and seats a fifth passenger. Its European brother is 163 inches long, 70.1 inches wide, and 65.4 inches tall; which puts it in Mini Countryman territory.

Quality

Chrysler's poor reliability ratings haven't improved much over the years. Its main failings continue to be an unreliable drivetrain, so-so electronics, prematurely worn brakes, and shoddy body workmanship. Although the June 2013 J. D. Power Initial Quality ratings for Chrysler models beat the industry average (113), with 109 problems per 100 units – its Jeep (118), Dodge (130), Ram (132) and Fiat (154) brands finished in the bottom 12, though all brands improved on their last year's scores.

Top Problem Areas on 2013 New Models

1. Built-in voice recognition frequently doesn't recognize or misinterprets commands
2. Built-in Bluetooth mobile phone/device frequent pairing/connectivity issues
3. Excessive wind noise
4. Materials scuff and/or soil easily
5. Navigation system is difficult to use or poorly located

Source: J.D. Power and Associates

Pentastar V6

Owner feedback confirms that the Pentastar V6 engine head gasket failures continue unabated and now affect Chrysler's 2013 engines. Inasmuch as the 2014s return relatively unchanged, it's likely the engine problems will be carried forward. Here's what one 2013 Wrangler owner posted on *wranglerforum.com*:

I just bought a 2013 Wrangler Sport, at the end of September, it now has 6400 miles on it and the dealer just finished replacing BOTH heads, yes BOTH heads, with NEW ones. I took it in because it would barely idle, it had a MIL code of P0300 (multi-cylinder misfire)! Wow, I now have a brand new Jeep that has a REBUILT motor in it! So, my guess is, they still have not resolved the head problem. The build date on the door is August 2012. I have not picked it up yet, so I don't know how we'll it will run.

Chrysler came out in 2010 with its Pentastar V6 engine that is already showing serious reliability problems, although the company has minimized the extent of the engine failures and has tried to put some of the blame on owners.

Nevertheless, Chrysler is replacing under warranty defective cylinder heads on its Pentastar V6 engines with what it calls "more robust" parts. To its credit, Chrysler says it will pay for rentals if the engines are fixed under warranty.

Independent repairers say the failures are widespread. Early signs of the problem are an engine ticking noise, increased gas consumption, loss of power, and stalling-out. Also, the Check Engine light illuminates on all affected engines.

Chrysler blames the engine failures on a combination of factors that include the type of fuel used, owner driving habits, and how well the vehicle was maintained. Owners call this corporate nonsense. They say Chrysler's decision to install more durable engine components in the Pentastar V6 certainly gives credibility that the engine problem is factory-related.

Unfortunately, Pentastar engine problems aren't limited to defective head gaskets. Engine techs at *Flatratetech.com*, a website run by independent auto repairers, say the valve guides have been problematic for some time:

The exhaust valve guide is too sloppy, and allows the valve to wobble. Usually it's the number three or five cylinder, but it's not isolated to those two.

The stakes are high for Chrysler because the 3.6L Pentastar V6 powers most of its vehicle lineup. It's the standard powerplant in some minivans, the Grand Cherokee and Wrangler, Chrysler 300, and Dodge Charger sedans and Journeys, and this fall will be available on the 2013 Ram 1500 pickup. And Chryslers are not the only affected vehicles. Volkswagen's Routan minivan, a Chrysler Town & Country clone, uses the same Pentastar, and VW owners are asking for similar warranty coverage for the problem.

bad buy

The Chrysler 200.

RATING: *200*: Below Average (2011-14); *Avenger, Sebring*: Not Recommended (1995-2013). Used models are poor buys, despite their "bargain" price tag. 2010 was the Sebring's last model year; the 200 is a reworked Sebring in disguise. **Road performance:** Considerably improved in 2011 with stiffened body mounts, a smoother suspension, a raised roll centre, an upgraded rear sway bar and tires, improved noise reduction, and a softened ride. The base 4-cylinder engine coupled to the Jurassic 4-speed tranny is a puny performer and lacks reserve power for passing and merging. **Strong points:** A more stylish appearance; a gentler, more comfortable ride; better handling; and a classier, quieter interior. V6 engine gives plenty of power. Easy access to the interior. Standard side curtain airbags and electronic stability control. **Weak points:** The 6-speed transmission shifts are harsh and too frequent. Only average fuel economy. Uncomfortable front seats have insufficient thigh room. Interior feels small, closed in. Smallish trunk. **Major redesign:** *Avenger*: 2008, 2011; *Sebring*: 2001, 2007, and 2011. **Highway/city fuel economy:** *2.4L 4-speed auto.:* 6.7/9.9 L/100 km. *2.4L 6-speed auto.:* 6.4/10.5 L/100 km. *3.6L 6-speed auto.:* 6.8/11L/100 km. *Convertibles: 2.4L 4-speed auto.:* 6.9/10.3 L/100 km. *2.4L 6-speed auto.:* 6.8/11.5 L/100 km. *3.6L 6-speed auto.:* 6.8/11L/100 km. **Best alternatives:** The Mazda3, Honda Accord, and Hyundai Elantra.

Prices and Specs

Prices (Soft): *LX:* $19,995, *Touring:* $22,995, *Limited:* $26,995, *Convertible LX:* $29,995, *Convertible Touring:* $36,495, *Convertible Limited:*$38,495; *Avenger SE:* $19,995, *Avenger SXT:* $23,995, *Avenger SXT V6:* $25,200, *RT:* $28,995 **Freight:** $1,400 **Powertrain (Front-drive):** Engines: 2.4L 4-cyl. (173 hp), 3.6L V6 (283 hp); Transmissions: 4-speed auto., 6-speed manumatic **Dimensions/capacity (sedan):** Passengers: 2/3; Wheelbase: 108.9 in.; H: 58.4/L: 191.7/W: 72.5 in.; Headroom F/R: 3/3.5 in.; Legroom F/R: 42.4/36.2 in.; Cargo volume: 13.6 cu. ft.; Fuel tank: 62L/regular; Tow limit: 1,000 lb.; Load capacity: 865 lb.; Turning circle: 36.5 ft.; Ground clearance: 6.1 in.; Weight: 3,590 lb.

SAFETY: Limited three-quarter rear visibility. NHTSA awarded the 2001-13 Sebring and Avenger five stars for frontal crash safety and three and four stars for side and rollover protection. The 200 model got four stars for overall crash protection. IIHS rates the 200 sedan and convertible "Good" in front, side, rollover, roof strength, and rear crashworthiness tests.

ALERT! Pentastar V6 head gaskets may be problematic for all model years. Be on the lookout for a suspension "death wobble" after passing over potholes, etc.

200/Avenger/Sebring Profile

	2004	2005	2006	2007	2008	2009	2010	2011	2012
Used Values ($)									
200	—	—	—	—	—	—	—	11,500	13,500
Avenger SE	—	—	—	—	6,000	6,500	8,500	11,000	13,000
Sebring	2,000	2,500	3,500	4,500	5,500	7,500	10,000	—	—
Convertible	3,500	4,500	6,000	—	9,500	10,500	14,500	—	—
Recommended	★	★	★	★	★2	★2	★2	★2	★2
Reliability	★	★	★	★	★	★2	★2	★2	★3

SECRET WARRANTIES, INTERNAL BULLETINS: 2007-08—Tips on silencing noisy seats and rear suspension rattles. Sunroof water leaks. Rear-door glass comes out of its track; won't roll up. Engine surge or gear hunting upon deceleration. Steering honk, moan, or grinding sound when making left turns (replace the power steering fluid reservoir). Broken transmission gearshift-lever interlock spring retainer hook "freezes" lever in Park position. Customer Satisfaction Notification Program K16, dated August 2010, says steel reinforcement clip will be installed for free, if needed. **2007-09**—Difficult to fill fuel; nozzle shut off. Horn honks or moans on hard left-hand turns. **2007-10**—AC leaks water onto passenger floor. Lower door hinge popping, groaning noises. **2008**—Hard starts; no-starts. **2010**—Cold start is followed by rough idle. Automatic transmission transfer gear beating noise. Rear-door glass may make a "shuttering" noise when raised or lowered. Trunk release operates even though vehicle is locked. **2011**—RPM fluctuations and hard starting are addressed in TSB# 18-028-11, issued May 27, 2011. Both problems are reimbursable under warranty. **2011-12**—Hard shifting can be resolved by reflashing the PCM (under warranty), says TSB# 18-020-12. **2012-13**—A poor upshifting automatic transmission is covered in TSB# 21-013-12, issued November 10, 2012. **2013**—There's a free fix under warranty for off-centre steering wheels.

CHARGER/CHALLENGER ★★/★★★

RATING: *Charger:* Below Average (all years), because it costs more, depreciates faster, and elicits more safety-related complaints than its cheaper, high-performance brother. *Challenger:* Average (all years). In a nutshell, the Challenger remains the premiere muscle car with a retro look and a small horsepower edge over its Dodge rival, while the Charger continues as Dodge's slightly higher-priced muscle car, now sporting an 8-speed automatic transmission. Both cars offer a choice of the Hemi or the head gasket-challenged Pentastar V6. **Road performance:** In past model years, the Challenger's lack of agility made it more of a Clydesdale than a "pony car," but recent suspension and steering tweaks have made the car more responsive. The Charger's performance is also better than average, particularly with the 8-speed automatic transmission. **Strong points:** These are comfortable, spacious, and affordable sports cars with a healthy dose of muscle car flair (especially the 2012 Challenger). Challenger's bigger back seat and larger trunk give it an edge when compared with the Chevrolet Camaro and Ford Mustang. The infotainment system, unlike Ford/Lincoln's, is first-class. It's undeniable that both cars have exceptional styling, horsepower to burn (as in, "What do you mean the fuel tank is on empty again?"), and attitude. **Weak points:** A stiff, jarring ride, handling that's not particularly agile, overly assisted steering that requires constant correction, and marginal rear headroom. The Challenger is in dire need of an interior facelift similar to the Charger's. There are many quality issues that mostly concern the 305 hp 3.6L V6 and powertrain dependability has come under fire from owners of 2009-12 models. Drivetrain electronics, airbags, steering, brakes, suspension, and fit and finish all need to be checked carefully prior to buying any used model. **Major redesign:** *Charger/Intrepid:* 1998, 2006, 2011; *Challenger:* 2008. **Highway/city fuel economy:** *Charger 3.6L:* 7.3/11.7 L/100 km. *Charger 5.7L:* 8/13.5 L/100 km. *Charger 5.7L AWD:* 8.5/14.4 L/100 km. *Challenger 3.6L:* 7.3/11.7 L/100 km. *Challenger 5.7L, man.:* 8.2/13.8 L/100 km. *Challenger 6.4L, SRT8:* 8.8/15.1 L/100 km. *Challenger 6.4L, SRT8 auto.:* 9.2/15.6 L/100 km. **Best alternatives:** The Chevrolet Camaro and Hyundai Genesis. Why not the Mustang? Way too many safety-related defects and internal service bulletins decrying the 'Stang's poor highway performance and abysmal reliability.

Prices and Specs

Prices (Soft): *Charger SE:* $29,995, *Charger SXT:* $32,745, *Charger SXT Plus:* $34,745, *R/T:* $37,995, *R/T AWD:* $39,996, *SRT8:* $47,995, *Challenger SXT:* $26,995, *Challenger SXT Plus:* $28,995, *Challenger R/T:* $36,695, *Challenger R/T Classic:* $38,690, *Challenger SRT8:* $47,995 **Freight:** $1,400 **Powertrain (Rear-drive /AWD):** Engines: 3.6L V6 (292 hp), 3.6L V6 (305 hp), 5.7L V8 (370 hp), 5.7L V8 (375 hp), 6.4L V8 (470 hp); Transmissions: 5-speed auto., 8-speed auto.; Challenger: 6-speed man., 6-speed auto.

Dimensions/capacity: Passengers: 2/3; Wheelbase: 116 /120 in.; *Charger:* H: 58/L: 200/W: 75 in.; *Challenger:* H: 57/L: 198/W: 76 in., Headroom F/R: *Charger:* 3/2.5 in.; *Challenger:* 3.5/2 in.; Legroom F/R: *Charger:* 41.5/28 in.; Cargo volume: 16 cu. ft.; Fuel tank: 68-72L/regular; Tow limit: *Challenger:* Not recommended, *Charger:* 1,000 lb.; Load capacity: 865 lb. est.; Turning circle: 41 ft.; Ground clearance: 4.5 in.; Weight: *Challenger:* 3,720-4,140 lb., *Charger:* 3,728-4,268 lb.

SAFETY: *Charger:* Four stars for frontal collision and rollover protection and three stars for side crashworthiness. 2005 and earlier models did almost as well, except that side passenger protection earned three stars. The IIHS rates recent model Chargers "Good" for frontal, side, and head-restraint protection and roof strength. *Challenger:* Since 2009 NHTSA has given five stars for front and side crashworthiness and four stars for rollover resistance.

ALERT! Can you read the dash gauges during daytime driving?

Charger/Challenger Profile

Used Values ($)	2004	2005	2006	2007	2008	2009	2010	2011	2012
Charger SE	—	—	4,500	5,500	6,500	9,000	11,500	15,000	18,000
SXT AWD	—	—	—	6,000	8,000	11,000	15,500	—	23,000
SRT8	—	—	10,000	11,500	14,000	18,000	24,500	—	36,000
Challenger SXT	—	—	—	—	—	12,500	16,000	19,000	19,500
SRT8	—	—	—	—	—	22,000	27,000	33,500	38,000
Recommended	★	★	★	★	★	★	★	★	★
Reliability	★	★	★	★	★	★	★	★	★

SECRET WARRANTIES, INTERNAL BULLETINS: Long crank time and RPM fluctuations; reardoor; wind noise; and light to moderate paint defects. **2005-10—***Charger:* Inoperative door locks remedy found in TSB# 08-061-12, issued November 29, 2012. **2011-12—**A front end clunk can be silenced by replacing both the left and right side front tension struts (under warranty), says TSB# 02-005-12. Automatic transmission controls cause a shudder, shift concern; deck lid spoiler rattle, chatter; front-door wind noise; battery drain; radio powers itself on with the ignition off; fix for the rear chime; false chime from the blind spot system; trunk won't open with passive switch; and coolant leaks. **2012—**There's a free fix under warranty for front shocks that may be out of specification (TSB# 02-006-12, issued October 13, 2012). **2011-12—***Challenger:* Intermittent no-start; automatic transmission malfunctions; booming noise at idle; door glass self-cycling/battery drain; passive door handles inoperative; and deck lid and trunk can be opened without the key fob nearby. Incorrect ride height can be fixed by replacing the right and left rear spring.

RATING: Average (2011-14); *Magnum:* Not Recommended (all years). Introduced as a 2005 model, this large rear-wheel drive station wagon was dropped at the end of the 2008 model year. It was Dodge's first car to use the new Chrysler LX platform, shared with the Chrysler 300 and Dodge Charger. **Road performance:** Here's your dilemma: The relatively new Pentastar 3.6L V6 gives the car power and fuel economy it has always lacked, but skimps on reliability; the V8 has much more power, but it guzzles fuel. Early 300 models provide so-so handling that was improved with the 2011 models. The touring model gives a smoother, more-comfortable ride than does the Magnum, 300M, or 300C. **Strong points:** You will enjoy a remarkably quiet, luxurious, and spacious (up front) interior, and a large trunk. Uconnect infotainment system works flawlessly and is easily mastered. The Garmin-based navigation system is one of the most intuitive systems available. **Weak points:** Subpar powertrain electronics and head gasket failures with the Pentastar powerplant. Mercedes-sourced electronics have had serious, head-scratching reliability glitches that defy correction. Airbag and engine warning lights are constant and not always meaningful. Limited backseat head- and legroom. Options can send the already-high base price soaring. Hemi-equipped models are overpriced, and the 300's resale value falls as quickly as Montreal's mayors. Standard towing capability is less than one would expect from a reardrive. **Major redesign:** 1999, 2005, and 2011 (no more wagons). **Highway/city fuel economy:** *3.6L:* 7.3/11.7 L/100 km. *5.7L 300C (cylinder deactivation):* 8/13.5 L/100 km. *5.7L AWD:* 8.7/13.4 L/100 km. Owners report that real-world fuel consumption for both engines is far more than these estimates. **Best alternatives:** Honda Accord Crosstour, Hyundai Azera, Subaru Forester or Legacy, Toyota Avalon, and Sienna.

SAFETY: Impressive crashworthiness, says NHTSA, which gave the 2001-04 models four stars for frontal and side crash protection. The 2005-09s earned five and four stars, while the 2010 through 2013 cars got five stars in all categories. Recent models tested by IIHS also garnered top scores.

ALERT! Before purchasing any one of these models, have an independent garage check the brake calipers and rotors (pull the wheels), the steering assembly, and the condition of the transmission fluid. Also, ensure that the tilted head restraints aren't a pain in the neck (especially on the 2009 and later SRT8).

Prices and Specs

Prices (Very Negotiable): *Touring:* $32,745, *Limited:* $35,745, *C:* $39,995, *AWD:* $41,995, *S:* $35,995, *AWD:* $37,995, *V8:* $39,995, *V8 AWD:* $41,995, *SRT8:* $48,995 **Freight:** $1,400
Powertrain (Rear-drive /AWD): Engines: 3.6L V6 (292 hp), 5.7L V8 (363 hp); 6.4L V8 (465 hp) Transmissions: 5-speed auto., 8-speed auto.
Dimensions/capacity (base): Passengers: 2/3; Wheelbase: 120 in.; H: 58.4/L: 199/W: 75 in.; Headroom F/R: 3/2.5 in.; Legroom F/R: 41.8/40.1 in.; Cargo volume: 16.3 cu. ft.; Fuel tank: 68L/regular; Tow limit: 2,000 lb.; Load capacity: 865 lb.; Turning circle: 41 ft.; Ground clearance: 4.7-5 in.; Weight: *300:* 3,961-4,513 lb.

300/300C/Magnum Profile

Used Values ($)	2004	2005	2006	2007	2008	2009	2010	2011	2012
300 Touring	—	3,500	4,000	5,000	7,000	8,500	12,500	17,000	20,500
300C, Limited AWD	—	5,000	6,500	8,000	9,500	12,500	17,500	24,500	23,500
Magnum SE	—	4,000	5,000	5,500	6,000	—	—	—	—
SRT8	—	6,500	8,500	10,500	13,500	—	—	—	—
Recommended	★	★	★	★	★	★	★	★	★
Reliability	★	★	★	★	★	★	★	★	★

SECRET WARRANTIES, INTERNAL BULLETINS: 2005-10—Inoperative door locks remedy found in TSB# 08-061-12, issued November 29, 2012. **2006-10**—Lower door hinge popping, groaning. **2007-10**—Harsh 4-3 shift; poor shift quality. **2008-09**—How to reduce engine whistling. **2009**—Poor steering wheel returnability. **2010**—Inoperative side windows and MIL light warnings. MIL light may be signaling the need to install a shim onto the thermostat, or replace the thermostat housing. **2011-12**—Radio malfunctions; a fix for water infiltrating into the mirror turn-signal housing; Forward-Collision warning system light comes on when no threat is imminent; airbag light also activates for no reason; hard starts and no-starts; car may not shift from Neutral to Drive; warning chime that there is another vehicle in close proximity may malfunction; poor headlight and side light illumination; rear-view and side-view mirrors give too dark an image; fuel spills out after refueling; computer malfunction causes excessive amounts of fuel to be dumped into the engine cylinders.

CARAVAN, GRAND CARAVAN/TOWN & COUNTRY ★★★/★

RATING: Average (2011-14); Not Recommended (1990-2010). The 2011 refinements corrected many of these minivans' past deficiencies. As for long-term servicing, it seems repairs and parts aren't a problem. **Road performance:** The tight chassis and responsive steering provide a comfortable, no-surprise ride. 2011's stiffer springs have greatly improved handling and comfort. Manoeuvring around town is easy, though high-speed merging with a full load takes some skill. The 2011 Pentastar V6 has been very problematic. The engine tends to run roughly and suddenly lose power, and the transmission shifts erratically, mostly due to poorly-calibrated electronics. Power steering is vague and over-assisted as speed increases. Downshifting from the electronic gearbox provides practically no braking effect. The brake pedal feels mushy, and the brakes tend to heat up after repeated applications, causing considerable loss of effectiveness (fade) and warping of the front discs. The ABS has proved to be unreliable on older vans and costly to repair. **Strong**

points: Very reasonably priced and subject to deep discounting. Rapid depreciation lures bargain hunters who faint at the first tranny repair bill. Lots of innovative convenience features; user-friendly instruments, controls; and infotainment features. **Weak points:** A sad history of chronic powertrain, AC, ABS, suspension (Ram and Jeep "death wobble"), and body defects that are exacerbated by the automaker's hard-nosed attitude in interpreting its after-warranty assistance obligations ("Let them burn!" First Jeep recall response.). **Major redesign:** 2001, 2008, and 2011. **Highway/city fuel economy:** *Caravan 2.4 4-cylinder:* 11.8/8.2 L/100 km. *Caravan 3.0 V6:* 12.7/8.3 L/100 km. *Caravan 3.3 V6:* 12.2/8.2 L/100 km. *Grand Caravan 3.3 V6:* 12.9/8.5 L/100 km. *Grand Caravan 3.8 V6:* 13.2/8.7 L/100 km. *Town & Country 2.7:* 15.5/10 L/100 km. *Town & Country 4.0:* 12.2/7.9 L/100 km. *Town & Country AWD:* 13.6/9.1 L/100 km. *3.6L:* 7.9/12.2 L/100 km. **Best alternatives:** First, think small and consider the six-passenger Mazda5. Honda's Odyssey should be your next choice, with the Toyota Sienna placing third. Full-sized GM rear-drive vans are also worth looking at. They are more affordable and practical buys if you intend to haul a full passenger load or do regular heavy hauling, are physically challenged, use lots of accessories, or take frequent motoring excursions. Sure, they're less fuel-efficient, but they are are often discounted over 30 percent. Don't splurge on a new luxury Chrysler minivan: Chrysler's upscale Town & Country may cost up to $10,000 more than a Grand Caravan yet be worth only a few thousand dollars more after six years on the market.

SAFETY: 2010-13s were given NHTSA's top, five-star rating for frontal and side crashworthiness; rollover resistance earned four stars. Earlier 2002-09 models also earned impressive scores. 2001 and earlier Caravans weren't as safe. IIHS ranks frontal offset, side impact, roof strength, and head-restraint protection as "Good."

ALERT! The chrome ring around the passenger-side heater deck may cause a distracting reflection in the side-view mirror in the Town & Country; the backup camera image is too dim in daytime to be useful; and the third-row seat belt is a hostage-taker.

Caravan/Grand Caravan/Town & Country Profile

	2004	2005	2006	2007	2008	2009	2010	2011	2012
Used Values ($)									
Caravan	3,000	3,500	4,000	5,000	—	—	—	—	—
Grand Caravan	3,500	4,000	4,500	5,500	6,000	7,500	9,500	17,500	16,500
Town & Country	4,000	5,500	6,000	7,500	11,500	14,500	18,500	23,000	27,000
	—	6,500	8,500	10,500	13,500	—	—	—	—
Recommended	★	★	★	★	☆	☆	☆	☆	☆
Reliability	★	★	★	★	★	★	★	☆	☆

Prices and Specs

Prices (Very Negotiable): *Grand Caravan Cargo:* $29,495, *SE:* $27,995, *SXT:* $30,995, *Crew:* $33,995, *R/T:* $38,795, *Town & Country Touring:* $39,995, *with leather:* $41,995, *Limited:* $45,995 **Freight:** $1,400 **Powertrain (Front-drive):** Engine: 3.6L V6 (283 hp); Transmission: 6-speed auto. **Dimensions/ capacity:** Passengers: 2/2/3; Wheelbase: 121 in.; H: 69/W: 77/L: 203 in.; Headroom F/R1/R2: *Grand Caravan:* 3/3/1.5 in., *Town & Country:* 3/3/1.5 in.; Legroom F/R1/R2: *Grand Caravan:* 41/30.5/27 in., *Town & Country:* 41/31/25 in.; Cargo volume: 61.5 cu. ft.; Fuel tank: 76L/regular; Tow limit: 3,800 lb.; Load capacity: 1,150 lb.; Turning circle: 41 ft.; Ground clearance: 5 in.; Weight: *Grand Caravan:* 4,600 lb., *Town & Country:* 4,755 lb.

SECRET WARRANTIES, INTERNAL BULLETINS: 2008—Harsh shifting. Abnormal front brake pad wear. Outside sliding-door handle is inoperative in freezing temperatures. Roof rack howling sound. Howl, honk from the front windshield. Front door rattle or window won't roll down. Exhaust system rattle, clunk. Slow fuel tank fill; pump shuts off prematurely. **2008-09**—Roof rack crossbar adjuster corroded/seized. **2008-10**—Front wheel bearing growling, humming will be corrected by the free replacement of the front wheel bearings under a 5-year/145,000 km "goodwill" warranty extension, as outlined in TSB #02-003-11, published September 29, 2011. Power steering fluid leaks. An inoperative power sliding door may only require a reflashing of the sliding-door computer module. **2009**—Remedy for front brake squeal, pulsation. **2009-10**—Correction for sliding-door binding. **2009-11**—A front end vibration or short front brake pad life may require installing new brake linings and replacing both brake rotors under warranty (TSB# 05-005-12, issued September 20, 2012). **2010**—Silencing transfer-gear bearing noise. **2011-13**—Erratic automatic transmission shifting may be corrected by flash reprogramming the Powertrain Control Module (PCM) with new software covered by the 8-year Emissions warranty.

RAM 1500/2500 PICKUP ★★★★

The Ram.

RATING: Above Average buy (2013-14); Below Average (1994-2012); Average (1981-93). Recent model Rams are dramatically improved after the truck lineup was lost in the wilderness following its 1994 redesign. Reliability has improved and powertrain failures are less frequent, but still no where near the quality of most Asian products. Nevertheless, Ram pickups are unique: They are the only models with a half-ton 1500 with a diesel engine, or a coil-sprung 2500 Heavy Duty pickup. When equipped with a manual tranny and a diesel engine, Rams are adequate for most chores, even with their "death wobble" suspension/steering assemblies for which most affected models have been recalled. **Road performance:** Compare the stability and ride with Asian trucks, and you will be impressed by the newest Ram's better handling and more comfortable ride. Mercifully, this may mean the end of the Chrysler/Ram "death wobble," where the truck loses steering control after passing over potholes or uneven terrain. **Strong points:** In a recent comparison test run by *Consumer Reports* magazine, Ram was ranked "Recommended" after beating out the Ford F-150 and Toyota Tundra. Only the Chevrolet Avalanche and Silverado/Sierra out-pointed the Ram (by a few points). The test Ram was a four-wheel-drive 1500 Crew Cab, with an optional 5.7L Hemi V8 coupled with a more efficient 8-speed automatic transmission. This setup provided seamless power along with a 15 mpg fuel economy rating. The lockable "Ram box" storage compartment keeps items secure and out of the weather. **Weak points:** The Pentastar and 8-speed tranny have yet to prove they are dependable performers. So far, Pentastar hookups with 6-speeds aren't that impressive. The fuel-thirsty Hemi V8 isn't a wise choice, either. Its cylinder-deactivation feature is helpful, but not very. The Hemis are also complicated to service, and parts are often backordered. The "Ram box" takes up some of the bed width. Two other minuses: a high step up and a heavier than usual tailgate. **Major redesign:** 1981, 1994, and 2013. The wimpy 2012 V6 had only a 4-speed automatic. Carried over this year is the 305 hp 3.6L V6, which, with 305 hp, is up 42 percent over the old 3.7L. Add the 8-speed automatic combined with the peppier V6, and you won't need a V8. In addition to the 2014 Ram's 1500 EcoDiesel and new engine and suspension options for the heavy-duties, there's also an all-new 6.4L Hemi V8 used with the 4500 and 5500 models. This will give buyers two different horsepower and torque ratings with the 6.7L Cummins engine and two gasoline engines with two different horsepower ratings (at less than 10,000 pounds GVW, it's 410; more than 10,000 pounds GVW it's 367). Chassis cabs get reinforced steel frames to allow for much bigger payloads and trailer towing. **Highway/city fuel economy:** *3.9 4x2:* 15.9/11 L/100 km. *5.2 4x4:* 18.9/13.1 L/100 km. *Hemi V8 with Multi-Displacement System:* 13.9/8.8 L/100 km. *V6:* 12.2/8.1 L/100 km. Pre-2006 models' average real-world fuel consumption has been reported at 21 L/100 km. **Best alternatives:** Honda Ridgeline and the Nissan Frontier. Chevrolet's Silverado and the GMC Sierra are the best Detroit alternatives to the Ram. Ford's F-Series was also redesigned at the same time as the Ram with a more solid-feeling structure and larger cabs and cargo beds, as well as additional compartments and dividers. Ford F-Series trucks took a big step forward on the powertrain front with its introduction of the twin turbocharged EcoBoost V6 and a strong new base V8 engine. On the other hand, the redesigned 2011 and 2013 Heavy Duty (HD) versions are much more refined than the 2014 Silverado Sierra, even though the HD versions may have a less accommodating, less comfortable crew cab.

SAFETY: NHTSA gives 2003-10 models five star crash protection scores with four stars awarded for rollover resistance. Earlier models also had above average scores through 2000. *All 2010 1500 models:* IIHS gave frontal crash protection and head restraints a "Good" rating. IIHS gave side crash protection a "Marginal" rating. Many owner reports of mediocre braking. If you are a short driver, you may not be able to see over the raised hood.

ALERT! The 2013 Rams arrived late to the market and haven't been tested much, nor have the dealer mechanics had much experience with the new hi-tech features. Smart buyers will wait for a better-built second-series Ram that will reach dealer lots in late spring, or buy the much improved 2014 Ram. Be wary of "pain in the neck" front head restraints. They could be a dealbreaker. Check them out during the test drive, or rent the truck for a weekend. Look for paint flaws, particularly on the hood.

Ram 1500/2500/3500 Pickup Profile

	2004	2005	2006	2007	2008	2009	2010	2011	2012
Used Values ($)									
1500 ST 2X4	4,000	4,500	5,000	5,500	6,500	7,500	9,000	11,500	14,500
1500 ST 4x4	5,000	—	7,500	7,000	8,500	10,000	11,500	14,500	17,500
2500 ST 2X4	5,500	6,000	7,000	8,000	10,000	12,000	14,000	16,000	18,000
2500 ST 4x4	—	7,500	9,000	10,000	12,000	14,500	16,000	18,500	21,000
Recommended	★1	★2	★2	★2	★2	★2	★2	★2	★2
Reliability	★1	★1	★1	★1	★1	★1	★1	★2	★3

SECRET WARRANTIES, INTERNAL BULLETINS: 2006-08—Horizontal paint etching. **2007**—Automatic transmission torque converter shuddering. Transmission defaults to neutral. **2009**—Steering wander may require installation of a steering shaft kit. Under a special warranty extension campaign, Dodge will replace free of charge torn seat cushion covers or seat cushions. Hood squeaking, creaking sound on turns or when passing over bumps. AC hissing noise. **2009-10**—Quad rear doors won't lock or unlock. Water leaks diagnostic tips. Under Customer Satisfaction Notification K23, Dodge will replace a corroded front bumper for free. No mileage or time limitations have been imposed. Another Campaign will tackle poor AC performance by replacing defective air door actuators free of charge. **2009-11**—Excessive steering wheel vibration on the 1500 model may require a new steering wheel assembly under warranty, says Chrysler. Fuel filler housing pops out of opening. A wind noise from the front door area can be silenced by adding more soundproofing material under warranty. **2011-12**—Excessive transfer case noise when shifting from Drive to Neutral can be remedied by installing a revised separator plate into the transmission valve body (reimbursable under warranty, says TSB# 21-010-12, issued July 16, 2012).

JEEP

All Jeeps are rated Below Average buys because they are unreliable and aren't very durable. Apart from fire-prone fuel tanks and biodegradable bodies, the entire Jeep lineup for the past several decades has been bedeviled by powertrain, fuel system, electrical system, brakes, suspension, and fit and finish deficiencies. Depreciation? A 2009 Grand Cherokee Laredo that cost $41,245 new, now sells for $14,500. OUCH!

WRANGLER	★★

RATING: Below Average (all years). The *Dirty Harry* of off-road prowess; an unreliable, macho *poseur* as a daily commuter (*"Was that five head gaskets or six, punk?"*). Jeeps are all about cachet and cash. The cash is needed to pay for the biodegradable 3.6L V6 repairs and to correct the Salvador Dali-inspired fit and finish. Yet, in spite of its dated design, the Wrangler is one of the most off-road-capable Jeeps ever made. That's it. The little SUV falls far short when driven on-road. **Road performance:** This entry-level Jeep's impressive "bush" performance is taken away by its overall poor reliability and dangerous on-road performance, highlighted by the powertrain suddenly jumping out of gear when the outside temperature drops, or the steering and suspension going into a "death wobble" after passing over potholes or speed bumps. Plus, its short wheelbase, loud and porous cabin, and mediocre highway performance makes the Wrangler annoying at best as a daily commuter and outright uncomfortable as a road trip vehicle. The V6 engine is powerful enough for most chores, but fuel economy suffers with the automatic 5-speed. Handling is compromised by vague steering and low cornering limits

Prices and Specs

Prices (Firm): *two-door Sport:* $19,345, *four-door Unlimited:* $24,445, *two-door Sahara:* $26,245, *two-door Rubicon:* $29,245, *four-door Unlimited Rubicon:* $34,495 **Freight:** $1,400 **Powertrain (Rear-drive / part-time/full-time AWD):** Engine: 3.6L V6 (285 hp); Transmissions: 6-speed man., 5-speed auto. **Dimensions/capacity (base):** Passengers: 2/3; Wheelbase: 116 in.; H: 71/W: 74/L: 173 in.; Headroom F/R: 5.5/5 in.; Legroom F/R: 41/28 in.; Cargo volume: 34.5 cu. ft.; Fuel tank: 70L/regular; Tow limit: 3,500 lb.; Load capacity: 850 lb.; Turning circle: 43 ft.; Ground clearance: 8 in.; Weight: *Sport:* 3,849 lb., *Rubicon:* 4,165 lb.

(standard stability control is a plus). A rigid frame makes for a stiff, jiggly ride and clumsy handling. **Strong points:** The Wrangler comes with a roomy, plush cabin with plenty of headroom. Unlimited models with four doors have 1.6 inches more legroom in the back and lots of cargo space. **Weak points:** All Wranglers sell at their full list price and are not likely to be discounted by much as the year progresses. Getting in and out takes some acrobatics and patience; the two-door interior isn't very uncomfortable; and there is only a small amount of cargo room in the back. **Major redesign:** 1997 and 2007. A 2014 model redesign is rumoured. If it is redesigned, stay away the first year. **Highway/city fuel economy:** Fuel economy? Much less than advertised (don't believe government-posted figures). *3.6L V6 man.:* 9.3/12.7 L/100 km. *3.6L V6 auto.:* 9.5/12.6 L/100 km. **Best alternatives:** Honda CR-V or Element, Hyundai Tucson, Nissan Xterra, Subaru Forester, and Toyota RAV4. Remember, none of these other models do as well as the Wrangler off-road.

SAFETY: 2007-14 models not crash-tested by NHTSA, though rollover resistance predicted to be average from 1997 through 2014. 1997-2006 models earned four-star scores, but driver frontal crash safety was given only two stars on 1994-1996 models.

ALERT! Owners report that the Wrangler's off-road prowess is compromised by poor original equipment tires and thin body panels. Although there's not much you can do about the body panels, *www.tirerack.com* can give you invaluable, unbiased tips on the best and cheapest tires for the kind of driving you intend to do.

Wrangler SUV Profile

	2004	2005	2006	2007	2008	2009	2010	2011	2012
Used Values ($)									
X/Sport	4,000	4,500	5,000	5,500	6,500	8,500	11,500	14,000	16,500
Sahara	—	—	6,000	6,500	9,000	12,000	16,500	19,500	22,500
Rubicon	5,000	5,500	6,500	7,000	10,000	13,600	17,500	21,000	24,500
Unlimited TJ, X, Sport	5,500	6,500	7,500	8,000	8,500	11,000	14,500	18,500	20,500
Recommended	★	★	★	★	★	★	★	★	★
Reliability	★	★	★	★	★	★	★	★	★

SECRET WARRANTIES, INTERNAL BULLETINS: 2007-09—Excessive steering vibration when passing over rough surfaces. Difficult fuel fill. Wind noise and water leaks from the windshield/soft top header. **2007-10**—Manual transmission pops out of First gear when upshifting. Hard starts, no-start, or dead battery. Special Campaign #J34 for free replacement of the steering damper hardware. **2008-10**—Warranty is extended to 7 years/70,000 miles to cover the replacement of the automatic transmission cooler line on vehicles equipped with a 3.8L engine. **2009-10**—Transmission fluid may overheat; a chime will be installed to alert the driver when this happens. This is a Customer Satisfaction Program, not a safety recall. **2010-11**—Chrysler will repair, free of charge, a noisy right rear door latch. **2011-12**—Countermeasures to eliminate engine misfiring. Manual transmission pops out of gear (TSB #21-002-12, issued January 12, 2012). Light to moderate paint imperfections. Water leak onto front floor.

GRAND CHEROKEE ★★

RATING: Below Average, for two important reasons: First, during the past decade the Grand Cherokee has been beset with chronic automatic transmission, engine head gasket, brake and electrical system defects in addition to abysmally bad fit and finish. Take, for example, the fact that Jeep placed 27th out of 33 brands in J.D. Power and Associates' ranking of initial quality released in June 2010. Second, this year's 2014 model is mostly a carryover of the 2012, except for a diesel option, which is noted for some of the same powertrain and body deficiencies decried in the past. *Lemon-Aid* has learned from 42 years of rating Chrysler cars and trucks

220

Prices (Firm): *Summit Laredo:* $37,995, *Laredo X:* $43,185, Summit *Limited:* $47,195, *Summit Overland:* $50,195 **Freight:** $1,400 **Powertrain (Rear-drive/part-time/full-time AWD):** Engines: 3.0L V6 turbodiesel (240 hp), 3.6L V6 (290 hp), 5.7L V8 (360 hp), 6.4L V8 (470 hp) Transmissions: 5-speed auto., 6-speed auto., 8-speed auto. **Dimensions/capacity (base):** Passengers: 2/3; Wheelbase: 114.8 in.; H: 69.4/W: 84.8/L: 189.8 in.; Headroom F/R: 4/3.5 in.; Legroom F/R: 41/28 in.; Cargo volume: 36.3 cu. ft.; Fuel tank: 80L/regular; Tow limit: 3,500-7,200 lb. (the higher towing capacity applies to the 4x2 model); Load capacity: 850 lb.; Turning circle: 37.1 ft.; Ground clearance: 11.1 in.; Weight: *Sport:* 3,849 lb., *Rubicon:* 4,165 lb.

that revamped Chrysler models can be much more problematic than previous models, so don't be too quick to jump on the redesigned 2014 bandwagon. **Road performance:** The Grand Cherokee is built on a proven rear drive unibody platform that the Mercedes-Benz ML has used for years; when combined with front and rear independent suspension systems, the result is enhanced on-road handling and comfort. A small turning circle enhances maneuverability. On the other hand, the 3.6L V6 has to be pushed to move this heavy SUV and its lack of midrange torque makes for scary passing maneuvers. The 5-speed transmission often goes gear-hunting over hilly terrain. Low-range gearing for off-road driving is lacking on most models. **Strong points:** The 290 hp Pentastar V6 boosts power with 80 horses more than the previous 3.8L V6 engine. The cabin is quiet and well-appointed with high-quality materials. **Weak points:** Grand Cherokees sell at a premium; a good reason to wait until mid-2014 for prices to settle down. The engine, automatic transmission, and electrical system have shown some quality glitches in each first-series production. Fit and finish is quite poor (especially the doors), and the touch screen radio isn't user-friendly. Owners report engine surges when brakes are applied and that the soft brake pedal, doesn't provide much stopping power until halfway through its travel. The 6-speed manual transmission sometimes pops out of gear and the automatic transmission slips erratically in and out of Second gear, suddenly downshifts, or leaks fluid. **Major redesign:** 1999, 2005, and 2011. The 2014 Grand Cherokee offers an EcoDiesel V6 engine that, according to U.S. tests, gives 22-30 mpg in city/highway use; the Selecterrain system receives multiple upgrades on four-wheel-drive Grand Cherokees, and the much-praised Uconnect infotainment system is offered for the first time. **Highway/city fuel economy:** *3.6L:* 8.9/13L/100 km. *5.7L:* 10.6/15.7 L/100 km. No independent diesel data, yet. **Best alternatives:** Don't waste your money on the short-lived 2013 version; a second-series 2014 or later diesel would be a better investment. This will give the factory more time to get the 2014 redesign bugs fixed. If you don't have the patience to wait, consider a Honda CR-V or Element, Hyundai Tucson, Subaru Forester, and Toyota RAV4. Remember, none of these other models can follow the Grand Cherokee off-road, but on the other hand, they won't be following it to the repair bay, either.

SAFETY: NHTSA gives the 2011-14 models five stars for side-impact crash protection, four stars for side protection, and three stars for rollover resistance. The 4x4 model has a similar rating, except that rollover resistance was a bit better, at four stars. 2001-04s were given a "marginal" rating for frontal offset protection and three stars for full-frontal crashworthiness. The IIHS awarded a "Good" ranking for roof strength, frontal offset, side, and head restraint effectiveness.

ALERT! 1993-98 models may have fire-prone fuel tanks: Chrysler will install a free hitch, if needed. Safety advocates say the hitch will be ineffective. Make sure the headlights provide sufficient illumination during a night road test; many dissatisfied drivers wish they had tested this before buying their Grand Cherokee.

Grand Cherokee Profile

	2004	2005	2006	2007	2008	2009	2010	2011	2012
Used Values ($)									
North/Laredo V6	3,000	4,000	6,000	9,000	12,000	15,000	20,000	22,500	26,500
V8	—	—	—	—	—	—	21,000	24,000	28,000
SRT8	—	—	8,000	11,500	14,500	19,500	26,500	—	42,500
Limited V6	3,500	4,500	7,500	10,500	14,500	19,500	26,500	29,000	34,000
Overland V6	—	—	7,500	12,000	15,000	20,500	—	33,500	38,500
Recommended	★	★	★	★	★	★	★	★	★
Reliability	★	★	★	★	★	★	★	★	★

SECRET WARRANTIES, INTERNAL BULLETINS: 2011—A shudder or bump felt through the steering wheel under moderate braking and/or driving over rough roads may require a new intermediate steering column shaft covered by warranty. **2011-12**—Excessive transfer case noise when shifting from Drive to Neutral can be remedied by installing a revised separator plate into the transmission valve body (reimbursable under warranty, says TSB# 21-010-12, issued July 16, 2012). **2012**—Troubleshooting engine misfiring and power loss. Engine power sag, hesitation may be fixed by replacing the power control module. A shudder felt when accelerating, decelerating, or when coasting may require only the reflashing or changing of the drivetrain control module. Power liftgate won't open or close. A rear shock absorber buzz, squeak, or rattle may signal the need to replace both rear upper shock mounts. Excessive exhaust noise can be corrected by replacing the exhaust pipe/catalytic converter assembly. Light to moderate paint imperfections.

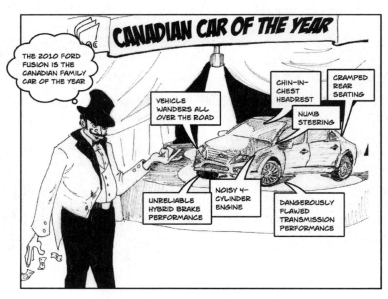

Sadly, automakers have had to "pay to play" the Car of the Year game.

EcoBoost Stalling

Ford Motor Co. is being sued by three vehicle owners in Ohio because of alleged defects in the automaker's six-cylinder EcoBoost engine. According to the lawsuit, the 3.5-liter V6 EcoBoost engine "contained serious latent design, manufacturing, or assembly defects" that cause vehicles to shake, misfire and rapidly lose power.

Ford knew of the problem, the suit says, because it published several technical service bulletins and suggested potential fixes to dealers covering the F-150.

The V6 EcoBoost has been offered in the 2010-13 Ford Flex crossover and Taurus SHO, 2010-13 Lincoln MKT crossover and MKS sedan, 2011-13 F-150 pickup, and 2013 Ford Explorer Sport.

The National Highway Traffic Safety Administration has received nearly 100 complaints about the engine, the lawsuit states.

VINCE BOND JR.
AUTOMOTIVE NEWS, MAY 15, 2013

Less Quality, More Sales

It doesn't make sense. J.D. Power and Associates' 2012 Initial Quality Study (IQS) blasts Ford over its poor quality and complicated MyFord Touch and MyLincoln Touch electronic systems and other controls. The company's dual clutch automatic transmission has also been singled out as being balky and unpredictable. Owners say the Fiesta and Focus Power Shift automatic transmission is particularly troublesome and are lodging class action lawsuits alleging that Ford's C-Max and Fusion hybrid fuel savings claims are as believable as Senator Mike Duffy's expense reports. And, to cap it all off, the Ford's Lincoln division is on life-support.

Bye-bye Town Car. You were too good for Lincoln.

Yet, the automaker has had record sales for 2013 with customers standing in line to buy new Fiesta and Focus compacts. Evidently, there is such a pent up demand for new cars that shoppers aren't as concerned about safety, quality, or reliability as they are about price, fuel economy, and cachet.

FORD SYNC(R) – UNABLE TO LOCATE VEHICLE, GPS ISSUES
SERVICE BULLETIN NO.: 12-11-2   DATE: 11/15/12

GLOBAL POSITION SATELLITE MODULE – TRAFFIC DIRECTIONS AND INFORMATION/ NAVIGATION – UNABLE TO LOCATE VEHICLE – BUILT ON OR BEFORE 5/14/2012.

FORD: 2010-211 Fiesta, Focus, Mustang; 2010-12 Fusion, Taurus; 2010 Explorer Sport Trac; 2010-11 Explorer; 2010-12 E-Series, Edge, Escape, Expedition, F-150, F-Super Duty, Flex; **LINCOLN:** 2010-12 MKS, MKZ; 2010-11 MKX; 2010-12 Navigator; **MERCURY (U.S.):** 2010 Milan, Mountaineer; and 2010-11 Mariner.

ISSUE: Some 2010-12 vehicle equipped with SYNC non-navigation and MyFord Touch or MyLincoln Touch and built on or before 5/14/2012 may exhibit a voice prompt indicating SYNC Service's Traffic, Directions or Information (TDI) is unable to locate the vehicle or a Global Position System (GPS) issue is present. Vehicles equipped with MyFord Touch/ MyLincoln Touch and Navigation may exhibit a screen message indicating navigation stopped functioning contact your dealer, GPS has red strike through X, Navigation unavailable is displayed in the upper right hand corner of the display screen, and/or the last known vehicle location may be displayed instead of current location.

"For Pete's sake, honey, will you ask someone for directions."

Some of Ford's latest model offerings fall far short of the company's carefully orchestrated hype. Highway performance is much less than promised, head restraints are poorly designed, interior instruments and controls are far from user-friendly, high-tech communication and navigation gizmos are needlessly complicated, and quality control is woefully inadequate (see the reports on "lag and lurch" self-destructing manual transmissions in the Mustang section and failure-prone automatics in the Fusion ratings). Yet, Ford's products represent the best of what was formerly called the Detroit Big Three – shows how far the benchmark has been lowered.

In the past decade, powertrain defects, faulty suspensions and steering components, and premature brake wear and brake failures were the primary concerns of Ford owners. The company's engine and automatic transmission deficiencies affected most of its products, and these deficiencies have existed since the early '80s, judging by *Lemon-Aid* reader reports, NHTSA complaints, confidential Ford internal documents, and technical service bulletins. And we aren't talking about mechanical and electronic components only; Ford's fit and finish has traditionally also remained far below Japanese and South Korean standards.

Ford's much ballyhooed, redesigned 2011 Explorer handles less like a truck and provides better fuel economy now that Ford has replaced its body-on-frame platform with a car-like unibody chassis. Unfortunately, the reworked Explorer also brought with it serious performance and quality control deficiencies decried by both *Consumer Reports* and *Motor Trend*. Surprisingly, *Consumer Reports* gave the Explorer an easier time than *Motor Trend* did in this May 2011 article:

> We didn't like driving the Explorer very much. . . . Massive, freaky, comical torque steer (the vehicle pulls to one side when accelerating). The big Ford also rode worse than much of the competition. . . . We also had issues with the seating position . . . the chassis needs some refinement. . . . Car feels wobbly at speed—not confidence inspiring. . . . The MyFord Touch system shut down for about 60 seconds, taking away all climate, stereo, phone, and navigation controls.

Consumer Reports' June 2011 edition confirmed many of *MT*'s findings: *CR* points out that the 6-speed automatic transmission shifts slowly at times, the engine is noisy, handling is mediocre with excessive body roll when cornering, and the slow steering transmits little road feedback. Interior ergonomics and comfort apparently wasn't Ford's "Job 1" with the reworked Explorer, either. The driving position is described as "flawed," with limited footroom, a poorly placed footrest, and pedals that are mounted too close together. Front seat cushions felt narrow and too short; rear cushions too hard, too low, or too short. *CR* rated fit and finish as average, and the MyFord Touch system was judged to be overly complicated, with the Sync-voice-command system often misunderstanding simple commands.

EcoBoost

Get used to the term "EcoBoost." It is used by Ford to describe a new family of turbocharged and direct-injected 4-cylinder and 6-cylinder gasoline engines that deliver power and torque consistent with larger displacement powerplants. Engines using the EcoBoost design are touted to be 20 percent more fuel-efficient than naturally aspirated engines. Ford says the EcoBoost's power output and fuel efficiency rival hybrid and diesel engine technology, and the company intends on using it extensively in future vehicle applications.

Unfortunately Ford's EcoBoost engine may be more of an empty "eco-boast" that an authentic fuel-saver, as *Consumer Reports* dubs the turbocharged system:

> Its 25 mpg overall places it among the worst of the crop of recently redesigned family sedans. The Toyota Camry, Honda Accord, and Nissan Altima, all with conventional 2.4- or 2.5-liter four-cylinder engines, get an additional 2, 5, and 6 mpg, respectively. And all accelerate more quickly.

Owners claim in several lawsuits that Ford knew the Fusion and C-Max hybrids would never match the glowing mileage figures hyped by the automaker (*editorial. autos.msn.com/2013-ford-c-max-hybrid-review):*

> I thought my 2013 C-MAX would be a Prius Killer? NOT! As a returning Ford buyer I feel deceived. I want to support US companies and US jobs. What was Ford thinking when they published 47/ 47/47 estimates? Based on the advertised EPA estimates, I would have been ok with low 40's but 28-33 mpg is not even in the ballpark. This is not an issue about EPA testing standards, but rather an issue about setting false customer expectations in order to promote sales. Ford's "47MPG" marketing campaign tarnished what should have been the roll out of a truly remarkable vehicle, the C-MAX. Real world MPG estimates should have been promoted in the mid-30's.

Ford may yet improve overall quality by joining the competition and shifting its product mix to smaller vehicles that use more-reliable Japanese components and are assembled more cheaply in Mexico or offshore. Like most major automakers, the company is copying more fuel-efficient European designs, importing some models directly from Europe, then transferring their production to North America. By selling and building worldwide models that are virtually identical, Ford can keep production costs down and quickly get to market better-performing, more fuel-efficient models, and higher-quality vehicles.

Sure, Ford still makes some worthwhile vehicles like the Mustang and F-150 series and its quality control is still a bit better than Chrysler's, but the benchmark is low.

Fuel economy at all costs. This includes engine and transmission malfunctions, a cramped interior, and poor overall reliability. Buy a Honda Fit or Hyundai Accent, instead.

RATING: Below Average (2011-14). Available as a five-door hatchback or sedan, Ford is importing this little car from Europe until it can transfer production to North America. Interestingly Ford has never imported a European-derived vehicle that went on to become a success in North America. (Remember the Cortina? The Merkur XR4TI?) Poor quality, performance, and servicing afflicted most of these imports and sent them packing back to Europe. Will the Fiesta repeat history? Don't be the first to find out. **Road performance:** Good driving dynamics with responsive steering, easily-modulated brakes and nimble, better-than-average handling. Base engine could use more power for passing and merging and there's a choppy ride on uneven roadways. The PowerShift automatic transmission shifts erratically and unexpectedly. The car accelerates best with the manual gearbox. **Strong points:** Stylish with plenty of high-tech interior features and great gas mileage with a manual gearbox. There is also just adequate space in the front of this five-seater for the driver and passenger (the Honda Fit provides more room for passengers and cargo). Little noise intrudes into the well-appointed cabin. A tilt and telescopic steering wheel, height-adjustable driver's seat, and capless fuel filler also come with the car. A relatively high ground clearance reduces "belly drag" in the snow (an inch higher than the Toyota Yaris and VW Jetta). **Weak points:** Owners report that the automatic transmission cuts gas mileage by almost 15 percent. Rear passenger space is cramped; even Honda's Fit has more storage space than the Fiesta five-door hatchback. Drivers find the head restraints force a chin-to-chest driving position that's so uncomfortable they're removing the head restraints altogether. Audio control takes getting used to. Seats could use a bit more lumbar and thigh bolstering. Armrest is too far forward on the Fiesta's door. Rear seatbacks may not lock into position, allowing any cargo to fly forward as a deadly projectile in a sudden stop. Limited cargo and rear seat space. The dash houses angled keys that look good but lack functionality. Owners report following failures: Airbags failed to deploy; fuel leaked under the car; oil pan, water pump, and front crank seal leaks; engine stalling and surging along with poor transmission performance; electrical shorts; excessive steering-wheel vibration; noisy brakes; and various fit and finish deficiencies (for example, door panel fell apart). **Major redesign:** The 2012-14 models aren't very different from each other; for sport car thrills, the new 2014 ST is fast and smooth. Wait until spring models arrive to give Ford a few extra months to fix the ST's factory-related bugs. **Highway/city fuel economy:** *Man.:* 5.3/7.1 L/100 km. *SFE auto:* 4.9/6.8 L/100 km. *Auto.:* 5.1/6.9 L/100 km. **Best alternatives:** GM Sonic, Honda Civic (except 2012) or Fit, Hyundai Accent or Elantra, Kia Rio, Mazda2 or Mazda3, and Nissan Versa. The Ford Focus is the better buy, if you must buy a Ford. Its fuel economy is similar, and you get a more comfortable ride with more room.

SAFETY: A nice array of safety features and airbags are everywhere. All Fiestas earned four stars for frontal crash protection and rollover resistance and garnered five stars for side crashworthiness from NHTSA. IIHS gave it top marks in frontal offset, side, and rear impact occupant protection, as well as protection from excessive roof intrusion into the cabin.

ALERT! Brake and accelerator pedals are placed too close together; be wary of the front head restraints:

> The headrest is causing me to have headaches due to the forward leaning position of the headrest. I have tried all the situations of the seat and it is the same for all of them. I am 5'2" and in my research have found most other short people have the same issue

SECRET WARRANTIES, INTERNAL BULLETINS: 2011—Customer Satisfaction Program 11B31 (secret warranty) calls for a free upgraded clutch replacement on the DPS6 automatic transmission. Engine stalling and surging along with poor transmission performance may be due to a malfunctioning transmission control module. Automatic transmission grind or rattle noise in 2nd, 4th, or Reverse gear. Poor or no engine start, or transmission engagement. Engine block heater coolant leakage

Prices and Specs (2011-14 Profile)

New 2013-14 Prices (Firm): *Sedan S:* $14,000, *Sedan SE:* $15,999, *Sedan ST:* $23,024, *Hatchback SE:* $16,001, *Titanium:* $19,000; **2012:** *Sedan S:* $9,500, *Sedan SE:* $12,000, *Hatchback SE:* $12,500, *Sedan SEL:* $14,000, *Hatchback SES:* $14,500; **2011:** *Sedan S:* $8,500, *Sedan SE:* $10,500, *Hatchback SE:* $11,000, *Sedan SEL:* $12,500, *Hatchback SES:* $12,500 **Freight:** $1,750 **Powertrain (Front-drive):** Engine: 1.5 3-cylinder (123 hp), 1.6L DOHC 4 (120 hp); Transmissions: 5-speed man., 6-speed manumatic. **Dimensions/capacity:** Passengers: 2/3; Wheelbase: 98 in.; H: 58 /L: 173.6/W: 66.8 in.; Headroom F/R: 5/1.5 in.; Legroom F/R: 42.2/31.2 in.; Cargo volume: 12.8 cu. ft.; Fuel tank: 45L/regular; Tow limit: Not recommended; Turning circle: 34.4 ft.; Ground clearance: 6.7 in.; Weight: 2,578 lb.

and spillover into the spark plug well. Some Fiestas may exhibit an oil leak at the cylinder head oil galley located behind the exhaust cam phaser. On Fiestas equipped with manual windows, the window glass may suddenly drop due to a defective window regulator (a warranty item, for sure). AC condensation may collect on the front passenger floor. **2011-12**—Automatic transmission fluid leak from the clutch housing will require a major repair covered by the base warranty (TSB #12-4-6, issued April 20, 2012). Some 2011-12 Fiestas vehicles equipped with a manual transaxle may exhibit a transmission disengagement from reverse gear on high tip-in RPM (2500-3000 RPM). Steering column pop, clunk, knock during slow-speed turns. **2011-13**—AC lack of heat; blower motor frozen in cold weather. This may be caused by snow entering through the cowl top area. The snow melts and the water enters the blower motor and refreezes during a below freezing overnight soak. The blower motor fuse at location F4 in the Power Distribution Box may also be open (repair covered under the base warranty).

FOCUS

RATING: Not Recommended (2012-14); Above Average (2011); Average (2005-10); Not Recommended (2000-04). **Road performance:** This small car is fun to drive and a fairly good highway performer when the transmission is working properly – which isn't often. Like the Fiesta's similar transmission, overall performance both on the highway and in town is hampered by a failure-prone, poorly designed, and often badly-calibrated PowerShift automatic that stumbles and surges. Its deficiencies compromise safety and fuel economy and lead to white-knuckle driving when merging or when slowing down. Nevertheless, the car usually gives a smooth, supple ride, shows excellent handling and road holding, and provides a commanding view of the highway. **Strong points:** Stylish, with a well-appointed interior and plenty of high-tech options. Very reliable from 2005-11, which is all the more surprising because the 2000-04 models were such stinkers. **Weak points:** Infotainment controls are distracting, uncooperative, and glitch-prone. Backseat legroom is minimal. What a difference a few years make; good thing *Lemon-Aid* is an annual guide, because the redesigned 2012-13 Focus has been transformed back into its lemony former state. 2011 Focus posted only 13 safety incidents and *Lemon-Aid* recommended the car. Not this year. The 2012 has attracted 210 complaints (100 would be average), and the 2013 has already recorded 54 complaints – too many, too

Prices and Specs

Price (Negotiable): *Sedan S:* $14,869, *Sedan SE:* $16,219, *Hatchback:* $17,020, *SEL:* $18,444, *Hatchback:* $19,245, *Titanium:* $21,114, *Hatchback:* $21,648, *Electric:* $41,199 **Freight:** $1,500 **Powertrain (Front-drive):** Engine: 2.0L DOHC 4 (160 hp), Electric motor (143 hp); Transmissions: 5-speed man., 6-speed auto. **Dimensions/capacity:** Passengers: 2/3; Wheelbase: 104.3 in.; H: 57.8/L: 178.5/W: 71.8 in.; Headroom N/A; Legroom F/R: 43.7/33.2 in.; Cargo volume: 13.2 cu. ft.; Fuel tank: 47L/ regular; Tow limit: Not recommended; Turning circle: 36 ft.; Weight: 2,970 lb.

early. The car's deficiencies are legion – mostly related to the powertrain (engine and transmission), brakes, electronics (infotainment) and electrical systems, steering, and fit and finish. **Major redesign:** 2000 and 2012 models. **Highway/city fuel economy:** *Man.:* 5.6/8 L/100 km. *Auto.:* 5.8/8.2 L/100 km. **Best alternatives:** Take a good look at the Honda Fit, Hyundai Accent or Elantra, and Mazda3 for exceptionable performance, cabin space to comfortably seat five, high fuel economy, and a reasonable price.

SAFETY: NHTSA gives the 2000-10 models three to five stars for frontal/side crashworthiness and rollover resistance. The 2000 and 2001 two-door models only got one star for passenger side-impact protection. IIHS gave its top rating ("Good") for frontal offset, rear, and side crash protection and roof strength. However, head restraints receive criticism for being angled downward too sharply, forcing the head to bend forward.

ALERT! Watch out for the driver head restraints pushing your chin to your chest, especially with the Recaro seats on the ST.

Focus Profile

	2004	2005	2006	2007	2008	2009	2010	2011	2012
Used Values ($)									
S	3,000	4,000	4,500	5,000	6,000	6,500	8,000	9,500	12,000
SE	3,500	4,500	5,000	5,500	6,500	7,500	9,500	12,000	14,000
SEL	—	—	—	—	—	8,500	11,000	13,000	15,500
Recommended	★	★	★	★	★	★	☆	☆	★
Reliability	★	★	★	★	★	★	★	☆	★

SECRET WARRANTIES, INTERNAL BULLETINS: 2008-10—Ignition key binds in the ignition cylinder. **2008-11**—An underbody squeak or creaking noise may be silenced by replacing the parking brake cables and routing eyelets (December 16, 2011, TSB #10-24-06). Paint damage? Here is Ford's "secret warranty" that will pay for a new paint job. Shh! (See Part Three, under the Art of Complaining, Mediation and Arbitration.) **2009-10**—A fix for inoperative door locks. **2011**—Ford says excessive road wander, steering drift, or uneven rear tire wear may require the installation of a new right rear lower control arm (January 25, 2011, TSB #11-1-1). **2012**—AC Engine controls/drivability issues. Automatic transmission controls – various drivability concerns. Free transmission clutch replacement. Steering wander. Front-end crunching, creaking when passing over bumps. MyFord Touch glitches. Loss of steering power assist. Erratic fuel gauge readings. Fixing a depression in the hood's surface.

PAINT DEGRADATION/ROAD ABRASION

BULLETIN NO.: 10-15-6   **DATE: AUGUST 16, 2010**

2008–11 Focus

ISSUE: Some 2008–11 Focus vehicles may experience paint damage or road abrasion on the rocker panel and on the side of the vehicle located slightly ahead of the rear tires on both 2 door and 4 door models. Rocker Panel, 1/4 panel, dog leg and/or rear door, dependent on model. This has been reported in geographical areas that commonly experience snow and ice conditions and use various forms of traction enhancers.

ACTION: Follow the Service Procedure steps to correct the condition.

NOTE: Per the warranty and policy manual paint damage caused by conditions such as chips, scratches, dents, dings, road salt, stone chips or other acts of nature are not covered under the warraty. However, paint abrasion at the dog leg area due to the above circumstances is a unique condition on the focus and, as a result, repairs are eligible for basic warranty coverage.

FUSION/LINCOLN MKZ

RATING: *Fusion:* Below Average (all years). *MKZ:* Above Average (all years). A fusion of Dr. Jekyll and Mr. Hyde. Lincoln's Dr. Jekyll prescribes good acceleration and fair handling; steering that is tight, precise, and vibration-free; and 4-cylinder and V6 engines that are adequate, but not as thrifty or dependable as presented. The Fusion's Mr. Hyde gives you a 19th century automatic transmission that's cursed; a dysfunctional infotainment system; a car that runs off in all directions; and braking that's far scarier than anything Robert Louis Stevenson could imagine. **Road performance:** *Fusion:* Good acceleration and fair handling; steering is tight, precise, and vibration free; and the 4-cylinder and V6 engines borrowed from Mazda are competent. Added rigidity and additional chassis tweaking have resulted in a car that will seat five passengers (four in comfort) and corner reasonably well. On 2013s, AWD is again available, a fuel-saving engine stop-start system is standard on 1.6L models, and hybrid buyers get a new 2.0L. An Atkinson-cycle 4-cylinder replaced the outgoing 2.5L. The high-performance Fusion ST uses a refined version of the EcoBoost 2.0L powerplant. Some negatives: Fusion carries a dangerously flawed automatic transmission; brake performance is unreliable; and the car tends to wander all over the road. *MKZ:* The Lincoln accelerates and handles without a hitch. Ride comfort and interior amenities are average. **Strong points:** Stylish. Overall reliability (except for the automatic transmission) is average with the Lincoln MKZ. It can run on one or both of its power sources and requires no plug-in charging. **Weak points:** Cramped rear seating and tilted-forward head restraints can be pure torture; owners say the front seats are painful to sit in due to a hard block within the seat. An accident survivor says Lincoln airbags failed to deploy, and both front seatbacks collapsed in a rear-ender. Fusion owners say the knee airbag restricts brake pedal access and the brakes are too weak. Chronic automatic transmission failures and erratic shifting with the Fusion: Sudden stalling when the car is underway; Hybrid brake pedal is mounted too close to the accelerator pedal. Fuel economy estimates (Hybrid included) can't be trusted. **Major redesign:** *Fusion:* 2006 and 2010 models; *MKZ:* 2006. NHTSA recorded 1018 safety-related complaints on the redesigned 2010 Fusion when 150 would be normal, the 2011 model is at the 266 complaints mark, while the 2012 only has posted 87 complaints. The 2013s? They account for a respectable 24 safety-related incidents – well below the 50 complaint-per-year average. Hopefully, this shows Ford has a handle on quality control after seven years of building trash. Only ten complaints have been posted relative to the 2010 Lincoln, while the 2013 gets by with only two safety complaints. **Highway/city fuel economy:** *2.5L:* 6.9/9.4 L/100 km. *Auto.:* 6.9/9.4 L/100 km. *3.0L:* 7.3/11.1 L/100 km. *3.0L AWD:* 7.8/11.8 L/100 km. *3.5L AWD:* 8.3/12.7 L/100 km. *Hybrid:* 5.4/4.6 L/100 km. **Best alternatives:** *Fusion:* Honda Accord, Hyundai Elantra or Tucson, Mazda6, and Toyota Camry. *MKZ:* Toyota Avalon, BMW 5-Series, and Mercedes-Benz E-Class.

SAFETY: NHTSA gives the 2006-14 Fusion/MKZ four to five stars for crashworthiness, although the 2011-12 MKZ earned only three stars for passenger side-impact protection. IIHS ranked the 2012 Fusion/MKZ "Good" for roof strength, frontal offset, side, and rear crash safety. Owners note poor visibility through the rear windshield.

ALERT! Super-fast depreciation that's an asset when buying used, but a liability come trade-in time.

Fusion/Lincoln MKZ Profile

	2006	2007	2008	2009	2010	2011	2012
Used Values ($)							
S	—	—	—	—	—	12,500	14,500
SE	4,500	6,000	7,000	9,500	11,000	14,500	16,500
SEL	5,000	6,500	7,500	10,500	11,500	15,500	18,500
SEL V6	6,000	7,000	8,000	10,500	13,500	17,500	20,500
HYBRID	—	—	—	—	14,400	18,500	21,500
MKZ	7,500	9,000	10,500	13,500	18,500	23,000	26,500
HYBRID	—	—	—	—	—	23,500	28,000
Recommended							
Fusion	★	★	★	★	★	★	★
MKZ	☆	☆	☆	☆	☆	☆	☆
Reliability							
Fusion	★	★	★	★	★	★	★
MKZ	☆4	☆4	☆4	☆4	☆4	☆5	☆5

SECRET WARRANTIES, INTERNAL BULLETINS: 2006-11—*Fusion, MKZ:* Vehicles may exhibit a single rear wheel stud fracture. A small number of rear brake rotors may have been manufactured with a wheel mounting face that is not flat. **2007-11**—*Fusion, MXZ:* Vehicles equipped with AWD systems and built on or before 8/13/2010 may exhibit a driveline vibration or a howl noise at highway speeds in cold temperatures. **2010**—*Fusion, MKZ:* Vehicles equipped with AWD may exhibit a shudder/chatter/vibration driveline sensation during a tight turn, or a thump/clunk noise on light acceleration. These symptoms may also occur under 40 mph (64 km/h), on tip-in, driving uphill, or towing under heavy acceleration. **2010-11**—Vehicles may experience a leaking/stuck canister purge valve. This condition may cause various intermittent driveability symptoms without any diagnostic trouble codes (DTC). The condition may also cause driveability symptoms with malfunction indicator light on with DTCs P144A, P2196, P2198, P1450, or P0456. **2011-12**—Sync infotainment functionality concerns. **2010-12**—Transmission fluid leak from the left hand halfshaft seal. This may be due to seal and/or bushing wear caused by the halfshaft surface finish.

MUSTANG ★★★★

Ford's 2011 rear-drive Mustang came with a much-needed 305 hp V6 engine that reignited the Camaro-Mustang battle.

RATING: Above Average (2011-14); Average (2001-10). The Mustang has been downgraded this year due to a flood of owner complaints relating to chronic manual and automatic transmission failures and "shift lag," "unfixable" electrical shorts, electronic module malfunctions, and rattling door panels. **Road performance:** Fast acceleration and impressive handling and braking. The V8 is a pocket rocket. The automatic transmission robs the engine of some of its performance; and the manual tranny is more responsive with crisp short-throws. **Strong points:** Base models come equipped with a host of safety, luxury, and convenience features. There's easy access into the interior and comfortable, upright front seating gives an excellent view of the road. Resale value is better than average. **Weak points:** A poorly performing manual transmission; an automatic transmission that "hunts" for the proper gear. Limited rear seat room, and poor quality fit and finish is unimpressive. **Major redesign:** 1994, 2005, and 2011. There was a huge horsepower boost on the base 2011 Mustang that turned a wimpish 210 hp V6 into a sizzling 305 hp. Incidentally, the 2011-12 GT500 ratcheted up performance by a few notches, too, with an aluminum-block engine that produced 550 hp. Other goodies on the 2011-12 Mustangs: A new limited-clip differential, larger brakes (taken from the 2010 GT), electronic power steering, a retuned suspension, stiffer rear anti-roll bars, and convertibles get less body flexing through the use of shock-tower braces. Another big change: Fold-down rear head restraints to improve visibility. **Highway/city fuel economy:** Fuel consumption is cut in the new 3.7L V6 (manual) to a frugal 6.9/11.2 L/100 km. *3.7L V6 auto.:* 6.4/10.7 L/100 km. *3.7L V6 convertible auto:* 7.8/11.9 L/100 km. *5.0L V8 man.:* 7.7/12.2 L/100 km. *5.0L V8 auto.:* 7.9/11.8 L/100 km. *5.4L V8 man.:* 8.8/14.5 L/100 km. **Best alternatives:** The resurrected Camaro is looking better and better as it boosts horsepower and offers more standard gear. Forget about the Dodge Challenger. Its 250 hp engine and heavy body take it out of the running. In summary, four fun and reliable competitors are the Chevrolet Camaro, Hyundai Genesis, 2012 Infiniti G25 or G27, and Mazda Miata. The special-edition Boss 302 Mustang will not be returning to the 2014 lineup.

SAFETY: NHTSA gives 2012-14 Mustangs four stars for overall crashworthiness and five stars for rollover resistance. 2001-10 models are rated five stars for frontal offset crash protection. 2001-04 models merited three stars for side-impact crashworthiness while the 2005-10 models earned four to five stars. The IIHS's rating is not as positive. Although frontal offset collision protection and head restraints were rated "Good," side crashworthiness was ranked only "Acceptable." Ironically, the convertible version, a car style that usually doesn't do well in crash tests, outperformed the two-door model with a "Good" rating in all three categories.

ALERT! Invest in an anti-theft system (one that includes an engine immobilizer) and good tires recommended by *www.tirerack.com*. Stay away from the notchy, erratic-shifting 6-speed Getrag manual transmission. It has performed poorly on 2011-12 models and the jury's still out on the 2013s (see *mustangsdaily.com/blog/2011/11/09/ford-responds-to-nhtsasinvestigation-of-the-mustangs-mt82-6-speed-transmission*).

Prices and Specs

Prices (Firm): *Coupe V6:* $23, 999, *V6 Premium:* $26,999, *V6 Premium Convertible:* $31,999, *Coupe GT:* $39,299, *Convertible GT:* $44,299, *Boss Coupe:* $48,799, *Shelby GT500:* $61,549, *Shelby GT500 Convertible:* $66,249 **Freight:** $1,500 **Powertrain (Rear-drive):** Engines: 3.7L V6 (305 hp), 5.0L V8 (402 hp), 5.0L V8 (444 hp), Supercharged 5.8L V8 (650 hp); Transmissions: 6-speed man., 6-speed auto. **Dimensions/ capacity:** Passengers: 2/2; Wheelbase: 107.1 in.; H: 55.8/L: 188.5/W: 73.9 in.; Headroom F/R: 5/1 in.; Legroom F/R: 39.5/23 in.; Cargo volume: 13 cu. ft.; Fuel tank: 60.1L/regular; Tow limit: 1,000 lb.; Load capacity: 700 lb.; Turning circle: 33.4 ft.; Ground clearance: 5.7 in.; Weight: 3,585 lb.

My 2012 Mustang GT was most likely totaled tonight when the transmission did not allow a shift into 5th gear. It slid into 3rd [gear] and caused the wheels to spin resulting in the car fishtailing and hitting a tree in the median.

Mustang Profile

	2004	2005	2006	2007	2008	2009	2010	2011	2012
Used Values ($)									
Coupe	4,500	6,000	7,000	9,000	10,500	11,500	14,500	17500	16,500
Coupe Premium	—	—	—	—	—	—	—	—	20,500
Convertible	6,500	7,500	8,500	12,000	13,000	14,500	17,500	21,500	24,500
Coupe GT	7,500	8,500	9,500	12,500	13,500	16,500	20,500	24,500	28,500
Convertible GT	8,500	10,500	13,000	15,500	17,000	20,000	24,500	29,500	34,000
Coupe Boss	—	—	—	—	—	—	—	—	38,500
Shelby Coupe	—	—	—	17,500	21,500	25,000	33,500	40,000	46,000
Coupe Cvt.	—	—	—	21,000	24,500	29,500	38,000	45,000	52,000
Recommended	☆	☆	☆	☆	☆	☆	☆	☆	☆
Reliability	☆	☆	☆	☆	☆	☆	☆	☆	☆

SECRET WARRANTIES, INTERNAL BULLETINS: 2005-12—May have a major fluid leak from the rear axle vent. **2011-12**—Sync voice recognition system may ignore your voice … "Hello, Hal, do you hear me?" Manual transmission may be difficult to shift in cold weather. Front-end suspension may produce a grunt, creak, chirp, or squeak. **2012**—Engine cold start-up ticking noises with 3.5L and 3.7L engines; the repairs require installing a camshaft kit that takes two hours of labour. Automatic transmission fluid leak from the bell housing. Squealing, squeaking rear brakes.

RATING: Above Average (2004-14). After its 2013 model overhaul, the 2014 arrives relatively unchanged. The decade-old Escape is a good buy, with many standard features and reasonably good overall reliability, but it was in dire need of the 2012 redesign to save fuel, provide a roomier interior, and improve ride and handling. The Escape Hybrid was dropped after the 2012 model year in favour of two direct-injected and turbocharged 1.6L and 2.0L EcoBoost 4-cylinder engines that use less fuel than the 2012 model. The 2013 model also features improved interior space and technology, and accessibility that tops the previous model and much of the competition. **Road performance:** Improved considerably. The new Escape is much more agile and comfortable now that it shares its underpinnings and the majority of its suspension components with the new Focus. **Strong points:** Peppy performance and a roomy, well-finished interior that provides lots of high-tech content and plenty of cargo space. *Hybrid:* Surprisingly for a vehicle that has such a complicated electrical system, there aren't any complaints concerning the hybrid components. One would normally expect to see, on average, 50 or so reports per model year. Owners do report some brake failures. **Weak points:** Owners are complaining EcoBoost engines don't always deliver the promised fuel savings and work poorly with automatic transmissions. **Major redesign:** 2001, 2008, and 2013 models. The 2013's powertrain is causing some headaches for first-year buyers stuck with factory-related snafus relating to the more refined EcoBoost engines, transmissions, and electronic modules. Actually, if you can afford to wait, get a 2014 version next summer. **Highway/city fuel economy:** *FWD, 2.5L:* 6.3/9.5 L/100 km. *FWD, 2.0L:* 6.7/9.5 L/100 km. *AWD, 2.0L:* 6.9/9.8 L/100 km. *2012 Hybrid:* 6.5/5.8 L/100 km. *Hybrid AWD:* 7.4/7 L/100 km. **Best alternatives:** Chevrolet Equinox, GMC Terrain, Honda CR-V, Hyundai Tucson, Kia Sportage, Mazda CX-5, Nissan Rogue, and Toyota RAV4. If you want a cheaper Escape twin, shop for a Mazda Tribute. Taken off the market in 2011 and morphed into the CX-5, the Tribute has all the attributes of the Escape, but with less fit and finish glitches.

SAFETY: NHTSA gave the 2013 and 2014 Escape five stars for side crashworthiness and four stars for side and rollover protection. 2011 and 2012 models earned Average crashworthiness scores (three stars) in all categories. The IIHS gave its top rating ("Good") to the 2009-13s for frontal offset protection; 2005-08 models were ranked "Acceptable," and the 2001-04s got a "Marginal"

Prices and Specs

Prices (Negotiable): *S FWD auto.:* $22,204, *SE FWD auto.:* $26,080, *SE 4×4 auto.:* $28,038, *SEL FWD man.:* $30,263, *4×4:* $32,221, *Titanium 4×4:* $35,514 **Freight:** $1,500 **Powertrain (Front-drive):** Engines: 1.6L 4-cyl. (173 hp), 2.0L 4-cyl. (231 hp), 2.5L 4-cyl. (168 hp); Transmission: 6-speed manumatic **Dimensions/capacity:** Passengers: 2/3; Wheelbase: 106 in.; H: 66.3/L: 178.1/W: 72 in.; Headroom F/R: 7/4.5 in.; Legroom F/R: 43/36 in.; Cargo volume: 35 cu. ft.; Fuel tank: 62L/regular; Tow limit: 2,000 lb.; Load capacity: 825 lb.; Turning circle: 37 ft.; Ground clearance: 7.9 in.; Weight: 3,598 lb.

rating. 2013 models were rated "Poor" in small overlap front crashes. Side crash scores were "Good" for 2001-13 Escapes with airbags; "Poor" for 2001-07 without airbags. Roof strength was rated "Marginal" on the 2008-12s, while the 2013 models excelled in the same test. Rear crash protection for 2005-08 models was judged "Acceptable" and 2009-13 Escapes merited a "Good" designation.

ALERT! Airbags fail to deploy, driver's seat collapses, or seat belt latch pops open; spontaneous windshield cracks and sunroof/side window shattering; distorted windshields; and liftgate glass exploded.

Escape Profile

Used Values ($)	2004	2005	2006	2007	2008	2009	2010	2011	2012
Escape XLS 4x2	3,000	3,500	4,000	4,500	5,500	—	—	—	—
4x4	3,500	4,000	4,500	5,500	—	—	—	—	—
XLT 4x2	4,000	4,500	5,500	6,000	7,000	7,500	10,500	13,000	17,500
4x4	4,500	5,000	6,000	6,500	7,500	8,500	11,500	14,500	19,000
Hybrid 4x2	—	5,000	6,000	6,500	7,500	10,000	15,000	22,000	26,500
4x4	—	6,000	7,000	7,500	8,500	12,000	16,000	23,500	28,000
Recommended	☆	☆	☆	☆	☆	☆	☆	☆	☆
Reliability	★	★	★	★	★	★	★	★	★

SECRET WARRANTIES, INTERNAL BULLETINS: 2008-09—Steering column pop, clunk when turning. All instrument cluster warning lights come on intermittently. Uncommanded liftgate opening or closing. Exterior heated mirror glass cracking. Front grille chrome peeling. **2008-10**—Steering wheel vibration can be remedied by installing a special damper Ford has devised. Special Ford fix for steering column pop or clunk. Windows squeak, grind when operated. Ignition key binds in ignition cylinder. Washer nozzles leak fluid onto the hood. Poor radio reception. **2009**—Ford Customer Satisfaction Program #10B15100419-001 (secret warranty) was set up April 19, 2010, to cover the cost of reprogramming the Power Control Module to reposition the solenoid regulator valve and eliminate bore wear. Mechanics are also empowered to replace the valve body, overdrive, and forward clutch. Ford says these measures are needed to increase the transmission's durability. If Ford says no to a free repair, ask them to apply the Emissions Warranty and threaten to go to small claims court with their own service bulletin as proof. Automatic transmission fluid leaks from the dipstick tube. Exterior door handles may be hard to open and may not be flush. **2009-10**—Automatic transmission sticks in Fifth gear (reprogram the power control module). A harsh-shifting automatic transmission requires the same remedy. Harsh engagements, shifts, or starts in Fifth gear from a start signal; there's an open signal in the output shaft speed sensor or the main control lead frame connector. Automatic transmission axle shaft seal fluid leak. AWD models may produce a vibration, rumble, and/or excessive exhaust noise in cold temperatures. **2009-11**—The rear axle may produce a "hoot" noise on light acceleration just before the 1-2 shift. **2012**—Transmission fluid leakage. .5L engine drone or rattle. 2.0L and 2.5L engines may constantly cause the MIL light to come on. Harsh or delayed shifts. Broken liftgate window. Water leaks from the liftgate area.

EXPLORER ★★

RATING: Below Average (2012-14); Not Recommended (2002-11). A middle of the pack, clumsy gas hog that's underpowered with the optional 4-cylinder EcoBoost engine, uses a dysfunctional MyFord Touch electronics interface, and is uncontrollable when the steering fails. Problematic quality control and poor highway performance hobble what should have been Ford's best SUV. **Road performance:** The Explorer's unibody construction cuts weight and gives car-like road manners to the SUV. It offers front-drive, AWD, or FWD that can be left engaged on dry pavement, and has a low-range gear for off-roading. Downshifts can be slow and abrupt, and braking may be hard to modulate on hills. **Strong points:** Average performance and reliability with the V6; an optional fuel-efficient turbocharged 4-cylinder is also available. Abundant high-tech features, and an upscale cabin. **Weak points:** Transaction prices are too high; bundled options are especially pricey; the longer you delay your purchase, the better quality you'll likely find as Ford tackles quality and design deficiencies that usually hang around for a few years on new designs. The most likely areas of concern for the next several years: Costly powertrain failures in addition to faulty brake, electrical system, steering and suspension components, and subpar body construction. We are also seeing electronic devices that are distracting and failure prone; a dash offering a confusing array of small buttons, crowded displays, and redundant controls; and head restraints that are literally a pain in the neck. The cabin is an adequate size, but it's not quite as roomy as what is offered by the Dodge Durango, Ford Flex, or Chevy Traverse. Cargo space is the smallest of the group, and the third row is somewhat cramped. **Major redesign:** 1995, 2002, 2006, and 2011 models.

Prices and Specs

Prices (Very Negotiable): *Base FWD:* $29,539, *EcoBoost FWD:* $30,399, *Base V6 4WD:* $32,769, *XLT V6 FWD:* $33,690, *XLT EcoBoost FWD:* $34,550, *XLT V6 4WD:* $37,360, *Limited V6 FWD:* $38,407, *Limited EcoBoost FWD:* $39,267, *Limited V6 4WD:* $42,077, *Sport:* $41,545 **Freight:** $1,500 **Powertrain (Front-drive /4×4/ AWD):** Engines: 2.0L 4-cyl. (240 hp), 3.5L V6 (290 hp); *Sport:* 3.5L twin-turbo V6 (350 hp); Transmission: 6-speed auto. **Dimensions/ capacity:** Passengers: 2/3/2; Wheelbase: 112.6 in.; H: 70.4/L: 197.1/W: 79 in.; Headroom F/R1/R2: 5.5/3,5/3 in.; Legroom F/R1/R2: 42/27/27 in.; Cargo volume: 42 cu. ft.; Fuel tank: 70.4L/regular; Tow limit: 5,000 lb.; Load capacity: 1,570 lb.; Turning circle: 39.2 ft.; Ground clearance: 7.6 ft.; Weight: 4,557 lb.

Highway/city fuel economy: *3.5L V6:* 8/11.9 L/100 km; *4x4:* 8.8/12.5 L/100 km. **Best alternatives:** Honda CR-V or Ridgeline, Hyundai Tucson or Santa Fe, and Toyota RAV4.

SAFETY: NHTSA gave the 2001-14 Explorers between three and five stars for rollover resistance and front/side crash protection, except for 2001-03 models which scored only two stars in rollover resistance. IIHS scored frontal offset protection as "Good" with 2002-13 models; 1995-2001 Explorers earned just "Acceptable" scores. Side protection was "Good" for 2011-14 and "Acceptable" for the 2006-10 Explorers. Head-restraint effectiveness was "Acceptable" and roof strength was deemed "Good." Head restraints were "Good" on 2004-08 models; "Acceptable" on the 2009-10s, and "Good" on the 2011-14 Explorers.

ALERT! Some things to check out at the dealership: Drivers say there's insufficient footroom (the brake and accelerator pedals are mounted too close to each other); narrow, poorly cushioned seats lack sufficient thigh support; and the small rear window cuts visibility. Other criticisms: The head restraints are literally a pain in the neck and can be dangerous if the airbags deploy; mediocre automatic transmission performance and fit and finish deficiencies; sunvisors are poorly designed; driver's foot presses on the foot rest bar when braking; sudden power-steering failure; and worst of all, under hard acceleration, the driver has to contend with sudden, unintended acceleration accompanied by loss of brakes.

Explorer Profile

	2004	2005	2006	2007	2008	2009	2010	2011	2012
Used Values ($)									
Base 4x2	—	—	—	—	—	—	—	17,500	20,000
XLT	—	—	—	—	—	—	—	22,500	26,000
4x4	4,500	5,500	6,500	7,500	9,500	13,500	17,500	23,000	28,000
Recommended	✰	✰	✰	✰	✰	✰	✰	✰	✰
Reliability	✰	✰	✰	✰	✰	✰	✰	✰	✰

SECRET WARRANTIES, INTERNAL BULLETINS: 2011-12—Intermittent front brake squeal; forward centre console storage bin door hard to open. Interior rattle or buzz; and front bumper creaking. **2012**—Power liftgate malfunctions.

F-150 PICKUP ★★

RATING: Average (2011-14); Below Average (2001-10). The F-150 has seen the best of times and the worst of times. It's coming out of a 2009 sales slump that almost forced the company into bankruptcy and the company's stock is nudging $17 a share after having reached a pre-recession high of $40. Contrary to Ford's ads, quality has taken a beating as references to serious engine and electronic deficiencies are showing up all over the Internet, in confidential service bulletins, and in courtrooms. **Road performance:** Handling is a breeze, although the ride is a bit stiff; best in its class for towing. On the downside: The powertrain is rough and loud, and braking is just acceptable. **Strong points:** Powered by Ford's 365 hp 3.5L Ti-VCT EcoBoost V6 engine and mated to a 6-speed automatic transmission. Look for a lavishly appointed cockpit, heated and cooled memory seats, ambient lighting, a moonroof, a rear-view camera, a multi-media hub, a Sony audio system, Sync with MyFord Touch, and voice-activated navigation connected to Sirius Travel Link. Offers lots of upgrade options, a roomy cab with plenty of convenient storage bins, a power-opening centre rear window, and a spring-assisted tailgate. **Weak points:** High sticker price; less comfortable than comparable models; and long-term reliability doesn't look promising until the F-Series' redesign of the 2015 models. Then shoppers would be wise to wait a year for the inevitable factory-related "bugs" to be worked out. This is especially important because these trucks have disappointed owners after each redesign since the mid-'80s. **Major redesign:** 1987, 1992, 1997, 2004, and 2009. The F-150 will be completely redesigned for the 2015 model year. **Highway/city fuel economy:** *3.5L V6:* 9/12.9 L/100 km; *6.2L V8:* 11.4/16.9 L/100 km; *3.5L V6 4x4:* 9/12.9 L/100 km; *6.2L V8 4x4:* 12.7/18.3 L/100 km; *3.7L V6:* 8.9/12.9 L/100 km; *3.7L 4x4:* 9.8/13.4 L/100 km; *5.0L V8:* 9.7/13.9 L/100 km; *5.0L V8 4x4:* 10.5/15 L/100 km; *Raptor 6.2L V8 4x4:* 14.2/19.1 L/100 km. **Best alternatives:** Chrysler's Ram equipped with a Cummins diesel and a more-reliable manual transmission, GM's Silverado or Sierra base models or HD series, Honda's Ridgeline, and Nissan's Titan. Nissan's Frontier or King Cab are also worth considering.

SAFETY: NHTSA gave the 2013-14 F-150 five stars for side crashworthiness and four stars for frontal collision protection and rollover resistance. Earlier models scored between three and five stars through

Prices and Specs

Prices (Soft): *F-150 Regular:* $21,549, *F-150 Super Cab:* $23,947, *Super Crew Cab:* $31,129, *F-250 XL 4x2 Super Duty Regular Cab:* $35,499, *Super Cab:* $38,599, *4x4:* $38,899 *Crew Cab long bed:* $40,599, *XLT 4x2 Crew Cab long bed:* $46,849, *Lariat 4x2 Crew Cab long bed:* $55,049, *Crew Cab:* $28,781, *F-350 Regular:* $26,230, *Super Cab:* $28,466, *Crew Cab:* $29,928, *F-450 4x2:* $41,968, *F-450 4x4:* $45,064 **Freight:** $1,500 **Powertrain (Rear-drive/ Part-time 4x4/AWD):** Engines: 3.6L V8 (248 hp), 4.6L V8 (292 hp), 5.4L V8 (310 hp), 6.2L V8 (411 hp), 6.4L V8 diesel (350 hp), 6.7L V8 diesel (385 hp), 6.8L V10 (362 hp), 3.5L V6 (365 hp); EcoBoost: 3.7L V6 (302 hp), 5.0L V8 (360 hp), 6.2L V8 (411 hp); Transmissions: 4-speed auto., 5-speed auto., 6-speed auto., 6-speed man. **Dimensions/capacity:** Passengers: 2/1 up to 3/3; Wheelbase: 121 in.; H: 69/L: 201/W: 77 in.; Headroom F/R: 70/5.5 in.; *F-250:* Headroom F/R: 6/6 in.; Legroom F/R:40/29.5 in.; *F-250:* Headroom F/R: 6/6 in.; Legroom F/R: 40/30.5 in.; Fuel tank: 98.4L/regular, Raptor: 94L/regular, Harley-Davidson: 136L/regular; Tow limit: *F-150:* 5,400 lb.; *F-250:* 12,500 lb.; Load capacity: 1,480–5,100 lb.; Turning circle: 48 ft.; Ground clearance: 8.5 in.; Weight: 5,620 lb.

1992, except for 2001-03 4x4 models that earned only two stars for rollover resistance. IIHS also gave the 2005-13 F-150 top marks ("Good") for frontal offset crashworthiness; 1997-2003s were judged "Poor" performers. Side impact protection with the 2009-14 models was judged to be "Good." Roof strength on the 2011-14s was also rated "Good." The best ("Good") head restraints were found on the 2009-14 versions; the worst results were with the 2004-08s ("Marginal" to "Poor").

ALERT! Owners confirm some headrests are uncomfortable and dangerous:

> Headrest forces driver's chin into the chest. Dealer stated that this is the new safety design. Headrests are non-adjustable. Also, they are very wide and, in conjunction with the frame post at the rear of the doors, create a blind spot on both sides of the pickup.

Ford's new EcoBoost engines have been heralded as providing plenty of turbo power and using less fuel than previous powerplants. This is true, but these redesigned engines have a nasty habit of losing power when most needed, thereby exposing passengers and pedestrians to serious injury or death.

> Major safety issue with F150 EcoBoost trucks. Hundreds of owners with this issue: [*www.blueovalforums.com/forums/index.php?/topic/49606-f-150-ecoboost-shutter*] while taking off from T-intersection and turning left crossing oncoming traffic the truck started to take off then lost all power for approximately 3–5 seconds. This left my family and I sitting in the oncoming traffic lane on a blind corner. The truck did not die (I thought it did), I mashed the accelerator to the floor and the truck did not respond whatsoever. My wife was screaming frantically at me asking what I was doing while I attempted to get the truck to move out of the oncoming lane. After approximately 5 seconds the truck regained power and accelerated normally. This has occurred 3X now and I am afraid to drive the truck but do and my wife will not drive it at all.

F-150 Pickup Profile

	2004	2005	2006	2007	2008	2009	2010	2011	2012
Used Values ($)									
Base 4x2	4,500	5,500	6,500	7,500	8,500	11,000	14,500	16,500	18,500
F-250 XLT	5,500	6,500	7,500	8,500	10,000	13,500	16,000	18,000	19,500
Recommended	★	★	★	☆	☆	★	★	☆	☆
Reliability	★	★	☆	☆	☆	☆	☆	☆	☆

Note: After each redesign, quality suffers.

SECRET WARRANTIES, INTERNAL BULLETINS: 2005-10—Uncommanded TCC application on the 1-2 shift, causing hesitation and or lack of power. **2009**—Harsh shifting at low speeds. **2009-10**—F-150, 250, 350, and F-Super Duty vehicles equipped with a 4.6L 3V or 5.4L 3V engine may emit a low frequency engine knocking noise at hot idle. 6R80 transmission bulkhead connector sleeve leaking fluid. Shudder, vibration on moderate acceleration. Before springing for costly repairs, simply ask mechanic to adjust the rear axle pinion angle under warranty. Water stains the rear portion of the headliner due to the high mounted stoplamp assembly leaking water. ater leak at satellite antenna. Remedies for Sync phone problems affecting most of Ford's lineup. The new SYNC service Microphone kit now includes a voltage filter incorporated into the jumper harness. The foam seal detaches between the instrument panel and the windshield glass (covered under a "goodwill" extended warranty on a case-by-case basis. Likely a sure-fire winner for small claims court). Headline droops, sags at rear of roof opening panel. **2009-10** F-150; and **2011** F-250 and F-350—Vehicles may exhibit an audible clicking noise in the engine compartment and/or a hard start after refueling with diagnostic trouble codes (DTCs) P0144A, P0171, P0174, P0316, and/or P1450. **2010**—A service kit has been released to assist in repairing of the 4R75E transmission in 2008 Mark LT, 2008-10 F-150, E-Series, 2008-211 Crown Victoria, Grand Marquis and Town Car vehicles that exhibit a grinding, whine-type noise, vibration and/or gear slippage while driving or a loss of reverse resulting from a planetary gear assembly failure. **2011-12**—Vehicles equipped with a 3.5L gasoline turbocharged direct injection (GTDI) EcoBoost engine may exhibit an intermittent engine surge during moderate to light loads at cruise, stumble and/or misfire on hard acceleration after an extended drive at highway speeds during high humid or damp conditions. This could result in a steady or flashing malfunction indicator lamp (MIL). **2013**—More troubleshooting tips for MyFord Touch and MyLincoln Touch infotainment feature.

GENERAL MOTORS

Doing Things Half-Right

"The new blood is still doing some of the same old GM stuff on the product side," Mr. Hall, managing director of the auto consulting firm 2953 Analytics said. GM has had success with totally new products, like its Cadillac ATS sedan and Buick Encore sport utility vehicle. But revamped versions of bellwether Chevrolet models like the Malibu and Impala have fallen flat."

BILL VLASIC
NEW YORK TIMES, JUNE 6, 2013

Sorry, Bill, but the 2014 Impala has just been voted "best sedan tested" by *Consumer Reports* and General Motors is riding high

GM's Corvette brings new meaning to "topless."

going into 2014 with sustained sales over the past several years that puts the company back in the black at almost pre-recession levels. Additionally, the company's stock, worthless going into its 2009 bankruptcy, is at a post-recession high of $37.44 (September 24, 2013) after topping $33 following GM's November 2010 IPO. Hmmm...over $4 bucks profit per share after almost three years?

Moreover, there's not any cheering from the thousands of sacked workers and small suppliers who were never paid a dime of what they were owed by GM and couldn't get bankruptcy protection or a handout from Ottawa or Washington. Their future? No job and little money, while incompetent and negligent GM executives are rewarded with "golden parachutes" worth millions of dollars.

Best- and Worst-selling GM Cars in Canada

Sales	Model	YTD	YTD % Change	Sales	Model	YTD	YTD % Change
#5	GMC Sierra	14,396	+ 8.9	#102	Chevy Spark	967	—
#5.1	GMC Sierra Crew Cab	8904	+ 12.6	#105	Buick Encore	894	—
#5.2	GMC Ext. Cab	4330	+ 9.7	#108	Cadillac SRX	885	- 0.1
#5.3	GMC Reg. Cab	1162	- 14.6	#109	Buick Enclave	884	+ 13.2
#10	Chevy Silverado	11,901	+ 7.7	#110	Chevy Traverse	882	- 1.9
#10.1	Chevy Silverado Crew Cab	7106	+ 13.6	#114	Cadillac ATS	862	—
#10.2	Chevy Silverado Ext. Cab	3660	+ 3.2	#128	Chevy Camaro	622	- 36.
#10.3	Chevy Silverado Reg. Cab	1135	- 9.2	#150	Buick LaCrosse	405	-58.2
#12	Chevy Cruze	9843	+ 2.5	#155	GMC Yukon	374	-6.0
#21	Chevy Equinox	5478	- 20.0	#158	Chevy Tahoe	338	-31.3
#36	GMC Terrain	3592	- 3.3	#160	Chevy Suburban	327	-4.9
#40	Chev Sonic	3128	+ 19.0	#167	Buick Regal	294	-64.3
#51	Chevy Malibu	2778	+ 69.8	#168	Cadillac Escalade	293	-13.1
#65	Chevy Trax	2139	—	#168.1	Cadillac Escalade	147	-33.2
#79	Chevy Impala	1897	- 41.9	#168.2	Cadillac Escalade EXT	99	+70.7
#83	Buick Verano	1777	+ 23.9	#168.3	Cadillac Escalade ESV	47	-20.3
#89	Chevy Avalanche	1421	+ 43.1	#170	Cadillac XTS	290	—
#94	Chevy Orlando	1277	- 41.4%	#172	Cadillac CTS	287	-68.0
#95	GMC Acadia	1270	+ 9.4	#176	GMC Yukon XL	247	-21.1

Sales	Model	YTD	YTD % Change	Sales	Model	YTD	YTD % Change
#178	Chevrolet Volt	241	+14.8	T232	GMC Canyon	24	-96.5
#210	Chevy Colorado	96	-87.0	T243	Chevy HHR	3	-97.2
#225	Chevy Corvette	50	-41.9	T243	Buick Lucerne	3	-99.3

YTD means through April 2013. "Sales" is ranking among 247 Canadian nameplates.

Sources: *www.goodcarbadcar.net, automakers, and Lemon-Aid*

Quality

Generally, new and redesigned vehicles tend to have more problems than carry-over models that undergo fewer design, engineering and equipment changes.

GM quality has definitely improved. Not across the board, but in key areas like fit and finish, fuel economy, and infotainment features.

IPhone Beats Automakers in Navigation

One exception, though, is GM's much-criticized $1,500 dashboard-embedded navigation system, complete with an 8-inch screen and a $50 update fee for downloading updates through OnStar. Users say they can get better navigation assistance and fresher data from their iPhone's free navigation application, attaching it to the dash with suction cups, and angling it for better viewing. When you leave the car, you take the phone with you.

Drivers are also using smartphone social networking nav map apps like Waze, that report accidents and traffic jams and send re-routing instructions to save time. Garmin and Tom Tom offer similar apps. No wonder 47 percent of drivers have switched over to smartphone nav apps.

Keep these iPhone advantages in mind when a dealer or private seller tries to get a higher price for a car equipped with a "factory" navigation system.

Of course, GM still has serious powertrain, electrical system, and fuel system shortcomings, but despite the above glitches, General Motors now ranks near the top of J.D. Power's annual Initial Quality Index survey, while Ford continues to be dragged down by its unreliable electronic features and unjustified fuel-economy claims. Chrysler's momentum has been sustained by its improved quality control and popular truck offerings.

Power concludes that almost two-thirds of problems reported on 2013 models were design errors rather than factory-related defects – things drivers considered not faulty but still difficult to understand or operate. Subsequent surveys show design difficulties are the hardest to rectify by dealers, hence Ford's infotainment nightmare.

Let's look at the quality of these quality surveys.

Power's three-month study is its weakest survey based on random responses from only 83,000 consumers who bought or leased 2013-model light vehicles within the past 90 days. The other annual Power quality survey, which looks at owners who have driven their vehicles several years, has much more probative weight. Nevertheless, companies that fall in ranking during the initial 90 days, rarely do well in the longer study.

Consumer Reports' annual survey is based upon over a million subscriber responses who have owned their vehicles for two to seven years and is broken down into different vehicle components. *CR*'s findings have been criticized for "cherry-picking" Northeastern United States resident-subscribers with a fixed mindset who probably bought vehicles recommended by the consumer group, engendering conclusions reflecting the magazine's published reports.

J.D. Power and Associates 2013 U.S. Initial Quality Study

2013 ranking (problems per 100 vehicles)							
Porsche	80	Hyundai	106	BMW	114	Ford	131
GMC	90	Kia	106	Volvo	114	Ram	132
Lexus	94	Mercedes-Benz	106	Smart	115	MINI	135
Infiniti	95	Audi	108	Land Rover	116	Nissan	142
Chevrolet	97	Cadillac	108	Jeep	118	Mitsubishi	148
Acura	102	Buick	109	Volkswagen	120	Fiat	154
Toyota	102	Chrysler	109	Mazda	125	Scion	161
Honda	103	Lincoln	113	Subaru	128		
Jaguar	104	Industry Average	113	Dodge	130		

Top three models per car segment

	Highest Ranked		
City Car	Smart Fortwo	Chevrolet Spark*	
Sub-Compact Car	Mazda MAZDA2*	Hyundai Accent*	Honda Fit*
Compact Car	Honda Civic*	Toyota Corolla*	Honda Insight
Compact Sporty Car	Mazda Miata*	Volkswagen Eos	Volkswagen GTI*
Compact Premium Car	Acura TL*	Infiniti G*	Cadillac CTS
Compact Premium Sporty Car	Porsche Boxster	Nissan Z	BMW Z4
Midsize Car	Toyota Camry*	Hyundai Sonata	Buick Regal
Midsize Sporty Car*	Chevy Camaro* Ford Mustang*		
Midsize Premium Car	Hyundai Genesis Sedan*	Mercedes-Benz E-Class Sedan/Wagon*	Jaguar XF Lexus GS*
Large Premium Car	Lexus LS*	Audi A8	Porsche Panamera
Midsize Premium Sporty Car*	Porsche 911*		
Large Car	Chevrolet Impala*	Hyundai Azera*	Chrysler 300 Series

	Highest Ranked		
Sub-Compact CUV	Buick Encore* Kia Sportage*	Nissan JUKE*	
Compact CUV	Honda CR-V*	Toyota FJ Cruiser*	Chevy Equinox*
Compact MPV*	Kia Soul*	Mazda Mazda5*	
Midsize CUV	Nissan Murano	Buick Enclave*	Hyundai Santa Fe
Midsize Premium CUV	Infiniti FX*	Lexus GX*	Porsche Cayenne
Minivan	Chrysler Town & Country	Honda Odyssey*	
Large CUV*	Chevrolet Tahoe*	Toyota Sequoia*	
Large Premium CUV*	Cadillac Escalade*	Mercedes-Benz GL-Class*	
Large Light Duty Pickup	Chevy Avalanche* GMC Sierra *	Chevy Silverado*	
Large Heavy Duty Pickup*	Chevy Silverado*	GMC Sierra*	

Sources: J. D. Power, Bloomberg, and *Lemon-Aid*. Models marked with an * are considered good buys by *Lemon-Aid*.

2014 New Models

GM will launch 18 new vehicles for 2014, more than any other automaker, and will continue as a smaller, leaner organization with fewer brands, dealers, and workers. In other words, the automaker plans to make more money, selling fewer cars, while relying on sales incentives like free two-year maintenance, 96-month financing, and adding more standard features. Furthermore, GM is targeting Ford's pickup lead and fuel-economy by introducing redesigned 2014 model full-sized pickups that will exceed the fuel economy of Ford's F-Series trucks by about one mpg (independent Canadian tests not yet available). In effect, the 2014 non-turbo, two-wheel-drive 4.3L EcoTec3 V6 Silverado and Sierra will get an estimated 18 mpg in city driving and 24 mpg on the highway.

SONIC ★★★★

RATING: Above Average (2012-14). Basically a second-generation Aveo, the Sonic offers more refinement, enhanced crashworthiness, better performance, and impressive fuel economy. It fits into GM's small car lineup between the Spark and Cruze and proves that cheap subcompact cars don't mean you have to endure an uncomfortable ride and white-knuckle highway performance. **Road performance:** Fast and smooth acceleration; the optional turbocharged 1.4L engine has more torque and a nicely refined power curve. Steering is precise and responsive, with no torque steer pulling the car to the side when accelerating, however, some reports of excessive steering shake. **Strong points:** Reasonably priced, refined, and well appointed. The interior is comfortable and practical, with little noise intrusion into the cabin. Sedans are about a foot longer than hatchbacks. Production has moved from South Korea to the States. **Weak points:** Firm pricing. The hatchback's load floor is quite high – the Honda Fit is more useful and versatile. Mushy brakes and chronic rear brake squeal (corrosion). Owners also report that the front passenger-side airbag sensor doesn't recognize that the seat is occupied; car rolls backwards when stopped on a hill, even though Hill Holder is engaged; the transmission sometimes hesitates before shifting; and the front end of the vehicle is too low and drags on the ground when passing over uneven terrain. **Major redesign:** Not before the 2015 model year. **Highway/city fuel economy:** *RS 6-speed man.:* 5.9/8.1 L/100 km. *RS 6-speed auto.:* 7.6/8.7 L/100 km. **Best alternatives:** Honda Fit, Hyundai Accent, Mazda2, Nissan Versa, and Toyota Yaris.

SAFETY: 2012-14 models earned five stars from NHTSA for front, side, and rollover crash protection. IIHS also gave its "Good" top score for frontal offset, side, rear, and roof crashworthiness. 2014s will include a standard driver-side power door-lock switch, and an optional Rear Vision camera, plus, an Advanced Safety Package that includes Forward Collision Alert and Lane Departure Warning.

ALERT! Owners note that the Sonic wanders with original equipment tires and wheels; consider getting better quality alternatives.

SECRET WARRANTIES, INTERNAL BULLETINS: 2011— Power Tires leak air or suddenly go flat (clean and resurface the wheel bead seat). A drivetrain clunk noise heard when shifting is an acceptable characteristic of GM transmissions, says TSB #01-07-30-042G, issued September 22, 2011. Automatic transmission clunk noise. Engine hesitation at start-up requires reprogramming the engine control module. **2011-12**—*Sonic and Volt;* **2012**—*Verano and Camaro*—The driver airbag assembly may not be fastened to the steering wheel assembly as intended. **2012**—Campaign – Rattle or clunk noise during turns or over bumps may require the free replacement of the stabilizer bars which may have lower ball joint boots that are subject to water and dirt intrusion. As a result, contamination within the boot may cause the joint to loosen due to rust, causing wear between the ball stud and socket. Fuel Pipe Quick Connect Replacement Campaign. These vehicles may have an engine idle that is rough and/or stalls immediately after engine start in an outside temperature range 20-30 Celsius degrees.

Prices and Specs

Prices (Firm): *LS Sedan:* $14,495; *LT:* $16,495; *LTZ:* $20,495; *LS Hatch:* $15,495; *LT Hatch:* $17,495; *LTZ Hatch:* $20,995 Used prices are simple to calculate: 2012s have depreciated about 25 percent; 2013s: 15 percent. **Freight:** $1,500 **Powertrain (Front-drive):** Engines: 1.8L 4-cyl. (138 hp), 1.4L 4-cyl. turbo (138 hp); Transmissions: 5-speed man., 6-speed man.,6-speed auto. **Dimensions/ capacity:** Passengers: 2/3; Wheelbase: 99.4 in.; H: 59.7/L: 173.1/W: 68.3 in.; Headroom F/R: 5/2.5 in.; Legroom F/R: 41.8/34.6 in.; Cargo volume: 14.9 cu. ft.; Fuel tank: 45L/regular; Tow limit: Not recommended; Load capacity: 895 lb.; Turning circle: 17.3 ft.; Ground clearance: 4.9 in.; Weight: 2,727 lb.

CRUZE ★★★

RATING: An Average buy (2011-14). A turbocharged 2.0L 4-cylinder diesel engine will be gradualy phased in through a limited number of cities in North America. Diesel fuel economy is estimated by the U.S. EPA at a combined 34 mpg with an automatic transmission (Canadian data not yet available). **Road performance:** A peppy, smooth, and efficient turbocharged engine, plus good steering and handling. The firm suspension makes you feel every bump in the road. **Strong points:** An upscale interior, large trunk, quiet cabin, and comfortable front seats. The Eco model gives impressive fuel economy. **Weak points:** The Bluetooth feature often disconnects during phone calls; cramped rear seating with seat cushions set too low; limited storage area; a boring exterior; and unproven long-term reliability. Owners report sudden, unintended acceleration, "lag and lurch" when accelerating; airbags fail to deploy when they're needed; floor mats slide up under the pedals; loss of braking when backing up or underway (vacuum pump suspected); axle seal leaks; chronic automatic transmission failures and malfunctions (often caused by a faulty transmission control module); excessive headlight glare from the rear-view mirror; the rear-view mirror vibrates constantly; power steering failures; and in one incident, the steering wheel came off in the driver's hand. **Major redesign:** None. 2014 is to be the Cruze's final model year. **Highway/city fuel economy:** *Eco 1.4L man.:* 4.6/7.2 L/100 km. *Eco1.4L auto.:* 5.1/7.8 L/100 km. *1.8L man.:* 5.4/7.8L/100 km. *1.8L auto.:* 5.6/9.2 L/100 km. **Best alternatives:** Some good alternative models are the Honda Fit, Hyundai Accent, Mazda2, and VW Jetta (with a more-reliable manual transmission).

SAFETY: All model years ranked five stars for frontal and side protection; rollover resistance scored four stars. IIHS rates frontal, side, head-restraint, and roof crash protection as "Good." Rear-view mirror blocks the view through the front windshield.

ALERT! Fuel economy with entry-level models isn't extraordinary; consider the diesel option.

Prices and Specs

New 2013-14 Prices (Firm): *LS:* $14,995, *LT Turbo:* $19,335, *LT Turbo+:* $20,530, *ECO:* $20,795, *LTZ Turbo:* $25,445; **Used prices (2012):** $10,500, *LT Turbo:* $13,500, *LT Turbo+:* $14,000, *ECO:* $14,500, *LTZ Turbo:* $17,500 **Freight:** $1,750 **Powertrain (Front-drive):** Engines: 1.8L 4-cyl. (136 hp), 1.4L turbocharged 4-cyl. (138 hp); Transmissions: 6-speed man., 6-speed auto. **Dimensions/capacity:** Passengers: 2/3; Wheelbase: 105.7 in.; H: 58.1/L: 181/W: 70.7 in.; Headroom F/R: 6/30 in.; Legroom F/R:43/26 in.; Cargo volume: 15 cu. ft.; Fuel tank: 59L/regular; Tow limit: 1,000 lb.; Load capacity: 900 lb.; Turning circle: 35.7 ft.; Ground clearance: 6.5 in.; Weight: 3,056 lb.

SECRET WARRANTIES, INTERNAL BULLETINS: 2011—Power-steering fluid leaks. Shock absorber/strut fluid leaks; tire slowly goes flat. Automatic transmission clunk noise. Engine hesitation at start-up requires reprogramming the engine control module. **2011-12**—Uneven brake pedal feel. This bulletin provides a service procedure to reprogram the Electronic Brake Control Module. **2012**—Engine hesitation at start-up under high accessory loads requires reprogramming of the ECM under the Emissions Warranty.

MALIBU/HYBRID ★★

RATING: Below Average Buy (1997-2014). This bland, unpopular mid-sized car helped push GM into bankruptcy a few years back, and, unlike the much-improved Impala, Malibu continues to disappoint. Its poor fuel economy, non-existent quality control, and mediocre highway performance made the car so unwanted that even fleet buyers are turning them down. By the time GM began improving the 2008 Malibu and Impala, the company had lost the public's confidence and shut its doors. Hybrid: Average (2008-10). The Hybrid arrived as a 2008 model and uses a 2.4L 4-cylinder gas engine with an electric motor/generator. The 4-banger is mated to a 4-speed automatic. It is classified as a "mild" hybrid because it can't run solely on its battery. Despite its complexity, there have been few owner complaints targeting the Hybrid models. The biggest disappointments so far is that the car loses power at times, comes close to stalling, and fuel consumption is far higher than the figures touted by Environment Canada and GM (8.5/6.2 L/100 km). *CanadianDriver.com* tested the Hybrid and found it burned an average of 11 L/100 km. **Road performance:** The base 4-cylinder engine with an automatic transmission is barely adequate for highway driving with a full load. Nevertheless, the car does give a comfortable though firm ride and offers better-than-average handling, thanks to its independent suspension. **Strong points:** Well-appointed, with many advanced high-tech features; adequate passenger and luggage space; few squeaks and rattles; higher-grade materials used in the interior; and the Eco's high fuel economy. **Weak points:** As with earlier redesigns, expect premature brake wear, electrical shorts, and powertrain failures. Less rear legroom than in other cars in this class; transmission makes the Eco model feel sluggish; and overpriced bundled option packages. The car, despite its restyling, still seems to be more plastic than metal and the controls appear to be a bit more complicated than those used in previous

> ### Prices and Specs
>
> **Prices (Very Negotiable):** *LS:* $24,995, *LT:* $26,325, *Eco:* $27,940, *LTZ:* $30,650, *LTZ Turbo:* $30,925 **Freight:** $1,800 **Powertrain (Front-drive):** Engines: 2.4L 4-cyl. (182 hp), 2.5L 4-cyl. (197 hp); Transmission: 6-speed auto. **Dimensions/capacity:** Passengers: 2/3; Wheelbase: 107.8 in.; H: 57.6/L: 191.5/W: 73 in.; Headroom F/R: 3.5/3; Legroom F/R: 42.1/36.8; Cargo volume: 14 cu. ft.; Fuel tank: 61L/regular; Tow limit: NR; Load capacity: 905 lb.; Turning circle: 18.7 ft.; Ground clearance: 5 ft.; Weight: 3,500 lb.

years. **Major redesign:** 1997, 2004, 2008, 2013, and a 2014 "refresh." Four redesigns in six years and buyers remain unimpressed. 2014 models boast a restyled front end, an upgraded interior, and a more fuel-efficient powertrain. Will these changes improve Malibu's fortunes? Not likely. Keep your powder dry for at least six months until Malibu's changes have been owner-tested. **Highway/city fuel economy:** 2.4L: 6.5/9.5 L/100 km. 2.4L 6-speed: 5.9/9.4 L/100 km. V6: 7.8/12.2 L/100 km. 2014 fuel economy may increase 3-5 percent, thanks to start-stop feature and variable valve lift control. The Hybrid's real fuel economy isn't much more than what the 4-cylinder-powered Hyundai Sonata and Toyota Camry provide. **Best alternatives:** The Honda Accord has more usable interior space, is much more reliable, and has quicker and more-accurate steering; Hyundai's Elantra is cheaper and just as well put together, and Toyota's Camry is plusher, though not as driver-oriented. Other cars worth considering are the Mazda3 or Mazda6 and Nissan Sentra. Another possibility is the much improved Chevy Impala, a slightly larger and higher-priced in-house competitor. Look for generous sales incentives on the Malibu in early 2014.

SAFETY: Beginning with the 2004 models, NHTSA has awarded the Malibu its five-star crashworthiness score for frontal and side protection and four stars for frontal rollover resistance. 2002-04 models ratings slipped a bit to three and four stars. 2001s were four-star rated except for side protection which scored only two stars. IIHS says frontal offset, side, rear, and roof crash protection is "Good."

ALERT! Consider the standard 2.5L-equipped models, instead of snapping up the more expensive, feeble, and untested mild-hybrid Eco version. In fact, the base model offers the same fuel economy at a lower price.

Malibu Profile

Used Values ($)	2004	2005	2006	2007	2008	2009	2010	2011	2012
LS	3,000	5,000	5,500	6,000	7,000	8,000	10,500	13,500	16,000
LT	3,500	5,500	5,500	6,000	7,500	8,500	11,500	14,500	17,000
LTZ	—	—	6,000	6,500	8,500	10,000	16,500	17,500	19,500
MAXX LT	5,000	6,000	6,500	7,000	8,000	—	—	—	—
Hybrid	—	—	—	—	7,500	9,500	12,500	—	—
Recommended	☆	☆	☆	☆	☆	☆	☆	☆	☆
Reliability	☆	☆	☆	☆	☆	☆	☆	☆	☆

SECRET WARRANTIES, INTERNAL BULLETINS: 2004-08—Front-end clunk or rattle when passing over small bumps at low speeds. **2005-08**—2005-06 G6, Malibu, and Malibu Maxx; 2008 G6, Malibu, Malibu Maxx, and Aura may have a sudden loss of steering power-assist. Under Special Coverage Adjustment #10183, dated July 20, 2010, GM will replace the failed components free of charge up to 10 years/100,000 mi. (160,000 km). **2006-07**—TSB #10134A, published August 24, 2011, says that cars with the 2.2L 4-cylinder engine and those with the 2.4L 4-cylinder with 4-speed automatic transmission may have a deteriorating catalytic converter, causing the engine light to illuminate. The warranty is extended to 10 years/192,000 km. for 2006-07 Cobalt, G4/G5, and Ion. **2011**—Power-steering fluid leaks. Airbag warning light comes on intermittently (likely caused by a loose, missing, or damaged connector position assurance retainer). Shock absorber fluid leaks. Wet front or rear passenger-side carpet (this condition may be caused by a plugged HVAC evaporator drain – in some cases, water from the HVAC system will drain back though the front of the dash). Clunking automatic transmission shifts are called "normal" by GM. **2013**—Inoperative voice recognition feature.

IMPALA/ALLURE/LACROSSE ★★★★ / ★★ / ★

bad buy

Again, Consumer Reports shocked the car industry with a car report, earlier this year. This time with an unexpected rave review of the redesigned 2014 Chevrolet Impala – calling it the "best new sedan tested." It's the first time in at least 20 years that an American sedan has been so positively rated by CR.

For the first time in two decades, one of Detroit's Big Three has beaten the likes of Japan's and Europe's best to win the top spot among all sedans from *Consumer Reports*. In fact, using *CR*'s point system, only the $90,000 Tesla S luxury electric car and the BMWi did better in their categories. Last year's Impala scored 63 out of 100 points and the 2014 version stunned the motoring press with a score of 95. Impala got such high marks for its comfy ride, agile handling, spacious cabin, peppy acceleration and big trunk. Concludes *Consumer Reports*:

Impala is competitive with cars that cost $20,000 more, including the Audi A6 and Lexus LS460L, as well as the recently reviewed Acura RLX and Jaguar XF.

RATING: *Impala*: Above Average (2014); Below Average (2006-13); Not Recommended (2000-05). Over the past decade, Impala has become one of GM's least competitive products and was almost culled from the herd years ago. GM knew that keeping the Impala without major upgrades soiled the Chevrolet brand and gave Ford's Fusion and Chrysler's 200 a big sales boost. General Motors is fighting back with this year's Impala. It has spent millions upgrading the car in almost every way to make it leap past its sorry history with fine handling and even better styling. *Allure/LaCrosse and Lucerne*: Below Average (2006-14); Not Recommended (2000-05). There is very little "new" in the 2014 LaCrosse, wait until the 2015 model year when GM will either update or drop the model, as it did with the 2011 Lucerne. LaCrosse and Lucerne are similarly equipped large front-drive sedans that are hobbled by mediocre road performance and poor quality control. The discontinued Lucerne is the larger of the three cars and the model that had accumulated the most performance- and safety-related complaints. **Road performance:** The V6 provides smooth acceleration and works well with the 6-speed automatic transmission, though it could use more high-speed torque. Handling and ride are better than average, owing to recent suspension and steering refinements. A few years ago, the mid-sized LaCrosse was completely restyled and its four-wheel independent suspension was retuned to improve the ride and handling. The available AWD system employs a limited-slip differential to send torque to whichever wheel has more traction for better control on slippery roads. **Strong points:** *Impala:* Comes with an array of standard features and a refined interior. Both cars provide a comfortable ride, and have an easily accessed interior and rear seatbacks that fold flat, opening up cargo storage space. Plenty of rear seat room with both models. Crash safety is exceptionally good since 2000. *LaCrosse:* Adequate rear legroom, and a front bench seat. LaCrosse also has a much better reliability record than the Impala. **Weak points:** Rear seating is uncomfortable for all three and obstructs rear visibility due to the tall, wide rear-seat head restraints. Says one owner of a 2012 LaCrosse:

> The "Blind Spots" on this vehicle are outrageous. The front seat head restraints are so big it is not possible to look out the driver's side rear window when backing up. I would remove the headrests to make the car safer for others (the ones you can't see), but they cannot be removed. The deck lid is so high that the rear-veiw mirror shows only one half of the outside — the rest of the mirror shows the interior of the car. The pillar between the rear side windows and the back window is so wide this also obscures the view when backing up.

Other shortcomings: engine rear main seal leak; loud engine knocking, ticking noise; chronic stalling; car was parked with transmission in "Park," and it rolled away; wheel lug nut studs snap off. **Major redesign:** 2000 and 2006; *Impala:* 2014. **Highway/city fuel economy:** *Impala 3.5L:* 6.7/10.8 L/100 km. *3.9L:* 7.4/12 L/100 km.

LaCrosse 2.4L: 6.5/10.8 L/100 km. *3.6L:* 7.3/12.2 L/100 km. *AWD 3.6L:* 7.7/12.7 L/100 km. **Best alternatives:** The 2014 model is a game changer. GM's redesign had made it one of the top three full-sized sedans money (just a little money) can buy. Wait for the better-made mid-2014 to arrive. In the meantime, there's always tried and proven Honda Accord, Mazda6, Hyundai Elantra, and Toyota Camry or Avalon. Those wanting a bit more performance should consider the BMW 3 Series. More room and better performance can be had by purchasing a Hyundai Tucson or a Honda CR-V.

SAFETY: NHTSA gave the 2014 Impala and LaCrosse a five-star overall crashworthiness, except for four stars for rollover resistance. 20012-13 versions got four – star scores across the board. However, year 2000-11 models posted impressive four- and five-star rankings. IIHS judged front, side, and rear crashworthiness as "Good" on the 2012 Impala, while roof strength and rear crash protection (head restraints) were judged to be only "Acceptable." The 2012 LaCrosse was rated as "Good" by IIHS for front, side, roof, and rear crashworthiness. Additional safety features, like a lane departure warning system and blind-spot detection are available. Low resolution rear-camera display may disappoint some; excessive brake fade after successive stops.

ALERT! *Impala:* During the test-drive listen for an annoying high-pressure fuel pump knocking/ticking when accelerating. GM bulletins say "Tough! That's the way we build them." When stopped at a red light, brake pedal may slowly drift toward the floor, allowing the car to roll. Distorted windshield may skew your view of the road; headache-inducing. *LaCrosse:* Can you adjust to the front pillar partially obstructing your view?

Impala/Allure/LaCrosse Profile

	2004	2005	2006	2007	2008	2009	2010	2011	2012
Used Values ($)									
Impala LS	3,500	5,000	5,500	6,000	7,000	8,000	12,000	14,500	17,500
LT	—	—	6,000	6,500	7,500	8,500	12,500	15,500	18,500
LTZ	—	—	6,500	7,000	8,000	9,500	13,500	17,000	26,500
SS	5,000	6,500	7,500	8,000	10,000	12,000	—	—	—
Allure/LaCrosse	4,000	5,500	6,500	7,000	8,000	9,500	14,000	18,000	22,500
AWD	—	—	—	—	—	—	15,500	20,000	26,000
Recommended	★	★	★	★	★	★	★	★	★
Reliability	★	★	★	★	★	★	★	★	★

Prices and Specs

Prices (Very Negotiable): *Base Impala LS:* $28,300, *LT:* $29,290, *LTZ:* $34,450; *Base LaCrosse:* $36,195, *AWD:* $42,965 **Freight:** $1,745 **Powertrain (Front-Drive/AWD):** Engines: *Impala:* 2.5L (195 hp), 3.6L V6 (305 hp), 3.9L V6 (230 hp), 5.3L V8 (303 hp); *Hybrid:* 2.4L (182 hp); *LaCrosse:* 2.4L 4-Cyl. (182 hp), 3.0L V6 (255 hp), 3.6L V6 (280 hp); Transmissions: *Impala:* 4-speed auto.; *LaCrosse:* 6-speed auto. **Dimensions/capacity:** Passengers: 2/3; Wheelbase: *Impala:* 110.5 in.; *LaCrosse:* 111.7 in.; *Impala:* H: 58.7/L: 200.4/W: 72.9 in.; *LaCrosse:* H: 58.9/L: 197/W: 73.1 in.; Headroom: F/R: 3.5/3.5 in.; Legroom F/R: 44/31 in.; Fuel tank: 64L/regular/premium; Cargo volume: 11 cu. ft.; Tow limit: NR; Load capacity: *Impala:* 905 lb., *LaCrosse:* 905 lb.; Turning circle: 38.8 ft.; Ground clearance: 6 in.; Weight: *Impala LS, LT:* 3,555 lb., *LTZ:* 3,649 lb.; *LaCrosse CX:* 3,948 lb.

SECRET WARRANTIES, INTERNAL BULLETINS: 2005-07—Automatic transmission shudder when accelerating. **2005-08**—Countermeasures for harsh shifting and slipping. Repair for a steering column clunk heard when turning. **2005-09**—Automatic transmission slips in gear; left-side axle seal leaks (see bulletin). Wind noise diagnostic tips. Airbag warning light comes on intermittently. **2005-11**—Reduced power, as MIL alert lights up (see bulletin). **2006-09**—Airbag warning light stays lit. **2007-09**—Steering gear mount to frame may make a pop, creak, or click noise. **2008**—Power steering leak may require the replacement of the steering gear cylinder line. Tips on reducing tire vibration. **2008-09**—Poor AC performance. Inaccurate fuel gauge readings. **2008-09**—V8 engine oil leak from the rear cover assembly area. **2009**—V8 engine valve tick noise remedy (replace the valve lifters). *Impala:* **2006-08**—GM bulletin #08-06-04-039, published August 7, 2008, says that if the car cranks but won't start, the likely culprit is a blown fuel pump fuse. Coolant leaks that can cause engine overheating usually require that the engine head gasket be replaced. Again, this is a warranty item that is often covered up to 7 years/160,000 km under "goodwill" warranty extensions. **2006-09**—Rear suspension creak, clunk, pop noise. Power-steering noise reduction measures. **2007**—Troubleshooting wind/road noise. **2007-08**—Engine squealing on start-up. AC won't maintain desired temperature. Ignition key cannot be removed. No shift out of Park. Undercar noises. Rear speaker rattling. **2008**—Inaccurate fuel gauge readings. **2011**—Automatic transmission clunks when shifted. Power-steering leakage. Airbag warning light comes on intermittently. Shock absorber fluid leaks. Tires slowly go flat. *Lucerne:* **2006-08**—Inoperative Park Assist feature. Frayed headliner (front edge). **2006-09**—Airbag warning light stays lit (replace the right front seat belt buckle). Vehicle pulls to the right when accelerating. Bump, clunk on slow speed turns. Front door won't open or unlock. Inoperative inside and outside rear door handles. Hard to view instrument panel cluster in sunlight. Hard starts, no-starts (repair and re-route transmission wiring harnesses). **2006-11**—Reduced power as MIL alert lights up. **2007-10**—Low-speed automatic transmission moan or whine noise. **2009**—Parking Assist gives erratic visual and audio warnings.

2009-10—Engine coolant leaks (replace coolant crossover pipe gaskets). Campaign and service bulletin number: #10142, dated May 12, 2010, provides for the resecuring of the electronic brake control module at no charge to the vehicle owner. Courtesy transportation will also be provided. This is not a recall. Oil leak at the front of the engine (replace the front cover seal). **2009-11**—Procedures outlined to reduce front brake rotor noise and pulsation.

CAMARO ★★★★

RATING: Above Average. The base 2014 model gets a revised front end, larger grille and improved seats. A reworked Z/28 arrives next summer with a 500 hp V8 engine. **Road performance:** Impressive V6 and V8 acceleration with reasonable fuel economy and nice steering/handling. **Strong points:** Interior trim looks and feels to be of better quality, and the seats provide good lateral support and are easy to adjust. Very few serious reliability complaints. **Weak points:** No headroom; if you are 6'2" or taller, your head will be constantly brushing up against the headliner; rear seating is a "knees-to-chin" affair; not much cargo room; small trunk and trunk opening. Owners report and *Consumer Reports* confirms that fit and finish glitches are everywhere; exterior styling seems to have been slapped together by a committee; the rear, especially, is ugly and obstructs rear visibility; plus, the car is set too high to look "sporty." **Major redesign:** 1993 and 2010. The next redesign is scheduled for the 2016 model year and will include a weight reduction of 15 percent across GM's lineup. The car will pick up the same 2.0L turbocharged engine used by the ATS, in addition to the new 5.2L V8 that powers GM's trucks. **Highway/city fuel economy:** *3.6L V6:* 7.1/12.4 L/100 km. *Auto.:* 6.8/11.4 L/100 km. *SS man. and 6.2L V8:* 8.2/13.2 L/100 km. *Auto.:* 8/13.3 L/100 km. **Best alternatives:** Camaros are "hot," and this year's sales have beaten the equally popular Ford Mustang by a small margin. Smart buyers will wait on the more reasonably priced, leftover models available in the spring of 2014.The Hyundai Genesis Coupe, Mustang, and Mazda Miata are good second choices. When comparing the Mustang and Camaro for overall reliability, the Camaro has a slight edge due to the 'Stang's infotainment, powertrain, and fit and finish deficiencies. 2002 and earlier Camaros are cheap project cars that sell for $5,000 to $8,000,

Prices and Specs

Prices (Very Negotiable): *1LS man.:* $28,200, *2LS auto.:* $29,400, *1LT man.:* $30,110, *2LT man.:* $34,390, *1SS:* $39,580, *2SS:* $39,580, *1LT Conv.:* $36,300, *2LT Conv.:* $40,250, *1SS man.:* $38,350, *2SS auto.:* $43,220, *1SS Conv.:* $44,820, *2SS Conv.:* $49,100 **Freight:** $1,500 **Powertrain (Rear-drive):** Engines: 3.6L V6 (323 hp) • 6.2L V8 (400-426 hp), 6.2L supercharged V8 (580 hp); Transmissions: 6-speed man., 6-speed auto. **Dimensions/capacity:** Passengers: 2/2; Wheelbase: 112.3 in.; H: 54.2/L: 190.4/W: 75.5 in.; Cargo volume: 11. cu. ft.; Headroom F/R: 3.5/0 in.; Legroom F/R: 40/22 in.; Fuel tank: 71.9L/regular; Tow limit:1,000 lb.; Turning circle: 37.7 ft.; Weight: 3,769-3,849 lb.; Fuel tank: 64L/regular/premium; Cargo volume: 11 cu. ft.; Load capacity: 730 lb.

depending upon whether you pick up a base, no frills model or a V8-equipped convertible (prices can be confirmed on the Internet at VMR Canadian Used Car Prices). Another Camaro advantage over the Mustang is the less likelihood of finding rust rot in the rocker (door) panels and trunk.

SAFETY: NHTSA awarded the 2012-14 models its top five-star rating for frontal, side, and rollover crashworthiness. Earlier models going back to 1991 are rated mostly four and five stars in overall crash protection. IIHS hasn't yet crash-tested the Camaro. Reports that the passenger-side airbag doesn't recognize the seat is occupied.

ALERT! Listen for front strut shock noise when passing over uneven terrain or small bumps. Some drivers also report that the steering gives way to any imperfections in the road.

Camaro Profile

	2010	2011	2012
Used Values ($)			
Camaro LS	14,000	17,500	20,500
LT	14,500	18,500	21,500
SS	19,500	24,500	29,000
Convertible LT	22,500	26,500	30,000
Convertible SS	—	29,500	34,000
Recommended	★	★	★
Reliability	★	★	★

SECRET WARRANTIES, INTERNAL BULLETINS: 2011—Automatic transmission makes a clunk sound when shifted. Recalibration of the electronic brake control module to improve cold weather braking performance. Power-steering fluid leaks; moisture from vent when AC is on/carpet may be wet. Lower rear window seal loose or missing. Side window glass won't clear moulding. Tips on removing scratches and scuffs on the radio display screen. Door light bar inoperative or loses intensity. Noisy six-way power front seats. Rear bumper facia contacting body/paint peeling. Door and quarter panel paint appearance. Convertible top spots, indentation/damage. **2011-12**—Convertible top headliner tears near the support brackets; excessive wind intrusion. **2012**—The correction for an airbag warning light that stays on for no reason. This fix will be done for free until April 30, 2014. Evaporative Emission Canister Vent Solenoid Valve Replacement under warranty.

CORVETTE

★★★

According to the *New York Times,* "General Motors recalled 22,000 Corvettes because the roof might fly off, and what do you think kicked the company into action? Complaints on the National Highway Traffic Safety Administration website from owners? Was it the safety agency itself, worried about the complaints? Concerns raised by the Federal Aviation Administration? Nope. it was the Japanese Ministry of Land Infrastructure and Transport, unhappy about the problem on imported Corvettes."

RATING: Average; a brawny, bulky sport coupe that's slowly evolving into a more-refined machine. But quality control continues to be subpar, and safety-related transmission and body deficiencies are common. The Corvette does deliver high-performance thrills – along with suspension kickback, numb steering, and seats that need extra bolstering. Overall, get the quieter and less temperamental base Corvette; it delivers the same cachet for a lot less money. **Road performance:** A powerful and smooth powertrain that responds quickly to the throttle; the 6-speed gearbox performs well in all gear ranges and makes shifting smooth, with short throws and easy entry into all gears. Easy handling; enhanced side-slip angle control helps to prevent skidding and provides better traction control. No over-steer (in fact, steering is a little vague), wheel spinning, breakaway rear ends, or nasty surprises, thanks partly to standard electronic stability control. Better-than-average braking; the ABS-vented disc brakes are easy to modulate, and they're fade-free. **Strong points:** The car has a relatively roomy interior, user-friendly instruments and controls, and lots of convenience features. There's a key controlled lockout feature that discourages joy riding by cutting engine power in half. All Corvettes are also equipped with an impressively effective PassKey theft-deterrent system that uses a resistor pellet in the ignition to disable the starter and fuel system when the key code doesn't match the ignition lock. Cars equipped with manual transmissions get a Performance Traction Management system that modulates the engine's torque output for fast starts. This feature also manages engine power when the driver floors the accelerator when coming out of a corner. **Weak points:** The car is so low that its front air dam scrapes over the smallest rise in the road. Expect lots of visits to the body shop. Limited rear visibility; inadequate storage space; poor quality powertrain; mediocre fit and finish; cabin amenities and materials aren't up to the competition's standards. The Corvette's sophisticated electronic and powertrain components have low tolerance for real-world conditions. **Major redesign:** 1997, 2003, 2008, and 2014 (Stingray). The seventh generation Stingray is now faster, fuel-efficient, more powerful, more refined, and offers a much better interior (smaller steering wheel and better seats). The new 6.2L V8 coupled to a 7-speed manual transmission produces 455 hp (with cylinder deactivation). **Highway/city fuel economy:** *6.2L man.:* 7.7/12.9 L/100 km. *Auto.:* 8.1/14.3 L/100 km. *7.0L man.:* 8.2/14.2 L/100 km. *Auto.:* 8.2/14.2 L/100 km. *ZR1 man.:* 10.2/15.5 L/100 km. **Best alternatives:** Other sporty models worth considering are the Ford GT or Shelby GT500 Mustang and the Porsche 911 or Boxster. The Nissan 370Z looks good on paper, but its quality problems carried over year after year make it a risky buy, much like Nissan's attractively styled Quest.

SAFETY: No crashworthiness or rollover data available from NHTSA or IIHS.

ALERT! A word about the ZR1: It's like buying shares in Dell Computer – don't! A 2010 ZR1 that sold new for $128,515 is now worth $70,000. The Z06, although not quite as fast as the Dodge Viper, is the fastest model found in the Corvette lineup (0-100 km/h in 3.6-4.2 seconds). It's also the lightest Z06 yet, thanks to the magic of Detroit reengineering. Instead of just adding iron and components to carry extra weight, GM has reinforced the rear axle and 6-speed clutch, installed coolers everywhere, adopted a dry-sump oil system to keep the engine well oiled when cornering, and added wider wheels and larger, heat dissipating brakes. These improvements added about 50 kg of weight, which was trimmed by using cast-magnesium in the chassis structure and installing lighter carbon-fibre floorboards and front fenders. Net result: A monster Vette that is rated for 300+ km/h and weighs less than the base model. To be honest, the Z06 chassis isn't very communicative to the driver, so the car doesn't inspire as much driving confidence as does the European competition, although it does feature standard stability control for when you get too frisky. Keep in mind that premium fuel and astronomical insurance rates will further drive up your operating costs.

Corvette Profile

Used Values ($)	2004	2005	2006	2007	2008	2009	2010	2011	2012
Coupe	16,000	21,000	20,000	21,500	24,000	27,000	33,000	40,000	47,000
Convertible LT	18,000	23,000	22,000	24,000	27,000	34,000	39,000	48,000	57,000
Z06	18,500	—	25,000	27,500	29,000	42,000	48,000	60,000	68,000
ZR1	—	—	—	—	—	58,000	71,000	87,000	98,000
Recommended	☆	☆	☆	☆	☆	☆	☆	☆	☆
Reliability	☆	☆	☆	☆	☆	☆	☆	☆	☆

Prices and Specs

Prices (Very Negotiable): *1LT:* $50,575, *2LT:* $52,720, *3LT:* $56,570, *4LT:* $60,070, *Grand Sport:* $56,975, *Convertible:* $77,040, *Grand Sport Convertible:* $83,740, *Z06:* $95,705, *ZR1:* $128,600 **Freight:** $1,745 **Powertrain (Rear-drive):** Engines: 6.2L V8 (430 hp), 7.0L V8 (505 hp), 6.2L V8 Supercharged (638 hp); Transmissions: 6-speed man., 6-speed auto. **Dimensions/capacity:** Passengers: 2; Wheelbase: 106 in.; H: 49/L: 175/W: 73 in.; Headroom: 3.5 in.; Legroom: 43.5 in.; Cargo volume: 11 cu. ft.; Fuel tank: 68.1L/premium; Tow limit: Not recommended; Load capacity: 425 lb.; Turning circle: 42 ft.; Ground clearance: 4.5 in.; Weight: 3,280 lb.

SECRET WARRANTIES, INTERNAL BULLETINS: 2005-12—Be wary that top doesn't lift off while driving. Snap, pop, creak, or rattle noise from lift-off roof panel while driving (verify condition and perform appropriate repairs). **2005-13**—Folding top contacts stowage compartment lid (tonneau) and/or tonneau contacts rear window during top operation (verify condition and perform appropriate adjustments). **2011**—Wheel hop and differential chatter, under-hood rattle, engine tapping noise, and automatic transmission clunks. Power-steering and shock absorber fluid leakage. Airbag warning light comes on intermittently. Cracks in transparent removable roof panel. Convertible headliner frayed at outer edges. Troubleshooting tips for eliminating various noises from lift-off roof while driving. **2012-13**—Campaign allows for the free replacement of the air inlet grille panel.

CONVERTIBLE TOP COVER SEPARATION

DATE: JULY 1, 2010

BULLETIN NO.: 08312A

CUSTOMER SATISFACTION, CONVERTIBLE ROOF COVER SEPARATION – INSTALL NEW RETAINER BRACKET

2008-09 Chevrolet Corvette With Manual or Power Roof Convertible

CONDITION: Certain 2008 and 2009 model year Chevrolet Corvette manual or power roof convertible vehicles may have a condition in which the fabric roof cover may begin to separate from its retainer bracket near the top edge of the windshield. When the vehicle reaches speeds of approximately 100 mph (160 km/h) or greater, the roof cover could begin to pull away from the retainer bracket and, depending on the speed of the vehicle and duration at that speed, could tear to the rear glass. If this were to occur, the headliner would remain intact and the roof cover would not separate from the vehicle.

CORRECTION: Dealers are to install a new design retainer bracket.

CADILLAC CATERA/CTS ★ / ★★★

RATING: Average. The CTS is the successor of GM's Catera, a mid-size, entry-level luxury sedan imported from 1997-2001 in Germany, as a rebadged variant of the Opel. It was noted for serious reliability problems and mediocre performance. CTS continues that tradition with a wimpy V6 and a problematic powertrain. Unfortunately, as Cadillac reinvents itself in a futile attempt to lure younger buyers, its cars are becoming more complex and less distinctive. **Road performance:** Competent and secure handling; a pleasant ride; three manually tuned suspension settings for all tastes; and available AWD. The 3.6L V6 is smooth and adequate, if not pushed. **Strong points:** Roomier cabin than with other cars in this class (the Sport Wagon's generous cargo space is especially noteworthy); a tasteful, well-appointed interior loaded with high-tech gadgetry. **Weak points:** Not as agile as its rivals; poor rear visibility; and an awkward driving position caused by uneven pedal depth and limited knee room due to the intrusion of the centre stack. Rear occupants have tight seating. Owners also complain of embarrassingly evident fit and finish defects and frequent electronic module malfunctions. Rear-seat access requires some acrobatics due to the low rear roofline, and the rear seatback could use additional bolstering. Also, the trunk's narrow opening adds to the difficulty of loading bulky items. **Major redesign:** 1997, 2003, 2008, and 2014. The 2014 CTS is lower, longer, and sleeker as it moves up to mid-sized. **Highway/city fuel economy:** *3.0L:* 7.2/11.23 L/100 km. *3.6L:* 6.9/11.4 L/100 km. *3.6L AWD:* 7.9/13 L/100 km. *CTS-V man.:* 10.5/14.9 L/100 km. *CTS-V auto.:* 11/17.5 L/100 km. **Best alternative:** Acura TL SH-AWD, BMW 3 Series, Hyundai Genesis, Infiniti G37, and Lincoln MKS or Town Car.

SAFETY: NHTSA gives the CTS four and five stars in crash tests going back to 2003. IIHS awarded its top rating of "Good" for frontal offset, side, roof, and rear (head-restraint) crashworthiness.

ALERT! Buy the cheaper 2013 model this spring when Asian competition heats up, forcing prices down and leading to more generous customer rebates and dealer sales incentives. Think carefully about whether you want AWD: That option will cost you about $4,500 more with the base 3.0L engine or $2,600 when coupled to the 3.6L engine.

Cadillac Catera/CTS Profile

	2004	2005	2006	2007	2008	2009	2010	2011	2012
Used Values ($)									
Sedan	16,000	21,000	9,000	10,500	12,500	14,500	18,000	22,000	26,500
Coupe	—	—	—	—	—	—	—	24,000	28,000
Wagon	—	—	—	—	—	—	19,000	23,000	27,500
CTS-V	7,000	8,000	11,000	12,500	—	23,500	32,000	39,500	48,000
Recommended	✩	✩	✩	✩	✩	✩	✩	✩	✩
Reliability	✩	✩	✩	✩	✩	✩	✩	✩	✩

SECRET WARRANTIES, INTERNAL BULLETINS: *All models/years:* Reverse servo cover seal leak. Paint delamination, peeling, or fading. *CTS:* **2003-07**—Remedy for a front seat cushion that pops, creaks, and moves sideways on turns. **2003-12**—Drivetrain chatter or rear axle clunk: Replace the rear differential fluid. **2005-11**—Loss of engine power may be caused by water intrusion into the instrument panel (TSB #07-06-04-019D). **2008-09**—Clunk noise while turning, or automatic transmission extension housing leaks. Front brakes squeal when braking. GM suggests owners replace the brake pads with Kit #PN 25958115). Owners should ask for a partial reimbursement. Front seat lateral movement, clunking. Front door window drops incrementally. Rear door windows may go down by themselves. Front door latch freezing "Customer Satisfaction" policy: At no charge, dealers are to seal the latch housing on both front doors to prevent water intrusion. **2008-10**—Front door window is slow or noisy when activated. **2008-11**—Noise heard when shifting between Reverse and Drive. Inoperative low-beam headlights. **2008-12**—Front seat lateral movement/clunking noise. **2011**—Tire slowly goes flat. Slow, noisy operation of the front door glass. Power steering/shock absorber leaks. The airbag warning light comes on intermittently. An easy, inexpensive way to eliminate a chatter-type noise or rear axle clunk.

Prices and Specs

Prices (Very Negotiable): *Coupe RWD:* $42,860, *Coupe AWD:* $44,675, *3.0L Sedan:* $37,095, *AWD:* $41,420, *3.0L Wagon:* $44,130, *AWD:* $46,755, *3.6L Performance Wagon:* $50,760, *Performance AWD Wagon:* $53,795, *CTS-V Coupe:* $71,250, *Sedan:* $72,565 **Freight:** $1,745 **Powertrain (Rear-drive/AWD):** Engines: 3.0L V6 (270 hp), 3.6L V6 (304 hp), 6.2L V8 (556 hp); Transmissions: 6-speed man., 6-speed auto. **Dimensions/ capacity:** *(Base CTS)* Passengers: 2/3; Wheelbase: 113 in.; H: 58/L: 192/W: 73 in.; Headroom F/R: 3/1.5 in.; Legroom F/R: 44/28.5 in.; Cargo volume: 14 cu. ft.; Fuel tank: 70L/ premium; Tow limit: 1,000 lb.; Load capacity: 890 lb.; Turning circle: 38 ft.; Ground clearance: 5 in.; Weight: 3,940 lb.

CHATTER TYPE NOISE/REAR AXLE CLUNK

BULLETIN NO.: 10-04-20-001D

DATE: NOVEMBER 08, 2011

REAR AXLE CLUNK AND/OR CHATTER TYPE NOISE ON TURNS (DRAIN/REFILL REAR DIFFERENTIAL FLUID)

2003-12 Cadillac CTS, Sport Wagon (Including V-Series and Export); 2004-09 Cadillac SRX (Including Export); and the 2005-10 Cadillac STS (Including V-Series and Export) Equipped with Limited Slip Differential (RPO G80).

CONDITION: Some customers may comment on a clunk and/or chatter type noise from the rear of the vehicle while making turns. This condition may be worse on vehicles built prior to the 2008 model year. Carbon-faced clutch plates were introduced into production in the 2008 model year and have decreased the likelihood of the clutch plate chatter.

CAUSE: This condition may be caused by slip/stick of the posi-traction clutch plates due to insufficient limited-slip axle additive. As plates slip and stick, a jumping or jerking feel occurs accompanied by a clunk noise.

CORRECTION: DO NOT remove the differential cover. It is not necessary to flush the old fluid from the differential. Drain and refill the rear differential with fluid, GM P/N 88862624 (in Canada, 88862625). Refer to the Axle Lubricant Change procedure in SI. This fluid includes a friction modifier already added with a different formulation that lasts longer and does not break down over time.

EQUINOX/TERRAIN ★★★★★/★★★★★

good buy

The Chevrolet Equinox.

RATING: Recommended. **Road performance:** These tall wagons handle very well, provide a comfortable ride, and are easily controlled with precise steering. Thrilling acceleration with the V6 and manual transmission; the 4-cylinder engine and automatic gearbox are acceptable and fairly quiet, but the V6 is the better performer with little fuel penalty. The most important change among model years is the choice of a potent 301 hp 3.6L V6; which has 14 percent more horsepower and 22 percent more torque than the 3.0L V6. Interestingly, fuel-economy figures for the 3.6L are the same as with the 3.0L. **Strong points:** The Terrain shares its basic design and powertrain with the Chevrolet Equinox. Besides a plethora of airbags, the Terrain also comes with ABS, traction control, and an antiskid system. A rear-view camera is standard on all Terrain models. Acceptable handling and braking combined with a comfortable ride. Plenty of passenger room; a quiet interior; most controls are well laid out; very comfortable seating. **Weak points:** The 4-cylinder engine comes up short when passing other vehicles or merging into traffic; handling is better with the Honda competition; tall head restraints cut rear visibility; the dash buttons all look the same; cheap-looking, easily scratched, and hard-to-keep-clean door panels and dash materials. Overall reliability has been only average: The transmission, suspension, electrical, and fuel systems have been problematic, and fit and finish continues to get low marks. Not quite as much cargo space as seen in some rival makes; and some dash controls are difficult to reach. **Major redesign:** 2005 and 2010. **Highway/city fuel economy:** *2.4L auto.:* 6.1/9.2 L/100 km. *AWD:* 6.9/10.1 L/100 km. *3.0L auto.:* 8.1/12.4 L/100 km. *AWD:* 8.6/12.9 L/100 km. **Best alternatives:** Honda CR-V, Hyundai Tucson, Mazda CX5, Nissan Rogue, Subaru Forester, and Toyota RAV4.

Prices and Specs

Prices (Firm): *LS:* $26,315, *AWD:* $28,885, *2LT:* $30,955, *LT w/1LT:* $29,920, *LT w/2LT:* $31,720, *AWD:* $37,425, *LTZ:* $35,900, *AWD:* $37,850, *Terrain: SLE-1:* $28,695, *AWD:* $30,645, *SLE-2:* $31,040, *AWD:* $32,990, *SLT-1:* $32,665, *AWD:* $34,615, *SLT-2:* $37,145, *AWD:* $39,000, *Denali:* $39,830, *AWD:* $41,780 **Freight:** $1,500
Powertrain (Front-drive /AWD): Engines: 2.4L 4-cyl. (182 hp), 3.6L V6 (301 hp); Transmission: 6-speed auto. **Dimensions/capacity:** Passengers: 2/3; Wheelbase: 112.5 in.; H: 66.3/L: 187.8/W: 72.5 in.; Headroom F/R: 5/4 in.; Legroom F/R: 43/31 in.; Cargo volume: 33.5cu. ft.; Load capacity: 1,070 lb.; Fuel tank: 59L/regular; Tow limit: 3,500 lb.; Turning circle: 40 ft.; Ground clearance: 7.8 in.; Weight: 3,786 lb.

SAFETY: NHTSA gives the 2005 through 2014 models top marks (four and five stars) for crash protection. After testing the Equinox and Terrain, IIHS gave them both a "Good" designation for frontal, side, roof, and rear (head-restraint) crash protection.

ALERT! These cars are hobbled by the turbocharged 4-cylinder engine; go for a V6-equipped version.

Equinox/Terrain Profile

	2004	2005	2006	2007	2008	2009	2010	2011	2012
Used Values ($)									
4x2 LS	4,000	4,500	5,000	5,500	6,000	7,000	10,500	14,000	16,500
LT V6	—	—	—	—	—	—	12,000	16,500	21,500
LS 4x4	—	—	—	5,500	7,000	8,000	12,000	15,500	18,500
LT	—	—	—	6,000	7,500	9,000	13,000	18,000	22,000
Recommended	★3	★3	★3	★4	☆	☆5	☆5	★4	☆5
Reliability	★2	★2	★3	☆	☆	☆	★4	★3	★4

SECRET WARRANTIES, INTERNAL BULLETINS: 2007-12—*Acadia, Enclave, Equinox, OUTLOOK, Terrain, Torrent, Traverse, and VUE*—Transfer case fluid leak. **2007-13**—*Avalanche, Escalade, Sierra, Silverado, Suburban, Tahoe, and Yukon*—Tapping/clicking/ticking noise at windshield area. **2010-12**—*Avalanche, Equinox, Escalade, Sierra, Silverado, Suburban, Tahoe, Terrain, Yukon, and Yukon Denali*—Roof panel flutters/rattle noise when doors close. **2011**—Automatic transmission clunks when shifting. Troubleshooting tips to plug transfer case fluid leaks. Power steering, shock absorber leaks. Tire-pressure monitor system update for Canadians only. **2012-13**—*Equinox, LaCrosse, Malibu ECO, Regal, Terrain, Verano*—Voice recognition feature inoperative.

ACADIA/ENCLAVE/TRAVERSE

RATING: Above Average. These are practically identical seven- and eight-passenger crossover SUVs, with the Traverse being the most recent addition in 2009 with the other models launched in 2008 (Enclave) and 2007 (Acadian), respectively.

The Buick Enclave (top), Chevrolet Traverse (centre), and GMC Acadia (bottom) are all quite similar midsize SUVs that are reasonably reliable and well appointed. The downside: Poor fuel economy, and a sticker price for the Enclave that's easily 20 percent higher than its worth. Consider the cheaper Chevrolet Traverse, GMC Acadia, or a remaindered 2009 Saturn Outlook.

Road performance: The smooth-running 3.6L V6 has plenty of power for most chores and isn't as fuel-thirsty as other SUVs in the same class; a taught and comfortable ride; and standard stability control. On the negative side: The automatic transmission sometimes hesitates when shifting. **Strong points:** Strong acceleration; many powertrain configurations; a quiet interior; good towing capability; parts aren't hard to find and are reasonably priced; mechanical/body failures aren't excessive; and repairs can be done by independent garages. **Weak points:** Side airbags sometimes fail to deploy; transmission oil leaks and malfunctions; fuel-pump flow module fails, making the engine run rough or stall; inaccurate fuel gauges; a noisy, failure-prone suspension; and headlight failures. Middle-row passenger windows vibrate and make a loud noise when partially rolled down; excessive seat creaking and squeaking and overall fit and finish is subpar. **Major redesign:** *Acadia*: 2007; *Enclave*: 2008; and *Traverse*: 2009. **Highway/city fuel economy:** *Front-drive*: 8.4/12.7 L/100 km. *AWD*: 9/13.4 L/100 km. **Best alternatives:** The 2010-14 models are your best buys for the lowest price/highest quality advantage now that GM has corrected some of the first-year production quirks. Higher fuel prices and new products are also pushing leftover SUV and truck base prices way down; $15,000 discounts are commonplace. The Ford Flex, Honda Pilot, Hyundai Veracruz, and Mazda CX-9. If you don't mind downsizing a notch, consider the Ford Edge, Hyundai Santa Fe, and Nissan Xterra. Be wary of the Saturn Outlook. It has many identical features and components, but not the equivalent quality nor reliability.

SAFETY: Since 2007 NHTSA has gave these vehicles five stars for overall crashworthiness. IIHS awarded the trio identical "Good" ratings for front, side, roof, and rear collision crash protection. Side panels create a huge blind spot and there's limited rear visibility.

ALERT! Again, those pesky head restraints can make your driving a living hell if you are not the ideal size. Check this out with a test drive. Stay away from Firestone and Bridgestone original-equipment tires; *www.tirerack.com* is your best contact for dependable and well-performing tires.

CHATTER TYPE NOISE/REAR AXLE CLUNK

BULLETIN NO.: 10-04-20-001D

DATE: NOVEMBER 08, 2011

TRANSFER CASE FLUID LEAKAGE AT THE LEFT HAND WEEP HOLE OR BETWEEN TRANSFER CASE TO TRANSMISSION INTERFACE (REPLACE TRANSFER CASE INPUT SHAFT SEAL-LEFT OR TRANSFER CASE O-RING SEAL)

2008–12 Buick Enclave; 2008–09 Chevrolet Equinox Sport; 2009–12 Chevrolet Traverse; 2010–12 Chevrolet Equinox; 2007–12 GMC Acadia; 2010–12 GMC Terrain; 2008–09; Pontiac Torrent GXP; 2007–10 Saturn Outlook; 2008–10 Saturn; VUE; and 2007–09 Suzuki XL-7 models equipped with 6T45/70/75 Automatic Transmission RPOs MHC/MH4/MH6 for GM or AF33-5 AWD/PTU Automatic Transmission (RPO M45) for 2007–08 Suzuki and Getrag 760 or 790 Power transfer case.

CONDITION: Some customers may comment on a fluid leak from the automatic transmission or transfer case area. Upon further diagnosis, the technician may find fluid leaking between the transmission to transfer case interface or from the transfer case left hand weep hole.

Acadia/Enclave/Traverse Profile

	2004	2005	2006	2007	2008	2009	2010	2011	2012
Used Values ($)									
Acadia SLE	—	—	—	8,500	11,000	12,500	17,000	21,500	25,500
AWD	—	—	—	9,500	11,500	14,000	18,500	23,500	27,500
SLT	—	—	—	11,000	12,000	14,500	20,500	27,000	32,000
AWD	—	—	—	12,500	13,000	15,500	22,000	28,500	33,500
Denali	—	—	—	—	—	—	—	33,000	40,000
Enclave	—	—	—	—	12,500	14,500	19,000	24,500	29,000
AWD	—	—	—	—	13,500	16,000	20,000	26,000	31,000
Traverse LS	—	—	—	—	—	12,500	16,500	21,000	24,500
AWD	—	—	—	—	—	13,500	18,000	22,500	26,500
Recommended	☆3	☆3	☆3	☆4	☆4	☆5	☆5	☆5	☆5
Reliability	☆2	☆3	☆3	☆4	☆4	☆4	☆5	☆5	☆5

Prices and Specs

Prices (Very Negotiable): *Enclave 2×4 CX:* $43,750, *AWD:* $46,750, *Traverse 1LS 2×4:* $35,910, *AWD:* 38,910; *LT:* $38,570, *AWD:* $41,570, *AWD:* $41,570, *LTZ:* $47,835, *AWD:* $50,835, *Acadia: SLE-1:* $38,440, *AWD:* $41,440, *SLE-2:* $41,010, *SLT-1:* $46,450, *AWD:* $49,450, *SLT-2:* $50,005, *Denali:* $58,090 **Freight:** $1,500 **Powertrain (Front-drive/AWD):** Engine: 3.6L V6 (288 hp); Transmission: 6-speed auto. **Dimensions/ capacity:** *Enclave* Passengers: 7/8; Wheelbase: 119 in.; H: 70/L: 201.5/W: 78 in.; Headroom F/RR: 3.5/4/0 in.; Legroom F/RR: 41.5/30/24 in.; Cargo volume: 44 in. (behind 1st row).; Load capacity: 1,335 lb.; Fuel tank: 83L/regular; Tow limit: 4,500 lb.; Turning circle: 40.4 ft.; Ground clearance: 8.4 in.; Weight: 5,100 lb.

SECRET WARRANTIES, INTERNAL BULLETINS: 2007-10—Warranty coverage on the water pump shaft seals of several GM crossovers are being extended to ten years or 120,000 miles. In TSB #13091 issued on May 20, 2013, GM said the seal might fail and cause coolant leaks. Affected models: 2007-10 GMC Acadias and Saturn Outlooks; 2008-10 Buick Enclaves; and 2009-10 Chevrolet Traverses. Should the leak develop, a new water pump will be installed. 2011—Engine won't shut off. Electrical/water issues. Troubleshooting tips to plug transfer case fluid leaks. Power-steering, automatic transmission clunks. Steering-column squeak or rattle. Shock absorber leaks. Tires slowly go flat. Second-row "Easy Entry" seats may not work.

ELECTRICAL – ENGINE WON'T SHUT OFF/ELECTRICAL ISSUES

BULLETIN NO.: 08-08-57-003C

DATE: JULY 15, 2011

FLOOR WET UNDER CARPET/ENGINE CONTINUES TO RUN WITH KEY OFF/POSSIBLE NO CRANK/NO START/COMMUNICATION LOSS/VARIOUS ELECTRICAL CONCERNS (SEAL SEAM)

2008-12 Buick Enclave; 2007-12 GMC Acadia; and the 2007-10 Saturn Outlook.

CONDITION: Some customers may comment on any, or a combination of, the following conditions:
- Evidence of a water leak at the right side A-pillar and/or the right front floor is wet under the carpet.
- Various electrical concerns such as: Engine Continues to Run with Key Off/Possible No Crank/No Start/Communication Loss/Various Electrical Concerns, which may be a result of a water leak on the IP BEC.
- Other electrical related conditions that may be communication issues between certain electrical modules due to water dripping on the IP BEC.

CAUSE: Water from the right front sunroof drain hose exits the vehicle through the plenum (upper arrow) and may re-enter through the un-sealed seam at the front of the dash. In more current models and years, sunroof drain hose and windshield related issues have sometimes been found to be a source of a water leak in the A-pillar area. This water can also sometimes leak on the IP BEC and/or onto the floor area.

RATING: An Above Average buy (2008–14); Average buy (1999–2007). These large SUVs are for those who need rugged, truck-like capabilities, a nine-passenger capacity, and lots of cargo space. All three vehicles are practically identical, though the Escalade comes with a 6.2L V8 and a plusher interior and is also more gadget-laden.
Road performance: Surprisingly good handling for an SUV this large. Comfortable for highway cruising, and pretty agile around town as well. The Tahoe now comes with only a 320 hp 5.3L V8 hooked to a 6-speed automatic transmission. The former Hybrid model is not available for the abbreviated 2014 model year and may be dropped with the next-generation vehicle. **Strong points:** Strong acceleration; many powertrain configurations; standard stability control; a quiet interior and comfortable ride; good towing capability; parts aren't hard to find and are reasonably priced; and repairs can be done by independent garages. Very few reliability problems since the last redesign in 2007. A hybrid version is available. **Weak points:** Extremely poor fuel economy; rapid depreciation; small third-row seat sits too low and doesn't fold into the floor; long braking distances; and terrible fit and finish. Specific problem areas include loss of brakes; faulty powertrain, suspension, and climate controls; chronic electrical shorts, and various body glitches. **Major redesign:** *Escalade:* 1999, 2002, and 2007. *Suburban, Tahoe, and Yukon:* 2000 and 2007. The 2014 fourth generation Cadillac Escalade and its Chevrolet/GMC clones will be based on the new truck platform used in the next generation Chevrolet Silverado. They will likely feature a 6.2L V8 EcoTec3 engine, and sport a revised exterior and interior to distinguish the Escalade from its Suburban, Tahoe, Yukon, and XL brothers. As with all redesigns, buy the second year's "debugged" production. **Highway/city fuel economy:** *Escalade AWD:* 10 /15.3 L/100 km. *Escalade AWD auto.:* 13.8 /21.2 L/100 km. *Escalade Hybrid AWD:* 8.5/10.4 L/100 km. The other model spin-offs are within the same range. **Best alternatives:** Many SUV buyers can't resist the options and end up buying much more car than they need. Question the need for 4x4. If the weather is that bad, maybe you should stay at home. Did you know sunroofs are usually much more trouble than they're worth (shattering when a door is closed, or when the temperature drops, leaking, whistling)? Or, that most extras aren't worth much come trade-in

Prices and Specs

Prices (Negotiable): *Escalade EXT Base:* $84,955, *Escalade Luxury:* $91,855, *Platinum:* $108,205, *ESV:* $88,685, *EXT:* $79,945, *Escalade Hybrid:* $95,110, *Suburban 2X4 LS 1500:* $52,220; *Tahoe LS 2X4:* $49,555; *LT:* $54,960; *Tahoe Hybrid 2×4:* $68,815, *4x4:* $761,800, *Yukon SLE 2X4:* $49,555, *4x4:* $54,015, *Denali AWD:* $73,355, *Hybrid 2X4:* $68,815, *4×4:* $71,800, *4x4 Denali:* $80,557 **Freight:** $1,500
Powertrain (Front-drive/AWD): Engines: 5.3L V8 (320 hp), 6.2L V8 (403 hp), 6.0L V8 (332 hp); Transmissions: 6-speed auto., CVT **Dimensions/capacity:** Passengers: *Escalade:* 3/3/2; *Tahoe:* 3/3/3; Wheelbase: *Escalade:* 116 in.; *Hybrid:* 202.5 in.; H: 74.3/L: 202.5/W: 79 in.; Headroom F/RR: 3/3.5/0 in.; Legroom F/RR: 40/27/28.5 in.; Cargo volume: 46.5 cu. ft.; Load capacity: Fuel tank: 98L/regular; Tow limit: *Escalade:* 8,100 lb.; *Hybrid:* 5,600 lb.; Maximum load: *Escalade:* 1,330 lb.; *Hybrid:* 1,484 lb.; Turning circle: 40.4 ft.; Ground clearance: 9 in.; Weight: *Escalade:* 5,691–5,943 lb.; *Hybrid:* 6,116 lb.

time. Plus, the extra money for a "loaded" SUV or truck could be put to paying off the loan, fuel economy will suffer from the extra weight and 4x4 option, and a smaller car is easier to unload. If there's a need to trade up look at cheaper alternatives. For example, you can get eight-passenger seating and better fuel economy and manoeuvrability in the cheaper Chevy Traverse. Other good choices are the Buick Enclave, Chevrolet Avalanche, Equinox or Terrain, Ford Flex, GMC Acadia or Traverse, Honda Pilot, Hyundai Santa Fe, Mazda CX-5 or CX-9, and Toyota Highlander. The Ford Flex and the Mazda CX-9 get good fuel economy and are easier to drive, and their third-row seating outclasses what GM offers. Plus, crossover SUVs are available with AWD, which can provide a good amount of all-weather capability. In the new year, prices will fall and many of these large SUVs will sell with almost a third off their original price.

SAFETY: 2000-14 models have earned top marks of four and five stars, except for three-star rollover resistance performance. Hasn't been tested by IIHS.

ALERT! Keep a wary eye on the rear hatch when loading or unloading cargo:

2011 Cadillac Escalade power rear cargo door is a serious safety hazard. Son was seriously hurt at airport luggage claims when a power rear cargo door was closing, came down on his head and face without warning of any kind that this door was closing. The door is so large and heavy as it comes down, it's fast and does not retract back up when it hits something. The driver had no warning that a person was behind him as he closed the door.

Escalade/Hybrid/Suburban/Tahoe/Yukon Profile

Used Values ($)	2004	2005	2006	2007	2008	2009	2010	2011	2012
Escalade	8,500	11,000	14,000	17,000	22,000	36,000	38,500	47,500	56,000
ESV	—	—	—	18,000	24,000	31,000	39,500	49,500	58,500
EXT	—	—	—	17,500	22,000	27,000	35,000	44,500	52,000
Hybrid AWD	—	—	—	—	—	—	39,000	52,000	62,000
Suburban	6,000	8,000	10,000	12,000	14,500	16,500	23,000	29,000	32,000
Suburban AWD	7,500	9,000	11,000	16,000	21,000	22,000	25,000	30,000	34,000
Tahoe	6,000	7,500	8,500	9,500	10,500	12,500	18,000	25,000	29,500
Tahoe AWD	—	—	—	10,500	11,500	14,500	21,000	26,500	32,500
Hybrid	—	—	—	—	10,500	15,500	24,000	27,000	41,000
Hybrid AWD	—	—	—	—	11,000	16,500	25,500	35,000	43,000
Yukon	6,000	7,000	8,000	9,500	10,500	12,500	19,000	25,000	30,000
Yukon AWD	—	—	—	6,000	14,000	19,500	26,000	27,000	32,500
Hybrid	—	—	—	6,000	10,500	15,000	25,000	30,000	31,000
Hybrid AWD	—	—	—	6,000	11,500	17,500	33,000	35,000	43,500
Recommended	☆	☆	☆	☆	☆	☆	☆	4	☆
Reliability	☆	☆	☆	☆	☆	☆	☆	☆	☆

SECRET WARRANTIES, INTERNAL BULLETINS: 2011—Engine knocking on a cold start (GM says, "Don't worry, be happy"). Power-steering, shock absorber leaks. Airbag warning light comes on intermittently. Airbag isn't flush with the dash. Exhaust leak, rattle, and rumble noise. Tapping, clicking. and ticking noise at windshield area. Sun visor fails to stay in the up position. Sticking, binding door mounted seat switches. Front-door window regulator squeaks. Third-row seat hard to remove and install. Front seat cushion cover becomes detached and warped. Wavy front or rear fender liners.

SILVERADO/SIERRA ★★★★★

RATING: Recommended (2008-14); Above Average (1999-2007) . General Motors introduced its first pickup truck in 1930 and the "Silverado" name was used only to detail the trim for the Chevrolet C/K pickup trucks and Suburbans from 1975 through 1999. These pickups have been essentially the same for their entire history, except for the 2014's redesigned 1500 model. The Silverado today is seen as the "standard" version aimed for use in agriculture, while the Sierra targets industrial workers and truck aficionados who want a bit more luxury. GM's pickup quality and performance have improved dramatically since its 2008 redesign and the company no longer needs a "twin-brand" gimmick to sell trucks and SUVs. All the more reason why GM should merge GMC with Chevrolet. Money saved could go into the major truck and SUV redesign planned for the 2015 models, following an abbreviated 2014 model year 1500 series to match the improvements now seen with GM's Heavy Duty (HD) series. **Road performance:** Since its 2007 model redesign, the Silverado handles much better, offers more usable power, and gives a more-controllable ride (no more "Shakerado"). Nevertheless, annoying and dangerous powertrain glitches remain, making GM's 2014 "freshening" and 2015 model redesign imperative. These owners' reports are typical of many other complaints that target the powertrain's "Reduced Power Mode" feature and assorted engine/transmission malfunctions:

> I have had a recurring problem with my new 2012 Chevrolet Silverado 1500 LT (5.3 liter engine) going into "Reduced Engine Power Mode" which also results in the disabling of stability control and traction control. This is a dangerous condition in that it results in a loss of power while operating the vehicle upon the roadway. An authorized repair facility has replaced the number one and two throttle sensors, the accelerator pedal assembly, the throttle body, the alternator, the computer, and a large ground wire behind the dash. A GM engineer has flown in and now the repair center is replacing the engine wiring harness. The vehicle (which was purchased less than three months ago) has been out of service for approximately 30 days. In researching this matter I have found that Chevy has had an ongoing problem with this in various vehicles in its product line since 2003. Although several service bulletins have been produced there does not seem to be a consensus regarding the cause of this problem. All of the parts associated with trouble codes C0242, P2127, and P2138 have been replaced without result. This condition could result in the affected vehicles being rear-ended, or, because of the loss of stability and traction control, result in a rollover. This needs to be addressed immediately.

Transmission shifts hard from a complete stop as 1st gear was being engaged. Drove it until break-in period was over and took it back to the dealer where the transmission body and valves were replaced. Now getting more problems with the transmission shifting between gears at a speed of 35-45 mph [56-72 km/h]. Transmission disengages and I have no power going to the wheels, like it shifts to Neutral for 5-10 seconds. This will cause an accident if transmission does not reengage while driving in traffic you will get rear ended.

Ford's F-Series and the Dodge Ram 1500 have had many recent refinements, sport better interiors and more capable powertrains that give a comfortable ride. But, from a quality and dependability standpoint, GM products have excelled. The company says its upcoming redesigned models will be radically improved, as the 2014 Impala has been. The new pickups will carry more powerful, fuel-efficient EcoTec engine trains and updated interior appointments. The Silverado 1500 Hybrid has a 6.0L V8 that pairs with an electric motor, producing 332 hp. It can run on one or both of its power sources depending on driving demands, and doesn't need to be plugged in. The Hybrid has a continuously variable automatic transmission and a maximum towing capacity of 6,100 lb. **Strong points:** *1500:* Comfortable seating; a quiet interior; lots of storage capability; generally good crashworthiness scores; and acceptable fuel economy with the 6-speed automatic transmission coupled to the 5.3L V8. *2500.* These heavy-duty work trucks are built primarily to be load carrying vehicles capable of working off-road; the independent front end improves handling and smoothes out the ride. The standard engine is a powerful 360 hp 6.0L V8 backed up by a 397 hp 6.6L turbodiesel. On the other hand, the GM Allison transmission dates to the late '40s, yet it hasn't performed as well as Ford's TorqShift 6-speed found in the Super Duty models. **Weak points:** *1500:* Powertrain smoothness and reliability doesn't measure up to what the Honda Ridgeline and Nissan Titan can provide, especially when comparing the performance of the V8 4x4 model. GM Duramax-equipped pickups need diesel exhaust fluid (urea) refills every 8,000 km (5,000 mi.). This is more frequent than the oil change one usually does every 12,000 km (7,500 mi.). Furthermore, the urea-filling process can be costly. **Major redesign:** *Silverado/Sierra 1500:* 1999, 2007, and 2014-15. This year's re-engineered 1500 model carries a new 355 hp V8 that gets better gas mileage than Ford's F-Series pickup. Silverado also has a larger cargo bed, more payload capacity, and can now tow up to 11,200 lb. The tailgate is easier to use, it has a lower step-in height than the rivals and there are steps to make it easy to climb into. **Highway/city fuel economy:** *4.3L 2WD:* 10/14.1 L/100 km. *4.3L 4WD:* 11.3/14.9 L/100 km. *4.8L 2WD:* 10.6/14.7 L/100 km. *4.8L 4WD:* 11.1/15.4 L/100 km. *5.3L 2WD:* 10.1/14.5 L/100 km. *5.3L 4WD:* 10.3/14.7 L/100 km. *6.2L AWD:* 10.8/17.7 L/100 km. *Hybrid 2WD:* 9.2/9.8 L/100 km. *Hybrid 4WD:* 9.8/10.5 L/100 km. **Best alternatives:** Any 1999-2013 GM pickup will do, if cost is your primary concern. The Honda Ridgeline and Nissan Titan are good first choices, while the Nissan Rogue remains a competent crossover SUV with power and storage space to spare.

Ford trucks still have some problems to work out. But Chrysler's new suspension gives it one of the smoothest rides of any full-size pickup, and its Laramie Longhorn trim is well worth the extra cost. The company has also made important strides in quality control. Ford's F-150 trucks are comfortable to drive; and the EcoBoost engine promises good fuel economy (a promise not realized say owners). On the other hand, Ford's low quality and dependability ratings make its best-selling trucks also-rans in this year's *Lemon-Aid* ratings, where GM and Chrysler take the number one and two spot for most value for your buck.

SAFETY: NHTSA gave the redesigned 2014 Silverado/Sierra five-star overall crash protection scores; redesigned Ram and Ford F-150 trailed. 2010 through 2013 Silverado 1500 and Hybrid got a four-star score for overall crash safety; earlier 1500 models got even better crash ratings. Silverado 2500 series test results for 2012-14 models are much lower (two to four stars). Earlier pickups and other models weren't tested. IIHS has given the Silverado 1500 a "Good" rating for frontal offset protection and an "Acceptable" score for side-impact crashworthiness and head-restraint effectiveness. IIHS says the 1500's roof crashworthiness merits a "Marginal" rating. Seat pelvic-thorax and side curtain airbags are available but aren't standard on the 2500HD; Ford Super Duty trucks have them as a standard safety feature.

ALERT! Diesel owners can save money buying urea at independent retailers. Save your money; buy an almost identical, but much cheaper, 2013 base 1500 series, or HD if you need the additional power. If there are no more models left in stock, wait for a second-series 2015 built in the late spring or summer of 2014. The 2015 models get all the improvements.

Silverado/Sierra Profile

	2004	2005	2006	2007	2008	2009	2010	2011	2012
Used Values ($)									
Silverado 1500 4x2	8,000	10,000	12,500	8,000	9,000	10,000	13,000	16,500	19,500
Hybrid	—	—	—	5,500	—	16,000	22,000	27,000	34,000
Sierra	—	—	—	8,000	9,000	10,000	13,500	16,000	19,000
Hybrid AWD	—	—	—	—	—	16,000	21,500	27,500	32,500
Recommended	☆	☆	☆	☆	☆	☆	☆	☆	☆
Reliability	☆	☆	☆	☆	☆	☆	☆	☆	☆

SECRET WARRANTIES, INTERNAL BULLETINS: 2009-13—Brake-induced pulsation/vibration felt in steering wheel, rumble noise from underbody during downhill descent (verify condition and replace front brake pads). GM admits this is a factory goof-up, so ask for a free pad replacement within two years, or a refund of 50%

Prices and Specs

Prices (Very Negotiable): *1500 WT Standard Cab 4x2:* $28,600, *LT Standard Long Cab 4x2:* $32,430, *Standard Cab 4x4:* $36,580, *Hybrid:* $47,715 **Freight:** $1,500 **Powertrain (Rear-drive/4x4):** Engines: 4.3L V6 (195 hp), 4.8L V8 (302 hp), 5.3L V8 (315 hp), 6.0L V8 (360 hp), 6.2L V8 (403 hp), 6.6L V8 TD (397 hp); *Compressed Natural Gas (CNG):* 6.0L V8 (279 hp); *Hybrid:* 6.0L V8 (332 hp), 6.6L *Diesel* (397 hp); Transmissions: 4-speed auto., 6-speed auto., *Hybrid:* CVT **Dimensions/capacity:** Passengers: *1500:* 2/1, *2500:* 3/3; Wheelbase: *1500:* 144 in., *2500:* 133.6-167 in.; *1500:* H: 74/L: 230/W: 80 in., *2500:* H: 77/L: 240/W: 80 in.; Headroom F/R: *1500:* 6.5/6 in., *2500:* 6/5 in.; Legroom F/R: 41.5/29 in., *2500:* 40.5/27 in.; Fuel tank: 129L/ regular; Tow limit: *Hybrid:* 6,100 lb., *1500:* 7,500 lb., *2500:* 13,600 lb.; *HD Turbo Diesel:* 15,600 lb.; Load capacity: *1500:* 1,570 lb., *2500HD:* 2,485 lb.; Turning circle: *1500:* 50 ft., *2500:* 55 ft.; Ground clearance: 9.5 in.; Weight: *1500:* 5,435 lb., *2500:* 6,920 lb.

thereafter. **2011**—Airbag light comes on intermittently. Side roof-rail airbags may not deploy as designed, says GM Customer Satisfaction Campaign bulletin #11288 (shh…it's a "secret warranty" – the fix is free). Automatic transmission clunks when shifted. Rear suspension clunk and squeaks. Rattle noise from wheel or hubcap. Underbody pop, clunk when turning. Rear leaf-spring slap or clunk noise. Exhaust leak, rattle, or rumble. Front-door regulator squeak. Tapping, clicking, or ticking at the windshield area. Shock absorber and power-steering leaks. Sun visor won't stay up. Water leaks through the headliner near the sunroof. Tires may slowly go flat. Warped or wavy fender liners. Rear-view mirror shake. Front brake vibration. **2011-12**—*Express, Savana, Sierra, Silverado, Suburban, and Yukon XL*—Free fix to correct a rear axle grinding noise/vibration. Program is in effect until April 30, 2014, after which an extension can be requested through any small claims court.

BULLETIN NO.: 10-08-58-001F

EXCESSIVE WIND NOISE FROM REAR INTERIOR

DATE: DECEMBER 14, 2011

2007-12 Chevrolet Silverado and 2007-12 GMC Sierra

CONDITION: Some customers may comment on hearing excessive wind noise coming from the rear interior of the vehicle.

CAUSE #1 (2007-10 MODEL YEARS ONLY): This condition may be caused by a void in the body filler within the C-pillar.

CAUSE #2: This condition may be a result of the design of the body rear panel acoustic insulator that is mounted behind the rear seat. The insulator could be one of several early designs (1 or 2 in the above graphic), which demonstrated a lesser success of minimizing noise.

GM has allowed this problem to continue for the past six model years – from before to after bankruptcy. Can you blame motorists who say Detroit automakers still consider quality to be "job last"? This service bulletin is proof the company is negligent and, under the implied warranty (see Part Three), must foot the bill for any repair – long after the normal warranty has expired.

ASIANS ON THE DEFENSIVE

Help! Toyota has been hijacked by pirates!
(That's why their trucks are rust-cankered, their brakes fail,
and their cars accelerate on their own, right?)

Suzuki is gone, Mitsubishi is wobbly, and Toyota is losing sales to stiff competition from the Ford Fusion, Honda's redesigned Accord, and General Motors' Cruze compact. Not even hybrids offer a safe port in spite of rising fuel costs. Prius sales have tumbled 8.4% for the first-quarter of 2013.

And, to add insult to poor sales, traditional car quality survey "bottom-feeders" have risen to the top of many car-buying lists. For example, GM's "bland leading the bland" Impala and Chrysler's 1500 Ram pickup – with no pick up – have morphed into "Recommended" buys, praised by auto critics and independent consumer groups, alike, for their quality, performance, and styling.

Declining sales are a wake-up call to automobile manufacturers that buyers won't accept cars that accelerate on their own, suddenly lose their brakes, or transform rear-end collisions into inescapable infernos. Chrysler CEO Sergio

Chevrolet's unwanted Impala (above) and Malibu came within a hair's breadth of getting the axe. Malibu is still on the scaffold.

Marchionne learned that lesson earlier this year when massive protests and U.S. government intervention forced him to recall 2.7 million fire-prone Jeep Grand Cherokee and Liberty models.

As Toyota settles its unintended acceleration lawsuits for $1.3 billion in the States and gives Canadians practically nothing, South Korean and American manufacturers move ahead with new products that are reasonably priced and stop and go as they should. Of course, all carmakers love to fib about their fuel economy figures, but that's a far cry from being run over by your own car.

So in a nutshell, the temporary pain of lost sales has had a cleansing effect that eventually leads to improved quality and better performing, safer vehicles at lower prices.

Get used to it. It's called competition.

ACURA

Acura, Honda's luxury division, has sold a variety of models in Canada, mostly as upscale Hondas with a luxury cachet. There is the entry-level ILX compact and the discontinued CLX (a TSX sport sedan), the TL performance luxury sedan (a ZDX four-door sport coupe), the RL luxury performance sedan – replaced by the RLX – (a turbocharged RDX luxury crossover SUV), and the MDX luxury SUV. All but the TSX, and the recently revamped MDX, are rated in the Appendix.

Acuras are good buys, but let's not kid ourselves – most Acura products are basically fully loaded Hondas with a few additional features and unjustifiably higher prices.

Automobile magazine calls Acura "a lost brand" – a harsh judgement of the first Japanese nameplate (four years before Lexus) to take on the U.S. luxury market with the popular 1986 Legend and Integra. The brand is now less distinctive than it once was when Acura was a showcase for advanced technology. It has lost its leadership edge and now offers what everybody else provides, at a discount. One Acura owner puts it this way in The Temple of VTEC, an Internet forum for Acura (and Honda) owners:

The Acura Question has been discussed here *ad nauseam*, amongst the North American contingent and elsewhere ... It's no secret that while Acura sales are 'ok', the brand has been lost for years with no direction and, quite frankly, no soul, flip-flopping between strategies, gaining no traction ... A rebadged Civic ILX or a rebadged Euro Accord TSX just will not cut it anymore in what has become a crowded very competitive field of players. We're not in the same time and place when an Integra with Civic internals could eat its competitors for lunch.

Acura has moved away from affordable, nimble, sporty cars to be a builder of high-end SUVs like the MDX – its bestseller that accounts for one-third of all Acura sales. Despite the fact that Acura and Honda dealers have abhorred real price competition for years, declining sales during the past few years have forced them to give sizeable rebates and other sales incentives to customers to keep market share. In their own right, maintenance costs are low, depreciation is generally slower than average, though there are some exceptions, and reliability and quality are much better than average. What few defects Acuras have are usually related to squeaks, rattles, minor trim glitches, and accessories such as the navigation, climate control, and sound systems.

Here's a tip for penny-pinchers: Despite being the best-selling vehicle in Acura Canada's lineup, Honda axed the Acura CSX after the 2011 model year and replaced it with the Civic-based ILX (see Appendix I "Reviews and Previews"). Smart shoppers should consider buying a fully loaded 2011 CSX Sedan Tech, with some remaining warranty, for $16,500, a "steal" for a car that originally sold for $25,790.

And, speaking of the warranty, Acura has extended its warranty to cover an automatic transmission judder (shake) that may also damage the transmission torque converter (see below).

WARRANTY EXTENSION:TORQUE CONVERTER
PRODUCT UPDATE: PCM UPDATE FOR LOCK-UP CLUTCH FUNCTION

CSC-10049199-8317   SEPTEMBER 2012

VEHICLES AFFECTED: MDX 2007-09, RL 2009-10, and TL 2009-11
This letter is to notify you of a warranty extension and product update on your Acura.

WHAT IS THE REASON FOR THIS PRODUCT UPDATE?
A transmission judder (vibration) may sometimes be felt while driving between 20-45 mph. To minimize the opportunity for judder to occur, a software update for the transmission is available. If you do not feel the transmission judder, the software may prevent it from occurring. If the transmission software is not updated, the transmission may become damaged.

WHAT IS THE REASON FOR THIS WARRANTY EXTENSION?
If the judder goes away or never appears, no action is required on your part. If the judder appears or comes back after the product update is applied, the torque converter may need to be replaced. To ensure your confidence in your vehicle, American Honda is extending the warranty on the torque converter to 8 years from the original date of purchase or 105,000 miles, whichever comes first. This warranty extension provides coverage for the original owner and any subsequent owners.

TSX ★★★★

RATING: Above Average (2011-14); Average (2004-10). An entry-level luxury car that debuted as a 2004 model and may be in its last year on the market. **Road performance:** Essentially a European Accord, the TSX provides a mildly sporty performance due to its firm suspension that's compromised by vague steering (an RL drawback, as well). Good handling with very little body lean, though there's a slight tendency to understeer (the car turns wider than the driver wants it to). The sport suspension produces a slightly jittery ride, while the responsive 6-speed manual and 5-speed automatic transmissions keep power flowing smoothly in all gear ranges. The fuel-frugal 4-cylinder is loud and underpowered until it gets into the higher rpms; the overpriced optional V6 tames the torque curve but adds a pinch of torque-steer wandering. It doesn't give you sportier handling than the 4-banger, though the car is generally sportier than the TL, yet it isn't as harsh as the discontinued high-performance RSX. **Strong points:** Powerful V6; slick-shifting automatic transmission; generously appointed; instruments and controls are well laid out; good navigation system controls; comfortable front seats; brakes are easy to modulate, producing short, controlled stops; impressive fit and finish; and reasonable fuel economy. **Weak points:** Premium fuel negates the small engine's fuel-sipping savings; cabin centre console houses too many buttons; the interior is a bit snug, especially in the rear; rear seats have insufficient thigh support; lots of road noise in the cabin; trunk hinges limit utility; and the low roofline hampers rear access. Owners also report: A chronic "lag and lurch" when letting off the accelerator; excessive steering vibration with the wagon; noisy brake pads, and premature brake caliper and rotor wear; paint peeling and spotting; and malfunctioning power accessories and entertainment systems. **Major redesign:** 2004, and 2009. **Highway/city fuel economy:** *4-cyl. man.:* 6.8/9.9 L/100 km, 42/29 mpg. *4-cyl. auto.:* 6.2/9.3 L/100 km. *V6 auto.:* 7.0/10.7 L/100 km. **Best alternatives:** Audi A4, BMW 328i, Infiniti G37, Lexus IS 250 or 350, and Lincoln MKZ. The BMW 3 Series and Mercedes C-Class look good but the cars aren't as reliable as the TSX and will likely cost a bundle to maintain. The TSX's size and good looks outclass the TL by far, and the V6 puts it about where the former TL was in size and power.

SAFETY: NHTSA crash tests awarded the 2013 TSX five stars for rollover resistance. Occupant protection in offset, side, and rear crashes are "Good," according to IIHS. Roof strength was also rated "Good."

Prices and Specs

Price (Firm): *Premium:* $33,990, *TECH package:* $38,290, *V6 TECH package:* $42,090 **Freight:** $1,895
Powertrain (Front-drive/awd): Engines: 2.4L 4-cyl. (201 hp), 3.5L V6 (280 hp); Transmissions: 5-speed auto., 6-speed man. **Dimensions/capacity:** Passengers: 2/3; Wheelbase: 107 in.; H: 57/L: 186/W: 73 in.; Headroom F/R: 3.5/3 in.; Legroom F/R: 40.5/26.5 in.; Cargo volume: 13 cu. ft.; Fuel tank: 70L/premium; Tow limit: 1,000 lb.; Load capacity: 850 lb.; Turning circle: 36.7 ft.; Ground clearance: 5.9 in.; Weight: 3,440 lb.

ALERT! When you consider the 2013 TSX's price is about $10,000 more than a base Honda Accord, you have to ask yourself, "What the hell am I doing?" – especially, since the difference narrows down to just $5,000 with the 2011s. Other things to be wary of: Overly sensitive seat sensors that disable the airbag, even when an average-sized adult is seated and poorly-performing Bridgestone/Firestone original equipment tires (consider Michelin, Yokohama, or Pirelli rubber). Finally, remember that a cheaper, almost-identical 2012 model gives you a cornucopia of standard safety, performance, and convenience features – like stability and traction control, and head-protecting side airbags.

TSX Profile

	2004	2005	2006	2007	2008	2009	2010	2011	2012
Used Values ($)									
Base	8,000	9,500	11,000	12,000	13,000	14,500	17,000	20,500	23,500
Premium	—	—	—	—	—	16,000	19,000	22,000	25,500
Tech	—	—	—	—	—	17,000	20,500	24,500	28,500
Tech V6	—	—	—	—	—	—	22,000	26,500	31,000
Recommended	★	★	★	★	★	★	★	★	★
Reliability	★	★	★	★	★	★	★	★	★

SECRET WARRANTIES, INTERNAL BULLETINS: 2009-10—A popping or clicking that comes from the lower area of the steering column when turning the steering wheel may be silenced by replacing the steering column. If the engine rattles during a cold start-up, it's likely the variable valve timing control (VTC) is defective, says TSB #10-024, issued October 6, 2012. Hood flutters at highway speeds. Fuel fill door may be hard to open. **2009-11**—Door lock makes a high-pitch whine or doesn't work. **2009-12**—A popping or clicking from the left or right rear of the vehicle when driving over bumps or through dips may require the installation of a wedge between the sheetmetal panels (in the inner side sill) that make up the jack point. **2010**—Starter motor grinds in cold weather (problem also affects the 2011 RDX). Honda recommends replacing the starter motor under warranty. **2010-11**—Acura admits responsibility for bubbled dashboards caused by insufficient die temperature during the manufacturing process. **2012**—The retractable master key does not lock in its extended position.

MDX

RATING: Above Average (2007-14); Average (2001-06). **Road performance:** Good highway performance with commendable acceleration, nice handling, and better braking "feel" than with the 2013s. Although steering is more responsive, the returning 6-speed automatic transmission isn't as efficient as the 7- or 8-speeds

Prices and Specs

Prices (Negotiable): *Base:* $53,190, *TECH package:* $58,690, *Elite package:* $63,390 **Freight:** $1,895 **Powertrain (AWD):** Engine: 3.7L V6 (290 hp); Transmission: 6-speed auto. **Dimensions/capacity:** Passengers: 2/3/2; Wheelbase: 111 in.; H: 67.6/L: 194.3/W: 77.2 in.; Headroom F/RR2: 4.5/4 /0 in.; Legroom F/RR2: 41./28.5/24 in.; Cargo volume: 45.1 cu. ft.; Fuel tank: 72.7L/premium; Tow limit: 5,000 lb.; Load capacity: 1,150 lb.; GVWR: 5,732 lb.; Turning circle: 37.6 ft.; Ground clearance: 8.2 in.; Weight (SH-AWD): 4,255 lb.

offered by German competitors. However, this year's larger wheelbase and improved suspension help improve the ride quality and extra inches in length provide greater cargo capacity. Less width also aids parking. **Strong points:** Loaded with goodies; above-average reliability; a roomy interior, plenty of interior comfort and top-quality body and mechanical components. Engine and road noise intrusion into the cabin has been muted. Also new this year is rear and middle seats that fold flat and give easier rear seat access. **Weak points:** Overpriced and overweight; the rear third seat remains for kids only; the dash console isn't user-friendly; audio and navigation systems are needlessly complicated; and fuel consumption is on the high side. 2014 models have ten fewer horses. Owners report noisy brake pads and premature brake wear; and malfunctioning power accessories and entertainment systems. **Major redesign:** 2001, 2007, and 2014. **Highway/city fuel economy:** 9.6/13.2 L/100 km (2013 model). The 2014's ten fewer horses and other refinements are expected to increase fuel economy by almost 15 percent. **Best alternatives:** The BMW X5, Buick Enclave, Chevrolet Traverse or Terrain, Infiniti FX35, and Lexus RX series. Would you like comparable Asian performance and reliability for $15,000 less? Try a Honda Pilot (the MDX's cheaper cousin), a Nissan Xterra, or a Toyota Highlander. The Volvo XC90 and Mercedes ML320, ML350, or ML550 have adequate cargo room with all the rows down, but they have neither comparable cargo room behind the second row nor quality control and dealer servicing. Furthermore, now that Volvo has been sold to Chinese interests, Volvo sales and servicing in North America may become problematic.

SAFETY: NHTSA gives 2001-13 models four and five stars for occupant crash protection. IIHS says rear, offset, side, and roof protection are "Good." IIHS qualifies 2001–12 models' frontal offset, side protection, and head restraints as "Good." One discordant note: 2003-06 model head restraints were judged to be "Poor."

ALERT! This mid-size SUV's sporty suspension may not sit well with passengers who expect a smoother ride; 2014 model provides a smoother ride. The Lexus RX is much smoother, even over the roughest roads. Another advantage of the RX is its lower starting price and reasonable fuel economy for an AWD. 2000-03 models had failure-prone automatic transmissions and so-so reliability.

MDX Profile

	2004	2005	2006	2007	2008	2009	2010	2011	2012
Used Values ($)									
MDX	8,000	10,000	13,000	15,500	17,500	21,500	29,000	35,000	41,000
Touring/Tech	10,000	11,500	14,000	17,000	19,000	23,000	31,500	38,000	43,500
Elite	—	—	—	18,500	20,500	25,000	33,500	41,000	47,500
Recommended	★	★	★	★	★	★	★	★	★
Reliability	★	★	★	★	★	★	★	★	★

SECRET WARRANTIES, INTERNAL BULLETINS: 2007-10—Warranty extension for a steering wheel that's hard to turn. Honda is extending the warranty on the power steering pump to seven years from the original date of purchase or 100,000 miles, whichever comes first. A water leak at the rear of the moonroof signals the need for a moonroof drain channel seal. **2007-11**—With a normal engine oil level, a "check engine oil level" message appears on the MID or the navigation screen. The low oil pressure indicator on the instrument panel may also be on. Honda will replace the engine oil pressure switch. **2010-11**—If the front or rear seat stays hot after the seat heater is turned off, the heater switch has to be replaced. **2012**—Running board step plate pad doesn't lay flat and the master key won't lock in the extended position. **2013**—The front brakes may squeal when applied. In TSB #13-020 issued on April 13, 2013, Acura said the noise was caused by glazed brake pads. Replacing the pads and installing new pad return springs should resolve the problem.

HONDA

Picking Up the Pieces

Honda, Nissan, and Toyota were the auto manufacturers hit hardest by natural disasters in Japan a few years ago, yet all three companies are rebounding with a sales surge that's breaking records in North America.

New or used, Honda's Fit offers bulletproof reliability, superior driving performance, and excellent fuel economy, all at a reasonable cost.

Honda's increased sales this year has been helped along by a number of new products like the redesigned 2014 Fit small compact and the company's "freshening" of its much-maligned compact Civic, which lost favour with many shoppers following its "decontenting"

2012 redesign. All this thanks to a strong pent-up demand for cars and trucks, increased competition, more sales incentives and leasing deals, cheaper, longer auto loans, and lots of new product. And, in an effort to shorten its supply chain, more than 87 percent of the Honda and Acura models sold in North America are now made in North America, up from 84 percent a year earlier.

Auto shoppers are still casting a wary eye at Honda's recent lowered quality ratings from different independent consumer groups which concluded the automaker had been "coasting" on its previous high ranking by putting less into its 2012 cars to boost profits. Now with a much lower Yen to keep prices down and by focusing on top-quality, feature-laden products ("hey, free backup cameras for all"), Honda's 2014 models are set to do some serious damage to competitors like Mazda, Nissan, Toyota, and the Hyundai/Kia duo.

FIT ★★★★

RATING: Above Average (2008-14); Average (2007). Slotted below the Civic, the Fit is a good choice among small compacts. Indeed, it ranked first out of 41 affordable small cars rated by U.S. News & World Report based on the analysis of 37 published reviews and test drives and other reliability and safety data. **Road performance:** Plenty of smooth, quiet power with either the manual or automatic transmission; handles and brakes like a sports car. The accelerator may be too sensitive and cause the car to over-accelerate. Handling is easy, but side winds require constant steering corrections. The ride is also somewhat choppy due to the car's small size. Unintentional drifting at highway speeds. **Strong points:** The 2014 Honda Fit is small on the outside but big on the inside. It sips fuel and still performs well. Its 1.5L engine isn't in the big leagues, but you will seldom realize you're driving a mini-compact. Innovative seats allow you to lift the rear seat's base up against the backrest to make room for bulky items, or the seat can be folded flat, which doubles the cargo space. You can even configure the seats to make a small bed. Buy the cheaper, practically identical 2013 version, since Honda won't revise the present model until mid-2014 when it gets ten more horses and other powertrain upgrades. Honda offers lots of standard features; outstanding resale value; good interior ergonomics; ample and flexible interior space; quality craftsmanship; and good resale value. **Weak points:** Engine struggles going uphill with a full load; a busy ride; front seats aren't height-adjustable; and more legroom is needed for taller passengers. Headlights may not project far enough into the distance. Road debris easily destroys the AC condenser – an expensive repair not covered under warranty, says one angry Honda owner in this NHSTA-logged complaint:

There are "vents" which lie below the license plate holder near the road, wide enough to fit a fist and the length of the front bumper. This allows all kinds of road debris to enter and hit the A/C condenser only inches behind the opening. This damage has been reported on a number of websites from model year 2008 to 2011. A similar issue has also been reported in a number of other Honda car models, including the CR-V and the Odyssey, which resulted in a successful class action lawsuit. Honda, however, still does not provide a grill or other form of protection despite the reported problem and does not cover the repairs with their bumper to bumper or Honda care warranties.

Barely a handful of complaints were logged by NHTSA for the 2011-13 models when 50 per model year would be the norm. On older models, owners report sudden acceleration and airbag failures; windshield stress fractures; seat belts break, and the tire jack may bend sideways when lifting the car; periodic brake failures; paint chipping and premature cosmetic rusting; insufficient legroom causes drivers to apply the brakes and accelerator at the same time; the dashboard's elevated design obstructs forward visibility; some transmission seal leaks; a weak AC; a small gas tank; a fuel sloshing noise heard under the front seats; squeaky brakes; the vehicle tends to sway and wander when buffeted by moderate side winds; jerky acceleration when driving in traffic; excess gear shifting over hilly terrain; some interior engine and road noise; and some paint peeling and delamination. **Major redesign:** 2007 and 2009. **Highway/city fuel economy:** *Man.:* 5.7/7.2 L/100 km. *Auto.:* 5.5/7.1 L/100 km. Interestingly, tests prove the automatic gearbox is more fuel-efficient than the manual transmission. Whichever transmission you choose, owners say fuel economy claims are overstated by Honda. **Best alternatives:** Other good econocars are the Honda Civic (except the 2012 model), Hyundai Accent or Elantra, Mazda2 or Mazda3, and Nissan Versa. Mercedes' Smart Car and Toyota's Yaris aren't as refined as the Fit.

SAFETY: Comparatively few complaints have been posted on NHTSA's *safercar.gov* website. NHTSA gives the 2011-13 models four stars for occupant protection in all types of collisions. Earlier 2007-10 models provide five-star frontal and side protection and score four stars for rollover resistance. IIHS ratings are "Good" for offset frontal, side, rear, and roof crashworthiness. Traction control and an anti-skid system are available, but only on the more expensive models. Safety-related complaints include airbags that fail to deploy, "touchy" brakes, and a narrow view out the rear window. Owners also report some brake failures, sudden unintended acceleration, and extreme side wind sensitivity when cruising on windswept roadways. Also, side visors can't block the sun shining through the side windows for small-statured occupants and rear seat belts ratchet tighter around children.

ALERT! Welcome to head-restraint hell on some models:

> The head rest pushes my head forward and strains my neck to the point that I either have to sit upright away

Prices and Specs

Prices (Firm): *DX:* $14,580, *LX:* $16,980, *Sport:* $18,880 **Freight:** $1,495 **Powertrain (Front-drive):** Engine: 1.5L 4-cyl. (117 hp); Transmissions: 5-speed man., 5-speed auto. **Dimensions/capacity:** Passengers: 2/3; Wheelbase: 98 in.; H: 60/L: 162/W: 67 in.; Headroom F/R: 5.5/4 in.; Legroom F/R: 45/27 in.; Cargo volume: 24 cu. ft.; Fuel tank: 41L/regular; Tow limit: No towing; Load capacity: 850 lb.; Turning circle: 34.3 ft.; Weight: 2,450 lb.

from the seat or stretch my neck far out in pain. Either way it is not safe, whether in case of accident or generally for my health. With no cool-off period on new cars in California, I cannot return the car, which at this point has 12 miles [19 km] on it, so I am forced to drive unsafely. I ran Google search for Honda head rest complaints and found out that customers have been complaining about Honda's new head rests for the same very reason since 2007 for most of their models—from Accord and Odyssey to Fit.

What makes the matter worse is that you cannot reverse the headrest as there are grooves only on one of the two support poles. By making head restraint extremely uncomfortable to use, Honda is forcing its customers to drive unsafely, specifically without head restraint. I spoke to [the] service manager at my dealer and he told me that Honda does not have adjustable or reversible head restraints.

He is also aware of the complaints from the customers. Solution should be easy to implement by making the head rest reversible for those like me with neck or back problems. I drove Hondas for 18 years and cannot believe that Honda has not responded to 3 years of continuous complaints.

Fit Profile

	2007	2008	2009	2010	2011	2012
Used Values ($)						
DX	5,000	5,500	6,000	7,500	8,500	10,500
LX	6,000	6,500	7,000	9,000	10,500	12,500
Sport	7,000	7,500	8,500	10,000	11,500	14,500
Recommended	★	★	★	☆	☆	☆
Reliability	★	★	★	☆	☆	☆

SECRET WARRANTIES, INTERNAL BULLETINS: 2009-10—The front windshield has a vertical crack starting at the bottom, above the cowl, near the middle. Honda will replace the windshield as a "goodwill" gesture. Cite TSB: #12-006, published January 21, 2012. This defect is not an insurance claim. Honda is responsible 100 percent and must pay supplementary transport while car is out of service. Fix for a fuel filler door that won't open. **2009-11**—Floor carpet wears out prematurely. The legal principle of "reasonable durability" comes into play here. **2012**—Running board step plate pad doesn't lay flat. The master key won't lock in the extended position.

CIVIC ★★★★★

RATING: Recommended (2013-14); Below Average (2012): Above Average (2001-11). **Road performance:** These cars are noted for good acceleration and a smooth-shifting automatic transmission. Some minuses are mediocre handling, a choppy ride, and vague steering:

My 2012 Honda Civic LX Coupe has extremely vague steering feel at speeds greater than 55 mph [89 km/h], causing excessive and repeated correction to maintain proper course. The car also veers to the right on a regular basis causing me to direct the steering wheel towards the left to continue driving straight. The dealer has performed a 4-wheel alignment twice without resolution.

Strong points: 2013 and 2014 models have regained the quality and performance edge that was lost with the 2012 redesign. Instruments and controls are easily accessed; a tilt/telescoping steering wheel is standard; and interior space is more than adequate for most adults. Civics also have a strong resale value. **Weak points:** The 2012s aren't as reliable, or perform as well, as other model years. Brakes require a long stopping distance, and interior materials look and feel cheap. **Major redesign:** 2001, 2006, and 2012. **Highway/city fuel economy:** *1.8L (140 hp) man.:* 5.4/7.4 L/100 km. *Auto.:* 5.7/8.2 L/100 km. *2012 Hybrid:* 5.3 L/100 km (combined highway/city). **Best alternatives:** Chevrolet's popular fuel-efficient Cruze, or revamped 2013 Chevrolet Impala, the fuel-efficient and more aggressively styled Hyundai Elantra, a peppy and stylish Mazda3, the "pocket rocket" Kia Forte, or a larger and less expensive VW Jetta.

SAFETY: NHTSA awarded the 2012 four-door Civic five stars for front and side crash protection and four stars for rollover resistance. The two-door version got a four-star rating across the board. The 2011s didn't do as well: Four stars for front protection and rollover resistance, and only two stars for side crashworthiness. The 2013 models have yet to be tested. IIHS results for the 2012 SI's rear crash protection were "Good." The 2012 four-door Civic received a "Good" rating in all categories. The 2011 two-door was "Good" in frontal offset crash tests and "Acceptable" for side protection. The coupe's steeply raked front windshield cuts forward visibility. Owners report seat belts tighten progressively when connected; the airbag warning light stays lit even though an adult passenger occupies the seat; and many instances of inadvertent side airbag deployment, or airbags failing to deploy in collisions:

I was trying to back into a parking space with my 8-month-old 2012 Honda Civic. As I took my foot off the gas pedal to put the car into reverse and before I could step on the brake, the car surged forward at a tremendous rate of speed, jumped a curb and went straight into a brick building. The car bounced backwards onto the parking lot and I was able to step on the brake and regain control. This happened in a matter of a split second with no time to jam the brake on as the car lurched forward. Even though the car jolted tremendously, the airbag did not go off, but a service light came on the dash board indicating "Check Airbag System."

Other common safety-related failings are fractured front tie rods, causing complete steering loss; sudden acceleration or surging when the AC or heater is engaged, or when the steering wheel is turned sharply; car veers sharply to the right when braking; and the brake and accelerator pedal are mounted too close together and the premature replacement of brake pads and discs:

My Honda Civic has only 13,000 miles [21,000 km] on it and my brake pads have already worn down to nothing and had to be replaced yesterday. The repair guy told me there is absolutely no way that at such low miles that this should have happened. There must have been a problem with the original breaks on my car and $378 later, I already had to replace them.

Often the vehicle hesitates when accelerating from a stop or there's engine surging when exiting an off-ramp or when the brakes are applied:

Car suddenly stops dead while accelerating to make left-hand turn. It will resume acceleration only after a four-second pause. Turning into oncoming traffic with a dead vehicle is going to cause an accident involving injuries or death. This is the third time that this incident has occurred to my vehicle. The Honda dealer cannot find the cause.

Body fit and finish and accessories are also problematic: A-pillar, dash, or sunroof rattles; windows bind or come out of run channels; doors and trunk lid are hard to close; inoperable fuel-door handle; body and bumper paint peeling and cracking; poorly mounted driver's seat; inoperable door locks and power windows; trunk cannot be opened from the cabin area; a driver-side window that won't roll back up; sun visors that fall apart; an erratic fuel gauge, speedometer, and tachometer; an interior light that hums as it dims; lousy radio speakers; water leaks through the door bottoms, from the tail light into the trunk, and onto the driver-side footwell carpet; windows that often come off their tracks; trunk springs fail; exterior and interior lights dim to an unsafe level; heated side mirrors gradually lose their reflective ability; and the AC condenser is easily destroyed by road debris.

ALERT! The head restraint pushes the driver's head too far forward:

I have tilted the seat back as far as I safely can and still be able to drive. I am [a] 53 year old female, 5'3" tall, and wear bifocals. I am having difficulty focusing from tachometer to speedometer to road because I cannot [move] my head to use the right part of my glasses to see. I cannot tilt my head back at all because of the headrest. I also experienced a headache that evening as well due to eye strain. The NHSTA changed their headrest regulations in 2008. Test dummies for large males were used and then standards were put in place. After spending

Prices and Specs

Prices (negotiable): *DX:* $15,440, *LX Coupe:* $18,590, *EX-L, Sedan:* $25,240, *Si Sedan:* $26,191 **Freight:** $1,495 **Powertrain (front-drive):** Engines (2012 Hybrid): 1.5L 4-cyl. (110 hp) plus electric motor (23 hp), 1.8L 4-cyl. (140 hp), 2.4L 4-cyl. (201 hp); Transmissions: 5-speed man., 5-speed auto., 6-speed man., CVT auto. **Dimensions/capacity:** *Sedan:* Passengers: 2/3; Wheelbase: 105.1 in.; H: 56.5/L: 177.3/W: 69 in.; Headroom F/R: 5/2.5 in.; Legroom F/R: 41/27 in.; Cargo volume: 13 cu. ft.; Fuel tank: 50L/regular; Tow limit: 1,000 lb.; Load capacity: 850 lb.; Turning circle: 35.4 ft.; Weight: 2,725 lb. *2012 Hybrid:* Passengers: 2/3; Wheelbase: 105.1 in.; H: 56.5/L: 177.3/W: 69 in.; Headroom F/R: 5/2.5 in.; Legroom F/R: 41/27 in.; Cargo volume: 11 cu. ft.; Fuel tank: 47L/regular; Tow limit: N/A; Load capacity: 850 lb.; Turning circle: 35.4 ft.; Weight: 2,853 lb.

thousands of dollars on a new car, I am unable to safely drive it. I have to either remove, turn around, or jerry-rig a remedy for the headrest in order to drive and not suffer neck, back, shoulder, and visual pain. The cost is my safety in an accident. Or, I can leave the headrest and drive with my posture in a horrid position. I cannot sit up straight, my head is forced downward so I cannot use my bifocals properly, and I cannot tilt the seat back any further and still see over the dashboard.

Civic Profile

	2004	2005	2006	2007	2008	2009	2010	2011	2012
Used Values ($)									
Sedan DX	4,000	4,500	5,000	5,500	6,000	6,500	8,000	9,000	10,000
Sedan DX-G	—	—	—	6,500	7,000	7,500	9,500	12,000	—
Sedan LX	4,500	5,000	6,000	7,000	8,000	—	—	—	12,500
Si	—	7,500	—	—	9,500	11,000	13,500	16,500	18,500
Hybrid	5,000	5,500	6,000	6,500	7,500	8,500	—	—	19,000
Coupe LX	4,500	5,000	6,000	7,500	8,500	9,100	11,500	—	13,000
Si	—	7,000	8,000	9,000	10,500	11,500	14,000	17,000	18,500
Recommended	☆	☆	☆	☆	☆	☆	☆	☆	★
Reliability	☆	☆	☆	☆	☆	☆	☆	☆	★

SECRET WARRANTIES, INTERNAL BULLETINS: All models/years: Most Honda TSBs allow for special warranty consideration on a "goodwill" basis, even after the warranty has expired or the car has changed hands. Referring to the "goodwill" euphemism will increase your chances of getting some kind of refund for repairs that are obviously related to a factory defect. Seat belts that are slow to retract will be replaced for free under Honda's seat belt lifetime warranty, says TSB #03-062, issued September 16, 2003. Paint defect claims require an accompanying digitized (2 MB) photo before they can be considered. Tips for submitting a successful paint claim can be found in TSB #10-002, published January 20, 2010. **2006-08**—Some Civic models may be eligible for an extended warranty related to uneven rear tire wear. In TSB #13-047 Honda said the uneven tire wear on 2006-07 Civics and 2006-08 Civic Hybrids might be caused by incorrect rear suspension geometry. Repairs include new upper control arms. *Hybrid:* **2006-07**—Hybrids that lose power when accelerating need three different software updates. This will be done under a "goodwill" warranty at no charge to the customer, says Honda Service Bulletin #09-058, published July 30, 2009. Honda's 2006 Civic software update caused a dramatic drop in fuel economy. Accord Hybrid owners say they are also getting poor gas mileage, since the same revised engine/IMA battery software was installed in their Hybrids to extend IMA battery life. **2006-09**—Engine overheats or leaks coolant because the engine block is cracking at the coolant passages. Honda will install a new engine block assembly free of charge under a "goodwill policy," as stated in its TSB #10-048, issued August 17, 2010. The sunvisor may come apart or split with use. American Honda has extended the warranty on its sunvisors to seven years from the original date of purchase or 100,000 miles, whichever comes first. **2006-10**—Hood paint cracking. Cite Honda TSB #12-049, issued August 24, 2012: "On some 2006-10 Civics that are painted blue (paint code B-529P) or black (paint codes B-92P and NH-731P), the exterior paint on the hood and the leading edge of the front fenders may crack. American Honda is extending the warranty on the paint on the hood and tops of the front fenders on affected vehicles to 7 years from the original date of purchase with no mileage limit. If this extended warranty has already expired based on the original date of purchase, American Honda is further extending the warranty 6 months from the mailing date of the notification letter." This TSB is critical as a benchmark by Honda for any paint claims targeting other models, colours, model years, or automakers. Again, the legal principle of "reasonable durability" and negligence applies. Torn engine mounts cause a rattle or a knock coming from the right front of the vehicle when driving over bumps at 15-20 mph (24-32 km/h). It is likely the passenger's side hydraulic side engine mount is cavitating and making a rattling sound, or it is torn and making a knocking sound. It needs to be replaced under an extended warranty. Cite Honda TSB #06-060, issued December 24, 2010. **2006-11**—There may be a pop or clunk from the front suspension area when driving over bumps. This usually occurs after completing a tight (full lock) turn and the front bump stops become dislodged and then pops back into place. Cite TSB #078, issued March 2, 2012. **2006-11**—Trunk lid repaint warranty extension. Dissimilar metals in the chrome trim and the trunk lid, along with road salt, may create a very low electrochemical reaction that forms corrosion, rust spots, or stains on the trunk lid. Honda is extending the warranty on the trunk lid to seven years from the original date of purchase says TSB #13-004, issued January 3, 2013. **2012**—Running board step plate pad doesn't lay flat. The master key won't lock in the extended position. Rear spring upper mounting cushion may not be properly installed.

A/T, CTV START CLUTCH WARRANTY EXTENSION

BULLETIN NO.: 07-049

DATE: FEBRUARY 8, 2008

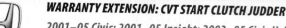

WARRANTY EXTENSION: CVT START CLUTCH JUDDER
2001–05 Civic; 2001–05 Insight; 2003–05 Civic Hybrid

NOTE: Because of a class action settlement, the warranty extension coverage for CVT start clutch judder on 2002–05 Civic GXs and HXs with CVT, 2003–05 Civic Hybrids with CVT, and 2002–05 Insights with CVT purchased or leased between April 13, 2002, and November 7, 2006, is 7 years or 105,000 miles [170,000 km], whichever occurs first. For more information, refer to Service Bulletin 06-085, Warranty

EXTENSION: Vehicle Warranty Mileage.

On affected vehicles, a momentary judder may be felt after accelerating from a stop, but only up to about 15 mph [24 km/h]. The most likely cause of the judder is a worn start clutch in the CVT (continuously variable transmission). To increase customer confidence, American Honda is extending the warranty for this potential problem to 7 years or 100,000 miles [160,000 km], whichever comes first. This extended warranty covers only CVT start clutch judder below 15 mph and CVT drive belt slippage (see Service Bulletin 07-050).

ENGINE OVERHEATS/LOSES COOLANT

BULLETIN NO.: 08-044

DATE: JULY 30, 2009

ENGINE OVERHEATS OR LEAKS COOLANT

2006–08 Civic—ALL except GX, Hybrid, and Si

SYMPTOM: The engine is leaking coolant and may be overheating.
PROBABLE CAUSE: The engine block is cracking at the coolant passages.
CORRECTIVE ACTION: Install a new engine block assembly.
WARRANTY CLAIM INFORMATION:

OP#	Description	FRT
111100	Install a new engine block assembly	12.0
Q	Add for alignment	0.4

IN WARRANTY: The normal warranty applies.
FAILED PART: P/N 10002-RNA-A00
H/C 8143323
DEFECT CODE: 07601
OUT OF WARRANTY: Any repair performed after warranty expiration may be eligible for goodwill consideration by the District Parts and Service Manager or your Zone Office. You must request consideration, and get a decision, before starting work.

CR-V ★★★★★

RATING: Recommended (2007-14); Above Average (2001-06). A Honda bestseller, the CR-V has distanced itself from the Toyota Sienna and enhanced the driving experience by making a driver-communicative SUV that is as reliable as it is cheap to service. **Road performance:** A smooth-running 4-banger handles most chores well, but owners could use a bit more grunt for merging and tackling steep grades with a full load. Also, owners say a persistent hesitation before acceleration problem crops up from time to time. The 5-speed automatic transmission performs flawlessly, and braking is first-class. The ride is firm but comfortable, though the steering is a bit stiff and vague. High-speed cornering is not recommended, due to excessive body lean. Also, annoying highway noises are omnipresent when at cruising speeds. **Strong points:** The 2014 CR-V has more legroom than ever before, thanks to the roomy rear seats that recline and slide independently and fold down

Prices and Specs

Prices (Firm): *LX:* $25,990, LX 4WD: $28,140, *EX:* $28,940, EX 4WD: $31,040, *EX-L 4WD:* $33,240, *Touring:* $35,140 **Freight:** $1,395 **Powertrain (Front-drive/AWD):** Engine: 2.4L 4-cyl. (180 hp); Transmission: 5-speed auto. **Dimensions/capacity:** Passengers: 2/3; Wheelbase: 103.1 in.; H: 66.1/L: 177.8/W: 71.6 in.; Headroom F/R: 4/4 in.; Legroom F/R: 40.5/29 in.; Cargo volume: 36 cu. ft.; Fuel tank: 50L/regular; Tow limit: 1,500 lb.; Load capacity: 850 lb.; Turning circle: 39 ft.; Ground clearance: 7.2 in.; Weight: 3,404 lb.

to create a flat cargo floor. The lift-up tailgate is much more convenient than the swing-out version used in previous years. **Weak points:** Styling is confused, with rear-quarter styling trumping a decent outward view. Key frequently gets stuck in the ignition; driver's side window suddenly shattered; electrical system shorts; premature brake wear; airbags fail to deploy; AC condenser is destroyed by road debris (a chronic failure on most of Honda's lineup); bent wheel studs can easily snap; brake rotors wear out prematurely; the engine oil pan leaks; the driver's and passenger's sun visors fall out of their mounting; windshield washer nozzles freeze up in cold weather; omnipresent vibrations, rattles and clunking, knocking sounds. **Major redesign:** 1997, 2002, 2007, and 2012. **Highway/city fuel economy:** *Front-drive:* 7.1/9.8 L/100 km. *AWD:* 7.5/10.1 L/100 km. Expect a tad more fuel economy with the 6-speed automatic. **Best alternatives:** The CR-V's biggest competitor is the Toyota RAV4. If you don't mind going downscale a bit, consider a Hyundai Tucson.

SAFETY: NHTSA gave the 2013 CR-V five stars for frontal and side crash protection and four stars for rollover resistance. IIHS awarded the 2012 model its top rating of "Good" in frontal offset, side, and rear impacts, and also for roof strength. Sudden, unintended acceleration has some owners requesting a little "intended" acceleration: There are reports that when the accelerator is pressed hard, there is a loss of power and downshifting is delayed, just when extra power is needed. Traction control has also been a problem with earlier models.

ALERT! Again, painful head restraints.

CR-V Profile

	2004	2005	2006	2007	2008	2009	2010	2011	2012
Used Values ($)									
EX/LX	4,500	5,000	6,000	7,000	8,000	9,000	10,500	14,500	17,500
4x4	—	—	—	7,500	8,000	10,000	12,000	16,000	19,500
EX	6,500	7,000	8,000	—	—	10,500	13,000	17,000	21,000
4x4	—	—	—	8,500	9,500	11,500	14,000	18,500	22,500
EX-L	—	—	—	9,000	10,000	12,000	14,500	19,500	23,000
Touring LX	—	—	—	—	—	—	—	—	24,500
Recommended	☆	☆	☆3	☆4	☆5	☆5	☆5	☆5	★1
Reliability	☆	☆	☆3	☆4	☆4	☆5	☆5	☆4	★2

SECRET WARRANTIES, INTERNAL BULLETINS: All years: Keep in mind that Honda service bulletins almost always mention that "goodwill" extended warranties may be applied to any malfunction. **1999-07**—Vehicle pulls/drifts to one side. **2005-06**—Front suspension clicks while driving over bumps or turning. **2007**—Power steering pump seizure. Honda will cover the cost of this repair under Campaign #08-070. Inoperative power windows. Low Tire Pressure light stays on. Distorted image in driver's side mirror. Wiper won't park or turn off. **2007-08**—Poor AC performance on acceleration; AC hoots or whistles. Headliner rattles or buzzes when driving. Tailgate rusting near licence plate trim. Exhaust system squeaks. False low tire pressure alert. **2007-09**—Inoperative windshield washer pump. Roof rack whistling at high speeds. **2007-11**—Rear brakes grind or thump. A new brake pad will fix the problem says Honda's TSB #10-020, published May 20, 2011. **2008**—Cold engine whine may be corrected by replacing the engine oil pump. **2008-09**—Headliner sagging near the liftgate. **2010-11**—Fluid leaks from rear of vehicle. Low power on acceleration requires only a software update, says Honda. **2011-12**—An engine oil leak at the rear of the cylinder head cover may be caused by a defective No. 5 rocker shaft holder. The left rear wheelwell doesn't have enough seam sealer, which may allow water to leak into the interior under the rear seat. Honda has set up a free repair campaign to apply sealer. A loss of power when accelerating may be caused by faulty PGM-FI software.

ACCORD/CROSSTOUR ★★★★ / ★★★

RATING: Above Average (2010-14); Below Average (2008-09); Above Average (2001-07). The 2013-14 models have much more content, but Honda is still working on serious factory-related glitches related to the 2013 redesign – one of which is a deadly "lag and lurch" powertrain malfunction, posted at safercar.gov by this owner of a 2013 Accord:

> This was instance #3 and worst occurrence. Stopped at traffic light, made a left turn when break in traffic, half way into turn engine lagged with no response like it shutdown, then took off. Almost T-boned by oncoming traffic. Lag between start of turn and then engine response was at least 2-3 seconds. Same issue has happened 2 times before. Both of those instances were right turns on red, with no oncoming traffic. Even though no traffic was coming, the concern is that the lag/dead response worries me and creates a safety issue. Have spoken with 3 Honda service advisors that have not heard of the issue and because it is intermittent don't know what they could do. They stated clearly that unless they could recreate the issue, it would be difficult to troubleshoot it. I have searched the Internet forums and found similar occurrences with other Honda owners, not only of the Accord but also the Crosstour.

Past Honda redesigns always took a year or two to get the factory kinks corrected (look at the 2008 redesign quality decline) and we shall see next year if this is still the case. Interestingly, the Accord and Crosstour have registered much fewer safety complaints over the past four years. **Road performance:** Excellent acceleration with all engines. The Accord also handles and rides well, thanks to large tires, a sturdy chassis, and standard stability control. Like most Hondas, this is a driver's car, while its primary competitor, the Toyota Camry, is more of a mobile cocoon. Honda's Sport and Touring model offers 18-inch alloy wheels, fog lights, 10-way power driver's seats, a spoiler, dual chrome exhausts, paddle shifters (CVT models only), a stiffer tower strut bar, and retuned suspension and steering. Crosstour: More responsive handling, comfort, and a car-like driving position. A competent performer that suffers from a large turning radius, a confusing dash, and not as much cargo space expected of a wagon. **Strong points:** A well-designed family car, the Accord was last redesigned for the 2013 model year and jumped leagues ahead of the competition by giving owners superior road performance and a roomy interior with loads of safety and convenience features thrown in. If you want good fuel economy and performance with a conventional powertrain, choose one of the two 4-cylinder engines. The V6 is a bit of a gas hog and is necessary only for highway travel with a full load. Ride comfort and responsive handling are assured by a suspension and steering set-up that enhances driver control. And what about space? Recent model Accord sedans are roomier than ever before, with interior dimensions and capacity that provide more interior space than you'll likely need. Fast and nimble without a V6, this is the mid-sized sedan of choice for drivers who want maximum fuel economy and comfort along with lots of space for grocery hauling and occasional highway cruising. With the optional V6, the Accord is one of the most versatile mid-sized cars you can find. It offers something for everyone, and its reasonable resale value after five years means there's no way you can lose money buying one. **Weak points:** Mediocre fuel economy with the V6, and some road noise intrusion into the cabin area. An astoundingly high number of performance and reliability defects on the 2008-09 models, with apparently biodegradable brakes topping the list. Chronic radio malfunctions. Annoying windshield dash reflection; distorted windshields; and creaks and rattles. "Hey, wanna $500 deal on a new AC condenser?"

Air conditioner condenser damaged due to road debris. Vehicle design is poor leaving the condenser unprotected from road debris. Grill opening is large with no screen or mesh in front of the condenser. Repair cost is $786.

Crosstour: The four-year-old Crosstour is billed as a "crossover utility vehicle," which is Honda-speak for a high-riding hatchback family station wagon equipped with four-wheel drive capability. This five-seater Accord spin-off offers a disappointing 22 cubic feet of cargo space and 51.3 cubic feet with the rear seatbacks folded. Strut towers intrude into storage space, and the sloping rear-end styling compromises the Crosstour's utility. **Highway/city fuel economy:** *2.4L 4-cylinder auto.:* 5.8/8.8 L/100 km. *3.5L V6 6-speed man.:* 7.8/12.6 L/100 km. *Auto.:* 6.7/11 L/100 km. *Crosstour auto. 2WD:* 7.2/11.5 L/100 km. Auto. 4WD: 8/12.3 L/100 km. **Best alternatives:** BMW 3 Series, Hyundai Elantra or Sonata, Mazda6, and Toyota Camry. Crosstour: Nissan Murano, Subaru Outback, and Toyota Venza.

SAFETY: Accord has earned five-star crashworthiness scores from NHTSA for front, side, and rollover protection since 2002. Earlier models, through 1998 merited three- and four-star crashworthiness scores. Side protection for 1997 and earlier models was scored three stars. The car was also given a "Good" rating by IIHS for head-restraint effectiveness, frontal offset, side, rear, and roof crashworthiness. *Crosstour:* NHTSA scores: five stars for frontal and side occupant crash protection and four stars for rollover resistance. IIHS rated frontal offset, side, and rear crashworthiness as "Good"; roof crash protection was "Mediocre." Many owner reports of airbags that explode for no reason or fail to deploy, brake failures, and sudden, unintended acceleration. Limited rear visibility and poorly-designed, ineffective side mirror (see below):

ALERT! Low-beam headlights give insufficient illumination. During the test drive, make sure the seat and head restraint design don't cause neck or back pain (a complaint over the past several years):

I bought a 2013 Honda Accord knowing that there have been complaints online about the headrest issue, but brief test drives prior to purchase don't fully reveal the extent to which this is a safety defect. An Acura (also made by Honda) dealer even told me that Acura had had these same complaints for several years, but modified the headrest design in the 2013 models to correct the flaw. Honda has not done this yet, though. I test drove many other manufacturers' cars and they comply with federal regulations without such an obvious design problem. I'm 5'4" and sit up straight when driving, which means the head restraint continually bumps or pokes the back of my head while providing no back support at all — which is itself a safety defect in a crash. So is the fact that it pushes my head so far forward that it impedes good visibility when I turn my head to look back over my right shoulder. Slumping causes back, shoulder and neck pain, untenable on a road trip and also impedes visibility. Earlier model head-restraints that don't have this issue won't fit due to different center-to-center post measurements, so there are no available parts to replace the existing restaint (I tried — even with one in my older Acura). I have read online forums in which desperate Honda drivers describe bending the posts or making other modifications to relieve their pain while driving. They shouldn't have to and this could jeopardize their safety.

Prices and Specs

Prices (Firm): *Accord Coupe DX:* $26,290, *EX-L Navi:* $29,990, *EX-L V6 Navi:* $35,390, *Accord Sedan LX:* $23,990, *Sport:* $25,490, *EX-L:* $29,090, *V6:* $32,790, *V6 Touring:* $35,290; *Accord Crosstour EX-L:* $34,990, *EX-L 4WD:* $36,990, *EX-L 4WD Navi.:* $38,990 **Freight:** $1,640

Powertrain: *Accord front-drive:* Engines: 2.4L 4-cyl. (185 hp), 2.4L 4-cyl. (189 hp), 3.5L V6 (278 hp), Hybrid 2.0L 4-cyl. (196 hp); Transmissions: 6-speed man., 6-speed auto., CVT; *Crosstour Front-drive/4WD:* Engines: 2.4L 4-cylinder (192 hp), 3.5L V6 (271 hp); Transmission: 6-speed auto. **Dimensions/capacity:** *Accord Sedan:* Passengers: 2/3; Wheelbase: 110.2 in.; H: 58.1/L: 191/W: 72.6 in.; Headroom F/R: 5/2 in.; Legroom F/R: 41/30 in.; Cargo volume: 16 cu. ft.; Fuel tank: 65L/regular; Tow limit: 1,000 lb.; Load capacity: 850 lb.; Turning circle: 37.7 ft.; Weight: 3,236-3,298 lb. *Crosstour Sedan:* Passengers: 2/3; Wheelbase: 110.1 in.; H: 58.1/L: 196.8/W: 74.7 in.; Headroom F/R: 6.5/3.5 in.; Legroom F/R: 41.5/30 in.; Cargo volume: 25.7 cu. ft.; Fuel tank: 65L/regular; Tow limit: 1,500 lb.; Load capacity: 850 lb.; Turning circle: 40.2 ft.; Ground clearance: 8.1 in.; Weight: 3,852-4,070 lb.

Accord/Crosstour Profile

	2004	2005	2006	2007	2008	2009	2010	2011	2012
Used Values ($)									
Coupe SE/EX	5,000	6,500	8,000	8,500	10,000	11,000	13,000	15,500	18,500
EX V6/EX-L V6 Nav.	—	—	—	9,500	12,000	13,500	17,000	21,000	25,500
Sedan LX/SE	5,500	6,500	7,000	7,500	8,500	9,500	11,500	13,500	17,500
EX	7,000	8,000	9,000	—	—	11,000	13,000	15,500	19,000
EX-L V6 Nav.	—	—	—	—	12,000	14,000	17,000	21,500	25,500
Crosstour EX-L	—	—	—	—	—	—	15,000	18,500	22,500
EX-L Nav.	—	—	—	—	—	—	17,000	21,000	26,000
Hybrid	—	—	—	—	—	—	8,000	8,500	9,500
Recommended	✩	✩	✩	✩	✩	✩	✩	✩	✩
Reliability	✩	✩	✩	✩	✩	✩	✩	✩	✩

SECRET WARRANTIES, INTERNAL BULLETINS: 2003-08—The 6-speed manual transmission grinds when shifted into Third gear, pops out of Third gear, or is hard to shift into Third gear. **2003-09**—Power-steering moan/whine. **2005-10**—Silencing a chirp coming from the engine timing belt area. **2007**—A fix for the manual transmission grinding or popping out of Third gear (TSB #08-020, dated July 18, 2008). Inadequate AC cooling. Noisy rear window regulator. **2008**—Excessive oil consumption. Road debris continues to damage expensive AC compressors. Engine rattles on cold start-up. Blower motor noisy or inoperative. Carpet on the passenger's side pulls out from under the door sill trim. If an owner reports a front brake squeal or judder, Honda will refinish the front brake discs and install new brake pads under a "goodwill" warranty, says Honda Service Bulletin #09-096, published December 24, 2009. **2008-09**—Troubleshooting an engine whining noise and a steering clicking. Fix for an engine that ticks or knocks at idle. **2008-10**—Honda extends its brake repair up to the 2010 models and states the normal warranty applies. This admission of a part failure or of a "defect" gives rise to Honda's liability beyond its normal warranty limitations under the legal *implied* warranty. That's the case to make in small claims court, should Honda reject your claim. *Hybrid:* **2006-07**—Hybrids that lose power when accelerating need three different software updates. This will be done under a "goodwill" warranty at no charge to the customer, says Honda Service Bulletin #09-058, published July 30, 2009. Honda's 2006 Civic software update caused a dramatic drop in fuel economy. Accord Hybrid owners say they are also getting poor gas mileage, since the same revised engine/IMA battery software was installed in their Hybrids to extend IMA battery life. **2012**—Running board step plate pad doesn't lay flat. The master key won't lock in the extended position.

ODYSSEY ★★★★★

RATING: Recommended (2012-14); Above Average (2009-11); Average (1997-08). 2014s get a new 6-speed automatic transmission, revised exterior styling, and an upgraded instrument cluster and dash controls. The Odyssey outclasses Toyota's Sienna in driving pleasure and is just a bit more reliable. In a Sienna, the driver is "driven;" in an Odyssey, the driver is more actively involved in the overall performance of the vehicle. There have, however, been frequent reports of safety- and performance-related failures, notably involving the electrical system, and this is likely to occur more frequently with future redesigns. Of particular concern are airbag malfunctions, brake defects leading to sudden brake loss, and the frequent replacement of the brake calipers and rotors. **Road performance:** Plenty of power for high-speed merging and lots of mid-range torque means less shifting when the engine is under load. Car-like ride and handling. Unlike with the Sienna, all-wheel drive isn't available and there is some tire rumble, rattling, and body drumming at highway speeds. **Strong points:** The Odyssey has a lean look, but the interior is wide and long enough to accommodate most large objects. Sliding doors are standard equipment, and if you buy the EX version, they will both be power-assisted. Sufficient power is supplied by a competent V6, which includes variable cylinder deactivation to increase fuel economy. The engine's ability to automatically switch between 6-cylinder and 3-cylinder activation, depending on engine load, may cut gas consumption by up to 10 percent. The Odyssey has remained relatively unchanged since the 2011s got a restyled interior and wider/lower exterior; a reworked front end; and user-friendly instruments and controls. The wider interior houses a versatile second-row bench seat that spreads the seats out and uses a total of five latch positions for child seats, as well as more ample third-row seats. If you need extra cargo space, you can easily fold the third-row seats, add the cargo, and bring the kids up into the second row. Additional comfort and infotainment features include an HDMI port; a wide screen to play one movie for all or play two separate video feeds simultaneously (copying Toyota's Sienna); a removable console with a hidden bin; and a small cooler in the central stack of the dash. Honda also boasts that not only has its 4-cylinder engine fuel economy improved, but its 3.5L V6 is more fuel-frugal than the Sienna's 4-banger. The brakes were made larger, and independent rear suspension was added (see www. odyclub). **Weak points:** Fuel consumption isn't as low as Honda touts, despite its innovative cylinder deactivation system. Second-row head restraints block visibility; front passenger legroom is marginal, owing to the restricted seat travel; and it's difficult to calibrate the radio without taking your eyes off the road. The storage well won't take any tire larger than a "space saver," meaning you'll carry your flat in the back. Sometimes AC comes on and won't shut off, plus many complaints of road debris destroying the AC condenser. **Major redesign:** 1999, 2005, and 2011. **Highway/city fuel economy:** 8.5/13.3 L/100 km. *EX-L & Touring:* 7.8/2.3 L/100 km. **Best alternatives:** For better handling and reliability, the closest competitor to the Odyssey is Toyota's Sienna minivan. One major difference between the two models is the seating. Toyota's are like La-Z-Boy armchairs and are a chore to remove. Honda seats are more basic and are easier to install or remove. The Mazda5 and Chrysler's Caravan are worth considering for different reasons. The Mazda5 has less room but burns less fuel (without a high-tech engine add-on), and Chrysler's many minivan defects can be an annoyance and a budget-buster as well, but they are dirt-cheap, offer lots of room for people and things, and have plenty of convenience and safety features. The Kia Sedona minivan is also a decent choice. If you're looking for lots of towing "grunt" and plenty of usable space, rear-drive GM full-sized vans are fairly reliable vehicles that often carry sizeable discounts in the summer of the following year. Try to resist the gimmicky video entertainment, DVD navigation system, and expensive leather seats. See if you can trade the original-equipment Firestone or Bridgestone tires for something better (check with *www.tirerack.com*).

 SAFETY: Impressive NHTSA crash safety scores: top five-star score in all crash categories, except rollovers (four stars), going back to the 1998 model. IIHS rates as "Good" the frontal, side, rear, and roof crash protection. Odysseys are very reliable and safe. In fact, the 32 owner safety-related complaints registered by NHTSA for the 2012 model is only one-third the average most vehicles elicit at 50 per model year. Nevertheless, the few safety-related failures listed *are* scary. For example, look at these two reports just entered in the 2013 model NHTSA database: "Airbags didn't deploy after a severe rear-ender and after hitting a deer and failure to deploy was accompanied by brake loss." Brakes are another major problem area highlighted: sudden brake loss after the VSA light comes on (some dealers suggest unplugging the VSA); brake loss when backing out of a parking lot; brake pedal sometimes sinks to the floor; premature front brake wear and excessive noise; and a history of mushy braking. On other model years we see warped airbag covers; early engine failure; severe drivetrain judder and bucking felt when accelerating uphill; electrical malfunction-caused stalling in traffic; third row cup-holder area panel gets so hot passengers could be burned; and the van's headlights often blind oncoming drivers' eyes. Older models have even more to be wary of: automatic transmission breakdowns; transmission slams into gear or suddenly locks in low gear while the vehicle is underway; erratic downshifts; steering pulls continually to the right; premature replacement of the front strut assemblies; poor handling in snow, despite traction control; windshield shattered on its own; third-row folding seat collapsed and broke a child's

Prices and Specs

Prices (Negotiable): *LX:* $29,990, *EX:* $33,990, *EX RES:* $35,490, *EX-L RES:* $40,990, *Touring:* $46,990 **Freight:** $1,495 **Powertrain (Front-drive):** Engine: 3.5L V6 (248 hp); Transmission: 5-speed auto. **Dimensions/capacity:** Passengers: 2/3/3; Wheelbase: 118.1 in.; H: 68.8/L: 202.1/W: 77.1 in.; Headroom F/R1/R2: 2.5/5/3.5 in.; Legroom F/R1/R2: 41/32/29 in.; Cargo volume: 61.5 cu. ft.; Fuel tank: 80L/regular; Tow limit: 3,500 lb.; Load capacity: 1,340 lb.; Turning circle: 36.7 ft.; Ground clearance: 5 in.; Weight: 4,387 lb.

fingers; the side sliding door frequently malfunctions by closing unexpectedly, opening when the vehicle is underway, and failing to retract when closing on an object; the EXL's running board can be dangerously slippery when wet; and reports of some near-falls and many bruised shins.

ALERT! During your test-drive see if the van has a tendency to lag and lurch when accelerating, or the emissions warning light comes on intermittently. Some owners say the headlights don't project far enough – check that out, too.

Odyssey Profile

	2004	2005	2006	2007	2008	2009	2010	2011	2012
Used Values ($)									
DX/LX	6,000	7,000	8,000	9,000	10,000	12,000	15,500	18,000	22,000
SE/EX	6,500	7,500	9,000	10,000	12,500	14,000	17,500	20,500	24,50
EX-L Res	7,000	8,000	10,000	11,000	13,500	15,500	20,500	26,000	30,500
Touring	—	—	—	12,000	14,500	17,000	24,500	30,000	36,500
Recommended	★	★	★	★	★	★	★	★	★
Reliability	★	★	★	★	★	★	★	★	★

SECRET WARRANTIES, INTERNAL BULLETINS: All years—Honda TSBs allow for special warranty consideration on a "goodwill" basis by the company's District Service Manager or Zone Office. There's an incredibly large number of sliding-door problems covered by a recall, and a plethora of service bulletins too numerous to print here. Ask Honda politely for the bulletins or "goodwill" assistance. If refused, subpoena the documents through small claims court, using NHTSA's complaint and service bulletin summaries as your shopping list. **1999-2003**—Deformed windshield moulding. **1999-2006**—Troubleshooting vehicle pull or drift to one side. **2003-07**—Honda has a secret warranty extension that covers paint defects up to seven years (no mileage or prior ownership limitation), says TSB #08-031, issued January 8, 2010. Although this service bulletin is specifically for blue metallic paint defects, the coverage can be easily extrapolated to cover any other Honda colours, as indicated in TSB #10-002 "Paint Defect Claim Information," issued January 20, 2010. **2005**—Windshield noise remedy. Correction for middle-row seat that won't unlatch. **2005-06**—Noise remedy for the power steering, front brakes, front wheel bearings, windshield, sliding door, and exhaust system. **2005-07**—Drivetrain ping, squeal, or rattle. Power steering pump whine or buzz. Power seat won't move forward or backward. **2005-09**—Engine timing belt chirp. Sliding door doesn't open all the way. Power door locks continually lock while driving. **2005-10**—If the steering wheel is hard to turn at low speeds, Honda will replace the steering pump for free up to 7 years/100,000 miles (TSB 11-039, available in the U.S.). **2007**—

Delayed First gear engagement. Insufficient AC cooling at idle. **2007-08**—If the brake pedal feels low and spongy, the dealer should replace the ABS/TCS or VSA modulator control unit under warranty, says Honda TSB #07-045 issued March 5, 2009. **2008**—Engine knocking or ticking at idle. **2008-09**—Water accumulates in the inner tail lights in the tailgate. **2008-10**—Gap between the front passenger's airbag lid and the dashboard. Front door glass opens/closes slowly or sticks. **2008-12**—Remedy for engine ticking at idle.

ENGINE TICKING OR KNOCKING AT IDLE

BULLETIN NO.: 08-017

DATE: NOVEMBER 23, 2011

PROBABLE CAUSE: The rocker shaft bridge has excessive clearance which causes the rocker shaft to rotate and make noise.

CORRECTIVE ACTION: Loosen and retorque the rocker shaft bridge bolts.

PILOT ★★★★★

RATING: Recommended (2001-14). **Road performance:** The second-generation Pilot has grown into a large-sized people carrier that offers adequate power for highway cruising, superb handling, and a fairly comfortable ride. Some minuses: mediocre acceleration when fully loaded and so-so braking. **Strong points:** Pilot's a mouse that sometimes roars and at other times squeaks. Truck-like on the outside, but a much tamer vehicle when you look closely and get it on the road. It combines car-like comfort and handling in a crossover package where ride comfort, utility, and passenger accommodations are foremost. A versatile interior that could be more refined; plenty of passenger space; seating for up to eight; the third-row seat folds flat into sections to free up storage space; and there's a small storage area in the floor. Chock full of safety and convenience features and the GPS and voice operation feature are easy to use – with a little practice. Overall reliability has been better than average. **Weak points:** Unimpressive fuel economy – the much-heralded cylinder deactivation system doesn't save as much fuel as Honda fantasizes. Interior plastic materials and overall fit and finish aren't up to Honda's reputation for quality, and some road noise is omnipresent. The centre console and other controls' many buttons can be confusing to operate until you've mastered the layout. **Major redesign:** 2003 and 2009; next important redesign is scheduled for the 2015 model year. **Highway/city fuel economy:** *Front-drive:* 8.7/12.7 L/100 km. *AWD:* 9.1/13.1 L/100 km. **Best alternatives:** GM's heavily discounted Tahoe and Yukon SUVs are selling at bargain prices. A GM Terrain or Traverse would also be worth considering.

SAFETY: NHTSA gave the 2011-14 models four stars for frontal and rollover protection, and five stars for side protection. 2003-10 Pilots have even better scores; five stars for both frontal and side impacts and four stars for rollover protection. IIHS gave the Pilot its top "Good" rating in all crash categories, except for roof strength on the 2009-11 models, which were judged "Marginal" and 2003-05 Pilot head restraints which were rated both "Poor" and "Marginal." Although owners reported only 124 complaints to NHTSA during the past three years (most vehicles average 50 reports a year), some of the reported incidents are quite serious threats: airbags failed to deploy; fuel leak under the vehicle; sudden, unintended acceleration and brake failure; transmission lurches back and forth between Fourth and Fifth gear; mushy brakes that lose pressure; electrical failures leading to stalling and hard starting:

> I was told not to bother to bring it in for service each time it stalled because they were waiting for a recall/fix from corporate. After six weeks, multiple stalls, which were all reported to my dealer as requested, dealer agreed to trade my vehicle in for a different Pilot. Within less than 24 hours of owning this second 2012 Honda Pilot, my new car stalled. I have recently been on YouTube and discovered that this is a common problem with the 2012 Honda Pilots, and has also been reported with some 2011 Honda Pilots.

Front wheel fell off; and several owners warn that unprotected wiring in the undercarriage area could be life-threatening if damaged:

> Wheel sensor wires on 2011 Honda Pilots are exposed and unprotected under the vehicle which when damaged, disable anti-lock braking system (ABS), vehicle stability assist (VSA), and the variable torque management (VTM-4) systems. Exposed wires are prone to be cut or damaged by road debris and hazards. Due to the wire being exposed, it was damaged and caused an out-of-pocket expense of approx. $266.00 to repair.

Other owner complaints include: Automatic transmission fluid leaks; secondary hood latch failed when passing over rough roads; rear tailgate window exploded while vehicle was parked in a garage (window was replaced under warranty, which

Prices and Specs

Prices (Negotiable): *LX:* $34,820, *LX 4WD:* $37,820, *EX 4WD:* $40,720, *EX-L 4WD:* $43,020, *EX-L res 4WD:* $44,620, *Touring 4WD:* $48,420 **Freight:** $1,495 **Powertrain (Front-drive/AWD):** Engine: 3.5L V6 (250 hp); Transmission: 5-speed auto. **Dimensions/capacity:** Passengers: 2/3/3; Wheelbase: 109.2 in.; H: 71.0/L: 190.9/W: 78.5 in.; Headroom: F/R1/R2: 40/39.8/38.2 in.; Legroom: F/R1/R2: 41.4/38.5/32.1 in.; Cargo volume: 18 cu. ft.; Fuel tank: 79.5L/regular; Tow limit: 3,500-4,500 lb.; Load capacity: 1,320 lb.; Turning circle: 36.7 ft.; Ground clearance: 8 in.; Weight: 4,319 lb.

shows Honda realizes this is a quality issue and not a routine insurance claim for damage caused from an outside source); original-equipment Goodyear tire sidewall failures; rear AC system will not shut off from the front control panel; and the driver's seat height adjustment lowers on its own while the Pilot is underway. Pilot dealer servicing has also been found wanting:

Spontaneous star crack in lower center windshield, spontaneous rear hatch and passenger door opening while driving with my young child in the rear passenger seat (with "locked" doors), transmission rattle upon slow acceleration or coast at second and third gears ... Honda dealer said call insurance about windshield, something must have "hit" windshield without me knowing it, said "found no abnormal noises" and "cannot duplicate" rattle noise because different people have different driving patterns, said "cannot duplicate" doors opening while driving, dealer did not "fix" any of these safety issues, just told us to pick up the car. ... After research on Internet, I believe these to be manufacturer defects.

ALERT! Pilot sales have rebounded this year, but dealers are willing to dicker a bit over prices, as Honda sweetens its leasing and financing deals. 2014s will be eligible for all kinds of automaker incentives that will drive down their prices during the first quarter of 2014. Be prepared to delay your purchase until then.

Pilot Profile

	2004	2005	2006	2007	2008	2009	2010	2011	2012
Used Values ($)									
EX/LX	6.500	8,000	9,000	11,000	12,000	13,500	18,500	23,500	27,500
4x4	—	—	—	12,000	13,000	14,500	19,500	25,000	29,000
EX-L Res	7,000	9,000	11,000	13,000	—	17,500	23,500	29,500	34,500
Touring	—	—	—	—	—	18,500	25,500	32,000	38,000
Recommended	★	★	★	★	★	☆	☆	☆	☆
Reliability	★	★	★	★	★	★	★	★	☆

SECRET WARRANTIES, INTERNAL BULLETINS: 2011-12—Engine ticking or knocking at idle (see Odyssey).

RIDGELINE ★★★★★

RATING: Recommended (2006-14); not only a top-performer, but well-appointed, and very reliable, as well. **Road performance:** Sustained and quiet acceleration; a smooth-shifting automatic transmission; and secure handling and good cornering control, thanks to communicative, direct steering and well-tuned shocks that also give a comfortable, supple ride. **Strong points:** The Ridgeline mixes performance with convenience. It's an ideal truck for most jobs, as long as you keep it on the highway. Off-road, this unibody pickup offers only medium performance relative to its nearest body-on-frame competitors, the Toyota Tacoma and the Nissan Frontier. Its long wheelbase and independent rear suspension give the Ridgeline an impressive in-bed trunk and excellent road manners, but make it difficult for the truck to traverse anything that's rougher than a stone road or has a breakover angle greater than 21 degrees. A friendly cabin environment where everything is easily accessed and storage spaces abound; a lockable trunk beneath the cargo bed; the tailgate opens either vertically or horizontally; and there's no intrusive wheel arch in the 5-foot-long bed. Reliability and overall dependability are legendary, and crashworthiness is exemplary. **Weak points:** High sales price which should come down this summer; excessive road noise; bed is too small for some needs; and don't get too confident when off-roading. **Major redesign:** 2006; the truck will go on hiatus until the redesigned 2016 model arrives. **Highway/city fuel economy:** 9.8/14.1 L 100 km. **Best alternatives:** Other pickups worth considering are the GM Silverado and Sierra duo, and Nissan Frontier.

SAFETY: Few safety-related incidents have been reported to NHTSA federal investigators or by *Consumer Reports* members within the last five model years. Also, internal manufacturer service bulletins show no major failure trends. Exceptionally high marks given by NHTSA for passenger crash protection: 2011-14 models earned four stars for rollover resistance, however, 2006-10 Ridgelines did much better, with five stars for frontal and side protection in addition to four stars for rollover crashworthiness. IIHS judged the truck "Good" in offset frontal, side, rear, and roof crash protection going back to the 2006 model year.

ALERT! Remember, small- and mid-sized pickups retain a higher resale value than most cars; it's the big rigs that depreciate the fastest, but also apparently last the longest, as well. So, even if you pay more than expected, you will recoup the difference by extending the trade-in time. Firestone and Bridgestone original-equipment tires will

Prices and Specs

Prices (Negotiable): *DX:* $34,990, *VP:* $36,690, *EX-L:* $41,490, *EX-L Navi.:* $43,690 **Freight:** $1,395 **Powertrain (Front-drive/4WD):** Engine: 3.5L V6 (250 hp); Transmission: 5-speed auto. **Dimensions/capacity:** Passengers: 2/3; Wheelbase: 122 in.; H: 70.3/L: 207/W: 69 in.; Headroom F/R: 6.5/4.5 in.; Legroom F/R: 42/28 in.; Fuel tank: 83.3L/regular; Tow limit: 5,000 lb.; Load capacity: 1,554 lb.; Turning circle: 42.6 ft.; Ground clearance: 7.5 in.; Weight: 4,504 lb.; GVWR: 6,051 lb.

not give you the best performance or durability; try to trade them for something better.

Ridgeline Profile

	2006	2007	2008	2009	2010	2011	2012
Used Values ($)							
LX/DX	10,000	11,500	13,000	15,000	18,500	24,000	28,000
VP	—	—	—	15,500	19,000	24,500	29,000
EX-L/Sport	11,500	12,000	15,000	17,000	21,500	27,500	29,500
EX-L Navi/Touring	—	12,500	15,500	18,000	22,500	28,500	33,000
Recommended	☆	☆	☆	☆	☆	☆	☆
Reliability	☆	☆	☆	☆	☆	☆	☆

SECRET WARRANTIES, INTERNAL BULLETINS: 2006-07—Automatic transmission is hard to shift into Fourth gear. Vehicle pulls, drifts to one side. Drivetrain ping, squeal, or rattle upon light acceleration. Rear differential noise, judder on turns. Steering wheel, interior squeaking noise. **2006-08**—Timing belt chirping. **2006-09**—Parking brake won't release in cold weather because of water infiltration. Noise and judder when turning. **2006-10**—Steering column clicking when turning. **2006-11**—Rear seat leg doesn't fold flat. **2009-10**—Headliner vibrates or rattles. Whistling from the front door windows. Gap between the front bumper and the fender/headlamp. **2009-11**—Tailgate won't open in swing mode; handle is stiff. Front seats squeak and creak.

HYUNDAI

Hyundai and its Kia lineup are racking up impressive sales across Canada for three reasons:

1. Their entry-level vehicles are relatively cheaper and loaded with more standard features when compared with the competition. Compare Accent, Genesis, and Tucson with other brands and laugh all the way to the bank.
2. Hyundai quality that was once a cruel joke played on Pony, Stellar, and Excel owners, now is recognized as better than average (except for the "wanderer" Sonata) – almost equal to the best that comes from Japan.
3. Hyundai's comprehensive base warranty is competitive with other automakers and its warranty performance is fair and relatively painless. The only exception has been Hyundai and its Kia brother's failure to quickly admit they lied when giving out fuel economy claims a few years back. Both companies subsequently set up compensation programs to satisfy owners.

Korean Quality?

Stop laughing. Wait until the Chinese get here.

Hyundai car quality over the past several decades has gone from risible to reliable, except for some redesigned models like the glitch-ridden 2011 Sonata. This general quality turnaround has been accomplished through the use of better-made components and corporate espionage.

Over a decade ago, Hyundai hired away a handful of Toyota's top quality-control engineers – and got a satchel-full of Toyota's secret quality-control documents in the bargain. Following a cease-and-desist letter from Toyota in 2006, Hyundai returned the pilfered papers and swore to Toyota's lawyers that they never looked at the secret reports stolen from the compakny (wink, wink; nudge, nudge).

Funny thing, though, Hyundai quality immediately improved; and Kia followed. Industry insiders say the privileged information was a major factor in Hyundai's leapfrogging the competition with better quality-control systems and more reliable components. How ironic, too, that Hyundai and Kia have copied the marketing strategy employed by Japanese automakers since the early '70s: Secure a solid beachhead in one car segment, like the Accent econocar, and then branch out from there with new models, like the Elantra compact and the Genesis sports coupe and sedan.

Hyundai redesigns its lineup every three years. Models that flop, like the Entourage minivan, Tiburon, and Azera, get dumped. The company also shares components with its Kia subsidiary to keep production costs down while raising Kia quality (yes, *Consumer Reports* now recommends the Kia Forte, Soul, and Sorento).

Hyundai Pony   Hyundai Genesis

"The $4,750 entry-level Pony was undoubtedly cheap and generally 'craptastic', but it was a beginning.
I knew a guy who drove one – and to say it was less than reliable would be an understatement."
(See "Hyundai Pony, 1984-87" at *www.autos.ca/forum/index.php?topic=73546.0.*) On the other hand,
Consumer Reports loves the Hyundai Genesis, which today costs seven times the original price of a Pony.
Says *CR*: "This upscale sedan delivers virtually everything a $50,000 sedan does, but for $10,000 less."

Has the Quality Bubble Burst?

Unfortunately, all is not rosy for Hyundai from a quality perspective. Its redesigned 2011 Sonata (the Kia Optima is the same car with different badging) is a mess – a potentially lethal mess – with over 500 safety-related complaints reported to NHTSA (100 complaints would be the norm after two years on the market).

Owners of 2011-13s decry sudden, unintended acceleration, malfunctioning powertrains, headlights that give inadequate lighting, and steering malfunctions that drive the Sonata to one side of the road or the other:

> 2012 Sonata will not drive straight, it pulls to the left mostly but also to the right. Basically the car swerves all over the road, especially at higher speeds. I took it back to the dealership and they told me all foreign cars drive like this. They adjusted the tire pressure but that did not solve the problem. I do not feel safe driving the car. Hyundai issued a service campaign to fix the 2011 Sonatas for this exact problem, why can't they just do the same for the 2012s?

> ...

> After purchasing the car new in Sept of 2011, we received notice from Hyundai advising of recall due to pulling while driving. We contacted the local dealer multiple times and were advised they were waiting on the technical specification on how to fix the problem. This has continued since November of 2011 (letter written June 12, 2012). The driving condition of the car has continued to decline and has even caused the front two tires excessive wear. The front tires already need replacement. The car drifts off to the right severely when you release the steering wheel, causing fatiguing of the arms due to continued correction of the steering.

To a lesser degree, similar safety problems (notably, steering malfunctions) have affected the Elantra. Could it be that Hyundai is following Toyota and Honda production practices a little too closely and is giving owners less content for more money?

During 2012, the South Koreans continued to invest heavily in North America as they trolled for dealers recently dumped by the bankrupt Chrysler and General Motors. They have brought out an extensive lineup of fuel-efficient new cars, minivans, and SUVs, and are targeting increasingly upscale customers without forgetting their entry-level base. For example, Hyundai has enhanced its luxury lineup with the Genesis luxury sedan and the Genesis Coupe, a Camaro/Mustang stalker. The 2012 Equus is a $64,499 (now worth $16,000 less, used), V8-powered, rear-drive luxury sedan aimed squarely at the BMW 5 Series and the Mercedes-Benz E-Class. Equus was developed on the rear-drive Genesis sedan platform, but the wheelbase was stretched by 10.9 cm (4.3 in.). It's 29 cm (11.4 in.) longer than the 2010 Mercedes E-Class. At the other end of the fuel economy spectrum, both Hyundai and Kia are focusing on fuel-frugal small cars and plan to offer drivers fuel-saving options that include smaller engines, direct-injection gasoline engines, plug-in hybrids, and fuel cell technology. Hyundai calls the fuel economy initiative "Blue Drive" – a fancy name for cheaper models with less content, less weight, and more miles per gallon. For example, Blue Edition models have a lower gear ratio and tires with less rolling resistance. Power windows and door locks, as well as other formerly standard amenities, will become optional, thereby trading convenience for cash savings. Hyundai is also giving each Sonata a Blue Link communications system that provides a direct connection to emergency services in the event of an accident. The feature also gives traffic and weather updates and allows owners easy access to roadside assistance. Smart phones can be connected with Blue Link to help owners locate their vehicle in large shopping malls or to follow "Junior" when he takes the car out on the weekend. The system can keep track of where the vehicle is being driven and how fast it's going.

"Hey son, I know you'll love this feature … son, son?"

ACCENT ★★★★★

RATING: Recommended (2012-14); Above Average (2006-11); Below Average (2001-05). **Road performance:** Good engine and automatic transmission performance in most situations; easy handling; a reasonably comfortable and quiet ride; a relaxed driving position with good visibility. Some drivers feel the engine could use a bit more torque and noise-vibration dampening and that the ride is a bit on the firm, jittery side. **Strong points:** Hyundai has transformed its entry-level Accent into a larger, upscale compact the same way the Civic was incrementally improved and enlarged to join the Accord in the family car class. All of these improvements have added to the Accent's base price over the years, however, it is still one of the cheapest and most reliable feature-laden small cars sold in North America. Carrying a homegrown direct-injection 1.6L 4-cylinder engine coupled to a standard 6-speed manual transmission (the 6-speed automatic is optional), the Accent offers bare-bones motoring, but includes many standard features found only on upscale cars such as a height-adjustable driver's seat, four-wheel disc brakes, active front head restraints, a tilt steering wheel, power locks, an incredibly good reliability record, with few complaints relative to safety or quality control; and it's cheap on gas. **Weak points:** Acrobatic rear-seat entry/exit with the hatchback; cramped rear seating; and some noise intrusion into the cabin. **Major redesign:** 2000, 2006, and 2012. **Highway/city fuel economy:** *Man.:* 4.9/6.7 L/100 km. *Auto.:* 4.8/7.8 L/100 km. **Best alternatives:** Chevrolet Cruze, Honda Fit or Civic (2011 or earlier), Mazda3, Nissan Versa or Sentra, Suzuki SX4, and Toyota Yaris.

Prices and Specs

Prices (Negotiable): *Hatchback L:* $13,699, *Auto:* $14,899, *Sedan L:* $13,299, *Auto:* $14,499, *GL:* $15,199, *Auto:* $16,399, *GLS:* $18,249 **Freight:** $1,495 **Powertrain (Front-drive):** Engine: 1.6L 4-cyl. (138 hp); Transmissions: 6-speed man., 6-speed auto. **Dimensions/capacity:** *Sedan:* Passengers: 2/3; Wheelbase: 101.2 in.; H: 57.1/L: 172/W: 66.9 in.; Headroom F/R: 4.5/2 in.; Legroom F/R: 41.8/33.3 in.; Cargo volume: 13.7 cu. ft.; Fuel tank: 43L/regular; Tow limit: N/A; Load capacity: 850 lb.; Turning circle: 34.1 ft.; Ground clearance: 5.5 in.; Weight: *L:* 2,396 lb., *auto:* 2,462 lb.

SAFETY: NHTSA crash tests give the 2012-14 Accent four stars for frontal, side, and rollover crash protection. 1996-2010 models did almost as well with three to five stars in overall crashworthiness. IIHS says moderate overlap frontal scores for the 2012 and 2013 models are "Good" and 2006-11 models are rated "Acceptable." Side impact results for the 2012 and 2013s are considered "Good," but the 2006-11s are rated as "Poor" performers. 2012-13 model roof strength is seen as "Good" while the 2006-11 models rate only "Acceptable". 2012-13 rear crashworthiness is "Good; 2010-11 versions are "Acceptable;" and 2006-09 Accents were judge "Poor." Owners report airbags may not deploy, sudden loss of power, and steering-wheel lock-up. Keep the car in the garage if you live in a woodsy area – rodents see your yummy wiring insulation as Tim Hortons take out. One owner reports that groundhogs love to snack on the car's undercarriage cables, thereby disabling the tranny and important dash gauges:

> I put down moth balls and fox scent to ward the hogs off, but they love Accent wires; losing the transmission and speedometer can make driving a little dangerous.

ALERT! Insist upon a spare tire instead of a tire repair kit.

Accent Profile

	2004	2005	2006	2007	2008	2009	2010	2011	2012
Used Values ($)									
HB /Sedan L	3,000	3,500	3,500	4,000	4,500	5,000	6,500	8,000	9,500
GL	3,500	4,000	4,500	5,000	5,500	6,000	7,500	9,000	10,500
GLS	4,000	4,500	5,500	6,000	6,500	7,500	9,000	10,500	12,000
Recommended	★	★	☆	☆	☆	☆	☆	☆	☆
Reliability	★	★	★	★	★	☆	☆	☆	☆

SECRET WARRANTIES, INTERNAL BULLETINS: 2008-11—Some 2008-11 Accents may have a rattle noise coming from underneath the vehicle near the front muffler pipe assembly. This bulletin provides a procedure to replace either the front muffler pipe hanger assembly or the front muffler assembly. **2011-12**—Harsh delayed shift diagnosis on the 6-speed automatic transmission. Reducing wind noise from the front door mirror area.

ELANTRA/TOURING

★★★★ / ★★★

RATING: Above Average (2009-14); Average (2002-08). **Road performance:** 4-cylinder engine has plenty of pep for daily chores and comes with a smooth-shifting 6-speed automatic transmission; however, the engine feels sluggish when in Active Eco mode, there's excessive engine noise when accelerating, and the steering pulls strongly to one or the other side. Good handling and a comfortable ride; electronic stability control comes with the SE trim. Touring: This compact wagon handles well and has excellent braking. Not as good a performer as the Elantra, though. First and Second gear are too far apart, the ride is quite firm, there's little steering feedback, and engine noise invades the cabin. **Strong points:** Elantra's sharp new styling breaks with its bland past and its roomy interior pushes the car into the mid-size category. A Touring wagon version arrived in early 2009. The 2011 revamping gave the car a more fluid, stylish exterior and a well-appointed and spacious interior; comfortable seats; a seatback that slides back far enough to easily accommodate drivers over 6 feet tall; and a classy, quiet interior. **Weak points:** Noisy brakes are sometimes a bit grabby and take some skill to modulate; a bit too much wind and road noise; and the dash vents would be more effective if they were mounted higher. Touring: Fuel economy isn't as good as the Elantra. **Major redesign:** 2001, 2007, and 2011. **Highway/city fuel economy:** *1.8L man.:* 4.9/6.8 L/100 km. *Auto.:* 4.9/69 L/100 km. *Touring 2.0L man.:* 6.4/8.9 L/100 km. *Touring auto.:* 6.5/8.7 L/100 km. **Best alternatives:** The Chevrolet Cruze, Honda Accord or Civic (2011 or earlier), Mazda3, Suzuki SX4, and Toyota Corolla.

 SAFETY: 2001-14 models are rated four and five stars for overall crashworthiness. Earlier models performed poorly in some of the crash tests. *Touring:* 2009-10 models garnered a four- and five-star ranking. IIHS says moderate overlap frontal scores for the 2004-13 Elantra models are "Good"; 2001-03 are "Poor"; and 1996-2000 versions are "Acceptable." Side impact results for the 2010-13 models are "Good;" 2007-10 are rated "Marginal,", and 2001-06 models are ranked as "Poor" performers. 2011-13s roof strength and rear protection is "Good." 2010 model rear protection is also "Good" and 2007-09 versions are "Acceptable." The worst rating is reserved for 2001-06 Elantras which were judged to give "Poor" protection. Safety-related complaints: Sudden engine shutdown on the highway; hood suddenly flew up while vehicle was underway; dangerous airbag deployment, or failure to deploy:

> Drivers side air bag deployed and metal bracket deployed with air bag from headliner area, also. It sliced my ear in half ... Could have been my neck ...

At other times, both airbags deployed for no reason; the airbag warning light and tire-pressure monitoring system alert come on for no reason; there was sudden, unintended acceleration accompanied by loss of braking capability; the cruise control suddenly reset itself to a higher speed; throttle sensor sticks when cruising; automatic transmission jumps out of gear; complete electrical shutdown; car may roll away even with the emergency brake applied; faulty electronic stability control; car idles roughly, then refuses to shift into Drive; sudden steering lock-up; the car continually pulls to the right or left: brakes freeze up when the vehicle is driven through snow; brake rotors rust prematurely producing a grinding noise;

Prices and Specs

Prices (Negotiable): *L Sedan:* $15,949, *L auto.:* $17,149, *GLS:* $19,949, *Limited:* $23,199, *GLS Limited/ Navigation:* $25,199, *GT GL man.:* $19,149, *GT GL auto.:* $20,349, *GT GLS man.:* $21,349, *GT GLS auto.:* $22,549, *GT SE auto.:* $24,349, *GT SE TECH:* $26,349, *Touring GL man.:* $18,199, *Touring GL auto.:* $19,399, *Touring GLS man.:* $20,649, *Touring GL auto.:* $21,849 **Freight:** $1,495 **Powertrain (Front-drive):** Engine: 1.8L 4-cyl. (148 hp); Transmissions: 6-speed man., 6-speed auto. **Dimensions/ capacity (Touring):** Passengers: 2/3; Wheelbase: 106.3 in.; H: 56.5/L: 178.3/W: 69.9 in.; Headroom F/R: 2.5/2 in.; Legroom F/R: 43.6/33.1 in.; Cargo volume: 14.8 cu. ft.; Fuel tank: 48L/regular; Tow limit: 2,000 lb.; Load capacity: 850 lb.; Turning circle: 34.8 ft.; Ground clearance: 5.5 in., Weight: 2,701 lb.

a history of front windshield cracks; windshield glare from defroster dish; sunroof implosions; can't trust the fuel gauge; Continental, Kumho Solus, and Hankook original equipment tires are noted for sidewall failures ("bubbling"); and large blind spots caused by the left and right front pillars:

The positioning of the rear view mirror only makes the right blind spot larger as there is only the space from the bottom of the mirror to the right pillar to view outside of the car. As a result, I almost hit someone crossing the street from my right to my left.

ALERT! Tire pressure sensors give false alerts. No need for optional equipment; Elantra comes with all the right standard features; one feature missing on some models – a spare tire and jack. Check it out.

Car dealers are allowed to sell Elantras with no spare tire or jack. Their policy is to only include a can of air which may or may not work when needed. They are also not keeping replacement tires in stock. This can of air is a hazard to keep in a car in Arizona when the temperatures in the summer reach 115 degrees [46°C]. And with the dealership not stocking the tires, my car was not drivable and strands the motorist.

Elantra/Touring Profile

Used Values ($)	2004	2005	2006	2007	2008	2009	2010	2011	2012
Sedan GL/L	3,500	4,000	4,500	5,000	5,500	6,500	7,500	9,000	11,000
GLS	4,000	5,000	6,000	6,500	7,000	8,000	10,000	12,000	12,500
LTD	—	—	—	7,000	7,500	9,000	11,000	13,000	15.000
Touring L	—	—	—	—	—	—	8,000	9,500	11,500
GLS	—	—	—	—	—	—	10,500	12,500	14,500
GLS Sport	—	—	—	6,000	7,000	9,000	11,000	13,000	16,000
Recommended	★	★	★	★	★	★	★	★	★
Reliability	★	★	★	★	★	★	★	★	★

SECRET WARRANTIES, INTERNAL BULLETINS: 2007-12—Troubleshooting hard shifts. **2010**—Some Elantra and Elantra Touring vehicles may exhibit a noise originating from the front struts when passing over bumps or dips at speeds of 10-16 mph. **2011-12**—Free rear door harness and centre muffler rattle noise repair. Excessive driveshaft noise (creaking or popping). Troubleshooting an automatic transmission that stays in Third gear, goes into "failsafe mode," or has an illuminated MIL alert. Touch screen new recalibration. **2011-13**—Hard starts may signal the need to clean the electronic throttle control (ETC) throttle body.

SONATA/HYBRID ★★/★★★

RATING: Below Average (2010-14); Average (2007-09); Below Average (2002-06). Like Honda, Hyundai cars don't tolerate redesigns very well (see Weak points and Safety, below). Nevertheless, it looks like Hyundai has been diligent in correcting some of its 2011 factory-induced deficiencies. *Hybrid:* Below Average (2012); Average (2013-14). Sonata's 2012 Hybrid debut was blasted by car columnists for its poorly-designed powertrain, inadequate braking, and fanciful fuel economy. The 2013-14 models seek to redress the earlier problems with a quieter and smoother-shifting transmission (no more buzzy drone), and a more refined clutch that smooths out the transition between gas and electric power. Braking is also more confidence-inspiring; the battery has a higher capacity and is smaller, freeing up some cargo space, and the car can reach 75 mph on battery power alone (engine power has been cut from 166 to 159 hp). **Road performance:** Sizzling, smooth V6 performance; acceptable handling; and a comfortable ride. The suspension is somewhat bouncy and noisy; there's too much body lean under hard cornering; and the steering lacks sufficient feedback. Many complaints of steering wander and pull. **Strong points:** V6 engine burns only a bit more gas than the 4-banger does. Well-equipped and stylish; user-friendly controls and gauges; spacious trunk, a conveniently low lift-in height; and a fairly quiet cabin that comfortably seats three in the back. **Weak points:** Noisy shocks/struts; owner complaints about problems that have been carried over from the 2011 model redesign. Sudden, unintended acceleration when passing other cars; same thing happens when shifting to Reverse; cruise control resets itself to a higher speed; and sudden hybrid engine failure due to water intrusion in rainy weather:

> Engine can easily become hydro-locked in heavy rain and road splash-back from other vehicles due to the design of the direct air intake of the Sonata Hybrid. With its design, it does not have any water baffles to prevent water from entering the air filter and once it enters the air filter box, there are no drain holes for it to drain out. This forces the water through the engine. This could lead to damage of the HEV system and battery pack.

Major redesign: 1999, 2006, and 2011. The 2014 model is expected to get a minor facelift and some upgrades. **Highway/city fuel economy:** *Auto. 2.0L:* 6.0/9.3 L/100 km. *Man. 2.4L:* 5.7/8.7 L/10 km. *Auto. 2.4L:* 5.7/9.4 L/100 km. *Hybrid:* 4.6/5.5 L/100 km.

Best alternatives: The Chevrolet Cruze, Honda Accord, Hyundai Elantra, Nissan Sentra, Mazda5 or Mazda6, and Toyota Camry.

 SAFETY: NHTSA awarded the 2013 Sonata five stars for side and rollover crashworthiness and four stars for frontal occupant safety. IIHS says the Sonata deserves a "Good" rating for front offset protection, head-restraint effectiveness, roof crush-resistance, and side-impact protection. This mid-sized sedan is a *Consumer Reports* top-rated pick and its sales, particularly since the 2011 redesign, have been spectacular. Unfortunately, not all model years are reliable or safe, judging from the following owner experiences with the 2011-14 versions: Sudden electrical shutdown; passenger side airbag disabled when normal-sized adult occupies the seat; airbags fail to deploy in a high-speed collision; parked vehicle rolled downhill, even though the transmission was left in Drive; manual transmission lunges forward when shifting from First to Second gear; poorly located cruise control Resume button inadvertently activates the feature; premature wearout of the rear brakes; low-beam headlights give inadequate illumination, left tail light fell out of its mounting inside the trunk due to the plastic mount crumbling; rear windshield exploded after door was closed; Hankook original equipment tires continue to fail due to sidewall bubbling; sun visors are not long enough (vertically) to keep sun from blinding the driver; the horn is weak, makes a short sound, and sometimes won't sound at all; and hard starts, no-starts:

> The only reliable solution for starting the car is to depress the brake pedal and depress the Engine Start button for a minimum of 10 seconds. I've placed the key fob in several locations in the car (dashboard, cup holder, smart key holder) with no repeatable success. After a visit to the dealership, they cannot find a problem. However, a search on the Internet shows other owners experiencing the same problem.

How could *CR* miss this? Probably because they did not compare their annual member survey comments with government NHTSA safety failure reports, nor with Hyundai's own confidential service bulletins.

Prior to the 2011 model's redesign, only a few dozen owner complaints would appear on NHTSA's safety database each year. For example, the 2010 model shows only 45 incidents reported where the four-year norm would be 200 reports. Contrast that with the redesigned 2011 model's profile up through August 2013. That model year alone elicited 569 safety-related reports posted on NHTSA's website. In the past, incremental powertrain, performance, safety, convenience, and styling changes were quickly corrected by Hyundai without provoking such large-scale owner dissatisfaction.

Is Hyundai fixing the above mentioned safety deficiencies? Apparently, yes, partly.

The 2012 and 2013 Sonata have been the object of only 103 and 67 safety reports, respectively. Does this mean it's safe to go out and risk buying a 2012 through 2014?

Not on your life.

There are still far too many safety failings on these cars like sunroof implosions and excessive steering wander and severe pulling to the right or left that come back year after year, as this owner of a 2013 Sonata bought last July 2013, confirms:

> I have had my 2013 Sonata Limited for two weeks. This is my third Hyundai vehicle after owning a 2011 Sonata Limited and 2007 Santa Fe. The steering in the vehicle weaves from left to right (does not track straight) and control of the car is jeopardized by the smallest road contours or gusts of wind requiring constant correction. As a result of the constant driving adjustments, I am experiencing fatigue and shoulder/neck soreness. Equally alarming, the lack of control is extremely noticeable on highways at increased speeds.

Prices and Specs

Price (Negotiable): *GL:* $22,699, *GL auto.:* $24,299, *GLS auto.:* $26,499, *Limited:* $29,899, *2.0T Limited:* $31,799 *Hybrid:* $28,999 **Freight:** $1,565
Powertrain (Front-drive): Engines: 2.4L 4-cyl. (198 hp), 2.0L 4-cyl. turbo (274 hp); Transmissions: 6-speed man., 6-speed auto.
Dimensions/capacity: Passengers: 2/3; Wheelbase: 110 in.; H: 57.9/L: 189.8/W: 72.2 in.; Headroom F/R: 3/3 in.; Legroom F/R: 45.5/34.6 in.; Cargo volume: 16.4 cu. ft.; Fuel tank: 70L/ regular; Tow limit: N/A; Load capacity: 860 lb.; Turning circle: 35.8 ft.; Weight: 3,161-3,316 lb.

ALERT! Check out front left side visibility and the headlight intensity:

> Low beams did not project adequately when driving up and down hills and driving around curves. The low beam headlight projection decreased up to 50% and sometimes more than 50% depending on the size of the hill or curve.

Sonata Profile

	2004	2005	2006	2007	2008	2009	2010	2011	2012
Used Values ($)									
GL	4,000	4,500	5,500	6,000	7,500	8,500	11,000	13,500	15,500
VE/GLS	—	5,000	6,500	7,000	8,500	—	—	16,000	18,500
GLX/LTD	4,500	5,000	—	—	9,500	11,000	13,500	17,000	20,000
Hybrid	—	—	—	—	—	—	—	18,500	—
Recommended	★2	★2	★2	★3	★3	★3	★3	★2	★2
Reliability	★3	★3	★3	★3	★3	★4	★4	★4	★5

SECRET WARRANTIES, INTERNAL BULLETINS: 2006-08—Engine hesitation and misfire repair tips. Remedy for seat creaking, squeaking. **2006-09**—Correction for a rough idle or display of the MIL warning light on vehicles equipped with the 3.3L engine. The oil temperature sensor may leak. **2006-10**—Steering squeaks when turning.

2007-10—Troubleshooting hard starts or a rough idle. **2008**—Correction for a steering wheel shimmy/vibration. **2009-10**—A cold weather no-start condition may require a new starter solenoid. A water leak onto the passenger side front floor is likely due to a kinked AC drain hose. **2009-13**—If the engine spins, but doesn't crank, replace the starter motor says Hyundai TSB #13-EE-001, issued February 2013. **2011-12**—Automatic transmission malfunctions caused by faulty solenoids and other electronic failures. The transmission may shift harshly, drop into a "safe" default mode, or hesitate between shifts.

GENESIS COUPE, SEDAN

RATING: Recommended (2011-14); Above Average (2009-11). Coupe or sedan? Both are excellent buys. The Genesis coupe and sedan are impressive upscale rear drive vehicles with different performance characteristics and widely varying retail prices. Any cheaper 2012 leftovers are not worth the 2013 upgrades you will miss. **Road performance:** The 3.8L engine gives breathtaking power to the coupe and quick acceleration when used with the sedan, although the sedan's 5.0L V8 is a real tire burner. The coupe's 4-cylinder turbo is both noisy and hooked to an imprecise 6-speed manual transmission; the optional 4.6L V8 is like having a sixth finger: It's there, but not all that useful. Expect the coupe to have a choppy, stiff ride, while the sedan has some body roll in hard cornering due to its more supple, "floaty" suspension (Infiniti and BMW models have stiffer suspensions that produce a more-secure feeling). **Strong points:** These luxury cars are loaded with high-tech safety gear and are generally well-appointed with first-class interior fit and finish; a quiet, vibration-free, and spacious cabin; and clear and easy-to-read gauges. The sedan has plenty of room fore and aft and has posted impressive crashworthiness rankings. The 2013s were restyled to look more aggressive, and their new powertrains pack more punch and a few more gears as well. For example, the Coupe's 3.8L V6 now generates 348 hp and the 2.0T is rated at 274 hp, a 30 percent increase over the previous engine. Cabin amenities have also been improved with easier-to-read gauges and extra seat bolstering. **Weak points:** Cramped rear seating with the coupe; navigation and audio system controls are cumbersome. Hyundai recommends premium fuel for extra horsepower from the 4.6L V8, but it's not worth the higher fuel cost for just a few more horses. V6 reliability is above average; V8s are average. Some early transmission failures. **Major redesign:** 2013. **Highway/city fuel economy:** *Coupe 2.0L man.:* 6.6/10L/100 km. *Coupe 2.0L auto.:* 6.7/10.5 L/100 km. *Coupe 3.8L man.:* 7.6/12 L/100 km. *3.8L auto.:* 7.3/12.2 L/100 km. *3.8L 8-spd. auto.:* 6.9/11.1L/100 km. *Sedan 3.8L:* 7.2/11.4 L/100 km. *Sedan 4.6L:* 8.1/12.6 L/100 km. *5.0L 8-spd. auto.:* 8.1/13.1 L/100 km. **Best alternatives:** *Sedan:* The BMW 3 Series, Ford Taurus, Lincoln MKS, Mercedes-Benz E-Class, and Toyota Avalon. *Coupe:* The Chevrolet Camaro and – for sheer sportster thrills without the bills – the Mazda MX-5.

SAFETY: NHTSA gave the 2011-13 models five stars for rollover resistance. The 2009-10 sedan and 2010 coupe have the top, five-star rating for front, side, and rollover occupant protection. 2009-13 Genesis models were top-scorers with the IIHS after earning a "Good" designation in the moderate frontal overlap crash test; 2009 models were judged "Acceptable." Side ratings for 2009-13: "Good;" roof strength: 2010-13: "Good;" 2005-09: "Poor;" and rear: 2009-13: "Good," There were less than 50 safety-related complaints posted during the past four model years – 200 would have been average. Owner reports include: Cruise control malfunctions; electronic stability control (ESC) locked driver's brakes when he was turning the vehicle; brake failures; various ESC and Bluetooth malfunctions; early replacement of the automatic transmission; loud manual transmission knocking while the clutch is disengaged and the transmission is in Neutral; steering tracks to the right or left; turn signal continues blinking after it is no longer needed; a small pebble damaged the AC condenser ($800); GPS and rear camera malfunction intermittently; windows and windshield produce a moldy-looking condensate; and the rear seat belt anchors are reversed.

ALERT! Fuel consumption figures are not to be believed; expect to get 20 percent less than what Hyundai promises.

Prices and Specs

Prices (Negotiable): *Coupe 2.0T: $26,499, auto.: $28,299, 2.0T GT man.: $31,149, 2.0T R-SPEC man.: $28,799, 3.8 man.: $32,999, 3.8 GT man.: $36,999, auto.: $38,799, Sedan: $39,999* **Freight:** *Coupe: $1,565, Sedan: $1,760* **Powertrain (Rear-drive):** Engines: 2.0L Turbo 4-cyl. (274 hp), 3.8L V6 (348 hp), 4.6L V8 (378 hp), 5.0L V8 (429 hp); Transmissions: 6-speed man., 6-speed manumatic, 8-speed manumatic **Dimensions/capacity:** *Coupe:* Passengers: 2/3; Wheelbase: 115.6 in.; H: 58.3/L: 195.6/W: 73.4 in.; Cargo volume: 15.9 cu. ft.; Fuel tank: 65L–73L/regular/premium; Tow limit: 5,000 lb.; Ground clearance: 5.2 in.; Turning circle: 36 ft.; Weight: 3,748 lb.

Genesis Profile

	2009	2010	2011	2012
Used Values ($)				
Coupe	—	13,500	15,500	18,000
GT	—	16,000	19,000	21,500
3.8	—	17,500	20,500	24,000
GT	—	18,500	22,500	26,000
Sedan	15,500	20,000	25,000	28,500
Tech	18,000	23,500	28,500	34,500
V8 Tech/V8 R-Spec	19,500	26,500	32,500	38,500
Recommended	☆	☆	☆	☆
Reliability	☆	☆	☆	☆

SECRET WARRANTIES, INTERNAL BULLETINS: 2001-12—Remedy for engine ticking at idle. A faulty transmission solenoid may activate the Check Engine alert and send the transaxle into "Fail-Safe" limp mode. Harsh, delayed shift diagnosis. A new touch screen recalibration. Coupe: Sunroof switch replacement campaign. Sedan: Troubleshooting speed sensor malfunctions (replace valve body assembly). **2009-12**—An inoperable or noisy A/C may require an A/C pulley disc limiter (Equus included). **2010**—No start in Park or Neutral. **2012**—Shift lever can't be moved out of Park.

TUCSON

RATING: Above Average (2011-14), Average (2004-10). **Road performance:** V6 engine provides smooth, sustained acceleration; sure-footed (thanks to the standard stability control); and effective, easy-to-modulate braking. Owners report the 4-cylinder engine struggles with a full load, the vehicle isn't as agile as others in its class, and the electric steering feels vague and lacks feedback at highway speeds. **Strong points:** The Tucson is Hyundai's compact crossover that was first introduced for the 2005 model year. It is smaller than the Santa Fe and built on the same Elantra-based platform as the Kia Sportage. It's reasonably priced and well equipped; has a roomy and easily accessed cabin; and above average reliability. **Weak points:** Stiff riding; poor styling limits cargo space; rear seat needs more bolstering for thigh support; some road noise; and advertised fuel economy shouldn't be expected. Automatic transmission jerks and slams into gear:

> Sudden downshifting with loud clunk and lurching of vehicle at 35 mph [55 km/h]. Felt as if I had been hit from behind by another vehicle. Instinctively hit the brakes and pulled over to check for exterior damage, and found none. Continued down the road and experienced unusual increases in rpms. When I arrived at my destination, the vehicle would not go in Reverse. Owned vehicle only 11 days. Incident occurred at 500 miles [800 km].

Major redesign: 2005, 2010, and 2014. **Highway/city fuel economy:** *2.0L man.:* 7.4/10.1 L/100 km. *Auto.:* 6.5/9.1 L/100 km. *2.4L man.:* 6.9/10 L/100 km. *Auto:* 6.3/9.5 L/100 km. *4WD auto.:* 7.1/10 L/100 km. **Best alternatives:** The Honda CR-V and Toyota RAV4.

Prices and Specs

Prices (Negotiable): *L man.:* $19,999, *auto.:* $22,899, *GL auto.:* $24,599, *GL AWD:* $26,599, *GLS:* $26,899, *GLS AWD:* $28,899, *Limited AWD:* $32,349, *Limited AWD Navi.:* $34,349 **Freight:** $1,595 **Powertrain (Front-drive/AWD):** Engines: 2.0L 4-cyl. (165 hp), 2.4L 4-cyl. (176 hp); Transmissions: 5-speed man., 6-speed manumatic **Dimensions/capacity:** Passengers: 2/3; Wheelbase: 103.9 in.; H: 65.2/L: 173.2/W: 71.7 in.; Headroom F/R: 5/4 in.; Legroom F/R: 41.2/38.7 in.; Cargo volume: 25.7 cu. ft.; Fuel tank: 58L/regular; Tow limit: 1,000-2,000 lb.; Load capacity: 860 lb.; Turning circle: 34.7 ft.; Ground clearance: 6.7 in.; Weight: 3,139-3,488 lb.

SAFETY: 2005-13 Tucsons scored a five-star crashworthiness rating for side-impact occupant protection and a four-star rating for frontal and rollover crashworthiness. 2010-13 Tucsons were top-scorers with the IIHS after earning a "Good" designation in the moderate frontal overlap crash test; 2005-09 models were judged "Acceptable." In the small frontal overlap test, the 2009-13 models got a "Poor" rating; side ratings: 2010-13: "Good;" 2005-09: "Acceptable;" roof strength: 2010-13: "Good;" 2005-09: "Poor;" rear: 2009-13: "Good;" 2006-08: "Poor." Owner safety-related complaints: Firewall insulation caught fire; rear window shattered spontaneously; key can be taken out of the ignition and transmission placed in Park and the Tucson will still roll downhill; loss of brakes for a couple of seconds after passing over speed bumps or small potholes; when accelerating to merge with traffic, the vehicle hesitates and then decelerates while the gas pedal is fully depressed; power steering seized; vehicle sways left and right while cruising; rear of the vehicle slides as if it were on ice; rear-tire lock-up; and speed sensor wires are vulnerable to road debris:

> Wires are located behind the tires and are fully exposed to road debris. They can be easily severed, thereby affecting ABS and traction control. The wire sticks out 3 inches in open air of the undercarriage and are located close enough to the tires that if they kick up any debris, it is in the direct path of the wire

ALERT! Does the car's rear styling cut your rearward visibility too much? Test the 4-cylinder engine for merging and steep grade performance. Also, check the steering performance and look for excessive road wander.

Tucson Profile

	2005	2006	2007	2008	2009	2010	2011	2012
Used Values ($)								
L	—	—	—	7,500	8,500	—	12,000	14,000
GL	5,000	6,000	6,500	8,500	9,500	11,000	14,000	16,500
GL AWD	—	—	7,000	9,500	10,500	13,000	15,500	18,500
GLS AWD	—	—	9,000	—	—	14,500	19,000	20,500
LTD AWD	—	—	—	10,000	11,500	18,000	20,500	23,000
Recommended	★	☆	☆	☆	☆	☆	☆	☆
Reliability	★	★	★	★	☆	☆	☆	☆

SECRET WARRANTIES, INTERNAL BULLETINS: 2005—Harsh automatic transmission shifting. **2005-08**—A humming noise may come from the 4x4 coupler. **2005-09**—No movement in Drive or Reverse. Fluid may leak from the area around the automatic transmission torque converter or between the transaxle and the transfer case. Correcting harsh gear engagement. Tips on silencing a rattling sunroof. **2006-**

07—Troubleshooting complaints relative to a cloudy paint condition. **2006-08—** Harsh, delayed shifting. **2008**—Self-activating antitheft alarm. Sunroof creaking, ticking. **2008-12**—Remedy for engine ticking at idle. **2010**—Troubleshooting harsh, delayed shifts by the automatic transmission. Incorrect operation of the transmission solenoids will cause the transmission to perform erratically and the Check Engine warning to light up.

SANTA FE

RATING: Recommended (2011-14); Above Average (2005-10); Average (2004-05); Below Average (2001-03). This SUV does almost everything right. **Road performance:** Acceptable acceleration with the base 2.4L 4-cylinder, but the 3.3L V6 gives you more usable power and acceptable fuel economy as well. You will also enjoy the smooth-shifting automatic transmission; fairly agile comportment; and a comfortable, controlled ride. Less enjoyable: The 2.4L four could use more low-end power; vague steering; and the ride quality may be too stiff for some. **Strong points:** The Santa Fe is a competitively priced family SUV that is at the small end of the mid-size sport-utility lineup. It offers impressive room, good build quality, and many standard safety and performance features that cost a lot more when bought with competing models. Revamped recently, the Santa Fe now has better-performing, fuel-thrifty powertrains and additional cabin space. A long list of standard equipment; standard stability/traction control and full-body side curtain airbags; a roomy interior that easily acommodates both passengers and cargo; enhanced by comfortable seats; simple, user-friendly controls; improved fuel economy, and better than average quality control. **Weak points:** You will have to get used to some annoying suspension and road noise. **Major redesign:** 2001, 2007 and 2013. **Highway/ city fuel economy:** *2.4L man.:* 7.7/11 L/100 km. *Auto:* 7.2/10.4 L/100 km. *2.4L 4WD:* 8.0/10.6 L/100 km. *3.5L:* 7.6/10.2 L/100 km. *3.5L 4WD:* 7.7/10.6 L/100 km. **Best alternatives:** GM Terrain, Traverse, Acadia, or Enclave; Nissan Xterra; and Toyota RAV4 or Highlander. Although the Santa Fe is 2.1 inches shorter than the Lexus RX330, its seats have more head, leg, and shoulder room than the RX, with additional room for an optional third-row seat, missing in the Lexus. The 2014 Hyundai offers six- or seven-passenger third row seating with its additional length and width.

SAFETY: NHTSA gave the 2002-13 models four- and five-star ratings in all crash categories; only exception was the 2012 with only two stars for side-impact protection. IIHS rated frontal, side, rear, and roof crashworthiness as "Good." Owners report: Sudden acceleration accompanied by loss of braking:

Driver was pulling into a parking space when Santa Fe suddenly surged or lunged forward and to the right causing car to jump over a concrete bumper and into another car parked at a 90-degree angle. After the accident investigation was cleared, driver proceeded to the local dealership. Enroute the Santa Fe would not shift out of low gear.

Prices and Specs

Prices (Negotiable): *2.4 Sport: $26,499, 2.4 Sport Premium front-drive.: $28,299, 2.0T Premium: $30,499, 2.4 Premium AWD: $30,299, 2.0T AWD: $32,499, 2.4 Luxury AWD: $33,899, SE: $35,299, Limited Navi.: $38,400* **Freight:** $1,595 **Powertrain (Front-drive/AWD):** Engines: 2.4L 4-cyl. (190 hp), 2.0L 4-cyl turbo. (264 hp), 3.3L V6 (290 hp); Transmission: 6-speed auto. **Dimensions/capacity:** Passengers: 2/3; Wheelbase: 106.3 in.; H: 67.9/L: 184.1/W: 74.4 in.; Headroom F/R: 6/4.5 in.; Legroom F/R: 41/28 in.; Cargo volume: 35.5 cu. ft.; Fuel tank: 75L/regular; Tow limit: 2,000 lb.; Load capacity: 930 lb.; Turning circle: 35.4 ft.; Ground clearance: 8.1 in.; Weight: 3,725-3,875 lb.

When accelerating, vehicle pulls sharply to the side; hesitation when accelerating; raw gas smell both inside and outside the vehicle; Santa Fe frequently shuts down when underway; a loud knock and transmission jerk occurs whenever the vehicle is first started; when shifting, the jerkiness of the transmission feels like someone is hitting the rear end; and loss of brakes, as the pedal descended to the floor.

ALERT! Take a night test-drive; headlight illumination may be insufficient:

> Low beam headlights illuminated, the contact experienced extremely poor visibility. When the contact drove down a hill, she stated that the headlights provided limited view. The high beam headlights had to be illuminated in order to see the road clearly.

Santa Fe Profile

	2004	2005	2006	2007	2008	2009	2010	2011	2012
Used Values ($)									
GL	4,000	5,000	6,000	7,000	8,500	9,500	12,500	14,500	17.500
GLS/Premium	4,500	5,500	6,500	—	—	—	—	17,500	20,500
3.3/3.5 FWD	5,000	6,000	6,500	7,500	9,500	11,000	14,500	18,000	22,000
2.4 AWD	—	—	—	—	—	—	—	19,000	22,500
3.3/3.5 AWD	—	—	—	8,000	10,000	13,000	16,000	19,500	23,500
Sport AWD	—	—	—	—	—	—	17,500	21,000	25,500
LTD/GLS/Sport AWD	—	—	—	9,000	12,000	11,500	18,500	23,000	27,500
Recommended	☆	☆	☆	☆	☆	☆	☆	☆	☆
Reliability	☆	☆	☆	☆	☆	☆	☆	☆	☆

SECRET WARRANTIES, INTERNAL BULLETINS: 2008-12—Tips on reducing excessive driveshaft noise (creaking or popping). **2010**—This bulletin provides a procedure to replace the intermediate shaft on some 2010 Santa Fe 2.4L 2WD vehicles with automatic transmissions (CAMPAIGN 102).

INFINITI

Unlike Toyota's Lexus division, which started out with softly sprung vehicles akin to your dad's fully loaded, rear-drive Oldsmobile, Nissan's luxury brand has historically stressed performance over comfort and opulence, and offered buyers lots of high-performance, cutting-edge features at what were initially very reasonable prices. But the company went more mainstream during the mid-'90s, and its vehicles became less original as they lost their price and performance advantage.

Goodbye, G25 (shown above); hello, Infiniti EV. The EV electric vehicle is innovative and unique. It uses many of the Nissan Leaf EV components and comes with a wireless charging system that makes a plug-in charger unnecessary. Owners can install a charging pad in their garage, driveway, or other parking space. They'll simply park over the pad and the charging system will take care of the rest. In the morning, the car can be driven away, fully-charged. Look for the 2015 EV in showrooms in mid-2014.

But Infiniti is fighting to get that performance edge back and is seriously considering launching a plug-in hybrid, mid-engine sports car and adding more high-performance models to its product mix. Jumping into a new product niche is the 2013-14 Infiniti JX/QX60, a $44,900 three-row crossover aimed at Acura and Audi customers. Infiniti's 2014 lineup begins with a name change for all models: Q for sedans and coupes and QX for crossovers and SUVs. The Infiniti Q50, formerly the G sedan, returns completely redesigned with a standard 328 hp 3.7L V6. A 360 hp-equipped engine also goes on sale in mid-2014 and features the first use of steer-by-wire in a mass-produced car (a dubious achievement, considering all of the electronic failures associated with drive-by wire powertrains).

Also new this year is the QX60 Hybrid, promoted as a more fuel-efficient version of the JX. V6 models retain the 260 hp 3.5L engine and the hybrid uses a 230 hp, supercharged 2.5-L engine. The 2014 gas-powered QX60 will be available in late fall, or you could buy now a similarly equipped, discounted 2013 JX35.

This year shoppers will also see greater stylistic differences between Nissan and Infiniti vehicles. Even though most models share the same platform, Infinitis usually add more powerful engines, more gears, more luxurious interior appointments, and steering and suspensions tweaked for sportier driving.

Although Infinitis are sold and serviced by a small dealer network across Canada, this limited support base hasn't compromised servicing availability, nor quality, for vehicles still on the market. But many discontinued models face long waits for replacement parts, a factor to seriously consider when buying a used

Infiniti. Fortunately, Infinitis are reasonably dependable (except for brakes, electrics, and body glitches), so there is less need for service and absolutely no need for an extra-cost extended warranty. The only two servicing drawbacks are that powertrain and body parts are sometimes in short supply and the use of complicated high-tech components drives up servicing costs by making dealer servicing mandatory and its complexity practically guarantees a higher failure rate.

G25/G35/G37 ★★★ / ★★★★ / ★★★★★

RATING: *G25:* Average (2011-12); *G35:* Above Average; *G37:* Above Average. **Road performance:** *G25:* This entry level sedan is fitted with a 218 hp 2.5L V6 that skimps on acceleration but burns about 15 percent less fuel. Generally, the car is fairly agile, quiet, and comfortable, but the engine is noisy when pushed. There is no manual transmission or sports package option. *G35:* Marking Infiniti's return to high-performance cars, the G35 borrowed Nissan's sporty 350Z platform, added a roomy cabin, and lots of rear-drive performance features for an affordable price. The sedan was refreshed inside and out in 2004 and the coupe in 2004 and 2005. In a class action settlement, the G35's standard Brembo brakes were dropped from the 2005 and 2006 models, and better brakes with larger discs were added. Owners had sued for compensation due to the premature wearout of brakes on 2003–04 models. The second-generation model is simply a G37 sedan with a smaller V6. A 2007 or later redesigned G35 is your best bet. You get a solid platform, more responsive handling, a powerful 306 hp 3.5L V6, less dated styling, and the use of better quality interior materials. *G37:* A powerful, smooth, and responsive powertrain; predictable, sporty handling; and a firm but comfortable ride. The convertible (325 hp) has five horses less than the coupe (330 hp) but lots more than you'll find with the competition. An IPL (Infiniti Performance Line) G Convertible joined the 2012 IPL G lineup with an array of special performance and luxury upgrades. **Strong points:** G25: Only a handful of owner complaints posted on the NHTSA (safercar. gov) website. **Weak points:** *All models:* Warped brake rotors and prematurely-worn pads; electrical and electronic system failures, defective tire pressure sensors, and, most surprising, mediocre fit and finish. The $1,950 freight and pre-delivery inspection fee is highway robbery. *G25:* You get less power and less equipment than with the G37, and the resale value for the 2012 has nosedived by $12,000 since this entry-level G-car was dropped in December 2012 after barely two years on the market. *G35:* Be wary of the poorly-designed unreliable manual tranny on the 2007 model. *G37:* There's a small rear seat and cargo area; towing is not advised; and the convertible model has even less room and has yet to be crash tested. The convertible has some body shake; engine tapping, clicking sound at start-up requires the use of a costlier "factory" oil; transmission suddenly downshifted to 15 km/h from 100 km/h:

> A chip was changed. However, the failure occurred three more times. The dealer then stated that the fluid in the vehicle was too full and was the cause of the failure.

The manual transmission gears grind when shifting, causing a delayed shift, especially in Sixth gear; transmission was replaced under warranty. The anti-traction feature activated on its own and caused the wheels to lock on a rainy day; defective Bridgestone Pole Position tires; tire pressure light did not come on when tire went flat; premature brake replacement; the area between the gas pedal and centre console gets quite hot; audio system malfunctions; and poor fit and finish. Incidentally, this car is not as much a "chick magnet" as it is a rodent attractant:

> Infiniti G37 has electrical wiring insulation made of soy-based polymer. Soy-based polymer is apparently biodegradable. The problem is that it is also attractive to rodents, who eat the wiring, creating electrical safety hazards. It also creates an economic stress on consumers and insurers who have to pay for repairs done to these automobiles, which Infiniti claims are not covered under any existing warranty.

Major redesign: 2007 and 2014. **Highway/city fuel economy:** *G37 3.7L 6-speed man.:* 7.9/12.3 L/100 km., *G37 3.7L 6-speed man. convertible:* 8.4/12.9 L/100 km., *G37 3.7L 7-speed auto. convertible:* 7.8/11.9 L/100 km., *G37 3.7L 6-speed man. coupe:* 7.9/12.3 L/100 km., *G37 3.7L 7-speed auto. coupe:* 7.4/11.0 L/100 km., *G37x 3.7L 7-speed auto.:* 7.8/11.7 L/100 km. **Best alternatives:** The G37 is a premium mid-sized car with SUV pretensions. It is sold as a two-door coupe, a four-door sedan, and a two-door convertible with a power-retractable hardtop. It targets shoppers who would normally buy the Acura RDX or the BMW 328i or X3. The convertible model is priced right within striking range of BMW's 328i/335i Cabriolet and the Lexus IS 250 or IS 350 convertible. The Mercedes-Benz CLK350 AMG Edition Cabriolet has priced itself out of that market.

 SAFETY: NHTSA gave the 2012 G25 five stars for rollover protection, while the 2008 G35 scored five stars in all categories. 2009-10 G37 models also earned five stars for occupant crash protection in all NHTSA categories; 2011-13 models were tested only for rollover protection, which was given five stars. IIHS found front overlap and side protection to be "Good," on the 2007-13 models and roof protection "Acceptable" for the same models years. 2011-13 G25s had no serious safety-related incidents reported to NHTSA. Head restraints were judged to be only "Marginal" with the 2007-13 G35s and "Poor" on the 2005-06 models. NHTSA files show the 2008 G35 elicited only 29 owner safety-related complaints: Driver's airbag failed to deploy; passenger-side airbag is disabled for no reason; chronic stalling; clutch sticks until it warms up; warped brake rotors and prematurely-worn brake pads; sudden wheel lockup when the anti-traction switch activates in rainy weather; doors won't lock or unlock due to faulty door actuators; and defective tire pressure sensors. 2011 G37 models generated 15 complaints: When the convertible top automatically folds into the trunk it doesn't retract if there is an object in the way, causing damage to the top and posing a safety hazard to children; sudden unintended acceleration; seat belt failed to lock in an emergency stop; long hesitation before accelerating:

The vehicle does not produce consistent and reliable response to throttle command when accelerating into and around traffic. On several instances, when pulling out of a driveway into oncoming arterial traffic, there has been no response to throttle input. A delay of 2-4 seconds has occurred and creates an extremely hazardous situation. This fault has also occurred at freeway speeds when attempting to pass from speeds between 40 & 75 mph!

. . .

As I was waiting to cross a major highway junction, I almost had a collision after crossing the highway due to what I suspect was a faulty transmission with hesitation in shifting. There was an SUV waiting to turn and while I had the right of way, they pulled off and as I had my chance to cross the 2-lane highway, they did too. I punched the gas and in the middle of the road, the engine took a few seconds to get into gear so I literally was in the road of oncoming traffic that was driving at speeds in excess of 55mph. It happened within 5 seconds but after I crossed avoiding a front and side collision, I pulled off the road because I was shaking.

Side mirrors become distorted in cold weather; and gas station automatic fuelling nozzles shut off after a few seconds. 2012 G37 has only six owner complaints: head restraints cause driver to sit in a chin-to-chest position which is painful and dangerous; hip pain caused by poor bolstering of the driver's seat; clutch pedal sticks; station automatic fuelling nozzles still shut off after a few seconds; vehicle suddenly accelerated while in Park with the engine running; engine also surges when braking (confirmed by TSB #ITBO7-048), or is slow to brake.

ALERT! $1,950 freight costs is literally highway robbery. Look for a discounted 2013 version, or save big bucks by shopping in the States for some of the pricier G37 models.

G25/G35/G37 Profile

	2004	2005	2006	2007	2008	2009	2010	2011	2012
Used Values ($)									
G25	—	—	—	—	—	—	—	21,500	25,500
AWD	—	—	—	—	—	—	—	23,500	27,500
G35	7,000	8,000	9,000	10,000	12,000	—	—	—	—
G37 Sedan	—	—	—	—	—	15,500	19,500	24,500	31,000
G37 Coupe	—	—	—	—	13,500	17,000	24,000	28,500	33,500
G37 Convertible	—	—	—	—	—	27,000	32,000	38,500	46,000
Recommended	☆	☆	☆	☆	☆	☆	☆	☆	☆
Reliability	☆	☆	☆	☆	☆	☆	☆	☆	☆

Note: Additional Infiniti ratings are in the Appendix.

SECRET WARRANTIES, INTERNAL BULLETINS: All models—Troubleshooting multiple transmission problems. Tips on reducing excessive driveshaft noise (creaking or popping). Steering pull/drift. Steering wheel is off-centre. Automatic transmission shifter boot may come loose. Drivebelt noise. Navigation screen goes blank (2010-12 models). Paint chipping off the edge of the trunk lid (2007-12 models). Steering noise on left turns (2012s). The warranty is extended under Campaign PO308 in relation to the radio seek function. *G25:* Shift issues (2011 models) Campaign PO385 relative to reprogramming the G25's engine control module (ECM). *G37:* Shift responsiveness issues (2009-12 models). Low battery, or no start (2008-10). Bluetooth voice recognition. Convertible top water leak at windshield header. AC blows warm air at idle. Door accent garnish replacements.

EX35/EX37 ★★★ / ★★★★★

RATING: *EX35:* Average (2008-12); *EX37:* Above Average (2013-14). Smaller than the Infiniti FX, the EX35 is essentially a G wagon priced in the same range as the Infiniti G series. Offering the room of a compact station wagon, the EX37 is a small, upscale SUV wannabe that targets shoppers who would normally buy the Acura RDX or the BMW X3. The EX and G series are entry-level Infinitis with the most to offer from a price and quality perspective – as long as you have short legs, don't mind limited headroom, or never ride in the EX's rear seat. **Road performance:** Not as sporty as Infiniti's sport sedans or some of BMW's crossovers; the latest EX performs like a car with power to spare, however; and the smooth, responsive manumatic transmission works flawlessly with the new V6 and 7-speed transmission. Overall, the car is much more agile, quiet, and comfortable than the G series. Wait until late-winter or spring for lower prices when extra rebates and other sales incentives kick in. **Strong points:** Larger V6 engine means there will be 28 more horsepower on tap in the EX37. Although it's not a car for serious off-road use, it definitely is a comfortable, well-equipped, and versatile vehicle for most driving needs. The new 7-speed manumatic may give a slight boost to fuel economy, but keep in mind that any new powertrain is a risky buy during its first year on the market. **Weak points:** A smallish interior makes the EX a four-seater; limited cargo space; back seat occupants must keep a knee-to-chin posture when the front seats are pushed all the way back; taller drivers will want more headroom (especially with the sunroof-equipped Journey model); voice recognition feature performs erratically; and fuel economy is unimpressive on pre-2013 models. Also, the larger, 18-inch wheels may make for a bumpier ride and also cut your gas mileage. **Major redesign:** 2008 and 2013. **Highway/city fuel economy:** *(2012) 3.5L 6-speed man.:* 8.5/12.3 L/100 km. (No federal-sourced fuel economy figures yet on the 3.7L 7-speed automatic transmission combo.) **Best alternatives:** Acura RDX, BMW 3 Series or X3, Lincoln MKX, and Lexus 350.

SAFETY: NHTSA gives the 2008-09 EX35 four stars for rollover and frontal-impact protection; five stars for side crashworthiness. 2011-12 versions scored four stars for rollover crash safety. The 2013 EX37 scored four stars for rollover protection. IIHS says the 2008-13 models have "Good" frontal overlap, side, rear, and roof crash protection. Right-rear visibility is compromised by right-rear head restraint and side pillar and some drivers find the accelerator and brake pedals are mounted too close together. Also, be wary of the Distance Control Assist or DCA. It creates a distracting "safety zone" around the vehicle and may apply the brakes or buzz an alert that could make matters worse. Plus, the system can malfunction if its sensors are snow covered. Almost no safety-related complaints posted at NHTSA relative to the 2008-13 E models.

ALERT! Beginning with the 2013 models, both the Infiniti EX and FX crossovers are powered by a much better performing 325 hp 3.7L V6, replacing the fuel-slurping 3.5L V6. Rebadged the EX37, don't be confused and buy a lesser-performing earlier model, unless you get a substantial discount and don't mind the mitigated performance with the 2012 and earlier versions.

Prices and Specs

Prices (Negotiable): *EX37 AWD:* $42,200 **Freight:** $1,950 **Powertrain (Rear-drive/AWD):** Engine: 3.7L V6 (325 hp); Transmission: 7-speed manumatic **Dimensions/capacity:** Passengers: 2/3; Wheelbase: 110.2 in.; H: 61.9/L: 182.3/W: 71 in.; Headroom F/R: 3/3 in.; Legroom F/R: 42/26 in.; Cargo volume: 24 cu. ft.; Fuel tank: 76L/premium; Tow limit: N/A; Load capacity: 860 lb.; Turning circle: 36 ft.; Ground clearance: 5.5 in.; Weight: 3,757-3,979 lb.

EX35 Profile

	2004	2005	2006	2007	2008	2009	2010	2011	2012
Used Values ($)									
EX35		—	—	—	—	14,000	16,500	21,500	26,000	31,000
Recommended		☆	☆	☆	☆	☆	☆	☆	☆	☆
Reliability		☆	☆	☆	☆	☆	☆	☆	☆	☆

SECRET WARRANTIES, INTERNAL BULLETINS: 2009-10—Some vehicles may have water entry into a wire harness which could cause an engine no-start condition or a warning light illumination when no warning issue exists. Infiniti will repair any damage and install a cover to protect the harness from water entry. This service will be performed at no charge for parts or labour. **2010-13**—Various navigation malfunctions. **2011-12**—Steering pull/drift, or steering wheel is off centre. Bluetooth voice recognition issues. Door accent garnish replacements.

KIA

Fuel-Economy Fraudster

We can't talk about Kia's lineup, without first exposing the company's spurious horsepower ratings and gas mileage lies. It's shameful that Kia, along with its parent company Hyundai, use bogus claims to sell cars. A class-action lawsuit has been launched in Ontario against Hyundai Canada and Kia Canada after the automakers were found to have overstated their vehicles' fuel mileage. London, Ontario-based law firm, Siskinds LLP, says it filed the legal motion against the two carmakers in Ontario, and expects similar lawsuits to be filed in Quebec and British Columbia.

The lawsuit comes just days after the companies announced they would reimburse the owners of more than 170,000 vehicles in Canada for the difference in the combined fuel consumption rating plus 15 per cent. The fuel mileage revelations came to light after a U.S. Environmental Protection Agency (EPA) audit found fuel economy was inflated by up to six miles per gallon on some vehicles. The affected vehicles for Hyundai are the 2010-13 Elantra, Sonata Hybrid, Accent, Genesis, Tucson, Veloster, Elantra Coupe, Elantra GT, and Santa Fe. For Kia, the affected vehicles are the 2010-13 Rio, Sportage, Soul, Soul ECO, and Optima HEV.

Kia has gone from buffoon to bestseller. Especially now that it doesn't make every model a failure-prone jack-in-the-box full of costly repair surprises, as it did five years ago. But, to carry the box metaphor farther, Kia's are like Forrest Gump's box of chocolates: "You never know what you're gonna get."

Buyers now have more confidence in Kia cars, SUVs, and minivans that have become more functional, fuel efficient, and stylish over the last few years. Hyundai and its Kia subsidiary are breaking sales records with a much improved lineup crafted during an economic recession and covering practically all the market niches, with the exception of trucks. While Hyundai goes upscale with high-tech and fuel-frugal models placed throughout its model lineup, Kia is putting its money into a more refined lineup of less-expensive, fuel-efficient vehicles that carry more standard features, are freshly styled, and have fewer reliability problems. Kia's also returning with some warmed-over models that offer nothing new other than revised grills and different tires like the Sedona minivan – axed for the 2013 model year, but back for 2014, with the same 2011-vintage 3.5L V6 coupled to a 6-speed automatic transmission, that delivers mediocre fuel economy and so-so highway performance.

Granted, Kia's quality has dramatically improved over the past few years, but serious safety- and performance-related defects keep appearing year after year. Sudden, unintended acceleration, powertrain failures, steering/suspension wander (a generic problem with many Hyundai/Kia models), and atrocious fit and finish haunt the entire Hyundai Kia lineup, along with automatic transmission and brake failures. And, both companies are chronic liars when it comes to engine power and fuel economy (but, so are Ford with its C-Max/Fusion fantasies and Honda's gas-gulping Hybrid models).

Ignoring the above deficiencies and prevarications, *Consumer Reports* has been recently won over by Kia's improved quality control after decades of listing most of the Kia lineup as "Not Recommended." *CR* has consistently criticized the automaker for making unreliable, unsafe vehicles. Now, in a surprising turnaround, it has many Kia models on its "Recommended" list published in April 2013.

And, that's the truth.

RIO/RIO5 ★★★★/★★★★★

RATING: Above Average (2011–14); Average (2009–10); Below Average (2007–08); Not Recommended (2000–06). The Rio sedan and Rio5 hatchback combine good fuel economy and interior room with useful standard features and a reasonable base price. **Road performance:** The 1.6L engine with the manual transmission is usually adequate for most chores; handling is exceptionally good, with plenty of steering feedback; good brakes; and a comfortable, though sometimes busy, ride. Slow acceleration with the automatic transmission; insufficient highway passing power; excessive engine noise at higher speeds; harsh ride when passing over small bumps. **Strong points:** Lots of standard features that cost extra on other cars; a well-equipped, roomy cabin housing good quality materials, user-friendly controls, and high-end electronics; strong brakes; and impressive fuel economy. Sharing the Accent platform and using more Hyundai components has undoubtedly improved Kia's quality, judging by J.D. Power survey results and the small number of owner complaints registered with NHTSA. In fact, the Rio and Rio5 have registered fewer owner complaints than the newer Kia Soul. **Weak points:** Automatic transmission malfunctions; poor fit and finish; premature brake repairs; electrical shorts; and trunk lid hinges intrude into the trunk area. **Major redesign:** 2001, 2006, and 2012. **Highway/city fuel economy:** *Man.:* 5.8/7.1 L/100 km. *Auto.:* 5.6/7.7 L/100 km. **Best alternatives:** The Chevrolet Sonic has a small performance edge and upfront occupant knee airbags. Honda's Fit is roomier, with versatile seating that accommodates five people. Other contenders: The Hyundai Accent, Mazda3, and Nissan Versa are more-refined small cars that offer better performance while also conserving fuel.

324

SAFETY: Crash protection is a mixed bag. NHTSA awarded the 2013 Rio five stars for side crash protection and four stars for frontal and rollover crashworthiness; earlier models through 2000 were generally positive with three- and five-star scores, except for the two-star rating for side protection on 2003-05 models. IIHS rates the 2011 Rio's frontal offset, rear, and roof crash protection as "Acceptable" and gives a "Poor" crashworthiness score for side collisions. Limited rear-corner visibility with the Rio5; airbags failed to deploy in a frontal collision; passenger-side airbag was disabled, even though an average-sized passenger was seated. Fuel hose vent line may leak fuel into the back seat area; sudden acceleration in Reverse, with loss of brakes; brakes locked up when applied; tie rod and ball joints broke away from the chassis while vehicle was turning; and the rear window shattered when the driver's door was closed.

ALERT! Taller drivers will appreciate the front headroom and legroom.

Rio/Rio5 Profile

	2004	2005	2006	2007	2008	2009	2010	2011	2012
Used Values ($)									
RS	2,000	3,000	—	—	—	—	—	—	—
Rio/Rio5 LX	—	—	—	—	—	—	—	—	8,500
EX	—	—	5,000	3,500	4,000	4,500	6,000	7,500	10,500
EX Luxury	—	—	—	—	—	—	—	—	13,000
EX Convenience	—	—	—	4,000	4,500	5,500	6,500	8,500	—
Rio5 Sport	—	—	—	4,500	5,000	6,000	8,000	10,000	—
Recommended	★	★	★	☆	☆	☆	☆	☆	☆
Reliability	★	☆	☆	☆	☆	☆	☆	☆	☆

SECRET WARRANTIES, INTERNAL BULLETINS: 2007-10—Kia will replace defective weather stripping for free up to five years/160,00 km (100,000 miles) under Campaign SA045. **2008**—Troubleshooting a rough idle. **2009**—"Goodwill" campaign to replace the fuel cap. **2009-10**—How to silence a rear strut creaking noise. *Spectra:* **2006**—Key sticks in the ignition. **2006-07**—Troubleshooting tips for automatic transmission 2-3 gearshift shock, slip, or flare. **2006-08**—Correcting a rough idle. **2009**—"Goodwill" campaign to replace the fuel cap and fix the window crank handle. **2010-13**—Poor windshield wiper performance can be fixed by replacing the washer pump inlet filter. **2011-12**—Troubleshooting instrument panel noise. Fixing an outside mirror cover gap. Steering-wheel noise and vibration repair tips.

SOUL ★★★★★

RATING: Recommended (2014); Above Average (2011-13); Average (2010). Fairly well equipped, the Soul is a cheap little four-door hatchback/wagon that combines safety with acceptable urban performance while keeping your fuel bills low. The best combination is the 2.0L engine hooked to a 6-speed manual transmission. The redesigned 2014 is much more practical than earlier models, offering a roomier cabin, and a more refined interior that houses additional infotainment and online connectivity features. **Road performance:** Some powerful engines and fuel-sipping powertrains (again, the 2.0L is a better choice for reserve power), although the base engine could use more grunt at low engine rpm; a compliant suspension, without undue body roll or front-end plow; and fairly agile cornering, with good steering feedback. A busy highway ride. **Strong points:** Inexpensive and well equipped with safety devices like ABS, stability control, six airbags, and active head restraints – features that are rare on entry-level small cars. User-friendly, simple controls; plenty of interior room, especially when it comes to headroom; excellent front and side visibility; and comfortable seats. **Weak points:** Omnipresent rattles; excessive wind and road noise; and many body, fit, and finish glitches. Poor-quality, easily broken, or prematurely worn interior items.

> The steering wheel was locked up and could only be turned if considerable force was applied to it. I carefully pulled over to the side of the road. The Kia dealer service shop ultimately had to replace the entire steering column to "fix" the problem. About two months later I was driving down the interstate and attempted to do a lane change. Again the electronic stability control falsely activated and caused me to collide with the vehicle directly in front of me. When the ESC activated, the steering wheel locked up and caused a sudden loss of control, resulting in the accident.

The AC defroster may not clear the windshield. Owners decry a plethora of fit and finish deficiencies, including excessive condensation in the headlights, chips in the glass and paint, and door panels that scratch with the slightest touch. Steering-wheel noise and vibration repair. Fuel economy is seriously overstated. **Major redesign:** 2014. **Highway/city fuel economy:** *1.6L man.:* 4.9/6.6 L/100 km. *1.6L auto.:* 4.9/6.8 L/100 km. Best alternatives: Other contenders are the Hyundai Elantra, Nissan Cube or Versa, and Toyota Corolla.

SAFETY: Soul does well in most crashworthiness tests: NHTSA gives the 2010-13 models four and five stars for overall crashworthiness. IIHS rates the 2010-13 Soul as "Good" in moderate frontal overlap, side, and roof crash protection. Small frontal overlap tests were ranked "Poor." Rio and Rio5 have registered far fewer safety-related complaints than the newer Kia Soul. Only 34 safety-related complaints reported to NHTSA, when 100 would have been normal for the 2012 model year. Airbags failed to deploy; brake pedal is too small; rear brake failure caused a rear-ender; automatic transmission slips and often sticks in gear or grinds when going into Second gear; sometimes the transmission suddenly downshifts for no reason; when the vehicle is shifted into Park, the doors are automatically unlocked; fuel spews out when refuelling; driver's door fails to latch; the steering column came off while the car was cruising on the highway; the electronic stability control may engage for no reason and lock up the steering. Poor rearward visibility through the small rear windshield and thick rear pillars.

ALERT! What? No spare tire? Tell the dealer this is a deal-breaker:

The 2012 Kia Soul does not come with a spare tire, instead it comes with a can of Fix-A-Flat and an air pump. There is no jack either. The flat may be fixed if the damage is on the tread and the hole is under ¼ inch in diameter. If the damage is on the sidewall or greater than ¼ inch, the vehicle has to be towed. For those people that have no cell phone or are in an area that gets no reception they will be stranded until another motorist comes along and these days most motorists don't stop for other drivers. Kia offers roadside assistance with the vehicle, but if you are traveling in a remote area, in the southwest (like Death Valley for example) what do you do without a spare? If your cell phone quits, you're done. Even if you have AAA, their driver will have to tow the vehicle as he won't have a spare either.

Prices and Specs

Prices (Firm): *1.6:* $16,795, *2.0 2U:* $19,195, *2.0 4U:* $22,895, *2.0 4U Luxury:* $25,595 **Freight:** $1,650
Powertrain (Front-drive): Engines: 1.6L 4-cyl. (138 hp), 2.0L 4-cyl. (164 hp); Transmissions: 6-speed man., 6-speed auto.
Dimensions/capacity: Passengers: 2/3; Wheelbase: 100.4 in.; H: 63.4 in./L: 162.2 in./W: 70.3 in.; Headroom F/R: 5/5.5 in.; Legroom F/R: 40/27 in.; Cargo volume: 24.5 cu. ft.; Fuel tank: 48L/regular; Load capacity: 850 lb.; Ground clearance: 6.5 in.; Turning circle: 34.4 ft.; Weight: 2,689-2,764 lb.

Soul Profile

	2010	2011	2012
Used Values ($)			
1.6	7,000	8,500	10,000
2.0 4d	8,500	11,500	13,500
Burner	9,000	12,000	15,500
Luxury	—	—	16,500
Recommended	★	★	★
Reliability	★	★	★

SECRET WARRANTIES, INTERNAL BULLETINS: 2010-13—Poor windshield wiper performance can be fixed by replacing the washer pump inlet filter.

FORTE 5/FORTE KOUPE ★★★★☆ / ★★★★★

good buy

RATING: Recommended (2014); Above Average (2010-13). The car's 2014 redesign blows away most of its earlier deficiencies. Kia slew the poor-quality dragon a few years back; now, Kia's roomy compact sedan, coupe, and hatchback have the engine, suspension, and equipment refinements the lineup lacked in the past. Among the various models, the hatchback is the most versatile for access and storage. **Road performance:** There are now three different engines with the 2014 and they all offer more than enough power for most driving needs. Handling is a breeze, thanks to the Forte's front-drive unibody frame and four-wheel independent suspension, which provide a firm and sporty ride with a minimum of noise, vibration, and harshness. Although the standard engine doesn't pack much of a punch, a smooth-shifting automatic transmission and confidence-inspiring handling produce a comfortable, though jittery, ride. **Strong points:** The restyled and redesigned 2014 Forte is longer, lower, and wider than its predecessor and loaded with standard features that are optional on other cars, like four-wheel disc brakes and easily accessed and intuitive controls, plus Bluetooth and steering wheel controls with voice activation. Nicely bolstered, comfortable front seats; lots of interior room; heated side-view windows; fewer rattles and body glitches; a large dealer network, with both Kia and Hyundai providing servicing; and a comprehensive base warranty. Overall quality is much improved, with few complaints posted on the NHTSA website. **Weak points:** Five passengers is a squeeze; steering wheel tilts but doesn't telescope (EX trim excepted). Minor audio and fit and finish complaints; major paint defects; and the windshield may not be installed securely at the factory:

Our technician was able to push most of the windshield out without having to cut the ure-thane bead. The urethane bead pulled right off the windshield, and was only adhered to about ⅓ of the windshield perimeter. This vehicle was not involved in an accident, but had it been, the windshield would not have remained intact. The safety of the vehicle occupants due to this factory-installed improper installation was compromised.

Major redesign: 2014. **Highway/city fuel economy:** *2.0L man.:* 5.7/8.1 L/100 km. *Auto.:* 5.5/8.0 L/100 km. *2.4L:* 6.2/9.2 L/100 km. **Best alternatives:** The Honda Fit and Civic, Hyundai Accent and Elantra, Kia Soul Plus, Mazda 2 and 3, and the Toyota Matrix (base model).

SAFETY: NHTSA gives the 2013 Forte four stars for front, side, and rollover crash protection. The 2010-13 models were rated "Poor" in IIHS's frontal small overlap crash test, however, they scored "Good" for side, rear, and roof crashworthiness.

ALERT! The Honda Fit might be a better choice. It's the roomiest hatchback in this class and is also the most versatile, thanks to seats that accommodate long and tall items. The Fit is also less expensive than the Forte hatchback, and is a better performer.

Prices and Specs

Prices (Firm): *LX man.:* $15,995, *auto.:* $17,195, *EX:* $18,595, *SX:* $23,095, *EX Koup:* $19,095, *auto.:* $20,295, *SX Koup:* $22,395, *auto.:* $23,595, *SX:* $22,395, *SX Luxury:* $24,695 **Freight:** $1,455 **Powertrain (Front-drive):** Engines: 1.8L 4-cyl (148 hp), 2.0L 4-cyl. (173 hp), 1.6L Turbo 4-cyl. (201 hp); Transmissions: 6-speed man., 6-speed auto. **Dimensions/capacity:** Passengers: 2/3; Wheelbase: 104.3 in.; H: 57.5/L: 178.3/W: 69.9 in.; Headroom F/R: 4/2.5 in.; Legroom F/R: 41/27.5 in.; Cargo volume: 15 cu. ft.; Fuel tank: 51.9L/regular; Load capacity: 850 lb.; Turning circle: 33.9 ft.; Ground clearance: 5.9 in.; Weight: 2,729-2,849 lb.

Forte 5/Forte Koup Profile

	2010	2011	2012
Used Values ($)			
LX	8,000	9,500	11,500
EX	9,000	11,000	13,500
SX	10,500	13,000	15,500
Koup EX	9,500	11,500	13,500
Luxury	—	14,000	16,500
Recommended	☆	☆	☆
Reliability	☆	☆	☆

SECRET WARRANTIES, INTERNAL BULLETINS: 2009-13—Poor windshield wiper performance can be improved by replacing the washer pump inlet filter. **2011-12**—An ECM software upgrade to address the MIL warning light coming on for no reason.

RATING: *Optima, Hybrid:* Below Average (2011-14). Optima's rating has been downgraded due to persistent steering failures, imploding sunroofs, and self-destructing engines, problems also seen with the Hyundai Sonata. **Road performance:** The base engine performs well, the ride is comfortable, and handling is secure. The optional 4-cylinder turbocharged engine is powerful and fuel efficient, but V6-equipped rivals give a smoother and quieter performance. Considerable body lean when turning. *Hybrid:* Minimal body roll when cornering, and an excellent ride. On the other hand, the electrically assisted steering is a bit numb, the powertrain's jerky when going from gas to electric power (see Secret Warranties, Internal Bulletins, below), and the regenerative brakes could be more responsive. **Strong points:** Nicely appointed; has good overall visibility; provides plenty of front headroom; uses firm, supportive front bucket seats with plenty of fore and aft travel; a spacious trunk; and posts better than average fuel economy figures with regular fuel. Another plus: Servicing can be done by both Hyundai and Kia dealers. *Hybrid:* Nicely styled and well appointed; intuitive, easily accessed controls; and plenty of room in front and back. **Weak points:** Mediocre braking; average rear headroom; excessive wind and tire noise; low rear seats; difficult rear access; trunk has a small opening; and fit and finish isn't up to Asian or European automakers' standards. *Hybrid:* Repair parts have been hard to find and can be costly. **Major redesign:** 2001, 2006, and 2011. **Highway/city fuel economy:** *2.0L auto.:* 5.8/9.2 L/100 km. *2.4L man.:* 5.7/8.7 L/100 km. *2.4L auto.:* 6.5/8.6 L/100 km. *Hybrid:* 4.9/5.6 L/100 km. **Best alternatives:** Consider the Chevrolet Cruze, Honda Accord, Kia Rondo, Mazda3, Suzuki Kizashi, and Toyota Camry.

SAFETY: NHTSA gave the 2013 Optima and Optima Hybrid five stars for front, side, and rollover crashworthiness. IIHS moderate frontal overlap tests rated the 2011-13 models "Good" and the small frontal overlap score for the same models was "Average." Side impact and roof protection were both rated "Good" as was the 2011-13 Optima head-restraint test. The front passenger seat is too low for some. Limited rear visibility:

> I purchased this new car in January and have had a difficult time adapting to the blind spots out of the rear window. The rear headrests of this car were designed too large. Even in the down position, these headrests block nearly two-thirds of the rear window visibility.

As with its Sonata cousin, the Optima pulls sharply to one side when accelerating:

> Vehicle hard to control and steer straight, especially at highway speeds. Severe pull to the left, though occasionally it drifts to the right. At city speeds, the steering problem is not as noticeable. I took the car to the dealer, and they checked the alignment. Minor adjustments, and tire inflation change, resulted in no significant change in the problem… It remains severe. If you let go of the steering wheel, then the car swiftly moves across to the left lanes.

Other scary failures: Airbags failed to deploy; sudden, unintended acceleration:

The contact owns a 2012 Kia Optima. While driving approximately 5 mph [8 km/h], the vehicle suddenly accelerated independently and crashed into the median. The vehicle was towed to the dealer for diagnostic testing where the technician advised that the front passenger side tire and axle would have to be replaced. The failure recurred four times. The fourth time the failure recurred, the contact crashed into another vehicle. The manufacturer refused to repair the vehicle because they stated there were no defects within the vehicle. Approximate failure mileage was 11,000 [17,700 km].

• • •

For 3 to 5 seconds, no response from engine at idle when accelerator depressed and the car is stopped (e.g., for traffic signal). Then, without warning, the engine went from idle (about 800 rpm) to rapid (surging) acceleration, often with screeching tires. This occurred each time I started from a stopped position.

Catastrophic transmission failure; a parked car will roll down an incline, despite being put in First gear or having the emergency brake engaged; driver-side floor mat bunches up around the brake pedal; Brake warning light comes on for no reason; side-view mirror fell off while driving along the freeway; no spare tire.

Prices and Specs

Prices (Negotiable): *LX:* $21,995, *LX+:* $25,795, *EX:* $26,795, *EX Turo:* $29,095, *EX Luxury:* $30,895, *SX:* $33,995 **Freight:** $1,455 **Powertrain (Front-drive):** Engines: 2.4L 4-cyl. (200 hp), 2.0L Turbo 4 (274 hp); Transmissions: 6-speed man., 6-speed auto. **Dimensions/capacity:** Passengers: 2/3; Wheelbase: 107 in.; H: 57.3/L: 190.7/W: 72.1 in.; Headroom F/R: 4.5/3 in.; Legroom F/R: 42.5/30 in.; Cargo volume: 15 cu. ft.; Fuel tank: 62L/regular; Tow limit: 2.4L: No towing, 2.7L: 1,000-2,000 lb.; Load capacity: 905 lb.; Turning circle: 35.8 ft.; Ground clearance: 5.3 in.; Weight: 3,206-3,385 lb.

ALERT! Despite the hype, real-world fuel economy is not all that impressive. Kia's mid-sized sedan is essentially a rebadged Hyundai Sonata.

Optima Hybrid

Kia's Optima Hybrid can be driven on battery power alone, or in blended gas-electric mode. When the car is stopped, the engine shuts off to save fuel. It uses a lithium polymer battery that will hold its charge up to 25 percent longer than hybrids with nickel metal hydride batteries.

The Hybrid also is one of the first full hybrid systems to use a typical automatic transmission – a compact 6-speed automatic that debuted on the 2011 Kia Sorento SUV. An external electrically driven oil pump provides the pressure needed to keep the clutches engaged when the vehicle is in idle stop mode.

Optima/Hybrid Profile

	2011	2012
Used Values ($)		
LX	12,500	15,000
LX+	15,000	17,500
EX	15,500	18,500
EX+	16,500	19,500
Hybrid	17,000	20,500
Premium	18,500	24,000
SX Turbo	20,500	24,000
Recommended	★	★
Reliability	★	★

SECRET WARRANTIES, INTERNAL BULLETINS: 2006-10—Poor windshield wiper performance can be improved by replacing the washer pump inlet filter. **2011-12**—An ECM software upgrade to address the MIL warning light coming on for no reason. The tire monitor system can be affected by radio signals. Remote Start system module software upgrade. Remedy for vehicles that stick in Park. *Hybrid:* Jarring gear shifting.

HYBRID SYSTEM – CHARACTERISTIC ACCELERATION FEEL

BULLETIN NO.: 115
DATE: MARCH 2012

CHARACTERISTIC ACCELERATION FEEL (OPTIMA HYBRID)

This bulletin provides information relating to the Optima Hybrid which features an advanced hybrid powertrain of the parallel variety. This means that the vehicle can operate under either electric power only ("EV Mode"), gasoline engine power only or a combination of the two ("HEV Mode"). The two power sources are selected automatically by an engine clutch which may provide a new and different driving feel to customers who are accustomed to conventional vehicles or other hybrid vehicles.

Part of this new driving feel is a slight oscillation in forward acceleration which may be described as a slight shudder, judder or jerking motion. This happens after the powertrain transitions out of EV Mode and into HEV Mode by engaging the engine clutch. This oscillation may occur in multiple situations but it is particularly noticeable when the following combination of events occur:

- After cold-start; and
- At low speed (less than 20 mph [32 km/h]); and
- Under light accelerator pedal input (less than 20%).

Oscillations under these conditions can be mitigated by temporarily turning off ActiveEco mode with the steering wheel-mounted eco button or by adjusting driving style (using different accelerator pedal inputs) when circumstances allow. Because the oscillation is reduced after vehicle warm-up the customer may elect to re-enable ActiveEco after the vehicle is warmed up, typically after 5-10 minutes of driving time.

> Based upon the technology used in the Optima Hybrid, this oscillation is a normal characterstic, is not an indication of a [defect] and is integral to the Optima Hybrid powertrain design that maximizes fuel economy and durability.

SPORTAGE ★★★★

RATING: Above Average (2011-14); Not Recommended (1993-10). A third-generation redesign turned this frog into a prince. The low rating for early models reflects the Sportage's serious steering problems, "jack-in-the-box" factory-related defects, and low crash test scores. **Road performance:** Kia's post-2010 Sportage comes with a lively 260 hp 2.0L turbocharged 4-cylinder engine, and lots of performance enhancements that set it apart from its twin, the Recommended Tucson. The boost in power is accompanied by a sport-tuned suspension with tauter shock and strut valving that makes for a stiff ride. The base engine on other models is a competent 4-banger that accelerates at a leisurely pace, though it's adequate for most driving chores. Early models aren't worth considering; acceleration and handling are mediocre and the driving "experience" includes moments of terror as the car wanders into oncoming traffic. Roadway feedback is barely noticeable, and the car exhibits excess body roll and, like the Optima, wanders all over the road in addition to pulling sharply to one side or the other. The part-time 4x4 system can't be used on dry roads. **Strong points:** Cheap, cheap, and cheap. **Weak points:** Cheap, cheap, and cheap. Interior hard plastic garnishments cheapen the look; the firm leather seats look good but are hard on the butt; noisy, ineffective brakes; brake pedal grip padding falls off; windshield cracking; minor problems with the audio system; cargo space and rear visibility compromised by the car's styling; and the subpar fit and finish produces lots of clunks and rattles. Excessive road noise. **Major redesign:** 1995, 2005, and 2011. **Highway/city fuel economy:** *2.4L man.:* 6.9/10 L/100 km. *2.4L auto.:* 6.2/9.4 L/100 km. *2.4L 4WD:* 7.0/9.9 L/100 km. *2.0L 4WD:* 7.7/10 L/100 km. **Best alternatives:** The Honda CR-V, Hyundai Tucson, Kia Rondo, Mazda Tribute, and Toyota RAV4.

SAFETY: NHTSA gives the 1997-2010 models three to five stars for overall crash safety; 2012 through the 2014s got four- and five-star scores for overall occupant protection. IIHS crashworthiness scores were as follows: moderate frontal overlap protection: 2011-13 models: "Good;" 2005-10 versions: "Average;" and 1998-2002s "Marginal." Small frontal overlap crash results on 2011-13 models: "Poor." Side impact test results on the 2011-13 models was rated "Good;" 2005-10s: "Average." Roof strength on the 2011-13 models: "Good;" 2005-10s were rated "Poor." Rear crash protection on the 2008-13s: "Good;" 2005 through some 2008s were rated "Poor."

ALERT! Hate to be a nag, but during your test drive, check the car for excessive wander or pulling:

Prices and Specs

Prices (Negotiable): *LX:* $21,995, *EX:* $27,595, *EX Luxury:* $34,095, *SX:* $37,395 **Freight:** $1,650
Powertrain (Front-drive/AWD): Engines: 2.4L 4-cyl. (176 hp), 2.0L 4-cyl. Turbo (256 hp); Transmissions: 6-speed man., 6-speed auto. **Dimensions/capacity:** Passengers: 2/3; Wheelbase: 103.5 in.; H: 66.7/L: 171.3/W: 70.9 in.; Headroom F/R: 5.5/4 in.; Legroom F/R: 42/29 in.; Cargo volume: 28 cu. ft.; Fuel tank: 58L- 65L/regular; Tow limit: 2,000 lb.; Load capacity: 925 lb.; Turning circle: 38 ft.; Ground clearance: 6 in.; Weight: 3,230-3,527 lb.

While travelling at highway speeds, or any speed above 50 km/h on a straight road, vehicle requires constant correction to track in a straight line. Without constant correction, the vehicle would leave the road surface. The resistance to steering pressure in correlation to speed does not seem properly programmed. The best way to describe this is to drive a car that would otherwise track down the road correctly, now throw control arms with worn out bushing and ball joints. It acts exactly like that, except a car with worn out control arm bushings and ball joints would in no way shape or form pass a safety inspection in any state. This problem, on trips over 45 minutes excessively fatigues the driver. (I thought I was going crazy on a 4.5 hour trip mostly expressway speeds). Over 110 km/h this problem seems to be eliminated…but not worth the endangerment to others using the roadway.

Sportage Profile

	2004	2005	2006	2007	2008	2009	2010	2011	2012
Used Values ($)									
LX	3,000	3,500	4,000	4,500	6,500	7,500	10,000	13,000	15,500
AWD	—	—	—	5,500	7,500	8,500	11,500	14,500	17,000
EX	—	—	—	—	—	—	21,500	15,500	19,000
AWD	—	—	—	—	—	—	—	17,000	21,000
Recommended	★	★	★	★	★	★	★	☆	☆
Reliability	☆	☆	☆	☆	☆	☆	☆	☆	☆

SECRET WARRANTIES, INTERNAL BULLETINS: 2006-13—Poor windshield wiper performance can be improved by replacing the washer pump inlet filter. **2011-12**—Outside radio signals may cause the tire-pressure monitoring system to malfunction. Steering-wheel noise and vibration repair tips.

A 2011 loser: Kia's Sorento... proof-positive that not all that is Asian is top-quality.

RATING: An Above Average buy (2012-14); Not Recommended (2011); A Below Average buy (2003- 10). The Sorento has proven that a good car that turns bad can become good again. The car represents good value in theory, with its strong towing capacity and excellent safety ratings. However, early models fall far short on reliability, safety, quality control, fuel economy, and ride quality. The 2011 redesign adopted a new unibody platform and an additional third-row seat, making the Sorento larger and much more reliable. **Road performance:** This is is an off-roader's delight, with low-range gearing and good ground clearance, but there's always that pesky reliability thing hitching a ride in the back of your mind. The base engine will do what is required. **Strong points:** Sorento is well-appointed and you get more SUV for fewer bucks. There's also a fairly roomy interior and good fit and finish. **Weak points:** Your off-roading fun may end as soon as the tranny, steering, or brakes give out. Life-threatening defects reported on the 2012 models: Sudden, unintended acceleration, as brakes wouldn't work and airbags failed to deploy; car stalls out when cruising; transmission hesitates or fails to upshift:

Transmission broken for the 4th time. Vehicle towed for 4th time.

• • •

The contact stated that the transmission failed to switch gears while driving 55 mph [88 km/h]. The contact had to shut off the engine to allow the vehicle to cool in order to proceed with driving. The vehicle was taken to the dealer for diagnosis where they were unable to diagnose or duplicate the failure. The vehicle was not repaired. The VIN is unavailable. The failure mileage was 3,000 [4,800 km].

• • •

On three occasions during the first month I owned the vehicle, I have experienced uncommanded downshift from 6th gear to 4th gear at speed. Transmission then locks in 4th gear until shut down and restarted. Very violent event when it occurs, with an instantaneous bang and corresponding immediate loss of speed.

Vehicle jerks, stutters, and stalls when accelerating:

Almost immediately started experiencing the occasional hesitation problem when pulling into traffic from a stop. On a couple occasions it put us in a very dangerous situation as we were crossing 2 lanes of traffic. Took the vehicle to dealer 4 times, they could not duplicate the problem. Finally they got us a 2012 near identical Sorento V6, and on the 3rd day had the same experience w/50 miles [80 km] on the vehicle. We now have 500+ [800 km] on it and have had a total of 7 similar situations.

Early brake wearout; chrome bezel instrument panel creates a painful and annoying reflection; rear sunroof exploded for no reason; headlight illumination is too short; sudden tire blowouts; and poor outward visibility:

New SUVs are adding huge pillars to the rear of vehicles, shrinking rear third windows, shrinking rear trunk door windows, pushing driver seats tightly up against the driver door—to shrink the car and boost gas mileage. On top of that, they are pursuing "quietness" & part of that is shrinking the exterior mirrors. Add this all up & you can hide a semi in the blind spot of this car. It was like driving a windowless cargo van w/o the big cargo van mirrors. The mirrors are small like what belongs on an economy car. Yes, my driver side mirror was well adjusted to only show a sliver of the vehicle. I just couldn't see. As I continued SUV shopping, I found this new design in many new SUVs. Gigantic blind spots are now the new design. I couldn't see to change into the left lane. When I looked over my shoulder my face was so close to the window, all I could see behind me were the separating pillars. Changing lanes was a guess.

Major redesign: 2003 and 2011. **Highway/city fuel economy:** *2.4L man.:* 7.4/10. 6L/100 km. *2.4L auto.:* 6.2/9.5 L/100 km. *2.4L 4WD:* 7.1/10.1 L/100 km. *V6 4WD:* 8.2/11.5 L/100 km. Fuel consumption is much higher than represented. **Best alternatives:** The Honda CR-V and Hyundai Tucson.

SAFETY: NHTSA gives five stars for side crash protection and four stars for frontal and rollover crashworthiness. IIHS scores the 2013 Sorento "Good" in all categories.

Prices and Specs

Prices (Negotiable): *LX:* $26,895, *LX V6:* $29,495, *EX:* $32,295, *EX V6:* $34,295, *EX V6 Luxury:* $38,795, *SX:* $41,295 **Freight:** $1,650 **Powertrain (Rear-drive/4WD):** Engines: 2.4L 4-cyl. (175 and 191 hp), 3.5L V6 (276 hp); Transmission: 6-speed auto. **Dimensions/capacity:** Passengers: 2/3; 2/3/2; Wheelbase: 106.3 in.; H: 68.7/L: 183.9/W: 74.2 in.; Headroom F/R/R2: 5.5/5.5/0 in.; Legroom F/R: 41/27/26 in.; Cargo volume: 37.5 cu. ft.; Fuel tank: 80L/regular; Tow limit: 1,650 lb.; Load capacity: 930 lb.; Turning circle: 38 ft.; Ground clearance: 7.5 in.; Weight: 3,571-3,682 lb.

ALERT! Sorento is a perfect example of how a redesign can screw up a vehicle's reliability and overall quality. The 2010 Sorento had only one safety-related complaint posted by NHTSA. However, the redesigned 2011 version generated 256 safety-related complaints, more than five times the average of 50 seen with other cars. Yet, the 2012 and 2013 models have elicited less than 50 complaints per year.

Sorento Profile

Used Values ($)	2004	2005	2006	2007	2008	2009	2010	2011	2012
L/LX/2.4	5,000	6,000	6,500	7,500	9,500	11,500	—	14,500	17,000
AWD	—	—	—	—	8,500	9,000	—	16,000	19,000
3.3/3.5	—	—	—	—	—	—	—	18,500	22,000
3.5 AWD	—	—	—	—	—	10,500	—	20,000	23,500
Recommended	★	★	★	★	★	★	★	★	☆
Reliability	★	★	★	★	★	★	★	★	☆

 SECRET WARRANTIES, INTERNAL BULLETINS: 2011-12—Steering-wheel noise and vibration repair. Transmission shift improvement. Steering wander or pull troubleshooting.

STEERING/SUSPENSION – PULL OR DRIFT CONCERN
BULLETIN NO.: CHA 033   DATE: JULY 2011

 SUB-FRAME AND SUSPENSION ADJUSTMENT FOR DRIFT CONCERN

This bulletin provides information related to a drift condition and adjusting/settling the suspension components under load as assembly variation can remain on the suspension. Camber and Caster may need slight adjustment depending on actual road conditions. To improve this condition the dealer is requested to first follow the TSB CHA 032 (Drift/Pull Diagnosis and Best Practices Tips) for specifications and if they are outside the parameters then perform the instructions as directed in this TSB.

LEXUS

Reliability, Luxury – and Stark Terror

No one had heard of Lexus vehicles suffering from sudden, unintended acceleration with attendant brake loss – until a few years ago. At that time, Toyota, the owner of the Lexus luxury brand, insisted the accidents and deaths were due to driver error. However, after some delay the automaker did a turnabout and in late

2009 recalled almost its entire Toyota lineup (4.4 million vehicles) to better secure floormats and fix a sticky throttle, while insisting that most of its higher-end Lexus models weren't involved.

This denial lasted until June 20, 2010, when the National Highway Traffic Safety Administration (NHTSA) asked Toyota to recall 2010 Lexus RX 350 and RX 450 H vehicles "for a serious safety issue involving potential pedal entrapment by the floor mat" – the same defect affecting vehicles involved in the 2009 recall campaign. Toyota has received complaints from consumers about floormat entrapment since 2004.

Lexus's impeccable reputation for quality and safety has taken a beating by the past several years' news barrage of owner complaints, recalls, and serial *mea culpas* issued by Toyota's president that "the company lost its way." You bet it has.

Take a look at this NHTSA-posted report of a "runaway" 2011 IS 250:

> Unintended accelerator event while driving up a steep hill, vehicle began to accelerate quickly on its own accord. While braking, the brakes went all the way to the floor and only served to destabilize the vehicle and slow it slightly. Tachometer was pegged at 6,000 rpm and the vehicle would not stop. After pushing the "start" button several times the vehicle shut down and was brought to a stop. This took almost two minutes and was extremely dangerous. Lexus inspected the vehicle and determined it operating as designed, with no manufacturing defects found. We sold this vehicle to the Lexus dealer for $26,000, well below the low Blue Book.

Former executives who have testified against the automaker say Toyota simply believes it is above the law – showing the same arrogant attitude it manifested earlier in Canada when it tried to fix new-car prices under an "Access" price scheme. Caught with its pants down by Ottawa anti-competition investigators who were acting on a *Lemon-Aid* complaint, Toyota paid a $2 million settlement to charity and beat the rap. In the States, the automaker paid almost $50 million for dragging its feet on recalls.

The combination of bad press, an economic recession, and Japan's Fukushima earthquake hasn't seriously hurt sales for either Toyota or Lexus. Luxury car sales took a hit during the first year, but the Lexus brand has bounced back sharply. Luxury car buyers, though, are no longer saying, "I'm gonna buy a Lexus." Instead, they are keeping an open mind, looking at vehicles offered in the luxury class, and then making their choice.

To make sure that choice is a Lexus, luxury car shoppers will be tempted by substantial rebates and other sales incentives throughout the 2014 model year. Plus, the automaker has promised to raise 2014 prices by only a few hundred dollars.

Lexus is a luxury automaker on its own merits, even though many models are mostly dressed-up Camrys. Unlike Acura and Infiniti, Lexus is seen by some as the epitome of luxury and comfort, with a small dab of performance thrown in. Lexus executives know that no matter how often car enthusiast magazines say that drivers want "road feel," "responsive handling," and "high-performance" thrills, the truth of the matter is that most drivers simply want cars that look good and that give them bragging rights for safety, performance, convenience, and comfort; they want to travel from point A to point B, without interruption, in cars that are more than fully equipped Civics or warmed-over Maximas. Lexus executives figure that hardcore, high-performance aficionados can move up to its sportier models and the rest will stick with the Camry-based ES series.

Although these high-end cars and SUVs do, in most cases, set advanced benchmarks for quality control, they don't demonstrate engineering perfection, as proven by a recent spate of engine failures, including sludge buildup and automatic transmissions that hesitate and then surge when shifting. And, yes, cheaper luxury cars from Acura, Hyundai, Kia, Nissan, and Toyota give you almost as much comfort and reliability, but without as much cachet and resale value.

Speaking of resale values, don't believe that buying a Lexus is akin to investing in an RRSP. Some models are money-losers. Take, for example, a 2010 entry-level ES 350: New, it sold for $42,900; today you can get one for about $15,500. What? A four-year-old Lexus selling for less than half its original value? Welcome to the real world.

Technical service bulletins show that recent Lexus models have been affected mostly by powertrain and electrical malfunctions, faulty emissions-control components, computer module miscalibrations, and minor body fit and trim glitches. To Lexus' credit, many owners haven't heard of these problems because Lexus dealers have been particularly adept at fixing defects early.

Most of the 2014 car and SUV models are carryovers from last year, so don't look for sweeping changes apart from cosmetic updates and refinements to existing technologies. Nevertheless, these are benchmark cars known for their comfort, convenience features, and good looks. Sports cars, they're not. But if you're looking for your father's Oldsmobile from a Japanese automaker, these luxury cars fit the bill.

When buying used, be especially wary of the redesigned 2010 "active" head restraints. Owners say the restraints push the driver's head down and forward, causing considerable neck and back pain. Worst of all, there is no fix for this problem that doesn't contravene U.S. and Canadian federal safety legislation.

Like Acuras and Infinitis, Lexus models may also suffer from some automatic transmission failures; engine sludge buildup (see *www.consumeraffairs.com/news 04/2007/01/toyota_sludge_settlement.html*); early rear main engine seal and front strut replacements (front struts are often replaced under a "goodwill" warranty); and front brake, electrical, body, trim, and accessory deficiencies.

Hybrids

Toyota and Lexus have been leaders in hybrid sales since the Prius was first launched in 2001. Lexus currently offers seven hybrids: The LS, GS, ES, IS, RX, CT and HS and industry insiders say it's a safe bet that Lexus will be releasing two new models in 2014.

The hybrid has gotten good marks for reliability and fuel consumption. Used, a 2013 ES 300h is worth between $37,000 and $39,000. Other vehicles worth considering are an all-dressed Toyota Camry, Avalon or Prius, the Acura TL, and the BMW 3 Series.

SECRET WARRANTIES, INTERNAL BULLETINS: *ES 350:* **2007-09**—Engine ticking noise. Upgraded front brake pads will reduce brake pulsation. Sunroof popping or creaking. Vehicle won't shift out of Park. **2007-10**—Rubbing noises from rear of vehicle. *GS 300/350:* **2006-10**—Front sway bar thumping noise. *LS 460/600h:* **2007-09**—Side window wind noise at highway speeds. Rear suspension rattle, knock. Uncomfortable lower seat cushion. Squawk from the brake actuator.

ES 300/330/350/300H

RATING: Average. An over-priced luxury sedan that's really a gussied-up Camry. There are two ES models: The naturally aspirated ES 350 and the ES 300h hybrid. They are practically identical at first glance – the hybrid model is distinguished by unique 17-inch alloy wheels, a rear decklid spoiler, and a fuel-frugal 2.5L Atkinson-cycle inline-four. The sixth-generation ES uses the Toyota Avalon platform and gains 1.7 inches of additional wheelbase (111 in total), 1 inch of additional length (192.7), and 0.8 inches of height. Lexus has managed to add 4 inches of additional rear legroom. **Road performance:** Good acceleration; a pleasantly quiet ride; steering feel is muted; and overall handling (excessive body roll) isn't as nimble as with its BMW or Mercedes rivals. There's a drive-select knob on the centre console that can be dialed to Normal, Eco, and Sport modes, and the steering and throttle response is altered to match your choice. Only problem: The differences between the Normal and Eco settings are more mental than mechanical. Dangerous erratically performing automatic transmission that hesitates and surges when shifting. **Strong points:** Aggressive styling and a well-appointed interior; lower curb weight and some engine tinkering nudges up fuel economy a bit; and better-than-average quality control. **Weak points:** Brakes are disappointing, in that the small discs are the same size as those found on the much lighter Camry and brake fade after successive stops is evident. The car is primarily a four-seater, as three adults can't sit comfortably in the rear; headroom is inadequate for tall occupants; trunk space is limited (low liftover, though); and some of the dash instruments and controls look a bit outdated. Fit and finish imperfections; Bluetooth cell phone voice distortion; and an inoperative moonroof. **Major redesign:** 2001, 2006, and 2013. **Highway/city fuel economy:** 7.2/10.9 L/100 km; *300h:* 4.7/5.1 L/100 km. **Best alternatives:** The early models are acceptable buys. Other choices: The Acura TL, BMW 3 Series, and Infiniti G35. Resembling an LS 400 dressed in sporty attire, the entry-level ES 300 was launched in 1992 to fill the gap between the discontinued ES 250 and the LS 400. In fact, the ES 300 has many of the attributes of the LS 400 sedan but sells for much less money. A five-passenger sedan based on the Camry, but 90 kg (200 lb.) heavier and with a different suspension and tires, it came equipped with a standard 3.0L 24-valve engine that produced 181-210 horses coupled to either a 5-speed manual or a 4-speed electronically controlled automatic transmission. Like some Infiniti models, however, the ES 300 hesitates and surges when accelerating. Headroom is also surprisingly limited for a luxury car. ES 330s came on the scene as 2004 models and offered buyers a more-powerful 3.3L V6 that produced more horses and a bit more torque. 2005 models got very little that was new, except for power front seats with a memory feature and power door mirrors that tilt down when in Reverse. The 2007 ES 350 arrived with new styling, more power, and additional features, but it remained an upscale Toyota Camry. It has a slightly larger wheelbase and a new 6-speed transmission, and is powered by a 272 hp 3.5L V6 instead of the ES 330's 218 hp 3.3L V6.

SAFETY: The 2013-14 models were given a five-star NHTSA rating for frontal and side crash safety and four stars for rollover resistance, while the 2012 version's side crash protection merited only two stars – unusually low for a higher-end car and four stars for front and side crashworthiness. 2007-10 models had high scores of four and five stars. IIHS gave 2007-13 models "Good" ratings for front, moderate overlap, side, and roof protection, but the 2012 got a "Poor" rating for small overlap crash safety. Head restraints were rated "Marginal" on the 2007-12s and "Poor" on the 2004-06 ES. Rear-corner visibility is hampered by the high rear end. Reports of sudden, unintended acceleration; stuck accelerator; automatic transmission shifts erratically, suddenly accelerates, or slips and hesitates before going into gear; car lurches forward when the cruise control is reengaged; brake failure and premature tire monitor system malfunctions; brake wearout; and radio system glitches.

ALERT! This entry-level front-drive comes with one of the rarest features of all: a spare tire.

> ### Prices and Specs
>
> **Prices (Negotiable):** *Base:* $39,500, *300h:* $43,900 **Freight:** $1,950
> **Powertrain (Front-drive):** Engines: 3.5L V6 (268 hp), *Hybrid:* 2.5L 4-cyl. (200 hp); Transmissions: 6-speed auto., *Hybrid:* CVT **Dimensions/capacity:** Passengers: 2/3; Wheelbase: 111 in.; H: 57.1/L: 193/W: 71 in.; Headroom F/R: 3/2.5 in.; Legroom F/R: 42.5/30.5 in.; Cargo volume: 15 cu. ft.; Fuel tank: 65L/regular; Load capacity: 905 lb.; Turning circle: 37.4 ft.; Ground clearance: 6.1 in.; Weight: 3,549 lb. *Hybrid:* 3,660 lb.

ES 330/350 Profile

	2004	2005	2006	2007	2008	2009	2010	2011	2012
Used Values ($)									
330/350	—	—	12,000	13,500	15,500	18,500	23,000	27,500	32,500
Recommended	★	★	★	★	★	★	★	★	★
Reliability	★	★	★	★	★	☆	☆	☆	☆

SECRET WARRANTIES, INTERNAL BULLETINS: 2011-12—Steering-wheel noise and vibration repair. Transmission shift improvement. Steering wander or pull troubleshooting.

IS ★★★★

RATING: Above Average (2011-14). Restyled and sporting an 8-speed automatic transmission, the 2014 IS uses the GS's platform, a stiffer suspension, and electrically-assisted power steering. The car is 3.4 inches longer, 0.4 inch wider, and 0.2 inch taller, with a wheelbase that's 2.7 inches larger. Interior improvements include more room, an enhanced telescopic steering column, improved seating, and touch-sensitive electronic climate controls. **Road performance:** The IS 350 has a competent standard 3.5L engine, but the IS 250's 2.5L feels rather sluggish when pushed. The larger engine has plenty of tire-smoking power and provides thrilling high-performance handling, but your thrills will come with a bone-jarring, teeth-chattering ride. Suspension is too firm for some and there's no manual transmission option. Handling on both the 250 and 350 models doesn't feel as sharp or responsive as with the BMW competition, owing in large part to an intrusive Vehicle Dynamics Integrated Management system that automatically eases up on the throttle during hard cornering. Emergency braking also isn't a confidence builder. **Strong points:** Targeting BMW's 3 Series, Lexus's entry-level IS 250 and IS 350 reardrive sport-compact sedans come with either a 204 hp 2.5L V6 or a 306 hp 3.5L V6. The F version ups the ante considerably with its 416 hp 5.0L V8 power-plant. Although Lexus lost some of its lustre after going through two years of safety-related recalls and increased competition from European and Japanese luxury carmakers, the nameplate continues to be a bestseller. Owner comments are still mostly positive, and the car's residual value has remained strong. The 2013 is wider, longer, and more solid-looking than previous models. It handles well and braking is exceptional. Interior amenities were also upgraded for 2013, including an optional navigation screen that is user-friendly and easily read. A low beltline provides a great view and the high-quality interior is relatively quiet. First-class fit and finish. **Weak points:** The navigation touch screen will suddenly shut off:

> There is a faulty connector on the 2008 IS 250 touch panel screen. The touch panel is a 4-wire resistive panel, taped to the LCD display. There's a four wire ribbon cable that is improperly bonded to the touch panel. Lexus quoted me $2,800 to fix this problem that is a common problem and a defect in their manufacturing.

The Vehicle Dynamics Integrated Management feature performs erratically. Cramped rear seating and limited trunk space on 2012s and earlier versions; convertibles lose almost all their trunk space when the top is lowered. Excessive window rattling when driving with the top down; transmission fluid leaks; and an AC-produced mildew odour (Lexus replaced the vehicle). Get used to paying top dollar for premium fuel and a sky-high freight charge when buying new. *IS F:*

A tiny cabin. **Major redesign:** 2001, 2006, and 2013. **Highway/city fuel economy:** *IS 250 man.:* 7.5/11.4 L/100 km. *IS 250 auto.:* 6.8/9.8 L/100 km. *IS 250 AWD:* 7.6/10.5 L/100 km. *IS 350:* 7.8/10.9 L/100 km. *IS 350C:* 7.9/11.5 L/100 km. *IS F:* 8.5/13.0 L/100 km. **Best alternatives:** Try the Acura TL, BMW 3 Series, and Infiniti G37. Audi's A4 would be a contender, if it wasn't for its recent redesign and attendant glitches, coupled to a less than stellar quality-control history. Audi's quality shortcomings are borne out in Consumer Reports' annual member surveys and in independent European consumer publications like Which? Car (*www.which.co.uk/cars/*).

SAFETY: NHTSA crash-tested the 2013 IS 250 and 350 for rollover protection only, and both cars scored four stars overall. The 2010 version posted similar results. IIHS-tested 2006-13 models earned "Good" ratings in moderate overlap frontal crashes and "Poor" in small overlap frontal tests. Side crash protection was "Good;" roof strength and head-restraints merited only an "Acceptable" score. Owner reports of sudden, unintended acceleration:

> On several occasions . . . the rpms increase randomly after the car has stopped and is stationary. The car inches forward and the driver has to apply more pressure on the brake pedal to make sure the car doesn't lurch forward and hit the car in front. The rpms go up almost 1000 rpms from idling. Happens in D and R. When turning on car, putting the gear [in] R, the car just lurches backwards unless the brake pedal is heavily [depressed]. This seems to be a software/ECM issue.

Also, many complaints of shattered sunroofs, premature brake wear, and the car jerking to one side when the brakes are applied. Automatic rear-view mirror dimmer takes up to seven seconds to dim trailing headlights and won't dim at all on roads with brightly lit overhead lighting. Poor instrument visibility:

> The visual displays on the center dashboard console indicating HVAC and audio information for the Lexus IS 250 C are so light as to be virtually invisible to the driver, particularly in bright sun and when the driver is wearing sunglasses.

ALERT! Expect $2,000-$3,000 discounts early in 2014, along with attractive financing and leasing deals as the European competition bounces back from its own economic woes and forces Lexus to add additional sales incentives.

Prices and Specs

Prices (Negotiable): *IS 250:* $34,500, *AWD:* $38,000, *250C:* $51,100, *IS 350:* $45,050, *350C:* $57,425, *IS F:* $69,950 **Freight:** $1,895 **Powertrain (Rear-drive/AWD):** Engines: 2.5L V6 (204 hp), 3.5L V6 (306 hp), 5.0L V8 (416 hp); Transmissions: 6-speed man., 6-speed auto. **Dimensions/capacity:** Passengers: 2/3; Wheelbase: 108 in.; H: 56/L: 180/W: 71 in.; Headroom F/R: 2/2 in.; Legroom F/R: 41.5/25.5 in.; Cargo volume: 13.0 cu. ft.; Fuel tank: 65L/premium; Tow limit: N/A; Load capacity: 825 lb.; Turning circle: 33.5 ft.; Ground clearance: 4.7-5.3 in.; Weight: 3,814 lb.

IS Profile

	2004	2005	2006	2007	2008	2009	2010	2011	2012
Used Values ($)									
IS 250	—	—	9,500	11,000	13,000	15,500	18,500	22,500	26,000
AWD	—	—	10,500	12,000	14,500	16,500	20,500	24,500	28,500
250C	—	—	—	—	—	—	29,000	35,500	40,500
350	—	—	—	14,500	20,000	22,500	27,000	32,000	36,500
300	6,500	8,500	—	—	—	—	—	—	—
AWD	—	—	—	—	—	—	—	33,500	38,500
350C	—	—	—	—	—	—	34,500	42,000	48,000
360 Sport	—	10,000	—	—	—	—	—	—	—
F	—	—	—	—	28,500	34,500	43,000	49,500	58,000
Recommended	☆	☆	☆	☆	☆	☆	☆	☆	☆
Reliability	★	★	★	★	★	★	★	★	★

SECRET WARRANTIES, INTERNAL BULLETINS: 2011-12—Fuel gauge indicates Empty when there is gas in the tank. Bubbled HID headlight housing.

RX 300, 330, 350/RX 400H, 450H ★★★★/★★★

RATING: *All Models:* Above Average (2011-14); Average (2000-10). Lexus invented the luxury crossover segment with the RX series in 1998, and since then it has been a perennial bestseller. Unfortunately, a decade ago, Lexus followed Toyota's example of cutting content to keep prices low, with the result that safety, and reliability suffered and owner dissatisfaction increased. Lexus is now recapturing market share by adding content, doling out sales incentives, and cutting new car prices. Of course these moves have brought down the price of used Lexus models, as well. *Lemon-Aid* alerted readers to Lexus safety hazards over a decade ago. Our ratings were lowered progressively since we noted that many models had engine sludge problems, dangerous engine surging and automatic transmission delayed shifts, sudden acceleration, unreliable brakes, inadequate and theft-prone headlights, and weak rear hatches that kept falling on people's heads. *RX 400h and 450h:* Above Average buy (2011-14); Average (2006; 2010). Fuel savings are a given with the hybrid, but you will pay a heavy purchase price in Canada (in the States, the car costs much less). Buying the RX in mid-2014 should save you about 15 percent. Resale value for the hybrid will drop faster as you get closer to the battery pack's warranty expiration – eight to ten years. Essentially a more fuel-frugal RX model with plenty of horsepower and full-time AWD, Lexus hybrids are ridiculously expensive and hazardous to drive. They can lose their brakes whenever passing over bumpy terrain, and their frequently delayed shifts and engine surges can be deadly either from a rear-ender when you stall, or from a T-bone collision that cuts your car in half as it suddenly accelerates into traffic. If you must go "green," get a cheaper used Ford Escape Hybrid or an all-dressed Prius RX. **Road performance:** Suspension is independent all around, and the progressive electronic power-steering system is speed-sensing for enhanced control. The front-drive and AWD RX models come identically equipped. Count on a smooth, car-like ride and a satisfying braking response and feel. Handling is not as positive; the car doesn't feel as agile as its competition. **Strong points:** Now in its third generation, the 2014 doesn't disappoint with its attractive styling, great safety ratings, lots of luxury in a spacious cabin, and adequate back-seat legroom. Also, the RX has excellent gas mileage for a luxury crossover. 2013s have increased cargo space over previous models. **Weak points:** No third-seat option; expensive options packages; modest cargo capacity; and excessive road noise. There's less steering feedback when compared to the RX 450h. Owners also report excessive dust/powder blows from the AC vents; tire monitor system malfunctions; inoperative moonroofs; the vehicle pulls to the right; audio system glitches; and poor fit and finish. *Hybrid:* Slow acceleration; the car takes more effort to turn; and the Remote Touch multifunction joystick and screen are distracting features. **Major redesign:** 1999, 2004, and 2010. **Highway/city fuel economy:** *RX 300:* 9.7/13.0 L/100 km. *RX 330:* 9.0/12.8 L/100 km. *RX 350:* 8.2/11.6 L/100 km. *RX 400h:* 8.1/7.5 L/100 km. *RX 450h:* 7.2/6.6 L/100 km. **Best alternatives:** There's not much new with the 2014 model; go for a much cheaper 2013 or earlier version, instead. Other vehicles to consider: The BMW 5 Series, GM Acadian or Traverse, Honda Pilot, Hyundai Santa Fe Limited or Veracruz SE, Nissan Murano SL or Xterra, and the Toyota Highlander Limited.

SAFETY: The 2013 models earned four-star crash scores from NHTSA for frontal and rollover crash resistance and five stars for side crash safety. IIHS gave the 2012 RX a "Good" ranking across the board.

ALERT! During the test drive, pay careful attention to how the RX 450h 4×4 "On Demand" feature performs (see below and Weak points and Safety (above)). Hybrid suddenly accelerated as it was being parked, brakes were ineffective, and the front tire exploded. Car surges forward when the brakes are applied. RX 450h brake failures are similar to those reported on the Prius:

> I wanted to alert you that other hybrid models that were manufactured with the same braking system as the Prius suffer the same issue. I have a 2010 Lexus 450h RX and its brakes disengage when I am driving on bumpy roads and over pot holes. I live in a northeastern city with many bumps and my brakes stop working often and as a result I have to slam them on much more quickly.

The 4×4 system doesn't perform as advertised:

> The RX 450h is downright dangerous. The 4 wheel drive does not switch "on demand" as the advertising says. I live in snowy Massachusetts and do not need permanent 4 wheel

drive, but it is essential when the roads are full of snow or ice. I was puzzled at first that the 4 wheel drive only actuated under 25 mph [40 km/h]. I tested it on sharp corners in the snow: the back slid out; and on faster, gradual corners: the car side slipped. Never did the 4 wheel drive switch on and correct the slide. I looked in the manual for the method to manually activate 4 wheel drive but couldn't find it. I contacted Lexus. They said that I should use the snow switch. This is a menu item which annoyingly [must] be switched on every time you drive. It didn't work, as it only changes the gear and acceleration characteristics like any other winter/summer switch. They also said that it should work at high speeds when more power is needed. I tried that and found that at 60 mph [95 km/h] if I absolutely floored the accelerator on a steep hill the 4 wheel drive would switch on briefly.

Prices and Specs

Prices (Negotiable): *RX 350:* $44,950, *F Sport:* $57,900, *450h:* $56,750 **Freight:** $1,950 **Powertrain (Front-drive/AWD):** Engines: 3.5L V6 (275 hp), Hybrid: 3.5L V6 (295 hp); Transmissions: 6-speed auto., CVT **Dimensions/capacity:** Passengers: 2/3; Wheelbase: 108 in.; H: 67/L: 188/W: 74.2 in.; Headroom F/R: 3/4.5 in.; Legroom F/R: 41.5/28.5 in.; Cargo volume: 40 cu. ft.; Fuel tank: 70L/regular; Tow limit: 3,500 lb.; Load capacity: 825 lb.; Turning circle: 37.1 ft.; Ground clearance: 7.3 in.; Weight: 4,178 lb.

ALERT! Stay away from sunroof-equipped models. Not only is it a non-essential feature and often failure-prone, but it also comes in packages that include other frivolous features. Also, be wary of the Adaptive Cruise Control; it may operate erratically and can be costly to troubleshoot and repair.

RX 300, 330, 350/RX 400h, 450h Profile

	2004	2005	2006	2007	2008	2009	2010	2011	2012
Used Values ($)									
300	—	—	14,000	—	—	—	—	—	—
330	10,000	12,500	15,000	—	—	—	—	—	—
350	—	—	—	15,500	17,500	22,000	26,000	31,000	36,500
400h	—	—	15,500	16,000	20,000	22,500	—	—	—
450h	—	—	—	—	—	—	32,000	41,000	47,500
Recommended	☆	4	4	☆	☆	☆	☆	☆	☆
Reliability	☆	☆	☆	☆	☆	☆	☆	☆	☆

SECRET WARRANTIES, INTERNAL BULLETINS: *All models/years:* There are dozens of bulletins that address the correction of various squeaks and rattles found throughout the vehicle. **2003-10**—Windshield ticking. **2004-06**—Rear door-stay improvement. Unacceptable power backdoor operation. Fuel tank shield rattle. **2004-07**—Troubleshooting dash rattles. **2004-08**—Front power seat grinding, groaning. **2004-09**—Transmission fluid or gear oil leaks from the transfer case vent. Plugging water leaks at the liftgate area. **2004-10**—Remedy for brake rattle, buzz heard near the driver's side dash. Power back door noise. **2006-09**—Multiple warning lights; can't shift out of Park. Moonroof auto-close function inoperative. **2007**—Engine timing cover oil leaks. Engine squealing. Moonroof rattle. **2007-08**—Oil leak from the engine camshaft housing. Replace engine VVTI oil hose free of charge. **2007-09**—Driver's door rattle. **2007-10**—Engine ticking noises. **2007-11**—Oil control valve will be replaced under warranty. **2008-09**—Transfer case fluid leak. **2010**—Steering groan when turning the steering wheel. Front seat track noise. **2010-11**—Steering column rattle. *450h:* **2010**—Steering groan when turning the steering wheel. **2011-12**—Fuel gauge indicates Empty when there is gas in the tank. Bubbled HID headlight housing. Inoperative smart key. Insufficient charging.

Mazda has lots to smile about. Four decades ago, it was a marginal automaker selling cheap, hard-to-service, here-today-gone-tomorrow rustbuckets. But during the past decade Mazda trimmed its Ford ties and improved the quality of its lineup, and it now specializes in peppy, fuel-sipping small cars, family sedans, a bestselling six-passenger mini-minivan, and a number of popular SUV crossovers.

MAZDA

Mazda Is All Smiles

Mazda sales have been on a roll for the past five years and the company wants to keep the momentum by updating its vehicles more often than the traditional third-year makeover. The Mazda6 and CX-5, for example, will get new interiors and restyled front ends next year, only 18 months after the Mazda6 was revamped and about two years since the CX-5 was launched. Additionally, a redesigned CX-9 crossover will highlight the 2016 model year along with an eye-popping next-generation MX-5 Miata.

Mazda's past is a story of missed opportunities. It snared the rights to the innovative Wankel rotary engine from GM (destined for the Vega and Astre) that had a reputation for being relatively small and powerful – but at the expense of poor fuel efficiency. Mazda put the Wankel in its RX-7 series of roadsters (1978–2002) and its RX-8 sports cars (2004–10) and was fairly successful in marketing the cars to the high performance crowd. But once North American fuel prices soared and gas station lineups stretched for blocks, Mazda switched gears, dropped the Wankel, and went back to building conventionally powered, non-descript econocars.

Ford saved Mazda from bankruptcy in 1994 by purchasing part of the company and sharing the production of their cars and trucks. Mazda soon turned profitable through better management and a popular new array of small cars and trucks made in partnership with Ford. The company's sole minivan, the MPV, was both a quality and performance boondoggle and never got any traction. It was put out of its misery in 2006. Mazda went back to its small-car roots with last year's brand-new $13,995 Mazda2, a four-door hatchback powered by a 100 hp 1.5L 4-cylinder engine with a standard 5-speed manual transmission or optional 4-speed automatic. It gets 7.2 L/100 km (39 mpg) in the city and 5.6 L/100 km (50 mpg) on the highway (see Appendix I for a rating summary).

Fast and Frugal

Mazda's 2014 product lineup is going to be augmented by four new models scheduled to be introduced later in the year. First, we have the return of the redesigned CX-5, followed by the all-new Mazda6 which will arrive late next year with a sportier appearance and more fuel-efficient engines. Additionally, Mazda is expected to launch redesigned versions of the Mazda3, MX-5, and CX-9. *Automotive News* says, all the models will have Skyactiv technologies and ride on lightweight platforms.

The slightly upscale Mazda3 does everything the Mazda2 doesn't. There's plenty of interior room, and the powertrain performs flawlessly. In fact, this little pocket rocket, marketed as an urban runabout, remains on back order, due to the performance crowd support since its debut as a 2004 model. This peppy and fuel-efficient compact takes Mazda back to its compact-car roots and adds some performance thrills to its fuel-saving powertrain. Recently the "3" was restyled, the suspension stiffened to enhance handling, and a third engine, a 155 hp 2.0L 4-cylinder, was added along with Mazda's new Skyactiv fuel-saving feature that was introduced last year and expanded to the 2014 models.

In March 2012, Mazda launched the CX-5, its smallest SUV, equipped with a 148-155 hp 2.0L 4-cylinder engine. A 2.2L diesel version is planned for later this year. The CX-7 increased in size last year, when it replaced the larger CX-9.

MAZDA3 ★★★★★

good buy

RATING: Recommended. A fuel-efficient compact with a performance edge. The Mazda3 five-star rating hasn't changed during the past several years mainly due to the absence of owner complaints and its superior highway performance. The Mazda3 is an econobox with flair that pleases commuters and "tuners" alike. The car offers spirited acceleration and smooth, sporty shifting. Handling is enhanced with a highly rigid body structure, front and rear stabilizer bars, a multi-link rear suspension, and four-wheel disc brakes. Interior room is quite ample with the car's relatively long wheelbase, extra width, and straight sides, which maximize headroom, legroom, and shoulder room. There is an outrageously high $1,495 freight fee you shouldn't pay. Heck, just across the border Mazda charges Americans only $795. So, by driving 80 kilometres, smart shoppers can save $700, plus another $500 due to the lower price on the American side. The cheaper and virtually identical 2012 version is recommended but hard to find as higher gas prices stampede buyers toward anything that is fast and frugal. Hatchback models give you the most versatility. **Road performance:** Good powertrain set-up, with plenty of reserve power for passing and merging; easy, predictable handling; good steering feedback; small turning radius; rear multi-link suspension gives the car great stability at higher speeds. **Strong points:** Spacious, easy-to-load trunk; user-friendly instruments and controls; and better-than-average workmanship. **Weak points:** The Mazda3 has a history of automatic transmission malfunctions (but no more than with Honda or Toyota models) and prematurely worn-out brake rotors and pads. A small trunk; limited rear footroom; excessive road noise intrudes into the cabin. Some owners have reported premature wearout of brake pads and rotors, accompanied by an annoying grinding sound and pulling to one side when the brakes are applied; brake rotors are easily grooved; dash and door gaps (2014); rear glass window may explode in chilly weather:

Morning: 16 degrees F [−9°C]. Approached my car in the morning and heard a crackling noise. I thought the sound was ice. I started the car and the rear defogger. As I sat in my driveway … approximately 30 seconds after turning on the defogger … the rear glass exploded with a loud noise. … The car is 4 months old and under warranty. … I called Mazda and was told that this is due to outside influence (i.e. the same as if a tree branch fell on the car). He indicated that I should expect that this could happen in the cold weather. I cannot believe that I should expect that my rear window can explode in cold weather.

Prices and Specs

Price (Firm): *GX sedan:* $16,295, *Auto.:* $17,495, *GX Sport:* $17,495, *Auto.:* $18,695, *GS sedan:* $19,595, *Auto.:* $20,795, *GS Luxury:* $21,690, *Auto.:* $22,890, *GT sedan:* $24,425, *Auto.:* $25,625, *MazdaSpeed:* $29,695 **Freight:** $1,495 **Powertrain (Front-drive):** Engines: 2.0L 4-cyl. (155 hp), 2.5L 4-cyl. (184 hp); Transmissions: 5-speed man., 6-speed man., 5-speed auto., 6-speed auto. **Dimensions/capacity:** *Sedan:* Passengers: 2/3; Wheelbase: 106.3 in.; H: 57.3/L: 181/W: 70.7 in.; Headroom F/R: 4.5/3 in.; Legroom F/R: 41/25 in.; Cargo volume: 12 cu. ft.; Fuel tank: 55L/regular; Load capacity: 850 lb.; Turning circle (hatchback): 34.2 ft.; Ground clearance: 6.1 in.; Weight: 2,799 lb.

(Note: in the above-cited incident, the car owner could have easily sought restitution from small claims court on the grounds that the "balance of probabilities" points to a defective rear window.) Front passenger-side airbag may be disabled even though an average-sized adult is seated; manual transmission clutch failure; and the rear sway bar link nut may loosen, causing a clunking sound to be heard coming from the rear undercarriage when the car passes over bumps or rough roads. **Major redesign:** 1999, 2004, 2010, and 2014. The restyled 2014 is wider and shorter, offers more safety features, comes with two fuel-efficient Skyactiv engines (seven more horses with the 2.0L engine; 17 more with the 2.5L), a new interior, and an upgraded infotainment system. **Highway/city fuel economy:** *2.0 man.:* 5.9/8.1 L/100 km. *2.5 man.:* 6.9/10.2 L/100 km. **Best alternatives:** A 2013 Honda Civic.

SAFETY: NHTSA's front-impact crashworthiness rating for the 2013 model is five stars, rollover resistance earned four stars, and side protection scored only three stars. IIHS gave the 2012 Mazda3 its top, "Good" score for frontal offset, head-restraint, and rear crash protection. Roof strength was also rated "Good." A high deck cuts rear visibility.

ALERT! The Mazda3 is a theft magnet. Invest in an engine disabler and GPS tracker.

Mazda3 Profile

	2004	2005	2006	2007	2008	2009	2010	2011	2012
Used Values ($)									
300	—	—	14,000	—	—	—	—	—	—
330	10,000	12,500	15,000	—	—	—	—	—	—
350	—	—	—	15,500	17,500	22,000	26,000	31,000	36,500
Recommended	☆	☆	☆	☆	☆	☆	☆	☆	☆
Reliability	☆	☆	☆	☆	☆	☆	☆	☆	☆

SECRET WARRANTIES, INTERNAL BULLETINS: 2001-13—Tips on eliminating excessive sulfur odours. **2004-11**—Remedy for intermittent no starts in Park. **2004-12**—Correction of brake judder, or dragging. **2006-13**—Troubleshooting a clunk, bang, or jolt from the front of vehicle upon takeoff. Fuel gauge indicates Empty when there is gas in the tank. Bubbled HID headlight housing. Inoperative smart key; insufficient charging. **2010-12**—Corrective measures relative to cleaning rust on the bottom of the rear door guide. Bluetooth hands-free diagnostic tips.

MAZDA5

RATING: Above Average (2011-14); Average (2006-11). All the advantages of a small minivan, without the fuel penalty. Based broadly on the Mazda3, the Mazda5 carries six passengers in three rows of seats. Used mostly for urban errands and light commuting, this people-hauler employs a peppy, though fuel-frugal, 157 hp 2.5L 4-cylinder engine hooked to a standard 6-speed manual transmission or a 5-speed automatic. Apart from a restyled front end and interior, the 2014 is practically identical to last year's model. Consider buying a discounted, almost identical 2012 or 2013 version. **Road performance:** Agile, no-surprise handling. Drivers will find this Mazda a breeze to park and easy to manoeuvre with its tight turning radius and direct steering. The small 4-cylinder engine doesn't have much torque ("grunt," or pulling power) for heavy loads or hill climbing, and towing isn't recommended. Some body roll when cornering, and steering is somewhat vague. **Strong points:** This small minivan is a relatively tall and narrow car – it looks like a long hatchback – with a thick, obtrusive front A-pillar. Reasonably priced; decent fuel economy; a comfortable ride; dual sliding rear doors; an easy-access liftgate; and relatively quiet interior (except for omnipresent road noise – a common trait with small wagons). The cabin is roomy, and two wide-opening sliding doors make for easy access and are a great help when installing a child safety seat. Anothert advantage is that this mini-minivan is the perfect vehicle for servicing by cheaper independent garages. It hasn't changed much over the years, and its generic parts are available practically anywhere. **Weak points:** There isn't much room for passengers in the third-row seat, and the interior seats may be too firm for some. There's also a history of automatic transmission malfunctions (but no more than with Honda or Toyota vehicles), premature wearout of suspension components and brake rotors and pads. So-so fit and finish. Very few owner complaints recorded, except for the suspension, brakes, and fuel system (fuel pumps, mostly):

> The vehicle again suddenly shut down while driving on the highway. During this incident, not only was I about 80 miles [130 km] away from home, but I was traveling with 5 children in the vehicle! At this point, I became very concerned for the safety of my children in the car! The possibility that an accident could occur if my car lost power and another vehicle impacted the rear of the vehicle; or if I wasn't able to properly steer the vehicle was extremely high on such a busy highway!

Fit and finish glitches are quite common. Owners also report a few automatic transmission failures; transmission gear hunting and fluid leaks; power-steering malfunctions; electrical system shorts; rapid tire wear and the airbag warning light and Traction Stability Control (TSC) light may come on for no reason. **Major redesign:** 2006 and 2010. **Highway/city fuel economy:** *Man.:* 6.8/9.7 L/100 km. *Auto.:* 6.7/9.5 L/100 km. **Best alternatives:** Any Honda Civic but the redesigned 2012 model, Hyundai Tucson, and Toyota Corolla, Camry, or Matrix.

SAFETY: NHTSA's front- and side-impact crashworthiness rating for the 2010 model is five stars, and rollover resistance scored four stars.

Prices and Specs

Prices (Firm): *GS:* $21,795, *Auto.:* $22,995, *GT:* $24,395, *Auto.:* $25,595 **Freight:** $1,695 **Powertrain (Front-drive):** Engine: 2.5L 4-cyl. (157 hp); Transmissions: 6-speed man., 5-speed auto. **Dimensions/capacity:** Passengers: 2/2/2; Wheelbase: 108.2 in.; H: 64.1/L: 181.5/W: 68.7 in.; Headroom F/R1/R2: 4.5/4.5/2 in.; Legroom F/R1/R2: 41/29.5/22 in.; Cargo volume: 39 cu. ft.; Fuel tank: 60L/regular; Tow limit: No towing; Load capacity: 1,020 lb.; Turning circle: 37 ft.; Ground clearance: 5.9 in.; Weight: 3,408-3,465 lb.

ALERT! Mazda is mulling over the idea of replacing the spare tire with a repair kit in the trunk.

Mazda5 Profile

	2004	2005	2006	2007	2008	2009	2010	2011	2012
Used Values ($)									
300	—	—	14,000	—	—	—	—	—	—
330	10,000	12,500	15,000	—	—	—	—	—	—
350	—	—	—	15,500	17,500	22,000	26,000	31,000	36,500
400h	—	—	15,500	16,000	20,000	22,500	—	—	—
450h	—	—	—	—	—	—	32,000	41,000	47,500
Recommended	☆	☆	☆	☆	☆	☆	☆	☆	☆
Reliability	☆	☆	☆	☆	☆	☆	☆	☆	☆

SECRET WARRANTIES, INTERNAL BULLETINS: 2008-12—Bluetooth hands-free trouble-shooting. Headlights don't come on with parking lights. **2008-13**—Tips on getting rid of excessive sulfur odours.

MAZDA 626/ MAZDA6 ★★★★★

RATING: Recommended (2014); Above Average (2003-13); Average (2000-02). A car enthusiast's family sedan. Although earlier models weren't as refined or as sporty as the competition, notably, the Honda's Accord, the 2014 is an all-around winner. Its redesign makes the car roomier, acceleration smoother and more responsive, increases fuel economy, and adds more interior refinements. One caveat: Wait six months for the dust and prices to settle. You are likely to end up with a better made, cheaper car. **Road performance:** Good powertrain setup; very agile, with nice overall handling; responsive, precise steering; a tight turning circle; all independent suspension; and impressive braking. Ride quality is relatively firm. **Strong points:** Comfortable seating, and acceptable workmanship. High prices can be easily bargained down as the model year plays out. **Weak points:** Excessive road noise intrudes into the cabin; an unusually low roofline restricts access into the interior; the touch screen interface isn't user-friendly, nor as advanced as systems used by competitors, and the V6 can increase your fuel consumption by almost 20 percent. Mazda has a history of automatic transmission, suspension system, and fit and finish deficiencies. This is reinforced by owner complaints of minor problems with the transmission, electrical, and fuel systems. Also many reports of paint delamination and peeling. **Major redesign:** 1998, 2003, 2009, and 2014. Take note that the arrival of the 2014 Mazda6 diesel has been delayed until April 2014 due to problems with U.S. government emissions tests. **Highway/city fuel economy:** *2.5 man.:* 6.6/9.8 L/100 km. *2.5 auto.:* 6.5/9.4 L/100 km. *3.7:* 7.9/11.9 L/100 km. **Best alternatives:** Honda Accord, Hyundai Tucson, Nissan Altima, and Toyota Camry or Matrix.

SAFETY: NHTSA gives its top, five-star score to the 2013 Mazda6 for rollover protection, four stars for side crashworthiness, and three stars for frontal crash safety. Also, IIHS gives the 2012 its top, "Good" score for frontal offset and side occupant protection. Roof strength is rated "Acceptable," and head restraints get a "Marginal" score.

ALERT! For most people, the 4-cylinder engine has power to spare for most driving needs. Don't opt for a more expensive, less fuel-efficient V6 before test-driving a model with the smaller engine.

Mazda 626/Mazda6 Profile

	2004	2005	2006	2007	2008	2009	2010	2011	2012
Used Values ($)									
Mazda6 GS	4,000	5,500	6,500	8,000	9,500	10,500	12,500	15,500	18,000
GT	4,500	6,000	7,000	8,500	10,500	12,500	15,500	18,500	22,000
Recommended	✫	✫	✫	✫	✫	✫	✫	✫	✫
Reliability	✫	✫	✫	✫	✫	✫	✫	✫	✫

SECRET WARRANTIES, INTERNAL BULLETINS: 2003-12—Corrective repairs for brake judder or dragging. **2003-13**—Tips on eliminating excessive sulfur odours. **2007-11**—Excessive water/condensation in headlamps. **2009**—Poor AC performance; engine runs hot. Excessive manual transmission noise when shifting. Transmission servo-cover fluid leaks. Inaccurate fuel gauge. A Hyundai Campaign (MSP 22) will repair an electrical short that causes the wipers and headlights to work erratically. **2009-10**—Engine runs hot, poor AC performance. Manual transmission hard to shift into Third or Fourth gear. Diagnosing why the automatic transmission defaults to a "limp home" mode. Silencing drivetrain squeak noises. Premature front brake pad wear. Rear door locks inoperative in freezing temperatures. Front door speaker rattling. An electrical short circuit may cause the horn to intermittently self-activate. Rear taillight heat deformation. **2009-11**—Fix for front brakes that click or pop when applied. Repair tips for an inoperative sunroof. **2009-12**—Bluetooth hands-free troubleshooting. Improving poor AC performance. **2010**—Free fix for A-pillar water leaks. **2011-12**—Headlights may not come on with the parking lights. **2012**— Plugging water leaks from the left A-pillar/cowl area.

MIATA MX-5 ★★★★★

RATING: Recommended (1996-2014); Above Average (1990-95). Any discounted 2006-14 model would be an excellent buy, however, the 2012 version also includes electronic stability control – a good safety feature for any small sports car. For almost three decades, the Miata has proven to be an exceptionally fine-performing, time-tested, and reasonably-priced modern roadster. It's still a stubby, lightweight, rear-drive, two-seater convertible that combines new technology with old British roadster styling reminiscent of the Triumph, the Austin-Healy, and the Lotus Elan. It comes in a variety of trim levels: The three convertibles are the Sport, Touring, and Grand Touring. The fourth model is the Touring (Power-

Retractable) Hard Top. The lineup begins with the soft-top-only Sport; a removable hardtop is available as an option. All models come with a heated glass rear window. **Road performance:** Well-matched powertrain provides better-than-expected acceleration and top-end power at the 7000 rpm range; classic sports car handling; perfectly weighted steering with plenty of road feedback; and a firm but comfortable suspension. **Strong points:** It's amazing how well the MX-5 is put together, considering that it isn't particularly innovative and most parts are borrowed from Mazda's other models. For example, the engine is taken from the Mazda3 and Mazda6, and the suspension belongs to the RX-8. The MX-5 is shorter than most other sports cars; nevertheless, this is a fun car to drive, costing much less than other vehicles in its class. Impressive braking; mirrors are bigger and more effective than those found in most luxury sports cars; engine is fairly quiet, and little road noise intrudes into the cabin; instruments and controls are easy to read and access; good fuel economy; user-friendly trunk; manual top is easy to operate; very few safety- or performance-related defects; and a high resale value. **Weak points:** All the things that make roadsters so much "fun:" a compact cabin, difficult entry and exit, and a can of tire sealant instead of a spare tire. Some minor driveline, fuel system, and fit and finish complaints. Headlight beams blind oncoming drivers:

I have to apply tape over the driver side headlight to "fix" the problem and now I get zero bright beam flashes from oncoming cars. Other auto manufacturers offer the same type of lighting for their products, but they also install a dial that is used to adjust the light beams up and down. This car does not have such a device. Affixing an ugly piece of tape to my car is not what I expected when I paid $34,000 for this automobile.

Major redesign: 1999 and 2006. The 2006 redesign gave the car a firmer, more refined chassis, increased engine power, a larger interior, and better interior amenities. **Highway/city fuel economy:** *5-speed man.: 7.1/9.2 L/100 km. 6-speed man.: 7.1/9.7 L/100 km. 6-speed auto.: 7.2/10.1 L/100 km.* **Best alternatives:** The BMW Z cars, Chevrolet Camaro, Infiniti G37 Coupe, Mercedes-Benz SLK, and Porsche Boxster.

Prices and Specs

Prices (Firm): *GX:* $28,995, *Auto.:* $29,995, *GS:* $33,495, *Auto.:* $33,495, *GT:* $39,995, *Auto.:* $41,195 **Freight:** $1,695 **Powertrain (Rear-drive):** Engine: 2.0L 4-cyl. (167 hp); Transmissions: 5-speed man., 6-speed man., 6-speed auto. **Dimensions/capacity:** Passengers: 2; Wheelbase: 92 in.; H: 49/L: 157/W: 68 in.; Headroom: 1.5 in.; Legroom: 40 in.; Cargo volume: 5 cu. ft.; Fuel tank: 48L/regular; Tow limit: N/A; Load capacity: 340 lb.; Turning circle: 30.8 ft.; Ground clearance: 4.6 in.; Weight: 2,458–2,632 lb.

SAFETY: The 2005 earned five stars for rollover protection, four stars for frontal crashworthiness, and three stars for side-impact protection, but NHTSA hasn't crash tested the MX-5 since then. No IIHS crash scores. Restricted rear visibility with the top up.

ALERT! Car's a neon sign saying "come and get me" to thieves. An engine disabler and GPS tracker are your best anti-theft devices. Forget about lights, alarms, and steering-wheel locks.

Miata MX-5 Profile

	2004	2005	2006	2007	2008	2009	2010	2011	2012
Used Values ($)									
GX	5,500	7,000	9,000	11,000	12,000	13,500	16,500	19,000	20,000
GS/SV	6,000	7,500	9,500	12,500	13,500	14,500	18,500	22,000	23,000
GT	6,500	8,500	11,000	13,000	14,500	17,500	22,000	26,000	27,000
Recommended	★	★	★	★	★	★	★	★	★
Reliability	★	★	★	★	★	★	★	★	★

SECRET WARRANTIES, INTERNAL BULLETINS: 2006-12—Brake judder or dragging. **2006-13**—Clunk, bang, jolt from front of vehicle at takeoff is considered "normal" by Mazda. Dealing with excessive sulfur odours. **2007-12**—Silencing hardtop rattles at the windshield header. **2009-12**— Bluetooth hands-free troubleshooting tips. **2012-13**—Attending to leather seat wrinkles.

CX-5/CX-7/CX-9 ★★★★★

good buy

The Mazda CX-7.

RATING: *CX-5:* Recommended (2013-14); *CX-7:* Average (2007-10); Above Average (2011-12). *CX-9:* Above Average (2007); Recommended (2008-14). The CX-5 is a late arrival to the CX corral. It's a small SUV with taut handling and quick, responsive steering. Of course due to the car's size, the ride is a bit choppy and there is some road noise. CX-7 is a small five-passenger front-drive and AWD SUV crossover. It debuted as a 2007 model and was one of Mazda's bestselling models until it was axed in 2012. CX-9 is not an extended CX-7, yet. In fact, it shares its platform with the popular Ford Edge and adds a better interior in the process. Ford's DNA makes the "9" a quieter-running and more agile performer than its smaller brothers. There has been strong demand for both cars, and that may be their saving grace because the more CXs sold, the better servicing and supply should become. The ditching of the CX-7 has had little effect on CX-5 and CX-9 sales. **Road performance:** *CX-5:* The powertrain is adequate for most duties, but the engine quickly loses steam when merging with traffic or going up-hill with a load. In return, the car gives impressive fuel economy. *CX-7:* Mazda's first mid-size SUV since the Navajo was discontinued in 1994, the CX-7 is well equipped; turbocharged engine has power to spare; and excellent handling, with a relatively tight turning radius and responsive steering. Base engine is a so-so performer, and the turbocharged version is hampered by considerable "turbo lag," which increases the response time from the throttle to the engine. Both engines are also relatively noisy, with the 2.5L producing a coarse drone and the turbo powerplant emitting an annoying whine. Irregular roadways give occupants a shaky ride. *CX-9:* The Ford-sourced 273 hp 3.7L V6, introduced with the 2008 model, delivers plenty of power with little noise or delay. Handling is better than average, and the ride is fairly smooth and quiet over irregular terrain. **Strong points:** All models have better than average reliability. *CX-5:* Impressive fuel economy, a relatively roomy cabin, and simple controls. *CX-7:* Plenty of cargo room, and good all-around visibility. *CX-9:* Even roomier, with more headroom, legroom, and storage space. Instruments and controls are nicely laid out and not hard to master. Third-row seating is surprisingly acceptable. **Weak points:** *CX-7:* Ride comfort is so-so and may be a bit too firm for some; tall occupants may find headroom too limited; rear seating is a bit low and cramped; and interior garnishing seems a bit on the cheap side. Mediocre fuel economy; the turbo-equipped model requires premium fuel. Drivers have reported minor engine problems in addition to fuel system, brake, and fit and finish deficiencies. Excessive condensation in the front headlights; accelerator and brake pedals are mounted too close together; and persistent brake squeaking, groaning. *CX-9:* Braking distance is a bit long. Gas consumption

Prices and Specs

Price (Firm): *CX-5 GX FWD:* $22,995, *GS FWD:* $28,650, *GS AWD:* $30,250, *GT AWD:* $33,250, *CX-9 GS:* $33,995, *CX-9 GT:* $44,750 **Freight:** $1,695 **Powertrain (Front-drive/AWD):** Engines: *CX-5:* 2.0L 4-cyl. (155 hp) *CX-9:* 3.7L V6 (273 hp); Transmissions: *CX-7:* 5-speed auto., 6-speed auto.; *CX-9:* 6-speed auto. **Dimensions/capacity:** *CX-7 and CX-9:* Passengers: 2/3, 2/3/2; Wheelbase: 108.2 in., 113.2 in.; H: 52.7, 68/L: 184.3, 200.8/W: 73.7, 76.2 in.; Cargo volume: 29.9 cu. ft., 37.5 cu. ft.; Fuel tank: 69L, 76L/regular or premium; Tow limit: 2,000 lb., 3,500 lb.; Load capacity: 1,190 lb.; Turning circle: 37.4 ft.; Ground clearance: 8.1 in., 8 in.; Weight: 3,500-4,007 lb., 4,265-4,585 lb.

is relatively high. Among the few registered complaints, we find early brake wear, poor fit and finish, and audio system malfunctions. **Major redesign:** *CX-7:* Launched in 2007 and replaced by the 2013 CX-5. *CX-9:* 2008 engine swap. **Highway/city fuel economy:** *CX-7 2.5L:* 7.2/10.4 L/100 km. *CX-7 2.3L:* 8.7/12.2 L/100 km. *CX-9 front-drive:* 9.1/13.4 L/100 km. *AWD:* 9.6 /14.0 L/100 km. **Best alternatives:** The Chevrolet Equinox or Traverse, Ford Flex, GMC Acadia or Terrain, Honda Pilot, Hyundai Tucson or Santa Fe, and Toyota Highlander.

SAFETY: In NHTSA tests, the 2013 CX-5 side crashworthiness merited five stars, while frontal and rollover protection scored four stars each. The 2012 CX-7 and CX-9 rollover protection was rated four stars. Rear visibility is limited.

ALERT! Owners say gauges on the instrument panel are hard to read at night and in bright sunlight. Check it out.

CX-7/CX-9 Profile

	2007	2008	2009	2010	2011	2012
Used Values ($)						
CX-7	8,000	9,000	11,000	13,500	16,500	19,500
AWD	8,500	9,500	12,000	15,000	18,500	22,500
GT	9,000	10,000	—	—	—	—
AWD	9,500	10,500	13,500	18,500	22,500	27,500
CX-9	10,500	11,500	14,500	19,000	22,500	27,500
AWD	11,000	12,500	15,500	20,000	24,000	29,000
GT	11,500	—	—	—	—	—
AWD	12,000	13,000	17,000	22,500	27,000	33,000
Recommended	★	★	★	★	☆	☆
Reliability	★	☆	☆	☆	☆	☆

SECRET WARRANTIES, INTERNAL BULLETINS: 2006-12—Bluetooth hands-free troubleshooting tips. Silencing Bose speaker noise. Removing excessive sulfur odours. First aid for wrinkled leather seats. A remedy for excessive vibration from the floor or steering wheel during acceleration; front brake squeaking. *CX-5:* **2013-14**—Noisy front suspension struts may plague some CX-5 crossovers. In TSB #0200513 issued on May 24, 2013, Mazda said the knocking or squeaking noise was caused by a damaged strut bearing. A new bearing will restore the silence. *CX-7:* **2007-12**—Fixing a partly detached rear spoiler. **2010-12**—Door armrest trim peeling. *CX-7 and CX-9:* **2007-11**—These Mazdas may leak oil from the rear differential seal. In TSB #0300411 Mazda says the differential breather was placed too low and could easily become clogged by snow or water. A new differential with a raised breather covered by the breather boot will be installed for free on a case-by-case basis.

FRONT BRAKES SQUEAK ON BRAKE APPLICATION

BULLETIN NO.: 04-006/11   DATE: NOVEMBER 30, 2011

FRONT BRAKES SQUEAK WHEN APPLYING BRAKES

After parking in cold temperatures accompanied by a humid climate, some vehicles may exhibit a squeak from the front brakes during initial braking. This noise is caused due to deterioration of grease between the front disc pads, shims and the brake caliper. Customers having this concern should have their vehicle repaired using the following repair procedure.

REPAIR PROCEDURE: When you encounter a customer complaint, remove the disc pads (A) (right and left) and attach protectors to the original guide plates (B), then apply white grease to the location indicated on the caliper (C) and mounting support (D) according to the following procedures.

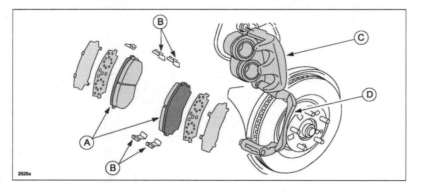

MITSUBISHI

Mitsus' new Mirage econobox: A Yogi Berra "déjà vu, all over, again" econobox? (See Appendix I.)

NISSAN

Nissan, Honda, and Toyota were hurt the most by the March 2011 Fukushima earthquake, a tsunami, and subsequent nuclear plant meltdowns in Japan. Nevertheless, all three companies have returned to normal production, with Nissan introducing a revised lineup of models that cover almost every marketing niche, with a few models that defy description (like the small Cube and Juke).

The Cube (above) ends its run this year.

The 2013 model year saw a redesigned Altima, Sentra, and Pathfinder and this year Nissan brings out more new products, like NV200 Compact Cargo commercial van, a stylish entry-level Versa Note hatchback, the reworked Rogue compact SUV, and an all-new Pathfinder Hybrid. Significant enhancements are offered in 2014 for Altima, Frontier, GT-R (including the limited production Track Edition and upcoming Special Edition Package), Versa Sedan, Xterra and 370Z NISMO.

On the infotainment front, Nissan will offer this year its all-new NissanConnect Apps smartphone integration platform on selected models like the Altima and Sentra. The company plans to expand this feature throughout its lineup by 2015.

Judging by the last few years of complaints sent in by *Lemon-Aid* readers and reports received by government and private agencies, Nissan quality control has picked up considerably, though owners still complain about fuel-delivery systems, brake and original-equipment tire durability, climate controls, and fit and finish. The Altima, Murano, and Rogue models continue to have the fewest complaints.

Nevertheless, Nissan pinches pennies when it comes to its "goodwill" extended warranties used to correct factory-related defects. For example, last year, the company extended its radiator warranty on 2005-10 Frontiers, Pathfinders, and Xterras to eight years or 129,000 km (80,000 mi) to fix a coolant-leak problem, caused by "a cracked oil cooler tube." Nissan assured owners it would cover "damage, repairs, replacement, and related towing resulting from this issue."

But the devil is most certainly in the details. What Nissan doesn't mention is that the radiator cooler tanks are rupturing, which forces the coolant into the transmission through the transmission cooler lines, causing the trannies to self-destruct in as little as 60,000 km (37,000 mi). Nissan insiders says the company is settling claims for transmission replacements on a "case-by-case basis." Angry Nissan SUV and truck owners faced with $6,000 (U.S.) repair bills want the eight-year extended warranty – extended – to cover transmission damage.

VERSA ★★★

RATING: Average (2007-14). The 2013 added a stylish exterior design, well-appointed interior, more standard features that would cost extra on competing models, and exceptional room for five adults. **Road performance:** Base engine lacks "grunt" at higher rpms and produces an annoying drone when pushed; the manual 6-speed is a bit clunky; the suspension is tuned more to the soft side; the rear drum brakes are less effective; there is no stability control on some models; and a 6-speed manual transmission is available, whereas most small cars offer only a 4- or 5-speed gearbox. The car's larger wheelbase makes for a smooth ride. The 1.8L 4-cylinder engine provides plenty of power, and handling is responsive and predictable, thanks to the tight, power-assisted steering and independent front suspension. **Strong points:** Good-quality interior appointments; tilt steering column. Versa offers a lot more interior room than what is found with other compact cars in its class, thanks to a tall roofline that also makes for easy access. Visibility is first rate, and there's minimal road noise. The fuel tank dwarfs the mini-car field, where most tanks are 45L; standard 15-inch wheels are used, versus the competition's 14-inchers; and the Versa carries a 122 hp engine, while the other micro cars get by with 103-110 hp powerplants. Very few owner complaints recorded. **Weak points:** Owners say real-world fuel consumption is about 20 percent higher than what is represented. Mediocre defrosting. No illumination of the unlock/lock tabs on the inside panel of the front doors:

All the doors lock automatically once the car is driven, I believe that the unlock/lock tabs need to be illuminated [so] that driver and passenger can quickly see the unlock tabs so we can get out of the car. We are literally locked into our cars and cannot see to get out of our car whenever it is dark.

Car can't be shifted into Reverse; it has to be turned off to unlock the doors; key sticks in the ignition, and complaints of hard starting; speedometer can't be read in daylight; and only the driver-side door can be unlocked from the outside. Owners also report some problems with the fuel and climate systems, paint, and body integrity. **Major redesign:** 2007 and 2012. **Highway/city fuel economy:** *1.6L man.:* 5.4/7.5 L/100 km. *1.8L man.:* 6.3/7.9 L/100 km. *1.8L auto.:* 6.2/8.5 L/100 km. 2014 Note: Combined gas mileage is 4.8L/100 km. **Best alternatives:** Get the 2013 hatchback coupled to a 6-speed manual transmission for the best

Prices and Specs

Prices (Negotiable): *1.6 S Sedan:* $11,898, *Note:* $13,348, *SV:* $13,878, *SL:* $16,378, *1.8 S Hatchback:* $14,678, *SV:* $15,678, *Hatchback SL:* $17,678, *Auto.:* $18,978 **Freight:** $1,567 **Powertrain (Front-drive):** Engines: 1.6L 4-cyl. (107 hp), 1.8L 4-cyl. (122 hp); Transmissions: 5-speed man., 6-speed man., CVT, 4-speed auto. **Dimensions/capacity:** Passengers: 2/3; Wheelbase: 102.4 in.; H: 60.4/L: 169.1/W: 66.7 in.; Headroom F/R: 5/3.5 in.; Legroom F/R: 40/30 in.; Cargo volume: 17.8 cu. ft., 13.8 cu. ft.; Fuel tank: 50L/regular; Tow limit: N/A; Load capacity: 860 lb.; Turning circle: 37 ft.; Ground clearance: 5 in.; Weight: 2,538-2,758 lb.

overall performance and highest residual value. Other contenders: Honda Fit, Hyundai Accent, and Mazda2.

 SAFETY: Not great crash protection scores. NHTSA gave the 2012-14 models four stars, but the 2011 version only scored two stars for overall crash safety. The 2012 merited three stars for front and side crash protection, while rollover resistance garnered four stars. Earlier Versas got better overall scores from NHTSA: Four and five stars: for the 2007-10s. IIHS's moderate overlap frontal test results on the 2007-12 models were "Good;" side impacts on the 2011-12s were "Acceptable," while 2007-10 versions were rated "Good." Rear impact protection for the 2007-13 models was judged "Good," while the same models' roof strength scored only an "Acceptable" rating.

ALERT! The 2013's slightly higher cost is justified by the car's added features and its relatively strong engine and roomy interior.

Versa Profile

	2007	2008	2009	2010	2011	2012
Used Values ($)						
S Hatchback	4,500	5,000	6,000	7,000	8,500	9,500
SL	5,000	6,000	7,000	8,500	11,000	12,000
S Sedan	4,000	4,500	5,000	5,500	7,000	8,000
SL	4,500	5,500	—	—	—	—
Recommended	☆	☆	☆	☆	☆	☆
Reliability	☆	☆	☆	☆	☆	☆

 SECRET WARRANTIES, INTERNAL BULLETINS: 2011-12—Troubleshooting a rear hatch that is difficult to close in cold weather. Diagnosing CVT oil leaks. Rear brake squealing. Front axle clicking. Front-seat creaking. Key sticking in the ignition, even though vehicle is in Park and shut off. Drivebelt noise troubleshooting tips. Repair tips for a malfunctioning fuel gauge. There's also a voluntary service program (Campaign #PM053) involving the free replacement of the instrument panel cluster and a free correction for seatbacks that won't recline.

SENTRA

RATING: Above Average (2013-14); Average (2008-12); Below Average. **Road performance:** The 2.0L engine is underpowered, but the 1.8L and 2.5L engines provide lots of power; manual transmission shifter's location may be too high and forward for some drivers; some body lean when cornering under power; occupants are treated to a quiet, comfortable, "floaty" ride; easy handling if not pushed hard; the rear end tends to fishtail a bit; some road wander; and long braking distances, probably due to the use of rear drum brakes instead of the more-effective disc brakes. **Strong points:** Unlike many bare-bones economy cars, entry-level Sentras offer dependable motoring with lots of safety, performance, and comfort. Besides making for a roomier interior, the large body produces a quieter, smoother ride. Plenty of cabin space, and the rear seat cushion can be folded forward, permitting the split rear seatback to fold flat with the floor; a commodious trunk; the locking glove box could house a laptop; and good quality control, with few safety- or performance-related defects. **Weak points:** Severe rear brake grinding and a noisy rear suspension head the list of complaints. Other reported failures: Faulty oil-pressure sensor gasket; engine piston slap; blown engine head gasket; ABS clanks, grinds, and causes excessive vibration when it is active; unstable front seats; driver's sun visor obstructs the rear-view mirror; bottom of the windshield may be distorted; tire-pressure indicator malfunctions. Problem areas also include fuel, climate, electrical, and audio systems, in addition to horrendous fit and finish deficiencies (a misaligned trunk lid and malfunctioning trunk locks, for example) that produce excessive rattling and water leaks into the interior. **Major redesign:** 2000, 2007, and 2013. The 2014s will get a recalibrated CVT transmission tuning while steering and suspension are retuned and the addition of front seat cushion storage pockets and an auto hazard warning signal. **Highway/city fuel economy:** *2.0L:* 6.4/8.4 L/100 km. *2.0L CVT:* 5.8/7.5 L/100 km. *SE-R:* 6.5/8.7 L/100 km. *Spec V:* 7.0/9.8 L/100 km. *1.8L CVT:* 5.8 L/100 km combined. Many owners say advertised fuel consumption figures aren't to be trusted. **Best alternatives:** Sentra's engine and body dimension improvements over the past few years have made it a good competitor for the Ford Focus, Honda Civic, Hyundai Elantra, and Mazda3.

Prices and Specs

Prices (Negotiable): *2.0:* $15,478, *Auto.:* $16,778, *2.0 S:* $18,878, *Auto.:* $20,178, *2.0 SL:* $23,278, *2.0 SR:* $20,178, *2.0 SE-R Spec V:* $23,478, *1.8 S:* $14,848, *1.8 SV:* $17,548 **Freight:** $1,567 **Powertrain (Front-drive):** Engine: 1.8L 4-cyl. (130 hp); Transmissions: 6-speed man., CVT **Dimensions/capacity:** Passengers: 2/3; Wheelbase: 106 in.; H: 59/L: 182/W: 69 in.; Headroom F/R: 6/2 in.; Legroom F/R: 41/26.5 in.; Cargo volume: 15 cu. ft.; Fuel tank: 50L/regular/premium; Tow limit: N/A; Load capacity: 850 lb.; Turning circle: 35.4 ft.; Ground clearance: 5.5 in.; Weight: 2,819-3,079 lb.

SAFETY: Four stars for overall crash protection were given by NHTSA to the 1991 through 2014 models. IIHS' moderate overlap frontal tests of the 2007-12 Sentras found them "Good," while side impact scores on the 2011-12s were rated "Acceptable;" and "Good" on the 2007-10 versions. Roof strength results on the 2007-12 models was scored "Acceptable." Head restraint protection varies considerably: 2013—"Good" and "Marginal;" 2010-12—"Acceptable;" 2007-09—"Good;" 2002-06—"Poor." Owner reports: Airbags failed to deploy; rear end of the car caught on fire; gas pedal is mounted too close to the brake pedal; sudden, unintended acceleration; defective computer module causes the vehicle to shut down; car can be started without driver's foot on the brake; the front side pillar obstructs the view of what lies ahead, and tall drivers will need to lean back to see the road more clearly. Car was shifted into Drive but went into Reverse instead; early replacement of Bridgestone Turanza EL400 tires; premature wearout of rear tires due to factory misalignment of the rear suspension; sudden brake loss; and brakes are hard to modulate, resulting in abrupt stops; and power-steering failures.

ALERT! Sentras are fast food mobile canteens for rodents:

> The contact owns a 2012 Nissan Sentra. The contact stated that the vehicle was parked when he noticed that mice were building nests inside of the heater vents. As a result, the blower motor failed. The vehicle was taken to an authorized dealer and the nests were cleaned out from the vents, however, mice continued to enter the vehicle and build nests inside of the heater vents.

Sentra Profile

	2004	2005	2006	2007	2008	2009	2010	2011	2012
Used Values ($)									
1.8/2.0	3,500	4,000	4,500	5,000	5,500	6,500	7,500	9,500	13,500
S	4,000	4,500	5,000	6,000	7,000	9,000	9,500	12,000	14,000
SE-R	4,500	5,000	6,000	6,500	7,500	9,500	10,500	14,500	16,500
SL	—	—	—	7,500	8,000	10,000	11,500	15,000	17,500
SE-R Spec V	5,000	5,500	6,500	8,000	8,500	9,500	12,000	15,500	18,000
Recommended	☆	☆	☆	☆	☆	☆	☆	☆	☆
Reliability	☆	☆	☆	☆	☆	☆	☆	☆	☆

SECRET WARRANTIES, INTERNAL BULLETINS: 2007-12—Front seats have a slight movement, or won't adjust. Troubleshooting an oil leak from the upper end of the oil cooler. **2011-12**—Correcting instrument cluster that may be too dim.

ENGINE – OIL LEAK FROM UPPER END OF OIL COOLER

CLASSIFICATION: EM10-002A   DATE: SEPTEMBER 6, 2011

ALTIMA SEDAN AND COUPE, SENTRA, AND ROGUE WITH FOUR-CYLINDER ENGINE OIL LEAK
2007-12 Altima Sedan; 2008-12 Altima Coupe; 2007-12 Sentra; and the 2008-12 Rogue

IF YOU CONFIRM: Oil is leaking from the upper end of the engine oil cooler.
ACTION: Reseal the oil cooler.

RATING: Not Recommended (2013-14); Average (2009-12); Not Recommended (2001-08). This car runs exceptionally well – when it runs. And, in a nutshell, that's the crux of its problem. Altima is beautifully styled and has all the performance features drivers and techno-philes could ever want. What the car lacks is quality, reliability and acceptable workmanship. This contradicts J. D. Power and Consumer Reports' high ratings for the model, but reinforces the owners' complaints and Nissan internal service bulletins studied by *Lemon-Aid*. Normally, even the best-made vehicles generate up to 50 NHTSA-registered owner complaints per model year. The reported life-threatening incidents for the 2013 model, as of August 2013, is 183 or almost four times the NHTSA "normal." And the car hasn't been out a full year. See for yourself at safercar.gov. Nissan's front-drive, mid-sized sedan stakes out territory occupied by the Honda Accord, Hyundai Sonata and Elantra, Mazda6, and Toyota Camry. The car's base 4-cylinder engine is almost as powerful as the competition's V6 powerplants, and the optional 270 hp 3.5L V6 has few equals among cars in this price and size class. And, when you consider that the Altima is much lighter than most of its competitors, it's obvious why this car produces sizzling acceleration with little fuel penalty. Four-wheel independent suspension strikes the right balance between a comfortable ride and sporty handling. The 3.5 S, 3.5 SE, and SR models add even more performance and luxury enhancements. **Road performance:** A powerful 4-cylinder engine delivers good fuel economy, and an even better V6 provides scintillating acceleration with only a small fuel penalty. When working properly (see below), the CVT transmission adds to overall driving comfort:

> The CVT transmission causes the vehicle to shutter and vibrate at light acceleration between 1200-2000 RPMs ... I have been told repeatedly that Nissan engineers are aware of the problem and are working on a solution. There are many, many complaints of this same issue on several websites ... They acknowledge the problem ... There answer is they have done the recommended service bulletins work sent to them from Nissan to repair this problem.

Handling is only so-so, though it is best with the soft-sprung 2.5 S, whereas the pricier 3.5 SE models come equipped with a firmer suspension and wider tires. **Strong points:** Good braking; well laid-out instruments and controls; and fuel frugal with the 2.5 engine, which also gives a better ride. Better-than-average interior room on 2013-14s. **Weak points:** Absolutely abysmal quality control; a small trunk; a snug interior with limited headroom and insufficient space for three (2012 and earlier models). **Major redesign:** 1998, 2002, 2007, and 2013. **Highway/city fuel economy:** *2.5:* 6.2/8.8 L/100 km. *CVT:* 6.0/8.7 L/100 km. *Coupe:* 6.3/9.0 L/100 km. *Auto.:* 6.2/8.9 L/100 km. *3.5 sedan:* 7.2/10.2 L/100 km. *Coupe:* 7.3/11.4 L/100 km *Auto.:* 7.3/10.2 L/100 km. *Hybrid:* 5.9/5.6 L/100 km. **Best alternatives:** Altimas depreciate quickly, making them poor new-car buys, but cheap used-cars. For example, a top-of-the-line 2008 Maxima SL that sold new for $41,498 now costs only $11,000 and can easily last another six years, if you can live with its defects. The larger redesigned 2013-14 Altima would be the model of choice, if not for its quality shortcomings. Stay away from leftover Hybrid models, though. They are no longer built and are overall poor performers. Other choices: The Honda Accord, Hyundai Elantra, Mazda6, and Toyota Camry.

 SAFETY: NHTSA gave the 2011-14 models four- and five-star scores following their crash safety tests. Earlier models through 2004 got similar high scores beginning in 1993, though the 1998 side-impact test only gave two stars for passenger protection. IIHS moderate overlap frontal crash safety tests scored the 2002-13 cars "Good;" 2000-01s were "Marginal." Small overlap performance was judged "Acceptable" on the 2007-13s and "Poor" for the 2004-06 models. Roof strength was "Good" for the 2013s; "Acceptable" for the 2007-12 models. Rear crashworthiness was judged "Good" for the 2013 model; "Acceptable" for the 2009-12; "Marginal" for the 2007-08s, and, again "Acceptable" for the 2005-06 models. NHTSA-posted safety complaints: Airbags failed to deploy; passenger-side airbag shuts off when the seat is occupied by a normal-sized occupant; and sudden, unintended acceleration:

> I used my automatic start … the car started and was warming up. As I approached my running car, I walked in front of the car to get around to the driver's side. I opened the driver's side door and the car accelerated and took off moving forward with nobody in it. I was holding onto the door chasing after my car trying to jump in and put my foot on the brake to stop the car. I was unsuccessful as the car ran into another car in the parking lot and came to an abrupt stop. My car was damaged and still running. The parked car that it hit was damaged. Upon impact, I was thrown against the open door and then onto the pavement on my back/right side. Many people were exiting church and gathered around. … It is fortunate that nobody was hit/run over by this "run-away" car.

Defective fuel-pump fuse makes it impossible to shut off the engine; vehicle may jerk violently when accelerating; abrupt downshifts; car "drifts" constantly; while cruising, car suddenly veered to the right as the steering froze; loss of power steering; transmission popped out of gear; premature clutch failure; loss of brakes; frequent AC, electrical, and fuel system failures; headlights don't cast a wide enough beam; windshield cracks for no reason:

> Please investigate if the windshields on 2013 Nissan Altima's are defective in nature. That is, do these windshields have a propensity to easily crack possibly due to weakness or defective manufacturing? Our 2013 Altima which has less than 3000 miles suffered a crack windshield passenger side. Other drivers have also seen this. (*www.carcomplaints.com/Nissan/Altima/2013/windows_windshield/windshield_cracked.shtml*) This does not appear to be an isolated incident.

And the ignition key may inadvertently start the car:

If you leave the key outside the vehicle and it is touching the vehicle, the push-button ignition will acknowledge the key and start the vehicle. According to the manual the key must be with you (inside) in order for the vehicle to start. There is no warning stating otherwise.

See Service Bulletin EM10-002A (dated September 6, 2011) under Sentra.

BRAKE MASTER CYLINDER

BULLETIN NO.: NTB12-001A   **DATE: APRIL 3, 2012**

VOLUNTARY SERVICE CAMPAIGN

2007–12 Altima Sedan & Coupe Brake Master Cylinder

INTRODUCTION: Nissan is conducting a Voluntary Service Campaign on Model Year 2007–12 Nissan Altima Sedan and Coupe vehicles to inspect the brake systems in vehicles with an illuminated brake warning lamp. If no leak is present, the reservoir will be topped off. If a leak in the brake master cylinder is identified, the brake master cylinder will be replaced for free.

Prices and Specs

Prices: *2.5 S:* $23,998, *Auto.:* $25,298, *3.5 S:* $28,498, *3.5 SR:* $32,098, *2.5 S Coupe:* $27,698, *Auto.:* $28,998, *3.5 SR Coupe:* $35,298, *Auto.:* $36,598 **Freight:** $1,595 **Powertrain (Front-drive):** Engines: 2.5L 4-cyl. (182 hp), 3.5L V6 (270 hp); Transmissions: 6-speed man. CVT **Dimensions/capacity:** *2.5S:* Passengers: 2/3; Wheelbase: 109.3 in.; H: 57.9/L: 190.7/W: 70.7. in.; Headroom F/R: 4.5/2 in.; Legroom F/R: 41.5/29 in.; Cargo volume: 7.4-13.1 cu. ft.; Fuel tank: 76L/regular; Tow limit: 1,000 lb.; Load capacity: 900 lb.; Turning circle: 34.6 ft.; Ground clearance: 5.4 in.; Weight: 3,168-3,492 lb.

ALERT! In your test drive, check out these three safety-related design deficiencies reported by other owners:

1. Painful front head restraints:

   The contact owns a 2013 Nissan Altima. The contact stated that the headrest caused the contact back pain, headaches and numbness in the arm. The contact took the vehicle back to the dealer where the dealer turned the headrest around. The contact stated that after the headrest was turned, there was no more pain.

2. A crooked driver's seat:

   The driver's seat is crooked—both across the back and across the seat. This means one's shoulders and torso are twisted and facing the center console, not the steering wheel. Hips are uneven with the right side significantly lower than the left. This is a very uncomfortable and painful position to be in. I have been informed by the dealership that all 2012 Altimas are like this and therefore it is not a warranty item! I have been able to determine the back of the seat is in fact crooked in the more than two dozen examples I have been able to check. However, the seat bottom is not supposed to sag or be uneven on either side. I've contacted Nissan North America and have been told the dealership is my only avenue to pursue a remedy. Due to the dealership's determination that the seat is supposed to be crooked, my choices are pay someone else or try myself to shim the entire seat or try to adjust the mechanism underneath to level the bottom. Nothing can be done about the seat back.

3. Brake and gas pedals that are mounted too close together:

My husband complained of this a few weeks ago when he drove my car because his shoe got caught on the brake pedal as he was lifting his foot off the gas pedal. Then, yesterday, the same thing happened to me. I nearly drove my car through the front of the daycare where I was dropping off my son. I am now aware of how extra-cautious I have to be when driving my car so this doesn't happen again. This has never happened to me with any other car. I've been driving for 25 years!

Altima Profile

	2004	2005	2006	2007	2008	2009	2010	2011	2012
Used Values ($)									
S Coupe	—	—	—	—	9,500	12,000	15,000	18,500	21,500
SE/SR	—	—	—	—	11,500	13,500	18,500	22,000	26,000
S Sedan	4,000	5,500	7,000	8,000	9,500	11,000	13,500	16,000	18,500
3.5 S	—	6,000	7,500	8,500	10,500	13,000	15,500	19,000	22,500
SE/SR	4,500	6,500	8,000	9,000	11,000	13,500	16,500	20,000	23,500
Hybrid	—	—	—	7,500	9,000	12,500	15,500	18,500	—
Recommended	☆	☆	☆	☆	☆	☆	☆	☆	☆
Reliability	☆	☆	☆	☆	☆	☆	☆	☆	☆

SECRET WARRANTIES, INTERNAL BULLETINS: 2007-12—Front seats bind, won't move fore or aft. Inoperative driver power seat lumbar support. **2008-12**—Buzzing wind noise from the A-pillar/mirror area. **2009**—Nissan set up a special Campaign (#PCO 44) to prevent the front windshield wipers from scraping the windshield. Parts and labour are Nissan's responsibility. Another Campaign (#PC005) provides free replacement of the rear suspension knuckle. **2011-12**—Oil may leak from the upper end of the engine oil cooler (see the Sentra profile). Steering/suspension drift. Sunroof water leak. Rear end clunking. Knocking on turns. Brake master cylinder may slowly leak fluid. **2013**—Shuddering at moderate speeds could indicate problems with the transmission torque converter in certain Altimas and Pathfinders. TSB #13-064A issued on June 13, 2013, says the shaking in 2013 V6-equipped models could be a sign that the torque converter is defective and needs to be replaced. The bulletin only covers a shudder occurring at 18-35 mph.

MAXIMA

RATING: Recommended (2007-14); Average (2005-06); Not Recommended (2004); Above Average (2000-03). Incredible! The 2013 Maxima generated only one safety-related NHTSA-registered complaint during last year, when 50 or so incidents would have been expected. Plus, the 2009 and earlier redesigns didn't produce more than a handful of complaints. Could it be that Nissan has finally shaken the poor-quality Quest and Altima monkeys off its back? Nevertheless, this front-drive, mid-sized model soldiers on as Nissan's luxury flagship, a competent and roomy sedan that's a mini-step above the bestselling Altima. The 290 hp 3.5L V6 is coupled to a continuously variable transmission, and the vehicle comes with an impressive array of standard equipment and a host of performance and safety features, such as large front brakes with full brake assist, a power driver's seat, xenon headlights, and 18-inch wheels. Granted, you get plenty of horsepower, comfort, and gadgets, but unfortunately the car isn't backed up with all the technical refinements and quality components provided by the competition. **Road performance:** The powerful V6 engine and smooth-shifting automatic transmission provide a comfortable, secure ride. Handling is compromised by steering that's overboosted at low speeds and then suddenly firms up. The 18-inch tires produce high-speed tire whine. **Strong**

Prices and Specs

Price (Negotiable): *3.5 SV:* $39,800 **Freight:** $1,620 **Powertrain (Front-drive):** Engine: 3.5L V6 (290 hp); Transmission: CVT **Dimensions/capacity:** Passengers: 2/3; Wheelbase: 109.3 in.; H: 57.8/L: 190.6/W: 73.2 in.; Headroom F/R: 4/2 in.; Legroom F/R: 42/30 in.; Cargo volume: 14.2 cu. ft.; Fuel tank: 70L/premium; Tow limit: 1,000 lb.; Load capacity: 900 lb.; Turning circle: 37.4 ft.; Ground clearance: 5.6 in.; Weight: 3,574 lb.

points: Good acceleration without guzzling gas; a quiet cabin; and comfortable, supportive front seats. **Weak points:** Tall occupants may find rear seating a bit cramped; interior materials are rather basic; small trunk opening limits what luggage you can carry; many incidents of the SkyView roof suddenly shattering; and premium fuel required. **Major redesign:** 2000, 2004, and 2009. **Highway/city fuel economy:** 7.7/10.9 L/100 km. **Best alternatives:** The Acura TSX, BMW 3 Series, Honda Accord V6, the Lexus IS 5-speed, Mazda6 GT V6, and Toyota Camry V6.

 SAFETY: 1995-2014 models earned four- and five-star scores for overall crashworthiness; 1990-94s' overall crash safety merited three stars. IIHS rates the 2004-13 models "Good" in moderate overlap front tests; 1997-2003 models rated "Acceptable;" and 1995-96s scored "Poor." Small overlap crashes with the 2009-13s produced "Acceptable" ratings. Side-impact protection was judged "Good" on the 2009-13 cars and "Marginal" on the 2004-08s. Roof strength with 2009-13 models was "Acceptable." Head-restraint effectiveness was rated "Marginal" on the 2007-13 and "Poor" on the 2004-06s. Owner-reported problems: Front airbags failed to deploy or the passenger-side airbag is disabled when the seat is occupied. This second problem represents the majority of owner complaints affecting Nissan's entire lineup over the past five years. C'mon Nissan, replace those sensors, as other automakers have done when faced with the same problem. By the way, the one safety-related complaint registered by NHTSA for the 2013? You guessed it. The passenser-side airbag disabled for no reason. Owners also say the car's low roofline complicates rear access and blocks visibility; an unstable driver's seat rocks back and forth; sometimes vehicle won't shift into Drive; engine surges when brakes are applied; drivers must constantly fight the steering wheel to keep from veering to the left or right; car would not shift out of First as the Check Engine warning light came on; electrical problems knock out the interior lights, door locks, and other controls; headlights may provide insufficient illumination; head restraints obstruct rear visibility, particularly when backing up; and the adjustable steering wheel may stick in its highest position.

ALERT! Only a small number of safety- and performance-related complaints have been reported to public and governmental agencies.

Maxima Profile

	2004	2005	2006	2007	2008	2009	2010	2011	2012
Used Values ($)									
SV	—	—	—	—	—	15,000	18,500	23,500	27,500
SE	5,000	6,500	8,000	9,000	10,500	—	—	—	—
SL	5,500	7,000	8,500	9,500	11,500	—	—	—	—
Recommended	★1	★3	★3	☆	☆	☆	☆	☆	☆
Reliability	★2	★3	☆	☆	☆	☆	☆	☆	☆

SECRET WARRANTIES, INTERNAL BULLETINS: 2000-03—Driver's seat won't go forward or backward. Abnormal shifting (the control valve assembly is the likely culprit, says TSB #NTB04-035). **2000-06**—Oil leaks from oil-cooler oil seal. **2002**—Erratic sunroof operation. Driver's power seat won't move forward or backward. **2002-03**—Hesitation on acceleration. Lack of engine power. Sunroof operates on its own. **2002-06**—How to silence an engine ticking noise. **2003**—Troubleshooting brake noise and judder. **2003-04**—Harsh 1–2 shifts. **2004**—Cold upshift shock; abnormal shifting. Fuel system misfires. Hard start after a cold soak. Engine won't crank in cold weather. Front brake noise. Water leaks from roof. Headlight fogging. Loose headliner. **2004-05**—Exhaust rattle/buzz when accelerating. Voluntary service campaign entails the free replacement of the rear suspension and bushing sealing for 13 years. If the subframe is too corroded, Nissan will buy back the car. **2004-06**—No-cranks in cold weather. Erratic gauge, AC operation. Front power-seat malfunction. Hard-to-move shifter. **2004-07**—Engine noise coming from the timing chain area. ABS activates when it shouldn't. Noisy driver's power seat. **2004-08**—Tire-pressure-monitor sensor may leak fluid. Inoperative power-door mirrors. Heat shield rattles. **2007-08**—Front suspension rattling. Inoperative lumbar support. **2007-09**—If the vehicle has low power accelerating to 80 km/h, the likely cause is a defective wheel speed sensor. Sunroof is inoperative or operates erratically. **2007-12**—Loss of power between 0-70 km/h. **2009**—Sunroof glass chatter, creaking, or popping. Sunroof wind noise. Power window "Up" and steering column adjustment may both be inoperative. Loose headliner. Front passenger seat shakes at highway speeds. Voluntary Service Campaign #PC005 to replace the steering knuckle for free. **2009-10**—Transmission "booming" countermeasures. Front power seats won't move. Driver's seat is wobbly. Can't turn ignition to the On position. Fuel gauge issues. **2009-11**—Silencing a rear end squeak or clunk heard when passing over bumps. **2011-12**—Steering pull/drift; door panel looks faded, discoloured. Rear-end squeak, clunk when driving over bumps. Driver's seat bottom shifts or rocks slightly.

CAMPAIGN PC005 – L/H REAR SUSPENSION KNUCKLE

BULLETIN NO.: NTB09-031   DATE: APRIL 23, 2009

2009 Maxima and 2009 Altima Sedan, Coupe, and Hybrid

INTRODUCTION: On some 2009 Altima and Maxima vehicles, the left hand rear suspension knuckle may not be manufactured to specification, which may result in noise or vibration under certain circumstances. Although no safety issue is presented, Nissan is conducting this service campaign to identify and replace those affected units. This service will be performed at no cost for parts or labor.

DEALER RESPONSIBILITY: Dealers are to inspect each vehicle falling within range of this campaign that enters the service department, and if necessary, perform the indicated knuckle replacement. This includes vehicles purchased from private parties or presented by transient (tourist) owners and vehicles in a dealer's inventory.

MURANO ★★★★

RATING: Above Average (2009-14); Average (2007); Below Average (2004-06); Not Recommended (2003). The mid-sized Murano continues to be the car-based "ying" to the Pathfinder's truck-based "yang." Both vehicles embody strong, in-your-face styling and are loaded with many standard safety, performance, and convenience features. **Road performance:** Nicely equipped with a refined, responsive powertrain that includes a smooth V6 coupled to a quiet CVT transmission; a comfortable, quiet ride; and no-surprise, responsive, car-like handling. **Strong points:** A plush, easily accessed, comfortable, and roomy interior; good fuel economy; and better-than-average reliability. **Weak points:** There is less cargo space behind the second row than what is available in competing models; limited rear visibility; save your loonies for gassing up with premium fuel. Frequent brake replacements (calipers and rotors) and poor body fit and finish, including paint defects and water/air leaks. Excessive vibration (sometimes fixed by reducing tire pressure from 41 psi to 36 psi); inoperative sunroof; and faulty sun visors that suddenly flop down, completely blocking visibility. **Major redesign:** 2003 and 2009. **Highway/city fuel economy:** 8.7/11.8 L/100 km, 32/24 mpg. **Best alternatives:** The Buick Enclave, GMC Acadia, and Hyundai Santa Fe.

SAFETY: NHTSA says the 2013 Murano merits five stars for side crash protection and four stars for frontal crashworthiness and rollover resistance. IIHS gives the 2012 Murano a "Good" rating for frontal offset, side, and head restraint protection. Roof strength is considered "Marginal." Airbags failed to deploy when needed; passenger-side airbag may be disabled when an average-sized occupant is seated; Airbag warning light comes on continually, even after multiple resets by the dealer; vehicle rolls down incline when stopped in traffic; Check Engine light comes on after each fill-up (cap must be carefully resealed); faulty transmission body causes the powertrain to vibrate when cruising; headlights may suddenly shut off; the Start/Stop ignition button can be accidently pressed, and this can suddenly shut down the vehicle in traffic; the tilt steering wheel may be unsafe in a crash; remote-controlled door locks operate erratically; and the sunroof may suddenly explode:

> Driving 30 mph [48 km/h] on open asphalt road, no cars ahead of me, no cars behind me, when I heard a loud explosion, similar to a shotgun blast. The moon roof had exploded. Appeared to be an upward explosion. Car taken to Nissan dealer for repairs. Damage was not caused from any flying objects. Has to be a defect.

Prices and Specs

Prices (Negotiable): *S:* $34,498, *SV AWD:* $37,548, *SL AWD:* $40,648, *LE:* $44,048 **Freight:** $1,650 **Powertrain (Front-drive/AWD):** Engine: 3.5L V6 (265 hp); Transmission: CVT **Dimensions/capacity:** Passengers: 2/3; Wheelbase: 111.2 in.; H: 68.1/L: 188.5/W: 74.1 in.; Headroom F/R: 3/3 in.; Legroom F/R: 40.5/28 in.; Cargo volume: 31.6 cu. ft.; Fuel tank: 82L/ premium; Tow limit: 3,500 lb.; Load capacity: 900 lb.; Turning circle: 39.4 ft.; Ground clearance: 6.5 in.; Weight: 4,034-4,153 lb.

ALERT! The Murano is known for its "lag and lurch" acceleration when ascending small inclines:

> At low speeds on a slight incline will not accelerate with input to gas pedal rpms will [increase but] vehicle will not respond then suddenly drivetrain will [respond] and engage (a slipping action) vehicle will suddenly launch forward with a slight bang and bucking.

Murano Profile

	2004	2005	2006	2007	2008	2009	2010	2011	2012
Used Values ($)									
SL/S	5,500	6,500	8,000	9,500	—	13,500	19,000	22,000	26,000
AWD SV	—	—	—	—	—	—	—	24,500	28,500
SL	6,500	7,500	9,000	10,500	—	14,500	20,000	26,000	30,500
SE/LE	7,000	9,000	10,000	11,500	—	17,500	23,000	29,000	33,000
Recommended	★2	★2	★2	★3	—	★4	★4	★4	★5
Reliability	★1	★1	★3	★3	—	★4	★3	★3	★3

SECRET WARRANTIES, INTERNAL BULLETINS: 2003-12—Troubleshooting a grinding, knocking noise from the rear on turns. **2011-12**—Intermittent power-steering noises; steering/suspension pull or drift diagnostics; Bluetooth voice recognition issues; and possible reasons for a faulty navigation screen.

NAVIGATION SYSTEM – SCREEN GOES BLANK

BULLETIN NO.: EL12-010   DATE: MARCH 16, 2012

NISSAN

2010-12 370Z Coupe and Roadster; 2011-12 Murano and Cross Cabriolet; and the 2011-12 Quest

IF YOU CONFIRM: The customer states the navigation display turns off, goes completely blank, or "blacks out" in DRIVE or REVERSE intermittently, and all functions of the audio system and heater/defroster/air conditioning work normally.

ACTION: Replace the AV display unit (also referred to as monitor or screen).

ROGUE

RATING: Recommended (2009-14); Above Average (2008). More car than truck. **Road performance:** This compact SUV is based on the Sentra sedan and gives car-like handling and better fuel economy than the competition that's still wedded to truck platforms. Nevertheless, the Rogue's car DNA becomes all the more evident as the engine protests going through the upper reaches of the CVT when accelerating. A redesigned 2014 model is expected to give the Rogue more horsepower and torque. **Strong points:** Standard features abound, with stability control, curtain airbags, active head restraints, and anti-lock brakes. Well-crafted interior, comfortable front seating, and impressive braking. Interestingly, fit and finish elicits few complaints, whereas this has been a chronic problem with Nissan's other models. **Weak points:** Some of the standard features are fairly basic, and those that are in the premium packages should be standard; engine sounds like a diesel when accelerating, and it could use a bit more "grunt;" lacks cargo space and rear-seat versatility. Poor rearward visibility. **Major redesign:** 2008 and 2014. The 2014 comes with third-row seating, better gas mileage, and a $3,000 higher price tag. **Highway/ city fuel economy:** *Front-drive:* 7.0/ 9.0 L/100 km. *AWD:* 7.7/9.6 L/100 km. **Best alternatives:** The Buick Enclave, GMC Acadia, and Ford Escape.

SAFETY: NHTSA gives the 2008-13 Rogue four and five stars for overall crashworthiness and rollover resistance. 2008-13 models were given IIHS's top "Good" rating for moderate overlap frontal crash protection; small overlap protection was "Marginal." Side crashworthiness was rated "Good" for 2006-13 models and roof strength was judged "Acceptable" for the 2008-13s. Head-restraint protection was judged to be "Good" for the 2008-13 models. Few safety-related complaints have been recorded since 2008, but some are deadly serious, like the following:

> I was on my way to work and had entered our parking lot and was ready to pull into a parking space. As I pulled in and was at a stop, my car suddenly accelerated and I was unable to stop it. I started to turn the wheel to the right because there was a 2010 Ford Explorer that was parked in front but unfortunately I hit the back end of the car and pushed it at least 30 ft dead straight. My car continued going to the right and over an island and by the time I got it to stop, the air bag had gone off. I'm not sure how this happened since I was stopped. There were two witnesses that saw my vehicle stopped and the next thing it accelerated. I know my foot was on the brake because I was stopped and ready to exit the vehicle, but it would not stop.

Transmission, steering wheel, gear shifter, and brake failures (brakes may also suddenly lock up):

> Nissan Rogue transmission failure at 16,000 miles [25,750 km]. Transmission began to make strange noises under load from the front end. Dealer replaced transmission and claimed there is no current recall. A check on the internet indicates the problem is pervasive.

Tire-pressure monitoring systems are so sensitive that they often give false alerts, so drivers end up ignoring them. Steering-wheel vibrations may numb your hands:

Prices and Specs

Prices (Negotiable): *S FWD:* 23,648, *S AWD:* $26,448, *SV FWD:* $26,548, *SV AWD:* $28,548, *SL AWD:* $33,514 **Freight:** $1,650 **Powertrain (Front-drive/AWD):** Engine: 2.5L 4-cyl. (170 hp); Transmission: CVT **Dimensions/capacity:** Passengers: 2/3; Wheelbase: 105.9 in.; H: 65.3/L: 182.9/W: 70.9 in.; Headroom F/R: 3.5/4 in.; Legroom F/R: 42/30 in.; Cargo volume: 28.9 cu. ft.; Fuel tank: 60L/regular; Tow limit: 1,500 lb.; Load capacity: 953 lb.; *AWD:* 1,026 lb.; Turning circle: 37.4 ft.; Ground clearance: 8.3 in.; Weight: 3,315-3,469 lb.

I think it's absurd my vehicle has 2,100 miles [3,380 km] on it and I've never owned a car that does this. You have to move your hands off the wheel because they go numb. I was told drive faster or take a different route to work.

Driver-side door handle broke, and it took over a month to get the part:

In the meantime, the only way to access my vehicle is by using the passenger side door and climb over the seats. If I were physically unable to climb over the seats, I would not be able to operate my vehicle. Fortunately, I am able, but if a person was not, they would either have to rent a vehicle or use some other means of transportation. I find this problem inexcusable. A simple door handle part must be sent from Japan to fix this problem.

ALERT! Owners say the sunroof doesn't open fully, and dealers say all Rogues are designed that way – check it out.

Rogue Profile

	2008	2009	2010	2011	2012
Used Values ($)					
S	7,500	9,500	13,000	15,500	18,000
AWD S/SV	8,500	10,500	14,500	18,500	21,500
AWD SL	10,500	11,500	15,500	21,500	24,500
Recommended	☆	☆	☆	☆	☆
Reliability	☆	☆	☆	☆	☆

SECRET WARRANTIES, INTERNAL BULLETINS: 2007-12—A leak from the oil cooler may be a problem on some Nissans. In TSB #NTB11015A, Nissan says the leak is from the upper end of the oil cooler. Door locks inoperative with Keyless Entry. **2008-12**—Troubleshooting a grinding, knocking noise from the rear on turns. **2011-12**— Inaccurate ambient display temperature. Troubleshooting water vapour in the exterior lights. Steering/suspension pull or drift diagnosis. Oil may leak from the upper end of the engine oil cooler (see Sentra profile). Noise when turning the steering wheel.

GRINDING/KNOCKING NOISE FROM REAR ON TURNS

CLASSIFICATION: RA09-004A   DATE: OCTOBER 5, 2011

2003-12 Murano (Z50, Z51) AWD ONLY and 2008-12 Rogue (S35) AWD ONLY

IF YOU CONFIRM: There is a grinding or knocking noise or vibration from the rear of the vehicle. **ACTION:** Remove the Rear Propeller Shaft and test drive the vehicle. If the noise/vibration DOES NOT stop: This bulletin DOES NOT APPLY. Refer to ASIST for further diagnostic assistance. If the noise/vibration DOES stop: Replace the Electrical Coupling Assy. (CPLG ASSY-ELEC) with the one from the Parts Information section of this bulletin.

FRONTIER ★★★★★

RATING: Recommended (2009-14); Above Average (2008); Below Average (2002-07). A gutsy, reliable pickup that's compact in name only. **Road performance:** Carries a powerful V6, with towing horsepower to spare; the 4-cylinder engine is acceptable for light chores; and handling is quick and nimble. **Strong points:** Well equipped; an accommodating interior, especially with the Crew version; plenty of storage in the centre console; and outstanding reliability. **Weak points:** Ride is a bit stiff; stability control is optional; rear seatroom is tight in the Crew Cab; and you'll need to eat your Wheaties before attempting to lift the tailgate. **Major redesign:** 1998 and 2005. **Highway/city fuel economy:** *2.5L man.:* 8.7/10.7 L/100 km. *2.5L auto.:* 9.2/12.6 L/100 km. *4.0L 4×2 auto.:* 9.2/14.2 L/100 km. *4.0L 4×4:* 10.4/13.7 L/100 km. *4.0L 4×4 auto.:* 10.4/14.7 L/100 km. **Best alternatives:** A cheaper 2013 Frontier will give almost everything that's offered with the 2014 version. Other choices are the Honda Ridgeline and Toyota Tacoma.

SAFETY: NHTSA gives the 2011-14 models, equipped with 4WD, four stars for rollover resistance; front-drives earned three stars. 2001-04 model scores varied between four and five stars. IIHS rates 2005-13 models moderate front overlap "Good;" 1998-2004s scored "Marginal." The 2010-13 models rated "Good" in side-impact crashes while the 2005-09 models were judged "Marginal." Roof crash protection was "Good" with the 2005-13 models, while head restraints were rated "Acceptable" with the 2010-13s and "Poor" in tests of the 2005-09 Frontier. Owner complaints: Passenger-side front airbag is disabled when an average-sized adult occupies the seat; airbags deploy for no reason:

> Myself and one passenger were off-roading in my 2012 Frontier PRO-4X going over a bumpy surface and without warning the side airbags went off! Luckily no one was injured, but we both got quite a scare due to the noise and lack of visibility. There is no damage to the front end nor were we at any degree of an angle. Yes it was bumpy but when you pay for a vehicle that states clearly off road on the side you expect it has the suspension to support the ride. The very last thing I was thinking of was the air bags, until they came out.

Delayed acceleration; faulty fuel-level sending unit sensor:

> I went online to *nissanhelp.com* after performing a search. I came across many others who have experienced the same problem. Apparently it has something to do

Prices and Specs

Prices (Negotiable): *King S 4×2:* $24,398, *SV 4×2:* $28,348, *4×4:* $30,348, *PRO-4X:* $33,298, *Crew SV 4×4:* $34,148, *PRO-4X:* $38,798 **Freight:** $1,595 **Powertrain (Rear-drive/AWD):** Engines: 2.5L 4-cyl. (152 hp), 4.0L V6 (261 hp); Transmissions: 5-speed man. 6-speed man., 5-speed auto. **Dimensions/capacity:** Passengers: 2/3; Wheelbase: 126 in.; H: 70/L: 206/W: 73 in.; Headroom F/R: 3/3.5 in.; Legroom F/R: 40/27 in.; Cargo volume: 60 cu. ft.; Fuel tank: 80L/regular; Tow limit: 6,100 lb.; Load capacity: 1,160 lb.; Turning circle: 43.3 ft.; Ground clearance: 8.7 in.; Weight: 4,655 lb.

with the fuel sending unit. A similar problem was found on the 2000–2004 Xterra models and a recall was performed when the vehicle would stop after not getting any fuel.

ALERT! Be wary of the front head restraints:

The contact owns a 2012 Nissan Frontier. The contact stated that the front driver's seat headrest could not be adjusted. The headrest was positioned downward, causing the driver's head to be forced to look down. The dealer was made aware of the failure and advised the contact that the headrest was designed in that manner and they could not compromise the design of the vehicle.

Frontier Profile

	2004	2005	2006	2007	2008	2009	2010	2011	2012
Used Values ($)									
4x2 XE/S	4,000	5,500	6,500	7,500	8,000	8,500	11,500	14,500	17,000
V6	—	—	7,000	8,000	9,000	10,000	13,500	17,000	20,500
Crew V6	—	—	7,500	9,000	10,500	11,500	15,500	19,000	22,500
4x4 SE/SV	—	7,000	8,000	8,500	10,000	11,000	16,000	19,500	23,500
Crew SE/SV	6,500	8,000	9,000	10,000	12,500	13,500	17,500	21,000	25,000
Crew PRO-4X	—	—	—	—	—	16,000	20,500	23,000	27,000
Recommended	★	★	★	★	★	★	★	★	★
Reliability	★	★	★	★	★	★	★	★	★

SECRET WARRANTIES, INTERNAL BULLETINS: 2007-12—Front seats bind, won't move fore or aft. Inoperative driver power for seat lumbar support. **2008-12**—Buzzing wind noise from the A-pillar/mirror area. **2011-12**—Oil may leak from the upper end of the engine oil cooler (see the Sentra profile). Steering/suspension drift; sunroof water leak. Rear end clunking, knocking on turns. Brake master cylinder may slowly leak fluid.

Subaru

An Extraordinary Ordinary Car

Even in these hard economic times, buyers are clamouring for Subaru's all-wheel-drive Forester, Impreza, and Legacy. And the company doesn't intend to risk its success with any dramatic changes. Except for a more aerodynamically-styled, more fuel efficient, and slightly larger Forester, Subaru's overall product lineup this year stands pat, with most of the redesigns and styling changes scheduled for the 2015.

Although all Subarus provide full-time AWD capability, studies show that most owners don't need the off-road prowess; only 5 percent will ever use their Subaru for off-roading. The other 95 percent just like knowing they have the option of going wherever they please, whenever they please – and they don't seem to care that an AWD burns about 2 percent more fuel. As one retired Quebec mechanic told me, "All-wheel drive simply means that you will get stuck deeper, further from home. It's no replacement for common sense."

FORESTER/IMPREZA WRX, STI ★★★★★ / ★★★★★ / ★★★

RATING: *Forester and Impreza:* Recommended (2005-14); Above Average (2001-04). *WRX and STI:* Average for all years. The Forester is a cross between a wagon and a sport-utility. Based on the shorter Impreza, it uses the Legacy Outback's 2.5L engine or an optional turbocharged version of the same powerplant. Its road manners are more subdued, and its engine provides plenty of power and torque for off-roading. The two "Boxer" 4-cylinder engines are both competitive in terms of power and fuel economy, despite being coupled to an outmoded 4-speed automatic transmission. The Impreza is essentially a shorter Legacy with additional convenience features. It comes as a four-door sedan, a wagon, and an Outback Sport wagon, all powered by a 173 hp 2.5L flat-four engine or a 224 hp turbocharged 2.5L. The rally-inspired WRX STI models have a more powerful turbocharged engine (a 305 hp 2.5L variant), lots of standard performance features, sport suspension, an aluminum hood with functional scoop, and higher quality instruments, controls, trim, and seats. **Road performance:** Good acceleration with the base 2.5L engine; however, the WRX STI and STI Limited models have even more powerful 305 hp engines. But with that power comes complexity – a complexity that requires good access to parts and servicing. *Forester:* Acceptable acceleration without any torque steer; the turbocharged engine is more robust, but fuel consumption increases and premium fuel is required; the 4-speed transmission is Flintstone-dated; competent, agile, and secure handling; and gives one of the smoothest rides in its class. The 2014 Forester XT turbo-equipped 2.0L develops 250 hp, up 11 percent over last year's 2.5L engine. Complementing the 2.0L is a 6- and 8-speed CVT transmission. *Impreza:* Not impressive performance. The base Impreza has to split its horsepower between all four wheels. (Yawn.) Some body roll when cornering, but the suspension smoothes things out nicely; the outdated 4-speed automatic transmission shifts roughly and wastes fuel, making the new CVT a must-have, though it augments engine noise; lots of road noise, too. *WRX and STI:* Quick acceleration with some turbo lag; solid handling; precise and responsive transmission, especially with the optional short-throw shifter; easy riding over bumps; good steering feedback; and some turbo whine at full throttle. **Strong points:** Full-time AWD; a roomy cabin; spacious rear seating; lots of storage space with the wagons; a nice control layout; good all-around visibility; and excellent quality control. The 2014 fourth-generation Forester has a roomier interior that offers more rear legroom and cargo space. **Weak points:**

Problematic entry and exit, some seats require additional lumbar bolstering and more height; hatchbacks have more wind and road noise; high-mounted cabin audio controls are hard to reach. Impreza interior materials look and feel cheap. WRX and STI bucket seats also need more lumbar support, and both cars require premium fuel. **Major redesign:** *Forester:* 1998, 2003, 2009, and 2014; *Impreza:* 1993, 2000, 2007, and 2011. **Highway/city fuel economy:** *Forester:* 7.4/9.9 L/100 km. *Auto.:* 7.5/9.9 L/100 km. *Impreza:* 5.9/8.3 L/100 km. *Auto.:* 5.5/7.5 L/100 km. *WRX:* 8.0/11.1 L/100 km. *STI:* 8.8/12.6 L/100 km. **Best alternatives:** If you don't really need a 4×4, there are some front-drives worth considering, like the Hyundai Elantra, Mazda6, and Toyota Corolla or Matrix.

SAFETY: Excellent crash scores. *Forester:* 2011-14 s earned four stars in all NHTSA crash scenarios; IIHS moderate overlap frontal, small overlap, side impact, and roof strength crash tests of 1999-2014s, confirmed the "Good" rating. 2006-14 Foresters gave a "Good" performance in head restraint protection, as well. *Impreza:* The 2012-14s earned four and five stars in various tests carried out by NHTSA; IIHS scores were identical to the Forester's rating. *WRX and STI:* Tested for rollover resistance only, but they each got five stars. *Forester:* Sudden, unintended acceleration while the vehicle was cruising on the highway; driver-side mirror and bracket detached and swung around wildly; and rear-view mirror also falls off. Cruise control malfunctions; smell of raw fuel permeates the cabin; front door corners can easily cut one's head when opened, due to their design. *Impreza:* WRX models have had fewer owner complaints (mostly paint, trim, and body hardware) than the STI, which has been afflicted with similar fit and finish deficiencies, plus engine, exhaust, and fuel system complaints. Also, reports of sudden, unintended acceleration:

Prices and Specs

Prices (Forester: Firm; Impreza: Negotiable): *Forester 2.5X:* $25,995, *Convenience Package:* $28,295, *Convenience with PZEV:* $28,995, *Touring Package:* $29,095, *Limited Package:* $33,395, *XT Limited:* $35,895; *Impreza 2.0i:* $19,995, *5d:* $20,895, *Touring Package:* $21,695, *Touring Package 5d:* $22,595, *Sport Package:* $23,895, *5d:* $24,795, *Limited Package:* $26,895, *Limited Package 5d:* $27,795; *WRX Sedan:* $32,495, *5d:* $33,395, *Limited 5d:* $36,395, *STI:* $38,195, *5d:* $39,095, *Sport-Tech Package:* $41,795, *5d:* $42,695 **Freight:** $1,695 **Powertrain (AWD):** Engines: *Forester:* 2.5L 4-cyl. (173 hp), 2.5L 4-cyl. Turbo (224 hp) and (250 hp with the 2014 model); *Impreza:* 2.0L 4-cyl. (148 hp); *WRX:* 2.5L 4-cyl. Turbo (265 hp); *WRX STI:* 2.5L 4-cyl. Turbo (305 hp); Transmissions: 5-speed man., 6-speed man., 4-speed auto., CVT **Dimensions/capacity:** *Forester:* Passengers: 2/3; Wheelbase: 103 in.; H: 66/L: 180/W: 70 in.; Headroom F/R: 6.5/6.5 in.; Legroom F/R: 41/29.5 in.; Cargo volume: 35.5 cu. ft.; Fuel tank: 64L/regular/premium; Tow limit: 2,400 lb.; Load capacity: 900 lb.; Turning circle: 38 ft.; Ground clearance: 8.9 in.; Weight: 3,064-3,373 lb. *Impreza:* Passengers: 2/3; Wheelbase: 104.1 in.; H: 57.7/L: 180.3/W: 68.5 in.; Headroom F/R: 6/3.5 in.; Legroom F/R: 43.5/35.4 in.; Cargo volume: 12 cu. ft.; Fuel tank: 64L/regular/premium; Tow limit: Not recommended; Load capacity: 900 lb., *WRX, STI:* 850 lb.; Turning circle: 37 ft.; Ground clearance: 6.1 in.; Weight: 2,910-3,384 lb.

While driving approximately 15 mph [24 km/h] on normal road conditions, there was sudden, aggressive, and forceful acceleration. The driver immediately depressed the brake pedal, but there was no response. The driver placed the gear shifter into Park, but the vehicle failed to slow down. The vehicle crashed into a brick wall. The failure occurred without warning. The police and ambulance were called to the scene and a police report was filed. The driver sustained severe back injuries. The vehicle was completely destroyed.

When accelerating, some model years have a serious shift lag, then the vehicle surges ahead; defective engine had to be replaced; head restraints push head forward at an uncomfortable angle, causing neck strain and backache; and the moonroof system cavity allows debris and small animals to enter between the headliner and interior walls – the perfect place for fungi and mould to incubate.

ALERT! Keep in mind, there is nothing remarkable about Subaru's lineup except for the inclusion of AWD in all models. If you don't need the AWD capability, you're wasting your money. Be wary of Subaru's high-performance WRX and STI models. They require special parts and specialized mechanical know-how that may be hard to find in these troubled economic times. Remember, WRX versions are expensive, problematic Imprezas, but when they run right, they'll equal the sporty performance of most of the entry-level Audis and BMWs – cars that cost thousands of dollars more. STIs are just a notch up on the WRX and not worth the extra cash.

Forester/Impreza WRX, STI Profile

	2004	2005	2006	2007	2008	2009	2010	2011	2012
Used Values ($)									
Forester 2.5X	4,000	5,500	7,500	8,500	10,500	12,500	15,000	18,000	20,000
2.5XT Touring	—	—	—	—	—	13,000	16,500	19,500	22,500
2.5XT/X LTD	—	—	9,000	—	—	14,000	18,000	21,500	24,500
Impreza	—	7,000	6,500	8,000	8,500	9,000	11,000	19,500	15,000
Touring	6,500	8,000	—	—	—	—	—	—	16,000
LTD	—	—	—	—	—	—	13,000	16,500	19,000
Wagon	—	—	7,000	—	—	—	—	13,000	15,500
WRX Sedan	—	—	8,500	9,500	11,000	13,500	17,500	21,500	24,500
WRX Wagon	—	—	9,000	—	—	—	—	22,500	27,000
STI Sedan/Wagon	—	—	13,000	9,500	12,000	—	—	26,500	30,500
Recommended (Forester)	★4	★	★	★	★	★	★	★	★
Reliability (Forester)	★3	★	★	★	★	★	★	★	★

LEGACY/OUTBACK ★★★★/★★★★★

RATING: *Legacy:* Above Average (2005-14); Average (2001-04). The most fuel-efficient mid-size AWDe sedan in North America, the 2014 Legacy is a competent full-time 4×4 performer for drivers who want to move up in size, comfort, and features. Available as a four-door sedan or five-door wagon, the Legacy is cleanly and conventionally styled. The redesigned performance versions of the Impreza will go on sale in early 2014. Subaru likely will drop the five-door and only produce a restyled WRX/STI sedan powered by a engine likely will be a high-performance version of the 2.5L 4-cylinder boxer that generating at at least 265 horses. *Outback:* Average; the car's greater number of safety complaints (related almost entirely to hesitation and stalling) shows sloppy assembly and the use of subpar components. Both cars are distinguished by their standard full-time AWD drivetrain. This AWD feature handles difficult terrain without the fuel penalty or clumsiness of many truck-based SUVs. Without it, the Outback would be just a raised wagon variant that's well equipped but outclassed by most of the import competition. **Road performance:** A refined and reliable AWD system; a well-balanced 6-cylinder engine; precise, responsive handling, and a comfortable ride; the GT handles best and has power to spare. On the downside: the base 2.5L engine remains a sluggish, noisy performer, despite the engine's three extra horses added this year, and the more powerful GT version is a fuel hog and available only with a manual gearbox. If you don't mind paying the fuel penalty, the 6-cylinder engine is quicker and quieter. *Outback:* This rugged SUV has all of the above and adds higher ground clearance. Handling degrades with extreme off-road use. **Strong points:** Interior materials and fit and finish have been substantially upgraded, and there's a spacious interior, with lots of cargo room (innovative under-floor, rear-car cargo storage area). *Outback:* An even roomier interior. **Weak points:** Fuel economy trails rivals like the Chevrolet Malibu, Ford Fusion, and Toyota Camry. Another mixed blessing: The stability control feature (VDC) adds exponential complexity to a vehicle that is already complicated to repair. Crosswinds require constant steering correction; excessive engine and road noise; limited rear access; front seats need more padding; interior garnishes look and feel cheap; the Mazda6 and Ford Fusion offer more cargo space; the V6 engine requires premium fuel; and these cars are very dealer-dependent for parts and servicing. God help you if you need parts when dealers are cutting back on inventory. **Major redesign:** 2000, 2005, and 2010. **Highway/city fuel economy:** *Legacy 2.5:* 7.4/10.6 L/100 km. *Auto.:* 6.5/9.2 L/100 km. *GT:* 8.0/11.5 L/100 km. *3.6R:* 8.2/11.8 L/100 km, 34/24 mpg. *Outback 2.5:* 7.4/10.6

L/100 km. *Auto.:* 6.9/9.5 L/100 km. *3.6:* 8.2/11.8 L/100 km. **Best alternatives:** The Honda CR-V, Hyundai Tucson or Santa Fe, and Toyota RAV4.

SAFETY: NHTSA awarded the 2011 Legacy four stars for front and side protection and five stars for rollover resistance; 2013-14s got five stars in all crash categories. Early Legacys have mostly five-star ratings from 2002 through 2011, except for three stars given for side protection with the 2003-04 models. The IIHS gave 2000-14 Legacys its top, "Good," rating for moderate overlap frontal crash protection; the 1995-99 models turned in an "Acceptable" performance. Small overlap tests results were also "Acceptable" on the 2013-14 models. Side impact tests also gave mixed results: "Good" for 2006-14 models; "Marginal" for 2005s. Roof protection on 2010-14 models was judged "Good," while rear crash safety was "Good" for 2010-14 Legacys and 2006-09 Outbacks. The 2005 Outback provided just "Acceptable" rear protection. Owners report the following safety-related concerns problems: *Legacy:* Sudden, unintended acceleration when in Park:

> The vehicle was in Park when it accelerated in reverse through a yard, crashing into a retaining wall.

Long delay to get up to speed when accelerating; engine may default to very low idle, almost to the point of stalling out; cruise control and brake failures; steering shimmy and wobbles, and car sways from right to left (partially corrected by replacing the steering-column dampening spring and force-balancing the tires); excessive steering wheel, clutch, and brake vibration; Airbag warning light comes on for no reason; and driver-side floor mats may "creep" toward the accelerator pedal. *Outback:* Sudden, unintended downshifting or accelerating:

> Situation: Travelling at 60 mph [97 km/h] up a steep hill in left passing lane. Cars following close, and cars in the right lane. For the first time (new car) I used the downshift paddle on the left side of the steering wheel to downshift to accelerate. I tapped it to downshift one gear. It instantly dropped to 1st gear. The engine rpms went to red line or above. The car decelerated dramatically, and I was tossed forward. I attempted to upshift using the right paddle but there was no response, and the car remained in first gear. The car behind nearly hit me. The only useful control that I had was the steering wheel (brakes or accelerator useless). Further, I assumed the brake lights were not lit. Due to the alertness of the driver behind and the drivers to my right as I slowed dramatically and got off the highway to the right shoulder, a serious accident was avoided.

• • •

> Ever since purchasing the 2012 Outback we have had a serious issue when using the paddle shifters to slow down for a stop. When the tach slows to about 1100 rpm in first or second gear the engine then accelerates to up to 2500 rpm, slowing down and then speeding up again then repeating the cycle over even if you apply the brakes. Sometimes it would just run at 2500 rpm until you braked to a stop.

Faulty cruise control/traction control:

Vehicle stopped cruise control & flashed Brakes & No Traction Control unexpectedly. Came close to a wreck shutting the vehicle down on the side of the road hitting various tire recaps & debris on the side of the road. Not told that this is a regular occurrence with this vehicle.

Passenger-side airbag may suddenly disable itself while vehicle is underway:

Prices and Specs

Prices (Negotiable): *Legacy 2.5i:* $23,495, *Convenience:* $25,995, *PZEV:* $26,695, *Touring:* $27,295, *Limited Package:* $32,495, *3.6R Limited:* $34,695, *Limited with Eyesight Option:* $36,195; *Outback 2.5i Convenience:* $28,495, *PZEV:* $30,495, *Touring Package:* $31,095, *Limited Package:* $36,295, *3.6R:* $34,495, *3.6R Limited:* $34,695, *(2012) GT navi.:* $38,595 **Freight:** $1,695 **Powertrain (AWD):** Engines: 2.5L 4-cyl. (173 hp), 2.5L 4-cyl.; Turbo (265 hp) 3.6L V6 (256 hp); Transmissions: 5-speed man., 6-speed man., 5-speed auto. CVT **Dimensions/capacity:** *Legacy:* Passengers: 2/3; Wheelbase: 108.2 in.; H: 59.2/L: 186/W: 72 in.; Headroom F/R: 6/3 in.; Legroom F/R: 43/30 in.; Cargo volume: 15 cu. ft.; Fuel tank: 70L/regular/premium; Tow limit: 1,000 lb.; Load capacity: 850 lb.; Turning circle: 36.8 ft.; Ground clearance: 5.9 in.; Weight: 3,273-3,522 lb. *Outback:* Passengers: 2/3; Wheelbase: 1,078 in.; H: 65.7/L: 188.1/W: 71.6 in.; Headroom F/R: 4/6 in.; Legroom F/R: 39.5/29 in.; Cargo volume: 36.5 cu. ft.; Fuel tank: 70L/regular; Tow limit: 2,700 lb.; Load capacity: 900 lb.; Turning circle: 39 ft.; Ground clearance: 8.7 in.; Weight: 3,540 lb.

Drove the car for approximately 45 minutes, made a quick stop with car turned off, when restarting car, air bag warning light came on and also the passenger side air bag light said it was off even though there was an adult passenger on that side of the car. Light stayed on even after restarting car, readjusting seat belts, etc. Drove with warning light on for about an hour.

Transmission slipped from Neutral to Drive:

I was setting the homelink mirror on my car to recognize a particular garage door opener. The mirror is powered so I needed to leave the car idling. I put the car in Neutral and began the programming process. The last step in the process is to engage the garage door opener from the motor head. To prepare to do this, I [exited] the car and moved on foot into the garage to look for a step ladder. As I was searching for a step ladder and after a period of at least one full minute, the automatic transmission slipped into "Drive" at which point the unoccupied car drove into the garage and hit the rear wall.

Chronic hesitation, stalling; steering shimmy, and wobble. Excessive wander over the roadway:

When driving on the highway the vehicle exhibits very poor straight line stability. Vehicle wanders within the lane and requires excessive steering wheel correction to maintain straight direction. Vehicle 500 miles [800 km] on it (350 driven by owner) but is now sitting in driveway for fear of personal safety if emergency maneuver is necessary on the highway.

ALERT! During the test drive, remember that owners say the head restraints force the driver's head into a painful and unsafe chin-to-chest position (worse for short drivers), a problem plaguing all

Subarus for several years. Running lights may not illuminate high or far enough, and headlights have a similar handicap. Owners have to pay up to $50 twice per year to have the federally mandated tire-pressure monitoring system reset when they change tires in the spring and fall.

Legacy/Outback Profile

	2004	2005	2006	2007	2008	2009	2010	2011	2012
Used Values ($)									
Legacy Sedan	4,000	5,500	6,500	7,500	9,000	9,000	12,500	14,500	17,500
LTD	—	6,500	7,500	8,500	11,000	12,500	18,000	19,500	23,000
Outback Sedan/wagon	4,500	6,000	7,000	8,000	9,500	10,500	15,500	18,500	21,500
LTD	—	7,000	8,000	10,500	13,000	14,500	20,000	23,500	29,500
Recommended	★★	★★	★	★	★	★	★	★	★
Reliability	★★	★★	★★	★★	★	★	★	★	★

SECRET WARRANTIES, INTERNAL BULLETINS: 2011-12—_Forester:_ TCM computer reboot to cure harsh shifting. TSB #02-113-11R, published January 26, 2011, addresses cold-start engine noise and suggests that the timing chain tensioner be changed. Excessive oil consumption, white exhaust smoke.

SUZUKI

The Suzuki SX4 (above) rides well, handles well, and crashes — not so well. See Appendix I.

TOYOTA

In a cryptic *mea culpa*, Toyota told *Automotive News* last August that it is setting aside rapid market share growth as a priority and will focus on "taking care of the customer" as its primary goal for 2014. Yet, that same month, the company stepped back from its assurances that sudden, unintended acceleration was a dead issue by stating it wouldn't sell its brake-override system as "safe stop" to avoid promising more than the mechanism could deliver for driver safety. What?

Sudden unintended acceleration, faulty airbags, and loss of braking combine to make crash survivability doubtful.

When Good Cars Go Bad

A quick glance at NHTSA's 2010 safety defects complaint log shows that the Camry, Corolla, and Prius are runaway bestsellers – "runaway" in the sense that you may find yourself an unwilling hostage in a car careening out of control with a stuck accelerator, no brakes, and limited steering. When running properly, though, Toyotas do hold up very well over the years, are especially forgiving of owner neglect, and cost very little to service at independent garages.

But as far as safety is concerned, Toyota's, "Oh what a feeling" jingle comes to mind – indeed, a "feeling" of fear and betrayal. I have recommended Toyota models since the early '70s, when the company first came to Canada. Their vehicles were reliable and cheap (though rust-prone), and most disputed warranty claims were paid without forcing customers to file small claims court lawsuits.

All this came to an end over a decade ago when bean-counters took over the company and adopted the mantra that profit and market share trump quality and fair prices.

In Canada, Toyota and its dealers subsequently used the Toyota Access program to keep retail prices artificially high. *Lemon-Aid* made a formal complaint to Ottawa, alleging Toyota price-fixing, and the next thing we knew, Toyota settled and agreed to give $2 million to a Canadian charity – without admitting guilt. Slick, eh? Price-fixing charges were never filed and Toyota prices have remained firm.

Fast-forward to Toyota's sudden-acceleration woes over the past two years. Although NHTSA-logged complaints confirm that Toyota reps stonewalled thousands of Toyota car and truck owners, these same Toyota executives, claims managers, and lawyers said they were unaware that the vehicles would suddenly accelerate out of control. Toyota's president cried as he testified before the U.S. Congress in 2010 when confronted with complaint records. Shortly thereafter, Toyota recalled almost its entire lineup to change floor carpets and throttles and paid almost $50 million (U.S.) in fines. In December 2012 another $1.6 billion was offered to Toyota owners in the States in a class action settlement.

Again, there was no admission of guilt, nor any confirmation by Toyota that its own internal service bulletins (published in *Lemon-Aid*) showed that 2002 and 2003 Camrys can suddenly accelerate due to defective computer modules.

After the congressional hearings, the U.S. government fined Toyota $49 million for dragging its feet in implementing the above recalls. In the meantime, owners swear that electronic component failures are the real culprit and Toyota still stonewalls their pleas. Toyota maintains that the problem isn't electronic-based, but just in case it's mistaken, a brake override feature has been added on all models. European vehicles have had this safety device as a standard feature for years. The problem is that some motorists driving Toyotas with the override feature added, say their cars still suddenly accelerate without warning.

Toyota's Quality Decline

Toyota's image as a builder of quality vehicles has been legendary, with *Consumer Reports*, J.D. Power and Associates, and the IIHS giving the company high marks for building reliable, crashworthy vehicles. Not so *Lemon-Aid*. Ten years ago we warned our readers that Toyota quality was declining; reports of "runaway" cars were coming in through NHTSA owner complaint Internet postings; and brakes failures were rampant. We immediately lowered our ratings on many Toyota models.

In the late '90s, Toyota's reputation took a battering when angry owners refused to pay $6,000-$9,000 to repair the sludged-up engines used on many Toyota and Lexus models. After first blaming the problem on poor owner maintenance, the automaker relented and quietly settled most claims.

One would think Toyota has learned to fess up when it messes up, but recent developments show the contrary. Remember the case of Mark Saylor, a California Highway Patrol officer who was loaned a Lexus ES350 by a San Diego dealer? The Lexus accelerated, flipped, and burst into flames. As the car careened out of control, the occupants dialed 911, and on the tape you can hear them screaming in terror. The dispatcher asks where they are passing, and Lastrella, Saylor's brother-in-law, is heard asking someone in the car where they are. He exclaims, "We're going 120 [mph]! Mission Gorge! We're in trouble – we can't – there's no brakes, Mission Gorge … end freeway half mile."

The dispatcher asks if they can turn the car off. Lastrella doesn't answer and says repeatedly, "We are now approaching the intersection, we're approaching the intersection, we're approaching the intersection."

The last sounds heard on the tape are someone saying "hold on" and "pray." Lastrella says, "Oh shoot … oh … oh." Then a woman screams.

Saylor, 45, his wife, their 13-year-old daughter, and Lastrella died in the crash on August 28, 2009.

Toyota blamed the driver, denied knowledge of similar incidents reported by other Toyota and Lexus owners, and refused to support its dealer, who claimed Toyota electronics were to blame for the crash. (The dealer was sued separately.)

Bowing to public pressure, the company finally paid $10 million to the officer's estate on February 25, 2011, in an out-of-court settlement. The automaker asked that a gag order be issued to prevent disclosure of the settlement sum. This was refused (*John Saylor v. Toyota Motor Corp.*, 37-2010-00086718, California Superior Court, San Diego County).

But the story doesn't end there.

Toyota rejected a petition from Phillip Pretty, the owner of a Ford Explorer that was hit by the above-mentioned, out-of-control Lexus speeding behind him at more than 160 km/h. Pretty was hospitalized with a concussion and injuries to a shoulder and knee. Toyota denied all responsibility – in the same accident it had paid $10 million a few months earlier to settle.

Lemon-Aid is skeptical of Toyota's claim that sudden acceleration is no longer a problem with its vehicles. There are too many complaints coming from owners of recalled models and service bulletins that point to an electronic failure in the throttle system.

"Lag and Lurch"

Toyota has systematically rejected owner complaints over dangerously defective drivetrains that possibly affect all of its 1999-2014 lineup. A look at NHTSA's safety complaint database shows a ton of complaints alleging these vehicles have an electronic module glitch that causes a lag and lurch when accelerating, decelerating, or turning.

Toyota knows that if it confirms the defect is electronic in nature, the company re-opens the sudden acceleration polemic and could be forced to replace electronic control modules on millions of vehicles – modules that cost far more than a floor-mat anchor.

A perusal of *Lemon-Aid* readers' letters and e-mails, as well as NHTSA reports, shows that other recent-model Toyotas have been plagued by engineering mistakes that put occupants' lives in jeopardy. These include Corollas that wander all over the road, Prius hybrids that temporarily lose braking ability, and trucks with rear ends that bounce uncontrollably over even the smoothest roadways. Other safety failures include engine and transmission malfunctions; fuel spewing out of cracked gas tanks; gauge lights that can't be seen in daylight; and electrical system glitches that can transform a sliding power door into a guillotine.

SECRET WARRANTIES, INTERNAL BULLETINS: 2006-09—*2006-08 RAV4, 2007-08 Solara, 2007-09 Camry, 2007-11 Camry Hybrid, 2009 Corolla, and 2009 Matrix.* The 2.4L 4-cylinder engine may be an "oil-burner." In TSBs SB002411 and SB009411, the company said the problem was traced to the piston assembly. Toyota will replace the pistons and rings on a "goodwill" case-by-case basis.

ECHO/YARIS ★★★★ / ★★★

RATING: *Yaris:* Average (2006-14); *Echo:* Above Average (2000-05). Echo's tall roof design gave the small car an airy, spacious interior that attracted tall drivers. Replaced by the unimpressive Yaris in 2006, Echo is distinguished by its competent highway performance, excellent view of the road, fuel-sipping engine, and above average reliability. Yaris, on the other hand, is a form-over-function econobox commuter, where a low price trumps style and driving pleasure. Not a sporty performer by any stretch. Positioned just below the Corolla, the Yaris manages to offer about the same amount of passenger space, thanks to a tall roof, low floor height, and upright seating position. The car also has a more modern look with its large windows, and additional legroom found on recent models. **Road performance:** Yaris feels underpowered, especially when equipped with the automatic transmission, which often doesn't downshift quickly or smoothly. A tall profile and light weight make the car vulnerable to side-wind buffeting and the base tires provide poor traction in wet conditions. Still, the Yaris passes over uneven terrain with less jarring movements than do other mini-compacts, and is quite nimble when cornering. Better road feel with SE models, thanks to electric power steering. **Strong points:** Lots of interior space up front; a nice array of storage areas, including a huge trunk and standard 60/40 split-folding rear seats; well-designed instruments and controls don't look as cheap as before; comfortable, high front seating; easy rear access; surprisingly quiet for a small car; and excellent visibility fore and aft. **Weak points:** Not overly generous with standard features. Interior ergonomics are subpar (an awkward seating position and poorly-placed centre gauges); interior materials look and feel cheap; and rear seating is cramped. There's also excessive torque steer (sudden pulling to one side when accelerating); some wind noise from the base of the windshield; the steering wheel is mounted too far away for some drivers; and gas mileage doesn't match the competition. **Major redesign:** 2000, 2006, and 2010. **Highway/city fuel economy:** *Man.:* 5.5/6.9 L/100 km. *Auto.:* 5.7/7.0 L/100 km. **Best alternatives:** The Honda Fit is the best of the competition – it's got more room and is a lot more fun to drive. Nevertheless, the Hyundai Accent, Kia Soul, Rio,

Prices and Specs

Price (Negotiable): *Hatchback CE 3DR.:* $13,990, *LE 5DR.:* $14,890, *SE 5DR.:* $18,990, *Sedan:* $14,400, *Convenience:* $15,990, *Enchanted:* $16,520 **Freight:** $1,425 **Powertrain (Front-drive):** Engine: 1.5L 4-cyl. (106 hp); Transmissions: 5-speed man., 4-speed auto. **Dimensions/capacity:** Passengers: 2/3; Wheelbase: 100.4 in.; H: 57.5/L: 169.3/W: 66.7 in.; Headroom F/R: 3.5/1.5 in.; Legroom F/R: 40.5/27 in.; Cargo volume: 13.7 cu. ft.; Fuel tank: 42L/regular; Tow limit: 700 lb.; Load capacity: 845 lb.; Turning circle: 30.8 ft.; Ground clearance: 5.5 in.; Weight: 2,315-2,355 lb.

or Forte hatchback, Mazda2 or Mazda3, and Nissan Versa are all worthwhile candidates.

SAFETY: *Echo:* Frontal collision and rollover protection for the 2001-05 models merited four stars, while side-impact protection was given three stars. *Yaris:* NHTSA gives the 2009-14 Yaris models four- and five-star ratings for crashworthiness; the 2007-09s were similarly rated, except that side protection was cut to three stars. IIHS scored front overlap crashworthiness and roof strength as "Good" on the 2007-12s, but head restraints got only a "Marginal" rating. Yaris owner safety complaints include airbags that fail to deploy; vehicle wandering all over the road, requiring constant steering corrections; and windows that spontaneously shatter.

ALERT! Steer clear of the poor-performing original tires. MSRP includes an "administration fee;" don't pay it.

Echo/Yaris Profile

	2004	2005	2006	2007	2008	2009	2010	2011	2012
Used Values ($)									
CE	—	—	4,000	4,500	5,000	5,500	7,500	9,000	10,000
LE	—	—	5,000	5,500	6,000	6,500	8,000	9,500	11,000
RS	—	—	5,500	6,000	7,000	7,500	10,500	12,500	15,000
Sedan	—	—	—	5,000	5,500	6,000	8,000	9,500	11,000
Echo	2,000	2,500	—	—	—	—	—	—	—
Recommended	☆	☆	★	★	★	★	★	★	★
Reliability	☆	☆	★	★	★	★	★	★	★

SECRET WARRANTIES, INTERNAL BULLETINS: *All models:* **2003-11**—Eliminating a windshield ticking noise. **2004-10**—Front seat squeak. *Echo:* **2002-05**—Fixes for a vehicle that pulls to one side. **2003-05**—AC evaporator leaks water into the cabin. *Yaris:* **2006-07**—Front windshield ticking noise. **2006-09**—Inability to shift out of Park. **2007**—Trunk lid full-open improvement. Engine compartment rattle heard when car is put in Reverse. Intermittent odour in the cabin. Paint staining along horizontal surfaces. **2007-08**—Water on front and rear carpets. Noise, vibration with the blower motor on. Rattle from the upper instrument panel area. ABS light stays on (corrosion alert). Noise, vibration on acceleration, or when shifting gears. **2007-09**—Engine noise, vibration when vehicle accelerates. Automatic transmission shift cable rattles when car in Reverse. **2007-10**—AC blower motor noise and vibration. **2007-11**—Front end clunk. **2011-12**—What to do if the passenger-side airbag OFF light comes on when the seat is occupied by an averaged-sized adult.

COROLLA/MATRIX/VIBE ★★★ / ★★★ / ★★★

RATING: Average (2011-14; 2008; 2002); Not Recommended (2009-10). Below Average (2003-07). What a disapointment! We are a year into Corolla's redesign and guess what incidents reappear in NHTSA's owner-reported, life-threatening defects compendium for the 2013 model – yep, faulty steering that causes the car to veer into traffic. Just like the falling headliners on its redesigned Avalon (see page 402) – Toyota doesn't always learn from its mistakes. Some minuses inherent in the car's redesign: The carryover rear drum brakes and torsion-beam rear suspension are pure Jurassic. The handling on the base and LE trim levels stumbles and wanders all over the roadway; and the near-vertical instrument panel is Austin Powers retro. Plus, the five-door Matrix is dead.

Geesh...

The contact owns a 2012 Toyota Corolla. The contact stated that while driving 55 mph, she attempted to turn left but the steering wheel pulled to the right. The contact stated that she applied the brakes but that caused both of the passenger side tires to become lifted off the ground. As result, the vehicle flipped onto the driver's side and rolled over several times.

• • •

The contact stated that while driving approximately 70 mph, the 2013 Corolla suddenly veered into another lane. The vehicle was taken to the dealer for diagnosis where the technician stated that there was an electronic steering failure but they were unable remedy the failure.

A step up from the Yaris, the Corolla has long been Toyota's conservative standard-bearer in the compact sedan class. Over the years, however, the car has grown in size and price, to the point where it can now be considered a small family sedan.

Matrix/Vibe: Corolla spin-offs that are Above Average buys (2004-13). These practically identical small front-drive or all-wheel-drive sporty wagons are crosses between mini-SUVs and station wagons, but they're packaged like small minivans. Unlike the Matrix, which has soldiered on, GM dropped Vibe from its lineup when it shut down the Pontiac division. The front-drive Matrix/Vibe is equipped with a 1.8L 132 hp engine, a 5-speed manual overdrive transmission, and lots of standard features; however, the weak, buzzy base engine can be felt throughout the car. The AWD models are about 10 percent heavier and are woefully power-challenged. If you really need a bit more horsepower, get a model equipped with the 2.4L 158-hp 4-cylinder, but keep in mind that there are safer, better-quality high-performance choices out there, such as the Honda Civic Si, Mazda5, or a base Acura RSX. Other front-drives worth considering are the Ford Focus, Honda Civic, Hyundai Elantra or Tiburon, Mazda3, Nissan Sentra, and Suzuki SX4. The Subaru Impreza and Forester are two other good choices for the AWD variant.

Road performance: Average acceleration requires constant shifting to keep in the pack; automatic-transmission equipped versions are slower still; clumsy emergency handling; and poor steering performance:

> The problem is the steering is dangerous over 65+ mph! The front end of the car feels like it floats at highway speeds. I have zero feeling of the road from my hands to the wheels. The car tracks and never stays true on the road. This is constant and not intermittent which means I am focusing more on the steering issue then on the traffic. I am either overcompensating for any slight movement of the steering wheel to barely touching the wheel to keep this car remotely driving straight in the center of the lane, and that doesn't help! It worsens at speeds of 75+ mph. Someone is going to get hurt! Please recall this EPS system now!!!

Strong points: The reworked 2013 Corolla has more interior space, provides a supple ride, and handles much better (except for its "Hail Mary" erratic steering) than previous models. User-friendly interior ergonomics are enhanced by the flat rear floor, which provides more room. **Weak points:** Lots of high-speed wander along with excessive wind and road noise; limited front legroom; and plastic interior panels and trim look cheap; harsh downshift when stopping; seat belt warning alarm isn't loud enough; instrument-panel rattling; front-seat squeaking, and the front power seat grinds and groans. Overall reliability is average to below average. **Major redesign:** 1998, 2003, 2009, and 2014. The 2014 Corolla gains four inches in wheelbase and overall length, with a longer wheelbase than a 1996-2001 Camry. Toyota also is offering an optional "Eco" version of the same engine with an additional intake-timing actuator that adds 8 horsepower and boosts highway fuel economy. **Highway/city fuel economy:** *1.8 man.:* 5.6/7.4 L/100 km. *Auto.:* 5.7/7.8 L/100 km. *2.4 man.:* 6.7/9.4 L/100 km. *2.4 auto.:* 6.5/9.4 L/100 km. **Best alternatives:** Some small cars that are good investments with dependable steering, windshields, and headliners include the Hyundai Elantra and Mazda3 and Mazda6.

SAFETY: NHTSA says the 2013 Corolla merits five stars for side crashworthiness and four stars for frontal and rollover occupant protection. The redesigned 2014 did worse, scoring a "Marginal" in IIHS' small overlap frontal crash test. NHTSA lists 621 safety-related failures for the 2010 model year alone, or four times what would be considered normal for three model years. Many complaints concern steering that allows the vehicle to wander all over the road (apparently, alignments and a new steering rack don't help). Sudden acceleration accompanied by total brake failure:

While driving 50 mph [80 km/h] the vehicle suddenly accelerated. As the vehicle is accelerating, the contact is trying to slow the vehicle down by applying the brakes. At this time the brakes are malfunctioning and increasing in speed. The contact was unable to slow the vehicle down and crashed into another vehicle.

Merchant Law Group has launched class proceedings (as a nation-wide class action on behalf of all Canadian owners and lessees of affected vehicles) alleging that 2009-10 Pontiac Vibes (equipped with an electronic throttle control system) may suddenly accelerate without driver input and against the intentions of the driver. Car speeds up or slows down on its own:

I see variations of about 500 rpm on the tachometer. Sometimes when letting off the throttle pedal, the car keeps going and doesn't get the message it's supposed to slow down. This is scary, it's almost like the car thinks it's on cruise control when it's not at all (here is a link to a forum where owners of 2011 Toyota Corollas describe exactly the same safety issue with the car: *www.corollaforum.com/showthread.php?p=285#post285*).

Sudden brake failure:

I went over a dip in the road at about 40 mph [64 km/h] and went to hit the brakes while taking a turn that was approaching a stoplight when the brakes would not let me push them down and would give me feedback as if ABS was active. After a couple seconds I was able to reapply pressure to the brakes to stop. This happened a total of eight times in 2,100 miles [3,380 km]. The car has been in some close calls, and all the incidents happened after hitting a dip while trying to reduce my speed from over 50 mph [80 km/h] to the time of hitting the dips.

Airbags fail to deploy:

The driver fell asleep at the wheel, awoke and tried to correct his lane position. Upon his attempt, the car could not be stabilized or controlled. This was a front end crash at a speed of approximately 50–55 mph going through a chain link fence, hitting hundreds of stacked lobster crates (like hitting a brick wall). The car was completely totaled, the driver had seat belt on. Not one air bag deployed. The driver side mirror smashed through the driver side window and a piece of wooden lobster crate with nails came through the front windshield and into the vehicle. This caused serious injury to the driver, severe facial and elbow lacerations, and major amounts of glass fragments in his body.

Driver cannot open the rear window with the other windows closed, as it produces a dramatic vibration and shaking inside the vehicle; mysterious windshield cracks; car parked on a small hill and with the parking brake applied will still roll away. Other safety-related reported with the 2013s: Airbag warning light comes on for no reason; sudden brake loss and unintended acceleration; rear defogger doesn't adequately clean the windshield; and the steering veers from one side to the other.

Prices and Specs

Prices (Negotiable): *CE:* $15,450, *S:* $20,605, *XRS:* $24,840 (2012) **Freight:** $1,425 **Powertrain (Front-drive):** Engine: 1.8L 4-cyl. (132 hp); Transmissions: 5-speed man., 4-speed auto., CVT **Dimensions/ capacity:** Passengers: 2/3; Wheelbase: 102.4 in.; H: 57.7/L: 178.7/W: 69.3 in.; Headroom F/R: 4/2 in.; Legroom F/R: 41/28 in.; Cargo volume: 12.3 cu. ft.; Fuel tank: 50L/regular; Tow limit: 1,500 lb.; Load capacity: 825 lb.; Turning circle: 37.1 ft.; Ground clearance: 5.8 in., XRS: 5.3 in.; Weight: 2,722 lb.

Corolla/Matrix/Vibe Profile

	2004	2005	2006	2007	2008	2009	2010	2011	2012
Used Values ($)									
CE	4,000	4,500	5,000	5,500	6,000	6,500	7,500	9,500	10,500
LE	4,500	5,000	6,000	7,000	8,500	9,500	11,500	13,000	15,000
XRS	—	5,500	7,500	—	9,500	10,500	12,500	14,500	17,500
Matrix Wagon	4,000	4,500	5,500	6,000	6,500	7,000	8,500	10,000	12,000
AWD	4,500	5,500	6,000	6,500	7,000	8,000	9,500	15,000	17,500
XRS/XR	4,500	5,000	6,000	8,500	9,500	11,500	13,500	16,000	18,500
Vibe Wagon	3,500	4,500	5,000	5,500	6,500	7,500	8,500	—	—
AWD	4,000	5,000	—	—	5,500	6,500	9,500	—	—
GT	4,500	5,500	6,000	—	—	8,000	10,000	—	—
Recommended	★	★	★	★	★	★	★	★	★
Reliability	★	★	★	★	★	★	★	★	★

SECRET WARRANTIES, INTERNAL BULLETINS: *All models/years:* Steering-column noise may require the replacement of the steering-column assembly. Toyota has developed special procedures for eliminating AC odours and excessive wind noise. These problems are covered in TSBs #AC00297 and #BO00397, respectively. *All models:* **2009**—According to TSBs #SB002411 and #SB009411, excess oil consumption in the 2.4L 4-cylinder engine was traced to the piston assembly. Toyota will replace the pistons and rings on a "goodwill" case-by-case basis. *Corolla:* **2002-04**—Troubleshooting tips for fixing a poorly performing AC. **2002-07**—Repair tips for correcting a severe pull to one side when underway (TSB #ST005-01). **2003-05**—Ways to silence front- and rear-door wind noise and a rear hub axle bearing humming. **2003-07**—Remedy for engine compartment squeaks and rattles. Rear hatch is slow to open. **2003-08**—Tips on silencing windshield, automatic transmission whistle or hoot, wind noise, and front brake rattling. **2003-11**—Remedy for a windshield ticking noise. **2004-06**—Front-seat movement correction. **2004-10**—Fixing front-seat squeaking. **2005-06**—Engine vibration/drone when accelerating.

Toyota's correction for hard starts (TSB #EGO53-06). Grill mesh available to protect the AC condenser from road debris. **2005-07**—Troubleshooting tips to fix a harsh-shifting automatic transmission and hard starts. **2009-10**—Poor steering feel. Steering clunk, pop noise. A-pillar rattles. Premature front brake pad wear (see TSB on following page). *Matrix, Vibe:* **2003**—Loose or deformed front or rear glass door run. AC doesn't sufficiently cool the vehicle. Headlights come on when turned off. **2003-06**—Correction for rear-end whining, humming, or growling. **2005-06**—Troubleshooting no-starts. **2009**—Harsh downshift when stopping. Instrument panel rattling. **2009-10**—No starts. Condensation dripping from the dome lamp. *Vibe:* **2003**—Transmission shifts too early when accelerating at full throttle and the engine is cold. Harsh shifting. Water leak from the A-pillar or headliner area. **2003-04**—Harsh 1-2 upshifts. Slipping transmission. **2003-08**—Silencing a hoot or whistle heard on light acceleration (replace the automatic transaxle cooler hoses).

BRAKES – PREMATURE FRONT BRAKE PAD WEAR

BULLETIN NO.: T-SB-0392-09   DATE: DECEMBER 3, 2009

TOYOTA

YEAR(S)	MODEL(S)	ADDITIONAL INFORMATION
2009–2010	Corolla	

APPLICABILITY: Some 2009–2010 model year Corolla vehicles may exhibit premature pad wear. Use the following replacement pads to address this condition.

PREVIOUS PART NUMBER	CURRENT PART NUMBER	PART NAME	QTY
04465-02240 (NAP)	04465-12630	Pad, Kit Disc Brake, Front	1
04465-02220 (JPP)			
04945-12100 (NAP)	Same	Shim, Anti-Squeal, Front	1
04945-02150 (JPP)	Same		1
N/A	08887-80609	Disc Brake Caliper Grease (50 g Tube)	1

CAMRY ★★★

RATING: Average. The Camry is another example of one of Toyota's "good" cars gone "bad." Nevertheless, Camry's rating has been upgraded one star for 2014 mainly because safety-related failures have declined, although there are some serious ones that remain. Another positive change is the addition of a brake/throttle override to combat sudden, unintended acceleration. **Road performance:** The 2012's redesign corrected most of the Camry's performance gaps, however vague steering causing excessive road wander remains a problem:

Steering is vague and not predictable. Never had a car with elec. steering. Car follows its own course. It takes a lot of attention to keep it on the road.

A retuned SE trim level delivers sporty handling; the base 4-cylinder is a competent, responsive performer; surprisingly, the 3.5L V6 powertrain set-up delivers fuel economy figures that are almost as good as the base 4-banger; although the ride has smoothed out, the SE suspension is a bit stiff. The 6-speed automatic transmission has a taller final drive ratio, which saves fuel, but slows acceleration. **Strong points:** There's a nice array of standard safety and convenience features that include a telescoping steering column, 10 airbags, stability control, antilock brakes, and four wheel disc brakes that are larger than those on the 2011 models. The cabin is quieter; instruments and controls are well laid-out in an interior that has a richer look and feel; and passenger and storage space is better than average. **Weak points:** Paint on the lower plastic bumper is easily chipped. Hybrid fuel economy is overstated by almost 30 percent, says Consumer Reports and many others. Frequent failures of the engine cam head, which is often back ordered; inaccurate speedometer readings; gasoline in the fuel tank hits the tank baffle with a loud bang; driver-seat lumbar support may be painful for some drivers; a strong "out-gassing" odour may permeate the cabin; windows often stick in the up position; and some complaints of Hybrid AC failures. **Major redesign:** 1998 and 2005. **Highway/city fuel economy:** *Hybrid:* 4.9/4.5 L/100 km. *XLE:* 5.1/4.7 L/100 km. *2.5:* 5.6/8.2 L/100 km. *3.5 V6:* 6.4/9.7 L/100 km. Owners say fuel-economy figures are much lower than advertised. **Best alternatives:** The Honda Accord, Hyundai Elantra, Mazda5 or Mazda6, and Nissan Sentra or Altima. Stay away from the optional moonroof: It robs you of much-needed headroom and exposes you to deafening wind roar, rattling, and leaks. Original equipment Firestone and Bridgestone tires should be shunned in favour of better-performing tires recommended by *thetirerack.com*:

The car has Bridgestone Turanza EL 400–02 tires, which had 689 miles [1,109 km] on them. The rear driver-side tire failed at 60 mph [96 km/h] when the tread split. After reading all the similar complaints by other Toyota car owners, I believe these tires are dangerous. After a very ugly discussion with the dealership, the one tire was replaced, but Toyota would not replace the remaining three.

SAFETY: NHTSA gives the Camry and its Hybrid variant four stars for side crashworthiness and rollover resistance and three stars for frontal crash protection. IIHS also gives the Camry its top rating for frontal offset, side, and roof crash protection. IIHS rates head-restraint effectiveness as only "Marginal." The same safety-related failures are reported year after year and will likely increase with the 2013 redesign. These defects can be especially lethal to older drivers with slower reflexes. Indeed, probably few Camry drivers have the necessary driving skills to confront excessive steering wander, engine surging, or delayed transmission engagement when accelerating, merging, passing, or turning. As seen with other Toyota models (like the 2010 Prius, which has received 1,700 complaints), sudden, unintended acceleration without any brakes has been the top reported problem with Camrys for many years, with an added twist – they still speed out of control after having recall work done to correct the problem:

> Entering a driveway at 2 mph the car accelerated to approximately 30 mph and struck a brick wall. The air bags deployed causing injury and the car was totaled.

Other safety problems reported: Airbags fail to deploy; when accelerating from a stop, the vehicle hesitates, sometimes to a count of three, before suddenly accelerating; and when decelerating, the vehicle speeds up, as if the cruise control were engaged. The close placement of the brake and accelerator pedals also causes unwanted acceleration due to driver error; however, this cannot explain the large number of incidences of sudden acceleration reported. Transmission shift lever can be inadvertently knocked into Reverse or Neutral when the vehicle is underway; harsh shifting; vehicle may roll backwards when parked on an incline; and electronic power steering operates erratically and is sometimes unresponsive. There have also been reports that the steering constantly pulls the car to the left, into oncoming traffic, no matter how many alignments you get; the centre console below the gear shift becomes extremely hot; Hybrid's low beam lights are inadequate for lighting the highway; excessively bright LED tail/brake lights will impair the vision of drivers in trailing vehicles; and wheels may lock up. Reports of the front windshield cracking from the driver-side upper left corner and gradually extended toward the middle of the windshield. Glass sunroof implodes and in one incident the rear window exploded while the vehicle was stopped in traffic; front windshield distortion looks like little bubbles are embedded in the glass; rear windshield distortion when viewed through the rear-view mirror during night driving; the passenger-side windows may fall out; rear window-defrosting wires don't clear the upper top of the windshield; and head restraints obstruct driver's rearward vision. Trunk lid "beans" people when the weak struts fail:

> A short time after I took delivery of the car, I parked it on my driveway which has a small climb to the garage. The car was parked with the rear end lower than the front. When I opened the trunk to unload it and released the trunk lid it came down and hit me in the head. It happens every time when the trunk is opened under the same conditions and sometimes when the car is level. Obviously the trunk lid needs a tighter spring.

ALERT! Many owners say the Camry is a "rat hostel:"

> While driving 40 mph [64 km/h], the driver noticed a rat crawled from under the passenger seat into the glove compartment and into the air conditioner. The [sight] of the rat almost caused the driver to crash. The contact was able to get the rat out of the vehicle. Two days later the contact took the vehicle to the dealer to repair the back seat and the seat belt that the rat has chewed through and also clean the air conditioner.

Can you endure the severe wind buffeting if driving with one window open?

The wind buffeting that occurs in this car is unbearable. This causes an unsupportable pressure that you feel in your ears and head. Speaking while one of the rear windows is open is also impossible because our voices will echo.

Make sure there's no rear window defroster line reflection at night:

The rear window reflects all the defroster lines when a car is behind you. So when looking out the rear window and there is 1 car you see 20 lines of lights and if there [are] 2 cars you see 40 lines of lights and so on.

. . .

The contact owns a 2012 Toyota Camry. The contact stated that when looking out of the rear window, the defrost lines going across the window and the tint caused the contact to see multiple headlights. The contact stated that one headlight would appear as twenty various headlights, disorientating the driver. The contact took the vehicle to multiple dealers and was told that the design was normal.

Also, inspect the factory-ordered window tinting. Check out the tint in the day and at night before purchase:

The contact stated that she was unable to see out of the factory rear window tint. The vehicle was taken to the dealer. The dealer confirmed the failure was with the factory window tint.

Camry Profile

	2004	2005	2006	2007	2008	2009	2010	2011	2012
Used Values ($)									
LE	4,000	5,500	7,000	8,500	9,500	11,000	13,000	15,000	17,000
SE V6	—	—	—	10,500	12,000	14,000	15,500	18,500	22,500
XLE	—	—	—	—	—	—	17,500	20,000	23,500
XLE V6	5,000	7,000	8,000	11,500	13,500	15,500	19,500	22,500	26,500
Hybrid	—	—	—	9,000	11,000	12,500	15,500	17,000	19,000
Recommended	★	★	★	★	☆	☆	☆	☆	☆
Reliability	★	★	★	★	☆	☆	☆	☆	☆

SECRET WARRANTIES, INTERNAL BULLETINS: 2004-05—Correction for drifting or pulling into oncoming traffic involves installing new springs and struts. **2004-08**—Front seat squeaking. **2006-09**—No shift from Park; multiple warning lights come on. **2007**—Engine oil leaks from the timing cover. Rough idle, stalling; shift flare. **2007-08**—No crank; engine starts and dies. Premature brake pad wear; squeaking rear brakes. Excessive steering-wheel vibration, flutter, and noise. Instrument panel rattle. Frame creaking noise. Rear suspension squeaking, rubbing. Engine oil leak from camshaft housing. Engine ticking noises. Torque converter shudder. Moonroof knocking when underway. Troubleshooting brake pulsation/vibration. Rattle from trunk area. **2007-09**—Silencing engine ticking and floor pan creaking. Inoperative moonroof. **2007-10**—Braking vibration, pulsation can be reduced through the use of new brake pads and brake rotor R & R. Work should be paid for by Toyota, whether vehicle was bought new or used. A rattle or buzz coming from the driver's side dash may require an updated vacuum check valve. Tips on correcting a roof knocking sound. Intermittent noxious AC odours. Loose sun visor mounts. **2007-11**—Uneven rear brake pad wear. Water leaks from sunroof onto headliner and into footwell area. **2008-09**—TCM update for shift improvements. **2008-10**—Ignition coils may need replacing if the MIL alert is illuminated. **2010-11**—Wheel cover ticking, creaking. *Camry:* **2007-09**—The 2.4L 4-cylinder engine burns oil rapidly. *Hybrid:* **2007-09**—No shift from Park; multiple warning lights come on. Water leaks onto headliner and footwell area. Inoperative moonroof. **2007-10**—Ways to fix a knocking sound from the roof area. **2007-11**—The 2.4L 4-cylinder engine burns oil rapidly. **2011-12**—Passenger-side airbag OFF light will come on even though the seat is unoccupied. Uneven rear brake wear. Insufficient alternator charging may be corrected with an updated pulley assembly. Remedy for a front/rear suspension noise that occurs when passing over bumps in the road. A front door trim panel rattle. Underbody rattling. Troubleshooting a windshield back glass ticking noise.

Prices and Specs

Prices (Negotiable): *LE:* $25,310, *Convenience:* $26,700, *SE:* $27,755, *LE V6:* $29,020, *XLE:* $31,235, *SE V6:* $34,255, *XLE V6:* $36,410, *Hybrid:* $31,310 **Freight:** $1,490 **Powertrain (Front-drive):** Engines: 2.5L 4-cyl. Hybrid (200 hp) 2.5L 4-cyl. (178 hp) 3.5L V6 (268 hp); Transmissions: 6-speed auto. CVT **Dimensions/capacity:** Passengers: 2/3; Wheelbase: 109.3 in.; H: *Camry:* 57.9, *Hybrid:* 57.9/L: 189.2/W: 71.7 in.; Headroom F/R: 5/2 in.; Legroom F/R: 42/29 in.; Cargo volume: *Camry:* 15 cu. ft., *Hybrid:* 10.6 cu. ft.; Fuel tank: *Camry:* 66L, *Hybrid:* 65L/regular/premium; Tow limit: *Camry:* 1,000 lb., *Hybrid:* Not advised; Load capacity: 900 lb.; Turning circle: 36.1 ft.; Ground clearance: *Camry:* 5.3 in., *Hybrid:* 5.9 in.; Weight: *Camry:* 3,190 lb., *Hybrid:* 3,638 lb.

PRIUS ★★

The Toyota Prius C.

RATING: *Prius:* Below Average. We know the problems: Sudden acceleration, no brakes or weak brakes, and a cruise control that doesn't turn off are scary enough. But what about a steering column that becomes unhinged? Or head-spinning depreciation. Did you know that a 2007 Prius that sold for $31,280 is now worth barely $12,000? That alone wipes out most fuel savings. *Prius C:* Below Average. Hope springs eternal. We expect the C model to be a better-built petite Prius, but the jury's still out. The best priced hybrid around, this little hybrid is Not Recommended until it shows us more after its first year on the market. **Road performance:** Slow-steering, has lots of body roll when cornering, and is prone to stalling. Braking isn't very precise or responsive, and the car is very unstable when hit by crosswinds. Highway rescuers are wary of the car's 500-volt electrical system, and take special courses to prevent electrocution and avoid toxic battery components. **Strong points:** Good fuel economy and acceleration in most situations with only little cabin noise. **Weak points:** The car is too darn dangerous to drive; owners are still reporting that the brakes give out when they pass over a bump in the road. Poor performance in cold weather; battery pack will eventually cost about $3,000 (U.S.) to replace; fuel consumption may be 20 percent higher than advertised; 50 percent depreciation after five years; higher-than-average insurance premiums; dealer-dependent servicing means higher servicing costs; rear seating is cramped for three adults; sales and servicing may not be available outside large urban areas; and the CVT cannot be easily repaired by independent agencies. Inaccurate fuel readings; hands-free phone system is inordinately complicated to use; musty AC smell; noisy rear brakes; and the driver-side seat can't be adjusted away from the steering wheel. Toyota sells four Prius models in Canada: The base Prius, PriusV wagon, Prius C subcompact (set on the Yaris platform), and the incoming Prius

Plug-in Hybrid. Toyota's latest third-generation Prius uses a 1.8L DOHC 16-valve 4-cylinder engine. It may sound hard to believe, but the bigger engine doesn't have to work as hard. So at highway speeds, the lower rpms save about 1.3 km/L (3 mpg). With the debut of the Prius V five-door wagon, Prius is now approaching the Camry in size, and its powerplant is more sophisticated, powerful, and efficient than what you get with similar vehicles in the marketplace. Interestingly, because the car relies primarily on electrical energy, fuel economy is better in the city than on the highway – the opposite of what one finds with gasoline-powered vehicles. An electric motor is the main power source, and it uses an innovative and fairly reliable CVT for smooth and efficient shifting. The motor is used mainly for acceleration, with the gasoline engine kicking in when needed to provide power. Braking automatically shuts off the engine, as the electric motor acts as a generator to replenish the environmentally unfriendly NiMH battery pack. The Solar Panel option uses solar energy to keep the vehicle cool when it's parked. Do the math: You will spend a lot of money upfront to save a little money later on. After two decades you may break even. One surprising statistic comes from R.L. Polk, an automotive marketing research company based in the United States. Polk's August 2012 study found only 35 percent of hybrid owners purchased another gas-electric vehicle when trading in during 2011. Repurchase rates varied across hybrid models, with the highest percentage of hybrid loyalty going to the Toyota Prius. Removing Prius from the mix shows a repurchase rate under 25 percent. Prices are relatively firm due to the 2012 improvements. Wait until the new year to allow prices to settle down a bit. Major redesign: 1998 and 2005. **Highway/city fuel economy:** 4.0/3.7 L/100 km. **Best alternatives:** Honda Fit or Insight, Hyundai Accent, and Nissan Versa. In a Prius-versus-Insight matchup, the Prius gets better fuel economy but is more expensive; the Insight,despite its fewer horses, is more fun to drive, though it's not as fast as the Prius. On the other hand, the Nissan Insight or Leaf won't abduct you at high speed, or send you head-on into a guard-rail with no brakes.

 SAFETY: NHTSA gave the 2013 Prius a five star rating for side crash protection, and four stars for front-impact and rollover crashworthiness. *Prius, Prius V,* and *C:* IIHS gave all three 2012 models its top, "Good," rating for frontal offset, side, roof, and head-restraint protection. Sun reflects into the driver's eyes:

My 2012 Prius V has a serious reflection in the point of view of the side view mirrors, when the front windows are rolled up, and the sun is high noon (+-5 hours) position. This is caused by the white dash trim that the sun hits.

Furthermore, the low driver's seat impedes visibility:

The driver's seat does not raise far enough to allow shorter drivers to see over the dash board, base of windshield and rear of hood. This prevents shorter drivers from being able to see the ground anywhere near the car. Giving the drivers a 2 dimensional view of the traffic and objects between 3 and 5 feet high. Anything below 3 [feet] tall is not visible for 30 to

50 feet in front of the car. The raised belt line is also causing this problem of 2 dimensional views versus 3 dimensional views. This is a serious safety issue. It could be fixed with increased travel height for the driver's seat. As I have had to offer several friends chair cushions to prop them up so they could see.

Only 15 safety-related complaints have been posted against the 2012 Prius, while over 1,800 incidents were reported on the 2010 model; 50 reports would be average. Almost all of the earlier complaints concern sudden acceleration, loss of brakes, and cruise control failures. A major complaint with the 2012s is the sudden loss of Drive or Reverse:

> Car becomes immobile – will not shift into Reverse or Drive. Computer keeps sending the message to put it in Park and depress brake, but once that is done, any attempt to shift into Reverse or Drive triggers the message, endlessly. The problem is apparently intermittent. Occurred for two hours yesterday, after occurring to a lesser extent in preceding days (in the days preceding the total breakdown, I was able to shift after a slight delay and a few attempts). The dealership to which I had it towed said it was fine today. Everything checks out. This is a safety hazard because the car can be in an unsafe position when it becomes immobile. I was partly out of a parking space, somewhat blocking traffic. The problem involves the computer and the transmission – at least.

The car is also extremely vulnerable to side winds, and light steering doesn't help much, causing the vehicle to wander all over the road and need constant steering corrections. Owners of 2012 models continue to report brake failures when their car accelerates out of control. This occurs despite Toyota's much-vaunted brake/throttle override:

> As I was approaching a turn I began to brake and the brakes failed. I tried pressing the brake pedal harder and making sure that I had proper foot placement and it felt like the car accelerated at that point. Since the car was not slowing down I was unable to make the turn and ended up crossing the road diagonally and going up onto the curb. Once the car was over the curb and in the grass the brakes finally engaged and the vehicle came to a stop.

Car lurches forward when brakes are applied; many reports of loss of braking even after having the recalled ECU replaced:

> Since Toyota updated the software for the recall, I still experience the same problem multiple times, and it is not only [happening] during slow and steady application of brakes, also [happening] when I use the brake in more sudden fashion even at moderate speed (30-40 mph [48-64 km/h]).

Cruise control doesn't disengage quickly enough:

> I have to press the brake harder than any prior vehicles I have owned to kill the cruise control and if I release the brake before the cruise control is released then the car lurches forward.

Many other people have experienced this issue and have documented their experiences on the forum *priuschat.com*. They have even fixed the problem themselves by moving the cruise control disengagement closer to the top of the brake pedal.

The steering column may fall out of its mount:

My wife and 2 daughters were driving on Interstate 90/94 when the entire steering column slowly dropped. I double checked the lever underneath to adjust it, but that was tight. I could see wires and bolts where the column had been dropped several inches. I lifted the column up and thought it would lock in or click back in place. When I did this, the entire column collapsed in my lap. An alarm sounded and I had no control of the steering while going 110 [km/h].

Transmission sometimes goes into Reverse when shifted into Drive, or goes into Drive when Reverse is selected; traction control engages when it shouldn't; airbags failed to deploy; and the headlights go on and off intermittently.

ALERT! Okay, the fuel savings are exaggerated, but how about running out of gas?

When driving, dashboard [reads] "Hybrid system not working. Pull over..." This was 7/3/2012. It had run out of gas even though there were 2 bars out of 10 still present on gas gauge. On 7/30/12 later this happened again with 4 bars showing. Got the fuel sensor and gauge replaced on 7/30/12. 8/14/12 with 3 bars showing, cruising range of 60 miles and having gone 480 miles the same warning "Hybrid system not working...." I was able to get to a gas station before running out of gas. The Prius manual states the tank holds 9.5 gallons. Filling up the tank took 9.91 gallons. There is clearly something wrong.

During the test drive, verify if you can drive safely with the car's blind-spots:

There are very dangerous blind spots on both rear driver and passenger sides of the Prius V. Vehicles located near the mid to rear of the car cannot be seen in mirrors or by glancing over the shoulder when changing lanes. I have had numerous near collisions due to this design defect.

Finally, check that your child's safety seat can be safely installed in the Prius V – some can't:

The latch system design on the seats on the new Prius V is flawed. Instead of having four latch points, one set of two for the left seat and one set of two for the right seat, they have only three latch points, one in the middle of the left seat, one in the middle of the right seat and one in the middle of the car. Our child safety seat has

Prices and Specs

Prices (Negotiable): *Prius C:* $20,950, *Prius C Technology:* $23,160, *Base Prius:* $25,995, *Moonroof Upgrade Package:* $29,295, *Touring Package:* $29,550, *Technology Package:* $34,080 **Freight:** $1,490 **Powertrain (front-drive):** Engine: 1.8L 4-cyl. (134 hp); Transmission: CVT **Dimensions/capacity:** Passengers: 2/3; Wheelbase: 106.3 in.; H: 58.3/L: 175.6/W: 68.7 in.; Headroom F/R: 4/2 in.; Legroom F/R: 40.5/30 in.; Cargo volume: 15.7 cu. ft.; Fuel tank: 45L/regular; Tow limit: No towing; Load capacity: 810 lb.; Turning circle: 34.2 ft.; Ground clearance: 5.5 in.; Weight: 3,042 lb.

three buckles designed to work with the latch system, one on the left, one on the right and a top tether. The left and right buckles cannot attach to the same latch point because then the child safety seat will pivot.

Prius Profile

	2004	2005	2006	2007	2008	2009	2010	2011	2012
Used Values ($)									
Base	4,000	5,500	7,000	8,500	10,500	12,000	14,500	17,000	20,000
V	—	—	—	—	—	—	—	—	20,500
Recommended	★	★	★	★	☆	☆	☆	☆	☆
Reliability	★	★	★	★	☆	☆	☆	☆	☆

SECRET WARRANTIES, INTERNAL BULLETINS: *All years:* It is surprising that with so many serious consumer complaints and recall campaigns, most Prius service bulletins are bereft of any reference to major deficiencies. **2000-08**—Multiple warning lights on; vehicle won't shift out of Park. Steering pulls to the right. **2003-08**—Windshield back glass ticking. **2004-07**—According to Limited Service Campaign #A0N, Toyota will replace the water pump free of charge until November 30, 2013. There is no mileage limitation. **2004-08**—Troubleshooting an engine knock and inaccurate fuel gauge readings. Intermittent instrument display in cold weather. **2006-09**—Toyota has a Customer Support Program to provide reimbursement to new and used Prius owners for the full cost of replacement of HID headlight control ECUs for 2006-09 Prius vehicles. Additionally, Toyota will offer the difference in cost between the original Prius HID bulb suggested retail price of $300 (U.S.) per bulb and the currently reduced suggested retail price of $150 per bulb (maximum value $150 per bulb). **2010**—Warped engine cover. **2011-12**—An extended warranty (Limited Service Campaign) covers repairs to the Lane-Keeping Assist feature until May 31, 2015. *2012 Prius V:* Under SC-C0F1204241-002, Toyota will replace free of charge the exhaust gas control actuator which may leak coolant. This Service Campaign will apply until May 31, 2015. Abnormal noise when brake pedal is released. Excessive roof sun shade noise. Cleaning tips to keep the HV battery cooling fan at peak efficiency. Troubleshooting rear windshield ticking.

AVALON ★★★★

RATING: Above Average (2009-14; 1995-2004); Average (2005-08). The last redesigned Avalon would be a Recommended choice if not for its serious fit and finish deficiencies. How many luxury cars have headliners that fall down, a seriously distorted windshield view, or reflective interior trim that blinds drivers?

Nevertheless, the revised 2013-14 Avalon is a relatively reliable luxury sedan with more compact dimensions, a lighter curb weight and a Camry Hybrid powerplant. Restyled with cleaner lines like those of the Audi A7, the interior has been reworked to increase headroom and trunk capacity, make controls easily accessible, add more supportive seats, and give the cabin a high-end look. **Road performance:** A smooth and responsive powertrain that provides quick acceleration combined with good fuel economy; acceptable handling and the ride is both comfy and quiet. Some negatives: a mushy brake pedal and ultra-light steering that can degrade handling. **Strong points:** This five-passenger, near-luxury, front-engine, front-drive, mid-sized sedan offers more value than do other, more expensive cars in its class. A roomy, limousine-like interior with reclining backrests and plenty of rear seat room and storage space; large doors make for easy front- and rear-seat access; comfortable seats; user-friendly controls; exceptional reliability; and good resale value. **Weak points:** Excessive interior noise; a suspension that may be too firm for some; and serious fit and finish deficiencies. Practically all owner complaints unrelated to safety concerns, poor fit and finish, and water leaking into the cabin. Other concerns include engine and rear windshield/window ticking; a front power-seat grinding, groaning noise; transmission control module (TCM) updates needed to improve shifting; problems with the trunk opener; and sunshade switches that are located too close together. Buying an Avalon means you are getting the equivalent of an entry-level Lexus: It performs well, is loaded with safety, comfort, and convenience features, and costs thousands of dollars less than a Lexus. **Major redesign:** 1994, 1999, 2005, and 2013. **Highway/city fuel economy:** 7.0/10.7 L/100 km. Expect actual fuel consumption to be about 20 percent higher than advertised. **Best alternatives:** Other choices to consider are the Honda Accord V6, Hyundai Genesis, Mazda6, and Nissan Altima.

SAFETY: NHTSA gave the 2005-10 Avalon five stars for front and side crash protection and four stars for rollover resistance; 2013s had five star for overall crash safety. IIHS rates the 2000-13 Avalon as a "Good" performer in moderate overlap frontal crash tests; earlier models through 1995 didn't do as well. Side impact protection was "Good" for 2011-13 models. Rear (head restraint) crash protection was judged to be "Good" for the 2009-13 models, while 2001-08 Avalons turned in "Poor" crash results. Here are some of the many safety-related failures reported by owners: Sudden unintended acceleration; rear-corner blind spots and excessive rear windshield glare and distortion:

> Failed component in this vehicle, as well as every other 2013 Toyota Avalon, has a distorted rear window and one cannot get a clear view of what is behind. All lines are zig-zag and everything behind is fuzzy.

Loss of brakes; driver's seat belt may not retract; water leak from the roof staining the headliner; headliner falls down; takes months to get it corrected:

Purchased showroom 2013 Toyota Avalon with headliner in the rear dropped down. This is brand new ... I was told that probably some kids have pulled the headliner down while in showroom. Waiting for resolution I decided to read on common problems and low and behold! Toyota, you had better get this fixed immediately before there is an accident due to headliner obstructing the drivers view. How fast this is resolved is going to determine how I speak about Toyota and future purchases! Get after it! Next up, seat back covers also was blammed on kids in showroom pulling them down. I looked at the design and see how sorry the engineering is.

Other reported driving hazards: "Lag and lurch" when accelerating; when cruise control is engaged, applying the brake slows the car, but as soon as the foot is taken off the brake, the car surges back to its former speed; vehicle rolls backward when parked on an incline; "chin-to-chest" head restraints; a defective telescopic steering-wheel lever may cause the steering wheel to collapse towards the dash when the vehicle is underway; steering column is unusually loose; "outgassing" produces an interior film that coats the windows, seriously distorting visibility; newly designed high-intensity discharged headlights only partially illuminate the highway; and electrical shorts that may suddenly shut down dash lights.

ALERT! What is Toyota doing selling Bridgestones, instead of Michelin or Pirelli tires with this car? Ask for a replacement set. Serious glare and reflections throughout the car due to the trim and other instruments: A "must-check" during the test-drive:

Avalon dashboard trim causes a dangerous reflection of sunlight directly into driver's eyes. During mid-day sun, blinding beams of sunlight bounce off several areas of the mirrored-chrome-coloured plastic trim that surrounds the dashboard and wraps around the instrument cluster. Sunlight is reflected off chrome trim beneath the tachometer and speedometer. Blinding sunlight also reflects off trim on both sides of the steering wheel, and other points across the trim depending on time of day and direction of car, sunlight bounces off different places on the trim because the trim is beveled, instead of a vertical surface, it focuses the sunlight directly back into the driver's eyes. Drivers need to regularly glance down at the instrument cluster and reflected sunlight from that area and other sections on the dash is dangerously distracting.

Prices and Specs

Prices (Negotiable): *Base:* $42,000 **Freight:** $1,650 **Powertrain (Front-drive):** Engine: 3.5L V6 (268 hp), *Hybrid:* 2.5L 4-cyl. (200 hp); Transmissions: 6-speed auto., CVT auto. **Dimensions/capacity:** Passengers: 2/3; Wheelbase: 111 in.; H: 57/L: 195/W: 72 in.; Cargo volume: 16 cu. ft.; Fuel tank: 70L/regular; Headroom F/R: 3/2.5 in.; Legroom F/R: 41/31 in.; Tow limit: 1,003 lbs; Load capacity: 875 lb.; Turning circle: 36.9 ft.; Ground clearance: 5.3 in.; Weight: 3,497 lb.

Avalon Profile

	2004	2005	2006	2007	2008	2009	2010	2011	2012
Used Values ($)									
XL/Touring/Base	5,500	7,500	9,000	12,000	14,000	17,000	21,500	26,000	29,500
XLS/Premium	6,000	8,000	9,500	12,500	14,500	18,000	23,000	—	—
Recommended	☆	☆	☆	☆	☆	☆	☆	☆	☆
Reliability	☆	☆	☆	☆	☆	☆	☆	☆	☆

SECRET WARRANTIES, INTERNAL BULLETINS: 2005-09—Front power seat grinding, groaning. **2005-11**—Sunroof leaks at headliner and floor areas. **2006-07**—Harsh shifting. **2007**—Rough idle, stalling. **2007-08**—Steering-wheel flutter; body vibration. **2008-10**—High-beam headlight failures will be covered by Toyota's base warranty and, thereafter, by a "goodwill" policy. Claimants should refer to TSB #004410, published January 27, 2010. If Toyota rejects the claim, go immediately to small claims court. The company's service bulletin admits Toyota goofed. **2008-11**—Underbody rattling noises. **2009-11**—Front, rear knocking noises when passing over bumps.

SIENNA

RATING: Recommended (2012-14); Above Average (2009-11); Average (2007-08); Not Recommended in view of more than 1,644 reports of life-threatening failures for the 2004 model alone (1998-2006). There has been an astounding decrease in serious safety-related complaints since the dark days of 2004 and later models. Interestingly, the Sienna's 2011 redesign did not produce an inordinate number of owner complaints. **Road performance:** Smooth (most of the time) 3.5L V6 powertrain performance; and optional full-time AWD; standard stability control. Handling isn't as sharp and secure as some of the competing vans. Sienna is in the top of its class when all systems are working correctly, but when they don't:

> Joining highway in a situation where vehicles giving way ... braking then acceleration repeatedly, transmission refused to downshift on kick down, vehicle would not accelerate, actually slowed significantly forcing following vehicles to brake. Vehicle eventually began to pick up speed. Generally poor response from transmission in all modes. Transmission drops out of drive at low speeds causing engine to race before taking up Drive, very hard to operate vehicle smoothly. Excessive engine vibration and noise.

Strong points: Toyota's redesigned, third-generation Sienna has become more car-like than ever in its highway handling and comfort, while offering a larger, restyled interior. It is sold in a broad range of models, and stands out as the only van with an all-wheel-drive option (though this is not recommended). It's now available only with a 6-cylinder engine and as a seven- or eight-passenger carrier. Toyota built the Sienna for comfort and convenience. Sienna's V6 turns in respectable acceleration times, and the handling is also more car-like, but not as agile as with the Odyssey. **Weak points:** Recommended options are bundled with costly gadgets; an unusually large number of body rattles and assorted other noises. The 2013s aren't as versatile or as reasonably priced as Chrysler's vans. How's this for "spin control?" Toyota says slimmer seats and controls add to the feeling of "roominess." No matter how they spin it, the interior looks less luxurious than before, cabin noise levels are higher, and fit and finish is far from acceptable. Avoid models equipped with the under-powered, noisy, 4-cylinder engine. **Major redesign:** 1998, 2004, and 2011. **Highway/city fuel economy:** *(2012) 2.7L:* 7.5/10.4 L/100 km. *3.5L:* 8.1/11.5 L/100 km. *AWD:* 9.0/12.8 L/100 km. The 2.7L 4-cylinder engine burns almost as much fuel as the V6. **Best alternatives:** Toyota promises to keep 2014 prices near last year's levels, making this year's lineup a better buy from a price perspective. As far as quality is concerned, it would be wise to delay your purchase a few months to take advantage of fewer factory-related glitches with later versions. Faster than average depreciation is another important factor to consider. For example, a 2009 LE seven-passenger AWD Sienna that sold for $37,420 now sells for $15,000. If an independent mechanic OK's the deal, this could be a bargain for used car buyers. Other choices: Honda's Odyssey and the Mazda5 (a mini-minivan). Chrysler's minivans bring up the rear of the pack due primarily to their Pentastar V6 and automatic transmission failures. Why not Nissan's Quest? The Quest's persistent powertrain and fit and finish deficiencies over the years preclude the van's purchase until we see if the upcoming redesign removes or exacerbates these deficiencies.

SAFETY: NHTSA gives the 2011 through 2014s four and five stars for crashworthiness in all categories;1998-2010 Siennas did even better, with five-star scores following almost every crash test. IIHS gives the 2005-13 Siennas its top, "Good," rating for moderate overlap frontal offset crash safety; side protection was also judged "Good" with the tested 2005-13 models. Roof protection for 2011-13s was rated "Good," however , head restraint protection on the 2005-10 models earned a "Poor" score, while the 2011-13 versions were "Good." Be wary of the power-sliding door and power-assisted rear liftgate. The doors can crush children and pose unnecessary risks to other occupants, while the liftgate can seriously injure anyone standing under it. Go for Michelin or Pirelli original-equipment tires; don't buy Bridgestone or Dunlop run-flats. Believe it or not, 2012 Siennas *continue* to suddenly accelerate and lose braking capability, in spite of Toyota's brake/throttle override feature:

> The contact owns a 2012 Toyota Sienna. The contact was driving 15 mph when the vehicle suddenly accelerated. The contact attempted to stop the vehicle but the brakes would not respond. The contact had to shut the vehicle off while it was moving to stop the vehicle from accelerating and avoid a possible crash. The failure mileage was 2,800 miles.

The contact stated that as he approached a stop light, he suddenly experienced sudden acceleration and there was an increase in the engine rpms up to 8,000 rpms. The contact forcefully applied the brakes and shifted into Neutral. The vehicle then decelerated and the contact drove home slowly. The dealer was notified and towed the vehicle in for a diagnostic test. They were unable to diagnose a failure and attributed it to a driver's error. The manufacturer was notified and offered no assistance. The failure mileage was 900 miles.

When the brakes *do* work, and are applied, the driver's seat moves forward; cruise control won't turn off; brake failure:

At around 5 pm on a clear Monday evening I went to turn left into a parking spot. I stepped on the gas and nothing happened, I let up a bit and stepped again and my Sienna shot forward. I slammed on the brake halfway into the parking spot and ran into the tree in front of the van.

Airbags don't deploy when needed; power-sliding rear doors and power rear hatch are two options known more for their dangerous malfunctions than their utility:

My 17-month-old's head got jammed between the right rear wheel and the right rear door panel while the electric door slid open. Even though my wife pulled on the door handle the door kept sliding open. My baby's head was crushed between the tire and door panel. This is a very unsafe design as my wife tried to stop the door from sliding back and the door kept moving.

• • •

My 2-year-old daughter got her leg caught in the back part of the sliding door of a 2011 Toyota Sienna. She was inside the car. The door was opened. Her leg fell into the space while the door was opening. The door opened as far as it could and constricted her leg. Her leg was so constricted we could not reposition her body to open the door. ... She was trapped (screaming) for 20–25 minutes. Her leg was cold and turning blue before it was freed. ... I'm very concerned about the design of the door. I've looked at other minivans (even the same make and model but different year) and they don't have the gap in the back part of the door like the 2011 Toyota Sienna.

• • •

Couple of months after I got the car, there were several incidents [in which] me and family members were hit on our heads and shoulders by self closing liftgate [and we] didn't know what the cause was. After researching about this problem, Toyota had recalled Sienna in the past about this same problem for older models for faulty strut used for power liftgates.

In another reported incident, a driver accelerated to pass another car, and his Sienna suddenly accelerated out of control, while the brakes were useless. Brakes

Prices and Specs

Prices (Negotiable): *Base:* $28,140, *V6:* $29,140, *LE 8-pass.:* $32,905, *LE AWD 7-pass.:* $35,730, *SE V6 8-pass.:* $37,205, *XLE V6:* $39,740, Limited AWD: $41,425 **Freight:** $1,635 **Powertrain (front-drive/AWD):** Engine: 3.5L V6 (266 hp); Transmission: 6-speed auto. **Dimensions/capacity:** Passengers: 2/3/2; 2/3/3; Wheelbase: 119.3 in.; H: 69.5/L: 200.2/W: 78.2 in.; Headroom F/R1/R2: 3.5/4/2.5 in.; Legroom F/R1/R2: 40.5/31.5/2.5 in.; Cargo volume: 39.1 cu. ft.; Fuel tank: 79L/regular; Tow limit: 3,500 lb.; Load capacity: 1,120 lb.; Turning circle: 36.7 ft.; Ground clearance: 6.2 in.; Weight: 4,189–4,735 lb.

can take a couple of seconds before they engage; the slightest touch of the gear shifter causes a shift into Neutral or Reverse; airbags fail to deploy; multiple warning lights come on, and the vehicle cannot shift; sunroof may spontaneously explode; front windshield distortion:

I noticed a distortion across the lower 3" of the windshield. It is very distracting, as the paint stripes on the road "bend" towards the driver. It's worse at night.

Excessive rear-view mirror vibration; factory-installed TV screen obstructs the field of vision through the rear-view mirror; rear tires quickly wear out; front passenger seatback tilts forward when braking and second-row seats may be unstable.

ALERT! The run-flat tires are fast-wearing and expensive to replace. There have also been many owner reports that the brake and accelerator pedals are mounted too close together; see if this affects your driving during the dealership test-drive:

The contact owns a 2012 Toyota Sienna. The contact stated that when attempting to brake or accelerate, both pedals would be depressed simultaneously. The contact stated that the two pedals were too close in proximity. The manufacturer and the dealer were notified of the failure, but denied any assistance with repairs to the vehicle. The vehicle was not repaired. The failure mileage was 60 miles and the current mileage is 1,300 miles.

Sienna Profile

	2004	2005	2006	2007	2008	2009	2010	2011	2012
Used Values ($)									
CE	4,000	5,500	6,500	8,500	9,500	11,500	14,500	19,000	22,500
LE AWD	4,500	6,500	8,000	10,500	12,500	15,000	17,500	24,500	28,500
XLE	5,500	7,000	9,500	11,000	13,500	16,500	—	26,000	31,000
Recommended	★1	★1	★1	☆3	☆3	☆4	☆4	☆4	☆5
Reliability	★2	★2	★2	☆3	☆4	☆4	☆4	☆4	☆5

SECRET WARRANTIES, INTERNAL BULLETINS: All years: Sliding-door hazards, malfunctions, and noise are a veritable plague affecting all model years and generating a ton of service bulletins. Owner feedback confirms that front brake pads and discs are often replaced under Toyota's "goodwill" policy if they wear out before 2 years/40,000 km (in spite of Toyota's pretensions that brakes aren't a warrantable item) and the customer is adamant that the brakes aren't "reasonably" durable. Rusting at the base of the two front doors will be repaired at no cost, usually with a courtesy car included. **2003-09**—Upper, lower windshield ticking noise. **2004**—Rear disc brake groan (TSB #BR002-04). Intermediate steering shaft noise on turns. Front-door area wind noise (TSB #NV009-03). Power-sliding door inoperative, rattles (the saga continues). Back door shudder and water leaks. Seat heaters operate only on high. **2004-05**—Remedy for hard starts in cold weather. Transmission lag, gear hunting. Premature brake pad wear. Fuel-injector ticking. Inoperative AC light flashing. AC blower or compressor noise; seized compressor. **2004-06**—Silencing engine ping, knock. Power-hatch door shudder and leakage. Power-sliding door rattles. Excessive steering effort in high road-salt areas. **2004-07**—Back power-sliding doors are hard to close. Back power-door shudder. **2004-08**—Front power-seat grinding, groaning. Remedy for front brake pads that wear out prematurely. **2004-10**—Front seat squeaking. Sliding doors don't operate smoothly (change the lock assembly). Sliding-door rattle. Brake rattle, buzz from driver's side of the dash. **2007**—Inoperative front, sliding-door windows. Front-seat squeak. **2006-09**—No shift from Park. **2007-08**—Engine compartment squeaking. **2011-12**—Engine ticking; more ticking from the windshield/back glass. Transfer-case fluid leaks. Water puddles in the van's rear storage area near the back door. Insufficient alternator charging may require an updated pulley assembly.

RAV4 ★★★★

RATING: Above Average (2009-14); Below Average (2006-08); Average (1996-2005). This SUV crossover combines a car-type unibody platform with elevated seating and optional AWD. Although classed as a compact SUV, the RAV4 is large enough to carry a kid-sized third-row bench seat, giving it seven passenger capacity. A powerful V6 makes this downsized SUV one of the fastest crossovers on the market. **Road performance:** 4-cylinder acceleration from a stop is acceptable with a full load; excellent V6 powertrain performance; transmission is hesitant to shift to a lower gear when under load, and sometimes produces jerky low-speed shifts; some nose plow and body lean when cornering under power; and some road and wind noise. Good handling and a comfortable, and relatively quiet ride are big improvements over earlier, more firmly sprung models. **Strong points:** Lots of sales incentives available. Base models offer a nice array of standard safety, performance, and convenience features, including electronic stability control and standard brake override; RAV4 seats five, but an optional third-row bench on Base and Limited models increases capacity to seven; comfortable seats; a quiet interior; cabin gauges and controls are easy to access and read; exceptional reliability; and good fuel economy with the 4-cylinder engine (the V6 is almost as fuel frugal). **Weak points:** Resale value is only average. (A "Strong Point" for used SUV shoppers!)

Practically all of the owner complaints unrelated to safety involve poor fit and finish and audio system malfunctions. Some drivers say they are sickened by a sulphur smell that invades the interior. Owners also deride the flimsy glove box lid, loose sun visor, constantly flickering traction control light, sticking ignition key, uncomfortable head restraints, squeaks and rattles from the dashboard and rear-seat area. **Major redesign:** 2001 and 2006. **Highway/city fuel economy:** *2.5L:* 6.9/9.4 L/100 km, 41/30 mpg. *2.5L AWD:* 7.2/9.7 L/100 km. *3.5L:* 7.4/10.7 L/100 km. *3.5L AWD:* 7.7/11.7 L/100 km. Owners say fuel economy figures are too high by 15 percent. **Best alternatives:** Other vehicles worth considering are the Honda CR-V, Hyundai Tucson, and Nissan X-Trail.

SAFETY: NHTSA gives the 2012-13 RAV4 five stars for side crashworthiness and four stars for frontal and rollover protection. 2014s earned five stars for side crash safety; four stars for rollover protection. IIHS rates 2004-13s "Good" in moderate overlap front crash tests; 2001-04 models were judged "Acceptable," and 1996-2000 models were considered "Poor." Since 2009, the RAV4 has elicited only a handful of safety-related complaints, which is impressive for such a popular SUV. Among the incidents reported, we see the return of sudden, unintended acceleration (even after recall repairs were done) and loss of braking:

> After attempting to drive in reverse out of a parking space with the brake pedal engaged, the vehicle suddenly accelerated and crashed into a parked vehicle. A police report was filed. The driver sustained bruises to her leg. The vehicle was taken to the dealer who was unable to diagnose the failure. The failure and current mileage was 4,620 miles. The consumer stated the vehicle changed gears on its own, and the gas pedal went to the floor on its own as well.
>
> . . .
>
> The contact owns a 2012 Toyota RAV4. The contact stated that upon shifting into Drive, there was a rapid increase in the engine rpms and the vehicle began to surge forward. The contact applied excessive pressure to the brake pedal, but the engine continued to rev. Another individual opened the doors and turned off the ignition.
>
> . . .
>
> My 2012 has done this virtually from day 1. When braking, there is a sudden acceleration for 1/4 to 1/2 second at the time the transmission downshifts. I also notice it while driving at high speeds and braking. It is more dangerous at slower speeds especially when braking at a light with someone in front of you. It feels like you are pressing both the brake and accelerator at the same time. It does not do this all the time. Maybe once or twice a day. I think it has to do with how hard you brake and what speed you are going. It is most noticeable just before you come to a stop. It always happens just as the transmission automatically downshifts and most noticeable when it downshifts to Second or First. I notice it when braking say from 65 to 55 mph as well, but the sudden acceleration at that speed has no or minimal affect and is not that noticeable.

Other reports: Fire erupted in the engine compartment; steering angle sensor malfunction causes the vehicle to stall out; a "thumping" rear suspension noise; cracking front windshields:

> Vehicle is only a few weeks old and the windshield began developing a crack from the passenger side spreading towards the center of and down towards the bottom of the passenger side.

Original-equipment Yokohama tires may blow out their side walls; and the defroster/air circulation system is weak; and wide rear roof pillars that obstruct visibility. And, the mice are back! Rodents routinely enter the vehicle at will through the clean-air filter. One dealer suggested owners buy mouse traps or adopt a cat:

> Check Engine light indicated. The car was taken to the dealer, where the dealer mentioned, "Evidence of rodent/ small animal has chewed wiring harness at connector completely through." The car will need a new wiring harness.

ALERT! The Sport model has an option that uses run-flat tires and dispenses with the tailgate-mounted spare tire. Stick with the regular tire: It's cheaper and less problematic. If you come across a substantially discounted 2012, buy it. The 2013s don't offer much more.

RAV4 Profile

	2004	2005	2006	2007	2008	2009	2010	2011	2012
Used Values ($)									
Base 4x2	—	—	—	—	—	—	13,000	16,000	19,000
Base 4x4	4,500	—	7,000	8,500	9,500	10,500	14,000	17,500	21,000
Sport V6	5,000	—	7,500	9,500	11,500	13,000	15,500	20,500	24,000
LTD V6	—	7,000	8,000	10,000	12,500	13,500	18,000	22,500	28,000
Recommended	★3	★3	★2	★2	★2	☆	☆	☆	☆
Reliability	★4	★4	★2	★2	☆4	☆	☆	☆	☆

SECRET WARRANTIES, INTERNAL BULLETINS: 2002-06—Correction for vehicles that pull to the right when accelerating. **2003-11**—Windshield ticking noise considered a factory-related problem (T-SB-0142-08, published July 29, 2008). **2004-10**—Front-seat squeaking. **2006**—Engine timing cover oil leaks. **2006-07**—Automatic transmission shift lever doesn't move smoothly. Water leaks onto the passenger floorboard. Front-door locks may be inoperative in cold weather. **2006-08**—Engine compartment squeaks. Steering clunk, pop, knock. **2006-09**—Engine ticking noise. Multiple warning lamps lit; no shift from Park. Brake rattle, buzz heard from the driver's-side dash area. Inoperative moonroof. **2006-10**—No-crank, no-start requires the installation of a revised neutral switch assembly. Rough idle. Loose sun visor mount. Automatic transmission whining noise. **2007**—Paint stains on horizontal surfaces. **2008**—Water drips from the headliner near the A-pillar.

VENZA

RATING: Above Average (2010-14); Average (2009). Toyota's Venza is a five-passenger wagon sold in two trim levels that match the two available engines. Going into its fifth year, the car offers the styling and comfort of a wagon with the flexibility of a small SUV. This combination has proven itself to be relatively problem-free and a good highway performer. **Road performance:** Powerful and efficient engines; pleasant riding though the ride is stiff at times; and handling is acceptable, though there isn't much steering feedback. **Strong points:** Roomy interior; innovative cabin storage areas; an automatic headlight dimmer; easy entry and exit; and a low rear loading height. **Weak points:** No third-row seat; radio station indicator washes out in sunlight; and high-intensity discharge headlights are annoying to other drivers, are often stolen, and are expensive to replace. Resale value is lower than one would expect for a Toyota SUV. For example, a 2009 entry-level Venza that sold new for $28,270 is now worth only $15,000. **Major redesign:** 1998 and 2005. **Highway/city fuel economy:** *2.7L:* 6.8/10.0 L/100 km. *AWD:* 7.1/10.2 L/100 km. *3.5L:* 7.6/11.0L/100 km. *AWD:* 7.9/11.5 L/100 km. **Best alternatives:** The Ford Edge, Nissan Murano, and Toyota Highlander.

SAFETY: NHTSA gave the 2012 Venza a three-star rating for front crashworthiness, five stars for side protection, and four stars for rollover resistance. IIHS rated the vehicle as "Good" for frontal offset, side, roof, and rear occupant protection. Not a single safety-related incident reported with the 2012 Venza; only seven complaints were filed against the 2011 model. Sudden,unintended acceleration being the most life-threatening:

> We accelerated our Venza to match ongoing traffic speeds, when the throttle stuck wide open and was increasing in speed, I stepped on the brakes, which failed to respond. I then checked the cruise control, to see if I had inadvertently engaged it, but I had not. I then started to pump the accelerator pedal with extreme force, and after numerous pumps, the throttle disengaged.

Transmission would not go into Reverse; the Hill-Start Assist feature doesn't prevent the car from rolling back when stopped on a hill in traffic:

I feel Toyota should immediately send out a safety notice requiring all employees be briefed about the Hill-Start Assist feature, how it doesn't activate automatically, and how to activate the feature when stopped on an uphill slope.

Airbags failed to deploy; brakes don't immediately work when slow and steady pressure is applied; sometimes, after the brakes are applied, the car won't accelerate; automatic rear hatch can crush a hand if it is caught when the hatch is closing; seat belt began strangling a three-year-old, who had to be cut free; sunroof exploded; the radio overheated up to 63 degrees C (145 degrees F); and chin-to-chest head restraints:

> The head rest on my vehicle pushes my neck forward into an extremely uncomfortable position. This cannot be adjusted. As a 5'4" female, I was having to seek medical treatment for neck and shoulder pain following long trips. I have reversed the head rest so that I can continue to drive my car. I am now concerned about the safety of this in the event of an accident (whiplash), but feel like I have no choice. Severe neck pain was interfering with ability to turn my head while driving.

ALERT! Yikes! Not the poorly designed head restraints, again!

> The headrest for the front seats on the Venza makes these seats the most uncomfortable I have ever sat in, let alone drive. I am only 5'4" tall and the way the headrest lands, it pushes my head forward when I drive. I end up with both a headache and a neck ache whenever I drive. It appears this vehicle was designed for someone taller, perhaps a man. The headrest needs to be redesigned for someone of my stature. I would gladly pay for another headrest if one was available. But the bottom line here is that once again the needs of women (shorter than men) are not what is driving the design. I expect more from all car manufacturers. It is time to recognize that women make up 51% of the population.

Venza Profile

	2009	2010	2011	2012
Used Values ($)				
Base	11,500	15,000	18,500	22,000
V6 AWD	13,500	17,500	22,000	25,500
Recommended	☆	☆	☆	☆
Reliability	☆	☆	☆	☆

Prices and Specs

Prices (Negotiable): *Base front drive:* $29,310, *AWD:* $30,760, *V6:* $30,800, *AWD:* $32,250 **Freight:** $1,635 **Powertrain (Front-drive/AWD):** Engines: 2.7L 4-cyl. (182 hp), 3.5L V6 (268 hp); Transmission: 6-speed auto. **Dimensions/capacity:** Passengers: 2/3; Wheelbase: 109.3 in.; H: 63.4/L: 189/W: 75 in.; Cargo volume: 33 cu. ft.; Fuel tank: 67 L/regular; Headroom F/R: 5/4.5 in.; Legroom F/R: 41/30 in.; Tow limit: 2,500-3,500 lb.; Load capacity: 825 lb.; Turning circle: 39.1 ft.; Ground clearance: 8.1 in.; Weight: 4,125 lb.

SECRET WARRANTIES, INTERNAL BULLETINS: 2007-11—Some vehicles equipped with 2GR-FE/FXE towing package engines may exhibit an oil seep from the engine oil cooler pipes. **2009-10**—Wind noise from the front door area can be silenced by adding weather stripping. This repair is covered by Toyota's 36-month/60,000 km warranty. If that warranty has expired, argue that "reasonable durability" is at least five years and ask for partial compensation. Rear end squawk noise on bumps. **2009-11**—Correction for a steering column rattle. The abnormal noise may be caused by rear coil spring contact with the lower strut seat due to a displaced or damaged rear coil spring lower insulator. An updated rear coil spring lower insulator is available for this condition. **2009-13**—Drivers may hear a "pop" noise from the steering column when turning the steering wheel sharply during low speed maneuvers. Some Venzas equipped with 2GR-FE engines may exhibit difficulty restarting in sub-freezing temperatures (approximately -4°F [-20°C] and lower). A new Engine Room Junction Block Assembly is available to address this condition. Some vehicles equipped with the 1AR-FE engine may exhibit one or more of the following conditions: An inoperative A/C while the vehicle is stopped, or rising engine temperature when stopped. Some vehicles may exhibit a condition where the seat heater is inoperative. Replace the seat heater assembly at Toyota's expense. Cold start engine knock/rattle. **2013**—Entune infotainment/navigation issues and concerns.

HIGHLANDER

RATING: Above Average (2009-14); Average (2001-08). A crossover alternative to a minivan, this competent, refined, family-friendly SUV puts function ahead of style and provides cargo and passenger versatility along with a high level of quality. The car has been downgraded due to the resurgence of brake failures and complaints of sudden, unintended acceleration. **Road performance:** Powerful engines and a smooth, refined powertrain; the Hybrid can propel itself on electric power alone; a quiet interior enhances the comfortable ride; and responsive handling. **Strong points:** Roomy second-row seating is fairly versatile. Third-row seating is much improved with the bigger 2014 version. **Weak points:** The third-row seat is a bit tight and doesn't fold in a 50/50 split. **Major redesign:** 2000 and 2007. **Highway/city fuel economy:** 7.3/10.4 L/100 km. *V6:* 8.8/12.3 L/100 km. *Hybrid:* 8.0/7.4 L/100 km. **Best alternatives:** From the Detroit SUV side, try the Buick Enclave, Chevrolet Traverse, Ford Flex, and GMC Acadia. A good Asian SUV is the Honda Pilot. The Honda Odyssey is the only suitable Asian minivan choice. V6-equipped models best represent the Highlander's attributes, as the Hybrid models' higher prices will take years to offset in fuel savings.

SAFETY: NHTSA gives the 2005-14 Highlander and its Hybrid variant four stars for frontal crashworthiness and rollover resistance; five stars were awarded for side impact protection. IIHS rates the 2001-13s as "Good" in providing occupant protection in moderate overlap frontal crashes. Side and roof protection were also judged "Good" for the 2008-13 models. Head restraints were rated "Good" for the 2008-13s and "Poor" for the 2004-07 models. NHTSA's safety-defect log sheet shows only 27 complaints registered against the 2012-13 models. Nevertheless, lag and lurch acceleration, unintended acceleration and brake failures are front and centre:

> The contact owns a 2012 Toyota Highlander. The contact stated that while attempting to park with the brake pedal depressed, the vehicle suddenly accelerated and went over the curb. The contact applied the brake with both feet and shifted into Park in order to bring the vehicle to a complete stop.

• • •

> The contact owns a 2012 Toyota Highlander. The contact stated that while driving at 40 mph, she attempted to brake but the vehicle accelerated rapidly instead. She attempted to apply the brake, however the brake pedal had become very stiff. She had to apply extreme pressure to the brake and the vehicle stopped 15 feet later. She shifted into Neutral and turned the vehicle off. The vehicle was taken to the dealer for diagnosis where the contract was informed that there was an idle up clutch defect, which occurred at low speeds and when the air conditioner was activated. The dealer would not repair the vehicle. The manufacturer was notified but offered no assistance. The vehicle had not been repaired. The current mileage is 6,800 miles.

• • •

> My Highlander was at the airport for three days parked. When I was leaving the lot I was driving slow in the lot to pay my parking. When I got out of the lot to mainstream traffic I tried to accelerate and the car would only go slow as I kept pushing the throttle. There were cars on both sides of me with no one in front and then the car just took off. It did startle me because I was not expecting this. Thank god no one was in front of me because I am sure I would not have reacted fast enough to stop because of the rapid acceleration. Something is wrong with the throttle in these vehicles. I did not take it in because I am sure they would not have been able to reproduce the problem. This has only happened once and I hope it doesn't happen again.

• • •

> While pulling into parking space in private shopping mall at slow rate of speed the vehicle suddenly and without warning rapidly accelerated forward into vehicle parked directly in front of my vehicle. My vehicle went up and over parked vehicle causing damage to both vehicles. No one was hurt in this accident and no police report was made as it was on private property. Complaint was made to

---

Prices and Specs

Prices (Negotiable): *Base:* $31,675, *V6 4WD:* $35,925, *Limited V6 4WD:* $45,075, *Hybrid:* $42,990, *Hybrid Limited:* $51,950 **Freight:** $1,635 **Powertrain (Front-drive/AWD):** Engines: 2.7L 4-cyl. (187 hp), 3.3L V6 (270 hp), 3.5L V6 (270 hp); Transmissions: 5-speed auto., 6-speed auto., CVT **Dimensions/capacity:** Passengers: 2/3/2, *Hybrid:* 2/3; Wheelbase: 110 in.; H: 69.3/L: 188.4/W: 75.2 in.; Cargo volume: 37.5 cu. ft.; Fuel tank: 72.5L/regular; Headroom F/R1/R2: 3.5/5/0 in. (Ouch! Third-row seat is for only the very young or very short.); Legroom F/R1/R2: 41.5/32/23.5 in.; Tow limit: 3,500-5,000 lb.; Load capacity: 1,200 lb.; Turning circle: 38.7 ft.; Ground clearance: 8.1 in.; Weight: 4,050-4,641 lb.

Toyota who investigated and Toyota determined that no vehicle defect or design existed and refused to offer any assistance. My wife who was driving the vehicle has never had an accident and swears as to the fact. She did not contribute at all to this accident. Toyota is marketing a defective vehicle which will eventually and unfortunately result in death or serious injury if they are not now held accountable.

Other incidents: Airbag failed to deploy; transmission will not hold car parked on an incline; speedometer overstates the car's true speed by about 3 mph; sudden brake failure; brake and steering both went out as driver was making a turn; engine replaced after overheating, due to road debris damaging the radiator; engine loses power in turns; and windshield distortion.

ALERT! Don't open the window while underway:

> While driving on the highway, my son opened the rear passenger window. When he opened the window the noise and pressure on our ears was unbearable, it was like an extremely loud helicopter noise. We even tried opening other windows in the car to reduce the pressure and noise, while the noise and pressure were reduced it was still very loud and distracting. I called the Toyota dealer where we bought the car and he said all cars do that and to just open another window to relieve pressure. When I told him we tried that and it did not work he did not have any other answers. The dealer gave me a phone number to Toyota service, I called them and the rep said she had checked and they have never heard of anything like that. After checking on the Internet I have found multiple instances where other people have had this issue, the noise is so loud it actually hurts your eardrums.

Highlander Profile

	2004	2005	2006	2007	2008	2009	2010	2011	2012
Used Values ($)									
Base	5,000	6,000	—	—	—	—	—	20,500	24,000
AWD	—	7,000	8,000	9,500	12,500	14,000	17,500	23,500	28,000
Base Hybrid	—	—	8,500	10,000	12,500	15,000	21,000	26,500	32,000
Recommended	★	★	★	★	★	☆	☆	☆	☆
Reliability	★	★	★	★	★	☆	☆	☆	☆

SECRET WARRANTIES, INTERNAL BULLETINS: 2011-12—Insufficient alternator charging may require an updated pulley assembly. Procedures needed to fix a loose roof drip moulding.

TACOMA ★★★

RATING: Average (2011-14); Below Average (1995-2010). This cheap light-duty, basic truck would have been rated higher if it weren't for the Tacoma's infamous hazardous drivetrain, decade-old lag and lurch transmission, and sudden unintended acceleration problems spilling over into the 2011-14 lineup. Plus, Toyota's entry-level pickup isn't as utilitarian as its predecessors or some of the competition (watch the payload), but it has sufficient power and is relatively inexpensive if not too gussied up. **Road performance:** Well-chosen powertrain and steering set-up; ideal for off-road work with electronic stability control and the optional suspension; good acceleration, although delayed transmission engagement and excessive drivetrain vibration are still present. Very responsive handling over smooth roads; over rough terrain, the ride can be jolting and steering control reduced. If you decide to go for the optional off-road suspension, you will quickly notice the firmer ride and increased road feedback. The driving position seems low when compared with the competition. **Strong points:** A well-garnished, roomy interior; plenty of storage space; and good reliability. **Weak points:** Excessive driveline vibration:

> Toyota has included this model in the technical service bulletin for the shudder. However, the dealership and Toyota fail to tell you about the known problems with the truck before they sell it to a sucker like me. Additionally, there is a vibration from the front end when I apply the brakes, especially when braking from high speeds. I took it back to the dealership and they had the technicians go through the instructions in the technical service bulletin. The technicians confirmed the shudder, and the service manager said there is no fix for the problem.

Shaking drivetrains and bad gear boxes (transmission pops out of gear); premature wearout of the brake rotors and drums; squeaking, howling rear brakes; AC malfunctions; noisy fuel pump; suspension bottoms out at 300-500 lbs; instrument panel is poorly-lit; loose front passenger seat; and some fit and finish complaints. **Major redesign:** 1995 and 2004. The 2014 will have a late introduction; changes are uncertain. **Highway/city fuel economy:** *2.7:* 7.8/10.5 L/100 km. *Auto.:* 7.9/11.0 L/100 km. *AWD:* 9.1/12.0 L/100 km. *4.0 4×4:* 10.8/14.7 L/100 km. *Auto.:* 9.9/13.4 L/100 km. **Best alternatives:** Look for a nearly identical 2012 model discounted by about 15 percent. Other choices: The Chevrolet Terrain and Traverse, Nissan's Frontier and X-Trail, and the Toyota Tacoma.

SAFETY: 2004-14 models get a four- and five-star rating across the board from NHTSA. IIHS "Good" designation for 2005-13 models' moderate overlap front collision protection and 2009-13 side protection. Roof strength was judged to be "Marginal" with the 2005-13 models, while rear crashworthiness was scored "Good" for the 2009-13s equipped with bucket seats. 2005-08 models equipped with similar bucket seeks were rated "Marginal." Only 27 life-threatening incidents were registered on the 2012-13 models where 50 reports per year would be the average. But the same safety hazards reappear year after year. Airbags fail to deploy; sudden unintended acceleration accompanied by loss of braking ability; truck surges forward when stopped; brakes come on by themselves when turning and there is no brake light warning:

> Reported phenomenon with my 2013 Tacoma has occurred 10 times within the previous 5000 miles. When entering a turn with no brakes applied, most commonly a cloverleaf, the vehicle stability control will engage and apply then breakes in the middle of the turn. No brake lights are displayed so vehicles behind are not aware of the sudden slowing.

> *www.tacomaworld.com/forum/suspension/41215-lift-vsc-answer.html* ...

> *www.tacomaworld.com/forum/2nd-gen-tacomas/167922-who-has-problems-after-3-less-lift-vsc-who-doesnt.html* ...

> *www.tacomaworld.com/forum/2nd-gen-tacomas/272560-abs-activates-occasionally-after-front-end-lift.html* ...

> *www.tacomaworld.com/forum/2nd-gen-tacomas/92474-recalibrating-vsc-why-how.html*

Spare tire fell off the vehicle in traffic; false low-pressure tire alerts:

> The dealer suggested that I try driving on different roads and to take another route home. The dealer also stated that radio signals are causing the light to flash. My 2013's mileage: 158 miles.

ALERT! Payload capacity may be overly optimistic:

> My 2012 Toyota Tacoma TRD Off Road does not meet its payload capacity. It has a limit of 1240 lbs and routinely bottoms out with 300–500 lbs in the bed of the truck. Toyota knows about the issue on its 2005-11s [and] has issued TSBs on the leaf springs but refuses to solve the issue on the new 2012 trucks.

Tacoma Profile

	2004	2005	2006	2007	2008	2009	2010	2011	2012
Used Values ($)									
Acces Cab 4x2	4,500	5,500	5,500	6,000	6,500	8,000	10,500	13,000	15,500
4x4 SR5	—	—	—	8,000	9,000	10,000	12,500	15,000	17,500
V6	5,500	7,000	8,000	9,000	10,000	12,000	15,500	17,500	21,000
Double Cab/SR5	—	9,500	10,000	11,500	13,500	14,500	18,500	25,000	25,000
PR/TRD	—	10,000	11,500	12,500	14,500	15,500	19,500	23,500	26,000
Recommended	★	★	★	★	★	★	★	★	★
Reliability	★	★	★	★	★	★	★	☆	☆

Prices and Specs

Prices (Negotiable): *Access Cab 4×2:* $22,100, *4×2 SR5:* $24,125, *4×4:* $26,450, *4×4 SR5:* $28,325, *4×4 V6:* $26,900, *4×4 V6 SR5:* $29,200, *V6 TRD offroad:* $31,950, *Double Cab V6:* $28,500, *Double Cab V6 TRD Sport:* $31,950 **Freight:** $1,635 **Powertrain (Rear-drive/AWD):** Engines: 2.7L 4-cyl. (159 hp), 4.0L V6 (236 hp); Transmissions: 5-speed man. 6-speed man., 4-speed auto., 5-speed auto. **Dimensions/capacity:** Passengers: 2/2; Wheelbase: 127.8 in.; H: 70/L: 208.1/W: 75 in.; Fuel tank: 80L/regular; Headroom F/R: 4/3 in.; Legroom F/R: 42.5/28 in.; Tow limit: 3,500-6,500 lb.; Load capacity: 1,100 lb.; Turning circle: 44.6 ft.; Ground clearance: 8.1 in.; Weight: 4,115 lb.

SECRET WARRANTIES, INTERNAL BULLETINS: 2005-12—Passing over rough surfaces may produce a steering shaft rattle. **2005-13**—A rear differential whine at 50-60 mph may be heard by some owners of Tacoma pickups. In TSB #005713 issued on April 26, 2013, Toyota said the noise could occur in 2005-13 models with the 5-speed automatic transmission that were not equipped with limited-slip or locking rear differentials. Replacement of the differetial is the cure. **2011-12**—Bouncy rear suspension ride with a heavy load can be corrected by installing free upgraded rear spring assemblies up to 3 years/36,000 miles.

EUROPEAN VEHICLES

Mice ate my Audi TT ($18,250).

hitchhikinganimals.blogspot.com/2009/10/mice-ate-my-car-support-group-needed.html

TECHNICAL BACKGROUND: Animal damage primarily occurs on easily accessible, exposed cables and on thin cables. To avoid future animal bites, advise the customer to clean the engine compartment. Electrical deterrents and cable protection have proven effective, but 100% protection cannot be guaranteed. **WARRANTY:** This damage is due to outside influence and is not covered by any Audi warranty.

Audi of America
2012 memo to dealers

Slow European Sales

Europe's in a financial meltdown, and its automobile industry reflects this. On both sides of the Atlantic, European automakers are having their worst sales slump in a decade and turning to China as a safe haven.

German car makers are the major exception. BMW and Daimler remain profitable in part because they are taking market share from the other manufacturers by offering luxury vehicles at a middle-class price. Volkswagen/Audi is also a major winner after holding the line on prices and discounting its high-end models.

Hard times in Europe impact Canadian new car buyers in two ways:

1. European manufacturers are offering deeper cuts to Canadians in the new year through the use of low-cost financing, dealer discounts, and manufacturer rebates. Volvo will likely join the Daimler, BMW, and VW/Audi parade to lower prices, while Land Rover, Jaguar, and Porsche will likely

both gouge and cut. Fiat, on the other hand, is on the ropes in Europe and will probably stand pat on prices in Canada or increase them only slightly.

2. Cross-border shopping will surge as buyers of high-end European cars and SUVs flock to the States to take advantage of cheaper prices. This is already happening, says Statistics Canada in a cross-border travel report issued August 2012, which found Canadian residents took nearly 2.8 million overnight trips abroad in June, the highest monthly figure since record keeping began in 1972.

EUROPEAN "ORPHANS"

Orphans are those vehicles that have been sold by their parent builder, or, as in Volvo's case, sold twice to different automobile manufacturers. Usually when this occurs, the purchased companies dwindle into bankruptcy or irrelevancy after a few years. It happened with American Motors, Bricklin, Chrysler, DeLorean, and Saab, and may also bring down Volvo, an automaker with some good cars, that's still struggling.

There are many problems with buying orphan models. First, there's the high cost of servicing, due to increased costs for parts that become rarer and rarer. Second, it's incredibly difficult to find mechanics who can spot the likely causes of some common failures; there isn't a large pool of them who work on those vehicles all the time, and those who can work on them don't have current service bulletins to guide them. There's also an absence of secret ("goodwill") warranties to pay for work outside of the warranty period, because the automaker will have dropped the warranty extensions along with the models.

LUXURY LEMONS

European vehicles are generally a driver's delight and a frugal consumer's nightmare. They're noted for having a high level of performance combined with a full array of standard comfort and convenience features. They're fun to drive, well appointed, and attractively styled. On the other hand, you can forget the myth about European luxury vehicles holding their value – most don't. They're also unreliable, overpriced, and a pain in the butt to service.

Sales/Rating of European Cars Sold in Canada (YTD August 2013)

Sales of 256 Models	Model	Sales of 256 Models	Model	Sales of 256 Models	Model
#14	Volkswagen Jetta*	#36	Volkswagen Golf*	#58	Fiat 500 *Fiat 500*
#35	BMW 3-Series*	#53	Mercedes-Benz C-Class*		*Fiat 500C*

Sales of 256 Models	Model	Sales of 256 Models	Model	Sales of 256 Models	Model
#65	Volkswagen Passat	#142	Land Rover Range Rover Evoque	#201	BMW 6-Series
#68	Audi Q5	#147	Land Rover Range Rover Sport	#202	Audi TT*
#70	BMW X3	#150	Smart Fortwo	#203	Land Rover LR4
#71	Volkswagen Tiguan	#154	Volvo S60*	#206	Fiat 500L
#76	Mercedes-Benz GLK-Class*	#164	Audi A6*	#208	Jaguar XJ
#81	Audi A4*	#165	BMW 1-Series	#211	Porsche Panamera
#93	Mercedes-Benz M-Class	#175	BMW X6*	#212	BMW Z4*
#94	Mini Cooper	#176	Porsche 911	#215	Audi A8
#102	BMW X1	#181	Audi A7	#217	Porsche Cayman
#105	Mercedes-Benz B-Class*	#183	Volkswagen Eos*	#218	BMW 7-Series*
#108	BMW X5*	#185	Volvo XC90	#224	Mercedes-Benz G-Class
#110	Mercedes-Benz E-Class, CLS-Class*	#186	Land Rover Range Rover	#225	Jaguar F-Type
#117	Volkswagen Beetle	#187	Volvo XC70*	#226	Mercedes-Benz R-Class
#123	Audi A5*	#189	Jaguar XF	#228	Volkswagen Routan
#126	Mercedes-Benz GL-Class*	#190	Audi A3*	#230	Volvo C70
#127	BMW 5-Series*	#194	Land Rover LR2	#234	Audi R8
#133	Volkswagen Touareg	#195	Mercedes-Benz SL-Class	#235	Jaguar XK
#135	Porsche Cayenne	#196	Porsche Boxster	#240	Mercedes-Benz SLS AMG
#137	Audi Q7*	#198	Volvo C30*	#243	Volvo S80
#138	Volvo XC60*	#199	Mercedes-Benz S-Class & CL-Class	#250	Mercedes-Benz SLR McLaren
#141	Mini Countryman	#200	Mercedes-Benz SLK-Class		

Source: Manufacturers and Polk
Note: * = Acceptable – Good Buys

This last point is important to remember because in hard economic times dealers skimp on parts inventories or mechanic training to adequately service what they sell. So, if you get a bad dealer, you will likely end up with a bad car.

Servicing problems and costs can be attenuated by purchasing a model that's been sold in relatively large quantities for years and has parts that are available from independent suppliers. If you insist on buying a European make, be sure you know where it can be serviced by independent mechanics in case the dealership's service becomes "lemony." Interestingly, independent BMW, Mercedes, Volkswagen, and Volvo garages seem to be fairly well distributed, while Jaguar, Saab, and Smart repairers are found mostly in the larger cities, if at all.

So what's wrong with European cars? First, they can't compare to cheaper Asian competitors in terms of performance and durability. Who wants a Mercedes when offered a Lexus? Why get a dealer-dependent and quality-challenged VW Passat when you can have more fun with a Mazda3 Sport (even with its stupid grin on the front grille)? Second, when times get tough, European automakers get out of town or go belly up. Remember ARO, Dacia, Fiat, Peugeot, Renault, Saab, Skoda, and Yugo? Finally, European vehicles require constant, expensive maintenance that rivals the cost of a week in Cannes. Shoppers understandably balk at these outrageously high prices, and European automakers respond by adding complicated, failure-prone electronics that drive up servicing costs even more.

British independent automotive journalist Robert Farago, former editor of the *Truth About Cars* website (*www.thetruthaboutcars.com*), writes:

> Once upon a time, a company called Mercedes-Benz built luxury cars. Not elk aversive city runabouts. [An allusion to the Smart Car.] Not German taxis. Not teeny tiny hairdressers' playthings. And definitely not off-roaders .... In the process, the Mercedes brand lost its reputation for quality and exclusivity. In fact, the brand has become so devalued that Mercedes themselves abandoned it, reviving the Nazi-friendly Maybach marque for its top-of-the-range limo. Now that Mercedes has morphed with Chrysler, the company is busy proving that the average of something good and something bad is something mediocre.

You won't read this kind of straight reporting from the cowering North American motoring press, as they fawn over any new techno-gadget-laden vehicle hailing from England, Germany, or Sweden. It's easy for them; they get their cars and press junkets for free.

Lemon-Aid readers who own pricey European imports invariably tell me of powertrains that stall, China-made DSG transmissions that jump out of gear, nightmarish electrical glitches that run the gamut from annoying to life-threatening, and computer malfunctions that are difficult to diagnose and hard to fix. Other problems noted by owners include premature brake wear, excessive brake noise, AC failures, poor driveability, hard starts, loss of power, and faulty computer modules leading to erratic shifting. Plus, servicing diesels has gotten costlier and more complicated, now that a urea tank has to be refilled regularly – only by the dealer. Yikes!

Urea is needed for diesels in higher concentrations than
your body produces … wink, wink, nudge, nudge.

SERVICE WITH A SHRUG

Have you visited a European automaker's dealership lately? Although poor servicing is usually more acute with vehicles that are new on the market, it has long
been the Achilles' heel of European importers. Owners give European dealerships
low ratings for mishandling complaints, for inadequately training their service
representatives, and for hiring an insufficient number of mechanics – not to mention for the abrasive, arrogant attitude typified by some automakers and dealers
who bully customers because they have a virtual monopoly on sales and servicing
in their regions. Look at their dealer networks, and you'll see that most European
automakers are crowded in Ontario and on the West Coast, leaving their customers
in eastern Canada or the Prairies to fend for themselves.

NOT RECOMMENDED/UNRATED EUROPEAN MODELS

Lemon-Aid doesn't give a "Recommended" rating to vehicles built by Jaguar, Land
Rover, Saab (now bankrupt), Smart, or Volvo because there are better alternatives
available. Some of these brands have plummeting resale values and cannot be
serviced adequately by cheaper independent garages. Also, some of these brands
have been disowned by their parent manufacturers and sold for barely a third of
their value to Indian, Dutch, and Chinese interests. Their former owners couldn't
support the cost of ownership, and neither can you.

Jaguar and Land Rover

Not Recommended

Tata-owned Jaguar Land Rover is the exception; it is making money – profits up 29 percent for the third-quarter of 2013. On the heels of better sales in China and North America, Tata will expand in those regions to counterbalance India's severely-depressed economy and battered currency which con-

The Tata Nano is a primitive, no frills mini-compact. A radio and fire extinguisher are optional.

tributed to a third-quarter loss of 23 percent. Buoyed by the popular Land Rover Evoque, a Ford-conceived model, Tata has invested in improved quality control and continued to build its models in England, where it leaves most product decisions up to Jaguar Land Rover.

Jaguar sells eight models in Canada: XF: $53,500 (U.S. $46,975); XFR: $88,000 (U.S. $83,200); XJ: $89,000 (U.S. $73,200); XJL: $96,000 (U.S. $83,700); XK: $98,625 (U.S. $79,000); XKR: $109,125 (U.S. $97,500); and the XKR-S: $139,000 (U.S. $132,000). The new F-Type's prices are not as ridiculously high in Canada as we find with Jaguar's other models: F-Type: $76,900 (U.S. $69,000); F-Type S: $88,900 (U.S. $81,000); and the F-Type S V8: $92,000 (U.S. $88,900).

Three quick points about Jaguars and Land Rovers: first, as mentioned before, they are overpriced. Secondly, depreciation is so severe that a used Jaguar may look like a bargain, until you are faced with thousands of dollars in repairs from only one available dealer. Finally, most independent reliability surveys show both brands near the bottom of the list.

Land Rover sells six models in Canada: LR2: $40,000 (U.S. $37,295); LR4: $59,500 (U.S. $49,995); Range Rover: $98,300 (U.S. $83,545); Range Rover Evoque: $46,995 (U.S. $42,040); Evoque Coupe: $48,095 (U.S. $45,040); and the Range Rover Sport: $73,650 (U.S. $63,495).

Ideally, when buying a new or used vehicle you will want a vehicle that will hold its value in case you have to sell it quickly (say within three years, not much money will be lost through depreciation). As can be seen by the following table don't expect either Jaguar or Land Rover to give you a fair return on your investment.

2010 Jaguar and Land Rover (September, 2013)

JAGUAR			LAND ROVER		
Model	Cost	Used Value	Model	Cost	Used Value
XF	$61,800	$27,000	LR2	$44,900	$23,000
XFR	$85,300	$35,000	LR4	$60,000	$31,000
XJ	$88,000	$39,000	Range Rover	$93,800	$45,000
XJL	$95,500	$41,000	Rover Sport	$73,200	$37,000
XK	$95,500	$44,000			
XKR	$107,000	$51,000			

And, finally, there are good and bad Jaguars. The worst of the used lot are the failure-prone XJ and XF, followed by the X-Type and XJ. Only the XK stands out above the rest, while the jury is still out on the all-new F-Type. *Lemon-Aid* doesn't Recommend any Jaguar, new or used.

Jaguars are both beautiful and bad. Do you feel lucky? Jaguar's 2011 XF ($61,800 CDN in Canada; $53,000 U.S. in the States). Jaguar hopes that its offer of free maintenance will revive its sales in 2011. *Lemon-Aid* believes dropping the price in Canada by $15,000 would be a better idea.

Owner Comments

XF

I was driving with my 7-year-old son in the backseat (with booster). I went to accelerate and the pedal apparently got stuck. Harrowing experience to say the least. I saw the engine was revving very high and then thought it had dropped to a lower gear, but the speed kept increasing (rapidly). Tried using the brakes for 3-5 seconds, but it did not seem to do much.

• • •

My right ear was damaged by the explosion from the air bag deployment and now I have high shrill ringing 24/7 and can't sleep. I have been to hearing specialists and they say it is tennitus, but there does not seem to be any solution.

• • •

After depressing the brake pedal and activating the push to start feature the vehicle suddenly accelerated in reverse without any warning.

XJ

Contact owns a 2011 Jaguar XJ. The contact stated that when shifting into drive, the vehicle suddenly accelerated with the brake depressed. The brake pedal was depressed with extreme force and the contact shifted into park before the vehicle would stop.

• • •

The contact owns a 2011 Jaguar XJ. The contact stated that the heated windshield distorted his vision while driving. The street signs and lights also appear to have a halo and become blurry.

• • •

2011 XJ is exhibiting problems similar to those contained in NHTSA Campaign ID Number: 10V332000 for the XK and XF. Specifically, vehicle engine will stutter as if about to stall, which is most noticeable within the first 30 minutes after start up, but persists in varying degrees at all times, especially when idling. Problem is progressively worsening.

• • •

1) The TFT digital speedometer display will vanish without warning. When this happens, you have no idea how fast you are going. The problem usually happens when exiting a dark garage and entering daylight, but also has happened while on the highway. The digital dash will remain blank for up to 15 seconds usually before slowly reappearing. Problem does not happen all the time, but it is distressing and dangerous when it does. 2) Audio and navigation systems have become completely inoperative. When navigation was operating, it was directing you to make impossible driving maneuvers. 3) Power windows will not remain closed. 4) Numerous other problems, though not necessarily safety issues (have been reported to dealer).

XK

First episode I was slowing down to turn left and car turned off. I was able to restart car. Jaguar said they would update software. Second episode again I was turning left at low speed when car turned off. I tried restarting car twice and it would not start.

RANGE ROVER

The washer fluid spray nozzle does not provide suitable spray onto the windshield other than in park. Inadequate design, flow, spray pattern is causing a safety visibility issue. To clear the windshield in winter driving, I must pull over every 10-15 miles to spray window. This is a brand new vehicle design for Land Rover and an obvious safety issue.

EVOQUE

The contact owns a 2012 Range Rover Evoque. The contact stated that he started the engine and exited the vehicle when the vehicle independently rolled away and crashed into another vehicle. There were no injuries. The vehicle was taken to the dealer for inspection where they stated that the gear shift module needed to be replaced. ... The consumer discovered in case of an emergency, the transmission could not be locked up as in the case of brake failure or if the throttle by wire malfunctioned. He also found out, during his last visit to the dealer, the vehicle could not be placed in neutral if it was being towed.

. . .

While driving in rainy weather for approximately one hour, I went to accelerate to pass a car and there was a loss of power, amber warning light came on, engine light came on and I could not go faster than 35 mph. This could have caused a serious accident but I was able to slow down enough to get back in the slow lane. Car had to be towed to dealer the next day. The loner Evoque they game did the same thing in rainy weather.

. . .

My mother and I were driving to New England from Maryland through intermittent thunderstorms at speeds above 65 miles per hour. I attempted to accelerate to pass a vehicle when the engine began to lose power and took over 30 seconds to reach 40 miles per hour. I observed the speed warning light and the amber "Check Engine" light come on. I tried to accelerate to pull off of the road but could only drive approximately 35-40 miles per hour until the next exit which was over 2 miles ahead (as cars unsafely had to suddenly stop behind me on I-95).

LR4

Stopped at a stoplight behind another vehicle, when the engine suddenly revved and the vehicle took off. The vehicle suddenly accelerated on its own with a foot already on the brake. We continued to push on the brake and veered off to the side but clipped the vehicle in front of us. It was like we had no control over the vehicle.

RANGE ROVER SPORT

The car lost power & stopped suddenly when I was driving in a shopping plaza. Thank goodness I'm still alive! The car stopped in the front of Marshalls (so I have lots of witness). Peoples were trying to push my car to parking lot because the car blocked the traffic but we couldn't move the gear to N. I finally re-started it after more than 10+ times trying.

. . .

I was trying to part the car and was at a low speed. The brakes did not respond. I then stood up, holding onto the steering wheel. The car then stopped. A similar incident happened about three or four months ago when my husband was driving the car.

. . .

While driving vehicle straight on a 2-lane road, suddenly had to swerve left to avoid a car coming out of a parking lot without looking — and without any warning the power steering totally failed — and I could not pull the heavy truck back into the lane — and almost had a head-on collision!! More disturbing is the fact that upon inspection, Land Rover and the local dealer, Land Rover Main Line in PA, admitted this happened to another customer — but have no idea why this happened and can not assure that it is repaired!!!

...

While driving on highway at speed, the vehicle suffered a complete power failure. The headlights turned off, the engine shut down, the dashboard went dark, and the power steering failed causing me to swerve partially out of my lane (I was on a curve). The power then came back on and the vehicle resumed functioning normally.

...

The contact owns a 2011 Land Rover Range Rover Sport (N/A). While the contact was at a complete stop, he noticed smoke and a strong burning odor. The contact inspected underneath the hood with the gear placed in park and the engine in operation. There were small flames erupting from the bottom of the engine.

Saab

Not Recommended

Saab has passed away, but the coffin lid is rising slightly.

GM sold Saab in February 2010 to Spyker, a small Dutch company that made its name by building luxury high-performance cars that typically sold for $1 million apiece. Spyker never made a dime in sales, lost a restraint of trade lawsuit against GM, and shut the car plant down on April 2011, a year before declaring bankruptcy. Since then, GM has stepped in and assured Saab owners that anyone who bought the car with a GM/Saab warranty would have that warranty honoured by GM.

In the meantime, China-based National Electric Vehicle Sweden has bought Saab out of bankruptcy and says the Trollhattan plant is "practically ready" to begin building the mid-sized Saab 9-3. It will be very similar to the 9-3 that Saab stopped building in 2011 and will likely carry a be turbocharged powerplant. An electric version is planned for late 2014.

 SECRET WARRANTIES, INTERNAL BULLETINS: *All models sold originally by a GM/Saab dealer (up to 2009)*—**Problem:** All manufacturing defects covered by the original GM/Saab warranty. **Warranty coverage:** GM will honour warranty claims for Saabs at 179 certified dealerships in the U.S. and Canada. This includes second owners, as well. General Motors sold Saab in 2009 and assumes no responsibility, thereafter. Nevertheless, many Saabs built before this cutoff date still have plenty of of their warranties in force.

Volvo

The Volvo XC70 (above) is short on "Bling," but long on reliability and safety features.

Unrated

Volvo is on shaky ground now that it is owned by Geely, a Chinese truck manufacturer that has limited experience in automobile manufacturing and marketing and a track record in North America of only a few years. In the recent past, *Lemon-Aid* has rated the Volvo lineup "Not Recommended" for the same reasons that the uncertainties surrounding pre-bankrupt Saab earned that company a similar low rating.

Jeremy Cato, one of Canada's better auto writers, has also had his own misgivings about the company's future. He concludes that despite Volvo's emphasis on research and new products, Canada may not be much of a player in Volvo's future global growth plans (*www.theglobeandmail.com/globe-drive/driving-it-home/volvo-claims-it-has-a-plan-for-the-future/article8896220/*):

> I had all but given up on Volvo in Canada – and truthfully, Volvo in the rest of the world, too – when a prominent Volvo dealer approached me at the Toronto Auto Show. Do I want to meet the new Volvo Canada president? he asked.
>
> That would be Marc Engelen, who took over the top job in Canada on July 1. He replaced Jeff Pugliese, who seems to have been something of a disaster. But don't believe me; believe the numbers. Volvo Canada's sales were down 18.2 per cent last year, in a market that was up 5.7 per cent. Volvo sold 5,578 cars to Canadians last year. The premium car market in Canada is booming, yet Volvo's sales last year were a bust.

Worst of all, the company has a schizophrenic Board of Directors in place where some of the directors (led by the company's president) want to sell "bling" cars in the $1,000,000+ (U.S.) range in China, and the others want to sell safe, reliable, middle-class, family vehicles and shoot for volume in North America – the traditional Volvo way. This split has brought turmoil to the the 17-year-old Geeley enterprise which also faces the daunting task of integrating the Swedish and Chinese corporate cultures, with a little leftover Ford thrown into the mix – a task Chrysler was never able to accomplish with its Mercedes-Benz merger.

Volvo's greatest challenge, though, will be to make a profit from what had been a perennial money pit for Volvo decades ago, and even more so for Ford recently. Ford was hung out to dry when it sold off the dying brand to Geely: Originally purchased for $6.45 billion in 1999, Volvo was sold by Ford for a measly $1.5 billion

(U.S.). Having lost its quality edge after the Ford purchase, car shoppers have since been understandably leery of the company's products, which many feel are overpriced in Canada.

Lemon-Aid leaves Volvo's lineup "Unrated" this year and reminds readers that of the company's products sold in Canada, the S60, S80, XC60, and XC70 had the fewest "Troubles Spots" reported since 2007, according to *Consumer Reports'* annual survey. The C30, C70, and XC90 were seen as more troublesome. Finally, the 2013 Volvo S60 has been recognized as a Top Safety Pick by the Insurance Institute of Highway Safety (IIHS). Not surprising, since Volvo built its reputation upon the active and passive safety features its vehicle provide.

SECRET WARRANTIES, INTERNAL BULLETINS: 2007-10 S8; 2008-10 V70 and XC70, and 2010 XC60—*Problem:* Leaking coolant from the cylinder-head bleeder hose. Leakage may cause the engine to run hot and cause severe engine damage. *Warranty coverage:* According to Volvo Service Campaign #232, as announced in the company's November 30, 2010, internal dealer service bulletin, Volvo would replace the engine cylinder-head bleeder hose free of charge until November 30, 2012. Although this warranty extension has expired, Volvo has admitted negligence, opening the door for a refund to cover repair costs, or the replacement of the faulty hose.

"Green" Diesels

During the past few years, diesel emissions have been cleaned up to the point that environmentalists and economists alike see the increased use of diesel engines as the only way to gain time for the development of cleaner-burning fuel alternatives. Just don't look for big fuel savings in the interim.

Five Reasons a Diesel Is a Good Buy

1. **Improved highway mileage.** Diesels make sense for frequent long commutes without much stop-and-go traffic.
2. **Greater range.** Again, if long trips are your style, a diesel will mean less fill-up stops, although, you may lose some time finding a diesel outlet. In all-highway driving, the Cruze covered about 700 miles before needing a refill.
3. **More engine "grunt."** Turbocharged diesels have plenty of torque, making it easier to merge from an entry ramp, or pass other cars on two-lane secondary roads. Electric cars do this extraordinarily well; hybrids are laggards.
4. **Higher resale value.** Used diesels are easy to sell and they command a higher price, according to ALG, a firm that projects used-car values for use in leases. ALG says a three-year old VW Golf has a value of 61 percent of its original price, while a diesel version would be worth 5 percent more.
5. **Strong towing capacity.** With a diesel-powered SUV or truck, you don't need a gas guzzling V8 gas engine to pull a boat or trailer. A Jeep Grand Cherokee is rated up to 7,400 pounds – equal to the V8 gasoline model – but with better MPG.

Unless you travel more than 30,000 km a year, diesel cost savings may be illusory. Granted, there are usually fewer things that go wrong with diesel engines, and their fuel economy is 15-30 percent higher, but gasoline-powered Asian compacts are cheaper and much more reliable, their parts are easy to find and reasonably-priced, there are no extra-cost urea fill-ups, and they're almost as fuel-frugal, says *gasbuddy.com,* which pegs diesel fuel cost in Ontario at $1.10 to $1.30 a liter. In the States there is a considerable difference in the price of diesel fuel versus regular gasoline ($3.88 vs. a national average of $3.63 for regular gas).

All this is a moot point now that Asian and American automakers will have their own diesel-powered vehicles on the market for 2014: Namely, the Mazda6, Chevrolet Cruze, Jeep Grand Cherokee SUV, and a light-duty Dodge Ram pickup.

But keep this in mind: GM is offering just one Cruze Diesel model – fully loaded with features at $25,695 (U.S.), almost $3,000 more than a similarly equipped gasoline model. The EPA estimates that would require a payback period of ten years in gas savings to offset Cruze's extra purchase cost.

The other caveat is that none of these new entrants should be bought their first year on the market. Mechanics aren't yet familiar with them. Backup parts are still "in the pipeline," supposedly, and dealers aren't rushing to buy replacement parts until they sell their present stock. Wise shoppers will steer clear of these new diesel models, at least until mid-2014 when servicing know-how and parts distribution should have improved.

AUDI

From a quality and safety perspective, both Audi and BMW have reputations they don't deserve – Audi's aren't that bad; and Bimmers aren't that good. Saddled in the early '80s with a reputation for making poor-quality cars that would suddenly accelerate out of control, Audi fought back for two decades and staged a spectacular comeback with well-built, moderately priced, front-drive and AWD Quattro sedans and wagons that spelled "Performance" with a capital "P." Through an expanded lineup of sedans, coupes, and Cabriolets during the last decade, Audi gained a reputation for making sure-footed, all-wheel-drive, luxury cars loaded with lots of high-tech bells and whistles – and they look drop-dead gorgeous. Audi's quality control, servicing, and warranty support has not been first-class in the past, but it has gotten better lately as the company rebounds from the recession. Nevertheless, used Audis can be found at bargain prices, even among the models that have a relatively clean record. Take, for example, the TT: A 2008 TT Quattro Coupe that originally sold for $50,600 is now worth barely $19,000 after five years – a boon for used-car buyers with independent garage connections, but a bust for owners who bought new. The fact that Audi powertrains are covered under warranty only up to 4 years/80,000 km is far from reassuring, since engines and transmissions have traditionally been Audi's weakest components and many other automakers cover their vehicles up to 5 years/100,000 km. This worry is backed up by *Consumer Reports* surveys showing some powertrain problems with the entire Audi lineup.

No more Europe envy – additional diesel models are on their way to North America. The TDI should follow in the new year in both the Q5 and A6. Then, the A6, A8, and Q5 will gain a 3.0L TDI option in the 2014 models, which will debut sometime in late 2013. It's expected there will also be a diesel-powered A4 for 2015 and that the 2014 TT could include a diesel option, as well.

Audi launched four new 2013 models last year: The RS 5, S6, S7, and S8. The Q7 gained a new engine with new power figures and so far hasn't generated any serious customer complaints. The 2013 Q7 3.0L TDI got a slight power increase to 240 hp. The Q5 came out in the late fall with a 3.0L engine and a hybrid option. It has elicited a handful of owner complaints, inluding: Transmission failures; a noisy sunroof; Hybrid brake and accelerator pedals are mounted too close together; a child got locked inside; vehicle constantly drifts into oncoming traffic; and a "notch" feel appears at the 12 o'clock position on the steering wheel:

> It's almost impossible to maintain a straight direction without constantly adjusting the wheel from right to left. On several occurrences the wheel jerked to center uncontrolled. Turning the car off and back on will reset the issue and the occurrences are random. It is very annoying because the driver does not feel like you have control of the vehicle. In researching this issue I have found several other owners of the 2013 Audi Q5 that are having the same problem … Audi installed a new electromechanical steering system in the 2013 Q5 and apparently this is the source of the problem.

AUDI SECRET WARRANTIES, INTERNAL BULLETINS, SERVICE TIPS: *All models:* **1996-2010**—Silencing squealing brakes. **2000-08**—Hesitation on acceleration. **2000-10**—Low power, won't move after stopping. Inoperative keyless entry. Excessive oil consumption. **2005-10**—Noxious AC odours. **2005-13**—Remedy for squealing brakes. **2006-10**—Flickering interior lighting. **2007-10**—Multiple electrical malfunctions. **2009-11**—Steering squeak when turning. *A3:* **2005-10**—Headlights go on and off. **2005-11**—Sunroof noises. Inoperative windshield wipers. **2006-09**—No acceleration when shifted into gear. Inoperative low beams. Xenon headlights flicker and fail. **2006-10**—Cluster lights dim, flicker. Door electrical malfunctions. **2006-11**—Front suspension cracking, rubbing noise. Front, rear brake squealing. **2009**—Stiff steering. **2009-10**—Airbag light stays on. Hard start; timing chain noise. Automatic transmission control module update. Inoperative headlight washer system. **2010**—TDI catastrophic fuel-pump failure; sudden engine shutdown; metal shavings found in the fuel system (an $8,000 repair awaits). Automatic transmission suddenly downshifts to M1, inviting a rear-ender. *A4:* **2002-04**—Oil leak at camshaft adjuster. **2002-04**—Hard jerking in Reverse at idle. **2002-06**—Faulty glove compartment door. Noisy power steering. **2003-04**—Service campaign to replace the engine wire harness. **2005-06**—Remote won't lock/unlock doors. **2005-07**—Xenon headlights flicker and fail. **2005-08**—Remedy for a vehicle that pulls to one side. Dash clicking noises. Headlights vibrate. **2006-07**—Inoperative low beams. **2006-08**—

Front, rear brake squealing. Brakes moan when accelerating or turning. **2007**—Multiple electrical failures. **2009-11**—Sunroof noises, concerns. **2013**—Troubleshooting tips for automatic transmission harsh 1-2 upshifts or braking downshifts. Intermittent cruise control malfunctions. Water accumulation in Xenon headlights may cause serious electrical short-circuits elsewhere. A constantly lit ABS alert could mean the wiring harness is damaged. *A6:* **1998-2004**—Noisy power steering. **2005**—Fuel gauge reads empty with a full tank. **2005-06**—Rough-running cold engine. Inoperative sunroof. **2005-09**—Long warm-engine crank time. **2005-11**—Sunroof noises. Brakes moan when accelerating or turning. **2006-11**—Front, rear brake squealing. **2007**—AC doesn't cool. Loose, broken control knobs. **2008-09**—Erratic operating radio and door locks. *A4, A5, A6: Automatic transmission will not engage, or shifts only after key cycle.* **2013**—Coolant leak at water pump and hose area. *A4, A6, S6:* **2002-05**—Vehicles equipped with the Multitronic automatic transmission buck when accelerating. **2002-08**—Noisy power steering. Inoperative daytime running lights. **2005**—Cold engine stumble; warm engine stall. **2005-06**—Oil leak from oil filter housing. **2005-08**—Eliminating brake moan on low-speed turns. Front window reverses direction when closing. Inoperative sunroof switch. Inoperative One Touch window feature. **2005-09**—Long warm-engine crank time. **2005-10**—Headlights go on and off. **2006-08**—Brake squealing. **2007-08**—Paint spots or stains on upper surfaces. **2009**—Hard start; timing chain noise. **2009-10**—Airbag light stays on. *A6, S4:* **2002-06**—TSB #05-05, October 28, 2005, notes that in models equipped with 2.7L turbocharged V6 engines, a defective auxiliary coolant pump leaks coolant from the pump body; when pump fails, coolant light comes on, warning that continued driving could cause serious engine damage. Audi will install a repair kit free of charge up to 7 years/160,000 km. *A6, S4, S5 Cabriolet, Q5:* **2011**—TSB #131106 says that some models with 3.0L or 3.2L V6 engines may experience problems with the accessory drive belt or its guide due to a guide that is out of line, causing damage to the belt. Audi will do a free inspection of vehicles it suspects of having the problem and replace the guide and the belt for free as needed. *TT Coupe:* **2000-10**—Excessive oil consumption. **2002-11**—Front, rear brake squealing. **2004**—Front stabilizer bar upgrade to reduce noise. **2004-05**—Xenon headlight failure. **2004-06**—Momentary delay when accelerating. Vehicle won't go into gear. **2005-11**—Sunroof noises, concerns. **2006-09**—No acceleration when shifted into gear. **2006–10**—Cluster lights dim, flicker. **2007**—Inoperative windows, locks, and sunroof. **2007-08**—Inoperative One Touch window feature. **2007-11**—Interior buzzing vibrating noises. **2008-09**—Erratic radio and door locks. Inoperative low beams. Xenon headlights flicker and go out. **2007**—Loose, noisy air-intake duct. Rear suspension rumble, rattle. **2007-10**—Headlights go on and off. Inoperative headlight washer system. **2008-11**—Front suspension cracking, rubbing noise. **2009**—Hard start; timing chain noise. Stiff steering. **2009-13**—A coolant leak in some models may mean a new water pump is in order. In TSB #191336, issued on April 15, 2013, Audi said owners of 2009-13 A4, A5, Q5 and A6 models might notice leaks from the hose connecting the water pump to the heater core. Replacing the pump, hose and seal ring under this "goodwill" warranty" ought to correct the problem. Water pooling in xenon headlamp assemblies is covered in TSB #941314 issued on April 5, 2013. Audi said the headlight adjustment screw or the bonding channel between the housing and the lens might let water enter. The problem affects some 2013 A4, S4, A5, S5 and RS5 models. Replacing the headlamp assembly will prevent further leakage.

A3 ★★★★

RATING: Above Average, but only if you find good servicing and can keep the car six years or more to offset the high buy-in and depreciation loss. Based on the redesigned Volkswagen Golf, the A3 is Audi's entry-level, compact, four-door hatchback. It's a well-appointed, generously powered vehicle that arrived in the summer of 2005. This four-door hatchback is smaller and less costly than Audi's A4 compacts, and is just as much fun to drive. Since the 2014 cars are mostly carryovers from the 2012s, their prices haven't increased by much, and some models have been heavily discounted. **Road performance:** The car's a superb highway performer, thanks to its powerful and smooth-running engines and transmissions. Handling is crisp, steering is accurate, and cornering is accomplished with minimal body roll. **Strong points:** Loaded with safety, performance, and convenience features. Audi rates the A3 as capable of carrying five passengers; however, the three back-seat passengers had better be friends. **Weak points:** Fairly expensive for an entry-level Audi; on top of that, depreciation will likely be much faster than average, which increases your losses. Also, a freight fee that nudges $2,000 should be made a felony. Premium gas is required, and insurance premiums are higher than average. Navigation feature is confusing. Numerous factory-related problems affecting primarily the electrical system, powertrain, brakes, and accessories. Fit and finish are not up to luxury-car standards, either. **Major redesign:** 2006 and 2014. The restyled 2014 sedan will arrive at year's end and resemble the larger A4 and A6. Three engines will be used: a 2.0L TDI diesel, plus a 1.8L and a 2.0L turbocharged 4-cylinder gasoline engine. A more powerful S version will be available in the first quarter of 2014. **Highway/city fuel economy:** *2.0 front-drive man.:* 6.7/10.4 L/100 km. *2.0 front-drive auto.:* 6.9/9.4 L/100 km. *2.0 AWD:* 7.5/9.6 L/100 km. *TDI:* 4.7/6.7 L/100 km. **Best alternatives:** Acura TSX, BMW 3 Series, and a fully loaded VW Jetta TDI.

Prices and Specs

Prices (Negotiable): *2.0:* $34,100, *S tronic:* $35,700, *Quattro:* $37,500, *TDI:* $37,100 **Powertrain (Front-drive/AWD):** Engines: 2.0L 4-cyl. Turbo (200 hp), 2.0L 4-cyl. Diesel (140 hp); Transmissions: 6-speed man., 6-speed auto. **Dimensions/capacity:** Passengers: 2/3; Wheelbase: 101.5 in.; H: 56/L: 169/W: 69 in.; Headroom F/R: 4.5/2 in.; Legroom F/R: 42/25.5 in.; Cargo volume: 19.5 cu. ft.; Fuel tank: 55L and 60L/premium/diesel; Tow limit: Not recommended; Load capacity: 990 lb.; Turning circle: 35 ft.; Ground clearance: 4.3 in.; Weight: 3,219 lb.

SAFETY: No NHTSA crashworthiness data. IIHS "Good" designation for 2006-13 models' moderate overlap front collision protection, side protection, and roof strength; rear crashworthiness was scored "Good" for the 2008-13s, however, 2006-07 models were rated "Acceptable." Owners report sudden loss of diesel power when accelerating and the transmission engages and then disengages when accelerating from a stop or when parking:

> While pulling out into an intersection the DSG transmission briefly went into neutral and I saw the tachometer needle shoot up and heard the engine whine. I was in manual mode at the time. I down shifted and let off the gas and it re-engaged. The following day ... the same thing happened again. This time I was also in manual mode and was again pulling out into traffic from an almost complete stop. I have since learned that this is an ongoing and known issue with VW/Audi DSG transmissions.

ALERT! Canadian Audi dealers have had a very good sales year and are willing to haggle over prices to keep their inventory moving. Just be wary of bloated costs from bundled options, specious "administrative" fees, and usurious delivery charges.

A3 Profile

Used Values ($)	2006	2007	2008	2009	2010	2011	2012
A3 Sedan	8,500	10,000	12,500	14,000	17,500	23,000	25,500
AWD	—	11,500	14,500	15,000	19,500	24,000	28,,500
TDI	—	—	—	—	20,500	24,500	28,500
S-Line	11,500	—	—	17,500	20,500	24,500	30,000
TDI	—	—	—	—	20,500	25,000	31,000
Recommended	✩	✩	✩	✩	✩	✩	✩	✩	✩
Reliability	✩	✩	✩	✩	✩	✩	✩	4	4

SECRET WARRANTIES, INTERNAL BULLETINS: 2011-12—Tiptronic DSG transmission malfunctions can be corrected via a software upgrade. Parking Assist System false warnings. Bose Radio erratic sound volume. cannot pair Bluetooth phone to vehicle. Poor cell phone voice recognition. No-start due to discharged battery. Electrical malfunctions after window tint. Excessive engine noise. Front window binds or is noisy during operation. Inaccurate "distance to empty" display. Noises from the sunroof area. Disc brake squeal. Can't eject navigation DVD. Rattling, humming noise from speakers. Radio turns on/off, locks self-activates. Inoperative Remote key. Dash cluster lighting appears to flicker. Fuel system malfunction warning. Moisture accumulation in exterior lights. Expensive harness damage caused by rodent bites.

RATING: Average. Quality has improved measurably since 2003. Servicing is still spotty. On the positive side, so many of these vehicles have been sold for so long that sustained digging will usually find you the part and a mechanic who can service the vehicle competently. Plus, there has been a large reduction in safety-related problems reported by owners. This series of cars should be kept at least six years to compensate for their high initial cost and depreciation losses. **Road performance:** The base 2.0L engine provides gobs of low-end torque and accelerates as well with the automatic transmission as it does with the manual. The turbo-charger works well, with no turbo delay or torque steer. The manual gearbox, Tiptronic automatic transmission, and CVT all work flawlessly. Comfortable ride; exceptional handling, though not as sporty as Acura's TSX; acceptable braking performance. Not as fast as rivals; the ride is stiff at low speeds, and a bit firm at other times; some body roll and brake dive under extreme conditions; braking can be a bit twitchy. **Strong points:** Loaded with safety, performance, and convenience features, and you get lots of cargo room in the wagon. Safety-related complaints have dropped considerably. The new all-road Quattro offers more ground clearance than the A4 wagon (Avant) it replaces. **Weak points:** Limited rear seatroom (the front seatbacks press against rear occupants' knees); some tire drumming and engine noise. Owners report abysmal fit and finish. The electrical system is the car's weakest link, and it has plagued Audi's entire lineup for the past decade. Normally, this wouldn't be catastrophic; however, as the cars become more electronically complex and competent mechanics are fired as dealerships open and close, you're looking at a greater chance of poor-quality servicing, long waits for service, and unacceptably high maintenance and repair costs. Overpriced, with an outrageously high $2,000 freight charge and depreciation that is a wallet-buster. For example, a 2008 A4 that sold for $35,350 is now worth $12,500; and a 2008 S4 that once cost $70,400 now barely fetches $23,500. Not even high-performance S5 variants can escape value-robbing depreciation. The 2008 V8-equipped S5 coupe that originally sold for $66,000 is now worth $24,500. Worse yet, convertibles are no longer a safe haven, either: A 2010 S5 convertible that once sold for about $69,000 is now worth $40,000. Another expense to consider is the car's high maintenance cost, especially because of its costly dealer-only servicing. **Major redesign:** 1996, 2002, and 2009. The notchy steering can be caught during your road test: www.youtube.com/watch?v=mw9m2ncym4 shows you what to look for. **Highway/city fuel economy:** *2.0 front-drive man.:* 6.5/8.9 L/100 km. *2.0 front-drive auto.:* 7.0/10.0 L/100 km. *2.0 Quattro man.:* 6.5/9.5 L/100 km. *2.0 Quattro auto.:* 7.0/10.0 L/100 km. *A5 convertible:* 7.0/10.0 L/100 km. *A5 coupe man.:* 6.5/9.5 L/100 km. *S4 man.:* 8.1/12.2 L/100 km. *Auto.:* 7.9/12.1 L/100 km. *S5 convertible:* 8.1/12.9 L/100 km. *Coupe man.:* 9.4/15.1 L/100 km. *Auto.:* 9.8/12.8 L/100 km. New 3.0L engines have not been tested yet. Remember, AWD models exert a heavy fuel economy penalty for better traction. **Best alternatives:** Buy a 2013 model, and profit from Audi's decision to cut prices on leftover models. Better yet, buy one used, and save $10,000 and additional $2,000 freight fees, and more money when servicing it at an independent garage. S5 convertibles cost about $10,000 more than A5 convertibles mainly due to the V8 engine used by the S5. This is too much to pay for what is only a slightly better performer. Think twice about getting the power moonroof if you're a tall driver. If you like the S4 or S5 tire burners, also consider the BMW M3 convertible or 5 Series and the Porsche 911 Carrera. A4 alternatives are the Acura TL or TSX, BMW 3 Series, Hyundai Genesis, Infiniti G37, and Lexus ES 350 or IS series.

 SAFETY: 1996-2014 models get a four- and five-star rating across the board from NHTSA. IIHS "Good" designation for 2002-13 models' moderate overlap front collision protection; "Poor" for 2005-13s, in small overlap frontal collisions; and "Good" for 2005-13 models needing side protection. 2009-13 model roof strength was also judged to be "Good," while rear crashworthiness was scored also "Good" for the 2007-13s. NHTSA logs show few safety-related complaints. The smattering of reports show sudden, unintended acceleration; continued acceleration while braking; acceleration lag and engine surge; vehicle lunging every time the Tiptronic transmission is down shifted; stalling caused by faulty fuel injectors; CVT allows the vehicle to roll down an incline when stopped; and severe road wander.

Prices and Specs

Prices (Negotiable): *2.0 TFSI:* $37,800, *Quattro:* $39,700, *Quattro Tiptronic:* $41,300, *Allroad Quattro:* $45,100, *Premium:* $49,700, *Premium Plus:* $51,900, *S4 3.0 Quattro:* $53,000, *S4 Quattro S tronic:* $54,600, *Premium:* $57,800 **Freight:** $1,995 **Powertrain (Front-drive/AWD):** Engines: 2.0L 4-cyl. (211 hp), 3.0L SC V6 (333 hp); Transmissions: 6-speed man., 8-speed auto., 7-speed auto., CVT **Dimensions/Capacity:** *A4 Sedan:* Passengers: 2/3; Wheelbase: 110.5 in.; H: 56.2/L: 169.5/W: 71.8 in.; Headroom F/R: 3.5/2.5 in.; Legroom F/R: 41.5/24.5 in.; Cargo volume: 16.9 cu. ft.; Fuel tank: 62L/premium; Tow limit: Not recommended; Load capacity: 1,060 lb.; Turning circle: 37.4 ft.; Ground clearance: 4.2 in.; Weight: 3,665 lb.

After 3500 miles the vehicle developed a "notchy" sensation in the steering feel that varied in intensity and would occur at random times. This notchy sensation would occur any speed above 20 mph, as if switched on. When symptoms would occur there would be a heavy, notchy feeling on either side of straight steer that would take a lot of force to overcome and then once feeling like the wheel is over the notch, it would over correct making it difficult to maintain a lane. The steering wheel could not be placed in those notch positions, as if trying to drive using a click wheel. The notchiness is also felt throughout all wheel travel, not just on center, straight wheel. This makes staying on a given path difficult and unsafe. At random times steering felt so heavy that it felt like there was no power steering in maneuvers. Dealer has replaced the steering rack but the very next day the notchy steering symptoms reappeared randomly. There is no set of conditions to reproduce the problem, however turning the car off and on or turning the wheel lock to lock alleviates the symptoms. The symptoms have slowly increased in frequency since the replacement and occur at random times, especially during highway driving. This is the first year Audi has introduced electromechanical steering into their cars in the United States. This is potentially a new design flaw that has gotten through testing or a new production defect and should be investigated quickly. Many other 2013 Audi (varying models) owners have had the same issue.

Secondary radiator is easily damaged from road debris; sudden water pump failure; and the windshield wipers stop working when the vehicle comes to a stop. The following problems have all taken these cars out of service for extended periods in the past: Airbag fails to deploy; excessive steering shake due to a faulty lower control arm; engine, fuel-system (fuel-injectors, principally), and powertrain component failures; defective brakes; and chronic electrical shorts.

A4 Profile

	2004	2005	2006	2007	2008	2009	2010	2011	2012
Used Values ($)									
Sedan	5,000	7,500	9,000	11,000	13,000	16,500	21,000	28,000	32,000
Avant	5,500	8,000	10,000	11,500	13,500	17,000	23,500	28,500	33,000
S-Line	—	—	11,000	13,000	16,500	21,500	24,000	29,500	36,500
Recommended	★	★	★	★	★	★	★	★	★
Reliability	★	★	★	★	★	★	★	☆	☆

SECRET WARRANTIES, INTERNAL BULLETINS: 2002–06—Audi agreed to refund repair and other expenses to drivers who bought or leased 2002-06 Audi A4s and A6s with factory-installed CVTs. Owners said factory and design problems caused the transmissions to fail and that Audi was aware of the problems and hid them from consumers. **2009-13**—A coolant leak may signal the need for a new water pump. In TSB #191336 issued on April 15, 2013, Audi said owners of 2009-13 A4, A5, Q5, and A6 models might notice leaks from the hose connecting the water pump to the heater core. Replacing the pump, hose and seal ring ought to stop the dripping.

ELECTRICAL—HARNESS DAMAGE FROM ANIMAL BITES

BULLETIN NO.: 2021169/2

DATE: JULY 1, 2010

Audi

MODEL(S)	YEAR	VIN RANGE	VEHICLE-SPECIFIC EQUIPMENT
All Audi	2007–2010 2012–2015	All	Not Applicable
R8	2011	All	
A3	2011	All	
A4, S4	2011	All	
A4 Cabriolet	2011	All	
A5, S5	2011	All	
A5 Cabriolet	2011	All	
A6	2011	All	
Q5	2011	All	
Audi Q7	2011	All	

CONDITION: The customer may report:
- Engine warning light illuminated in IP cluster
- Reduced driving performance
- Engine does not start
- Coolant warning light illuminated
- ABS warning light illuminated
- Parking system warning illuminated in IP cluster
- Cable or rubber hose damages in the engine compartment.

TECHNICAL BACKGROUND: Animal damage primarily occurs on easily accessible, exposed cables and on thin cables. To avoid future animal bites, advise the customer to clean the engine compartment. Electrical deterrents and cable protection have proven effective, but 100% protection cannot be guaranteed. **WARRANTY:** This damage is due to outside influence and is not covered by any Audi warranty.

RECOMMENDED ANIMAL PROTECTION MEASURES: Electric deterrents. Similar to electric fences, these deterrents ensure effective and sustainable protection. Animals are driven away by harmless electric shocks.

Audis and Hondas represent a "Moveable Feast" to mice, rats, squirrels, etc. Rodent bites can cause up to $18,000 in wire/hose damage, make the car unsafe, and scare the dickens out of some drivers if "Mickey" decides to ride shotgun. Lawyers say Audi is 100% responsible for not building barriers to animal entry as other automakers have done. This means buying back the car, paying for rentals, tags, insurance, and inconvenience along with "mental distress" (See Sharman judgment in Part Three). "Honey, what just scurried under your seat?"

A6/S6/R8

RATING: Average. The A6 would have been rated higher if its build quality was better and its residual value didn't drop so much. Stick with Audi's simpler models. The A6 is a comfortable, spacious front-drive luxury vehicle that comes as a sedan or wagon. The sedan carries a standard 211 hp 2.0L four or an optional 310 hp 3.0L V6. Both engines are mated to a CVT or an 8-speed automatic transmission with manual-shift capability; Audi's Quattro all-wheel drive is also available. The Audi R8 is an all-wheel-drive, two-seat coupe with a mid-mounted engine. The entry-level 4.0L has a 420 hp V8 engine, but the 5.2L has a 550 hp V10. As with other Audis, depreciation is a value-killer. A 2008 (its debut year) top-of-the-line R8 coupe that sold new for $139,000 is now worth about $60,000 – a huge loss in just over five years. **Road performance:** A potent base engine that produces incredible acceleration times and gives excellent gas mileage, predictable handling, and good braking. The Servotronic steering is improved, but it is still the car's weakest feature. It is both over-boosted and uncommunicative in "Comfort" mode and ponderous and numb in its "Dynamic" setting. The V8 is a bit "growly" when pushed, and the firm suspension can make for a jittery ride. **Strong points:** Comfortable seating; interior includes a user-friendly navigation system and an analog/digital instrument panel that is a joy to behold and use; plenty of passenger and cargo room (it beats out both BMW and Mercedes in this area); easy front and rear access; and very good build quality. Dropping the failure-prone DSG automatic transmission in favour of the 8-speed automatic on the A6 was smart. The Avant wagon performs like a well-equipped sport-utility. Audi has never been a major player in the global mid-size luxury sedan market. For every A6 sold in 2010, Mercedes sold seven E-Series models and BMW moved five 5 Series sedans. This means you can haggle to your heart's delight because Audi dealers have a substantial profit margin, and they'll do almost anything to poach buyers from their competitors. **Weak points:** The restyling looks limp and dated: Overdone lights, ho-hum grille, and a painfully boring interior. Some tire thumping and highway wind noise; uncomfortable centre-rear seating; the wagon's two-place rear seat is rather small; and servicing can be problematic. And, if high servicing costs aren't enough, at the end of four years you may find your Audi is worth only a third of its original value. Non-safety related problems concern mostly the electrical and fuel delivery systems, in addition to scads of fit and finish deficiencies. **Major redesign:** 1998 and 2005. **Highway/city fuel economy:** *3.0:* 8.0/12.0 L/100 km. *4.2 Quattro:* 8.6/13.0 L/100 km. *3.0 Avant Quattro:* 8.6/13.0 L/100 km. *R8 4.2 Coupe man.:* 10.2/16.3 L/100 km. *Auto:* 11.4/17.0 L/100 km. *S6 5.2:* 10.0/15.2 L/100 km. **Best alternatives:** Although the base A6 2.0T models are cheaper and more fuel-efficient than many competitors,

Prices and Specs

Prices (Negotiable): *A6 2.0 Quattro:* $52,500, *Premium:* $58,500, *3.0:* $59,800, *R8 4.2:* $134,000 **Freight:** $1,995 **Powertrain (Front-drive/AWD):** Engines: 2.0L 4-cyl. (211 hp), 3.0L V6 (310 hp) 4.0L V8 (420 hp) 5.2L V10 (550 hp) Transmissions: 7-speed S tronic, 8-speed auto., 6-speed man. and S tronic, CVT **Dimensions/capacity:** Passengers: 2/3; Wheelbase: 114.7 in.; H: 57.8/L: 193.9/W: 73.8 in.; Headroom F/R: 3/3 in.; Legroom F/R: 41.3/37.4 in.; Cargo volume: 14.1 cu. ft.; Fuel tank: 75L/premium; Tow limit: Not recommended; Load capacity: 1,100 lb.; R8: 551 lb.; Turning circle: 39 ft.; R8: 38.7 ft.; Ground clearance: A6: 4.6 in.; S6: 4.6 in.; R8: 4.5 in.; Weight: 3,891 lb.

they are also the least powerful cars in the segment. *A6 4-cylinder:* This base model rivals the more-powerful BMW 528i. On the downside, the 528i's gas consumption can't match the A6. *A6 3.0T:* Infiniti's M37x is worth test driving. Other vehicles worth taking a look at are the Hyundai Genesis and Lexus GS.

SAFETY: No NHTSA crashworthiness ratings. IIHS "Good" designation for 2005-13 models' moderate overlap front collision protection; 1998-2004 A6 models were deemed "Acceptable." 2005-13s scored "Good" for side protection and roof strength was judged to be "Good" with the 2012-13 models, only "Acceptable" on the 2005-11s. Rear crashworthiness was "Good" for the 2007-13s; "Acceptable" for the 2005-07s, built before December 2006. Very few safety-related complaints have been recorded over the past two model years. Among the reports: Sudden, unintended acceleration; brakes barely stop the car at low speeds; power brake failure; and the brake and accelerator pedals are mounted too close together.

ALERT! The multi-tasking joystick control for all the entertainment, navigation, and climate-control functions can be confusing. It's similar in function to BMW's 2002 7 Series feature, based on Microsoft Windows CE. This failure-prone, non-intuitive feature gave knew meaning to the phrase "computer crash" and was quickly changed after it was panned as being dangerously distracting and confusing to operate.

A6 Profile

Used Values ($)	2004	2005	2006	2007	2008	2009	2010	2011	2012
A6 Quattro	4,500	5,500	5,500	16,000	19,500	23,000	28,500	39,500	42,500
AWD	—	—	—	—	—	24,000	32,000	—	—
S-Line	—	—	—	17,500	21,500	26,500	34,000	—	50,500
R8	—	—	—	—	59,000	66,000	86,000	108,000	117,000
S6	—	—	—	22,500	32,000	39,000	53,000	65,000	—
Recommended	★	★	★	★	★	★	★	★	★
Reliability	★	★	★	★	★	★	★	★	★

SECRET WARRANTIES, INTERNAL BULLETINS: 2002–06—Transmission repair refunds (see A4). **2011-12**—Countermeasure to prevent electrical harness damage caused by animal snacking.

The Audi TT.

RATING: Recommended (2008-12); Above Average (all previous years). TT models provide a nice balance of agility, comfort, and sleek styling. In essence, the car is a "chick magnet" that attracts classy chicks. The TT Coupe Quattro debuted in the spring of 1999 as a $49,000 sporty front-drive hatchback with 2+2 seating, set on the same platform used by the A4, VW Golf, Jetta, and New Beetle. *TT RS:* The series' most powerful model, the RS is powered by a 360 hp 2.5L 5-cylinder turbocharged engine hooked to a revised 6-speed manual transmission (there is no automatic). This little rocket goes from 0-60 mph in just 4.3 seconds, with a top speed of 174 mph [280 km/h]. An impressive performance appreciated mostly by gearheads. **Road performance:** The TT and TTS both come exclusively with the less reliable dual-clutch manumatic 6-speed transmission. The TT RS is available with a 6-speed manual transmission only. Be prepared for a surprisingly low resale value and handling that's not the equal of a Hyundai Genesis, Mazda RX8, or Porsche Boxster. **Strong points:** Beautifully styled and with better handling than most sporty cars, TTs are well-appointed and provide a tastefully designed interior; comfortable, supportive seats; and plenty of passenger and cargo space (especially with the rear seatbacks folded). **Weak points:** Poor rear and side visibility; a useless back seat; tough rear-seat access; awkward navigation system interface; and lots of engine and road noise. The hatch is heavy to raise, and a rear windshield wiper would be nice. These cars, like most Audis, don't hold their value well. Used bargains abound if you are an experienced Audi mechanic or have access to a competent independent repairer. **Major redesign:** 2000 and 2008. **Highway/city fuel economy:** *TT Coupe Quattro 2.0:* 6.4/9.1 L/100 km. *Roadster:* 6.4/9.1 L/100 km. *TTS Coupe:* 7.4/10.7 L/100 km. *Roadster:* 6.4/9.1 L/100 km. **Best alternatives:** A used TTS, priced thousands of dollars less and powered by a torquier small engine.

Other vehicles worth considering: The BMW Z Series, Hyundai Genesis Coupe, Infiniti G37 Coupe, and Mazda Miata. Think twice about getting a moonroof-equipped model if you're a tall driver.

SAFETY: No recent NHTSA or IIHS crashworthiness tests.

ALERT! Haggle for a 10 percent cut in the MSRP. Better yet, buy used. The TT's classic design doesn't betray the car's true vintage and three- to five-year depreciation tables take the sting out of the car's premium price.

TT Coupe/TT Roadster Profile

	2004	2005	2006	2007	2008	2009	2010	2011	2012
Used Values ($)									
Coupe	4,500	5,500	11,000	—	19,000	21,500	29,000	33,000	38,000
TTS	—	—	—	—	—	26,500	34,500	42,000	47,500
Roadster	—	—	—	—	22,000	23,500	31,500	34,500	40,000
TTS	—	—	—	—	—	26,000	37,000	44,000	50,000
TT RS	—	—	—	—	—	—	—	—	55,000
Recommended	☆	☆	☆	☆	☆	☆	☆	☆	☆
Reliability	☆	☆	☆	☆	☆	☆	☆	☆	☆

SECRET WARRANTIES, INTERNAL BULLETINS: 2011-12—Countermeasure to prevent electrical harness damage caused by animal snacking. Rattling, jarring engine noise. Disc brake squeal remedy. Door can be opened from the inside only. No-starts due to dead battery. Window tint causes electrical malfunctions. Inaccurate Distance to Empty display. False warnings from the parking-assist system. Radio turns on/off, locks self-activate. DSG transmission software update. Fuel-system malfunction alert. Dash cluster lighting flickers. Moisture accumulation in exterior lights, and possible harness damage from animal bites.

Prices and Specs

Prices (Negotiable): 2.0 Quattro Coupe: $48,400, S-Line: $49,900, TTS: $57,900, Roadster: $51,400, S-Line: $52,900, TTS Roadster: $62,200 **Freight:** $1,995 **Powertrain (Front-drive/AWD):** Engines: 2.0L 4-cyl. (211 hp), 2.0L 4-cyl. Turbo (265 hp), 2.5L 5-cyl. Turbo (360 hp); Transmissions: 6-speed man., 6-speed manumatic **Dimensions/capacity:** Passengers: 2/2; Wheelbase: 97.2 in.; H: 53.2/L: 165.2/W: 72.5 in.; Headroom F/R: 3.5/N/A in.; Legroom F/R: 41.1/29.3 in.; Cargo volume: 13.1 cu. ft.; Fuel tank: 55L/premium; Tow limit: No towing; Load capacity: 770 lb.; Turning circle: 36 ft.; Ground clearance: 4.4 in.; Weight: 2,965 lb.

BMW

BMW Strengths

Despite the hard economic times, and unlike Toyota and Honda, BMW has resisted the temptation to keep prices down by de-contenting its vehicles. In fact, the company is expected to hold the line on the cost of its 2014s by offering an array of discounts, rebates, and other incentives in the new year to keep its number-one spot in Canada's pantheon of luxury cars. Consumers haven't balked at BMW's high prices, yet, inasmuch as they are more attracted by the automaker's reputation (underserved) for offering well-built, nicely appointed cars with excellent handling and superior driving comfort. Entry-level shoppers have the 1 and 3 Series; families with more disposable income may opt for the 5 and 6 Series; and for those who have the cash to buy more comfort, convenience and snob appeal, there's always the flagship 7 Series. Sport-utility fans have four vehicles to choose from: The X1 "baby SUV," the compact X3, and the larger X5 and X6.

BMW Shortcomings

BMWs have excellent road manners and shout "Yes, I can!" Unfortunately, there's barely a whisper to warn you of a plethora of bizarre and deadly factory-related defects hiding in these beautifully-styled machines. These glitches are typical of what we find in many cheaper, entry-level European cars and SUVs. Owner surveys show, and internal service bulletins confirm, the cars are afflicted with chronic fuel and electrical system and powertrain deficiencies that can be quite expensive to troubleshoot and repair. Surprisingly, coming from a country that extols its German craftsmanship, BMW fit and finish is embarrassingly bad. Germany is also famous for its top electronics firms, but BMW electronic components head the list of parts most likely to cause owners grief. Three authoritative websites that list BMW problems and fixes are *alldata.com*, *safercar.gov*, and *www.roadfly.com*. Here are just a few incidents from BMW's "Dark Side" found at *safercar.gov*.

2007 X5 BMW: HOSTAGE TERROR

My wife and kids were in the vehicle while I went inside the store. After I got back to the vehicle, my wife told me she saw service lights. I try to start the vehicle and the vehicle wouldn't start. I drive screen faded in and out, windshield wipers move slow, and I saw various service messages. In the process of trying to start the vehicle, all doors locked. I tried to unlock the doors and wasn't able to. My family and I were trapped inside the vehicle with our kids. The emergency flashers worked as well as the horn. I notice the vehicle next to me (driver's side) was backing out. I honked the horn and banged on the window to get the passenger's attention. She was nice enough to notice and her husband got out of the vehicle and called 911. The good smaritan tried to unlock the vehicle from the outside without any luck. The vehicle started to fog up and it felt as if there was no air circulating inside the vehicle. I was parked in an area which was not well lighted and it was dark and raining outside. With a dark interior and no lights working inside the vehicle, I wasn't able to find the manual unlock in the back trunk area. About 8-10 minutes into this terrible ordeal, the doors unlocked automatically. BMW Service replaced the battery and wasn't able to reproduce the problem.

2005

When the rear locks get locked/jammed, do not have any manual override to open the back doors. My kids got trapped in and had to get out from the front door. There are lots of complaints like this on the Internet and the dealer says that there is a fault with the electrical connections to open the door.

2004

The extrenal driver door latch is not working, have to climb over from passenger side of vehicle, this is ridiculous.

2011 X5: QUIT STALLING, PAY UP!

Started the car and the engine light came on with "Engine Malfunction – Reduced Power" and drover a few hundred yards and then the car completely died. The 2011 BMW X5 35I Premium just died – no power whatsoever. Because there was no poer, the car could not be put into neutral to be put on a flatbed. The X5 had to be put on a crane and lifted onto a flatbed tow truck. (Engine replaced.)

2010 X5 DIESEL: WHAT'S THAT SMELL?

2010 BMW X5 3.5 Diesel was brought in for service to diagnose exhaust smell in the cabin. Diagnostics unveiled a cracked EGR Cooler that allowed raw exhaust fumes to enter the cabin.

"RAINDROPS KEEP FALLING ON MY DEAD"

2007 This is my second complaint of problems caused by water intrusion of my 2007 BMW X5. First complaint was the passenger-side floorboard carpet getting wet. Now, I have a problem with electrical components getting wet. My satellite radio receiver was destroyed by moisture.

NOT A HOT FOOT!

The contact owns a 2004 BMW X5. He started to smell something burning from under the driver's seat and found that there was a hole under the seat from the heated seat element. The contact then took the vehicle to the dealer where they replaced the heated seat element, but not the actual seat.

Owners also mention slow parts delivery; poor transmission performance with gear hunting and abrupt engaging, believed to be caused by a faulty mechatronic unit; premature fuel and water pump failures leading to stalling, no starts, and engine overheating; exhaust fumes that invade the cabin; faulty TPM tire sensors; no brake power assist; and high maintenance costs with dire consequence if not performed (simultaneous engine shutdown, and loss of brakes and steering):

> While driving my 2012 X5, the engine suddenly shut off along with power steering and power brakes. It started again and I took it to a BMW dealer that said I needed a $325 software update. I aksed if that meant my engine would shut off while driving should my software ever go out of date. They said yes, it happens but not on all software updates. They also said software updates come out about every 3 to 4 months meaning my engine could be shut off again at any time.

Finally, keep in mind that the base versions of these little status symbols are often more show than go, and just a few options can blow your budget. Adding to that, the larger, better-performing high-end models aren't worth their premium price and don't offer the same standard features found on cheaper Japanese and South Korean competitors.

SECRET WARRANTIES, INTERNAL BULLETINS, SERVICE TIPS: *All models:* Many of the service bulletins listed here apply to other cars in the BMW lineup, as well. If you want to check if there is an overlap that includes your car, ask a BMW dealer. If that doesn't work, go to *www.safercar.gov* and look up the service bulletins applicable to your car. As a last resort, pay $26.95 (U.S.) to ALLDATA (*www.alldatadiy. com/buy/index.html*) to get a digital copy of every bulletin applicable to your vehicle. *3 Series:* **2002**—Incorrect fuel gauge readings. Rattling, tapping engine noise. Troubleshooting navigation system malfunctions. No 1-2 upshifts. **2003**—Harsh 3-2 and 2-1 downshifts. **2004**—Delayed Park-Drive shift. Numerous malfunctions of telematics components. **2005-06**—Reduced engine power. **2007-10**—High-pressure fuel pump failue. BMW has extended the emissions warranty to 10 years/120,000 mi. (193,000 km), according to bulletin #SI B13 03 09, announced in BMW's November 2010 dealer letter. **2008**—Instrument cluster displays go blank. Intermittent engine valve lash adjuster noise. **2008-09**—Water leaks into footwell area. **2009**—Airbag warning light stays on. No start, or reduced engine power. Poor AC performance. Rattling noise from the radio area. No Reverse or Forward gear. An oil leak at the right-hand side of the V6 engine crankcase may require that the crankcase be replaced. Excessive engine vibration. Silencing brake squeak and squeal. No start, or false fuel reading. Steering column noises. Front suspension creaking and groaning. *5 Series:* **All years:** Water inside of headlight. Erratic performance of the navigation system. *525i:* **2006-07**—Troubleshooting AC compressor noise. *528i:* **2007-09**—Automatic transmission jolt or delay when accelerating from a stop. **2009**—Reduced engine power. Automatic transmission jumps out of Drive or Reverse into Neutral (requires a software adjustment). Troubleshooting front seat noise. Front brake squeak or squeal upon light brake application. An oil leak at the right-hand side of the V6 engine crankcase may require that the crankcase be replaced. Intermittent engine valve lash adjuster noise. Exhaust system vibration or drone at idle. Poor AC performance. Steering column noises. *530i: 2005-07*—Front brake squeak or squeal upon light brake application. Sunroof wind noise and water leaks.

3 SERIES/M SERIES

RATING: Above Average (2013-14); Average (2000-12). With BMW's recent mechanical upgrades, styling changes, and increased exterior and interior dimensions, the 3 Series has come to resemble its more-expensive big brothers, with super-smooth powertrain performance and enhanced handling (when working properly). Still, competitors deliver more interior room and standard features for less money. *M3:* Not Recommended; the transmission hesitation on acceleration or deceleration is too risky for high-performance driving demands. **Road performance:** Good acceleration; the 6-cylinder engines and the transmissions are the essence of harmonious cooperation, even when coupled to an automatic transmission – there's not actually that much difference between the manual and the automatic from a performance perspective. Light and precise gear shifting with easy clutch and shift action; competent and predictable handling on dry surfaces; no-surprise suspension and steering make for crisp high-speed and emergency handling; a somewhat harsh ride (but the M3 is harsher than most); lots of road feedback, which enhances rear-end stability; and smooth, efficient braking that produces short stopping distances. The optional Sport suspension does enhance handling and steering, but it also produces an overly harsh, jiggly ride on rough pavement. Wider tires compromise traction in snow. **Strong points:** Very well-appointed. **Weak points:** Seriously overpriced and depreciation is only slightly slower than with Audi's lineup. For example: The entry-level models keep their value reasonably well, but as you get into pricier BMWs, the depreciation is mind-spinning. For example, a 2008 BMW 323i that once sold for $35,900 is still worth about $14,500, but a 2008 750i that sold for $108,500 is now worth only $27,500. Ouch! Other complaints: Electrical and infotainment system , and some body trim and accessories are the most failure-prone components; engine overheating is a serious problem experienced by many owners; insufficient front headroom and seat lumbar support for tall occupants; limited rear seatroom and cargo area; tricky entry and exit, even on sedans; confusing navigation system controls; excessive tire noise, especially with the M3; radio buzz; and premium fuel is required. **Major redesign:** 1999, 2006, and 2012-13. **Highway/city fuel economy:** *323i:* 6.9/11.1 L/100 km. *Auto.:* 6.7/11.2 L/100 km. 328i: 7.0/10.9 L/100 km. *Auto.:* 6.9/11.3 L/100 km. *328i xDrive:* 7.6/12.2 L/100 km. *Auto.:* 7.8/11.9 L/100 km. *335i:* 7.9/11.9 L/100 km. *Auto.:* 7.6/11.9 L/100 km. *335i xDrive:* 7.9/12.2 L/100 km. *Auto.:* 7.9/12.2 L/100 km. *335d:* 5.4/9.0 L/100 km. *M3:* 9.7/15.3 L/100 km. *M3 Cabrio:* 10.1/15.7 L/100 km. **Best alternatives:** Smart BMW buyers will stick with the simple, large volume, entry-level models until the recession blows over. Other cars worth considering are the Hyundai Genesis Coupe or Sedan and the Lexus IS series. Stay away from the Turanza run-flats and Bridgestone tires:

> Bridgestone tire exhibits unsafe characteristics in wet weather, with noticeable drift and hydroplaning in any amount of standing water. The tire also flat spots every morning, especially in cool weather, but even in warmer weather as well, leading to vibrations in the initial miles of any drive. It is also especially harsh over roadway expansion joints, and is so loud on concrete pavement that it poses a safety hazard due to driver fatigue induced by the continuous noise.

 SAFETY: 1996-2014 models get a four- and five-star rating across the board from NHTSA. IIHS "Good" designation for 2000-13 models' moderate overlap front collision protection and 2006-13 for side crash safety. Small overlap front collision tests produced a "Marginal" score for 2012-13 3 Series models. Roof strength was judged to be "Good" with the 2012-13 models and "Acceptable" with the 2006-11 versions, while rear crashworthiness (head restraints/seats) was scored "Good" only for the 2009-13s. 2006-08 models were judge "Acceptable" but earlier models (2002-07) produced "Poor" rear crash scores. Keep this in mind when tempted to buy a cheaper earlier model. Safety-related incidents reported by owners: A fire originated in the fog light socket; premature tire wear – and owners are forced to pay for tire failures. *325i:* Excessive hesitation on acceleration:

> When the driver demands a sudden increase in acceleration, the car hesitates anywhere from 1.5 to 3 seconds. This is a dangerous condition when someone is making a left turn in traffic, or getting onto a highway, or passing on a 2 lane country road, etc. Other cars traveling at 60 mph [96.5 km/h] are moving at 88 ft./sec. [27 m/s]. The amount of leeway this car needs is much too excessive.

Bridgestone tire-tread separation and side wall buckling:

> Bridgestone Potenza RE050A run-flat tires. The tires buckled on the side wall after less than 8,000 miles [12,870 km]. Out of curiosity I checked the Bimmerfest (*www.bimmerfest.com/forums/showthread.php?t=146728*) forum and discovered this is a widespread problem among BMW owners.

328: Some of the failures reported during the past few years: Airbags fail to deploy; underhood fire ignited while car was parked; premature tire failure (bubbles in the tread); sudden acceleration; engine slow surge while idling at a stoplight; when accelerating, engine cuts out and then surges forward (suspected failure of the throttle assembly); severe engine vibrations after a cold start as Check Engine light comes on; poor rain-handling; First gear and Reverse are positioned too close together, as are the brake and gas pedals; sunroof spontaneously shattered; a rear-quarter blind spot with the convertibles; seat rails that project a bit into the foot area could catch the driver's feet; and the front passenger head restraint won't go down far enough to protect short passengers. *330i:* Side

Prices and Specs

Prices (Firm): *328i Coupe:* $44,300, *328i Convertible:* $57,300, *328i xDrive Sedan:* $46,200, *328i xDrive Coupe:* $46,800, *335i Coupe:* $53,400, *335i Convertible:* $68,900, *M3 Coupe:* $71,700, *M3 Convertible:* $82,300, *M5 Sedan:* $101,500, *M6 Coupe:* $124,900, *M6 Convertible:* $128,900 **Freight:** $1,995 **Powertrain (Rear-drive/ AWD):** Engines: 2.0L 4-cyl. (240 hp), 3.0L 6-cyl. (230 hp), 3.0L 6-cyl.Turbo (300 hp), 3.0L 6-cyl. Diesel (265 hp), 4.0L V8 (414 hp); Transmissions: 6-speed man., 8-speed auto. **Dimensions/Capacity:** Passengers: 2/3; Wheelbase: 109 in.; H: 56/L: 178/W: 72 in.; Headroom F/R: 3.5/2.5 in.; Legroom F/R: 40.5/27.5 in.; Cargo volume: 11 cu. ft.; Fuel tank: 63L/ premium; Tow limit: No towing; Load capacity: 1,060 lb.; Turning circle: 19.4 ft.; Weight: 3,485 lb.

airbag deployed when vehicle hit a pothole; vehicle overheats in low gears; and vehicle slips out of Second gear when accelerating. *335i:* Delay in throttle engagement when slowing to a roll and then accelerating; frequent false brake safety alerts; sunroof suddenly exploded; tires lose air due to defective tire rims; faulty fuel injectors; and engine stalling and loss of power, which was fixed by replacing the fuel pump – now exhaust is booming, fuel economy has dropped, and there's considerable "turbo lag" when accelerating. Many other cases of loss of power on the highway, or the high-pressure fuel pump failing, with some owners having to replace the pump four times. *335d:* After a short downpour, engine started sputtering. Dealer and BMW said there was water in the fuel and held the car owner responsible for the full cost of the repairs. *M3:* Tail light socket overheats, blowing the bulb and shorting other lights – costs $600 to rewire; vehicle loses power due to faulty fuel pumps; transmission hesitates when accelerating in Second gear (see *www.roadfly.com*).

ALERT! Short drivers report the head restraints are uncomfortable; check this out during the test-drive. Be wary of the diesel power option; the system is much more complicated to service and repair than earlier versions.

3 Series Profile

Used Values ($)	2004	2005	2006	2007	2008	2009	2010	2011	2012
Sedan 320i/323i/325i	6,000	8,500	10,000	12,000	14,000	16,000	20,500	24,500	27,000
328i	—	—	—	12,500	15,500	17,500	23,000	27,500	32,000
330/335i	—	10,000	12,000	14,500	18,000	22,500	30,000	36,000	40,000
Coupe 325i/328i	—	10,000	11,000	12,500	16,000	19,000	23,000	28,000	33,000
Cabriolet	—	12,000	14,500	18,000	22,500	26,500	33,500	40,000	46,500
M/M3	14,500	17,000	17,500	19,000	26,000	33,000	41,000	49,000	57,000
Recommended	★	★	★	★	★	★	★	★	★
Reliability	★	★	★	★	★	★	★	★	★

Note: 2007-12 M Series convertibles worth about $4,000 more than base models; no difference with 2006 and earlier versions.

SECRET WARRANTIES, INTERNAL BULLETINS: 2011-12—Reduced engine power. Buttons on iDrive controller don't work. Inoperative keyless system. Erratic operation of the wiper rain-light feature. Brake pedal squeaks. Troubleshooting tips to correct electrical failures that are often caused by a shorted fuel-sender harness. Intermittently inoperative cell phone. Odometer readings can't be recovered. Various audio system complaints. Radio continues to play after ignition is turned off. "Door open" displayed when door is properly closed. Key doesn't stay in ignition. BMW Assist doesn't work properly. AC howling or rough-running noise. Deteriorated headlight wiring. Headlight nozzle doesn't fully retract. Interior door handle paint peeling. Steering wheel leather peels from the rear. Engine whistling, hooting, or squealing.

ENGINE WHISTLING, HOOTING, OR SQUEALING NOISE

BULLETIN NO.: S1 B11 03 11   DATE: SEPTEMBER 2011

1 Series; 3 Series; 5 Series; 6 Series; X3; X5; X6; and Gran Turismo.

SITUATION: The customer states that a noise described as whistling, hooting or squealing can be heard from the engine compartment while the engine is running. The noise may be more apparent after the engine has reached operating temperature.

CAUSE: The noise is due to a manufacturing error in the rear crankshaft oil seal.

X3/X5/X6   ★★★

RATING: *X3 and X6:* Average. *X5:* Below Average through 2007; Average, thereafter. Here is where BMW took on the Asian automakers and came out second best. Despite BMW's recent sophisticated (and complicated) engineering, mechanical upgrades, styling changes, and increased exterior and interior dimensions, the X3, X5, and X6 SUVs are not very impressive from either a performance or a comfort/convenience perspective. Like most European offerings, these BMWs are overpriced and quickly lose their value. *X3:* A small crossover that has swelled to the size of the previous generation, X5. There is plenty of room for front passengers, while rear legroom is generous and well-paired with comfortable seating, making this one of the most family-friendly SUVs in its class. *X5:* BMW's first crossover SUV has been on the market since 1999. It's a mid-sized seven-seater that is quick to depreciate and has a poor reliability record that is worse than what owners have reported on the X1, X3, and X6. *X6:* An X5 spin-off that gives you many of the X5 advantages and fewer of the disadvantages, but in a larger box. **Road performance:** *X3:* A potent 6-cylinder and an efficient 4-cylinder engine; crisp handling; precise, predictable steering. Recent changes provide a more-forgiving suspension; a softer, less choppy ride; and more power-steering assistance. Unfortunately, the car's old nemesis – accelerator lag – is still present. Kickdown response suffers from a similar delay. Some help, though, is offered by leaving the transmission setting in Sport mode, which keeps the transmission in lower gear longer. Jerky stops, caused by the transmission's inherent imprecise shifting, compounded by the standard Brake Energy Regeneration system. *X5:* Engines deliver plenty of power, and there's a turbocharged diesel option; smooth, responsive power delivery; secure handling; and good steering feedback. *X6:* Billed as BMW's "sports activity" coupe because it's loaded with high-performance features. It carries a turbocharged 3.0L 6-cylinder engine or a powerful optional 4.4L V8 and is a bit taller than most coupes. Capable handling, the AWD system can vary the torque from side to side to minimize under-steer. Delayed throttle response continues to be a problem, and the 8-speed automatic transmission makes gearshifts less than luxurious. **Strong points:** *X3:* Abundant cargo space; good cabin access; and a quiet, nicely appointed interior, with a better integrated centre screen. The second-row seats have good leg and elbow room, and rear seating is relatively comfortable. *X5:* Comfortable first- and second-row seating; and a high-quality cabin. Suspension improvements have smoothed out the ride. *X6:* Comfortable front seats and solid construction. **Weak points:** Parts are scarce outside of major metropolitan areas, and independent mechanics who can service these vehicles are rare. Servicing deficiencies are accentuated by a weak dealer network and unreliable suppliers. Unbelievably fast depreciation. A 2010 X3 that once sold for $39,800 is now worth only $21,500. Hold on, it gets worse: A 2007 X5 sold for $61,900 new, yet its used value is now barely $17,500 – a tremendous six-year loss. Incidentally, the 2008 X6 (its debut year), sold new for $64,000, may eventually take the crown for possessing a reverse "Midas Touch." Its value five years later: $20,000. General complaints target the fit and finish, power equipment, audio system, fuel system, and transmission as most in need of special attention. *X3:* This little SUV with its somewhat narrow interior is way overpriced; options are a minefield of inflated charges; and mind-spinning depreciation makes Wall Street look tame. Reliability is compromised by powertrain deficiencies, serious fit and finish problems, audio system malfunctions, power equipment failures, and electrical system glitches. Although backseat legroom is adequate, the seat cushions are too low, forcing your knees to your chin. *X5:* A smallish cargo area; bundled options can be pricey; and there have been long-standing quality control issues with the fuel system (chronic stalling), brakes, powertrain, electrical components, climate control, body integrity, and fit and finish. The complicated shifter and iDrive controls can also be hard to master without a lot of patience and frustration; and the third-row seats are a bit cramped. *X6:* Insufficient back seat headroom with no adjustments; a small cargo area; hefty price; heftier weight; fit and finish glitches; and seats only four. **Major redesign:** *X3:* 2004 and 2011; *X5:* 2000 and 2007; *X6:* 2008. The second-generation 2015 X6 will be restyled more aggressively without losing its sloping roofline and occupants will have a roomier interior, thanks to increases in length, width, and height. BMW will likely ditch its powerful, gas-guzzling 4.4L V8. **Highway/city fuel economy:** *X3 28i:* 8.3/12.2 L/100 km. *X3 30i:* 8.2/12.5 L/100 km. *X5 30i:* 9.3/13.6 L/100 km. *Diesel:* 7.5/10.7 L/100 km. *X5 48i:* 10.2/15.6 L/100 km.

X5 M: 11.9/17.2 L/100 km. *X6 35i:* 10.0/14.4 L/100 km. *X6 50i:* 11.0/17.1 L/100 km. *X6 M:* 11.9/17.2 L/100 km. *X6 Hybrid:* 10.3/12.6 L/100 km. **Best alternatives:** *X3:* Buy the more fuel-efficient 2013-14 if gas mileage is your main concern, but give preference to the second-series model built in March 2013 or later to make sure the electronics are less glitch-prone. Or, pick up a less-expensive 2012 V6-equipped X3, sans the latest changes. The money saved could buy a lot of fuel. *X5:* If the reports of poor quality don't faze you, get an almost identical, cheaper 2012 version, as well. *X6:* A big, brash, and beautiful barge – for potentates and poseurs. Expect major discounting prior to the arrival of the redesigned 2015. If you don't need the extra room; take the savings and run. Also consider the Acura RDX and Honda's recently redesigned CR-V. Other worthy contenders: The GM Acadia, Enclave, Escalade, Terrain, or Traverse, and the Lexus RX Series.

SAFETY: The X3 and X6 haven't yet been crash tested, but NHTSA gave the 2010 X5 five stars for front and side crash protection and four stars for rollover resistance. IIHS "Good" designation for 2004-13 X3 models for moderate overlap front collision protection and 2008-13 side protection. Roof strength was also "Good" with the 2012-13 models, while rear crashworthiness was scored "Good" for the 2008-13s, and the 2004-07s posted "Poor" scores. *X5:* "Good" designation for 2001-13 X3 models for moderate overlap front collision protection and 2007-13 side protection. Rear crash protection was "Good" for 2008-13s, but surprisingly "Poor" for 2001 through 2007 models. *X6:* No crash-test results, yet, but poor rearward visibility noted. Owner complaints for the X3: Fewer than usual safety-related failures reported to the government, nevertheless, the safety implications are evident. Some examples: Wheel seized while car was parked; acceleration lag, and when the car does get up to speed, it veers to the right:

> Car veering to the right, increased on sudden stops; happens at various speeds. The prominent and dangerous condition is lag in acceleration. Sent the following e-mail to dealer & BMW along with 3 service reports from dealer attempts to address: "This X3 3.5i with all [its] electronic engine/drive train controls is a nightmare. It's a huge design flaw that is going to kill someone eventually. Yet again, yesterday, I felt unsafe due to the hesitation. The car didn't move for about a second or two when I tried to make a left turn in an intersection and then again when I was on the highway changing lanes. There were cars heading towards me but the initial distance was quite comfortable and safe. With the hesitation of the X3, I was actually in a panic and stepped really hard on the gas pedal to avoid a potential collision. And since then I have been stepping on the gas pedal much harder, guzzling gas, not to mention rough starts off of a full stop. I have seen countless Internet threads of people complaining about the same thing with the X3 model, both versions, however equipped. I would strongly suggest someone look at how this car's software is failing to function and fix this thing."

Car will roll backwards even if in Park; total shutdown of the electrical system:

> The windshield wipers don't work, the headlights operate sporadically, the power door locks and power windows do not operate, the A/C doesn't work, the horn honks periodically, the

tailgate won't open to facilitate replacement of fuses. The fuel gauge is inoperative and the cruise control doesn't work.

Run-flat tires are noted for their short tread life; steering failures on vehicles not included in prior steering recall; and car veers to the right with sudden stops. *X5:* Engine surges and stalls:

The vehicle sporadically suffers from engine failure when executing a sharp turn. This has happened so far on three separate and distinct instances during its first 1,000 miles [1,609 km] of service, under the operation of two different drivers, with several passenger witnesses on one occasion. When these failures happen, the vehicle engine stalls or otherwise shuts itself off, which leads to loss of power steering in mid-turn and loss of braking. The only way to recover control of the vehicle is to let it coast to a stop, then put the vehicle in Park, then push the ignition button to re-start the car.

• • •

I leased my 2012 BMW X5 35I in May 2011. I was driving on the interstate with 2 toddlers at around 65 mph [105 km/h], when the car suddenly lost power and the message displayed "Engine Malfunction, Reduced Power." I pulled over on the shoulder, and tried to re-start the

Prices and Specs

X3

Prices (Soft): *28i:* $42,450, *35i:* $47,400 **Freight:** $1,995 **Powertrain (Rear-drive/AWD):** Engines: 2.0L 4-cyl. (240 hp), 3.0L 6-cyl. (240 hp) 3.0L Turbo. 6-cyl. (300 hp) Transmission: 8-speed auto. **Dimensions/capacity:** Passengers: 2/3; Wheelbase: 110.6 in.; H: 67/L: 182.8/W: 74 in.; Headroom F/R: 4/3 in.; Legroom F/R: 41.5/27.5 in.; Cargo volume: 63.3 cu. ft.; Fuel tank: 67L/premium; Tow limit: 3,500 lb.; Load capacity: 905 lb.; Turning circle: 38.4 ft.; Ground clearance: 8.5 in.; Weight: 4,067 lb.

X5

Prices (Negotiable): *35d xDrive:* $61,800, *50i xDrive:* $75,700 **Freight:** $1,995 **Powertrain (Rear-drive/AWD):** Engines (Turbo): 2.0L 4-cyl. (240 hp), 3.0L 6-cyl. (300 hp), 4.4L V8 (400 hp); Transmission: 8-speed auto. **Dimensions/capacity:** Passengers: 2/3/2; Wheelbase: 116 in.; H: 70/L: 191/W: 76.1 in.; Headroom F/R: 3.5/3 in.; Legroom F/R: 40.5/26.5 in.; Cargo volume: 36 cu. ft.; Fuel tank: 93L/premium; Tow limit: 6,500 lb.; Load capacity: 1,290 lb.; Turning circle: 42 ft.; Ground clearance: 8.3 in.; Weight: 5,265 lb.

X6

Price (Negotiable): *35i xDrive:* $66,800, *50i xDrive:* $82,200 **Freight:** $1,995 **Powertrain (Rear-drive/AWD):** Engines (Turbo): 3.0L 6-cyl. (240 hp), 4.4L 8-cyl. (400 hp), 4.4L 8-cyl. (555 hp), 4.4L 8-cyl. Hybrid (480 hp); Transmissions: 6-speed auto., 7-speed auto., 8-speed auto. **Dimensions/capacity:** Passengers: 2/2; Wheelbase: 116 in.; H: 67/L: 192/W: 78 in.; Headroom F/R: 3.5/2.5 in.; Legroom F/R: 40/27.5 in.; Fuel tank: 85L/premium; Tow limit: No towing; Load capacity: 935 lb.; Turning circle: 42 ft.; Ground clearance: 8.5 in.; Weight: 4,895-5,687 lb.

car, but it wouldn't start. When it did start after multiple attempts, the car shook vigorously and then turned off. I initiated the SOS call via the BMW Assist feature in the car. For some reason, the call failed multiple times, and the data could not be transferred. When the call did go through, the car could not send my exact coordinates to the reps to help me get a tow truck. After trying for about 30 min to get help from the BMW Assist, I tried to restart the car, which started normally as if nothing ever happened. The in-built diagnosis said "All Systems OK." I got on the interstate, and as I reached around 60 mph [97 km/h], the engine stalled again with the same message. ... For the next 1.5 hours, I tried to call the BMW Assist over my phone to get help. They said the tow truck should come in the next hour. For about 2 hours, the 2 toddlers and 3 adults were sitting by the interstate. I then tried to drive at about 40 mph [64 km/h] and take the car to the dealer, only to be pulled over by the high-way patrol. The next day my wife took the car to the dealer, and the report sheet they provided said that the high pressure pump was faulty.

ALERT! The smaller X3's high buy-in puts it at a disadvantage against larger, mid-size luxury crossover SUVs like the Acura MDX and Lexus RX 350. But the X3 has a generous amount of passenger and cargo room, which outshines "compact" competitors like the Audi Q5 and Mercedes-Benz GLK350.

X3/X5/X6 Profile

	2004	2005	2006	2007	2008	2009	2010	2011	2012
Used Values ($)									
X3 2.5i/28i/30i	7,000	8,500	11,000	14,000	16,000	19,000	21,500	27,000	31,500
X5 3.0i/35i	8,500	10,500	13,500	17,000	19,500	25,000	32,000	38,500	45,000
M3/M	13,000	18,,500	22,500	—	—	—	51,500	64,000	73,000
X6 35i	—	—	—	—	20,000	26,000	34,500	42,000	49,000
Recommended	✩	✩	✩	✩	✩	✩	✩	✩	✩
Reliability	✩	✩	✩	✩	✩	✩	✩	4	4

SECRET WARRANTIES, INTERNAL BULLETINS: 2011-12—Oil leak from transfer case. **2013**—*X3:* Intermittently noisy cooling fan. Water leaks into the cargo area. In most cases, the customer is not aware of any water in the lower compartments of the cargo area, but complaints of an electrical malfunction or failure, as a result of water intrusion. Water leaks from A/C centre console into the left and right footwell. Condensation is leaking from the HVAC housing water drain connection (not fitted correctly). Various electrical system failures leading to no-starts. Repeated juddering or surging on acceleration. Intermittent loss of power. The EPDW (electropneumatic pressure convertor) for the turbocharger wastegate valve is binding internally. Vehicle drifts to the right when traveling straight ahead. Possible Causes: Tires or improper tolerance in the coil springs of the front axle. *X5:* Intermittent loss of power. Computer/controls. Idle may fluctuate or cut off. Various Faults Concerning the Automatic Tailgate Operation.

OIL LEAK FROM TRANSFER CASE

BULLETIN NO.: S1 B27 01 12

DATE: APRIL 2012

Model: X3, X5, and X6.

SITUATION: Oil is leaking from the transmission area, or oil seepage is noticed from the transmission/transfer case area during a service.

CAUSE: The leak can be misdiagnosed as a transmission fluid leak from either the mechatronics sleeve or transmission oil pan. The leak is actually coming from the transfer case (input or output shaft seal).

PROCEDURE: Before attempting to perform any repairs, check the fluid level in both the transmission and transfer case. If the level is low in the transfer case, repair as necessary. Delay in engine response may require recalibration of the software; engine whistling, hooting, or squealing; intermittent engine rattle upon cold start; noise from the transmission bell housing area; faulty various electrical/computer malfunctions; inoperative front window; free replacement of the right front window regulator under Service Action #214, published in March 2012; whistle noise from rear-view mirror; humming noise from front of car; AC blows warm air; wipers/washers self-activate, can't be shut off; revised sun visor repair instructions; Check Gas Cap alert; excessive door mirror vibration; inoperative cell phone; and leather peeling from the steering wheel.

MERCEDES-BENZ

"God-power" vs. Horsepower

The Mercedes-Benz E200 convertible belonging to the Rev. Hernando Fayid, a Catholic priest, was parked in Santa Marta, Colombia, Wednesday, bearing a for-sale sign. Father Fayid said he was selling the car after Pope Francis's recent statement that it wounded his heart to see a priest in a luxury car.

New York Times
http//.blogs.nytimes.com/2013/07/11/wheelies-the-holy-rolloer-edition/

Cutting Costs and Prices

Daimler AG, Mercedes' governing company, tripled its profits through the second quarter of 2013 – mostly generated by sustained cost cutting, a drop in reduced sales incentives, and a surprisingly sharp rebound in demand for new products from Chinese and North American car buyers. Moreover, M-B predicts its earnings in the second half of 2013 will be significantly better than in the first six months of the year. These profits are all the more remarkable in that North America, Europe, and Asia are in the midst of a recession where only the strongest brands (mostly German automakers) survive.

Shoppers want luxury, but they also want powerful, fuel-efficient, comfortable vehicles with a high-performance edge. Automobile alchemists capable of creating fast, fancy, and frugal cars will be the winners in 2013-14. Mercedes is doing just this.

High Profits, Small Lemons

Daimler AG, Mercedes' governing company, made a healthy profit in 2011, mostly generated by strong sales of the lucrative E-Class and S-Class models, a drop in costly sales incentives, and a surprisingly sharp rebound in demand from Chinese and U.S. car buyers.

The company has pulled off this turnaround by increasing sales of smaller and less expensive cars in the United States, while selling fewer – but larger and more expensive – models in Europe and Asia. This means we'll soon see new subcompacts, electric vehicles, crossovers, and a return to 4-cylinder engines that haven't been offered in years. Most of these front-drive minicars will be based on Daimler's new A/B platform.

Is it "Moose-Proof"?

Mercedes hasn't been vey good at making reliable or well-performing small cars and SUVs over the past few decades. Its first efforts with the C- and M-Class were flops and the jury is still out on the new compact B-Class entrants. Its first effort, the "Baby Benz" 190 was the Mercedes 190. The A-Class overturned in a 1997 test run called the "moose test," a performance exercise used for decades in Sweden that calls for the driver to suddenly change lanes while going 70-80 km/h (45-50 mph), as though trying to avoid hitting a moose. What shocked the West Germany-based Daimler dignitaries most was that the Trabant – a much older, widely mocked car from Eastern Germany – passed the test with flying colours.

Quality Concerns

Although Mercedes quality is improving, some models continue to do much worse than others. For example, the C-Class, E-Class, and GLK-Class still have a few quality shortcomings outstanding, like fit and finish and powertrain delays:

> I almost had two accidents due to the lag problems, and have attached a more detailed analysis for your review. Turbo Lag: This is the time it takes for the car to go from its naturally aspirated power to the full power of the car at full boost/peak boost is reached relatively low in the reverse range, but it is not instantaneous power like a naturallly aspirated engine. Throttle Lage: The drive by wire system has a bit of lag. Under certain conditions, I measured it at .2 of a second or so. Whatever the value, there is always lag there, and we are very sensitive to it. However, driving in S Mode vs E Mode does make somewhat of a difference. Nonetheless, the car always starts out in E Mode when I get in and start the car. We didn't purchase the car to always drive in S Mode. Transmission Lag: This I notice

significantly and it is, in my opinion, probably the most annoying to me. You'll notice this when stomping the pedal to the floor and then doing the wait … wait … wait … downshift. Even if this engine was running only on its naturally aspirated four cylinders, the transmission should respond immediately to a sure footed stomp to the floor with the quickness, as does my four cylinder RAV-4. However, the MB C-250 does not! In my opionion, you can reset the TCU all you want, the delay will remain.

Other models like the CLK, GL-Class, and M-Class SUV have a history of quality failures that can make your life miserable. Most ironic of all, the most expensive models like the S-Class can also be the most troublesome.

Selling for $91,850 to $210,900 (U.S.), the S-Class has the worst Mercedes reliability rating as measured by *Consumer Reports*' annual member survey. Way before *CR* got involved, everyone (except for some clueless buyers) knew that Mercedes' 1998 M-Class sport-utilities were abysmally bad. You couldn't have made a worse vehicle, judging by the unending stream of desperate-sounding service bulletins sent from head office to dealers after the vehicle's official launch. Two bulletins stand out in my mind. One was an authorization for dry-cleaning payouts to dealers whose customers' clothing had been stained by the dye from the burgundy-coloured leather seats. The other was a lengthy scientific explanation (which the Germans compose so well) as to why drivers were "tasered" by static electricity when entering or exiting their vehicles.

Car columnists have always known that Mercedes has made some bad cars and SUVs, but it took business reporters (not auto beat writers) from the gutsy *Wall Street Journal* to spill the beans. In a February 2, 2002, article titled "An Engineering Icon Slips," the *WSJ* cited several confidential industry-initiated surveys that showed that Mercedes' quality and customer satisfaction had fallen dramatically since 1999 – to a level below that of GM's Opel, a brand that had one of the worst reputations for poor quality in Europe. Industry insiders give different reasons for why Mercedes-Benz quality isn't world class. They say quality control has been diluted by M-B doubling its product lineup since 1997. Helpful, too, were the company's aggressive PR campaigns and the company mindset that blamed the driver rather than the product – both spectacularly successful in keeping the quality myth alive in the media until the *Wall Street Journal* broke its story. Neither mindset nor PR worked to mitigate owners' displeasure over M-B's engine sludge stonewalling, though. It cost Mercedes $32 million (U.S.) to settle with owners of 1998-2001 models after the company denied that there was a factory-related problem. Although Mercedes sales are on the upswing, its vehicles' residual values have fallen dramatically from the most expensive cars down to the base entry-levels. At the top end, a 2007 65 AMG S-Class Sedan that cost $229,900 new is now worth barely $31,000. Even the entry-level B-Class models feel the depreciation bite: A 2008 B-Class 200 that originally sold for $30,000 is now worth only $11,500, and a middle-range 2009 E-Class E320 BlueTEC sedan, once priced at $68,100, can now be bought for $24,500.

B-CLASS ★★★

RATING: Above Average (2012-14); Average (2006-11). Not up to the level of the Audi A3 and the recently introduced BMW X1. This is the second year of the car's redesign, which means, most of the first year's production errors have been corrected. Keep in mind, though, that most reworked Mercedes models do poorly integrating electronics and hardware during their first few years after a redesign. Further complicating the reliability and servicing is BMW's world-wide parts redistribution changes put in place this year. Owners in North America and Europe are grumbling that the new system is inefficient and parts are unduly delayed for even the most minor repairs. The parts are particularly hard to find in the States due to the B250's absence from the American market. This means possibly longer servicing waits in the States (a problem also facing Mercedes Smart owners), forcing prudent owners to plan Canada-only driving vacations. Audi, BMW, and VW competitors have nationwide servicing networks throughout the States. **Road performance:** Considering its small size, the "B" has an unusually large turning circle, which cuts its urban usefulness. The new 7-speed dual-clutch transmission, that replaces the previous year's inadequate CVT gearworks, delivers power smoothly and quietly. **Strong points:** More powerful, with greater fuel efficiency this year, thanks to turbocharging and the advent of an ECO stop/start feature that saves on gas in stop-and-go traffic. Occupant ingress and egress is much improved, and rear-seat passengers can sit in relative comfort. B250s are wider and longer, and have a stretched wheelbase, but they sit lower. Roomy, with lots of storage space, and feature-laden, with four-wheel disc brakes, stability control, seven standard airbags, upgraded suspension and steering, and a classier, more user-friendly interior. Impressive fuel economy. **Weak points:** The retail price could be trimmed by at least $5,000, making the car more competitive. Furthermore, shoppers would be wise to consider the equivalent Mazda or other Japanese or European compacts that can cost less and be serviced everywhere. Owners decry mostly fit and finish problems, electrical system shorts, and premature brake wear gripes. **Major redesign:** 2012. A B-Class Electric Drive is scheduled to arrive in Canada sometime in early 2014 as a 2014 model. The vehicle has a driving range of 200 km (124 mi) with a top speed of 150 km/h (93 mph). The battery can be charged at any standard public power outlet or rapid charging terminal. **Highway/city fuel economy:** 4.9/8.8 L/100 km. **Best alternatives:** Take a look at the BMW 1 Series, Kia Rondo, Mazda5, and Toyota Matrix.

Prices and Specs

Prices (Negotiable): *B250:* $30,500 (2014) **Freight:** Price includes $1,995 freight fee **Powertrain (Front-drive):** Engine: 2.0L Turbo 4-cyl. (208 hp); Transmission: 7-speed auto. **Dimensions/capacity:** Passengers: 2/3; Wheelbase: 106 in.; H: 61 /L: 172/W: 79 in.; Legroom F/R: 43/38.4 in.; Cargo volume: 23.5 cu. ft.; Fuel tank: 50L/premium; Tow limit: 3,307 lb.; Turning circle: 39.2 ft.; Weight: 3,252 lb.

SAFETY: Crashworthiness hasn't yet been tested. However, the turn signal and cruise control stalks have been repositioned to prevent misapplication.

ALERT! The paddle shifters take getting used to and may discourage spirited driving. Check out the left side-view mirror's blind spot.

B-Class Profile

	2006	2007	2008	2009	2010	2011	2012
Used Values ($)							
200	9,500	10,500	11,500	12,500	16,000	19,500	—
200T	10,500	11,500	12,000	14,000	17,500	22,000	—
Recommended	☆	☆	☆	☆	☆	☆	☆
Reliability	☆	☆	☆	☆	☆	☆	☆

SECRET WARRANTIES, INTERNAL BULLETINS: 2006-08—Owners report premature rusting of the rear hatch and door seams. Apparently, M-B is repairing the damage for free, on a case-by-case "goodwill" basis. Because the B-Class isn't sold in the States, there is no service bulletin repository to confirm what guidelines Mercedes is giving dealers.

C-CLASS

RATING: Average (2008-14); Below Average (2001-07). These little entry-level cars lack the simplicity and popular pricing found with the Japanese luxury competition; save up for an E-Class or a Hyundai Genesis. **Road performance:** A big improvement in power and handling with this year's adoption of V6 power. The ride is generally comfortable, though sometimes choppy, and braking is first-class. The light steering requires constant correction, and there's some tire thumping and engine and wind noise in the cabin. **Strong points:** Additional V6 power, and smoother shifting with the 7-speed automatic transmission. Plenty of high-tech performance and safety features; a good V6 powertrain matchup; available AWD; and an innovative anti-theft system. **Weak points:** Higher prices than are reasonable when compared with competitors and faster than average depreciation: A $41,000 2008 C300 Sedan is now barely worth $15,000. Owners report problems with the climate control systems, body hardware, and fit and finish, as well as complicated controls; limited rear-seat and cargo room; and tight entry and exit. Also, these cars are noted for being dealer-dependent for parts and servicing – a problem likely to worsen with this year's new powertrains and economic conditions that make dealers reluctant to invest in a large inventory. **Major redesign:** 2001 and 2008. **Highway/city fuel economy:** *C250, 1.8L:* 6.3/9.6 L/100 km. *2.5L:* 8.3/12.4 L/100 km. *Coupe:* 6.4/9.7 L/100 km. *C300:* 7.9/11.8 L/100 km. *4Matic:* 10.8/16.3 L/100 km. *C350:* 7.0/10.8 L/100 km. *4Matic:* 7.0/10.7 L/100 km. *4Matic Coupe:* 7.1/10.8 L/100 km. *63 AMG:* 10.4/16 L/100 km. *Coupe:* 10.4/16.1 L/100 km. *CL550:* 8.8/13.8 L/100 km. *CL600:* 11.2/18.1 L/100 km. *CL 63 AMG:* 9.3/13.8 L/100 km. *CL 65 AMG:* 10.9/17.4 L/100 km. *CLS 550 4Matic:* 8.2/12.7 L/100 km. *CLS 63 AMG:* 8.6/13.6 L/100 km.

Best alternatives: Take a look at the BMW 3 Series, or a Hyundai Genesis Coupe. The Bose sound system is a good investment.

SAFETY: NHTSA awarded 2002-14 C-Class models four and five stars for overall crash protection. IIHS crash tests gave top marks ("Good") for front moderate overlap protection from 2001 through 2013 model years and a "Poor" score for side crashworthiness. 2005-07 models rated "Acceptable" for side crash safety and "Good" for 2009-13 versions. Roof strength was judged "Good" from 2008 up to the 2013s and head restraints scored "Marginal" for the 2004-05s; "Acceptable" from 2006-07; and "Good" for the 2008-13s. Owner-reported safety failures: *C250:* Turn-signal control light is barely visible in daylight, and steering-column-mounted levers (cruise control, for instance) are hard to see behind the steering wheel. *C300:* Severe noise invades the cabin when the window is rolled down while driving (which seems unusual for a luxury German-made car):

> The contact owns a 2012 Mercedes Benz C300. The contact stated that while driving 35 mph [56 km/h], the rear passenger side window exhibited a loud, abnormal noise when opened. As a result, the contact experienced a temporary loss of hearing from the high pitch of the noise. The vehicle was taken to the dealer who stated that the loud noise was common for the vehicle.

ALERT! Average reliability, and unlike the B-Class B250, entry-level C-Class cars can be repaired anywhere.

Prices and Specs

Prices (Negotiable): *C250:* $37,300, *C300 4Matic:* $39,990, *C350 Sedan:* $44,750, *350 4Matic:* $47,700, *C63 AMG:* $65,300 **Freight:** Price includes $1,995 freight fee **Powertrain (Rear-drive/AWD):** Engines: 1.8L 4-cyl. (201 hp), 3.5L V6 (248 hp), 3.5L V6 (302 hp), 6.3L V8 (451 hp); Transmission: 7-speed auto.
Dimensions/capacity: Passengers: 2/3; Wheelbase: 108.7 in.; H: 56.9/L: 182/W: 70 in.; Headroom F/R: 2.5/1.5 in.; Legroom F/R: 42/26 in.; Cargo volume: 12.4 cu. ft.; Fuel tank: 62L/premium; Tow limit: Not recommended; Load capacity: 835 lb.; Turning circle: 35.3 ft.; Ground clearance: 4.2 in.; Weight: 3,565 lb.

C-Class Profile

	2004	2005	2006	2007	2008	2009	2010	2011	2012
Used Values ($)									
Coupe 230/250	5,500	7,500	10,500	—	—	—	—	—	28,000
320	—	7,500	—	—	—	—	—	—	—
AWD	—	8,500	—	—	—	—	—	—	—
350	—	—	—	—	—	—	—	—	35,000
AMG	—	—	—	—	—	—	—	—	44,000
Sedan 230/240	6,000	8,000	10,000	11,000	14,000	15,500	—	—	—
AWD	7,000	8,500	—	13,500	15,000	16,500	—	—	—
240	6,000	8,000	—	—	—	—	—	—	—
Wagon	6,500	8,500	—	—	—	—	—	—	—
AWD	7,000	9,000	—	—	—	—	—	—	—
250	—	—	—	—	—	—	21,000	24,500	27,000
AWD	—	—	—	—	—	—	22,500	26,500	30,000
280	—	—	10,000	11,500	—	—	—	—	—
AWD	—	—	11,000	12,500	—	—	—	—	—
300	—	—	—	—	14,500	17,000	22,500	25,500	—
300 AWD	—	—	—	—	15,500	18,500	24,000	27,000	32,000
320	6,500	—	—	—	—	—	—	—	—
AWD Wagon	7,500	—	—	—	—	—	—	—	—
350	—	—	11,500	12,500	16,000	18,000	27,000	29,000	33,000
AWD	—	—	12,000	13,500	17,000	19,500	25,000	31,000	35,000
AMG	—	—	—	—	—	27,000	34,000	42,000	47,000
Recommended	☆2	☆2	☆2	☆2	☆3	☆3	☆3	☆3	☆3
Reliability	☆2	☆2	☆2	☆2	☆3	☆3	☆3	☆3	☆4

SECRET WARRANTIES, INTERNAL BULLETINS: 2005—Engine oil leaks from the oil-level sensor. Harsh shifts with the automatic transmission. Transmission fluid leaks at the electrical connector. Inoperative central locking system and AC heater blower motor. Steering assembly leaks fluid. Sliding roof water leaks, rattling. Moisture in the turn signal lights and mirrors. Tail lights won't turn off; trunk light won't turn on. A Service Campaign calls for the free modification of the lower door seal. **2007**—Rough shifting. Automatic transmission shift chatter. Steering rack leaks. Inoperative AC blower motor. Remedy for brake squealing. Front-end/dash noise. Front axle knocking when parking. Torsion bar front-end creaking. Inoperative turn signals. Rear seatback rattle. Loose head restraint. Horn may not work due to premature corrosion of the assembly. *350:* **2009**—Oil leaks at the rear of the engine may be fixed by changing the camshaft cover plugs. Hard 1-2 shifts. Harsh engagement when shifting from Park to Drive. Delayed Reverse engagement. What to do if the automatic transmission goes into "limp home" mode. Front axle noise when maneuvering. Front axle dull, thumping noise when going over bumps. Front-end suspension or steering grinding noise. Front seat backrest noise. Interior lights flickering. Four-way lumbar support fails. Internal steering gear leakage. AC is inoperative or supplies insufficient cooling. *C250:* **2011-12**—Oil leakage at the seam between the automatic transmission and the transfer case housing. Suspension noise from front axle suspension struts on vehicles equipped with a 1.8L engine. Automatic transmission hard 2-3 upshift or slipping, no Third gear. **2013**—Oil loss in area of rear crankcase-transmission bell housing. Corrosion spreading under wheel hub sealing ring. Dirt and water are washed in front of the sealing ring of the wheel hub via the rpm sensor bore in the steering knuckle or through corresponding gaps between the anchor plate and steering knuckle. Corrosion forms on the contact surface of the sealing ring and spreads under the sealing lips. As a result, moisture can penetrate the wheel bearing and cause corrosion. Moisture in area of A-pillar trim/headliner at front left or right. Replace water drain grommet. Casting porosity in crankcase or leaks in oil filter housing (seal might be damaged at the oil filter housing plate). The steering boot heat shield with aluminum ring has loosened and is scraping on the steering shaft. *C300, C350, C63 AMG, and CL550:* Vehicle doesn't perform automatic engine stop. Repair tips for engine cylinder head cover leaks. Consumer electrical shutoff intermittently active. Automatic transmission switches to "limp home" mode for no reason. Automatic transmission hard 2-3 upshifts, slipping, or no Third gear. Oil leaks at the seam between the automatic transmission and the transfer case housing. Front suspension noise. Correcting various Parking Assist malfunctions.

E-CLASS ★★★★

RATING: Above Average for all years. Redesigned only a few times during the past decade, these family sedans, wagons, and convertibles manage to hold five people in relative comfort while performing acceptably well. Recently Mercedes added the E400 Hybrid, updated the engine in the E250 BlueTEC diesel, and now sells that model with optional AWD. The E63 high performance AMG sedan and station wagon are totally revamped. **Road performance:** Solid acceleration in the higher gear ranges; 4Matic all-wheel drive operates flawlessly; good handling, though not quite as crisp as with the BMW 5 Series; impressive braking with little brake fade after successive stops; and an acceptable ride, although the Sport model may feel too stiff for some. The car feels much slower than it actually is. **Strong points:** Well-appointed with many safety, performance, and convenience features; good engine and transmission combo; a relatively roomy interior (except for front headroom); lots of cargo room (with the 4Matic wagon); plush, comfortable seats; an innovative anti-theft system; and average quality control, though the AWD version generates more owner complaints. **Weak points:** E-Class cars have improved incrementally over the years, but they have also suffered from unreasonably high base prices, some content-cutting, overly complex electronics and fuel-delivery systems, and poor quality control. For example, the overly-complicated electronic control centre, and navigation system controls are hard to master. Other minuses: Transmission, brake system, and fuel pump malfunctions, diesel engine cabin noise; a surprisingly small trunk; and knee bolsters and limited headroom that will annoy tall drivers. Plus, the cleaner-burning diesel-equipped models require costly periodic urea fill-ups at the dealership. Instead, try to get urea off the shelf at auto supply outlets, and pour it yourself. You can save a few hundred bucks. A few years ago, Consumer Reports took its own diesel-powered Mercedes-Benz GL320 BlueTEC to a dealer because a warning light indicated that the SUV was low on AdBlue urea. The fill-up cost? $316.99! The GL needed 7.5 gallons, which accounted for $241.50 of the total bill ($32.20/gallon). Labour (twisting a cap and pouring) and tax accounted for the remaining $75.49. It took CR about 26,660 kilometres (16,565 miles) to run low on AdBlue, which means spending $1,457.80 on the stuff over 160,935 kilometres (100,000 miles). BMW covers this cost for its diesel powered vehicles up to 80,470 kilometres (50,000 miles). Faster than average depreciation can also be costly: A $58,600 2010 350 Coupe entry-level model is now worth $33,000 – great news if you are buying used, but depressing if the car was purchased new. **Major redesign:** 1996, 2003, 2007, and 2010, and 2014. The 2014s will be completely revised, with a new front end, the 3.5L V6 powering the E350 and the 4.7L twin-turbo V8 going into the E500 and E550. **Highway/city fuel economy:** *E350:* 8.3/12.7 L/100 km. *E550:* 8.6/13.8 L/100 km. *E63:* 10.2/16.5 L/100 km. **Best alternatives:** A discounted 2012 is your best bet. Again, old-time diesel lovers beware: Sure, they are quieter and less smelly but there is a price to pay. It is hard to find competent, inexpensive servicing by independent agencies. Choose instead, the Hyundai Genesis sedan or high performance coupe. They both have lower price tags, fantastic interiors, rear-drive power delivery, and powerful V8s. Other choices include the Acura RL, BMW 5 Series, Hyundai Equus, Infiniti M35x, and Lexus GS AWD.

SAFETY: NHTSA awarded the 2003-10 sedans four and five stars in all crash tests. IIHS test scores were just as impressive: 2000-13 versions received "Good" scores for front moderate overlap protection; 1997-99s were judged "Acceptable." Side and roof/rollover protection was "Good" from 2010 through the 2013s, though side crash protection was seen as only "Acceptable" for the 2007-09 versions. Head restraints were "Good" from 2006 though 2013, while earlier models tested "Acceptable." Owner safety complaints are few, but serious, like airbags failing to deploy in a collision; constantly stalling in highway traffic; original equipment Continental tire sidewall failures; frequent run-flat Bridgestone Turanza irreperable flat tires, says one owner:

> Tire repairman told me these run-flats are not flexible and have a very think sidewall so it gets punctured by the rim.

Interior dash vents and other vitems reflect sunlight onto the windshield and side mirrors; speedometer readings wash out in daylight; driver's seat belt vibrates continuosly against the shoulder; and an "exploding" sunroof:

> The panoramic sunroof exploded outward. When it occurred the sound was like someone fired a shotgun next to my head. I was driving northbound on I-25 just south of Denver. Had the fabric sunshade not been extended forward so it contained the glass the occupants in the car would have been showered with the sharp shards, which were so sharp the pieces that flew back on the back window and trunk lid left deep scratches on those surfaces. Not sure how much glass was thrown up into the air and impacted traffic behind the car. Think about a motorcycle rider being hit by these flying shards of glass. After the incident I looked online and found the following link, which details another incident in 2012 that seems to be exactly what I experienced on June 1: www.benzworld.org/forums/w251-R-class/1652488-exploding-sunroof.html.

ALERT! During your test drive, look for distracting side mirror reflections coming from the cabin and check out the front seat and seat belts for comfort:

Prices and Specs

Prices (Negotiable): *E300 4Matic Sedan:* $58,300, *E350 BlueTEC Sedan:* $65,600, *Coupe:* $61,400, *E350 4Matic Sedan:* $66,300, *4Matic Coupe:* $62,400, *4Matic Wagon:* $70,400, *4Matic BlueTEC Diesel:* $62,500, *E350 Cabriolet:* $69,200, *E550 Coupe:* $72,900, *4Matic:* $74,900, *E550 Cabriolet:* $79,900, *E63 AMG:* $99,700, *E63 AMG Wagon:* $102,300 **Freight:** Price includes $1,995 freight fee **Powertrain (Rear-drive/AWD):** Engines: 3.0L V6 turbodiesel (210 hp), 3.5L V6 (302 hp), 4.7L V8 (402 hp), 5.5L V8 (518 and 550 hp); Transmission: 7-speed auto. **Dimensions/capacity:** Passengers: 2/3; Wheelbase: 113.1 in.; H: 57.7/L: 191.7/W: 71.9 in.; Headroom F/R: 3/3 in.; Legroom F/R: 44/28.5 in.; Cargo volume: 16 cu. ft.; Fuel tank: 80L/premium; Tow limit: N/A; Load capacity: 960 lb.; Turning circle: 36.2 ft.; Ground clearance: 4.1 in.; Weight: 4,020 lb.

The 2012 EC50 interior dash vents (shiny items) are reflected onto the side mirrors making it dangerous when changing lanes because one cannot be sure what one is seeing in those lanes because the reflection is very pronounced. These vents and other dash items are also reflected on the windshield, almost like an obstruction when one is driving. In addition, the adjustable front seats are so uncomfortable that one is constantly adjusting the seat setting while driving.

E-Class Profile

	2004	2005	2006	2007	2008	2009	2010	2011	2012
Used Values ($)									
Coupe 300/350	—	—	—	—	—	—	33,000	40,000	48,500
Coupe 550	—	—	—	—	—	—	38,000	47,000	57,000
Sedan 280/300/320/350	9,000	11,000	13,000	15,500	19,000	22,000	—	—	—
Sedan 320/350 TEC	—	13,000	15,000	16,500	19,500	23,500	—	—	49,000
320/350 AWD	10,000	11,500	13,500	15,000	20,000	22,000	33,000	41,000	50,000
500/550 AWD	10,500	12,500	14,500	17,000	23,000	31,000	39,000	48,000	58,000
Cabrio 350	—	—	—	—	—	—	—	49,000	57,000
500/550	—	—	14,000	—	—	—	—	57,000	65,000
320/350 Wagon AWD	10,500	12,000	15,500	17,000	20,000	22,000	—	42,000	51,000
Amg	—	—	—	18,000	30,000	36,000	53,000	—	78,000
Recommended	✩	✩	✩	✩	✩	✩	✩	✩	✩
Reliability	✩	✩	✩	✩	✩	✩	✩	✩	✩

SECRET WARRANTIES, INTERNAL BULLETINS: 2004—No-starts. Harsh transmission shifts. Steering leaks. Sliding roof-rack cover cracks. Wheelhouse water drain modification. Rear axle rumbling. **2005**—Oil leaks from the oil-level sensor. Rough automatic transmission engagement, droning, buzzing noises. Transmission leaks fluid at the electrical connector. Campaign to check and repair possible automatic transmission pilot bushing leakage; another campaign concerns the free cleaning of the front axle carrier sleeve and bolt replacement; a third campaign will reprogram the battery control module; and a fourth campaign will inspect or replace the alternator/regulator. Foul interior odours. Steering fluid leaks and steering squeal when turning. Front-seat noise. Sliding roof water leaks, rattling. Moisture in the turn signal lights and mirrors. Rear seatback rattle. Loose passenger head restraints. Fanfare horns may not work due to premature wiring corrosion. *350:* **2006-07**—Rough transmission shifts. Upshift/downshift chatter or shudder. Front axle creaking, grinding, knocking noise when parking, and other front-end noises. Brake squeal. Steering-rack leaks. Rivet replacement to prevent water leakage. Inoperative AC, faulty blower motor, or compressor failure. False oil readings.

Inoperative turn signals. Loose front centre armrest falls off. *E350 Sedan and BlueTEC Diesel:* **2011-12**—Automatic transmission switches to "limp home" mode. Hard 2-3 upshifts, slipping, or no Third gear. Oil leakage at the seam between the automatic transmission and the transfer case housing. Also, the vehicle doesn't perform automatic engine stop. The front suspension may be noisy. Repair tips for Parking Assist malfunctions. **2011-13**— No crank/no start/intermittent no crank. **2013**—Navigation feature freezes/slow/delayed response. Battery discharged, vehicle does not start. Cause: Rotary light switch sending wrong signal after ignition Off.

VOLKSWAGEN

What Recession?

Volkswagen is one of the few automakers that have increased market share during the present worldwide recession. It has done this through a combination of diesel popularity, less exposure to the slumping American market than other automakers, the right mix of vehicles that responds well to up-and-down fuel prices, and a solid international footing. It has profitable operations in Latin America; an expanding presence in China, Russia, and India; and a dominant role in Western Europe, where it also markets its Seat and Skoda brands.

No 75th Anniversary Party for Beetle

Volkswagen has come a long way since production of what we know today as the Beetle was interrupted by World War II. Instead of making the *People's Car*, the factory churned out products for the military. In 1944, two-thirds of the factory's workers were forced labourers, according to German media. Volkswagen's Nazi past kept it from celebrating its 75th anniversary earlier this year.

VW's small, fuel-efficient cars and diesel-equipped lineup has touched a nerve with Canadian shoppers in much the same way as the company's first Beetle captured the imagination and support of consumers in the mid-60s. Building on that support, over the past few years Volkswagen has cut prices and features to keep its small cars affordable.

But quality has always been the company's Achilles' heel, from the first Beetle's no-heat heaters that your mom and dad will probably never forget, to gear-hopping, car-wrecking DSG transmissions afflicting Volkswagen's 2007-13 models:

> I own a 2009 Jetta TDI with a DSG transmission. I feel like I am going to get hit when I start from a stop. The transmission jumps and hesitates. It has been to the dealer without being fixed. It is terrifying to drive a car that may or may not accelerate, which also jumps in and out of gear!

We can all agree that Volkswagens are practical drivers' cars that offer excellent handling and great fuel economy without sacrificing interior comfort. But overall reliability goes downhill after the fifth year of ownership and servicing is often more competent and cheaper at independent garages, which have grown increasingly popular as owners flee more expensive VW dealerships.

Unfortunately, parts are fairly expensive, and both dealers and independent garages have trouble finding them due to VW's frequent addition of more-complex electronic and mechanical components as well as a chaotic parts distribution system, which has resulted from dealer and supplier closures during the ongoing recession.

With rare candor Volkswagen now admits that car buyers see its products as failure-prone, and the automaker vows to change that perception by building a more reliable, durable product and providing timely, no-return servicing. Taking a page out of Toyota's sudden, unintended acceleration/brake failure Congressional testimony several years back, Volkswagen says it is now paying more attention, sooner, to problems reported by fleet customers and dealers in order to find and fix problems before they become widespread among individual customers.

VW's quality control efforts seem to be working – more on some models than others. A check of the NHTSA owner complaints log at *safercar.gov* does show safety-related incidents have dropped during the last four years, probably as a result of the recall of the DSG transmission and subsequent "goodwill" warranty extension to address DSG claims. In spite of all these efforts, automatic powertrain-related problems are still the number-one failure reported to NHTSA's safety complaint website.

Four years ago, *Lemon-Aid* exposed the DSG problem and rated Audi and VW new and used models equipped with DSG transmissions as Not Recommended and we called for a warranty extension and recall. Since then, VW and Audi have recalled the tranny several times and extended the warranty to 10 years/100,000 miles on 2007-10 models.

Incidentally, Australian VW/Audi car owners, irate that VW stonewalled their DSG complaints, sought the help of local media. The *Sydney Morning Herald* and *The Age* championed their case, leading to Volkswagen pulling its advertising from both publications. Shortly thereafter, VW recalled the affected VW, Audi, and Skoda models.

For a copy of VW's extended warranty, go to *www.dsgproblems.co.uk/Volkswagen %20 of%20America%20Inc.pdf*.

Now there is fresh evidence that tranny failures have spread to the 2012-13 models.

Therefore, be wary in your choice of vehicle and persistent in pursuing your claim.

GOLF/JETTA ★★★

RATING: *All gasoline- and diesel-powered models equipped with the DSG automatic transmission:* Not Recommended, due to reports of serious, life-threatening powertrain and fuel-delivery defects. *Non-DSG transmission-equipped vehicles:* Average. **Road performance:** Drivetrain problems aside, these cars are good all-around front-drive performers when coupled to a manual shifter and adequate engine. The sporty GLI, with its turbocharged 200 hp 2.0L 4-cylinder engine, delivers high-performance thrills without much of a fuel penalty, and the 170 hp 2.5L 5-cylinder engine is well suited for city driving and most leisurely highway cruising, thanks mainly to the car's light weight and handling prowess. Be wary of models equipped with the wimpy 115 hp 2.0L 4-cylinder engine. The DSG's shifts are soft in full-auto mode, unreliable, stick in gear, and subject to a three- to ten-second lag when most needed, like on turns, merging from an on-ramp into traffic, passing on two-lane highways, or pulling away from a stop sign or traffic light:

> 2013 DSG Transmission Issues: When making a left hand turn across traffic, I coasted up to the light when it was my turn, then I pressed the accelerator and the car had no power. It crossed through the intersection at approximately 1 to 2 mph. It took 5 to 10 seconds for the power to return. It felt like if you are driving a manual transmission and have the car in 4th or 5th gear when trying to start moving. This has happened at quite a few intersections. Also it happened when I was accelerating then had to release the accelerator due to a vehicle slowing in front of me, I re-engaged the accelerator and there was no power for 5 to 10 seconds.
>
> • • •
>
> A two week old 2013 VW Jetta became stuck in reverse after being in park and then I tried to put it in drive in the middle lane of an extremely busy street in Brooklyn, NY. The car would not move from reverse and had to be towed away. I hear from others this is a known defect.
>
> • • •

We just bought a new 2013 Volkswagen Jetta Sports Wagon with a Diesel TDI engine and DSG transmission. Driving the car home from the dealer the transmission failed at 110 miles on the odometer. It has been towed to the dealer and they tell me that the mechatronic unit has failed. The sympton of the failure was that the transmission seemed to shift into neutral with no notice and the car had severally reduced power available (less than 10 mph). Research on the Internet shows that Volkswagen has had problems with this before. It seems very serious to me to have something like this fail on a brand new vehicle.

. . .

Jetta Hybrid. Loss of traction while ascending steep driveway. Never happened before even with another hybrid.

Strong points: "Practical and fun to drive" pretty well sums up why these VWs continue to be so popular – at least for the first couple of years. They offer an accommodating interior, plenty of power with the higher-end models, and responsive handling. Like most European makes, these VWs are drivers' cars with lots of road "feedback;" a comfortable ride; plenty of headroom, legroom, and cargo space; a standard tilt/telescope steering column; a low load floor; and good fuel economy. **Weak points:** Powertrains on the DSG-powered 2011 through 2013s are showing failures similar to the recalled 2007-10 models. Base Jettas come with a 115 hp 4-cylinder engine that is the runt of the litter. It fails to meet the driving expectations of most Jetta buyers, who want both good fuel economy and an engine with plenty of low-end torque and cruising power. Diesels with cruise control can't handle small hills very well, and often slow down by 10-15 km/h. Excessive engine and road noise; difficult entry and exit; and restricted rear visibility. Folding rear seats don't lie flat. Maintenance costs increase after the fifth year of ownership, it takes six years for fuel savings to equal the car's higher purchase cost; and depreciation accelerates as you approach the end of the four-year warranty, even with the always-popular Jetta. For example, a 2008 Jetta 2.0L turbocharged sedan that first sold for $27,475 is now worth only $10,500. Less than average annual maintenance cost while under warranty. After that, repair costs start to climb dramatically ... just replacing a fuse can be a head-scratcher: The GLI and TDI offer a DSG 6-speed dual-clutch automated manual that is fuel-frugal and a pleasure to drive ... when it's not hesitating, stuck in Reverse, falling into Neutral, or simply falling apart. Again, we raise the caveat that VW's relatively new diesel design will likely have higher servicing costs and parts availability problems. That said, auto analysts still maintain that diesel is the best alternative to paying high fuel prices that are nearing $1.35 a liter in some regions. Autoweek magazine concluded, "For comfort, quiet, and highway handling, our drivers found the TDI had significant advantages over every other car in the test. It would have been our choice, in other words, for an easy daytrip on the interstates, regardless of fuel economy. And we topped the hybrids by driving with just a little attention to fuel economy, not making it an obsession." **Major redesign:** *Golf:* 1999, 2006, and 2010.

Jetta: 1999, 2005, and 2011 *Eos:* 2007. **Highway/city fuel economy:** *Golf City 2.0L:* 7.0/9.8 L/100 km. *Golf 2.5L:* 7.0/10.4 L/100 km. *Auto.:* 6.9/9.2 L/100 km. *TDI:* 4.7/6.7 L/100 km. *Auto.:* 4.6/6.7 L/100 km. Jetta fuel economy should be similar. **Best alternatives:** VW says it will keep a lid on 2014 entry-level model prices, so there's little advantage in buying a 2013. However, the first batch of 2014 Golfs may have a water leakage problem. Auto Bild and Reuters report the seventh-generation Golf may have a faulty drainage tube in the air conditioning system that could leak water into the front passenger's footwell. VW is aware of the problem and is currently investigating. Price increases on 2014 higher-end versions may top a few thousand dollars. Stay away from the electric sunroof; it costs a bundle to repair and offers not much more than the manual sunroof. On top of that, you lose too much headroom and water/air leaks are common. Other cars worth considering are the Honda Civic and Civic Si or Accord, Hyundai Elantra, Kia Forte, Mazda6, Nissan Sentra, Suzuki Kizashi, and Toyota Corolla or Matrix.

 SAFETY: This is the deal breaker. Although many VW's will give you excellent crash protection, their inherent powertrain and fuel system failures will increase your chances of crashing. NHTSA gave the 2000-14 models its top four- and five-star scores in all crash tests; 1997-99 models earned three stars in most categories. IIHS crash test scores are also outstanding: 1999-2013 versions got a "Good" grade for front moderate overlap protection; 1994-98s were judged "Marginal;" and front small overlap protection was deemed "Marginal." Side and roof/rollover protection was rated "Good" from 2005 through the 2013s. Head restraints were "Good" from 2009 though 2013, earlier 2007-08s were "Marginal" and the 2005-06 sedans tested "Acceptable." Many of the NHTSA-posted complaints on 2013 and earlier models involve DSG transmission and high-pressure fuel pump failures:

> The car completely lost power while in motion and I had to pull off the roadway in heavy traffic. The dealer told me that the TDI (diesel) fuel system had a complete failure and imploded into many very small metal parts. VW is replacing the entire fuel system, but not the engine. I believe metal in the fuel lines is cause for a complete engine replacement as they cannot prove the contamination was limited to the fuel lines. The car is less than 4 months old and 5500 miles total.

Exhaust leaks on Jetta TDIs may send dangerous levels of exhaust gases into the cabin; some owners report hundreds of foggy-looking spots appear in the rear windshield:

> When these spots appear it is almost impossible to see out of this windshield or into it. This usually happens around dawn and around dusk though it has happened at other times of the day also. I have pursued having this problem resolved by contacting the dealer several times only to be told it is because of the window being polarizes. . . . You cannot see out of or in through the windsheild when these foggy spots are there. . . . The last time I heard from VW, they said they would tint the rear windshield so that I wouldn't see the problem. This does not make any sense. If you try to cover up the problem yu do not solve the problem.

The wheel rim may suddenly self-destruct if the tires are over-inflated:

The right front wheel on my 2012 VW CC shattered. My concern is focused on the safety of the wheel design and my belief that the overinflation of the tires contribute to rim failure. ... There were no visible defects in the road. ... While driving in the middle lane the car clearly came in contact with an irregularity, one that every car before and after was able to transverse without a problem. In my case the rim shattered and separated from the car causing a loss of control. My concern is twofold. One, the safety of the design and construction of the rim and the overinflation upon delivery of the tires which contributed to the weakness of the design.

Many of the same failures have been reported for almost a decade. Premature brake wear, electrical and electronic failures, and fit and finish defects are the top problems reported by the owners of the 2012 model. Fender sound system rattles (covered by a special service campaign). Water leaks are commonplace. *CC:* When coming to a stop, the car still inches forward; factory-installed GPS tells the driver to turn just moments before the turn must be made; the horn doesn't sound immediately; and the Low Tire Pressure warning indicator gives false alerts. Here are problems that are model-specific: *Golf:* Failure of the high-pressure fuel pump on diesel models is one cause of chronic stalling and unbelievably high repair bills reported for the past several model years:

At 6,519 miles [10,490 km], while about to enter the on-ramp of a local highway, the Check Engine light and glow plug indicator light began to flash. I was able to veer off the entrance ramp and continue down to the nearest safe parking lot area; as I pulled into the parking lot area, the vehicle shuddered and suddenly shut off. It would not re-start, and we had to arrange for a tow to a family member's house through our insurance company. In the morning we had a tow to our dealer set up through Volkswagen roadside service, who would not cover the entire cost of the tow to our preferred dealer, so we paid the difference out of our own pocket. I was notified by the dealer that the fuel pump (commonly referred to as HPFP) basically imploded and sent metal throughout the entire fuel system, which now needs to be replace. ... This is a design failure and/or oversight on the part of both Volkswagen and Bosch, the HPFP manufacturer. I am a veteran member of the TDI Club VW Diesel online community, and there is extensive information and documentation there of these repeated failures.

DSG automatic transmission failures have returned to haunt owners:

Leaving a parking lot in my 2012 Golf, put the gear into Reverse and was going forward. Put the gear in Parking 3X and back to Reverse 3X, but still going forward. Couldn't turn off the engine. Opened the door, and after maybe 10 minutes was able to turn off the engine, gave it a minute and then use the Reverse gear and it worked.

GTI: DSG transmission won't shift into gear, and sometimes the engine suddenly surges or stalls, accompanied by total brake failure:

During rush hour traffic, I had to slow down a little in order to allow the car next to me to pass so I could change lanes without hitting the car in front of me. The car seemed to shift into Neutral and did not respond when I hit the accelerator. The accelerator pedal actually sunk down to the floor with no response. After a few seconds, the transmission did shift into gear and took off too fast. In the meantime, I was almost rear-ended. This happens almost every day that I drive in heavy traffic. I can't control it so I have to make sure there is not a car within a mile behind me when I change lanes because the car frequently almost stalls. This also happens sometimes when I make a turn. It generally happens when I decelerate and then accelerate and the transmission is in Drive...The problem still occurs on an almost daily basis. The dealership told me to let them know if I still have the problem when I come back for the 10,000-mile service. I understand that this problem has been reported in GTIs with DSG transmissions since 2009, but VW still has not corrected it.

. . .

My 2012 6-speed has had two incidents – first, the car wouldn't engage into Reverse from a stop until the vehicle's ignition was turned off and on several times. Car operated normally for about 2 weeks. Second incident, car wouldn't engage into any gear while moving 10–15 mph [16–24 km/h] uphill while in First gear. During loss of powertrain, the engine revved in the 4000–5000 rpm range, smoke was visibly coming out of the engine bay and there was complete loss of brakes, including the emergency brake. The vehicle started to roll backward downhill and was stopped by turning the vehicle into the sidewalk. After 2 days of diagnostics, the technicians were not able to replicate the issue and concluded that the vehicle was operating within manufacturer specifications.

. . .

I was driving down the road and was coming to a stop sign. I had the clutch all of the way in and shifted into Neutral while slowing down, I put it into 1st gear with the clutch all the way in and the clutch engaged, causing the car to jerk violently. It went from 2200 rpm to over 6000 immediately. After getting stopped and in Neutral I released the clutch pedal for it to stay slammed to the floor. It would not go into First easily with the clutch all the way in.

Jetta: Starter/electrical fires due to starter overheating during attempts to start locked engine; chronic shudder and stalling upon acceleration or deceleration, often with no brakes:

After less than 3 minutes of operation, my 2012 Jetta will stall under a specific set of circumstances. The incidences (13 and counting in 2 months) always occur when in Second or Third gear at ~30–35 [mph]. The driver is slowing down (as to stop at a red light) and then accelerates (light changes to green). About 2–3 seconds after acceleration begins the engine stalls and must be restarted. The engine just cuts out during acceleration.

. . .

Purchased a VW Jetta SE on 7/20/12 and almost 1 month after the purchase I was driving on a local highway at apx. 50 mph [80 km/h] around 5:30 pm when car headlights blinked and car died (stalled). Attempted to re-start the car without any success. Since VW dealer was closed already—called a local auto shop and they towed [the] car to a shop to find [the] issue. Mechanic could not see anything obvious so he re-set a computer in my car and he was able to start it. Drove home. Later in the evening—drove to pick up some food and on the way home (inside a development)—while making a left turn at apx. 15–18 mph [24–29 km/h]—pressed brakes and realized I had none and at the same time car stalled and since it was raining and I was already slightly turning left—car slid in the direction on my turn and right rear tire hit the curb, tire fall off, car hit a street sign and an electric pole (both fell to the ground) and brought me to a complete stop on the grass.

Other things for Jetta owners to worry about: Sudden, unintended acceleration; complete loss of braking capability; Reverse lights don't work; fuel filler leaks because some gas pump handles don't fit into the fuel nozzle; left outside mirror blind spot cannot be adjusted; cracked fuel lines from the common rail on diesels; and chronic stalling:

Without warning, the engine shut down while driving down a busy road. Check Engine and Glow Plug warning light came on. Was just able to coast to the shoulder of the road. Car would turn over, but engine would not start. Car towed to dealer. Was told there was a catastrophic failure of the high pressure fuel pump, and metal shards were found throughout the fuel system. VW replaced the entire fuel supply system (including fuel tank) and fuel injection system.

Vehicle was idling on an incline with the brakes depressed, and it started rolling backwards, even though brakes were continuously applied; when stopped on an incline, the automatic transmission holds the car for only a few seconds before the vehicle starts rolling backwards; while attempting to start the vehicle, the steering wheel locked; premature replacement of the rear brakes; windshield distortion; roof design sends excess rainwater to the front windshield, and the wipers push large amounts of water into the driver's viewing range; wipers slow down as engine speed decreases; inoperative wiper motor; delayed horn response; premature original-

Prices and Specs

Prices (Negotiable): *Golf 3d:* $19,975, *5d:* $21,475, *Sportline:* $23,300, *Highline:* $23,980, *2.0 TDI:* $25,275, *2.5 Sportline Tiptronic:* $25,300, *2.5 Highline:* $26,475, *DSG:* $26,675, *2.5 Highline Tiptronic:* $27,875, *2.0 TDI Highline:* $28,775, *2.0 TDI Highline DSG:* $30,175, *GTI:* $29,375, *R:* $39,675, *Jetta:* $15,875, *2.5 Trendline:* $22,175, *Jetta TDI Trendline:* $24,475, *Jetta 2.5 Comfortline:* $24,875, *Jetta TDI Comfortline:* $27,175, *Jetta 2.0 Highline:* $29,075, *Jetta TDI Highline:* $30,875, *Jetta Wolfsburg:* $27,275, *GLI:* $27,475, *CC:* $35,125 **Freight:** $1,395 **Powertrain (Front-drive/AWD):** Engines: 2.0L 4-cyl. (115 hp, 2.0L TDI 4-cyl. (140 hp), 2.0L Turbo 4-cyl. (200 hp), 2.0L Turbo 4-cyl. (256 hp), 2.5L 5-cyl. (170 hp), 3.6L V6 (280 hp); Transmissions: 5-speed man., 6-speed man., 6-speed auto., 7-speed auto., 4 Motion all-wheel drive **Dimensions/capacity:** *Jetta:* Passengers: 2/3; Wheelbase: 104.4 in.; H: 57.2/L: 182.2/W: 70 in.; Headroom F/R: 4.5/2.5 in.; Legroom F/R: 43/30 in.; Cargo volume: 15 cu. ft.; Fuel tank: 55L/regular; Tow limit: 1,500 lb.; Load capacity: 1,070 lb.; Turning circle: 35.7 ft.; Ground clearance: 5.5 in.; Weight: 3,090 lb.

equipment tire failures; bubbling in the side wall of Continental original equipment tires; the muffler extends too far out from the underbody – one woman was burned on the leg while unloading groceries; and heated seats can catch on fire and give occupants much more than a "hot foot," as one owner so succinctly wrote to government investigators:

> My heated seats caught fire and burnt my ass!

ALERT! Before opting for the cheapest Jetta with its glacial 115 hp 4-cylinder engine, take it for a test drive and see if the reduced power is acceptable; guard againt tire over-inflation by garages; and don't pay last-minute $375 dealer "administration" or "processing" fees; they're scams.

Golf/Jetta Profile

	2004	2005	2006	2007	2008	2009	2010	2011	2012
Used Values ($)									
Golf CL/City	3,500	—	5,000	5,500	6,000	6,500	8,000	—	—
GL/GLI 4,000	5,000	5,500	—	10,500	12,500	—	—	—	
H/B Trendline	—	—	—	—	—	—	10,500	12,500	15,000
Highline	—	—	—	—	—	—	13,000	15,500	18,500
GL/Highline TDI	5,000	6,000	7,500	—	—	—	15,500	17,500	20,500
Wagon Trendline	—	—	—	—	—	—	11,000	13,500	15,500
Wagon Highline TDI	—	—	—	—	—	—	14,500	18,000	21,000
1.8T/GTI	5,000	6,000	7,000	8,000	10,500	12,500	15,500	19,000	22,000
Jetta GLI	—	6,500	—	9,000	—	—	—	—	19,500
City	—	—	—	6,000	7,000	7,500	—	—	—
GLS TDI/Wagon/Trendline	6,000	7,000	—	—	—	9,500	—	—	—
Sedan Trendline	—	—	—	—	14,500	9,000	11,500	9,500	10,500
2.5/Comfortline	—	—	6,500	8,000	9,000	10,000	12,500	12,500	14,000
1.8T/2.0T	4,500	5,500	7,500	8,500	10,500	—	—	—	—
TDI Comfortline	—	—	10,500	—	—	10,500	13,000	15,500	17,500
New Jetta	—	5,500	—	—	—	—	—	—	—
TDI	—	7,500	—	—	—	—	—	—	—
Recommended	★	★	★	★	★	★	★	★	★
Reliability	★	★	★	★	★	★	★	★	★

SECRET WARRANTIES, INTERNAL BULLETINS: 1995-2013—Squeak and rattle kit available. 1999-2013—(except Routan) Abnormal vibration when braking caused by excess corrosion or an out-of-round rotor; tackling unpleasant odours coming from the AC vents; reducing exterior light moisture accumulation, removing headlight lens blemishes; and servicing the cooling fan if it runs with the ignition turned off. **2003-10**—Headlights dim when vehicle is put into Idle. **2004-11**—DSG transmission lag and lurch troubleshooting (see *ALERT!* above). **2005-07**—Engine knocking noise. Rattle from front passenger-side floor area. **2005-08**—Trouble-shooting sound system malfunctions. Fix for an inoperative seat heater. Seized AC compressor. **2005-10**—Cooling fan runs on after ignition shut off. Poor heater output. **2006-08**—Ice deforms leading edge of doors. **2007-10**—AC blower motor operates on high speed only. **2008**—Loose door mirrors; incorrect fold functions. Engine cooling fan stays on. **2008-12**— Engine rattling noise correction. **2009-11**—No start, runs rough. *Jettas:* **2009-11** and *Golfs:* **2010-11**—(all with the 2.0L TDI engine) *VW* says it may have a remedy for diesels that won't start in cold weather. In TSB #2111-06 Volkswagen confirms that some vehicles might not start if left in temperatures below freezing. Moisture from the air intake may condense in the intercooler. VW suggests adding a cold weather intercooler kit, that will be provided free of charge on a case-by-case basis. **2013**—Engine intermittently shuts off immediately after starting. When restarted, the engine may exhibit rough idle for a few seconds. However, the engine does not shut off again on a restart. UV radiation can cause fading of the burred walnut veneer wood finish trim parts. Various door function control failures. Steering honking/squeaking noises. *Rabbit, GTI, R32:* **2010**—Noise from the B-pillar area. Front door gap causes some wind noise. Can't open liftgate after locking. **2010-11**—Poor front seat heater performance. **2011-12**—How to prevent electrical harness damage caused by animal snacking. If the heater doesn't blow hot enough, reboot the system with upgraded software. *Golf* – Tips on preventing windshield wipers from smearing the windshield. *Turbo diesels* – What to do about engine hesitation; harsh shifting in low gear and cold weather no-starts.

PASSAT ★★

RATING: Below Average. The Passat is an attractive mid-sized car that rides on the same platform as the Audi A4. It has a more stylish design than the Golf or Jetta, but it still provides a comfortable, roomy interior and gives good all-around performance for highway and city driving. The car's large wheelbase and squat appearance give it a massive, solid feeling, while its aerodynamic styling makes it look sleek and clean. Not recommend for driving or parking over hilly terrain (see the ALERT! section) or for drivers or passengers who are tortured by the poorly-designed head restraints:

> Recently I drove several new cars (the latest being the 2012 Passat) and found one common complaint: The headrests on these cars are tilted forward way too much with no adjustments available. My understanding is that NHTSA requires vehicles' headrests to be higher and close to the head to reduce whiplash injuries. How do you improve safety if it's impossible to find a comfortable driving position? The new headrest regulation forces the driver to slouch forward (and looking down) while driving, causing fatigue to set quickly. For me, the only way to find a comfortable position while driving these new Passats are by reclining the seat back excessively (so my head won't tilt forward). This, in my opinion, isn't safe since this position reduces the driver's alertness. With the active headrest technology, in my opinion the new headrest regulation is an easy and lazy way to reduce whiplash injury without proper research (i.e. only based on measurements with no regards to driver's comfort).

The fault isn't with government regulation, however, it's with VW's design engineers who picked the cheapest, most uncomfortable restraints possible – ones that would make the Marquis de Sade scream with joy (and pain). Ford had a similar inhumane design with its 2011 models until buyer protests forced the company to phase in versatile and comfortable head restraints later that year. **Road performance:** Impressive acceleration with the turbocharged engine hooked to the smooth-performing manual gearbox. The sophisticated, user-friendly 4Motion full-time all-wheel drive shifts effortlessly into gear; refined road manners; no turbo lag; better-than-average emergency handling; quick and predictable steering; handling outclasses most of the competition's; and the suspension is both firm and comfortable. Some negatives: Engine/automatic transmission hesitates when accelerating; excessive brake fade after successive stops; and you can't trust the speedometer reading:

> Vehicle does not show the true speed of the car. Speedometer is off by 7–8 kmh. @ 100 kms. VW does not accept that there is any problem.

Strong points: Well-appointed and holds its value fairly well. Quiet-running; plenty of passenger and cargo room; impressive interior fit and finish; and exceptional driving comfort. **Weak points:** In the 2011 J.D. Power Initial Quality Survey, VW scored 29th among 32 brands. Two years later, the same survey still put VW's models near the bottom third of the rankings at 23 out of 33 carmakers. Traditional deficiencies dating back to the 2006 model year include failure of the powertrain, fuel, and electrical systems, and various fit and finish flaws. Power windows freeze shut in cold weather. **Major redesign:** 1998, 2006, and 2012. **Highway/city fuel economy:** *2.5L:* 6.5/10.1 L/100 km. *Auto.:* 6.7/9.6 L/100 km. *3.6L:* 7.4/10.9 L/100 km. *TDI diesel:* 4.4/6.8 L/100 km. *Auto:* 4.9/6.9 L/100 km. **Best alternatives:** If you must have a Passat, get it used, without the DSG transmission, and with some warranty left. Other choices, the BMW 3 Series, Ford Fusion, Honda Accord, Hyundai Genesis, and Toyota Camry.

SAFETY: Good crashworthiness scores from both NHTSA and IIHS. NHTSA gave the 1995-14 Passats four and five stars for different crash scenarious and two to four stars for 1990-93 models. IIHS frontal moderate overlap tests of 1999-2013 Passats produced a "Good" rating; 1994-98s were rated "Marginal." Frontal small overlap tests qualified the 2013 performance as "Marginal." Side and roof strength were given a "Good" rating for the 2005-13 models, while the head restraints on the 2009-13s were rated "Good," "Marginal" (2007-08s), and "Acceptable" (2005-06 versions). Function is sacrificed to style with rear corner blind spots and head restraints that impede rear visibility. Owner safety-related complaints are down significantly; however, the failures reported relative to the powertrain are just as hair-raising as ever. In your test drive, check out the car's ability to parallel park on a hill, after first making sure there are no cars parked nearby that you might hit:

> Our new Passat has problem controlling the car while using Reverse on a hill. It appears that VW has tied the accelerator and braking function together in a way that the driver may lose control of the vehicle while in Reverse. If the brake is pressed, the accelerator is disengaged thus allowing the engine [to] fall to an idle and not develop any thrust. If the driver is using both feet to control the vehicle, left foot on the brake, right foot on the accelerator while depressing the brake, the engine develops no power even if the accelerator is depressed fully. By releasing the brake while the accelerator is depressed fully, the vehicle will lurch at full throttle in Reverse in an out of control condition until the driver realizes what is happening and removes their foot from the accelerator.

Some of the transmission failures are eerily similar to complaints heard from owners seven years ago. For example, delayed shifts and transmission fluid leaks that require a transmission transplant:

> The vehicle has a significant delay/hesitation upon initial acceleration (2.5L). This is dangerous when pulling into or across traffic. This issue is known to others and is reported elsewhere on the Web.

> ...

> As I was driving my new 2012 Volkswagen Passat from my house to my destination, my transmission fluid began to leak out onto the street. I had purchased the car eight days earlier which was a new car from the dealership which only had 2 miles on the car. The amount of miles I had put on the car was 500 miles [800 km] and the transmission fluid

leaked because of a malfunction inside of it. The car was under warranty and the dealership had to put a new transmission into my car because the old one had defective parts inside.

Fuel leaks within the first few months of ownership are also common:

I unlocked my 2012 Passat and opened the door to get some items from the car. Again, the sound of draining fluid could be heard and a strong odor of gasoline emitted from the vehicle. I checked underneath the car again, and a fresh pool of gasoline has formed. The gas is dripping from the passenger side, near the rear wheel. Needless to say, this is very disappointing, as the vehicle has only been driven for a little more than 1,000 miles [1,600 km].

ALERT! How'd you like to lose over half your Passat's value after barely three years? That's what would happen if you had bought a new 2010 Passat Comfortline sedan for $31,075. These cars are a favourite among thieves – whether for stealing radios, wheels, VW badges, or entire cars. (No, the delayed tranny shifts and fire-prone fuel system are *not* anti-theft measures.)

Passat Profile

	2004	2005	2006	2007	2008	2009	2010	2011	2012
Used Values ($)									
Base GLS	4,000	5,000	6,000	—	—	—	—	—	—
Base GLS TDI	6,000	8,000	—	—	—	—	—	—	—
Base/Sedan Trendline	—	—	7,500	—	9,500	10,500	14,000	—	16,500
Comfortline	—	—	—	—	10,000	11,500	15,000	—	20,000
TDI Trendline+	—	—	—	—	—	—	—	—	19,500
CC Spolrtline	—	—	—	—	—	12,500	16,500	21,000	25,000
CC Highline V6 AWD	—	—	—	—	—	14,500	22,500	29,000	34,500
Highline V6 AWD	—	—	—	—	—	15,000	—	—	—
Wagon Trendline	—	—	—	—	10,000	11,000	15,000	—	—
Comfortline V6 AWD	—	—	—	—	11,500	15,000	—	—	—
City	—	—	—	—	—	—	—	—	—
Comfortline/V6 AWD	—	—	—	—	12,000	15,500	—	—	—
2.5 Base	—	—	—	—	—	—	—	—	—
2.0T	—	—	8,000	9,000	—	—	—	—	—
Recommended	★	★	★	★	★	★	★	★	★
Reliability	★	★	★	★	★	★	★	★	★

Prices and Specs

Prices (Negotiable): *Trendline 2.5L:* $23,975, *Plus 2.5L:* $24,875, *Comfortline 2.5L:* $27,975, *Highline 2.5L:* $31,475; *Comfortline 3.6L:* $33,575, *Highline 3.6L:* $37,475, *CC:* $33,375, *VR 6:* $46,375, *Trendline diesel:* $27,475, *Comfortline diesel:* $30,575, *Highline diesel:* $33,775 **Freight:** $1,395 **Powertrain (Front-drive/AWD):** Engines: 2.0L 4-cyl. diesel (140 hp), 2.5L 5-cyl. (170 hp), 3.6L V6 (280 hp); Transmissions: 5-speed man., 6-speed man., 6-speed auto., 6-speed manumatic. **Dimensions/capacity:** Passengers: 2/3; CC: 2/2; Wheelbase: 106.6 in.; H: 55.9/L: 188.8/W: 73 in.; Headroom F/R: 4/3 in.; Legroom F/R: 43/29 in.; Cargo volume: 14.2 cu. ft.; Fuel tank: 70L/premium; Tow limit: 2,000 lb.; Turning circle: 38 ft.; Ground clearance: 4.5 in.; Weight: 3,853 lb.

SECRET WARRANTIES, INTERNAL BULLETINS: 1997-2009—Class action settlement results in Service Actions implemented 2007-08 to pay for and mitigate water damage to components and interiors of numerous models, and reimburse expenses. Service Action for owners and lessees of certain vehicles to modify leaking sunroofs, provide refunds, and update maintenance recommendations for drainage systems. Lawyers are litigating the inclusion in the settlement of all 1997-2009 models. (See *www.WaterIngressSettlement.com* or *www.volkswagen-classaction.com*.) **1999-2006**—Condensation inside exterior lights. **1999-2008**—Correcting excessive brake pulsation, vibration. **1999-008**—Inoperative heated rear glass lines. **2000-11**—Removing smelly odours from vents. **2003-10**—Excessive vibration when braking. **2004-11**—DSG delay on acceleration. **2005-10**—Cooling fan continues to run after ignition has been turned off. Poor heater output. **2006-07**—Airbag light constantly lit. Front suspension creak. **2006-08**—Front-seat creaking, cracking. Inoperative AC and seat heater. Seatback creaking; inoperative lumbar support. Front suspension knocking. Rear cupholder hard to remove. Back glass sunshade damaged or fails to work properly. **2006-09**—Wind noise from the top of the doors. **2006-10**—Inoperative front-seat back recliner. **2008**—Door mirrors loose or won't fold properly. Inoperative keyless remote. **2008-10**—AC blower motor only operates on high speed. **2008-11**—Silencing a front suspension knocking. **2008-12**—Rattling noise from engine, exhaust. **2011-12**—A transmission whistle or whine at highway speeds requires the installation of an updated shifter cable bracket. A harsh engagement from Park to Drive or Reverse may signal the need for a software update. **2011-13**—Possible oil leak from the oil filter housing. Troubleshooting tips to correct brake vibration/pulsation when brakes are applied. **2013-14**—Sunroof/sun shade won't open. Noise from the right-side door panel when driving.

Appendix 1
1990-2015 REVIEWS AND PREVIEWS

The discontinued 2012 Fisker Karma First Responder:
a $102,000 (U.S.) electric car that sells for $50,000 used.

In this Appendix we include thumbnail sketches of some of the vehicles that were passed over in Part Four, including models that have been axed, are relatively new to the market, or are scheduled to be introduced next year as 2015 models. We conclude with cheap older cars and trucks that are commonly called "beaters" or "minounes" in Quebec.

MOTOWN GETS ITS MOJO

2014-15 will be a milestone period as auto sales return almost to their pre-recession levels due to pent up buyer demand and a slew of new fuel-efficient, redesigned products. Compact cars are getting larger, while Cadillacs are downsized and go electric. Financing has been boosted to 96 months, GM and Chrysler pickups have rocketed to the top of *Consumer Reports'* best buy list and Chevrolet's Impala is hailed by *CR* as "the best sedan tested" by the consumer publication.

But the news isn't all positive. Thrice-divorced Chrysler has soured on Fiat's low estimate of Chrysler's value in a buy-out of UAW's interest and wants to initiate an initial public offering (IPO) where investors will bid up the price. Fiat CEO Marchionne is miffed at Chrysler's independence and has threatened to scuttle Fiat's relationship with the company. Strong words coming from the Italian automaker whose "rescue" of Chrysler in 2009 has morphed into the rescue of Fiat, after the company posted its lowest sales in over three decades.

And, then there's Ford, enjoying good sales, but bedeviled by several years of failure-prone infotainment systems that give wrong info, or simply ignore owner commands. Ford says it now has a fix for its high-tech electronic woes – buttons and knobs. *Lemon-Aid* always knew Ford would come up with a Better Idea.

New 2014 Models

MANUFACTURER	MODEL	MANUFACTURER	MODEL
BMW	3-Series GT, i3	Kia	Cadenza, Quoris
Cadillac	ELR	Mercedes-Benz	CLA
Chevrolet	SS	Mitsubishi	Mirage
Fiat	500L	Porsche	Macan

Redesigned 2014 Models

MANUFACTURER	MODEL	MANUFACTURER	MODEL
Acura	MDX, RLX	Land Rover	Range Rover Sport
Audi	A3	Lexus	IS
BMW	X5	Mazda	3
Cadillac	CTS	Mercedes-Benz	S-Class
Chevrolet	Impala, Corvette, Silverado	Mitsubishi	Outlander
Ford	Transit Connect	Nissan	Rogue, Versa Note
GMC	Sierra	Subaru	Forester, WRX
Infiniti	Q50 (G37)	Toyota	Corolla, Highlander
Jeep	Cherokee	Volkswagen	Golf, Gti
Kia	Forte, Soul		

Discontinued 2013 Models

MANUFACTURER	MODEL	MANUFACTURER	MODEL
Acura	ZDX	Ford	Mustang Boss 302
Aston	Martin Virage	Nissan	Altima Coupe
Audi	TT RS	Suzuki	Kizashi, SX4, Grand Vitara, Equator
Cadillac	Escalade EXT		
Chevrolet	Avalanche	Toyota	Matrix
Chevrolet	Corvette Z06, ZR1	Volvo	C30, C70

REDESIGNED AND NEW 2014-15 MODELS

The 2014-15 models listed below are either new to the market or scheduled to be redesigned. Several trends are easy to spot: More diesels, hybrids, and electric cars; downsized versions of popular compact cars; a return to turbocharged engines; and the gentrification of pickups.

It is also apparent that GM and Chrysler are the leaders in pickup performance and quality, having redesigned their base models this year. While GM extends it re-engineering to larger pickups next year, Ford won't have their improved F-Series on the market before 2015 (Ford's last redesign was in 2009).

American Automakers

CHRYSLER/DODGE/FIAT/JEEP—200, Cherokee, Durango, ProMaster City, and a subcompact Jeep

FORD/LINCOLN—Mustang, Transit Connect Van and Wagon, Edge, Expedition, F-150, and New Transit, MKC and Navigator

GENERAL MOTORS—Acadia, Colorado/Canyon, Cadillac ATS Coupe, Cadillac ATS V-Series, Cadillac ELR, Cadillac LTS, Cadillac SRX, Camaro Z/28, Enclave, Escalade, Cruze, Malibu, SS Sedan, Suburban, Silverado, Sierra 2500 and 3500, Tahoe, Terrain, Traverse, Verano, Volt, Yukon, and Yukon XL

Japanese Automakers

ACURA—MDX and TLX

HONDA—Fit, Fit Crossover, Odyssey, and Pilot

INFINITI—Q50, Q60 Coupe, QX60 Hybrid, and Q70 Hybrid

LEXUS—IS, NX 200t, and RC 350

MAZDA—Mazda6 diesel, CX-5, and Mazda2

MITSUBISHI—Mirage, Outlander hybrid, and Outlander Sport

NISSAN—GT-R Nismo, Juke Nismo, Maxima, Murano, Pathfinder hybrid, Versa Note, and Rogue

SUBARU—XV Crosstrek, Hybrid, WRK/STI, Outback, and Legacy

TESLA—Model X

Best Vehicles for Students, Families, and Seniors

Young drivers feel they are invulnerable to accidents and would never admit that they are poor drivers, or that they are more responsive to peer pressure than parental admonition. That's why you want to buy a car that gets top marks in crashworthiness and reliability, sips gas, and doesn't look like a Flintstone retread. Advanced safety features such as electronic stability control and full-torso side-curtain airbags are a plus. Large pickups or SUVs can be rollover-prone, hard to control on the highway, and carry too many distracting passengers. Sports cars beg to be driven too fast and inspire a false sense of confidence.

Check out these models for students:

Acura TSX	Honda Fit	Hyundai Tucson	Nissan Rogue
Chevrolet Camaro	Honda Civic	Kia Soul	Subaru Impreza/Outback
Ford Focus	Hyundai Accent	Mazda3	Toyota Matrix
Ford Mustang (auto.)	Hyundai Elantra	Mazda Miata	

Vehicles that are recommended for families and seniors have much in common: A reasonable price, good crashworthiness ratings, and dependable reliability are paramount. Your days of looking for a "chick magnet" are gone; appearance is not as important as access. Electronic stability control, full-torso side-curtain airbags, and no-hassle child safety seat installation are also a plus. Good visibility, maximum seat and head restraint comfort, a comfortable driving position, a spacious interior, and intuitive, easily-operated controls are key factors worth consideration. For more details as to what makes the ideal car for seniors, see page 33.

For the best models for families and seniors, check out these vehicles:

Acura RDX	Honda Accord	Honda Ridgeline	Mazda5
Chevrolet Silverado 1500	Honda CR-V	Hyundai Azera	Nissan Altima
Chrysler 1500 Ram	Honda Element	Hyundai Elantra	Subaru Forester
Ford Fusion	Honda Odyssey	Hyundai Genesis	Toyota Camry
GMC Sierra 1500	Honda Pilot	Hyundai Santa Fe	

Choosing the Right Car or Truck

The price of fuel is a wild card that affects new vehicle prices, depending upon how much fuel each model burns. As gasoline becomes more expensive, large trucks and SUVs become cheaper to buy as compacts and mini-compacts sell at a premium. However, once a barrel of oil goes below $100 (U.S.), small car sales wane and large cars, trucks, and SUV sales surge. This means you have to "time" the market.

Yes, these *are* volatile times; car and truck prices fluctuate dramatically and fuel costs change every day. Still, the longer you wait, the less you will pay, either through depreciation with both new and used cars, or through increased sales incentives (rebates, low-cost financing, and free maintenance) with new vehicles. You don't want the economic burden of buying a car that's on the market for the first time or one that has been radically changed this model year – the value of these vehicles is yet unproven. Nor should you invest in a vehicle that merely looks nice or is cheap if it doesn't have a positive reliability history. And you certainly don't want to overpay for a car or truck simply to be the first in your town with something "different" (remember the Chrysler PT Cruiser, Pontiac Aztek, and Smart car?). The uniqueness will pass; the repairs will remain constant.

Here are some choices worth considering.

Audi

A4 ALLROAD: Below Average. This is a comfortable and versatile $45,100 wagon that offers mediocre highway performance with its turbocharged four-banger and extra height. It also has a seemingly small interior, and an unjustifiably high retail price. Since this is an all-new model, wait for the improved 2014 version that will offer today's options as standard features. No crash data. The Acura TSX Sports Wagon and BMW 3-Series Sports Wagon are worthy alternatives.

Acura

ILX: Not Recommended. Acura's smallest sedan ($27,790), competitors have better performance, gas mileage, and cargo space. The sluggish base engine perks up only through the addition of the manual transmission. If you want more fuel economy, you'll

Acura ILX

have even less power to work with. Not a people-hauler. No changes expected for the 2014 model. The Buick Verano is a good alternative. **Crashworthiness:** Crashworthiness not tested yet.

RL: Above Average. The $69,690 flagship of the Acura fleet, the RL is loaded with intuitive (Hello, Ford?) high-tech gadgetry and premium luxury features that don't confound or distract the average driver. Except for some minor sound system glitches, the RL is flawless. **Crashworthiness:** NHTSA crash tested the 2012 RL for rollover protection and gave it a five-star rating.

RLX: Not Recommended during its first year on the market. Nevertheless, the advance showing of this impressive hybrid confirms the matchup of a solid V6 engine with electric motors and AWD. The untested powertrain hookup means prudent buyers should wait well into 2014 for early production problems to be corrected.

NSX: Not Recommended on the market. Predicted to arrive in mid-2014 as a 2015 model, the resurrected NSX (it was dropped in 2005) is estimated to cost $150,000 and be offered as a hybrid. It will employ a mid-mounted 3.7L V6 hooked to a twin-clutch 7-speed transmission, and an electric motor driving the rear wheels. Two more electric motors will spin the front wheels independently, delivering exceptional torque-vectoring to help pull the car around corners as well as the original NSX. The Sports Hybrid AWD system claims to deliver V8 performance with "better-than-four-cylinder" fuel economy (don't believe it).

Q5: Below Average. Audi's history of factory-related glitches and its "lag and lurch" powertrain are immediate turn-offs. **Price:** *2.0 TFSI Premium:* $41,200 (firm); *2.0 TFSI Premium Plus:* $45,300 (firm); *3.2 FSI Standard:* $45,500 (firm); *3.2 FSI Premium:* $49,900 (soft). The Q7's smaller brother debuted five years ago as a stylish five-passenger luxury crossover compact full of high-tech gadgetry, including an adaptive suspension that allows for firm, sporty handling, if so desired. The Q5 power comes by way of a 270 hp 3.2L V6 and the latest rear-biased version of AWD. **Crashworthiness:** NHTSA awarded five stars for front and side crashworthiness and four stars for rollover protection. IIHS gave its top, "Good," rating for frontal offset and side protection. Head restraint effectiveness is also rated "Good."

Q7: Average. These complicated five- or seven-passenger machines are made from bits and pieces of VW's other models. The Q7 offers both gasoline and diesel powertrains hooked to an 8-speed automatic transmission. **Price:** *3.0 TFSI:* $53,900 (firm); *3.0 TFSI Premium:* $59,000 (soft); *3.0 TFSI Sport:* $69,200 (soft); *3.0 TDI:* $58,900 (soft); *3.0 TDI Premium:* $64,000 (soft). **Crashworthiness:** NHTSA gives the Q7 five stars for front and side crash protection and four stars for rollover resistance. IIHS gives its top, "Good," score for frontal offset, side, and head-restraint protection.

BMW

1 SERIES: Below Average. Returning with minor trim changes, this little Bimmer is a joy to drive – when the powertrain, fuel, and electrical systems aren't acting up. Fit and finish isn't first-class, either, and servicing requires sustained dealer support. BMW's entry-level 128i and 135i include either a two-door coupe or convertible with a power-folding soft top. **Price:** *128i Coupe:* $35,800; *128i Convertible:*

$41,200; *135i Coupe:* $43,000; *135i Convertible:* $48,500. **Crashworthiness:** No crashworthiness data available. Owners report chronic fuel pump failures covered by a ten-year secret warranty:

> As I pulled out into the road, the Engine light came on and the car had reduced power. The car (with only 5500 miles [8,850 km] or so) was shaking violently when going under 10 miles [16 km] an hour. The RPMs fluctuated at idle to where the car almost stalled several times. I drove the 15 or so miles [24 km] home with my flashers on as the car was having trouble. The above is a description of a HPFP failure on the N54 engine. I would say many, many people get a bad fuel pump. BMW has covered the part for 10 years/120K miles [193,100 km], but it will fail again. There is no fix at this point. Just a new pump that eventually gives way. I know people who are on their 4th pump. Just do a Google search on "BMW HPFP" and see what comes up. The 1351, 3351, 5351 [and] Z4 351 all have the N54 engine, and they all suffer from this defect.

i3: Not Recommended. The BMW i3 is an urban electric plug-in car backed up by a scooter engine that will be launched as a 2014 model by the end of 2013. The car seats four, has the limited range of a Chevy Volt, and is as ugly as the Pontiac Aztek. There's also an optional 34-horsepower motorcycle engine that is mounted next to the electric motor. Its 2.4-gallon tank doubles the car's range, which is expected to attenuate driver "range anxiety" Really? **Price:** It sells for $42,275 (U.S.).

X1: Average. This is a rear-drive, small, luxury SUV, powered by a base 240 hp 2.0L turbocharged 4-cylinder or an optional 3.0L 300 hp V6, coupled to either a 6- or 8-speed automatic transmission. Test drivers recommend the 4-cylinder model for sportier performance. X1 has limited cargo space, tight rear seating, and costly, bundled options. The fuel-saving start-stop system is abrupt at times. **Price:** $36,900 ($30,650 U.S.) that drops to only $27,000 used (2013). It's priced lower than some competitors, but has fewer standard features. Buick's Encore is an alternative worth considering.

X4: Not Recommended. This is its first year on the market. The X4 is essentially to the X3 what the X6 is to the X5 – the same vehicle with a different roofline. It shares powertrains and almost everything else with the X3, including 4- and 6-cylinder gasoline and diesel engines. Six-and 7-speed dual-clutch transmissions will be standard; an 8-speed Steptronic transmission will be optional. **Price:** TBA. Smart shoppers will head straight for the practically identical X3 and save thousands. **Crashworthiness:** Unrated.

5 SERIES: Average (2011-14); **Below Average** (all earlier years). *5 Series GT:* Launched just a few years ago, this BMW has misjudged its market that wants conservatively styled sedans that don't have an ungainly liftback or a high load floor. Mercedes laughs all the way to the bank. The other models are beautifully-styled, roomy, problematic vehicles. Owners report frequent engine, transmission, and fuel system failures in addition to fit and finish glitches through the 2010 model year. For 2014, Canada gets a diesel-powered 535d xDrive version, equipped with a turbocharged 255 hp 3.0L inline-six that's paired with an 8-speed automatic transmission. While BMW claims the 535d can achieve fuel economy ratings as low as 4.5 L/100km – expect less. In what is mostly a carryover year, the rest of the 2014 BMW 5 Series lineup offers last year's range of engines that includes a 241 hp turbo four, a 300 hp turbo six, a 335-hp hybrid six as well as a twin-turbo, 445 hp 4.4L V8. **Price:** The 2014 price range is $55,000 to $77,000 for the sedan; $72,000 to $82,000 for the GT; and $68,150 for the new 535d xDrive. **Crashworthiness:** 2012-14 models have an overall five-star rating from NHTSA; 2008-10 versions have similar scores, except for passenger protection in a frontal collision that was given only three stars.

MINI COOPER: Average. Pain-in-the-butt kind of cute. This eye-catching classic British-cum-German car is a good highway performer, but high maintenance bills makes "cute" costly. Although the base Mini has an average reliability rating, the Cooper S has been much less reliable. **Price:** Clubman: $24,950; Convertible: $29,500; Coupe: $25,950; Hatchback: $23,600; and Roadster: $28,900. **Crashworthiness:** IIHS rates the Mini as "Good" for offset crash protection and head-restraint effectiveness; side crashworthiness was given an "Average" score. NHTSA says this little tyke merits a four-star rating for its frontal collision crashworthiness and five stars for side occupant protection and resistance to rollovers.

BMW's Mini: A "cute" low-quality performer that can burn you in a number of ways.

Buick

ENCORE: Above Average. The 2013 Encore is a small luxury SUV that is only slightly larger than the Chevrolet Sonic with which it shares its platform. Touted as a five-passenger SUV, the Encore can only sit four comfortably. Powered by the Sonic's optional 1.6L 140 hp turbocharged four, the Encore stresses fuel economy over speed. Nevertheless, Encores are flying off dealers' lots at the full MSRP price. **Price:** $26,895 for the base model. Forget haggling. **Crashworthiness:** Unrated.

VERANO: Average. The Verano doesn't have the luxury look or feel of some of its rivals. The $23,000 entry-level returns with no important changes, following its adoption of a new turbocharged 250 hp powerplant. Buick has outfitted the Verano with many of the suspension and body components used by the Chevrolet Cruze, but the Verano is much more than a warmed-over Cruze. It has its own style (please, get rid of the portholes on the hood), engine, and luxury features that sets it apart. However, this is not a quick car: the base 180-horsepower, 2.4L 4-cylinder engine will do 0-60 mph in about 9 seconds, but the responsive 6-speed automatic tranny makes those extra seconds uneventful. The suspension is softly sprung, without degrading handling. You also are treated to a quiet and luxurious cabin and generous standard features. **Price:** $22,595 for the base model. Only eight owner complaints have been posted by NHTSA for the 2012 Verano, when 50 would be the average: Rear window exploded as the door was shut; ineffective windshield wipers; all gauges suddenly went dark and engine lost speed; a rattling suspension noise when passing over uneven terrain and chronic stalling. **Crashworthiness:** Unrated.

Cadillac

ATS: Average. Essentially a compact Caddy. The ATS is a four-door, five-passenger compact luxury sedan that is Cadillac's smallest vehicle, slotted just below the CTS. Available in either rear- or all-wheel drive, the car comes with a 202 hp 2.5L 4-cylinder engine, but also offers a 272 hp 2.0L turbocharged Four, and a 321 hp 3.6L V6 – all paired to a 6-speed automatic transmission. A 6-speed manual transmission can be ordered with the 2.0L powerplant. **Price:** $35,000, which jumps to $40,000 for the AWD model. A used 2013 ATS shaves almost $10,000 off the base price. **Crashworthiness:** NHTSA gives the ATS five stars for overall crash protection. Owners report serious transmission shifting delay, steering malfunctions, and excessive shaking at idle or when passing over small bumps in the road:

> 2.5 litre engine at stop: Engine shakes for no reason. As usual take to dealer and can't find issue without a code. Now at 2572 miles still shakes and dealer says that all ATS do this so live with it. … Many other ATS customers have same issues. I see on Cadillac forum there seems to be a lot of frustration about lack of a fix.

ELR: Not Recommended during its first year on the market. A Volt in wolf's clothing, the ELR is an upmarket, plug-in hybrid that targets aging baby-boomers who want a sexy, luxury car that projects lots of cachet for lots of cash. The car will arrive in the spring and sell as a 2015 model. **Price:** Estimated to be between $65,000 and $75,000. Get this: Unlike Tesla's pure-electric Model S sedan, the ELR's gasoline engine that backs up its battery kicks in after 35 miles using electrical power. I repeat, you get to go 35 miles before your big Cadillac coupe switches over to its 1.4L 4-cylinder engine to keep the car moving. GEESH! The Chevy Volt (you can buy two for the price of one ELR), by contrast, can travel 64 km (40 miles) on electric power before it must use gas. **Crashworthiness:** Unrated.

SRX: Below Average. Base models are front-drive, while luxury versions include all-wheel drive; both are powered by a 308 hp 3.6L V6 hooked to a 6-speed automatic transmission, with a maximum towing capacity of 3,500 pounds. The 2014 version returns without any significant changes. Alternative vehicles are the Lexus RX or Acura RDX. **Price:** *FWD:* $41,780; and the *AWD (entry-level):* $48,000. Prices are very negotiable. Depreciation is unbelievable: A $50,000 2007 SRX is now worth barely $8,500. Other observations: The car is overpriced; the AWD model is slower to accelerate than the rear-drive, and the transmission often hesitates before downshifting; there's insufficient rear passenger room; poor fit and finish; costly, dealer-dependent servicing; and suspension may be too firm for some. Owners report the following safety related glitches, no doubt related to the SRX's redesign: Chronic stalling (the vehicle then proceeds to roll downhill); electrical malfunctions that knock out instruments and gauges as the car automatically switches to Neutral; automatic transmission sticks in low gear (vehicle has to be brought to a stop and restarted); hood release is located too close to driver's left foot; brakes grind as pressure is slowly lifted off the brake pedal; hard to get a spare tire. **Crashworthiness:** NHTSA has given its five-star crash-protection rating to the 2004-14 models.

Chevrolet

COLORADO/CANYON: Not Recommended. Performance and reliability aren't competitive with other vehicles in its class. **Price:** The 2012 Colorado/Canyon pickups are worth about $16,000; 2007s $10,000 less. Even for $6,000 these cars are no bargains. Main drawbacks are wimpy engines, poor handling, so-so reliability, and sloppy fit and finish. Pick up a 2010 Honda Ridgeline or Pilot for about $16,000. **Crashworthiness:** Surprisingly, these pickups garnered four- and five-star crash ratings from 2004-10, when tests were stopped.

EXPRESS/SAVANA: Recommended. These full-sized, rear-drive vans have been around forever. **Price:** *The Express sells for* $31,046 and the Savana costs only a few hundred dollars more. A 2010 is worth $12,000. These are easily accessed, capacious vans. And the good news doesn't stop there. With fuel prices going higher and the economy softening, these vehicles are turning into "blue-light specials" and are discounted by up to 25 percent at different times during the year, like in the dead of winter and just prior to the arrival of new models. Both vans are perfect recession buys because any independent garage can repair them, and most of their reliability issues aren't expensive to correct. Some weak areas: They are fuel-thirsty, are ponderous performers, and frequently are prey to water leaks. **Crashworthiness:** NHTSA gives the Express 1500 cargo van five stars for frontal protection; the 1500 passenger van also gets five stars for frontal protection and three stars for rollover resistance. The 2500 and 3500 12-passenger van and the 3500 15-passenger van earned three stars each for rollover resistance. But, as *Lemon-Aid* has reported before, 15-passenger vans can be killers due to their high propensity to roll over.

ORLANDO: Average. This Opel-inspired seven-seater combines reasonable fuel economy with a minivan passenger load in much the same way as the Mazda5, Kia Rondo, and my old favourite, the long-gone, greatly lamented Nissan Axxess. Thanks to its European DNA, the $20,000 Orlando rides and handles well and is reasonably fuel-efficient. Merging and hill-climbing with a full load are patience-building exercises due to the Orlando's sluggish 6-speed automatic transmission. Also, the third-row seats are suitable only for children. Reliability has been average. **Crashworthiness:** Unrated.

SPARK: Below Average. The Spark only has a puny 85 hp engine, yet doesn't get any better gas mileage than the 150 hp Honda Civic or 140 hp Chevy Cruze. This front-drive four-door hatchback is smaller than Chevy's Aveo subcompact. Since it's built by GM Daewoo, think of it as the Aveo's smaller brother. Light, direct steering is useful in the city and the car's $13,495 base price is quite reasonable. Accept the fact that this is a slow four-passenger urban econocar and you won't be disappointed. Five TV's *Fifth Gear* in Britain clocked the acceleration time for 0-100 km/h (0-62 mph) with the 1.0L and 1.2L engines. The results? 15.5 and 12.1 seconds, respectively, so bring along a good book and an hourglass. Some other faults: The steering is a bit light for highway driving; gear shifts are a bit clunky; steering column doesn't telescope; a harsh ride when going over uneven terrain; and refinement isn't what the Spark is best known for. Chevrolet plans to launch a Spark electric vehicle next year as a 2014 model. Smart shoppers will stay away during the car's first year on the market. **Crashworthiness:** Unrated.

VOLT: Not Recommended. Not an Electric Edsel, but close. Volt is GM's three-year-old electric compact four-seater. **Price:** Launched in Canada a year late, the 2012 model carried an astoundingly high starting price of $41,545. Disappointing sales forced GM to discount the car by $10,000 last August in addition to giving a provincial tax credit of up to $7,500. Still, the car is way overpriced if you consider a 2014 can be bought in the States for $28,000 once federal incentives are included. By the way a $42,000 2013 Volt is now worth $24,000. Ouch! **Crashworthiness:** NHTSA gave a five-star overall crashworthiness rating to the 2011-14s, while IIHS rated all Volts "Good."

So why isn't the car Recommended?

Here are some reasons: The car costs more than the Leaf, and $15,000 above a well-equipped compact with a gas engine. Canadian shoppers also say they are not seeing the promised discounts. Furthermore, owners of the 2012 are angry that they paid the full $41,000 price and they get practically apoplectic over their car's $20,000 current value (October 2013). Wait until they have to replace the battery.

GM's Volt has been a resounding flop: less than half of the number of cars projected have been sold. GM says the average Volt owner makes $170,000 per year.

Buying a Volt means you become the "captive customer" of a limited number of Chevrolet dealers; God help you if the car has an electrical short away from a large urban area. Also, owners report (*safercar.org*) that the Volt has these safety flaws: Front suspension may collapse; rear Reverse lights are too dim; rear windshield distorts the view; rear end "slips" when accelerating; and the charging system may overheat and short out. Also, if one leaves the car without powering down, it may keep running silently.

Chrysler/Dodge

100: Not Recommended. Expected to go on sale in late-2014 as a 2015 model, the 100 will be a spin-off of the Dodge Dart platform and built in Illinois. The hatchback version takes the place of the PT Cruiser and will be smaller and lighter than the Dart. **Price:** $16,000 to $18,000. **Crashworthiness:** Unrated.

DART: Above Average. The Dodge Dart is a much better performer than the Caliber it replaces. Buyers have the choice of one of three 4-cylinder engines: a 160 hp turbo 1.4L; a 160 hp 2.0L; or an 184 hp 2.4L. There are three choices of 6-speed gearboxes: one manual, one automatic, and one dual-clutch variant. The interior has some nice features like a central seat cushion that flips up to open a huge storage area for handbags, etc., and the user-friendly Uconnect media screen. **Price:** SE: $15,995; SXT: $18,595; Rallaye: $19,495; and the Limited: $23,245. A used 2013 Dart is worth about $11,000. Driving the Dart is a breeze, although the base 1.4L engine's turbo takes a bit of time to get the car up to speed. Going head to head with the Chevy Cruze, Ford Focus, Honda Civic, and Toyota Corolla, the Dart leads the pack for highway performance, especially with a manual transmission. Building on this advantage, 2014 Darts may offer a high-performance 300 hp SRT package complete with a 9-speed gearbox (OK, you can get up off the floor, now). **Crashworthiness:** NHTSA says the Dart's overall crash protection merits five stars; IIHS agrees that the car gives "good" crash protection, except for an "Average" score for small overlap front protection.

DURANGO: Below Average (2012-14); **Not Recommended** (1998-2011). The Dodge Durango is an SUV nightmare on wheels that has always been afflicted by serious powertrain, steering, electrical, brake, and climate system failures. A 1998 spin-off of the failure-prone Dakota pickup, the Durango has provided over the years three-row seating and several gas-guzzling V8s, that are underwhelming performers. Despite a 2004 and 2011 redesign, overall performance has improved only slightly and poor reliability continues to be troublesome. The ride continues to be truck-stiff, handling is ponderous, engines are noisy, and braking is far from a sure thing. The 2014 Durango features more aggressive styling, a new 8-speed automatic transmission, and an updated interior. **Price:** SXT: $38,5445 and Crew Plus V6: $46,845. A 2011 base Durango sells for $19,500. **Crashworthiness:** NHTSA says the 2012-13 Durango's overall crash protection merits four stars; rollover resistance scored only three stars. Surprisingly, 2001-09 models got higher safety ratings, except for a two-star rating for frontal crash protection (driver) given to the 2000 model year Durango.

Fiat

500: Average. After walking out on its U.S. and Canadian owners in 1984 and leaving them high and dry with worthless warranties and rust-cankered vehicles, Fiat announced a triumphant return to North America as Chrysler's saviour. When Fiat pulled out of North America, I was in the trenches as president of the Automobile Protection Association and remember only too well the many Fiat owners who were stunned that their rusty, unreliable, and unwanted pieces of crap would never be fixed. The CAW, UAW, Ontario provincial government, and Canadian federal government never lifted a finger to help owners of these rust heaps get their money back. Now Mexican workers are getting their salaries underwritten by our unions and governments. **Price:** $17,500-$19,000 for the base model and depreciation will shave over one-third of that value after two years (a 2012 base Fiat is worth about $11,000). **Crashworthiness:** NHTSA gave four- and five-star ratings to the 2013-14 Fiats, however, the 2012 earned an overall score of three stars and only two stars for side crash protection.

Ford

C-MAX HYBRID ENERGI: Not Recommended. Buy a Mazda5, instead. Part hatchback, wagon, and micro-van, the C-Max Hybrid is a tall five-seater powered by an electric motor and a 2.0L 4-cylinder gas engine. It is barely larger than a Ford Focus, but boasts more passenger volume than the Prius. **Price:** SE: $28,849; SEL: $31,849; and SEL Energi: $38,649. C-Max will operate electrically up to 100 kph, allowing the electric traction motor to power the vehicle, providing maximum fuel-efficiency. The car comes with two electronic features that may not yet be ready for prime time: the Microsoft-conceived Ford Sync voice command suite and the MyFord Touch infotainment system with touch-screen controls for audio, climate, and navigation. Some performance glitches: Poor gas mileage (Ford is refunding owners $500 for the extra fuel cost); no-starts; dead battery; fuel pump and radio turn themselves on overnite, while car is parked; navigation feature malfunctions; no spare tire; and the backup camera won't shut off. **Crashworthiness:** NHTSA four- and five-star ratings on 2013-14 models. Owners report sudden unintended acceleration; failure to go into Reverse:

> I put the car in Reverse to back out of the driveway and when I stopped, I couldn't go backwards. I pulled forward and parked. Pulled back again and the car didn't do it again. The engine light did come on and I took the car to the dealership. They had it for two weeks. Ford said it is a "Reverse Delay Problem" and they know about it. Ford is working on a fix. Ford is knowingly selling the C-Max with a drivetrain problem and does not consider the "Reverse Delay" a safety problem.

And stalling on the highway:

Driving in normal freeway traffic: Vehicle suddenly lost power and went into "Stop Safely Now" mode with wrench icon and red warning triangle. Vehicle retained minimal power availability and was eventually able to limp vehicle out of traffic and onto side road. Called two different dealers and was told to wait a few minutes and restart. After 10 to 12 minutes and three restart attempts, finally restarted with full functionality restored. Error again appeared just as I reached home.

ECONOLINE, E-SERIES: Average. These gas-guzzling, full-sized vans haven't changed much over the years and quickly lose their value, making them a better deal used. **Price:** *Commercial van:* $31,299; *Passenger van:* $36,399 (very soft). **Crashworthiness:** NHTSA gives the van three stars for rollover protection.

EDGE, MKX: Above Average. A five-passenger wagon/SUV crossover based on the same platform as the Fusion sedan, the Edge comes in either all-wheel drive (without low-range gearing) or front-drive. **Price:** $28,000-$46,500 (soft). **Crashworthiness:** NHTSA gives the Edge and MKX five stars for front and side protection and four stars for rollover protection. IIHS rated the Edge "Good" in front offset, side, and rear crashworthiness.

EXPEDITION: Below Average. This gas-guzzling, over-priced, full-sized SUV quickly loses its value and, like Ford vans, is a better deal bought used. **Price:** *XLT:* $47,000 (soft); *Limited:* $58,500 (soft); *4x4 Max Limited:* $61,000 (laughable). **Crashworthiness:** NHTSA gives the Expedition five stars for frontal and side crash protection. Three stars were awarded for AWD rollover resistance, but only two stars were given for front-drive rollover resistance. IIHS hasn't crash tested the Expedition.

FLEX: Above Average. This boxy front-drive, or AWD four-door wagon seats either six or seven passengers in three rows of seats. Power comes from a 262 hp 3.5L V6 mated to a 6-speed automatic transmission and an optional turbocharged 3.5L that unleashes 355 horses while mated to the same gearbox. **Price:** $29,999-$46,599 (soft). **Crashworthiness:** NHTSA gave the Flex five stars for front and side protection and four stars for rollover resistance.

Ford's $29,999 ($29,355 in the States) Flex is somewhat pricey, but it does offer car-like performance, SUV versatility, and excellent crashworthiness. A perusal of Ford service bulletins shows long-term reliability is still a question mark.

TAURUS: *2013 models:* **Average.** *2012 models:* **Below Average.** **Price:** $28,000-$48,200 (firm). A 2012 sells for $16,000. **Crashworthiness:** NHTSA gives the

Taurus four stars for overall crash protection. IIHS has awarded the car its top, "Good," rating for front offset, side, and rear collision occupant protection.

TRANSIT CONNECT: Below Average. Price: $27,000-$29,000 (soft). **Crashworthiness:** Good; NHTSA gives it five stars for protection from frontal- or side-impact injury, while IIHS has yet to test the van.

General Motors

DTS: Average. Essentially your father's comfortable, roomy, bouncy, and ponderous Oldsmobile with a Cadillac badge. **Price:** Dropped in 2011, that model year sold for $56,540 and is now worth $27,000. The $75,680 Platinum model sells for $38,000. There have been reports of airbags failing to deploy, loss of braking, and head restraints literally being a pain in the neck (try before you buy):

> Head rest is too far forward for his wife to drive the vehicle. … The consumer stated when his wife adjusted the seat for driving, the head rest forced her head down. The consumer stated all that needed to be done was to have the two head rest supports bent down backwards a little to solve the problem.

Crashworthiness: Good; four- and five-star protection ratings across the board.

STS: Below Average; dropped in 2011. **Price:** A 2011 that sold for $56,540 is now worth $27,000. **Crashworthiness:** NHTSA gave the STS four stars for frontal and side protection and five stars for rollover resistance.

SRX: Below Average. Base models are front-drive, while Luxury versions include all-wheel drive; both are powered by a 308 hp 3.6L V6 hooked to a 6-speed automatic transmission, with a maximum towing capacity of 3,500 pounds. **Price:** *Base FWD:* $40,495; *AWD (entry-level):* $45,300. **Crashworthiness:** NHTSA has given its five-star rating for front and side crash protection; rollover resistance received four stars.

HHR: Not Recommended. This five-passenger crossover compact wagon uses GM's Cobalt/Pursuit platform and a 4-cylinder engine. Dropped in 2011. **Price:** A $20,395 2011 model is now worth $11,500. **Crashworthiness:** NHTSA gives the HHR five stars for frontal- and side-impact occupant protection; rollover protection scored four stars.

Honda

CR-Z HYBRID: Below Average. Choose a cheaper second-series Hyundai Veloster instead. CR-Z is a sporty ("sporty" by hybrid standards, I suppose), two-passenger hybrid coupe equipped with a manual shifter; however, it doesn't come with the rev-happy performance we enjoyed with earlier sporty, fuel-frugal Honda runabouts, like the little CRX. A spin-off from Honda's "born again" Insight, the CR-Z has a shorter wheelbase, shorter length, and wider front and rear tracks than its cousin. Nevertheless, the Insight DNA is found everywhere in this little coupe. **Price:** $23,490; $19,200 in the States. *Strong points:* Fuel-efficient: EPA mileage figures will be 36 mpg in the city and 38 mpg on the highway. With the manual gearbox, predicted mileage falls to 31 mpg in the city and – thanks to the CVT – 37 mpg on the highway. *Weak points:* The CR-Z fuel economy numbers aren't all that impressive. Stylistically, this is not a pretty car. Its extremely short rear end and long front overhang are somewhat jarring, and the rear tail lights and liftgate window are Insight derivatives. The wheels need to be upsized to fill in the wheel-wells. **Crashworthiness:** NHTSA gives the car three stars for overall crash protection and five stars for rollover resistance.

INSIGHT: Average. One of the least expensive hybrids available in North America, the Insight was taken off the market in 2010. **Price:** A 2010 Insight is worth about $11,000, or less than half its original $24,000 MSRP. The first Insight hybrid had such a checkered reliability and performance history that Honda took it off the market for a few years. Its return was short-lived after Honda marketing gurus learned to their dismay that car buyers have long memories. **Crashworthiness:** NHTSA four- and five-star crash protection rating (2000-10 models).

Hyundai

EQUUS: Above Average (2011-14). The Hyundai Equus, the Latin word for "horse," is an upscale full-size luxury sedan that is Hyundai's largest and most expensive model. In 2009, the company released a new version on a rear-wheel drive platform aimed to compete with the BMW 7 Series, Mercedes S-Class, Audi A8, and Lexus LS. **Price:** $64,499. The car has been on the Canadian market since 2011 and that first-year model which retailed for $62,999, now sells for $38,000. **Crashworthiness:** Unrated by NHTSA, but the IIHS gives the car its top "Good" ranking in all of its crash-test scenarios. Owner safety complaints are sparse, with only six for the 2011 model. Still, the complaints are serious, like the following NHTSA-logged incident where the car's suspension suddenly collapsed:

Hyundai's Equus has been a slow seller; prices are soft.

While we were driving the car, the car's front suspension suddenly failed, the front collapsed and the body of the car nearly touched the ground on flat ground and dragged against the ground on inclines and declines. The wheels rubbed against the body of the car on turns and the car became very unstable and started to shake. This episode has occurred thrice despite manufacturer's repairs. This second episode resulted in mild whiplash.

. . .

The air suspension system failed and the whole car, mostly the front, dropped a number of inches. We could barely drive home and had to have the vehicle towed. Seems to be a very unsafe item. The first time it was the passenger side; second time it was the driver side.

Other failures include a fire that ignited from the interior wiring and the sudden shutting down of the instrument panel associated electrical components.

VELOSTER: Above Average. Surprisingly fuel-efficient; fuel economy rivals the Honda CR-Z Hybrid. A four-seater hatchback, this two-door sports coupe actually has a hidden rear passenger-side third door that gives access to the two rear seats. Parts and servicing aren't a problem since the Veloster shares most of the Accent's hardware and electronics, notably the 138 hp 1.6L 4-cylinder engine coupled to a 6-speed manual or automatic transmission. If its reliability matches the Accent, this small hatchback has lots of potential. **Price:** $22,000 for the base vehicle. Wait until the spring of 2014 for Veloster prices to settle lower (by about $1,500) and for the initial first-year production snafus to be corrected. A $19,000 2012 Veloster is now worth $12,000. **Crashworthiness:** NHTSA gives the car three stars for overall crash protection and five stars for rollover resistance.

Jaguar

F-TYPE ROADSTER: Jaguar makes a play to save its own soul with the introduction of the all-new 2014 F-Type roadster. It's a pure two-seater, powered by a new supercharged V6 that should make around 380 hp. With its small size, 8-speed ZF transmission and open cockpit, it's more Porsche 911 steak and potatoes than a high-end exotic. So expect it to be priced in the $80,000 range.

Jeep

JOURNEY: Not Recommended due to the Journey's poor reliability, wimpy engine, mediocre handling, and confusing base infotainment system. The 2013 model ranked 15 out of 21 in U.S. News and World Report ratings based on its analysis of 21 published reviews and test drives, and an analysis of reliability and safety data. Although the optional third row seating makes the Journey unique among compact SUVs, the base model can't match the performance or fuel economy of top-ranked rivals. **Price:** Base: $19,495; Crew: $25,545. **Crashworthiness:** 2004-10 models were five-star performers, except for a three-star score for the 2002-03 Liberty.

LIBERTY: Not Recommended. Introduced in 2002, the Liberty came on the scene equipped with several worthwhile features like an independent front suspension and rack-and-pinion steering. However, its interior is hard to access and relatively small and narrow, plus the ride is unsettled when passing over uneven terrain. As with most Jeeps, poor reliability is the Liberty's most serious problem. Owners complain about costly engine, transmission, electrical system, and AC failures. Premature brake disc and rotor replacements also figure prominently among owner gripes. **Price:** 2012 Sport: $19,500; Limited: $22,500. **Crashworthiness:** The 2012 Liberty's crash safety scores (mostly two- and three-stars) were worse than what earlier models had earned. 2004-10 models got mostly four- and five-star crash protection scores from NHTSA, with the exception of rollover protection which scored two stars (2002-03) and three stars (2004-10).

PATRIOT: Not Recommended. A spin-off of the Dodge Caliber and Jeep Compass, the Patriot arrived in 2007 and quickly sank out of sight. It's a small, upright SUV that comes equipped with the same anemic 2.0L and 2.4L engines that once powered the late, unlamented Caliber. Other shortcomings? A mediocre ride and so-so handling, fit and finish that's early Lada, and frequent brake, electrical, and powertrain failures. **Price:** Sport: $17,995; 4x4: $20,49; Limited 4x4: $26,695. A 2010 Patriot Limited 4x4 sells for $9,500. **Crashworthiness:** NHTSA awarded an overall score of four stars for crashworthiness to the 2007-14 models.

Kia

BORREGO: Below Average. Sold in Canada for only three model years (2009-11), the Borrego lacks the refined ride comfort and easy handling found in other luxury three-row SUVs, due to its truck-like body-on-frame construction. Cheap? No doubt about it: Prices range from $10,000 to $20,000 (2011). But, parts, repair agencies, and future buyers will be rare. Look to the 2011 Hyundai Santa Fe or Tucson and save $3,000 to $5,000. Vehicles with more car-like qualities are the Chevy Traverse, Honda Pilot, and Mazda CX-9. **Price:** A 2011 $39,000 Borrego now sells for $20,000. **Crashworthiness:** NHTSA gives the Borrego five stars for frontal and side occupant crash protection. Rollover protection was given four stars.

K900: Not Recommended. This isn't a remake of Disney's "101 Dalmatians" and, hopefully, this 2015 luxury car won't be a dog. Nevertheless, Kia is barking up a tall tree with a $50,000-$70,000 car that targets the Chinese Audi/BMW market. Why not Europe and North America? Because European automakers have a lock on those countries and China doesn't know much about Kia's poor-quality sordid past. The K900, sold as the K9 and Quoris in other markets, will carry the latest safety and luxury features and offer high performance with a 420 hp powerplant. It's similar in size to the BMW 7 series and targets both BMW and Audi's high-end sedans.

Land Rover

Not Recommended (all models). Both Rover and Jaguar are owned and built by India's Tata Motors, who purchased the companies in March of 2008. The $2.3 billion (CDN) purchase price is about a third of what Ford originally paid for the luxury nameplates. Nevertheless, Tata's "bargain" contributed to the company's first loss in eight years of $520 million (up to March 2009). Since then, Land Rover has had respectable sales, while being dragged through a sea of red ink due to Jaguar losses. Although the company is investing millions into Rover and Jaguar research, rumour has it that recession-pummeled Tata is looking for a white knight to take one or both companies off its hands.

Lexus

CT 200H: Above Average. A luxury sporty car, the CT 200h returns this year with an upgraded lateral performance damper system to minimize body vibration and increase overall ride comfort; an updated version of Lexus' Enform infotainment system meant to enhance the navigation system; and assorted interior improvements. Powered by advanced Lexus Hybrid Drive, to give better fuel efficiency in four option packages, including the F Sport package. **Price:** $31,450. **Crashworthiness:** No crash data, yet; no safety-related incidences logged by NHTSA.

Mazda

MAZDA2: Average. This subcompact five-seater (really, it's a four-seater) comes only as a four-door hatchback equipped with a 100 hp 1.5L 4-cylinder engine. The engine can be paired to either a 4-speed automatic transmission or a 5-speed manual gearbox. A success in Europe where it was known as the Demio, the Mazda2 – like the Honda Fit (Jazz) – has proven itself in other countries. **Price:** *GX:* $13,995; *GS:* $18,195. *Strong points:* Roomier in the rear than the Ford Fiesta and costs less. Highway/city fuel economy is quite good: *Man.:* 5.6/7.2 L/100 km, 50/39 mpg; *Auto.:* 5.8/7.3 L/100 km, 49/39 mpg. Highway and city driving is a breeze due to the car's superb handling and comfortable ride. Mazda's new vehicle launches have produced fewer first-year factory defects than Detroit-based and some Japanese and South Korean automakers like Daewoo/GM, Kia, Nissan, and Toyota. The 2008 Mazda2 garnered the highest rating of five stars for adult protection, a class-leading four stars for child protection, and a respectable two stars for pedestrian protection from the EuroNCAP ADAC-administered crash testing. Standard safety features include electronic stability control and curtain airbags. **Weak points:** Slow when carrying a full load; transmission needs more gears; and the interior is rather Spartan when compared with the competition. **Crashworthiness:** IIHS frontal offset and roof crash protection is rated "Good," while side and rear crashworthiness is judged "Acceptable." NHTSA gave the car a combined crashworthiness score of four stars.

Mercedes-Benz

ML 350: Not Recommended. In the past, these luxury SUVs weren't recommended due to their low quality and high cost. This year, 2012s aren't recommended for a different reason: They have been totally redesigned, and past experience tells us that M-B redesigns are usually accompanied by serious engineering faults and poor quality control. Plus, the ML Series is still way overpriced and loses its value quickly. In 2010 the Mercedes-Benz M-Class ranked 8th out of 15 luxury midsize SUVs in the *U.S. News and World Report*'s analysis of 64 published reviews and test drives, which included checks on reliability and safety data. This year's ML adopts the Grand Cherokee/Dodge Durango platform, which has been problem-prone on past Jeeps and Dodges. It will be powered by a new 302 hp 3.5L V6 or a 240 hp 3.0L V6 diesel. **Price:** $58,900 (ML350 BlueTEC) to $97,500 (ML63). Imagine spending that amount of money for an SUV that places in only the middle of the pack. By the way, these same two models can be found in the States for $50,490 and $92,590, respectively. **Strong points:** A luxurious interior; the ride is comfortable and quiet; handling is responsive and fairly predictable. Good off-road performance. **Weak points:** Not worth the asking price; quality will likely worsen with this year's redesign, and powertrain parts will be harder to find. The V6 is a competent but fuel-thirsty powerplant and the 7-speed gearbox may be rough-shifting. **Crashworthiness:** NHTSA gives the M-Class five stars for front and side crash protection and four stars for rollover resistance, while the IIHS ranked the 2010 and 2011 M-Class "Good" for frontal offset, side, and head restraint protection.

R-CLASS: Average. Mercedes first called this low-riding minivan a "sports cruiser" and when that was met with underwhelming enthusiasm, changed the name to "family cruiser" (anything to avoid the dreaded "minivan" moniker). Somber styling, awkward long rear doors, poor reliability, and a 7-speed transmission that "hunts" for the right gear. **Price:** R350: $57,800; Blue TEC: $58,900. How's this for rapid depreciation: A 2010 R350 that sold for $54,700 is now worth $26,000. The diesel version: $27,500. **Crashworthiness:** Unrated.

Smart Car (2004–13)

SMART: Below Average. This subcompact is highly dealer-dependent and seriously outclassed by the Honda Fit, Hyundai Accent, Mazda2, and Nissan Versa. **Price:** *Fortwo Coupe:* $13,990; *Passion:* $17,500; *BRABUS:* $20,900; *Passion Cabriolet:* $20,500; *BRABUS Cabriolet:* $23,900. **Strong points:** Once the car gets up to highway speeds (which may seem like it takes forever), it manages to keep up with traffic; fuel-frugal; highly practical for city driving and parking; good reliability reports; distinctive styling; its engine bay isn't as crammed as small cars' often are; responsive steering and transmission performance; and the ride is almost comfortable. Standard stability control, side airbags, and ABS. **Weak points:** You pay a maxi price for a mini vehicle that's less refined than cheaper Honda, Hyundai, Kia, Mazda, Nissan, Suzuki, or Toyota minicars; dealer-dependent servicing (trips must be planned carefully for servicing accessibility); slow acceleration from a stop; the automated manual shifter is annoyingly slow and rough; and you must use premium fuel. **Crashworthiness:** NHTSA gives the 2010 Smart four stars for frontal collision occupant protection, five stars for side protection, and three stars for rollover resistance. It also received "Good" ratings for front offset, side, and rear crash protection in IIHS tests.

Mitsubishi

MIRAGE: Below Average. Mitsubishi says its new Mirage econobox will fill a niche in the U.S. auto market for consumers looking for basic, efficient transportation at an affordable price. How's that for enthusiasm? Actually, Mitsubishi officials know the car is disappointing. Especially, when you consider there are many other models in its niche that are more refined and have a proven track record.

Why Mitsubishi's Mirage Is Doomed

	2014 Mitsubishi Mirage	2014 Chevrolet Spark	2014 Nissan Versa
Wheelbase	96.5 in.	93.5 in.	102.4 in.
Length	148.8 in.	144.7 in.	175.4 in.
Width	65.6 in.	62.9 in.	66.7 in.
Height	59.1 in.	61 in.	59.6 in.
Curb weight	1,973 lbs.	2,269 lbs.	2,363 lbs.
Base engine	1.2-liter 3-cyl.	1.2-litre 4-cyl.	1.6-liter 4-cyl.
Horsepower	74 hp @ 6,000 rpm	83 hp @ 6,400 rpm	109 hp @ 6,000 rpm
Torque, lbs.-ft.	74 @ 4,000 rpm	83 @ 4,200 rpm	107 @ 4,400 rpm
EPA mpg	34 city/42 hwy.	31 city/39 hwy.	27 city/36 hwy.
Base price	$13,790	$12,995	$12,800

Note: These are U.S. figures.

Mirage is an import from Thailand that was slightly re-engineered ("something old, something new") to suit North American market. To that end, Mitsubishi added extra materials to the instrument panel and the floor panels to reduce noise, vibration, and harshness. Bigger bumpers were also added. The car is small and light, seats four, measures more than a foot shorter than a Ford Fiesta, and comes with a 1.2L 3-cylinder engine that delivers 74 hp to the front wheels through a standard 5-speed manual or optional CVT transmission. Mitsubishi promises a highway/city fuel econmy rating of 40 mpg. **Price:** $14,000. **Crashworthiness:** Unrated.

Nissan

CUBE: Above Average. This is the five-passenger front-drive's sixth year on the Canadian market, and so far it has proven to be a reliable, though odd-looking, small car. The Cube is essentially a box on wheels that has plenty of room, but no personality. It is ugly stylistically and induces a feeling of instant claustrophobia. No 2012 changes are expected for this 122 hp 1.8L 4-cylinder-powered people-mover. **Price:** *Cube S:* $17,398; *Auto.:* $18,698; *SL:* $20,898; *Krom Edition:* $23,098. **Strong points:** The small number of complaints posted by NHTSA is surprising considering Nissan's history of churning out new and redesigned models before they have been "debugged." In comparison with the Kia Soul, the Cube is a better buy. Although the Kia is cheaper, neither the ride nor the handling can touch the Nissan. Then add the fact that the Cube has been proven in other countries (it's in its third generation), is highly reliable, and offers a high level of quality. As for the initial cash savings with the Soul, they will be wiped out by the Kia's higher rate of depreciation. **Weak points:** A wimpy engine and subpar fuel economy complement what Motor Trend calls "awkward proportions and asymmetric styling." **Crashworthiness:** Ratings have been quite positive. NHTSA gave the Cube five stars for side crash protection and four stars for frontal crashworthiness and rollover resistance. IIHS awarded the Cube "Good" marks in frontal offset, side, and rear occupant protection.

JUKE: Average. This funky-looking small wagon crossover makes no attempt to blend into the crowd; it also makes no attempt to provide an outstanding driving experience or offer good fuel economy, unlike the Mini Cooper. No, the Juke takes a cheap shot and targets young consumers who want a well-performing car with a unique look that will be a conversation starter and an attention-getter. *Car and Driver* believes the car's unique styling resembles a frog. Others say it looks like a crocodile. Esthetics aside, this front-drive, five-door compact crossover uses a direct-injection, turbocharged 188 hp 1.6L 4-cylinder engine coupled to a 6-speed manual or hooked to an optional CVT automatic transmission. All-wheel-drives use only an automatic shifter that splits engine power 50/50 between the front and rear wheels or the left and right sides. **Price:** *SV FWD:* $19,998; *Auto.:* $21,298; *SV AWD auto.:* $23,098; *SL FWD:* $23,548; *SL FWD auto.:* $24,848; *SL AWD auto.:* $26,648. **Strong points:** A reasonable front-drive price, without much difference in pricing between Canada and the States; excellent acceleration (hitting 62 km/h in 7.5 seconds – over a second quicker than the Honda CR-V); agile, with steering that is quick and sensitive; a comfortable ride; decent seating in front and back, complemented by reasonable storage space; a well-appointed interior; and Reliability hasn't been a problem during the Juke's first year. **Weak points:** Styling is weird (*autoblog.com* says it has a "Baby Predator" front end), and traction is quickly lost in fast starts or on wet highways. A recommended optional "integrated control" system can render the car more stable by uniformly setting the throttle, transmission, and steering response settings to Normal, Sport, or Eco modes. Rear seatroom is decidedly on the skimpy side, meaning anyone over six feet will feel cramped. **Crashworthiness:** Rated four stars for overall crash protection by NHTSA.

LEAF: Average. Nissan's first all-electric car. **Price:** $31,698. Interestingly, a 2012 Leaf that originally sold for $38,395, is now worth $16,500. **Strong points:** Good acceleration in city traffic; comfortable seats, with an interior about the size of a Toyota Prius; quiet running; great navigation feature that computes how far you can travel on a map of your current location. **Weak points:** Lethargic steering, excessive leaning when cornering, and a few, ahem, electrical problems. **Crashworthiness:** NHTSA says the Leaf gets a four-star rating for overall crash safety.

The Leaf is advertised as being able to travel up to 160 kilometres without stopping to recharge – a process the automaker tells us would normally take "only" eight hours on a 220-volt circuit (wink, wink; nudge, nudge). But, just after reassuring us with the above claims, Nissan then adds this caveat (i.e., don't believe what we just said): "Battery capacity decreases with time and use. Actual range will vary depending upon driving/charging habits, speed, conditions, weather, temperature, and battery age." Age, weather, temperature, speed? Yikes!

Consumer Reports (CR) comparison of the Leaf and Volt versus the most fuel efficient gasoline-powered automobiles available in the U.S. market in 2011 that CR tested. All prices are in US$.									
						Cost for trip miles			
Vehicle	Model year	Operating mode (powertrain)	Price as tested	CR overall fuel economy	Cost per mile	30 mi (48 km)	50 mi (80 km)	70 mi (110 km)	150 mi (240 km)
Nissan Leaf	2011	All-electric	$35,430	106 MPG-e (3.16 mi/kWh)	$0.035	$1.04	$1.74	$2.44	—
Chevrolet Volt	2011	EV mode (35 mi range)	$43,700	99 MPG-e (2.93 mi/kWh)	$0.038	$1.13	—	—	—
		Gasoline only (>35 mi)		32 mpg	$0.125	—	$3.19	$5.69	$15.69
Toyota Prius	2011	Gasoline-electric hybrid	$26,750	44 mpg	$0.086	$2.59	$4.32	$6.05	$12.95
Toyota Corolla	2011	Gasoline only	$18,404	32 mpg	$0.119	$3.56	$5.94	$8.31	$17.81

Notes: Graph supplied by Wikipedia. Costs for plug-in electric vehicles are based on the U.S. national average electricity rate of 11 cents per kWh and regular gasoline price of $3.80 per gallon.

Fortunately, *Consumer Reports* tested the Leaf's fuel economy in comparison with other similar cars and concluded that Nissan's figures were accurate. According to *Consumer Reports* as of December 2011:

> The Leaf has an out-of-pocket operating cost of 3.5 cents per mile (2.19¢ per km) while the heavier Chevrolet Volt has a cost in electric mode of 3.8 cents per mile (2.38¢ per km). These costs are based on the U.S. national average electricity rate of 11 cents per kWh and energy consumption was estimated from their own tests. The consumer magazine also compared the Leaf with the most fuel-efficient hybrid and gasoline-powered cars as tested by Consumer Reports. The results are summarized in the following table, and the analysis found that the Leaf's operating cost is much less than half of the gasoline-powered cars for trips up to 70 mi (110 km), which is close to the Leaf's maximum range. The Volt, while on EV mode, has a close cost per mile but as the distance is larger than its electric range of 35 mi (56 km), the Leaf advantage is similar to the other cars. Consumer Reports also noted that even with a much higher electric rate of 19 cents per kWh, such as rural Connecticut, the Leaf still cost about 20% less to operate than the Prius and around 50% less than the Corolla.

NV: Above Average. The NV (Nissan Van) represents Nissan's first attempt at breaking into the lucrative full-sized commercial van market monopolized by Ford and General Motors. There are two engines available: a 4.0L V6 and a 5.6L V8, both coupled to a 5-speed automatic transmission. Standard features include 17-inch steel wheels, fold-down passenger seatback, flat cargo floor, wide-coverage cargo area lighting system, water-repellent fabric on main seating surfaces, multifunction front layout and storage, multiple power outlets, cargo area side metal inner panels, multiple weld-nut attachment points for shelving and rack systems, recessed tie-down rings, a sliding passenger-side door, and wide-opening front and rear doors. **Price:** NV 1500: $30,998; NV 2500: $32,298; NV 3500: $34,448; NVP 3500: $37,898. **Strong points:** These vans combine convenience and utility, as well as roominess and comfort. There's a full-length cargo area inner panel to protect the outer walls from dents and dings from the inside, and there are multiple weld-nut attachment points for shelving and racks – again, requiring no sheet metal drilling. In addition, the NV's nearly vertical sidewalls maximize the usable cargo space. From the seats forward, the NV looks, acts, and feels like a pickup. You don't have to take apart the interior to access the engine and you don't have to worry about tucking your work boots into a cramped footwell. The U.S. EPA says gas consumption figures should average 21 mpg on a good day. **Weak points:** Since it is so new to the market, factory-related defects will likely be a problem and servicing will be slow due to back-ordered parts and mechanics' lack of familiarity with this new model. **Crashworthiness:** No crashworthiness data yet.

370Z, GT-R: Recommended. Nissan does have a couple of sports cars that are worth considering, although they have yet to be crash-tested. The 350hp V6-equipped 370Z is available as a $40,898 coupe or a $47,400 roadster. Is either model worth the price? Yes. Both are speedy and attractive alternatives to the Chevrolet Corvette, which costs much more. The Nissan GT-R ($99,500) is the first AWD sports car to be fitted with an independent rear axle and is powered by a 530 hp twin-turbo V6.

TITAN: Below Average. Buy a Chevrolet Silverado or Dodge Ram, instead. The Titan is a full-sized truck that hasn't been updated in over a decade. It is outclassed by the competition which offers more safety, performance, and convenience features, in addition to a more upscale interior. **Price:** King Cab S 4x2: $33,898; Crew Cab S 4x4: $39,898. **Crashworthiness:** NHTSA gives the 2012-14 Titan three and four stars for rollover protection; 2005-09 models earned five stars for frontal crash safety and four stars for rollover safety.

Porsche

BOXSTER AND 911: Below Average; CAYENNE: Average; CAYMAN AND PANAMERA: Not rated. Of these five cars, the Boxster and 911 owe their low rating to their high frequency of repairs and greater need for dealer servicing. **Price:** *Boxster:* $57,000-$71,000; *911:* $96,000-$206,000; *Cayman:* $60,000-$73,000; *Panamera:* $89,000-$184,000. Shop in the States and you will see savings of up to $40,000 (CDN). Porsche was forced to cut its Canadian prices by almost 10 percent when the Canadian dollar increased value in September 2007. As our dollar gets stronger once again, look for further price cuts. Adroit haggling should get you 20 percent off the suggested retail price. **Strong points:** A legendary racing cachet and excellent road manners. **Weak points:** Outrageously overpriced and a source of worry regarding service, repairs, theft, depreciation, high insurance costs, and premature wear and tear from cold and snow. Recent consumer complaints show that even the entry-level Boxster hasn't escaped the typical Porsche factory-induced defects affecting the engine, transmission, electrical system, brakes, and fit and finish. On the 911 and Cayenne, the powertrain, climate system, suspension, and fit and finish should be your main concerns. Making the reliability failings hurt more is the company's attitude that its cars are perfect, and what problems do occur are caused mainly by "driver abuse." Much to most owners' surprise and contrary to what Porsche dealers will tell you, Porsches *do* depreciate quickly. For example, a 2009 Boxster that originally sold for $58,400 is now worth about $26,000. All of the other Porsche models also lose much of their value during the first few years on the road. **Crashworthiness:** Not tested.

Saab

9-3, 9-4X, 9-5, AND 9-7X: Not Recommended "Distressed merchandise." With Saab thrown into bankruptcy, it is doubtful any Saab models will be built in the future. Saab dealers liquidated leftover Saabs at fire sale prices. Of course, no discount can compensate for poorly made cars hobbled by non-existent parts and servicing. Think Bricklin, Delorean, and early Fiats. The 9-3 is the automaker's entry-level model and represented 81 percent of the company's North American sales, while the 9-4X is a spin-off of the Cadillac SRX with different sheet metal, a 265 hp 3.0L V6, front-drive or all-wheel-drive power, and an Aero option that offered a 300 hp turbocharged 2.8L V6 AWD drivetrain. **Price:** A 2009 9-3 Aero convertible that sold originally for $59,000 is now worth barely $12,000. All models suffer from an abundance of defective components that imperil the cars' reliability and your own financial solvency. Be especially wary of powertrain, electrical, and fuel system breakdowns; brake failures; and poor fit and finish. Keep in mind that GM has promised to honour Saab's warranty on any new Saab sold by a GM dealer. **Crashworthiness:** NHTSA has given the 9-3 four stars for frontal crashworthiness and rollover resistance; side crash protection was awarded five stars. The 9-4X has shown good rollover resistance, while the 9-5 and 9-7X AWD remain untested by NHTSA. IIHS rated the 9-3's frontal offset, side, and rear crash protection as "Good." The 9-5's frontal offset crash protection was given a "Good" rating and side impact protection scored "Average." Head restraints were rated "Average." The 9-7X models got the worst scores among the Saabs tested by the IIHS; frontal offset protection was given an "Average," side crashworthiness was judged to be "Marginal," and restraints were rated "Poor."

Subaru

TRIBECA: A Subaru version of the ugly and unpopular Pontiac Aztek, the Tribeca's odd rounded styling and triangular grille has turned off buyers since the car was first launched in 2005. Now the car has a new look, but it, too, is failing to catch on with an unimpressed public. **Price:** $38,995. A 2010 Tribeca is worth $17,000. **Crashworthiness:** NHTSA gives the 2006-10 Tribeca five stars for overall crash safety; rollover protection was awarded four stars.

Suzuki

KIZASHI: Above Average. Sold for only three years (2011-13), this homeless, front-drive, five-door, compact crossover is more sizzle than steak and offers nothing exceptional for a $30,000 Suzuki. **Price:** A 2011 and 2013 are worth $14,500 and $22,000, respectively. Some good alternatives: The Acura TSX ($34,000) or the Subaru Legacy (*2.5i Sedan:* $24,000; *Sedan Sport:* $28,000). The Kizashi is a relatively well-equipped family sedan with standard electronic stability control. Handling is better than average, especially with the Sport model's precise steering. The trunk has a useful pass-through to the folded rear seats. A perusal of NHTSA owner-safety complaints and Suzuki's internal service bulletins shows no evidence of any quality problems. A few minuses: The car is an "orphan" abandoned by Suzuki early this year; insufficient power, a firm ride, and a narrow interior that's invaded by engine noise (especially with the Sport version). And speaking of the "sportier" Sport model, since when do a spoiler and five more horses (185) make a sports car? Furthermore, the 6-speed manual's long throws are annoying and the "gentle" gearing favours fuel economy over a sporty driving experience. The sunroof cuts into headroom, and rear seating is cramped. The 18-inch tires rumble on some road surfaces. **Crashworthiness:** NHTSA gives the car its top, five-star rating for front and side crashworthiness; four stars were awarded for rollover resistance. IIHS rated head restraints as "Good" and roof crashworthiness as "Acceptable."

Tesla

MODEL S AND MODEL X: Not Recommended (2013-14) during the car's first year on the market. The 2013 Tesla Model S electric car ($59,900-$94,900 (U.S.)) ranks 2 out of 10 super luxury cars based on *U. S. News and World Reports'* analysis of published reviews and test drives, as well as reli-

Tesla's Model S takes "Chick Magnet" to a whole new level.

ability and safety data. The top car: The gasoline-driven Mercedes-Benz S-Class ($84,007-$197,229 (U.S.)). Go figure. The Tesla's performance stats are astounding. It *is* the safest car in North America based on independent crash tests and Consumer Reports driving tests; its speed is hard to believe at 0-60 mph in 4.2 seconds; the car's battery range is 208 miles; and estimated EPA fuel economy is the equivalent of 94/97 mpg. So, why doesn't *Lemon-Aid* recommend the Tesla? Simple. Tesla owners are captive customers of a limited dealership network (Canada has only one factory dealer) and the car's real driving safety has yet to be determined. The recent incident where one Tesla quickly burned to the ground after running over road debris may mean nothing, or it could signal a serious danger that crashworthiness tests didn't check. If the car lasts two years on the market, it will change the automobile industry forever. In the meantime Hertz USA in Los Angeles and San Francisco is renting the Tesla Model S for $500 a day plus 0.49 per mile over 75 miles and $93.10 if you push the range.

Toyota

FJ CRUISER: Below Average for general use; **Average** for off-roading. **Price:** $33,440-$37,850 (negotiable). A 2007 and 2012 are worth $9,500 and $25,000, respectively. FJs are powered by a competent 258 hp 4.0L V6 that can be used for either two- or four-wheel drive. A 5-speed automatic transmission comes with both versions, and a 6-speed manual gearbox is available with the all-wheel drive. The Cruiser competes especially well off-road against the Ford Escape, Honda Element, Jeep Liberty or Wrangler, and Nissan Xterra. Off-roading should be a breeze if done carefully, thanks to standard electronic stability control, short overhangs, and better-than-average ground clearance. On the other hand, the FJ's turning circle is larger than those of similar-sized SUVs, making for limited maneuverability in close quarters. The rear side doors are taken from the Honda Element, which means rear and side visibility are severely restricted. There is also some side-wind vulnerability; a jiggly, busy ride; and annoying wind noises generated by the large side mirrors. Although touted as a five-passenger conveyance, a normal-sized fifth passenger in the back seat may consider litigation for cruel treatment. Front-seat headrests may be uncomfortably positioned for short occupants. Another minus is that premium fuel must be used to obtain mediocre gas mileage. **Crashworthiness:** A big surprise. Although NHTSA crashworthiness scores for front and side impacts are five stars, rollover protection merits only three stars. This is disappointing and is almost never seen with vehicles that are equipped with electronic stability control.

SOLARA: Recommended. Introduced in the summer of 1998 as a '99 model, the Solara is essentially a two-door coupe or convertible Camry that's longer, lower, and more bare-bones, with a more stylish exterior, sportier powertrain and suspension, and fewer quality problems. Most new Toyota model offerings, such as the Sienna, Avalon, and RAV4, are also Camry derivatives. The Solara was redesigned for 2004 and adopted the latest Camry sedan platform and upgrades. Convertibles arrived with seating for four instead of five and resembled the two-seat Lexus SC 430 hardtop convertible. The 2007 Solaras underwent a mild front and rear restyling, got standard side curtain airbags and a coloured rear spoiler, and dropped the SE V6 model. For 2008, the Solara's last model year, only the SLE remained. The 4-cylinder engine was replaced by the 3.3L V6, coupled to a 5-speed automatic transmission. **Price:** A 2008 Solara convertible that sold originally for $40,000, now costs $15,000. Relatively rare on the used-car market, you have a choice of either four or six cylinders. Unfortunately, vehicles equipped with a V6 also came with a gimmicky rear spoiler and a headroom-robbing moonroof. The stiff body structure and suspension, as well as tight steering, make for easy, sports-car-like handling with lots of road feel and few surprises. Unfortunately, the 4-cylinder base engine in pre-2007 models is wimpy and constantly reminds you and everyone else that it's a Toyota. Get the V6 instead. **Crashworthiness:** NHTSA gives the 2004-08 Solara five stars in all crash categories; 2003 models earned only three stars for side impact protection.

Volkswagen

THE "NEW" NEW BEETLE: Not Recommended. Volkswagen has taken the familiar Beetle design and literally flattened it to increase cabin and cargo space and added 3.5 inches to the car's length. **Price:** *Comfortline:* $22,175; *TDI Comfortline:* $24,175; used, these models sell from $5,500 (2007) to $15,500 (2012). Powered by an underwhelming, noisy 2.5L engine (a turbocharged variant is available); steering is over-assisted; the use of the failure-prone DSG dual-clutch automatic transmission doesn't bode well for long-term reliability; although diesel fuel economy is good, it's not as good as VW claims; the car is easily buffeted by crosswinds; large head restraints and large front roof pillars obstruct front visibility; limited rear legroom and headroom; and skimpy interior storage and trunk space. **Crashworthiness:** NHTSA gives the 2010-14 models five stars for side occupant crash protection and four stars for frontal and rollover crashworthiness. IIHS gives the 2010 New Beetle a "Good" rating for frontal offset crash protection and head restraint effectiveness, but cites side crashworthiness as "Poor."

EOS: Below Average. Watch out for the unpredictable, failure-prone transmission. Eos is agile, handles well, and provides a comfortable, taut ride. Braking is smooth, effective, and easy to modulate. The triumph of style over practicality: Limited interior access, rear legroom, and rear headroom; and excessive cabin engine noise. Owners give the Eos a below-average reliability score. **Price:** *Comfortline:* $39,875. 2007 and 2012 models sell for $10,000 and $27,000, respectively. **Crashworthiness:** NHTSA hasn't crash tested the Eos. IIHS gives the 2012 Eos its top, "Good" rating for frontal offset and side crashworthiness and head-restraint effectiveness. **ALERT!** Keep in mind that research shows convertibles driven with the top down contribute to premature hearing loss. (SORRY, WHAT WAS THAT? I CAN'T HEAR YOU!).

TOUAREG: Not Recommended. Price: $49,675-$63,800 (very soft). Recently redesigned, this SUV offers a 3.0L turbocharged V6 diesel mated to an 8-speed automatic transmission, in addition to the carried-over base 280 hp 3.6L V6. Next year's models will be equipped with a 380 hp 3.0L V6 hybrid powerplant that will cruise at 100 km/h on electric power alone. **Strong points:** Volkswagen's third-generation, mid-sized Touareg comes with lots of style, a plush and comfortable cabin, and some of the most impressive off-road capabilities in its class. **Weak points:** For those benefits, you pay an outrageously high price to get an SUV that doesn't offer third-row seating, has a pitifully poor reliability record, and has sky-high maintenance costs. Its problem areas include the powertrain, fuel, and electrical systems; brakes; and fit and finish. **Crashworthiness:** NHTSA gives the Touareg five stars for front and side crashworthiness and four stars for rollover resistance.

Volvo

Volvo is a car company without a country and with a limited future, like Saab, Jaguar, Land Rover, Smart, and, to a lesser extent, Chrysler LLC. The once-Swedish automaker is now owned by the Chinese firm Geely after living through a decade of "benign neglect" at Ford. Geeley wants Volvo's new models to cater to luxury-car buyers while the company's North American advisors want it to remain for mostly middle-class owners.

Geely's voice has prevailed; Volvo's future models will likely include more "bling, bling."

The Chinese takeover may annihilate what's left of the Volvo legacy. There's been a revolving door of Volvo executives coming and going and advertising agencies hired regionally with mixed messages. Hopefully, innovation and product improvements won't be starved from underfunding, and quality control will improve, even though Beijing's mindset may be more to "move the metal" and appeal to the $70,000 to $100,000 BMW/Audi Chinese crowd. Furthermore, additional performance features may price most Volvos out of reach for the average car buyer and make the cars almost impossible to service for the average mechanic. When it is found that a part is defective, its replacement may be back-ordered for weeks – if it can be found in Beijing, Detroit, or Sweden.

Recession-ravaged North American Volvo dealers have seen sales crater before and after the recession and both dealers and buyers are losing confidence in Volvo and loyal Volvo customers have lost confidence in a brand they once believed in; don't want to buy a car with a residual value that flows faster downhill than the Yangtze river. They long for that safe, solid, and understated New Democrat car that was always more Swedish than fashionable.

Bottom line: Don't buy any Volvo until we see where the company's headed in 2014.

Phil's "Beater" Beat 1970+

Automobiles are getting so complicated (infotainment and general electronic failures, 50-75 computer modules per vehicle, and high-tech emissions controls) that the average car owner has little choice for servicing and must go to the dealership where that vehicle was sold. This is a scary thought because it gives dealers a servicing monopoly and cuts out independent repairers who build their customer base through honest and competent service, and often serve as indispensable small claims court witnesses.

"Beaters" break automaker/dealer monopolies and allow motorists to go where service is the best and cheapest. Plus, the cars have been pre-rusted and a few more dents and scratches don't matter. There are plenty of cheap, reliable used cars, vans, and trucks out there that will suit your driving needs and budget. In the 1970s, the average car was junked after around seven years or 160,000 km (100,000 mi); two decades later, the average car was driven for almost eight years or 240,000 km (150,000 mi). Industry experts now say that most new models should last eleven years or more before they need major repairs. This means you can get good high-mileage vehicles for a few thousand dollars, and expect to drive them for five years or more.

But having said that, it can be tough to find a ten-year-old vehicle that's safe and reliable. Personally, I'd be reluctant to buy any decade-old vehicle from someone I didn't know, or one that has been brought in from another province. All of that accumulated salt is a real body killer, and it's just too easy to fall prey to scam artists who cover up major mechanical or body problems resulting from accidents or environmental damage.

Nevertheless, if you know the seller and an independent mechanic gives you the green light, you might seriously consider a ten-year-old, beat-up-looking car, pickup, or van (but heed my advice about old SUVs, following). Look for one of those listed in this appendix, or, if you have a bit more money to spend and want to take less of a risk, look up the Recommended or Above Average models found in Part Four.

Warning: No matter what you buy or how much you spend later on, you will remember your first "beater" as one of the best cars you ever owned.

Old Sport Utilities

Anyone buying a sport utility that's a decade old or more is asking for trouble, because many SUVs are worked hard off-road. The danger of rollovers for vehicles not equipped with electronic stability control is also quite high, particularly with Ford, Isuzu, and Suzuki versions; safety features are rudimentary, dangerous, and unreliable (especially airbags and ABS); overall quality control is very poor; and performance and handling cannot match today's models.

It's no wonder that many buyers are opting for new or almost-new SUVs manufactured during the past three years. During that time, prices came down considerably because more products were in the supply line, electronic stability control and full-torso side airbags were more widely available as standard features, and crashworthiness scores climbed higher.

Beaters You Will Love

Acura

The 5-cylinder **VIGOR** is a 1992-94 Honda Accord sedan spin-off that sells for $2,000-$3,000 and is rated an Above Average buy. This compact has power to spare, handles well, and has an impressive reliability/durability record. Problem areas: Excessive brake noise and premature brake wear in addition to fit and finish deficiencies. The 1992 Vigor turned in below-average crash test scores.

The 1989-95 **LEGEND** is an Above Average $2,500-$3,500 buy, but the 1986-88 model years are Not Recommended. Resale values are high on all Legend models, especially the coupe. Shop for a cheaper 1989 or later base Legend with the coupe's upgraded features and fewer reports of sudden, unintended acceleration. Pre-1990 Legends were upscale, enlarged Accords that were unimpressive performers with either of the two 6-cylinder powerplants. The 3.2L V6 that appeared in 1991 is by far a better performer.

Chrysler

DART, VALIANT, DUSTER, SCAMP, DIPLOMAT, CARAVELLE, NEWPORT, REAR-DRIVE NEW YORKER FIFTH AVENUE, AND GRAN FURY—Problem areas are electrical systems, suspensions, brakes, body and frame rust, and constant stalling when humidity is high. The Caravelle, Diplomat, and New Yorker Fifth Avenue are reasonably reliable and simple-to-repair throwbacks to a time when rear-drive land yachts

This is the 2014 Dart.

ruled the highways. Powered with 6- and 8-cylinder engines, they will run practically forever with minimal care. The fuel-efficient "slant 6" powerplant was too small for this type of car and was changed to a gas-guzzling but smooth and reliable V8 after 1983. Handling is vague and sloppy, though, and emergency braking is often accompanied by rear-wheel lock-up. Still, what do you want for a $300-$500 1984-89 "retro rocket"? Other problem areas include the carburetor (don't ask what that is; your dad knows), ignition, and suspension (premature idler-arm wear). It's a good idea to adjust the torsion bars frequently for better suspension performance. Doors, windshield pillars, the bottoms of both front and rear fenders, and the trunk lid rust through more quickly than average.

The **STEALTH** is a serious, reasonably priced sports car that's as much go as show. Although 1995 was its last model year in Canada, it was still sold in the United States as the Mitsubishi 3000GT. Prices range from $2,000-$2,500 for the 1991-93 base or ES model. A '95 high-performance R/T will go for about $3,500 – not a bad price for an old "orphaned" sports car, eh? Problem areas are engine, transmission, front brake, and electrical failures. The 1993 model excelled in crash tests.

Ford

MAVERICK, COMET, FAIRMONT, ZEPHYR, TRACER, (1964-2004) MUSTANG, CAPRI, COUGAR, THUNDERBIRD V6, TORINO, MARQUIS, GRAND MARQUIS, LTD, AND LTD CROWN VICTORIA— Problem areas are trunk, wheelwell, and rocker panel rusting as well as brake, steering, and electrical system failures. Price varies from $300 to $3,000 for the late-model, full-sized versions.

The 1990-97 **PROBE** is essentially a Mazda MX-6 sporty two-door coupe in Ford garb. It's quite reliable and gives better-than-average highway performance. Problem areas are AC, CV joints, and electrical and body glitches. Good crashworthiness ratings, but limited servicing support. Prices range from $1,000-$2,000.

General Motors

The **1982-96 CAPRICE, IMPALA SS, AND ROADMASTER** are Above Average-rated, comfortable, and easy-to-maintain large cars that have been off the market since the 1996 model year. Overall handling is acceptable, but expect a queasy ride from the too-soft suspension. The trunk is spacious, but gas mileage is particularly poor.

Despite the many generic deficiencies inherent in these rear-drives, they still score higher than GM's front-drives for overall reliability and durability. The Impala SS is basically a Caprice with a 260 hp Corvette engine and high-performance suspension. Good, cheap cars for first-time buyers, the 1991-93 models can be bought for $700-$1,000, while later models will cost $1,500-$2,000. Maintenance is inexpensive and easy to perform, and any corner garage can do repairs. Average parts costs can be cut further by shopping at independent suppliers, who are generally well stocked.

The 1991-96 models have shown the following deficiencies: AC glitches; prematurely worn brake (lots of corrosion damage), steering, and suspension components, especially shock absorbers and rear springs; serious electrical problems; and poor-quality body and trim items. Body assembly is not impressive, but paint quality and durability is fairly good, considering the delamination one usually finds with GM's other models. Wagons often have excessive rust around cargo-area side windows and wheelwells, and hubcaps on later models tend to fly off.

GM's 1984-96 rear-drive Cadillac **BROUGHAM** and **FLEETWOOD** are Above Average-rated luxury "land yacht" buys that sell for $2,000-$3,5000. Originally front-drives, these big sedans adopted the rear-drive, stretched platform used by the Buick Roadmaster and Chevrolet Caprice in 1993. Equipped with a 185 hp V8 mated to a 4-speed automatic transmission, all models came with standard traction control and anti-lock brakes. The rear-drive configuration is easy to repair and not hard to diagnose, unlike the cars' front-drive brethren. Other cars worth considering are Cadillac's DeVille and a fully loaded Ford Crown Victoria or Mercury Grand Marquis. The most serious problem areas are the fuel-injection system, which frequently malfunctions and costs an arm and a leg to repair; engine head gasket failures; automatic transmissions that shift erratically; a weak suspension; computer module glitches; brakes that constantly need rotor and pad replacement; poor body assembly; and paint defects. From a reliability/durability standpoint, the rear-drives are much better made than their front-drive counterparts.

Pontiac's 1991-95 **SUNBIRD** was GM's smallest American-built car, along with its twin, the Chevrolet **CAVALIER**. Available as two-door coupes, four-door sedans, and two-door convertibles, both models are Average buys. Nearly all Sunbirds were powered by a wimpy 96 hp 2.0L 4-cylinder engine as standard equipment, mated to a clunky, performance-sapping, fuel-wasting 3-speed automatic tranny. GT models featured a 165 hp turbocharged version of the same engine. Neither engine was very dependable. A better-quality, optional 140 hp 3.1L V6 came on the scene in 1991. In 1992, ABS became a standard feature, increasing the complexity and cost of brake maintenance for years to come. Not worth more than a few hundred dollars.

Honda

The 1984-91 **CRX** is a highly Recommended and seriously quick two-seater sports car – a Honda Civic spin-off that was replaced in 1991 by the less sporty and much less popular Honda del Sol. Prized by high-performance "tuners," a well-maintained CRX is worth between $2,500 and $3,000.

The 1985-2001 **PRELUDE** is an Above Average buy. It's unimpressive as a high-performance sports car, but instead it delivers a stylish exterior, legendary reliability, and excellent resale value. Preludes are, nevertheless, a bit overpriced and over-hyped; cheaper, well-performing makes such as the Ford Mustang or Probe, GM Camaro or Firebird, Mazda Miata, and Toyota Celica should be checked out first. Prelude repair costs are average, though some dealer-dependent repairs to the steering assembly and transmission can be quite expensive. Price: $3,000 to $3,500.

The year for big Prelude changes was 1997, while 1998-2001 models just coasted along with minor improvements (their prices vary from $4,000 to $7,000). The '97 was restyled and repowered, and given handling upgrades that make it a better-performing, more comfortably riding sports coupe. There's no crashworthiness data, though head-restraint protection has been given a Marginal designation. On these more-recent models, owners report that the engine tends to leak oil and crank bolts often loosen (causing major engine damage). AC condensers frequently fail after a few years and often need cleaning to eliminate disagreeable odours. Most corner mechanics are poorly equipped to service these cars, and the Automatic Torque Transfer System (ATTS) won't make their job any easier. Owners also report that a poorly designed clutch disc causes harsh shifting, and there have been clutch-spring failures.

Mazda

Sports-car thrills, minus the bills. The 1992-96 **MX-3**'s base 1.6L engine supplies plenty of power for most driving situations, and it's reasonably priced at $1,500. When equipped with the optional 1.8L V6 powerplant (the smallest V6 on the market at the time) and high-performance options, the car transforms itself into a 130 hp pocket rocket. In fact, the MX-3 GS easily outperforms the Honda del Sol, Toyota Paseo, and Geo Storm on comfort and high-performance acumen. It does fall a bit short of the Saturn SC because of its limited low-end torque, and fuel economy is disappointing. Reverse gear is sometimes hard to engage, and brake and wheel bearing problems are commonplace. Most of the MX-3's parts are used on other Mazda cars.

Toyota

All '80s and early '90s models are Above Average buys, except the **LE VAN**, which has a history of chronic brake, chassis, and body rusting problems. Chassis rusting and V6 engine head gasket failures are common problems with the 1988-95 sport-utilities and pickups (Toyota has paid for the engine repairs up to eight years). The **CELICA** is an especially fine buy, combining smooth engine performance and bulletproof reliability with sports-car thrills.

From its humble beginnings in 1979, the **SUPRA** became Toyota's flagship sports car by 1986, and it took on its own unique personality – with the help of a powerful 3.0L DOHC V6 powerplant. Supra prices range from a low of $4,000 for a '90 model up to $8,000 for a '97. It's an attractively styled high-performance sports car that had been quite reliable up until it caught the Corvette/Nissan 300ZX malady in 1993. Early models (pre-'93) are more reasonably priced and are practically trouble-free, except for some premature front brake wear and vibrations. On later models, owners report major turbocharger problems; frequent rear differential replacements; electrical short circuits; AC malfunctions; and premature brake, suspension, and exhaust system wear. The 3.0L engine is an oil-burner at times, and cornering is often accompanied by a rear-end growl. Seat belt guides and the power antenna are failure-prone. Body deficiencies are common.

Rated above Average, the **1999-2005 TOYOTA CELICAS,** all handle competently; the extra performance in the higher-line versions does come at a price, but this isn't a problem, given their high resale value ($10,000 for a 2005). Nevertheless, 1997 and later models sacrifice quality for performance. This is offset a bit by the proliferation of independent Toyota garages that perform most repairs for about a third less than what many dealers charge. Other vehicles to consider are the Ford Mustang, GM Camaro or Firebird, Honda Civic Si, Hyundai Tiburon, and Mazda3 or Miata. Incidentally, crashworthiness scores have generally been Above Average in most categories.

The early models saw engine failures caused by engine oil sludge (1997-2001 models), a problem once covered by Toyota "goodwill" (see the Sienna review in Part Four); brake pulsations and pulling to one side; rear defroster terminals breaking on convertibles; sunroof leaks; and smelly AC emissions.

Another subset of problems shows up on the redesigned 2000-05 models. This includes engine failures while driving ("weak" valves blamed), not much power when the accelerator is floored, stalling after a cold start, engine knocking, excessive oil consumption, early replacement of the belt tensioner and airflow meter, a failure-prone 6-speed transmission, insufficient AC cooling, lights dimming and heater lagging when shifting into idle, seat belt tabs that damage door panels, interior panels that separate, a driver's window that catches and doesn't go all the way up, a leaky convertible top and sunroof, drivebelt squeaks when turning, a squeaking gearshift lever, a grinding noise emanating from the front wheels and brakes, paint peeling, and limited rear visibility. The audible reverse alarm isn't Toyota's brightest idea: Audible only inside the vehicle, it adds a forklift cachet to your Celica.

A final Celica caveat: Keep your head up (or down, whichever the case may be). The rear hatch can "bean" you:

Rear hatch closes by itself. Dealer acknowledges problem but will not replace because it was not reported while still in warranty. The support arms are not strong enough to support the hatch. They have been discontinued and have been replaced with stronger ones. The hatch comes down without warning and could cause injury such as smash[ed] hands or fingers of children especially.

Toyota's 1991-99 **TERCEL** and **PASEO** models are Above Average buys, while the 1987-90 Tercel remains a good Average pick. Prices vary little: A 1992-1995 Tercel will cost $1,000-$2,000, while the 1996-99 versions sell for $2,000-$2,500. These economy cars are dirt cheap to maintain and repair, inexpensive parts are everywhere, and repairs can be done by almost anybody. Tercels are extraordinarily reliable, and the first-generation improvements provided livelier and smoother acceleration and made the interior space feel much larger than it was. Owners report these early models had hard-shifting automatic transmissions, premature brake and suspension component wearout, brake pulsation, leaking radiators, windshield whistling, and myriad squeaks and rattles. Be careful with very early models (1985-90). Updated 1995-99 Tercels are noted for sporadic brake, electrical system, suspension, and body/accessory problems. Frontal crashworthiness was rated two stars on the 1992 Tercel, four stars on the 1993-94, and three stars on the 1995-97. Head restraints were always rated Poor.

The Recommended 1996-99 Paseo is a baby Tercel. Its main advantages are a peppy 1.5L 4-cylinder engine, a smooth 5-speed manual transmission, good handling, a supple ride, great fuel economy, and above-average reliability. This light little sportster is quite vulnerable to side winds; there's lots of body lean in turns; there's plenty of engine, exhaust, and road noise; front headroom and legroom are limited; and there's very little rear-seat space. Generally, safety problems and defects affecting the Tercel are also likely to affect the Paseo.

Beaters You Will Loath

These cars will keep you eternally poor but healthy from your daily walks, and they'll quickly teach you humility – and mechanics.

AUDI FOX, 4000, AND 5000—Engine, transmission, and fuel-system problems; a combination of sudden acceleration and no acceleration.

BRITISH LEYLAND AUSTIN MARINA, MG, MGB, AND TRIUMPH—Electrical system, engine, transmission, and clutch problems; chassis rusting.

DATSUN/NISSAN 210, 310, 510, 810, F-10, AND 240Z—Electrical system and brake problems; rusting. Not worth buying at any price.

EAGLE MEDALLION, MONACO, AND PREMIER—These bargain-priced French American Motors *cum* Renault *cum* Chrysler imports – $500 for the Medallion and $1,000 for the Premier – had a 1988-92 model run. Sold through Chrysler's Renault connection, they're some of the most failure-prone imports to ever hit our shores.

FIAT—"Fix it again, Tony." All Fiat models and years are known for temperamental fuel and electrical systems and disintegrating bodies. Alfa Romeos have similar problems.

MERCEDES-BENZ 190E (1990-93)—Worth between $1,500 and $2,000, the "Baby Benz" was a flop from the very beginning. It was the company's smallest and cheapest sedan, powered by a 158 hp 2.6L 6-cylinder gasoline engine borrowed from the mid-size 260E sedan. A 5-speed manual transmission was standard, but most models were bought with the optional 4-speed automatic. A less-powerful, 130 hp 2.3L 4-cylinder engine was added to the 1991 model. Standard safety features were a driver-side airbag and ABS. Owners found the car to be both unreliable (automatic transmission, electrical and fuel system, and brake problems) and hard to service. Now, parts are almost impossible to find and mechanics run away when a 190E pulls into their service bay.

Chrysler

CRICKET, OMNI/HORIZON, AND VOLARÉ/ASPEN—Engine, brakes, and steering problems; chassis rusting.

CHARGER, CORDOBA, AND MIRADA—Brake, body, and electrical system problems.

The 1985-89 **LANCER** and **LEBARON** GTS may cost only $500-$700, but they're no bargain. In fact, they suffer from many of the same problems as the Aries and Reliant K cars and their 1989 replacements, the Spirit and Acclaim. Poor reliability causes maintenance costs to mount quickly. Turbo models are especially risky buys. Head gaskets are prone to leaks on all engines. Shock absorbers, MacPherson struts, and brakes wear out quickly. Front brake rotors are prone to rusting and warping. Crash test scores are below average.

Although they don't cost much – $300-$700, depending on the year – steer clear of 1983-89 **ARIES** and **RELIANTS.** Uncomplicated mechanical components and roomy interiors made these cars attractive buys when new, but they quickly deteriorated once in service. Both cars use dirt cheap, low-tech components that tend to break down frequently. They have also performed poorly in crash tests. Serious corrosion generally starts along the trunk line, the edges of the rear wheelwells, and the front fenders.

The 1990-98 **LASER** and **TALON** are Not Recommended, although the sporty Talons gave true high-performance thrills, just before they broke down. Maintenance and repair costs are much higher than average, mainly because of a scarcity of parts and a failure-prone and complicated-to-repair powertrain and emissions system.

Ford

CORTINA, PINTO, FESTIVA, (PRE-1980) FIESTA, BOBCAT, AND MUSTANG II—These over three-decade-old cars are disasters. Watch out for electrical system, engine, and chassis rusting – fire-prone Pintos and Bobcats are mobile Molotov cocktails. The German import Fiesta and the South Korean-built Festiva are two small imports that survived only a few years in Canada. Parts are practically unobtainable for both vehicles.

The 1994-97 Korean-built Ford/Kia **ASPIRE**'s size, engine, and drivetrain limitations restrict it to an urban environment, and its low quality control restricts it to the driveway. Be wary of brake, electrical, and fuel system failures. Parts are also hard to find. That said, you can pick up an Aspire dirt cheap for less than $500. In its favour, the car has consistently posted higher-than-average crash test scores.

Stay away from the Ford **CONTOUR** and **MYSTIQUE** (1995-99); they're two of the most failure-prone, hazardous vehicles you can buy. Industry insiders call the Mystique the "Mistake." The reason these cars are an even worse buy than the Taurus and Sable is that they've been taken off the market, drying up a minuscule parts supply and driving up parts prices (try $700 for an alternator). Resale values vary between $500 and $700.

General Motors

VEGA, ASTRE, MONZA, AND FIRENZA—Engine, transmission, body, and brake problems.

Cadillac **CIMARRON, ALLANTÉ, AND CATERA**—All gone; all bad. Overpriced, with poor-quality components. All front-drives suffer engine, automatic transmission, electronic module, steering, and brake problems, not to mention rust/paint peeling.

CITATION, SKYLARK, OMEGA, AND PHOENIX—Engine, brake, and electronic module problems; severe rust canker.

The Pontiac **FIERO,** sold from 1984 to 1988, snares lots of unsuspecting first-time buyers with its attractive sports-car styling, high-performance pretensions, and $500-$1,000 price. However, one quickly learns to both fear and hate the Fiero as it shows off its fiery disposition (several safety recalls for engine compartment fires) and its "I'll start when I want to" character.

Hyundai

PONY AND STELLAR—Two of the worst South Korean small cars ever imported into Canada. Their most serious problems involve electrical and fuel-system failures that cause fires, no-starts, stalling, and chronic engine hesitation. Stellars have irreparable suspension, steering, and brake deficiencies that make them dangerous to drive. Price: $300-$500.

The **EXCEL** is a low-tech and low-quality economy car that was orphaned in 1995. Resale prices are low ($300 for an '88; $1,000 for a '94). Likely problem areas are defective constant velocity joints, water pumps, oil-pan gaskets, oil pressure switches, and front struts as well as leaking engine head gaskets.

An Excel cross-dressing as a sports car, the 1991-95 **SCOUPE** ($1,500-$2,500) is essentially a cute coupe with an engine more suited to high gas mileage than hard driving.

Nissan

The 1989-96 **300ZX** is Nissan's answer to the Corvette, has everything – high-performance capability, a heavy chassis, complicated electronics, and average depreciation – resulting in a price range of $3,000-$3,500. Turbocharged 1990 and later models are much faster than previous versions and better overall buys. This weighty rear-drive offers a high degree of luxury equipment along with a potent 300 hp engine. Traction is poor on slippery surfaces, though, and the rear suspension hits hard when going over speed bumps. Crashworthiness scores have been average. The complexity of all the bells and whistles on the 300ZX translates into a lot more problems than you'd experience with either a Mustang or a Camaro – two cars that have had their own reliability problems but are far easier and less costly to repair. The best example of this is the electrical system, long a source of recurring, hard-to-diagnose shorts. Fuel injectors are a constant problem and guarantee sustained poor engine performance. The manual transmission has been failure-prone, clutches don't last long, front and rear brakes are noisy and wear out quickly, and the aluminum wheels are easily damaged by corrosion and road hazards. The exhaust system is practically biodegradable. The weird spongy/stiff variable shock absorbers and the glitzy digital dash with three odometers are more gimmicky than practical. Body assembly is mediocre.

Volkswagen

The original **BEETLE** was cheap to own but deadly to drive. Its main deficiencies were poorly anchored, unsafe front seats; a heater that never worked (fortunately, we were young and hot-blooded enough in those days to generate our own heat); fuel-tank placement that was dangerous in collisions; and poorly designed wheels and seat tracks.

The **CAMPER** minivan was safer but less reliable, with engine, transmission, fuel-system, and heater failings.

VW's 1987-93 **FOX** was the company's cheapest small car, combining good fuel economy with above-average road handling. An upgraded 5-speed manual transmission was added to the 1993 model year. This Brazilian-made front-drive never caught on because of its notoriously unreliable engine and transmission; quirky electronics; excessive road, wind, and body noise; atrocious fit and finish; and cramped interior (in the sedan). Parts are especially hard to find. Crashworthiness is way below average. Priced between $300 and $500, these cars are more skunk than fox.

VW's **SCIROCCO** is fun to drive but risky to own. Chronic breakdowns, parts shortages, and poor crashworthiness are just the beginning. Electrical short circuits, chronic fuel-supply problems, premature front brake wear, and fragile body parts are common owner complaints. Expect to pay $800.

Selling for $1,500 to $2,000, the 1990-95 **CORRADO** gives good all-around performance, with the accent on smooth acceleration, a firm but not harsh ride, and excellent handling with little body roll. So why is it Not Recommended? Poor reliability, hard-to-find parts, limited servicing outlets, and undetermined crash-worthiness.

Volvo

The 1989-93 **240 SERIES** is a Below Average buy, costing approximately $2,000. Avoid the turbocharged 4-cylinder engine and failure-prone air conditioning system. Diesels suffer from cooling system breakdowns and leaky cylinder head gaskets. The brakes on all model years need frequent and expensive servicing, and exhaust systems are notorious for their short lifespans. When a '79 Volvo 240 was crash tested, researchers concluded that both the driver and passenger would have sustained severe head traumas. The 1992-93 models, however, received excellent NHTSA crashworthiness scores.

Selling for $2,000-$2,500, the 1986-92 **700 SERIES** models are more spacious, luxurious, and complicated to service than the entry-level 240. The standard engine and transmission perform well but aren't as refined as the 850's. The 700 Series suffers from some electrical, engine cooling, air conditioning, and body deficiencies. Brakes tend to wear rapidly and can require expensive servicing. The 1988 model performed poorly in crash tests, while the 1991-92 versions did quite well.

NEW AND USED CAR CHECKLIST

Now, let's assume you're dealing with an honest seller and have chosen a vehicle that's priced right and seems to meet your needs. Take some time to assess its interior, its exterior, and its highway performance with the checklists below. If you're buying from a dealer, ask to take the vehicle home overnight in order to drive it over the same roads you use in your daily activities. Of course, if you're buying privately, it's doubtful that you'll get the vehicle for an overnight test – you may have to rent a similar one from a dealer or rental agency.

Here's how to check out a new or used vehicle without a lot of hassle. But if you are deceived by a seller despite your best efforts, don't despair. As discussed in Part Three, Canadian federal and provincial laws dish out harsh penalties to new- and used-car dealers who hide or embellish important facts. Ontario's *Consumer Protection Act* (*www.e-laws.gov.on.ca/html/statutes/english/elaws_statutes_02c30_e.htm*), for example, lets consumers cancel a contract within one year of entering into an agreement if a seller makes a false, misleading, deceptive, or unconscionable representation. This includes using exaggeration, innuendo, or ambiguity about a material fact, or failing to state a material fact, if such use or failure deceives or tends to deceive.

Just keep in mind these three points:

1. Dealers are *presumed* to know the history, quality, and true performance of what they sell.
2. Dealers and private sellers cannot mislead you as to the condition of what you are buying, although judges are more lenient with private parties.

3. Even details like a vehicle's fuel economy can lead to a contract's cancellation if the dealer gave a higher-than-accurate figure. In *Sidney v. 1011067 Ontario Inc. (c.o.b. Southside Motors) 15*, the plaintiff was awarded $11,424.51 plus prejudgment interest. The plaintiff claimed the defendant advised him that the vehicle had a fuel efficiency of 800-900 km per tank of fuel when, in fact, the maximum efficiency was only 500 km per tank.

Safety Check

1. Is the vehicle equipped with electronic stability control and full-torso side airbags, and has it earned a high crashworthiness ranking? Remember, a study by the Insurance Institute for Highway Safety (IIHS) found side airbags that include head protection cut a driver's risk of death almost in half for driver's side collisions. Another IIHS study concluded that electronic stability control reduces the risk of fatal single-vehicle crashes by more than half.
2. Is outward visibility good in all directions?
3. Are there large blind spots, like ones created by side pillars, impeding vision?
4. Are the mirrors large enough for good side and rear views? Do they block your view or vibrate?
5. Are all instrument displays clearly visible (not washed out) in sunlight? Is there daytime or nighttime dash glare on the windshield? Are the controls easy to reach?
6. Are the handbrake and hood release easy to reach and use? Will the handbrake hold the vehicle on a hill?
7. Does the front seat have sufficient rearward travel to put you at a safe distance from the airbag's deployment (about 30 cm/12 in.) and still allow you to reach the brake and accelerator pedals? Are the brake and accelerator pedals adjustable? Are they spaced far enough apart?
8. Are the head restraints adjustable or non-adjustable? (The latter is better if you often forget to set them.) Do they push your chin into your chest?
9. Are the head restraints designed to permit rear visibility? (Some are annoyingly obtrusive.)
10. Are there rear three-point shoulder belts, similar to those on the front seats?
11. Is the seat belt latch plate easy to find and reach?
12. Does the seat belt fit comfortably across your chest, release easily, retract smoothly, and use pretensioners for maximum effectiveness?
13. Are there user-friendly child-seat anchor locations?
14. Does the automatic side sliding door latch securely, and does it immediately stop when encountering an object as it opens or closes?
15. Do the rear windows roll only halfway down? When they are down, are your ears assailed by booming wind noise? Does it cause the vehicle to vibrate excessively?

Exterior Check

Rust

Cosmetic rusting (rear hatch, exhaust system, front hood, door jamb) isn't unusual on new cars that have been on the dealer's lot for some time. Minor rusting is acceptable and can even help push the price way down, as long as the chassis and other major structural members aren't affected.

Knock gently on the front fenders, door bottoms, rear wheelwells, and rear doors – places where rust usually occurs first. Even if these areas have been repaired with plastic, lead, metal plates, or fibreglass, once rusting starts, it's difficult to stop. Use a small magnet to check which body panels have been repaired with non-metallic body fillers. Use a flashlight to check for exhaust system and suspension component rust-out.

Catalytic Converter

Make sure the catalytic converter is present. In the past, many drivers removed this pollution-control device in the mistaken belief that it would improve fuel economy. The police can fine you for not having the converter, and you'll be forced to buy one (for $400+) in order to certify your vehicle.

Tires

Be wary of tire brands that have poor durability records. NHTSA's *www.safercar.org* will show you tire complaints and recalls, while *www.tirerack.com* will give you grass-roots owner experiences. Stay away from the Firestone/Bridgestone tires sold with many new vehicles; their poor reliability histories nearly guarantee future problems. Look at tire wear for clues that the vehicle is out of alignment, needs suspension repairs, or has serious chassis problems. Getting an alignment and new shocks and springs is part of routine maintenance, and it's relatively inexpensive to do with aftermarket parts. However, if your vehicle is an AWD or the MacPherson struts have to be replaced, you're looking at a $1,000 repair bill.

Accident damage

Most new cars have some shipping damage. In British Columbia, all accidents involving more than $2,000 in repairs must be reported to subsequent buyers.

Here are some tips on what you can do to avoid buying a damaged new or used vehicle. First, ask the following questions about the vehicle's accident history:

- Has it ever been in an accident? Was there a claim for transport damage when the vehicle was shipped from the factory? Can you show me the PDI (pre-delivery inspection) sheet? Do you have a vehicle history file?
- What was the damage and who fixed it?
- Is there any warranty outstanding? Can I have a copy of the work order?

- Has the vehicle's certificate of title been labelled "salvage?" ("Salvage" means that an expert has determined that the cost to properly repair the vehicle is more than its value. This usually happens after the vehicle has been in a serious accident.)

If the vehicle has been in an accident, you should either walk away from the sale or have the vehicle checked by a qualified auto-body expert. Remember, not all salvage vehicles are bad – properly repaired ones can be a safe and sound investment if the price is low enough.

What to look for

1. If the vehicle has been repainted recently, check the quality of the job by inspecting the engine and trunk compartments and the inside door panels. Do it on a clear day so that you'll see any waves in the paint.
2. Check the paint – do all of the vehicle's panels match?
3. Inspect the paint for tiny bubbles. They may identify a poor priming job or premature rust.
4. Is there paint overspray or primer in the door jambs, wheelwells, or engine compartment? These are signs that the vehicle has had body repairs.
5. Check the gaps between body panels – are they equal? Unequal gaps may indicate improper panel alignment or a bent frame.
6. Do the doors, hood, and rear hatch open and shut properly?
7. Have the bumpers been damaged or recently repaired? Check the bumper support struts for corrosion damage.
8. Test the shock absorbers by pushing hard on a corner of the vehicle. If it bounces around like a ship at sea, the shocks need replacing.
9. Look for signs of premature rust or displacement from a collision on the muffler and exhaust pipe.
10. Make sure there's a readily accessible spare tire as well as a jack and tools for changing a flat. Also look for premature rusting in the side wheelwells, and for water in the rear hatch channel.
11. Look at how the vehicle sits. If one side or end is higher than the other, it could mean that the suspension is defective.
12. Ask the seller to turn on the headlights (low and high beams), turn signals, parking lights, and emergency blinking lights, and to blow the horn. From the rear, check that the brake lights, backup lights, turn indicators, tail lights, and license plate light all work.

Interior Check

New vehicles often have a few hundred kilometres on the clock; used vehicles should have 20,000 km (12,500 mi) per model year. Thus, a three-year-old vehicle would ordinarily have been driven about 60,000 kilometres. The number of kilometres on the odometer isn't as important as how well the vehicle was driven and maintained. Still, high-mileage vehicles depreciate rapidly because most people consider them to be risky buys. On new cars, a few thousand kilometres showing may indicate the car was used as a demonstrator or sold and then taken back. Be suspicious. With used cars, subtract from your offer about $200 for each additional 10,000 kilometres above the average the car shows. Confirm the odometer figure by checking the vehicle's maintenance records.

The condition of the interior will often give you an idea of how the vehicle was used and maintained. For example, sagging rear seats plus a front passenger seat in pristine condition indicate that your minivan may have been used as a minibus. Delivery vans will have the paint on the driver's doorsill rubbed down to the metal, while the passenger doorsill will look like new.

What to look for

1. Watch for excessive wear of the seats, dash, accelerator, brake pedal, armrests, and roof lining.
2. Check the dash and roof lining for radio or cellular phone mounting holes (as used in police cruisers, taxis, and delivery vans). Is the radio tuned to local stations? If the radio is tuned for out of town stations, it could be an out-of-province car with a checkered history. Ask for more documentation as to previous ownership.
3. Turn the steering wheel. Listen for unusual noises and watch for excessive play (more than 2.5 cm/1 in.).
4. Test the emergency brake with the vehicle parked on a hill.
5. Inspect the seat belts. Is the webbing in good condition? Do the belts retract easily?
6. Make sure that door latches and locks are in good working order. If rear doors have no handles or locks, or if they've just been installed, your minivan may have been used to transport prisoners.
7. Can the seats be moved into all of the positions intended by the manufacturer? Look under them to make sure that the runners are functioning as they should.
8. Can headrests be adjusted easily?
9. Peel back the rugs and check the metal floor for signs of rust or dampness.

Road Test

1. Start the vehicle and listen for unusual noises. Shift automatics into Park and manuals into Neutral with the handbrake engaged. Open the hood to check for fluid leaks. Do this test with the engine running and then repeat it ten minutes after the engine has been shut down, following the completion of the test drive.
2. With the motor running, check out all controls, including the windshield wipers, heater and defroster, and radio.

3. If the engine stalls or races at idle, a simple adjustment may fix the trouble. But loud clanks or low oil pressure could mean potentially expensive repairs.
4. Check all ventilation systems. Do the rear side windows roll down? Are there excessive air leaks around the door handles?
5. While in Neutral, push down on the accelerator abruptly while paying attention to the colour of the exhaust smoke. Black exhaust smoke may require only a minor engine adjustment; blue smoke may signal the need for major engine repairs.
6. Shift an automatic into Drive with the motor still idling. The vehicle should creep forward slowly without stalling or speeding. Listen for unusual noises when the transmission is engaged. Manual transmissions should engage as soon as the clutch is released. Slipping or stalling could require a new clutch. While driving, make absolutely sure that a four-wheel drive can be engaged without unusual noises or hesitation.
7. Shift an automatic transmission into Drive. While the motor is idling, apply the emergency brake. If the motor isn't racing and the brake is in good condition, the vehicle should stop.
8. Accelerate to 50 km/h while slowly moving through all the gears. Listen for transmission noises. Step lightly on the brakes. The response should be immediate and equal for all wheels.
9. In a deserted parking lot, test the vehicle's steering and suspension by driving in figure eights at low speeds.
10. Make sure the road is clear of traffic and pedestrians. While driving at 30 km/h, take both hands off the steering wheel to see whether the vehicle veers from one side to the other. If it does, the alignment or suspension could be defective, or the vehicle could have been in an accident.
11. Test the suspension by driving over some rough terrain.
12. Stop at the foot of a small hill and then see if the vehicle can climb it without difficulty. Stop on a hill and see if the transmission holds the car in place without you giving it gas (a "hill-holder" feature).
13. On an expressway, it should take no longer than 20 seconds for most cars and minivans to accelerate from a standing start to 100 km/h.
14. Drive through a tunnel with the windows open. Try to detect any unusual motor, exhaust, or suspension sounds.
15. After the test drive, verify the performance of the automatic transmission by shifting from Drive to Neutral to Reverse. Listen for clunking sounds during transmission engagement.

Many of these tests will undoubtedly turn up some defects, which may be major or minor (new vehicles have an average of a half-dozen major and minor defects). Ask an independent mechanic for an estimate, and try to convince the seller to pay part of the repair bill if you buy the vehicle. Keep in mind that many three- to five-year-old vehicles with 60,000-100,000 km on their odometers run the risk of having an engine timing belt or timing chain failure that can cause several thousand dollars' worth of repairs. If the timing belt or chain hasn't been replaced, plan to do it and deduct about $300 from the purchase price for the repair.

It's important to eliminate as many duds as possible through your own cursory check, since you'll later invest two hours and about $100 for a thorough mechanical inspection. Garages approved by the Automobile Protection Association (APA) or members of the Canadian Automobile Association (CAA) usually do a good job. CAA inspections run from $100 to $150 for non-members. Remember, if you get a bum steer from an independent testing agency, you can get the inspection fee refunded and hold the garage responsible for your subsequent repairs and consequential damages, like towing, missed work, or a ruined vacation.

Appendix 11

TWENTY-TWO GAS-SAVING TIPS

All automakers build bad cars and trucks—some more often than others.
The trick is to know which models and years have the most problems.
Like wine, vintage is important.

...forget what biofuels have done to the price of foodstuffs worldwide over the past three years; the science seems to suggest that using ethanol increases global warming emissions over the use of straight gasoline.

Don't let anybody mislead you: The new push to get a 15% ethanol mandate out of Washington is simply to restore profitability to a failed industry. Only this time around those promoting more ethanol in our gas say there's no scientific proof that adding more ethanol will damage vehicles or small gas-powered engines. With that statement they've gone from shilling the public to outright falsehoods, because ethanol-laced gasoline is already destroying engines across the country in ever larger numbers.

City Garage manager Eric Greathouse has found that adding ethanol to the nation's gasoline supply may be a foolish government mandate, but it has an upside he'd rather not deal with. It's supplying his shop with a slow but steady stream of customers whose plastic fuel intakes have been dissolved by the blending of ethanol into our gasoline, or their fuel pumps destroyed. The average cost of repairs is just shy of $1,000.

www.businessweek.com/lifestyle/content/may2009/bw20090514_058678.htm

Before we tell you how you can cut your fuel costs, let's first explain why government fuel economy figures are always much better than the gas mileage you can count on.

Drivers are rightfully complaining that their real-world gas mileage is about 15 percent less than the "official" estimates given by Transport Canada and the U.S. Environmental Protection Agency (EPA). These figures are regularly included in published and online car guides, are posted on the window stickers of nearly every vehicle sold, and are showcased in automakers' advertising. Few people know that fuel economy tests are carried out primarily by the automakers under optimal conditions. The government retests 10-15 percent of the vehicles to keep the manufacturers honest, but motorists still complain their cars burn more fuel than advertised.

Ethanol: "Smoke and Mirrors"

Ethanol fuel is another "smart" government idea that has turned out to be a rathole down which Canadian and American taxpayers have poured billions of dollars. Several years ago, *Lemon-Aid* warned readers that ethanol would not save fuel and most certainly wouldn't make for a greener planet. Now we have confirmation that we were right in an article filed by Canwest News Service on October 2, 2009; it quotes a confidential memo sent to Natural Resources Minister Lisa Raitt by her deputy minister that says E85 fuel (85 percent ethanol and 15 percent ordinary gasoline) will do no good. In fact, Canwest concludes that E85 will bring no actual reductions in total greenhouse gas emissions, but will cost Canadian taxpayers $2.2 billion in federal subsidies, plus more from provinces – especially Ontario.

E85 has other drawbacks: You will pay more at the pump, despite huge subsidies given out to fuel companies by Ottawa; it burns 30 percent more fuel in cold weather; it's highly corrosive and requires rust-resistant tankers, storage tanks, pumps, and auto components; and in all of Canada, there are only four gas stations where you can buy E85. That means the estimated 300,000 E85 flex-fuel vehicles on the road today will likely never get near a filling station that can refuel their vehicle with the right product.

In the meantime, Canada's auto industry and its dealers are tuning Flex Fuel Vehicles (FFVs) to run on gasoline because they know widespread ethanol use will never happen and they don't want customers complaining that their cars' engines run poorly with gasoline.

Okay, now that we know ethanol and ethanol-fuelled vehicles aren't what they pretend to be, here are 20 real ways to cut your fuel consumption and save money.

1. **Buy a small 4-cylinder vehicle that has good crashworthiness and reliability ratings:** Generally, a vehicle with a minimum of 100 horses will get you around town and will be suitable for light commuting duties. I criticize VW for only offering 115 horses with the 2011 Jetta because I know Jetta buyers want more performance. Still, buying a low-horsepower car will cut your

fuel bills by one-third to one-half if you are downsizing from a V8 or a 6-cylinder engine – assuming that you will not load up the vehicle with fuel-burning accessories. Air conditioning and other electrical accessories will put a greater load on a vehicle's engine, and thus reduce its fuel economy.

WHY DREAD A HYBRID?

$8,000 (U.S.) BATTERY PACK

BATTERY DISPOSAL?

ELECTROCUTION DURING ACCIDENTS

EXPENSIVE

50% DEPRECIATION AFTER 3 YEARS

HIGH INSURANCE RATES

$30,000 FOR A PRIUS

FUEL SAVINGS OFF BY 40%

DEALER-ONLY SERVICE

A BETTER IDEA: A 2002 HONDA CIVIC ($9,000)...LEAVES $21,000 FOR FUEL!

2. **Stay away from hybrids and diesels:** You have to do a lot of driving to make a diesel or hybrid pay off. If you do go for a diesel, stay away from the ones made by Ford and GM and go with the Chrysler Cummins, but get extra powertrain protection. All three Detroit automakers have chronic diesel-injector problems on their trucks and SUVs, covered by secret repair warranties. And the situation won't get better. GM stopped its truck production for four months in 2010 to install more-complicated, urea-injecting emissions components on its diesel-equipped trucks. Hybrids are expensive, aren't as frugal as they pretend to be, keep you a captive customer, can be costly to service, and may be life-threatening. For example, only 60 volts across the chest can injure or kill, and a hybrid's NiMH battery can produce 270 volts. Furthermore, in a car accident with a hybrid, if the NiMH battery cable is damaged, heavy sparking can start a fire, toxic chemicals may be released, and the EMT rescuers must put on heavy rubber gloves before touching the car to extract passengers and get the car ready for towing. Getting this important NiMH battery information about hybrids from car dealers can be very difficult. There is also an economic angle: If your NiMH battery has an eight-year warranty, its replacement cost could almost equal the cost of the gasoline you saved. Interestingly, Nissan is thinking of selling separate battery pack leases for its Leaf electric car in order to strengthen the car's residual value as it nears the eight-year mark.

3. **Order a manual-transmission-equipped vehicle:** With rare exceptions, manual transmissions save fuel. How much depends on a number of factors, including the vehicle's size, the owner's driving style, and traffic conditions. Another benefit to manual transmissions is that they make you a more alert driver because you have to be constantly aware of traffic conditions in order to gear down to a stop or shift to accelerate. Interestingly, only 12 percent of the vehicles on North American highways use manual transmissions. In Europe, it's just the opposite – over 90 percent of drivers choose a manual gearbox.

4. **Get an automatic transmission with more gears:** If you choose an automatic, remember that a 5-speed tranny saves you more fuel than a 4-speed. Some high-end cars actually have 7-speed transmissions, and 8-speeds are being considered.

5. **Don't buy a 4x4 vehicle:** You will burn more fuel whether or not the 4x4 feature is engaged, because of its extra weight and gearing.

6. **Be wary of the cruise control:** It's a good idea to hold a steady speed on flat terrain, but if you're driving in a hilly area, the cruise control can actually make your gas mileage worse. In hilly conditions, if traffic permits, it's better to let the vehicle slow down a little on the uphill sections and then gain the speed back on the downhill side. If you use the cruise control in these conditions, it will floor the accelerator if necessary to keep your speed constant while going uphill.

7. **Use the AC sparingly:** Don't turn on the air conditioner as your first response to heat. Start your drive by slowly accelerating with the windows open to exhaust the hot air out of the rear windows, and then put on the AC if needed. This tactic will also enable the air conditioning to work faster and more efficiently when it is turned on. Having the AC off and the windows open will not save gas, however. Furthermore, driving any vehicle with a window or sunroof open will likely produce a painful roar in the cabin and cause excessive vibration in the steering.

8. **Keep your vehicle aerodynamic:** Resist the urge to attach accessories like roof racks, spoilers, and cargo carriers that hamper a vehicle's aerodynamics. Incidentally, pickup truck drivers won't save fuel by lowering the tailgate when driving on the highway. With the gate closed, air flows across the top of the bed and does not get caught by the tailgate. The airflow patterns are less efficient with the tailgate open or removed.

9. **Use the Internet to find cheap gas:** Websites like *www.GasBuddy.com* will show you which stations are selling cheaper fuel, sometimes up to 10 cents less than the average price. The Internet can also be helpful in calculating your real-world gas mileage and savings – *www.sciencemadesimple.net/fuel_economy.php* is an easy-to-use site to try.

10. **Use regular-grade fuel:** Unless the engine "knocks," using a higher-octane fuel than what is recommended by the manufacturer is foolish. Using premium fuel when the engine doesn't require it will not cause it to get better fuel consumption, and it may damage your emissions-control system. Some high-mileage vehicles, however, may need high-octane fuel if they "ping" (spark knocking) heavily on regular gas. Light knocking on acceleration is not a problem, but if the knocking continues at a constant speed, or if it's very loud, move up to a higher-octane fuel until it stops. Persistent, heavy knocking reduces an engine's efficiency and can damage it in extreme cases.

11. **Shop by price, not brand:** Gas is gas, and many different brands buy from the same refineries. Buy gasoline during the coolest time of day – early morning or late evening is best. During these times, gasoline is densest. Keep in mind that gas pumps measure volumes of gasoline, not densities of fuel concentration. It is also a smart idea to use credit cards that give cardholders cash rebates based on a percentage of their purchases.

12. **Coddle your throttle:** New vehicles don't usually attain their top mileage until they're broken in, which occurs at about 5,000-8,000 km (3,000-5,000 mi) of fairly gentle driving. Avoid the prolonged warming-up of the engine on cold mornings – 30-45 seconds is plenty of time. Also, don't start and stop the engine needlessly. Idling your engine for one minute consumes the amount of gas equivalent to the gas used when you start the engine. Avoid revving the engine, especially just before you switch the engine off; this wastes fuel needlessly and washes oil down from the inside cylinder walls, leading to the loss of oil pressure and premature wear. Lead-footed acceleration, heavy braking, and high-speed driving all increase gas consumption. The EPA estimates that jackrabbit starts and sudden stops can reduce fuel economy by as much as a third.

13. **Drive economically:** Driving at 110 km/h instead of 90 km/h will lower your car's fuel economy by 17 percent. Driving at fast rates in low gears can consume up to 45 percent more fuel than necessary. Don't worry about whether windows are opened or closed – tests carried out by *Consumer Reports* and others find it doesn't make any difference. Use only your right foot for both accelerating and braking. That way you can't accidentally ride the brake and use excessive gas.

14. **Get regular tune-ups, and change the oil and air filter frequently:** Don't let the Car Care Council and other trade groups convince you that more frequent tune-ups or adjustments will increase gas mileage. Once again, test findings show that the payoff is small – simply follow the instructions in the owner's manual. Malfunctioning emissions components, however, can burn lots of fuel. Have them "scope-checked" periodically by an independent garage, which will usually charge less than the dealer. Keep the brakes

properly adjusted, since dragging brakes increases resistance. Check your gas cap – one out of every five vehicles on the road has a gas cap that is either damaged, loose, or missing altogether, which allows gas in your tank to vaporize.

15. **Be tire-smart:** Inflate all tires to their maximum limits, and don't believe all the extended tire durability and fuel-saving claims made by sellers of nitrogen gas used in tire inflation. Each tire should be periodically spun, balanced, and checked for unevenness. Remove the spare tire; instead, keep a cell phone handy and join CAA. Changing a tire beside the road puts your life at risk, and it's a pain in the butt.

16. **Fight excess weight:** Remove excess weight from the trunk or the inside of the car, including extra tires, minivan back seats, and unnecessary heavy parts. Don't drive with a full fuel tank. Remember, carrying an extra 45 kg (100 lb.) in the trunk of your car may cut your car's fuel economy by 1-2 percent. An empty roof rack may cut fuel economy by 10 percent; fully loaded, it can reduce gas mileage by 18 percent. The further you run with the tank closer to empty, the further you run in a lighter car, thereby increasing the fuel mileage. Ideally, you never want to fill your tank more than a quarter- or half-tank full.

17. **Stay away from gas-saving gadgets:** They don't work, and they may cancel the manufacturer's warranty. Instead, park your car in the shade to reduce fuel evaporation, and buy a good windshield shade to keep the interior cool. Parking in your garage will help your car stay warm in winter and cool in summer, and you won't have to depend as much on your gas-guzzling air conditioning when you drive.

18. **Carpool:** Carpools reduce travel monotony and gas expenses – all riders chip in to help you buy and conversation helps to keep the driver alert. Pooling also reduces traffic congestion.

19. **Consolidate trips:** Combine several short errands into one trip, and combine private errands with business trips as a tax write-off.

20. **Fill up in the States:** Plan your trips to the States to include a fill-up on your return leg. Fuel costs a heck of a lot less there than it does in Canada.

21. **Look for false fuel economy settlements:** Take advantage of Honda, Hyundai, Kia, and Ford cash settlements for "misleading" high fuel economy claims.

22. **Sue, in provincial court if you don't get the promised gas mileage:** Use *Lemon-Aid*'s extensive misleading advertising jurisprudence found in Part Three.

Appendix III
SHOPPING AROUND

PRICES

Dealer profit margins on new and used cars vary considerably – giving lots of room to negotiate a fair price if you take the time to find out what the vehicle is really worth. A new vehicle's selling price as suggested by the manufacturer (MSRP) is just that – a suggestion. Most savvy buyers beat the MSRP by at least 10 percent by shopping when inventories pile up and automakers/dealers double-down on sales incentives (usually during the first quarter of the year).

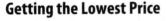

Getting the Lowest Price

If you want a low price and abhor dealership visits and haggling, search out a reliable new- or used-car broker. For years, *Lemon-Aid* has recommended Dealfinder, an Ottawa-based auto broker that helps clients across Canada. Go to *www.dealfinder. com* for all of the particulars. Ottawa-based Bob Prest, a small broker who believes in big discounts, has helped many people find great deals.

> To: Bob Prest <dealfinder@magma.ca>, August 30, 2010.
>
> Thank you so much! We picked up our new RAV4 today and are happy with the process. The salesman we had talked to previously took care of the details and we were pleased that he was not cut out of the transaction. Yet I know from past experience that we could never have negotiated such a good price… Thanks to Phil as well. His book was a big help.

For those readers who feel comfortable negotiating all of the transaction details with the dealer themselves, here's what to do.

1. Compare a new vehicle's "discounted" MSRP prices published on the automaker's website with invoices downloaded from the Automobile Protection Association (*www.apa.ca*), the Canadian Automobile Association (*www.caa.ca*), and a host of other agencies.
2. Check the prices you find against the ones listed in this book.

3. Pay particular attention to the prices charged in the States by accessing the automaker's U.S. website – just type the company name into Google and add "USA." For example, "GM USA" will take you directly to the automaker's American website, whereas "GM Canada" gives you the Canadian headquarters, models, and prices. If you find the U.S. price is substantially lower than what Canadian dealers charge, take your U.S. printout to the Canadian dealers and ask them to come closer to the American price. There is no reason why you should pay more in Canada. And this includes freight and pre-delivery inspection fees.

Real Trade-in Values

If you have a trade-in, it's important to find out its true value to decide whether selling it privately would put more money in your pocket than selling it to the dealer. Right now, there is a shortage of good three- to five-year-old used cars on the market and private buyers are paying a premium for them.

Problem is, how do you find how much your trade-in is worth? In the past dealers had a monopoly on this information because only they could afford the hundreds of dollars in annual subscription fees charged by the publishers of *Black Book* and *Red Book*. That has now changed with the advent of the Internet.

There is now an excellent alternative to the traditional *Red* and *Black Book* price guides. Go to *www.vmrcanada.com/* for free listings of trade-in values for 1984 to 2012 cars and trucks, reliability predictions, and three- to five-year residual value projections. Better yet subscribe to the publication in eBook format. A year's subscription for $9.95 (U.S.) is more comprehensive and much cheaper than either the *Black Book* or *Red Book* (although the other two publications give current new and used prices for 2013-14 models and are more popular with car dealers, insurance companies, and government agencies). The *Black Book* gives used values online for free at: *www.canadianblackbook.com/*; *Red Book*: *www.canadianredbook.com/* gives values online to subscribers for an annual fee of $195.95.

Now available in eBook format, *VMR Canadian Used Car Prices* delivers our unbiased, market-based values in an easy-to-use format. The smart PDF has a simple, built-in menu system incorporated with the Table of Contents, allowing fast and easy navigation to anywhere in the publication. Download it once to your computer or device and access it anytime, anywhere – just like a book. Only $9.95 (U.S.) for full year (published quarterly).

- Pricing directly from the Canadian market and in Canadian dollars
- Easy to use – Simple "one-button" navigation
- Use anywhere
- Universal PDF format
- "At a Glance" format
- Faster than an APP

- Print one page, several, or the whole book
- Only $9.95 (U.S.) for full one-year subscription, or single copy for $2.95.

Confidential Reliability Info

Unearthing reliability information from independent sources on the Internet takes a bit more patience. You should first wade through the thousands of consumer complaints logged in the NHTSA database at *www.safercar.org*. Next, use the NHTSA and ALLDATA service bulletin databases to confirm a specific problem's existence, find out if it's caused by a manufacturing defect, and learn how to correct it. Augment this information with tips found on car forums and protest/information sites. *Lemon-Aid* does this for you in its guides, but you can stay current about your vehicle's problems or research a particular failure in greater depth on your own by using the above search methods.

Automobile companies have helpful – though self-serving – websites, most of which feature detailed sections on their vehicles' histories and research and development, as well as all sorts of information of interest to auto enthusiasts and bargain hunters. For example, you can generally find out the freight fee before you even get to the dealership; sales agents prefer to hit you with this charge at the end of the transaction when your guard is down. As said earlier, cut the freight fee by 50 percent. Manufacturers can easily be accessed through a search engine like Google or by typing the automaker's name into your Internet browser's address bar followed by ".*com*" or ".*ca*". Or for extra fun and a more balanced presentation, type the vehicle model or manufacturer's name into a search engine, followed by "lemon," "problems," or "lawsuits."

Judgments OF THE
Supreme Court OF Canada

Decisions > Supreme Court Judgments > General Motors Products of Canada

Date: 1979-01-23

Report: [1979] 1 SCR 790

Judges   Laskin, Bora; Martland, Ronald; Spence, Wishart Flett; Pigeon, Louis-Philippe; Dickson, Robert George Brian; Estey, Willard Zebedee; Pratte, Yves

General Motors Products of Canada v. Kravitz, [1979] 1 S.C.R. 790

Date: 1979-01-23

General Motors Products of Canada Limited
(Defendant) Appellant;

and

Leo Kravitz
(Plaintiff) Respondent.

1978: February 14 and 15; 1979: January 23.

Present: Laskin C.J. and Martland, Spence,
Pigeon, Dickson, Estey and Pratte JJ.

ON APPEAL FROM THE COURT OF APPEAL FOR QUEBEC

Sale—Motor vehicle—Hidden defects—Legal warranty—
No-warranty stipulation—Conventional warranty—Liability
of manufacturer—Civil Code, arts. 1491, 1522, 1527 to 1530.

Court judgments are easy to find and often save you the expense of hiring a lawyer. This was
my first Supreme Court case where I acted as a pro bono witness for the car owner.

Cross-Border Shopping

Our Canadian loonie is worth about 97 cents to the American dollar – no justification for cars and trucks to sell for more than 20 to 30 percent higher in Canada than in Buffalo, Detroit, or Seattle.

But Canadians aren't as dumb as the automakers think.

Every time the loonie goes up in value, thousands of Canadians buy their new or used car across the border in the United States, where vehicles are 10-25 percent cheaper. For example, the Canadian dollar traded at par with the U.S. dollar in July 2008, and that year Canadian shoppers imported a record 240,000 vehicles from the United States into Canada. Imports slowed to a trickle in the first quarter of 2009 when the dollar dropped well below 90 cents (U.S.) (then, only 18,800 vehicles were imported). But, now with the Canadian dollar's value once again flying high, Canadian buyers are again flocking to dealer showrooms in the States.

Furthermore, dealers on both sides of the border are hungry for sales and aren't likely to knuckle under automaker pressure to refuse warranty repairs or service on cars purchased in the States, as they attempted to do a few years ago. Also, Transport Canada has made it easier to import new and used cars from the States, and businesses on both sides of the border have sprung up to facilitate purchases for Canadians. It's clear that getting a cross-border bargain is easier than ever. And most of us live within an hour's drive of the border.

Shopping Tips

Reported savings range from around 10 percent for subcompact and compact vehicles, compact SUVs, and small vans, to over 25 percent in the luxury vehicle segment. Most manufacturers honour the warranty, and many dealers and independent garages will modify cars to Canadian standards, including speedometer and odometer labels, child tether anchorage, daytime running lights, French airbag labels, and anti-theft immobilization devices. Some will complete the import paperwork for you. Again, whether it's worthwhile importing a car from the U.S. is a personal decision.

Keep in mind that there may be a few extra costs to consider. For instance, if the vehicle was not made in North America, you have to pay duty to bring it into Canada. Normally, the duty for cars is 6.2 percent of the value of the vehicle. There are also excise taxes on vehicles weighing more than 2,007 kg (4,425 lb). A listing of Canadian border crossing spots where you can bring in a just-purchased new or used car can be found at *www.ucanimport.com/Border_Crossing_Info.aspx*.

Consumer groups like Montreal-based Cars Without Borders and the Automobile Protection Association (*www.apa.ca*) say buying a car in the States as part of your vacation trip and driving it back to Canada or using an auto broker is a sure money-saver and easy to do. Canadian dealers say it's unpatriotic and not fair to dealers, and that U.S. cars have softer paint and weaker batteries.

Classic weasel-speak.

Ironically, in a U.S. class action settlement filed in 2011 (when cars bought in Canada were cheaper due to a depreciated Canadian dollar), Toyota paid $35 million in damages for conspiring to keep Canadian dealers from selling to Americans. And, here's the best part: The Canadian Auto Dealers Association shelled out another $700,000 for participating in the conspiracy with Toyota and other auto makers (*www.canadianexportantitrust.com/*):

> *Washington, DC:* Two proposed partial settlements of several class action lawsuits involving Toyota and the Canadian Automobile Dealer's Association (CADA) have been reached. The lawsuits allege certain automakers and trade associations conspired in violation of federal and state antitrust and consumer protection laws to prevent virtually identical, but cheaper, new cars from being exported to the United States from Canada, making new vehicle prices higher for U.S. consumers.

Toyota has agreed to pay $35 million for the benefit of a Class of people or businesses who bought or leased a new vehicle from January 1, 2001 to December 31, 2006. CADA has agreed to pay $700,000 for the benefit of the Class. Both Toyota and CADA have agreed not to conspire with others or share certain types of information with other automakers aimed at preventing Canadian new vehicles from entering the United States.

Talk about hypocrites, look at the court's documentary proof:

In furtherance of the conspiracy, the Conspiracy Defendants Controlled and limited the cross shipping of new motor vehicles from Canada to the US and from the US to Canada.

Beginning in at least December 2001, the Conspiracy Defendants communicated with one another through CADA and others and agreed amongst themselves and each other to act to prevent or limit the cross shipping of new motor vehicles across the Canada/US border.

For example, a memorandum of the Defendant Chrysler marked "Urgent" and dated December 20, 2001 from Lewis C. Scott, Daimler Chrysler's (as it then was) Zone Manager in Denver, Colorado to all dealers in the Denver zone, entitled "Imported Canadian Vehicles," states:

> Following is the latest information on the Canadian vehicle issue: Our management has spoken to the corporate headquarters of several of our competitors regarding this issue and have copies of their policies. The issue is currently being reviewed by our legal department, and it appears as though our policy will greatly mirror that of our competitors. The probability is that we will suspend the warranty on vehicles that come into the U.S. for retail sale....The plan is to have a detailed policy in place during the first quarter of 2002. (the "Chrysler Memorandum").

In May 2002, the Conspiracy Defendants' Defendant manufacturers' representatives gathered at the 2002 New York Auto Show in New York City and met with senior representatives of both CADA and others to discuss the export "problem." The Conspiracy Defendants Defendant manufacturers suggested that CADA's members police noncompliant dealers. The discussions also covered a proposed checklist of practices Canadian dealers could employ to stop export sales.

The Facilitators also assisted the Conspiracy Defendants Defendant manufacturers in their conspiracy to lessen competition and to unreasonably enhance prices for their product by assisting in the creation of a litigation defense fund for the protection of dealers that incurred costs or legal fees arising out of the Conspiracy Defendants' Defendant manufacturers' directives, and in furtherance of the conspiracy.

*www.jruslaw.com/classactions/carconspiracy/docs/cc_*
tetefsky_amended_fresh_statement_of_claim.pdf
Pages 23 and 30 of Tetesky vs. General Motors

These people aren't patriots; they're bums.

Canadian independent new- and used-car dealers aren't buying that argument; they are some of the biggest buyers of used cars in the States. For example, Advantage Trading Ltd. in Burnaby, B.C. (one of the largest importers on the West Coast), says they can get U.S. cars so cheaply that they can offer discounts to Canadians and still make a handsome profit. The only downside is that there is a shortage of some popular makes and models.

If you do decide to import a vehicle on your own, Transport Canada suggests you use the Registrar of Imported Vehicles' comprehensive and easy-to-follow checklist of things you must do (*www.riv.ca/ImportingAVehicle.aspx*).

- What to do before importing a vehicle
- What to do at the border
- What to do after the vehicle enters Canada
- What RIV fees will be applied
- Who to contact for vehicle import questions, including contact information for the Canada Border Services Agency (CBSA)

This list is all you need to import almost any car and get big savings. There are also independent resources listed at *www.riv.ca/HelpfulLinks.aspx* and *www.import-cartocanada.info/category/faq*. The latter site goes into even greater detail by answering these questions:

- Why buy a vehicle in the U.S. and import it into Canada?
- What are the differences between Canadian and U.S. vehicle MSRP prices?
- What vehicles can be imported into Canada?
- How long does it take to import a vehicle into Canada from the U.S.?
- What should I watch out for when purchasing a vehicle to import into Canada?
- What types of modifications are needed to import a vehicle into Canada?
- What kinds of documents do I need to import a vehicle into Canada?
- Do I have to pay tax when I import a vehicle into Canada from the U.S.?
- Do I have to pay duty when I import a vehicle into Canada from the U.S.?
- Is there anyone that can import the vehicle into Canada for me?
- Can I drive my U.S. vehicle into Canada without notifying U.S. Customs?
- Where can I cross the border to import a vehicle into Canada?
- What do I do at the border?
- What should I do when I arrive at home in Canada with my new vehicle?
- What happens if my vehicle fails federal inspection?
- What is a recall clearance letter?
- Can I import a vehicle into Canada that is over 15 years old?
- How do I import a vehicle into Canada from a country other than the U.S.?
- Which vehicle manufacturers honour warranties on vehicles imported into Canada?

RIGHTS, GRIPES, AND WEBSITES

Recent surveys show that close to 80 percent of car buyers get reliability and pricing information from the Internet before visiting a dealer or private seller. This trend has resulted in easier access to confidential price margins, secret warranties, and lower prices – if you know where to look.

CONSUMER PROTECTION

Automobile Consumer Coalition *(www.carhelpcanada.com)*

Founded by former director of the Toronto Automobile Protection Association, Mohamed Bouchama, the ACC's Car Help Canada website provides many of the same services as does the APA; however, the ACC is especially effective in Ontario and Alberta and uses a network of honest garages and dealers to help members get honest and fair prices for vehicles and repairs. The ACC has been particularly successful in getting new legislation enacted in Ontario and obtaining refunds for its members.

Automobile Protection Association *(www.apa.ca)*

A motherlode of honest, independent, and current car-buying information, the non-profit APA has been protecting Canadian motorists for over 40 years from its offices in Toronto and Montreal. This dynamic consumer group fights for safer vehicles for consumers and has exposed many scams associated with new-vehicle sales, leasing, and repairs. For a small fee, it will send you the invoice price for most new vehicles and help you out if you get a bad car or dealer. The APA also has a useful free online guide for digging out court judgments.

BBC TV's Top Gear *(www.topgear.com)*

Britain's automotive equivalent to CBC TV's *Marketplace*, *Top Gear* showcases the best and blows the whistle on the worst European-sold vehicles, auto products, and industry practices. Now that many new cars are being imported from Europe, it's prudent to find out how well they have performed in other countries. *Which?*

and *What?* are two British-based product review magazines that also give out useful performance and reliability information on most cars sold in Europe. *Which?* is published by the non-profit British Consumers Association – much like *Consumer Reports'* relationship with Consumers Union. All three magazines want you to subscribe before giving you detailed reviews. However, if you go to their online press releases, you will usually be able to get the info you need relating to their test findings.

Canadian Legal Information Institute *(www.canlii.org)*

Be your own legal "eagle" and save big bucks. Use this site to find court judgments from every province and territory all the way up to the Supreme Court of Canada.

CBC TV's Marketplace *(www.cbc.ca/marketplace)*

Marketplace has been the CBC's premier national consumer show for almost forever. Staffers are dedicated to searching out scammers, airbag dangers, misleading advertising, and unsafe, poor-quality products. Search the archives for auto info, or contact the show's producers to suggest program ideas.

Class Actions in Canada *(www.classproceedings.ca)*

After successfully kicking Ford's rear end over its front-end thick film ignition (TFI) troubles and getting a million-dollar out-of-court settlement, this powerhouse Ontario-based law firm got a similar settlement from GM as compensation for a decade of defective V6 intake manifold gasket failures. Estimated damages were well over a billion dollars. The firm has also worked with others to force Liberty Mutual and other insurers to refund money paid by policy holders who were forced to accept accident repairs with used, reconditioned parts instead of new, original-equipment parts.

Class Actions in the U.S. *(www.lawyersandsettlements.com)*

This is a useful site if you want to use a company's class action woes in U.S. jurisdictions as leverage in settling your own Canadian claim out of court. If you decide to go the Canadian class action route, most of the legal legwork will have been done for you. The site is easy and free to search. Just type in the make of the vehicle you're investigating and read the results.

Competition Bureau Canada *(www.competitionbureau.gc.ca)*

The Competition Bureau is responsible for the administration and enforcement of the *Competition Act*, the *Consumer Packaging and Labelling Act*, the *Textile Labelling Act*, and the *Precious Metals Marking Act*. Its role is to promote and maintain fair competition so that Canadians can benefit from lower prices, increased product choices, and quality services.

This website includes a handy online complaint form that gives Ottawa investigators the mandate to carry out an official probe and lay charges. Most auto-related complaints submitted to the Bureau concern price-fixing and misleading advertising. After *Lemon-Aid*, the APA, and Mohamed Bouchama from the ACC submitted formal complaints to Ottawa against Toyota's Access pricing program a few years ago, the automaker settled the case for $2.3 million. The Bureau agreed to drop its inquiry into charges that the automaker rigged new car prices.

Almost 28 years earlier, an APA complaint forced GM to pay a $20,000 fine for lying in newspaper ads, touting the Vauxhall Firenza's triumphant cross-Canada "reliability run." The cars constantly broke down, and one auto journalist brought along for the ride spilled the beans to Ottawa probers. GM took the car off the market shortly thereafter.

Consumer Affairs *(www.consumeraffairs.com/automotive/manufacturers.htm)*

Expecting some namby-pamby consumer affairs site? You won't find that here. It's a "seller beware" kind of website, where you'll find the scandals before they hit the mainstream press.

Consumer Reports and Consumers Union *(www.consumerreports.org/cro/cars.htm)*

It costs $6.95 (U.S.) a month to subscribe online, but *CR*'s database is chock full of comparison tests and in-depth stories on products and services. The group's $29.95 New Car Price service is similar to what the APA offers.

Protégez-Vous (Protect Yourself) *(www.protegez-vous.qc.ca)*

Quebec's French-language monthly consumer protection magazine and website is a hard-hitting critic of the auto industry. *Protégez-Vous* has supported the APA in testing dealer honesty and ratings of new and used cars in Quebec and throughout Canada. The magazine publishes dozens of test-drive results as well as articles relating to a broad range of products and services sold in Canada.

Supreme Court of Canada *(scc.lexum.umontreal.ca/en/index.html)*

It's not enough to have a solid claim against a company or the government. Supporting your position with a Supreme Court decision also helps. Three pro-consumer judgments rendered in February 2002 are particularly useful.

- *Bannon v. Thunder Bay (City):* An injured resident missed the deadline to file a claim against Thunder Bay; however, the Supreme Court maintained that extenuating factors, such as being under the effects of medication, extended her time to file. A good case to remember next time your vehicle is damaged by a pothole or you are injured by a municipality's negligence.

- *R. v. Guignard:* This judgment says you can protest as long as you speak or write the truth and you don't disturb the peace or harass customers or workers.

- *Whiten v. Pilot Insurance Co.:* The insured's home burned down, and the insurance company refused to pay the claim. The jury was outraged and ordered the company to pay the $345,000 claim, plus $320,000 for legal costs and $1 million in punitive damages, making it the largest punitive damage award in Canadian history. The Supreme Court maintained the jury's decision, calling Pilot "the insurer from hell." This judgment scares the dickens out of insurers, who fear that they might face huge punitive damage awards if they don't pay promptly.

AUTO SAFETY

Center for Auto Safety *(www.autosafety.org)*

A Ralph Nader-founded agency that provides free online info on model-specific safety- and performance-related defects.

Crashtest.com *(www.crashtest.com)*

This website has crash-test information from around the world. You can find additional crashworthiness data for cars just recently coming onto the North American market that have been sold for many years in Asia, Europe, or Australia. The Honda Fit (Jazz), Mercedes Smart, Magna's Opel lineup, and Ford's upcoming European Fiesta and Focus imports are just a few examples.

Insurance Institute for Highway Safety *(www.iihs.org)*

A dazzling site that's long on crash photos and graphs that show which vehicles are the most crashworthy in side and offset collisions and which head restraints work best.

SafetyForum *(www.safetyforum.com)*

The Forum contains comprehensive news archives and links to useful sites, plus names of court-recognized experts on everything from unsafe Chrysler minivan latches to dangerous van conversions.

Transport Canada *(www.tc.gc.ca/eng/roadsafety/safevehicles-defectinvestigations-index-76.htm)*

A ho-hum site that's in no way as informative as the NHTSA or IIHS sites. You can access recalls for 1970-2010 models, but owner complaints aren't listed, defect investigations aren't disclosed, and service bulletin summaries aren't provided. A list of used vehicles admissible for import is available at *www.tc.gc.ca/roadsafety/safevehicles/importation/usa/vafus/list2/menu.htm* or by calling the Registrar of Imported Vehicles (RIV) at 1-888-848-8240.

U.S. National Highway Traffic Safety Administration *(www.safercar.gov)*

This site has a comprehensive free database covering owner complaints, recall campaigns, crashworthiness and rollover ratings, defect investigations, service bulletin summaries, and safety research papers.

INFORMATION/SERVICES

Alberta Government's Vehicle Cost Calculator *(www.agric.gov.ab.ca/app24/costcalculators/vehicle/getvechimpls.jsp)*

Your tax dollars at work! This handy calculator allows you to estimate and compare the ownership and operating costs for any business or non-business vehicles. Eleven types of vehicles can be compared and the ownership cost can be calculated by modifying the input values. Alternatively, you may select the same model if you wish to compare one vehicle but with variations in purchase price, options, fuel type (diesel or gas), interest rates, or length of ownership.

ALLDATA Service Bulletins *(www.alldata.com/recalls/index.html)*

Free summaries of automotive recalls and technical service bulletins are listed by year, make, model, and engine option. You can access your vehicle's full bulletins online by paying a $26.95 (U.S.) subscription fee.

The Auto Channel *(www.theautochannel.com)*

This website gives you useful, comprehensive information on choosing a new or used vehicle, filing a claim for compensation, or linking up with other owners.

Auto Extremist *(www.autoextremist.com)*

Rantings and ravings from a Detroit insider.

Canadian Automobile Association *(www.caa.ca)*

The Canadian Automobile Association (CAA) performs a similar service to what the Alberta government offers. They track rising repair and maintenance costs as different vehicles age. Toronto-based DesRosiers Automotive Consultants says, by year five, the average annual repair cost of a vehicle is about $800; after seven years, expect to pay up to $1,100 annually.

GM Inside News *(www.gminsidenews.com/forums)*

Kelley Blue Book and Edmunds *(www.kbb.com; www.edmunds.com)*

Prices and technical info are American-oriented, but you'll find good reviews of almost every vehicle sold in North America – plus there's an informative readers' forum.

Online Metric Conversions *(www.sciencemadesimple.net/conversions.html)*

A great place to instantly convert gallons to litres, miles to kilometres, etc.

Phil Bailey's Auto World *(www.baileycar.com)*

Phil Bailey owns his own garage and specializes in the diagnosis and repair of foreign cars, particularly British ones. He's been advising Montreal motorists for years on local radio shows and has an exceptionally well-written and informative website.

Roadfly's Car Forums and Automotive Chat Rooms *(www.roadfly.org/forums)*

Another site that's no butt-kisser. Here you'll learn about BMW fan fires, upgrades, and performance comparisons. It also contains message boards for Bentley, Cadillac, Chevy, Jaguar, Lotus, Porsche, Mercedes-Benz, and others.

Straight-Six.com *(www.straight-six.com)*

Okay, for you high-performance aficionados, here's a website that doesn't idolize NASCAR, Earnhardt, or the Porsche Cayenne SUV (they call it the "Ca-Yawn").

Women's Garage *(www.womensgarage.com)*

Three Canadian mechanics with a combined 100 years' experience set up this site to take the mystery out of maintaining and repairing vehicles. Don't be deterred by the site's title – men will learn more than they'll care to admit.

Finally, here are a number of other websites that may be helpful.

- *forum.freeadvice.com*
- *www.lexusownersclub.com*
- *www.benzworld.org/forums*
- *www.bmwboard.com*
- *www.bmwnation.com*
- *www.carforums.com/forums*
- *www.consumeraffairs.com/automotive/ford_transmissions.htm*
- *www.datatown.com/chrysler*
- *www.epa.gov/otaq/consumer/warr95fs.txt*
- *www.flamingfords.info*
- *www.ford-trucks.com/forums*
- *www.hotbimmer.net*
- *www.ptcruiserlinks.com*
- *www.troublebenz.com/my_opinion/actions/links.htm*
- *www.vehicle-injuries.com*

Helpful Automobile Apps

Applications are little, self-contained programs that come with powerful web browsers to increase the functionality of modern "smart" phones. Apps allow users to do with the phone's browser in a few clicks whatever can be done with a desktop computer. The accessed information doesn't need a Bookmark or URL to be found and the image is enlarged to be easily read on the phone's screen.

In the "connect-me-now" world of communications, smart phones have replaced cell phones, MP3 players, global positioning systems (GPS), personal data assistants (PDA), and, in some cases, even computers. That's because these phones are much cheaper, multi-functional, and more mobile than most computers.

1. **Safer Car:** A free app downloaded from the NHTSA at *safercar.gov* for iPhone and iPod Touch devices, with development of an app for Android smart phones on its way. The Safer Car app allows you to receive immediate information on your phone when you register to receive safety updates. Other aspects of the Safer Car app include:
   - *Real time news:* The app forwards NHTSA safety headlines and information, including recalls on vehicles you own. You receive timely news that may bear on the safety of you and your family.
   - *Complaints:* With the Safer Car app, you can notify NHTSA of a complaint, concern, or safety issue you discovered with your car.
   - *Safety ratings:* Using the app, you can review and compare safety data for cars you own or are considering for purchase.
   - *Safety seats:* Information on safely installing child safety and booster seats is provided, along with help finding local support to have your seat checked or properly installed.

2. **iWrecked Auto Accident Assistant:** Available for free from *Apple.com* ITunes, the iWrecked application helps you make sense out of a stressful situation while protecting your rights by taking the "he said, she said" out of the experience. This app helps you document pertinent facts about the other parties involved, the vehicle description, witness names, addresses and comments, insurance contacts, and license plate and drivers license numbers. There is also a place to show photos of the damage and accident scene taken by your iPhone.

3. **Waze:** This powerful navigation app is not only free, but it works on both the iPhone and Android platform and is applicable to drivers on both sides of our border. Accident and construction delays are indicated in real time in both official languages. This is a full-fledged navigation application that threatens most automaker navigation devices that sell for thousands of dollars and cost up to a hundred dollars each time they are updated by the dealer. Waze allows drivers to report police or hazards, and see what other people have reported.

4. **GoPoint:** The free GoPoint app works with iPhones and uses a GoPoint cable (which costs $100, but can be purchased online for less) to plug into your car's On-Board Diagnostics (OBD) port to give you real-time information from the vehicle's built-in computer diagnostic system (see below). This is the sort of thing that your local mechanic will do using equipment that costs thousands of dollars, yet, your iPhone can do it for the cost of a cable and the time you spend downloading the application. Bosch offers a similar app for free, called fun2drive. It is downloaded from the Google Play Store or the Apple App Store (for iOS products).

5. **Gas Buddy:** An awesome free application for drivers who simply want the cheapest gas available, thereby, avoiding the annoyance of fueling up and then spotting cheaper gas a mile down the road. Gas Buddy quickly locates stations in Canada or the States with the most competitive price. It searches by city, zip code, or your nearest GPS-mapped location. Plus, Gas Buddy will map the route to the cheapest station and show what other amenities the station provides — such as a car wash, compressed air, ATM, convenience store, etc.

6. **Repair Pal:** This free iPhone app will quickly get you a repair estimate, and find a mechanic nearest your GPS location to do the work. Here's how it works: First, select the year, make, and model of your vehicle, and add your zip code or iPhone's GPS location. Next, pick, from a menu, the repair that needs to be done. An estimated price range from both dealerships and independent shops will appear shortly on your phone screen. This will be followed by a list of other things that could go wrong and a local mechanic's recommendation as to what should be tackled first. Repair Pal also provides a list of nearby shops, along with their star-based rating, and will map your route or call the garage automatically. And if more assistance is required, Repair Pal will connect you to roadside assistance or the manufacturer's customer assistance.

7. **iLeaseMyCar Pro:** This is an important $1.99 (U.S.) tool for iPhone users who aren't sure whether they want to buy or lease a new car. The application infuriates dealer salespeople because it quickly determines the monthly payment for an auto loan or lease down to the penny by using the same information found in dealership programs. If you are new-car shopping, this app can save your calculations on different vehicles so you don't get confused by all the figures. There is also a useful reverse lease/loan calculator that shows the selling price that will meet your desired payment.

8. **My Max Speed 2.0:** Using the accelerometer in an Android phone, this $4.99 (U.S.) application logs speed and location every 5 seconds and can export the data to a spreadsheet. It's a great way to monitor a teen's driving habits, or beat a traffic ticket. The app also shows where the vehicle has traveled and sends a message if the phone carrying the app travels outside a preset boundary.

9. **AccuFuel:** A $0.99 (U.S.) iPhone app that is primarily a fuel efficiency tracker that keeps a real time record of what you spend on fuel. Fuel use data is given in SAE, imperial, and metric units that can be stored for multiple vehicles.

10. **How about a Car:** A free application similar to AccuFuel, but designed for the android platform. It also tells you when to get your oil changed, check tire pressure, etc.

Breaking the EDR Code

Since 1996, cars sold in the U.S. have been required to provide a connection for mechanics and inspectors to measure what's going on electronically under the hood. The system, called On-Board Diagnostics generation two (OBD-II), uses a 16-pin connector mounted somewhere near the instrument panel to gather maintenance, component failure, and safety information and store it in a vehicle's "black box," much like airplane electronic data recorders (EDRs).

The problem is that, until recently, only dealers could read the codes and drivers paid dearly to have the EDR info decoded.

Fortunately, over the past half decade, the aftermarket has developed gadgets that use the OBD-II connection to transmit in real time uncoded stats, such as fuel economy, engine speed, temperature, and vehicle speed and pertinent safety information relative to airbag deployment and braking application. When this information is combined with a smart phone's accelerometer and GPS locating ability, you get a comprehensive view of your car's performance, efficency, safety-related defects, and emissions control malfunctions.

MODEL INDEX

Mercedes-Benz
C-Class *460*
Nissan Sentra *361*
Nissan Versa *360*
Subaru STI *377*
Toyota Camry *393*
Toyota Corolla *389*
Toyota Matrix *389*
Toyota Tacoma *417*
Toyota Vibe *389*
Toyota Yaris *387*
Volkswagen Golf *469*
Volkswagen Jetta *469*

BELOW AVERAGE

Buick Allure *251*
Chevrolet Malibu *249*
Chrysler 200 *207*
Chrysler Charger *209*
Ford Explorer *237*
Ford F-150 Pickup *238*
Ford Fiesta *226*
Ford Focus *228*
Ford Fusion *230*
Hyundai Sonata *307*
Jeep Grand Cherokee *219*
Jeep Wrangler *217*
Kia Optima *329*

Toyota Prius *398*
Volkswagen Passat *476*

NOT RECOMMENDED

Buick LaCrosse *251*
Cadillac Catera *259*
Chrysler Avenger *207*
Chrysler Caravan *212*
Chrysler Magnum *211*
Chrysler Sebring *207*
Chrysler Town &
Country *212*
Nissan Altima *364*